by George F. Thomas

RELIGIOUS PHILOSOPHIES OF THE WEST

CHRISTIAN ETHICS AND MORAL PHILOSOPHY

Religious Philosophies of the West

RELIGIOUS
PHILOSOPHIES
OF THE WEST

GEORGE F. THOMAS

Charles Scribner's Sons   NEW YORK

To my wife

Preface

In the writing of this book I have been indebted to so many persons that it would be impossible to list them all. I owe a special debt to my Tutor, the late Canon B. H. Streeter of Queen's College, Oxford, for introducing me to the philosophy of religion many years ago, to my teachers in the Departments of Philosophy at Yale and Harvard, and to my pupils at Princeton University and elsewhere with whom I have discussed problems of the philosophy of religion. I also wish to express my gratitude for the help I have received from several friends who have read one or more chapters of the book and have made valuable suggestions for their improvement: John Smith of the Department of Philosophy and William Christian of the Department of Religion at Yale University; Basil Mitchell, Fellow and Tutor in Philosophy at Keble College, Oxford University; Frederick Berthold of the Department of Religion at Dartmouth College; Hugh Kerr of the Department of Theology at Princeton Theological Seminary; Whitney Oates of the Department of Classics at Princeton University; Gregory Vlastos of the Department of Philosophy at Princeton University; and Philip Ashby, Horton Davies, Malcolm Diamond, and Victor Preller of the Department of Religion at Princeton University. The books and services of the libraries at Princeton University, Princeton Theological Seminary, and Dartmouth College have been generously put at my disposal. The book could not have been completed without the time made available by several leaves of absence from Princeton University and the support of my colleagues on the faculty there. Finally, I owe the greatest debt of gratitude to my wife who has encouraged me at every stage of the writing and has assisted me in ways too numerous to mention.

GEORGE F. THOMAS

Princeton, N.J.

Contents

Introduction

During the last generation most of the leading philosophers of Great Britain and America have shown little interest in the philosophy of religion. For some years after World War I, religion continued to claim the attention of a number of outstanding philosophers. Although the idealistic philosophy of religion of thinkers such as Josiah Royce had lost its appeal, Alfred North Whitehead manifested a strong interest in religious problems and was widely read. From the beginning of World War II, however, only a few creative books in the philosophy of religion were published. Neo-Thomists such as Etienne Gilson and Jacques Maritain produced a number of historical and constructive works which were respected by philosophers. In England, Austin Farrrer published a significant book in rational theology, *Finite and Infinite*. In America, Charles Hartshorne wrote *The Divine Relativity* and other books in which he applied the principles of process philosophy to religious problems, and Walter Stace in *Time and Eternity* sought to work out a synthesis of naturalistic philosophy with mysticism. But it must be confessed that these and other philosophical works on religion had a rather limited influence in philosophical circles.

The reasons for this neglect of philosophy of religion after World War II are many, but two stand out above the rest. The first is that many philosophers had embraced naturalistic or positivistic theories which were opposed to a religious interpretation of the world. The second is that there was a remarkable revival of interest in Christian theology between the two world wars, and this led to the development of a neo-orthodox Protestant theology based upon the biblical revelation and opposed to the philosophical approach to theology. In consequence, the philosophy of religion which had flourished in university departments of philosophy and in leading Protestant theological seminaries was thrust into the background or neglected altogether. While philosophers of the Left were indifferent or hostile to religion as a relic of the prescientific age, theologians of the Right shunned philosophy as useless and even dangerous speculation.

There have been recent signs that this situation is changing and that a renewal of interest in the philosophy of religion has begun. A few years ago a volume of essays on religious questions by a group of analytical philosophers in Great Britain was published by Antony Flew and Alasdair MacIntyre under the title *New Essays in Philosophical Theology*. It was followed by another series of essays written by Christian philosophers at Oxford University and edited by Basil Mitchell, *Faith and Logic;* by a book written by Ian Ramsey, *Religious Language*, in which he applied the method of linguistic analysis; and by John Hick's *Faith and Knowledge*. These and other essays and books indicate that in England the "linguistic veto" exercised by positivistic philosophers has lost most of its power. Among American philosophers there has also been a renewal of interest in religious problems during the last few years. As examples, we shall mention only Paul Tillich's *The Courage to Be, Dynamics of Faith,* and the third volume of his *Systematic Theology;* Charles Hartshorne's *The Logic of Perfection;* Walter Stace's *Mysticism and Philosophy;* John Smith's *Reason and God;* and John Wild's *Human Freedom and Social Order*. Such books as these clearly indicate that a climate of opinion more favorable to the philosophical approach to religion is emerging among both philosophers and theologians.

There are good reasons to welcome this recent development. Almost from the beginning of Western philosophy in ancient Greece, the criticism of popular religion has been one of the major sources of development in religious thought. As Xenophanes poured scorn upon the anthropomorphism of early Greek religion, Plato attacked the myths of the popular polytheism which pictured the gods as causing evil as well as good in the lives of men. In Jewish and Christian thought, also, philosophers have insisted upon the use of reason to challenge arbitrary and unworthy beliefs about God and His relation to man. Thus, philosophy has been a powerful force in the criticism of irrational elements in the great religions of the West.

Philosophy has also helped religion to achieve unity in its beliefs and to relate them to beliefs derived from other sources. Since the origin of religious beliefs is in religious intuition and imagination rather than logical thinking, they are often lacking at first in internal consistency and need to be brought into a coherent pattern by reason. Primary and essential beliefs need to be separated from secondary and nonessential ones, e.g., Christian belief in eternal life needs to

be distinguished from the mythological images in which it was originally expressed in order that religious people may not make presumptuous claims to detailed knowledge of the end of the world and
of the streets and walls of the Heavenly City. Thus, religious beliefs
can be purged of internal inconsistencies and naïve interpretations
with the help of philosophy. Philosophy can also assist in the process
of relating them to knowledge derived from science and other sources
and in making clear their implications for human life.

Equally important is the contribution of philosophy to religion in
providing it with concepts and principles for the interpretation of its
beliefs. Although the language of religion is usually concrete rather
than abstract, a religion as it develops inevitably seeks to express
its beliefs in conceptual terms for the purpose of clarifying and com-
municating them. Man is a rational being who seeks to understand
his faith as clearly as possible; he is also a social being who seeks
to share it with others as effectively as possible. Moreover, a religion
must come to terms with the philosophy of each age if it is not to
be divorced from the thought of the time. Thus, Jewish thinkers such
as Philo, Maimonides, and Martin Buber have sought to interpret
their religious faith under the influence of philosophies as diverse as
Platonism, Aristotelianism, and modern Existentialism. The use of
philosophy for these purposes is unavoidable if a religion is to express
its beliefs in terms relevant to the problems and needs of a particular
age. Men cannot live without a world view, and in every age they
are forced to choose between competing world views. For this reason, religion needs philosophy not only to purge it of unworthy beliefs through criticism and to help it attain consistency in its beliefs
but also to formulate a world view which will be compatible with
faith, and will at the same time commend itself to reason.

Nor can philosophy evade the responsibility of examining critically the claims of religious beliefs to truth. If a philosopher is to do
justice to all fields of human experience and thought, he must seek
to clarify the fundamental concepts and assertions of religion. It is
not enough for him to deal with ideas employed in the natural and
social sciences while ignoring those which express the religious dimension of experience. Moreover, if he develops a constructive philosophy which seeks to interpret reality as a whole, it is not enough
for him to formulate his system without taking account of religion
and then to add as an afterthought a perfunctory concluding chapter
to fit it into the system. For religion claims to provide an insight into
the nature of reality and life as a whole, and if a philosopher is to
interpret all aspects of experience he cannot treat it as unimportant.

Thus, both in clarifying the concepts employed in various fields of experience and in developing a constructive philosophy, the thought of a philosopher will be either enriched by a serious consideration of religion or impoverished by a neglect of it.

For these and other reasons, the philosophical approach to problems of religion is of vital importance for both religion and philosophy and the recent renewal of interest in it should be welcomed. However, the *function* of the philosophy of religion should not be misunderstood. Normally, new religious beliefs have originated not from the arguments of philosophers but from the insights of prophets, mystics, and founders of religions. The function of the philosopher of religion is not to discover new truths which will compete with and ultimately replace those of creative religious persons. It is to formulate clearly the beliefs which have arisen out of religious insights, to develop their implications for an understanding of the world and human life, and to inquire critically into their truth and value. In other words, the task of the philosopher of religion is not to construct a new religion based on reason alone which will supersede the religions of the past and present; it is to reflect upon the religious ideas and beliefs which have actually existed among men and to evaluate their claims. Of course, a philosopher may also be a theologian (Augustine, Aquinas) or a prophet (Kierkegaard), and he may discover new religious truths or gain a new understanding of old ones. Nevertheless, the philosopher's role as philosopher in relation to religious issues differs from that of others because he has a distinctive purpose and method. In the continuing drama of religious history, the philosopher does not take the lead but plays a secondary part. For if religion had not existed throughout the course of history as a living experience and way of life for multitudes of people, and if founders, prophets, and others had not expressed their religious experiences and beliefs in intelligible language, the philosopher would have nothing to deal with, no religious "data" to excite his interest and claim his attention. In short, the philosophy of religion has an important function to perform in the development of religion, but it presupposes the reality of religion and its task is primarily that of interpretation, criticism, and evaluation.

This book contains an exposition and critical evaluation of some religious philosophers and philosophical theologians of the West from Plato to Tillich. Its purpose is not to present a history of philosophical thought concerning religion, but to engage in a critical dialogue with a limited number of thinkers who represent different types of religious philosophy and offer different answers to the basic religious questions. For this reason, several thinkers who have made significant contributions to the philosophy of religion in the past have been omitted altogether, e.g., Anselm, Descartes, and Leibniz. Tillich is the only living philosopher who is critically evaluated in the book, since I hope to offer in a later volume a constructive treatment of some of the major problems and to come to grips with contemporary thought concerning them. However an Epilogue has been added which offers a brief account of several contemporary philosophical tendencies without attempting a critical evaluation of them. Its purpose is simply to give some indication of the present situation in which the philosopher of religion must face his task.

My primary aim has been to give a clear and comprehensive *exposition* of the religious philosophy of each thinker and sufficient *evaluation* to bring to light and sharpen some of the crucial issues raised by him. My reason for offering a thorough exposition of the position of each thinker is that some readers may not be familiar with the history of philosophy and theology. Consequently, I have usually, although not always, completed my exposition of a thinker's position before criticizing it.

If one is to separate truth from error in a religious philosophy, he must understand as a whole the philosophy of which it is a part. Some readers may wonder, for example, why a summary of Kant's theory of knowledge has been presented before his religious views are dealt with, or why a brief account of Whitehead's metaphysics precedes the discussion of his idea of God. The reason is simple: the *religious aspect* of a philosophy cannot be fully understood or justly evaluated apart from its relation to the philosophy as a *whole*. Indeed, a philosopher's answers to religious questions may be largely or even wholly determined by his theory of knowledge and metaphysics. Unfortunately, some philosophers of religion who have only a minor interest in general philosophy have attempted to confine their attention solely to religious questions. The result has usually been a superficial treatment of them in isolation from other questions which are closely related to them. It may require patience and effort for readers whose primary interest is in religious questions to study a religious philosophy in the context of the whole philosophy of which it is a part. But there are no short cuts to truth in the philosophy of religion.

Although the approach to religious issues through a careful study of classical philosophers and philosophical theologians is not popular with those whose interest is centered exclusively in contemporary movements, I believe that a thorough consideration of the best religious thought of the past is an invaluable preparation for fresh and independent thinking about religious problems in the present. I am convinced that the tendency to limit attention to contemporary writers and methods narrows the outlook of philosophers and prevents them from facing a number of important problems. At any rate, my own thinking has been stimulated and enriched by the thinkers who are discussed in the book, even by those with whom I most strongly disagree, and I believe that they are all worthy of careful study.

Religious Philosophies of the West

1 Theistic Idealism

PLATO

The development of Western philosophical thought concerning religion has been more profoundly influenced by Plato (428/7–348? B.C.) than by any other philosopher of the ancient world. Although the pre-Socratics had many interesting and significant things to say about the gods, it was Plato who defined the nature of rational theology and determined the direction of its later development. It is fitting, therefore, that we should begin our critical analysis of Western religious philosophies with Platonic Idealism.

After a brief account of Plato's attitude toward the popular religion of his time, we shall offer a broad outline of his theory of *Ideas* or Forms. This is essential not only because his theory of Ideas is the basis of his theory of knowledge and an important part of his metaphysics but also because his religious philosophy is centered to a considerable extent upon the relation of the soul to the Ideas which constitute the eternal realm of Being. Since the *soul* is also highly important in both his general philosophy and his religious and ethical theory, we shall next discuss its nature and its relation to the body, its spiritual development, and its hope for immortality. We shall then be in a position to consider the nature of the *cosmos* and the role of the gods in bringing it into being. Finally, we shall deal in some detail with Plato's conception of the nature of the *gods* and of the soul's relation to them. We shall conclude the chapter with an analysis of his major contributions to the philosophy of religion, especially to the development of Theism.

THE TRADITIONAL RELIGION

When Plato fell under the spell of Socrates and became a philosopher, the traditional polytheism of the Greeks was under heavy attack. The popular religion had lost its hold upon intelligent Athenians. The Homeric myths were being criticized as fanciful in their picture of the gods and immoral in their effects upon men. Xenophanes had ridiculed

1

naïve anthropomorphism, and Anaxagoras had scandalized conservative Athenians by asserting that the sun is a hot stone and the moon is
made of earth.[1] Some of the Sophists were claiming that moral rules
were not in accord with nature, *physis*, but were mere products of
convention, *nomos*. And Democritus had proposed a materialistic philosophy which explained the world in terms of atoms moving in space
without purpose. It is not strange that conservative citizens were
alarmed at the shaking of the religious and moral foundations of society and that one of the unjust charges against Socrates which led to
his execution was impiety.[2]

It was obviously impossible, even if it had been desirable, to coun-
teract these corrosive forces by an appeal to the authority of the past.
Although Plato was a deeply religious man, he was also a pupil of
Socrates and believed that every idea, however firmly established,
should be critically examined by reason. Thus, in the *Euthyphro*, one
of his early dialogues, he represents Socrates as subjecting the concept
of piety or holiness, *hosiotēs*, of a conservative Athenian to sharp criticism. When Euthyphro defines piety as that which is dear to or approved by all the gods, Socrates raises the question "whether the pious
or holy is beloved by the gods because it is holy, or holy because it is
beloved of the gods"[3] and complains that Euthyphro has offered an
"attribute" of holiness rather than its "essence" in his definition.[4] His
point, of course, is that acts of piety are not right from the mere fact
that they are commanded by the gods but because they are intrinsically right. Another definition by Euthyphro, i.e., that piety is a
form of ministration or service to the gods, is more promising, but it
raises questions he is unable to answer.[5] Although the dialogue ends
inconclusively, it has challenged a traditional conception of religion
which has led and still leads men to do many questionable acts. It has
also hinted at a truer conception of religion as service to the gods in
attaining worthy purposes, a conception which Plato develops in
later dialogues.

In the *Republic*, Plato makes a scathing criticism of the popular
polytheism. Many myths about the gods, he says, are immoral and
have serious moral consequences in the lives of their worshipers. He
offers two "rules and principles concerning the gods" which will enable
men to avoid these evils. The first is that God is good and is never the

---

[1] Plato, *Apology*, 26. Unless otherwise indicated, all quotations from Plato are
from the translation by B. Jowett (New York: Random House, 1937), 2 vols.

[2] For a general account of the religious situation in Greece at the time of Plato
see Friedrich Solmsen, *Plato's Theology* (Ithaca, N.Y.: Cornell University Press,
1942), Chap. 2.

[3] *Euthyphro*, 10.   [4] *Ibid.*, 11.   [5] *Ibid.*, 13.

cause of evil but only of good.[6] The second is that God is unchanging
and does not assume different forms.[7] For if God is perfect, He can
neither be compelled to change by anything external to Himself nor
will He change Himself since "if He change at all He can only change
for the worse." [8] The importance of these principles extends far beyond
Plato's criticism of polytheism. The first asserts that goodness is not
merely one among many attributes of God but His primary attribute
and that no quality or act should be ascribed to a divine being which
is not judged by reason to be good. Goodness rather than power is the
essence of deity. It was the influence of this principle which led later
Christian Platonists to reject the view of some theologians that God's
will is arbitrary and is not to be judged by moral standards. The
second principle rules out polytheistic myths in which the gods assume
human and animal forms to carry out questionable purposes, but it also
has a deeper meaning. In asserting that the gods cannot change, it
ascribes a fixed and consistent character to them. Thus it liberates men
from unworthy ideas of the divine will as arbitrary and capricious
impulse and enables them to conceive it as stable and dependable. On
the other hand, the assumption that God's perfection permits of no
change of any kind has created difficulties for Christian theology, since
it has often been interpreted in a static manner.

THE THEORY OF IDEAS

It is impossible to understand Plato's religious philosophy without
at least a brief reference to his theory of *Ideas* or *Forms*. An Idea, *idea*,
in the Platonic sense is not an idea in the subjective sense of a mental
state; it is an objective reality. It is most simply defined as a universal
characteristic which is present in and shared by all members of a class
of particulars. For example, courage is the quality in which all coura-
geous acts "participate," beauty the quality "shared" by all beautiful
things. We must be content with "opinion," *doxa*, concerning the objects we apprehend through the senses, since the objects of the sensible
world are always changing and their qualities do not remain the same.
But we can attain "knowledge," *epistēmē*, of the Ideas or Forms
through reason, since they are timeless and unchanging. Thus the
temporal world of Becoming, *genesis*, stands in contrast to the eternal
and immutable world of Being, *ousia*.

This contrast is heightened by the fact that the objects of the sensible world of Becoming are able to embody the Forms only imper-
fectly. For example, when we have a sense perception of sticks which

[6] *Republic*, Bk. II, 379.   [7] *Ibid.*, 380.   [8] *Ibid.*, 381.

appear to be equal, the reason is stimulated to conceive the Form of "equality," but the sticks themselves are only approximately equal.[9] Again, the experience of beautiful things leads the reason to an intuition of absolute beauty, but none of them is perfectly beautiful.[10] Hence the relation of particular objects to the universal Forms present in them is not one of full "participation," *methexis*, but one of "imitation," *mimēsis*. For the Forms are not only universals but also ideals, or norms to which particular things only approximate.

Finally, the Forms constitute a system in which they stand in definite relations to each other. Some Forms are compatible with and can be combined with one another, e.g., movement and being, but others are not, e.g., movement and rest.[11] Certain Forms such as being, sameness, and difference can be predicated of all Forms and hence can connect them with each other in a system. It is the task of philosophy not only to define each of the Forms but also to discover by dialectical reasoning its positive and negative relations to other Forms. The ultimate goal is to comprehend the whole system of interrelated Forms which constitute the intelligible world of Being. It is a hierarchical system in which the Form of the Good is supreme, according to the *Republic*.[12]

Although the perception of sensible objects can provide the occasion and stimulus for reason to conceive the Forms, Plato argues in the *Meno* that the act by which it knows them is one of "recollection," *anamnēsis*.[13] For we have once known the Forms but have lost our knowledge and have to recover it by being reminded of them. Recollection is possible because of the pre-existence of the soul in another life. According to a myth in the *Phaedrus*,[14] the souls of men once journeyed around the circuit of heaven under the leadership of the gods and contemplated the Forms. This was their true home and the source of their spiritual food. But they lost their wings and descended to the earth where they are now forced to live in bodies. They have all but lost the impression of the heavenly beauty upon which they once gazed and can recollect it only through the sight of earthly beauty which arouses love and awe in them. If this myth is to be taken seriously, the souls of men have known the Forms in a previous existence and need only to recover their knowledge by being reminded of them. It also seems to imply that the Forms have an existence independent of and separate from the particulars which exemplify or participate in them.[15]

---

[9] *Phaedo*, 74.   [10] *Symposium*, 210, 211.   [11] *Sophist*, 254.
[12] *Republic*, Bk. VI, 509.   [13] *Meno*, 86.   [14] *Phaedrus*, 244–257.
[15] W. D. Ross, *Plato's Theory of Ideas* (Oxford: Clarendon Press, 1953), p. 25.

They seem to constitute a supersensible realm of pure Being, eternal, immutable, and superior to the sensible things of time and change.

It is this theory of the *separate existence* of the Forms, *chōrismos*, which is the most famous aspect of Plato's philosophy. It is also the source of the conventional view of him as a metaphysical idealist who held that only the Forms are real and that sensible objects are unreal. According to this view, he had a contempt for the world of Becoming and sought to escape from its imperfections and evils by contemplating the Forms of the world of Being. In short, his religious philosophy was that of otherworldly mysticism.

There is an element of truth in this interpretation, but it is based upon only one side of Plato's thinking. It overlooks the fact that in the *Republic,* he contrasts Becoming not only with Being but also with Not-being and speaks of it as possessing "a place intermediate between pure being and the absolute negation of being." [16] This clearly implies that the world of Becoming is not unreal but is a mixture of reality and unreality. Through its participation in the Forms, it possesses order and at least relative value. Hence, the mind can ascend in its quest for truth from "opinion" concerning the objects of the world of Becoming, symbolized by shadows on the wall of a cave, to "knowledge" of the Forms of the world of Being, symbolized by objects lighted by the sun above the earth.[17] Similarly, in its love of beauty it can mount upward from the relatively beautiful objects of the world of Becoming to the absolute beauty of Being.[18] Thus, the dualism between Being and Becoming is not absolute, and the changing things of time possess meaning and value insofar as they imitate or participate in the unchanging Forms.

Plato goes even further in the *Sophist* and asserts that Being is not confined to the Forms alone but includes other kinds of reality also. To the "friends of the forms," the "Stranger" says, "O heavens, can we ever be made to believe that motion and life and soul and mind are not present with perfect being? Can we imagine that being is devoid of life and mind, and exists in awful meaninglessness an everlasting fixture?" [19] This assertion in one of his later dialogues of the reality of "motion and life and soul and mind" simply makes explicit and emphasizes the fact that from the first Plato regarded as real and important not only the Forms but also soul, together with motion and life of which it is the source, and mind which is its highest function. Therefore, it is essential to recognize that Plato's Idealism centers in soul and mind as

---

[16] *Republic,* Bk. V, 477.   [17] *Ibid.,* Bk. VII, 514–517.   [18] *Symposium,* 211.
[19] *Sophist,* 249.

well as in the Forms and that soul belongs in a sense to both the world
of Being and the world of Becoming and mediates between the two.

THE SOUL

The great worth of the soul is a major theme of the *Phaedo*. Although the primary problem discussed by Socrates and his friends in
that dialogue is the immortality of the soul, much of the argument
centers upon the nature of the soul. Socrates conceives of its relation to
the body in *dualistic* fashion. It is only externally related to its body,
living in it as in a tomb. Only when it is liberated from its body by
death can it fulfill its true destiny. For it is distracted by the senses and
appetites of the body from the activity of thinking, which is its highest
function, and from the moral virtue which depends upon knowledge.
Although it is entangled through sensation and appetite with the things
and values of the sensible world, its true essence is to be found in the
spiritual faculty of reason and its true home is the supersensible world
of Forms. Therefore, the philosopher or lover of wisdom will turn
away from the things of the senses and restrain his desire for worldly
values such as money and power in order to seek truth and virtue. This
"tendance of the soul" should be the primary concern of every man
because it is the true source of his happiness.

Plato has been justly criticized for this dualistic view of the relation
between soul and body and for the ascetic and otherworldly conception of life which is a logical consequence of it. It obviously corresponds to the contrast between Being and Becoming in his metaphysical Idealism. However, as that contrast is not absolute, so the dualism
in the *Phaedo* is mitigated in other dialogues. In the *Republic* the
soul is not identified with its rational aspect or function alone, but is
described as tripartite in its nature. In addition to its rational "part"
or function, it possesses an "appetitive" part and a "spirited" part, the
former of which is closely related to the body and the latter of which
is normally an ally of the rational part.[20] Similarly, in the *Phaedrus*,
the soul is symbolized by a charioteer driving two horses, one white
and noble and the other black and vicious.

The charioteer is reason, the ruling faculty in the soul, while the
white horse is the "spirited" part which obeys reason and the black horse
is the "appetitive" part which has to be forced by the whip to obey.
This tripartite view of the soul enables Plato to conceive of the good
life in less ascetic and otherworldly terms than in the *Phaedo*. It is no

---

[20] *Republic*, Bk. IV, 439–441.

longer to be attained by a harsh and rigid negation of sensation and desire, but by the control and direction of the two non-rational parts or functions by reason.

The arguments in the *Phaedo* for the *immortality* of the soul are not presented by Socrates as logical demonstrations like those of mathematics but as rational grounds of hope. As he faces death, he refuses to lament his fate and remains steadfastly cheerful to the end. Why should he fear death when he knows that the soul is spiritual and is quite distinct from the body? Has he not as a philosopher been daily practicing dying to the interests of the body by turning away from the senses and appetites and seeking wisdom and virtue? Why, then, should he fear the complete and final separation of the soul from the body which has been a prison preventing it from realizing its spiritual destiny? Since he has learned through his pursuit of truth and virtue that the soul has an affinity with the supersensible world of Being rather than with the sensible world of Becoming, does he not have every reason to hope that at death it will simply slough off its body and return to the world of the Forms and the gods, which is its true home? If it is to be rewarded or punished in the next life according to its deeds in this life, what has he to fear? How, then, can he better spend the hours of life remaining to him than by comforting his friends with words of hope and reminding them that they should so conduct themselves as to be worthy of a happy life after death? It is obvious from this that the hope of immortality, in Plato's opinion, has a profound bearing on the conduct of life. "It follows," says Taylor, "that the 'tendance of the soul' is incomparably the most serious of human interests, and the danger of neglecting this 'tendance' the most awful to which we can expose ourselves. . . . The value of faith in it is that it drives home the question what manner of man we ought to be if there is an endless future before us, and thus invests the choice for moral good or evil with an awful importance it would not otherwise have." [21]

It is generally agreed by most philosophers and theologians that the arguments of Socrates for immortality are not wholly convincing. However, they do show that the soul is worthy of surviving the dissolution of the body and that it may have the capacity to do so. Thus, they have value in that they offer reasonable grounds for hope. (1) One of the most interesting arguments is that, since there are absolute norms implied in judgments of truth and value and since these do not exist in the world of the senses, the soul must have known them in a pre-

[21] A. E. Taylor, *Plato, the Man and His Work* (New York: Dial Press, 1929), p. 207.

existent state. This is based upon the theory of recollection, of course, and stands or falls with it. But even if we do possess knowledge of norms not derived from sense experience, it is not necessary to account for it by postulating the pre-existence of the soul, since Kant and others have offered explanations of the *a priori* element in knowledge; and there is no positive evidence for pre-existence. (2) Another argument is from the contrast between the soul and corporeal things. While corporeal things are composite and hence divisible and corruptible, the soul is an uncompounded spiritual being and hence indivisible and incorruptible. Socrates seeks to prove its spiritual rather than corporeal nature by its affinity with the invisible and eternal Forms with which it is united in knowledge. This argument has value insofar as it indicates the *spiritual* nature of the soul by reference to the ideal nature of the objects it knows and the values it loves, but this does not prove that it is *eternal* like its objects. (3) A third argument seeks to refute the naturalistic view that the soul is only a "harmony" of the body and perishes with it. Socrates rightly points out that, since the soul is able to control the body, it cannot be a mere "harmony" of the body wholly dependent upon it for its existence. This argument is effective as an answer to views which reduce the soul to a mere epiphenomenon, because it shows that the soul is not a by-product of the body but has a distinctive life and activity of its own; but it does not show that it is a substantial entity which is wholly independent of the body. (4) Finally, Plato argues in the *Phaedrus* that whereas a thing which is moved by another in ceasing to move ceases also to live, the soul is a self-moving source and beginning of motion and hence must be uncreated. It follows from this, he says, that it must be indestructible. For if the soul as the source or beginning of motion were destroyed, there could be no beginning of anything and the universe would come to a standstill. But this proves only that *if* soul is the only source of motion and *if* motion is eternal, soul of some kind must always have existed and must continue to exist. Even if both of these assumptions are valid, the argument does not prove that individual souls are immortal but only that some kind of world soul must be eternal.[22]

Thus, Plato's arguments for immortality have value insofar as they indicate the spiritual nature of the soul, refute naturalistic attempts to reduce it to a mere function of the body, and emphasize its capacity to rule over the body. In this way, they prove the *possibility*, but not the *certainty*, of its survival of the death of the body. And Plato seems to claim for them only that they give support to the hope for immor-

[22] Frederick Copleston, *History of Philosophy* (London: Burns, Oates, and Washbourne, 1956), Vol. I, p. 214.

tality and render supremely important a life of wisdom and virtue like the life of Socrates for those who cherish that hope.[23]

By now it should be clear that the soul occupies a central position in Plato's philosophy. His interest is not only in the Forms but also in the soul's attainment of truth and virtue through its knowledge of the Forms. The discovery of the Forms is absolutely essential because personal morality and political justice alike depend upon conformity to the truth about reality. But Plato's interest in the Forms is motivated not only by the purely intellectual curiosity of the philosopher but also by the desire of the mystic to unite himself with the eternal and by the concern of a profoundly religious moralist and statesman to bring the personal and social life of men into conformity with the Good. In modern terms, his primary concern for truth as a philosopher is an existential one.[24]

THE COSMOS

Unlike many modern existentialists, however, Plato is convinced that man can attain authentic existence only by conforming his character and conduct to the structure and purpose of the cosmos of which he is a part. For this reason, cosmology is essential. There is already a suggestion in the *Phaedo* of the form his cosmology is to take. In a striking autobiographical passage, Socrates describes his disillusionment with the cosmologies he had studied as a young man because they did not give him a satisfactory explanation of natural events. When he heard of the new doctrine of Anaxagoras that "mind was the disposer and cause of all," he embraced it eagerly as it seemed to offer a teleological explanation of nature. "If mind is the disposer," he said to himself, "mind will dispose all for the best, and put each particular in the best place." [25] But he was disappointed when he found that Anaxagoras made no use of this principle in explaining natural events and depended like other cosmologists upon mechanical causes such as air and water. It was as if one should say that the reason Socrates was awaiting his death in prison instead of running away was the condition of his bones and muscles, "forgetting to mention the true cause, which

[23] According to some interpreters of Plato, however, certain of the arguments in the *Phaedo* were regarded by him as achieving demonstrative certainty if one accepts the hypothesis of the theory of Ideas upon which they are based, e.g., the pre-existence of the soul is as certain as the existence of the Ideas (76 1–77a).

[24] This aspect of Plato's thought has been treated in an interesting way in Robert Cushman, *Therapeia* (Chapel Hill, N.C.: University of North Carolina Press, 1958).

[25] *Phaedo,* 97.

is that the Athenians have thought fit to condemn me, and accordingly I have thought it better and right to remain here and undergo my sentence." [26] As a result of this disappointment, Socrates adopted another method of explanation which was based upon the fact that all things participate in Ideas or Forms and are best understood by reference to them. This did not mean that teleological explanation was to be abandoned, for there is a close connection between the end or "final" cause of a thing and its "formal" cause.

This suggestion in the *Phaedo* that the world should be explained teleologically by reference to Mind which realizes purposes through the Forms present in things is the basis of the cosmology Plato developed in his later dialogues. The presupposition behind that cosmology is that man knows the nature of things best as it is represented in himself, since he is a microcosm who includes in himself every kind and level of reality found in the macrocosm. Hence, the philosopher should take the nature of man as the key or clue to an interpretation of the cosmos, understanding the structure of the latter by analogy with that of man. For example, since the same elements which enter into the nature of the bodies of all animals, including our own, reappear in the constitution of the world, we may consider the world to be a body and our bodies to be "nourished" by, i.e., dependent upon, it.[27] Similarly, as our body has a soul, the body of the universe must have a soul, since there can be no other source for our soul.[28] For the same reason, our minds must come from "a presiding cause of no mean power, which orders and arranges years and seasons and months, and may justly be called wisdom and mind." [29] Moreover, as man's mind rules his body, "mind rules the universe." [30]

In the myth of the *Timaeus* a cosmology based upon such an analogy is developed to explain the order of the cosmos. Since the philosophical value of this myth has sometimes been questioned, it may be worthwhile to listen to what Plato himself says about it. "Wherefore, Socrates, if in our treatment of a great host of matters regarding the gods and the generation of the universe we prove unable to give accounts that are always and in all respects self-consistent and perfectly exact, be not then surprised; rather we should be content if we can furnish accounts that are inferior to none in likelihood, *eikotas,* remembering that both I who speak and you who judge are but human creatures, so that it becomes us to accept the likely account, *ton eikota mython,* of these matters and forbear to search beyond it." [31] Although

---

[26] *Ibid.,* 98.   [28] *Ibid.,* 30.   [30] *Ibid.*
[27] *Philebus,* 29.   [29] *Ibid.*   [31] *Timaeus* (Loeb ed.), 29d.

Plato in this passage admits that his mythical "account" is not always consistent or exact, he claims that it is the "likely" one, i.e., that it is as probable as any that finite man can attain. Therefore, although its mythical character will not allow us to take all of its details literally, we are meant to take it seriously.

The visible cosmos, we are told, came into existence as the creation of a divine *Dēmiourgos* or Craftsman who, motivated by the desire that all things should be as like himself as possible and guided by an eternal "Model" consisting of Forms, imposed order upon random and disorderly events in the "Receptacle" or *Space*. Although the myth represents the cosmos as coming into existence, many scholars think that Plato does not intend to assert that it had a beginning in time but is offering an analysis of the different factors which are necessary for the explanation of the world as we find it. Thus, it is a logical analysis and we are not meant to take literally the temporal order of events demanded by its mythical form. On the other hand, some scholars maintain that Plato meant his account of the beginning of the cosmos to be taken literally. They point out that he describes the origin of the cosmos as a beautiful and orderly whole as if it followed a condition of disorder. He also describes the heaven and time as "having been created together" to be a "moving image of eternity." [32] Thus, in contrast to the Craftsman and the Forms which are eternal, both the order of the cosmos and the time which measures its motions had a beginning.

Whatever one may think about this point, there is no idea of a creation *ex nihilo* in the Christian sense. The Craftsman does not create either the Forms in the "Model" or the "Receptacle." Both exist independently of him and he constructs the cosmos by imposing the former upon the latter and thereby bringing order out of chaos. This implies that he is not omnipotent since he is limited by factors independent of him. The myth also speaks of the Craftsman as being limited by "Necessity," *anankē*, so that "the creation is mixed, being made up of necessity and mind." "Mind, the ruling power persuaded necessity to bring the greater part of created things to perfection, and thus and after this manner in the beginning, when the influence of reason got the better of necessity, the universe was created." [33] "Necessity" here seems to refer not to natural law but to the fact that the original contents of the Receptacle act spontaneously in accordance with their properties and therefore are in a measure recalcitrant to the purpose of the divine Mind.[34] Nevertheless, Mind is able to perfect

[32] *Timaeus*, 37, 38.   [33] *Ibid.*, 48.
[34] Copleston, *History of Philosophy*, Vol. I, p. 248.

"the greater part of created things" not by force but by persuasion, transforming disorder into an orderly and beautiful cosmos which is a copy of the eternal Model.

THE GODS

The myth describes the divine *Craftsman* as creating a *World-Soul* "in origin and excellence prior to and older than the body" and diffusing it throughout the body of the world.[35] As we have seen, soul is regarded by Plato not only as the source of all motion and life but also as the seat of mind. Therefore, he accords the World-Soul primacy over the body of which it is the "ruler and mistress." The Craftsman also created "the heavenly race of the gods," i.e., the gods of the *fixed stars* and *planets*,[36] as well as the immortal part of human souls.[37] Then he entrusted to the gods he had created the task of making all the living creatures which are mortal, including the mortal parts of man.[38]

There has been much controversy over the question as to which of these divine beings Plato regarded as God. It is natural for Christian monotheists to suppose that the "Demiurge" or Craftsman is his God. According to A. E. Taylor, "this 'creator' or 'maker' is, strictly speaking, the only God, in our sense of the word, the dialogue recognizes. Later on we shall find the name *theos* given both to the world itself as a whole and to certain parts or denizens of it, but this must not mislead us. These *theoi* are all 'created'; their *raison d'être* is the will of the *Dēmiourgos*, who is thus distinguished from them as God is from 'creatures' in Christian theology." [39] But this interpretation overlooks the fact that Plato seems to be more concerned about the general nature of the divine than he is about the issue between monotheism and polytheism which is so important for Christian thought and that he often speaks indiscriminately of "the God" and "the gods" when he is referring to the divine element in the world.

For this reason Cornford holds that the Demiurge is only a mythical symbol for the divine Mind or Reason which works in the world for ends that are good. "He is mythical in that he is not really a creator god, distinct from the universe he is represented as making. He is never spoken of as a possible object of worship; and in the third part of the dialogue the distinction between the Demiurge and the celestial gods, whom he makes and charges with the continuation of his work, is obliterated. The evidences of design in the human frame are there attributed sometimes to 'the God,' sometimes to the celestial gods, who

---

[35] *Timaeus*, 34.   [36] *Ibid.*, 40.   [37] *Ibid.*, 41.   [38] *Ibid.*
[39] Taylor, *Plato*, pp. 441–442.

are the stars, planets, and earth." [40] Similarly Grube holds that the Demiurge is "the personification of the active principle of movement and causation, of the love of good which belongs to all the gods, as to all good souls." [41] He also identifies the Demiurge with the World-Soul and regards the heavenly gods and the immortal elements in human souls as simply "foci" or parts of the World-Soul.[42] Thus, all of the divine beings mentioned in the Timaeus become mythical symbols of divine Mind rather than distinct divine beings.

There is much to be said for this view. However, the description of the Demiurge as the creator of the World-Soul and the heavenly gods seems to manifest a tendency toward monotheism. If so, Plato may have been anticipating the later theistic distinction between God as transcendent to the world (the Demiurge) and God as immanent in it (the World-Soul and the heavenly gods). "But Plato would have had no motive," says Ross, "for introducing both an immanent world-soul and a transcendent divine Craftsman unless he had thought them both necessary to his account of the world as we know it." [43] Ross also refers to a passage in the Sophist which asserts that men, animals, and inanimate things are "known by us to be each and all the creation and work of God." [44] Moreover, general considerations suggest that Plato meant the Craftsman to be taken as more than a mythical symbol. "If the physical world is in its own right a jumble then it surely needs a supreme intelligence to order it, even though, when ordered, subordinate individual intelligences can sufficiently control the behavior of the piece of matter which they animate. . . . I think it would be contrary to the whole spirit of the doctrine to say that the craftsman is no more than a symbolic expression of the fact that the universe is rationally ordered. Corresponding to the timeless intelligible natures there exists the timeless mind which eternally comprehends them." [45] This seems to be the most reasonable view of the nature of the Craftsman, although the question cannot be answered conclusively since we do not know how Plato intended the details of his myth to be interpreted.

Although there is uncertainty about the proper interpretation of the Craftsman and his relation to other divine beings, it is clear that in the cosmology of the Timaeus divine Mind is an indispensable and primary factor. Indeed, if Theism is the belief that the world depends for

[40] F. M. Cornford, Plato's Cosmology (New York: Humanities Press, 1952), p. 38.

[41] G. M. A. Grube, Plato's Thought (London: Methuen, 1935), p. 169.

[42] Ibid.   [43] Ross, Plato's Theory of Ideas, p. 127.

[44] Sophist, 266.

[45] Ian Crombie, An Examination of Plato's Doctrines (London: Routledge, 1930), p. 391.

its order and value upon a divine Mind whose purpose is to realize good in the finite beings of the world, Plato is a theist. Moreover, since he holds that mind always resides in soul, and soul is the principle of life, it is clear that the divine Mind is not only intelligent but also *living*. It would be misleading to say that it is personal, for Plato has no explicit conception of personality as we understand it, but he ascribes attributes such as moral goodness and purpose to it which we would not ascribe to an impersonal principle.

What is the relation of the divine Mind to the Forms which are contained in the eternal Model of the cosmos? As we have seen, the Forms in the *Republic* constitute the world of Being which is contrasted with the world of Becoming but which is also the source of whatever reality is possessed by the latter. It is not surprising, therefore, that some interpreters of Plato have regarded the Craftsman and other divine beings of the *Timaeus* as mere personifications of the Forms. More especially, they have asserted that the Form of the Good, which in the *Republic* occupies the supreme position among the Forms, is really Plato's God. It is difficult to deny that Plato speaks of the Form of the Good in the *Republic* in religious terms. "You will agree," says Socrates, "that the Sun not only makes the things we see visible, but also brings them into existence and gives them growth and nourishment; yet he is not the same thing as existence. And so with the objects of knowledge: these derive from the Good not only their power of being known, but their very being and reality; and Goodness is not the same thing as being but even beyond being, surpassing it in dignity and power." [46] Here Plato represents the Form of the Good as the source of the being as well as the knowability of the world of Forms. According to Ross, this means that "all the Ideas are thought of as types of excellence, as species (as we may perhaps say) of the great generic Idea of excellence itself, and as intelligible only in the light of that Idea." [47]

But the primacy of the Form of the Good in the world of Forms does not imply that the Form of the Good is to be identified with God. As Ross says, "while any Idea, and therefore the Idea of Good, is for Plato always a *universal*, a nature, wherever he speaks of God he means a *being* having a nature, and in particular not goodness but a supremely good being. This is already clear in the *Phaedo* where in Socrates' account of his mental history, reason, i.e. the divine reason, is clearly distinguished from the good to which it looks in the government

[46] *Republic*, Bk. VI, 508, trans. F. M. Cornford (New York: Oxford University Press, 1950).

[47] Ross, *Plato's Theory of Ideas*, p. 43.

of the world." [48] To put it succinctly, a god for Plato is always a Soul, never a Form. However, the Good and the other Forms have an indispensable function in the cosmology of the *Timaeus*. The divine Craftsman constructed the cosmos because "he was good," and because he "desired that all things should be good and nothing bad, so far as this was attainable." [49] And he designed it as a copy of an eternal Model which consisted of "intelligible beings" or Forms. How then should we conceive of the relation of the gods to the Forms, especially the Form of the Good?

A clue to the answer may be found in a general comment of Grube's concerning Greek ideas of the gods. "Our word God," he points out, "is a synthesis of two concepts which the Greeks kept distinct and which are clearly differentiated in Plato. The divine has two aspects: the static and the dynamic. God may be looked upon as the ultimate reality, the highest form of being, the eternal absolute. We also speak of God as the creator, the first link in the chain not of existence but of causation, the maker, an active force causing movement and life." [50] In terms of this distinction, we may say that the "static" aspect of Plato's God is the Forms, especially the Form of the Good. But it is the "dynamic" aspect which he designates as "God" or "the gods," i.e., "those more personal beings, those more human forces personified in whom we find help and guidance in living the good life." [51] Following this clue, we may say that the Form of the Good and the other Forms are for Plato divine in the sense that they constitute the source of the *value* and *structure* of the cosmos, while the Craftsman and other gods are divine in that they provide the creative and purposive *activity* which is the source of the cosmos and which governs the lives of men. However, Grube's assertion that the Forms possess ultimate reality and that the gods are subordinate to them must be at least qualified. Certainly, the Forms have a more important position than the gods in the *Phaedo* and the *Republic*. However, the gods come into greater prominence in the later dialogues, and in Book X of the *Laws* the gods, which are perfect souls, occupy the central position.

The picture of the cosmos as grounded not on the blind and purposeless motions of material atoms but on the creative activity of divine Mind motivated by the purpose to bring into existence an orderly world in order to realize good has had a profound influence upon Western Theism, Christian and philosophical. Of course, from the per-

---

[48] *Ibid.* (italics added).   [49] *Timaeus*, 29, 30.
[50] Grube, *Plato's Thought*, p. 151.   [51] *Ibid.*, p. 152.

spective of Jewish and Christian monotheism Plato's Craftsman seems unsatisfactory. He is limited by the independent existence of the Forms which he copies, and by the necessity which prevents the perfect realization of his purpose. But the myth of God in his goodness shaping a beautiful and orderly world which "should be, as far as possible, like unto himself," has greatly enriched the Western religious tradition. As a result, Christian Theism at its best has insisted that God created the world not arbitrarily by the sheer power of His will but by rational will guided by Ideas which served as exemplars. Of course, it has modified the Platonic theory radically by denying the independent existence of the Ideas and affirming their existence only in the mind of God, and it has also affirmed the dependence of the matter of the world upon Him for its creation. But the image of the divine Craftsman creating an orderly cosmos in order to realize good in creatures distinct from himself has left an indelible impression upon the Western mind. And there have been philosophers such as Whitehead who have been more impressed by the picture of a God limited in His power and patiently "persuading necessity as far as possible" than by the orthodox view of an omnipotent God creating the world in obedience to His command.

RELIGION IN THE *LAWS*

In Book X of the *Laws,* Plato has given us his most complete and systematic discussion of the gods and their relation to men. As we have indicated, there were naturalistic philosophers who asserted that all changes in nature could be explained by material and mechanical causes without any reference to final causes or purposes. Although Socrates in the *Phaedo* had refuted arguments against immortality derived from this philosophy, a more complete answer to Materialism was needed. In Book X of the *Laws,* Plato offers an answer in the form of an argument for the primacy of soul over matter in the world and for the existence of gods as "perfect souls." Concerned about those who speak and act "insolently" toward the gods on the assumption either that they do not exist, or that if they do they take no care of man, or that they are easily appeased by sacrifices and prayers, he offers arguments to convince them that these are errors.[52]

The source of their belief that the gods do not exist is the doctrine that "the whole heaven has been created and all that is in heaven, as well as animals and all plants, and all the seasons come from these elements, not by the action of mind, as they say, or of any *God,* or from art, but . . . by *nature* and *chance* only." [53]

---

[52] *Laws,* Bk. X, 885.   [53] *Ibid.,* 889 (italics added).

They assert that "the gods exist not by nature, but by art, and by the laws of states, which are different in different places, according to the agreement of those who make them; and that the honorable is one thing by nature and another thing by law, and that the principles of justice have no existence at all in nature." [54] The influence of the materialists and the Sophists is evident in this doctrine. It rests upon the premise that nature consists of material elements and that the soul is formed from these; and it deduces from this the conclusion that the soul has a very subordinate place in the world and that moral judgments and religious beliefs are artificial products of convention.

Plato opposes to this theory the assertion that the soul is "among the first of things, and before all bodies, and is the chief author of their changes and transpositions," so that nature is "under the government of art and mind." [55] He bases this assertion on the fact that, unlike bodies which move other bodies but cannot move themselves, the soul is able to move itself as well as other things and hence is "the true principle of change and motion in all that is." [56] No attempt is made to prove that the soul alone can move itself and hence must be the beginning of motion in other things. Plato seems to depend for this premise upon the widespread Greek view that living things alone have the power to move themselves from within and that this power resides in their souls. He then proceeds to argue that, if the soul is prior to the body as the source of all motion and change, the reasonings, opinions, and desires of the soul are also prior to the body.[57] Hence the soul is the source not only of the motion but also of the order in the cosmos, directing all things by its "movements" of mind, deliberation, and will.[58] The conclusion that follows is that the heavens are moved and ordered by "perfect souls" or gods.[59]

Thus, Plato develops a cosmological and teleological argument for the existence of the gods as the cause of motion and change, on the one hand, and order and regularity, on the other. However, it must not be supposed that he has presented this argument merely to answer a metaphysical question concerning the First Cause of the cosmos. The discussion of the gods has arisen in the course of a dialogue dealing with political matters. Plato is concerned with atheism because it is a threat to the moral foundations of the state. It is not surprising, therefore, that he follows his proof of the existence of the gods with a refutation of those who say that the gods, even if they exist, pay no heed to men. Insofar as this view rests on the assumption that man is too small and insignificant for the gods to care for him, he answers it

[54] *Ibid.*   [55] *Ibid.*, 892.   [56] *Ibid.*, 894.   [57] *Ibid.*, 896.   [58] *Ibid.*, 897.
[59] *Ibid.*, 898, 899.

by affirming that "all mortal creatures are the property of the gods" and that "it would not be natural for the gods who own us, and who are the most careful and the best of owners, to neglect us." [60] To use human analogies, the physician, the pilot, and the general pay attention to small things as well as to great ones in carrying out their tasks. "Let us not, then, deem God inferior to human workmen, who in proportion to their skill, finish and perfect their works, small as well as great, by one and the same art; or that God, the wisest of beings . . . is like a lazy good-for-nothing, or a coward, who turns his back upon labour and gives no thought to smaller and easier matters, but to the greater only." [61] The assumption behind this argument is that God must be understood by analogy with the wisest and best of men and that His relation to His creatures must be at least as noble as that of conscientious human workers to their works. Plato's view of God at this point does not parallel or approximate the Christian view that God *loves* his creatures individually—indeed, he says clearly that God created the individual simply as part of the whole and for the sake of the whole [62] —but he at least implies that the goodness of God which led Him to create is also manifested in *caring* for His creatures.

Moreover, God exercises a kind of *moral government* in his dealings with man, "sending the better nature to the better place, and the worse to the worse, and so assigning to them their proper portion." [63] "When the king saw that our actions had life and that there was much virtue in them and much vice . . . and when he observed that the good of the soul was ever by nature designed to profit men and the evil to harm them—he, seeing all this, contrived so to place each of the parts that their position might in the easiest and best manner procure the victory of good and the defeat of evil in the whole. And he contrived a general plan by which a thing of a certain nature found a certain seat and room but the formation of qualities he left to the wills of individuals." [64] This moral government extends to the life after death and determines the destiny of men by the principle of justice. "O youth or young man, who fancy you are neglected by the Gods, know that if you become worse you shall go to the worse souls, or if better to the better, and in every succession of life and death you will do and suffer at the hands of like." [65] Moreover, although the wicked may prosper and be accounted happy by men, they cannot escape the working of divine justice by appeasing the gods with their gifts.[66]

Since the gods care for man and govern his destiny by moral principles, some interpreters have spoken of a Platonic doctrine of *provi-*

[60] *Ibid.*, 902.   [61] *Ibid.*, 903.   [62] *Ibid.*   [63] *Ibid.*   [64] *Ibid.*, 904.
[65] *Ibid.*, 905.   [66] *Ibid.*

dence. But it is misleading to ascribe to the gods in the *Laws* a provi-
dential direction of human life in the Christian sense of the term. In
general, although Plato uses certain terms which are similar to those
used by Christian thinkers, the similarity is far from complete and we
should be on our guard against attributing Christian ideas to him.
"For example, when the Demiurge is called the Father, he is so only
as the cause and origin of things, the creator. He is nowhere a father
in the sense of one who loves his children. We love the gods, or rather
the Ideas which the gods love also. But the gods do not love us." [67] As
the source of the natural and moral order, they are more to be revered
and imitated than to be loved. This may help to explain why Plato has
little to say about *prayer* as a personal relationship with the gods, despite his own deeply religious nature. Religious observance is primarily
a communal activity, and the *Laws* forbids all private religious ceremonies. Thus, the Platonic view of the gods differs substantially from the
biblical view of a personal God who loves His children like a Father,
enters into personal fellowship with them, and directs the course of
their lives by His providence.

Despite these limitations from the biblical point of view, Plato's
conception of the deity is one of the noblest of the ancient world, for
his gods are living, intelligent, and moral beings who are motivated by
goodness in their creation and moral government of the world. His
conception of *religion* is equally noble. Since the gods are uncompro-
misingly just, they will not be flattered by praises or bribed by sacrifices to withhold punishment from wicked men. The whole conception
of religion as a kind of bartering with the gods in which men buy their
favor with gifts is abhorrent to Plato. For true piety consists not in
seeking worldly benefits from the gods, but in serving their purposes
by imitating their rationality and goodness. Although each man is a
small and insignificant part of the universe, he has his share in realizing
its purpose and should always remember that he is taking part in a
great enterprise in cooperation with the gods.

There is an eloquent passage in the *Timaeus* in which Plato expresses this lofty conception of religion. "When a man is always occu-
pied with the cravings of desire and ambition, and is eagerly striving to
satisfy them, all his thoughts must be mortal. . . . But he who has
been earnest in the love of knowledge and true wisdom and has exercised his intellect more than any other part of him, must have thoughts
immortal and divine, if he attain truth, and insofar as human nature is
capable of sharing in immortality, he must altogether be immortal; and

---

[67] Grube, *Plato's Thought*, pp. 177–178.

since he is ever cherishing the divine power, and has the divinity within him in perfect order, he will be perfectly happy." [68] Thus, Plato returns to that "care" or "tendance" of the soul which he had emphasized in the *Phaedo*. For it is the heart of true religion as well as of morality. But he now proceeds to put it in the wider context of his cosmology by showing that the method one should follow in caring for his soul is to conform his thought and conduct to the cosmical order of which he is a part. "Now there is only one way of taking care of things, and this is to give to each the food and motion which are natural to it. And the motions which are naturally akin to the divine principle within us are the thoughts and revolutions of the universe. These each man should follow . . . and by learning the harmonies and revolutions of the universe, should assimilate the thinking being to the thought, renewing his original nature, and having assimilated them should attain to that perfect life which the gods have set before mankind, both for the present and the future." [69]

In this passage, Plato affirms both that there is a divine principle in the human soul and that it is nourished by study of and conformity to the divinely ordered and regular motions of the universe, i.e., those of the stars. Through the cultivation of the divine reason within themselves men should impose order upon the disorderly movements in their souls as the divine Craftsman has imposed Forms upon the random movements in space to create an orderly cosmos. This is a profoundly ethical conception of religion and it is firmly based upon a theistic cosmology. Moreover, the *Republic* and the *Laws* make it clear that the soul should seek wisdom and virtue not only for the sake of its own happiness but also for the sake of justice in the state and happiness for all its citizens.

If we bear this conception of religion in mind, we will not be tempted to dismiss Plato as an otherworldly visionary. Although there is an otherworldly element in his thought it is subordinate to his metaphysical Idealism and ethical Theism. As an idealist, he sees the order and value of the world in time and space as derived from its participation in eternal and unchanging Ideas or Forms. Since being is united with value in the Forms, he believes that the soul can realize its true destiny as a spiritual being only through knowledge of them by reason and conformity to them in conduct. His ethical Theism both supports and completes this idealistic world view and ethic. It explains the order and value of the cosmos as the work of a divine Mind giving form to

[68] *Timaeus*, 90.   [69] *Ibid.*

the world in order to realize good. It spurs the soul to base its life upon reason and virtue, and inspires it with a vision of its spiritual nature and kinship with the gods and the Forms. And it assures the soul that imitation of the gods through wisdom and virtue will bring true happiness in this life and beyond death.

Although we have emphasized the rational and ethical character of Plato's religion, there was also a *mystical* element in it. This mystical element was associated with the practice of philosophy and took the form of a vision of the Ideas rather than a union with the gods. In the *Republic,* the education of the future Guardians of the state culminates in a vision of the Idea of the Good; [70] in the *Symposium,* the ascent of the ladder of beautiful things ends in an intuition of absolute Beauty; [71] and in the myth of the *Phaedrus,* both the souls of men and the gods are nourished by contemplation of the Ideas as they move around the heaven.[72] Professor Gregory Vlastos has suggested [73] that Plato regarded the philosopher's vision of the Ideas as analogous to the vision or *epopteia* which was the culmination of the rites of the Eleusinian mysteries. He has also pointed out that there were great differences between them, since the philosopher's vision of the Ideas was personal rather than communal and was an intellectual experience which constituted intuitive knowledge. But it was also a passionate experience which brought the greatest delight, the philosopher's love for the Ideas being a kind of "madness" like that of the lover and mystic. Also, it resulted in a transformation of his personality and character, releasing him from his attachment to worldly things, enabling him to attain spiritual purity and peace, and preparing his soul for a return to its godlike state as an immortal being.

As we shall see, Plato's mysticism differed substantially from that of Neo-Platonic mystics such as Plotinus. For his mystical vision of the Ideas was not beyond thought and did not involve a loss of the individuality of the seer in his union with the seen. But the mystical vision was obviously of profound importance to Plato. Indeed, it can be argued that, while he felt reverence for the gods, he felt love only for the Ideas, so that his mysticism was at the center of his personal religion. There is truth in this view, but it would probably be more correct to say that his religion was like an ellipse with two foci: the *vision of the Ideas* which are the source of order and value in the world and the *imitation of the gods* who designed the cosmos, cause the regular motions of the stars, and govern the lives of men.

[70] *Republic,* Bk. VI, 507–509.   [71] *Symposium,* 211d–212a.
[72] *Phaedrus,* 246–247.   [73] In an unpublished paper.

THE CONTRIBUTION OF PLATO

The limitations of Plato's metaphysical Idealism and ethical Theism have often been pointed out, and we have mentioned some of them. Few philosophers would defend his theory that the Forms have a separate existence independent of the things which exemplify them, although many from Aristotle to the present have regarded the Forms which are immanent in actual things as essential elements in their being. Most philosophers have also rejected the dualism between the soul and the body which is found especially in the *Phaedo* and is never completely overcome. And theists, as we have seen, have never accepted the view that the Forms and the "matter" which the divine Craftsman brings together in shaping the cosmos have an existence independent of God.

Despite these and other weaknesses, the greatness of Plato's contribution to Western religious thought cannot be questioned. Perhaps we can best indicate its nature by referring to a well-known statement by Whitehead: "The safest general characterization of the European philosophical tradition is that it consists of a series of footnotes to Plato." [74] Whitehead makes it clear that he is speaking not of the philosophical system which is sometimes attributed to Plato but of the "wealth of general ideas" to be found in his writings. He speaks of three of these "general ideas" which have deeply influenced him in his own thought: the participation of actual things in eternal "potentialities of existence," which obviously correspond to Plato's Forms; the bringing together of actual things and these "potentialities" by "the divine element in the world"; and the attainment of ends of different kinds by means of this combination. [75] A brief consideration of these three ideas will indicate the general character of Plato's contribution.

The first idea is that the order and structure of the world of space and time has been made possible by the participation of actual things in eternal and timeless *Forms* or "potentialities." Whatever may be thought to be the status of the Forms in reality, the recurrence of qualities, relations, and patterns in things can be explained only by the fact that potentialities which are distinguishable from things have been actualized in them. It is doubtless true that the natural sciences repudiated the medieval attempt to explain natural things and events by reference to "formal causes" and substituted explanations by material

[74] Alfred North Whitehead, *Process and Reality* (New York: Macmillan, 1929), p. 63.
[75] *Ibid.*, pp. 63–64.

and efficient causes. But it must be remembered that natural science does not attempt to explain things as concrete realities but describes only those selected aspects of them with which its method can deal. Moreover, the basic reason for the criticism of formal causes was not that there are no universal or recurrent structures in nature, for natural science recognizes such structures, but that medieval science was so absorbed in the classification of things according to their forms that it neglected to investigate the material and efficient causes of them.

It was necessary for theistic thinkers after Plato to deny the separate existence of the Forms and their independence of God, for only in this way could the dualism between Forms and things and between Forms and God be overcome. Therefore, Augustine, Thomas Aquinas, and others fully accepted the reality of the Forms but regarded them as eternal Ideas in the mind of God. According to this view, God created the world in accordance with these Ideas as "exemplars." Once this change in the relation of the Forms to God had been made, it was possible for them to play an important role in the theistic interpretation of God and the world. The insight of the *Euthyphro*, that acts are not right because they are dear to the gods but that they are right in themselves and as such are dear to the gods, became the basis for the view that God does not determine what is good and evil arbitrarily by His will but that His will is governed by His knowledge of the intrinsic nature of good and evil. This view has enabled theists influenced by Plato to avoid the view that God's will is capricious and to conceive of Him as acting according to norms approved by His reason.

In the second place, Plato recognized the inability of the Forms to actualize themselves in things since they have no actuality and causal power in themselves, so that a *divine Mind* which has the power to actualize them is also essential for an understanding of the order and value of things. It was this insight, derived in part from Anaxagoras and Socrates, which made Plato one of the fathers of Western Theism. It is true, as we have said, that he seems to be more interested in the fact that divine Mind is the source of the cosmos than in the question as to whether there is only one God or there are many gods. But he sees clearly that the materialistic view which regards the world's order as a result of blind and purposeless matter is wholly inadequate, and he offers grounds for the theistic view that divine Mind seeking to realize good is the most reasonable alternative. Also, although he is fully aware of the dangers of crude anthropomorphism, he insists that we should base our conception of the divine Mind upon an analogy with human mind and purpose. In an ironical reference in the *Timaeus* to those who have constructed genealogies of the gods as if they were "speaking of what took place in their own family," [76] he acknowledges that men's knowledge of the traditional gods is limited. But he recognizes, as Book X of the *Laws* shows, that those who refuse to interpret the ultimate cause of the world in terms of mind and purpose, the highest thing we know, are likely to conceive it in terms of inanimate elements and blind forces. Therefore, he bases his explanation of the order and value of the world upon the belief that a divine Mind analogous to the human mind at its best disposes things in such a way as to realize its purposes. Thus, he was the first in the history of philosophy to present the rational grounds for Theism and to sharpen the issue between it and every form of Naturalism.

The third "general idea" of Plato which has profoundly influenced later philosophers is that the divine Mind is motivated in its realization of Forms in the world by the purpose to attain *values*. Although later theistic thinkers such as St. Augustine insist that God is not only the Designer but also the Creator of the world, Plato laid the foundation for their thought by his teleological explanation of cosmic order. This teleological view may be in Plato's mind when he speaks in the *Republic* of the Idea of the Good as the source of the being as well as the intelligibility of all the other Ideas, and it is at the heart of his assertion in the *Timaeus* that the Craftsman brought the cosmos into being because "he was good" and "desired all things should be as like himself as they could be." [77] For one of his fundamental insights is that being is inseparable from value and that no being can be understood without reference to the value which is realized in it. As we shall see, when value is divorced from being, being becomes meaningless and value is reduced to insignificance as a merely subjective and accidental aspect of things. Religion as well as morality suffers from such a divorce. If God is conceived as acting without purpose or for any purpose except the realization of good, He is degraded into an arbitrary will wielding His power not for the good of His creatures but to satisfy His own whims, or His will is believed to be "inscrutable" and to act for ends that are not approved by the moral consciousness.

While Plato's idealistic Theism emphasizes the eternal Forms, the divine Mind and the purpose to realize Good in the world, it does not deny the necessity and importance of *material* and *efficient* causes. In the *Phaedo* he speaks of material and efficient causes as necessary conditions or auxiliary causes and recognizes that ends cannot be attained without them. Again, in the *Timaeus*, he attempts to describe

[76] *Timaeus*, 40; cf. *Cratylus*, 400*de*.   [77] *Timaeus*, 29.

the various organs of the body, the processes involved in sight and hearing, and other natural phenomena as understood by the science of his time.[78] Material and efficient causes such as these he regards as "second and co-operative causes which God, carrying into execution the idea of the best as far as possible, uses as his ministers." [79] It is true that Plato is not as interested in these auxiliary causes as he is in the final causes of things which have their origin in mind. But he does regard them as necessary and there is no trace in him of the type of Idealism which treats nature as only an appearance of Absolute Mind or Spirit. It is also true that he sometimes seems to regard the body and matter in general as the source of evil, since the sensations and appetites which arise from the association of the soul with the body tend to distract the soul from its true good. But matter is not inherently evil, as in Manichaean dualism; it becomes a source of evil only when the soul refuses to order its appetites and actions by reason. Thus, although there is an element of dualism in Plato's Idealism, it does not lead him to the contempt for the world and the ascetic attitude toward the body which were characteristic of medieval monasticism.

Finally, Plato puts the *soul* and its *destiny* close to the center of his religious philosophy. As we have argued, it is a mistake to identify him exclusively with the theory of Ideas and to overlook his profound concern for the conversion of the soul from its obsession with sensible things and values to a primary interest in the spiritual life which is devoted to higher values such as truth and virtue. Although he emphasizes the mastery of reason over irrational appetite, his motive is the positive aspiration, *eros,* for truth, beauty, and moral goodness. Perhaps his most enduring contribution to Western man's understanding of religion is his conviction that religious belief must be supported by reason, on the one hand, and manifested in moral goodness, on the other. The soul is truly religious only when it has learned to turn away from worldly values such as riches and power and to devote itself to truth and goodness in imitation of the gods. Such a soul fulfills its spiritual nature and attains the highest happiness in this life; and it can look forward without fear to whatever lies beyond death.

[78] *Ibid.,* 43*ff.*   [79] *Ibid.,* 46.

2 Rational Theology

ARISTOTLE

As Plato was a pupil of Socrates and was inspired by his example to become a philosopher, Aristotle (384–322 B.C.) was for nineteen years a pupil of Plato in the Academy and developed his philosophy under the influence of his master. Some years after the death of Plato, however, he established a school of his own in Athens, the Lyceum, where he walked up and down with his pupils in the mornings discussing philosophical questions and in the afternoons or evenings expounded less difficult ideas in lectures to a larger audience.[1] His written works are mainly derived from notes used for his lectures and lack the literary mastery and dramatic quality of Plato's dialogues. But the analytical and critical power of his mind, the breadth of his intellectual interests, and his capacity to organize and systematize ideas make him one of the two greatest philosophers produced by ancient Greece.

Despite the fact that he has substantially influenced later religious thought, Aristotle seems to show little religious feeling in his mature writings. Although one of the charges against Socrates was impiety, the picture of him in Plato's dialogues is that of a deeply religious man who conceived of his vocation as inspired by the Delphic oracle, was guided on crucial occasions of his life by an inner voice or "daimon," and arranged just before his death for the offering of a cock to Asclepius. Again, while Plato was critical of the abuses of the popular polytheism, his interest in the gods is not merely that of a metaphysician seeking a First Cause of the world but is also an expression of existential concern for the perfection of the soul through its conformity to the divine purpose in the cosmos. In contrast, Aristotle seems to be indifferent to popular religion and even scornful of it,[2] and the Prime

[1] W. D. Ross, *Aristotle* (London: Methuen, 1930), p. 5.

[2] Aristotle, *Metaphysics*, Bk. XII, 1074b. Unless otherwise stated, the references to the *Metaphysics* and other treatises by Aristotle are to *The Works of Aristotle*, Eng. trans., ed. J. A. Smith and W. D. Ross (Oxford: Clarendon Press, 1908).

Mover who is the culmination of his metaphysics has little relation to men's religious needs.

Yet, paradoxical as it may seem, Aristotle has had a profound influence upon the rational theology of philosophers and even the theology of Jewish and Christian theologians. His proof of the existence of God, his conception of the relation of God to the world, his analysis of the soul, and his theory of the highest good of man have had a powerful effect upon Western religious thought. How are we to account for this paradoxical fact? In order to do so, we must consider his general philosophical position, especially his metaphysics, his physics, and his psychology; for his philosophy and the vision of the world and man which is expressed in it have had a peculiar fascination for thinkers with a less idealistic temper and outlook than Plato's.

We shall begin with his metaphysics. Aristotle's conception of Being as consisting of concrete individuals or substances rather than universal Ideas gives his metaphysics a naturalistic emphasis which is opposed to the idealistic world view of Plato. Also, his analysis of an individual being or substance as composed of form and matter and as developing from potentiality to actuality is of fundamental importance for an understanding of his religious philosophy. We shall next consider his philosophy of nature, with special reference to his theory of causes and his argument for a teleological as well as a mechanical explanation of nature. We shall then be in a position to understand his proof for the existence of an Unmoved Mover upon which nature depends, and his view of the soul. Finally, we shall consider his theory of the relation of value or good to reality and his conception of the highest good of man. Our critical evaluation will mainly consist of a comparison of his religious philosophy with that of Plato and a brief indication of his real contribution.

METAPHYSICS

The subject with which metaphysics is concerned, says Aristotle, is "being *qua* being," i.e., not being of this or that specific kind but being as such.[3] But his conception of "being" differs from that of Plato. For that which is being in the primary and most fundamental sense is not "Idea" or "Form" but "substance," *ousia*. Other categories or modes of being such as quality, quantity, and relation are secondary to substance and exist only in relation to it, but substance is "that which is not asserted of a subject but of which everything else is asserted."[4] For example, while a quality can exist only in a substance, a substance "can exist apart." When we say, "The apple is red," we mean that the apple

[3] *Ibid.*, Bk. IV, Chap. 1.   [4] Ross, *Aristotle*, p. 166.

is something which "has" the quality of red or which is the "substratum" in which the quality red inheres. It is an error to suppose, like some recent philosophers, that the emphasis of Aristotle upon the category of substance is due merely to the fact of grammar that predicates are asserted of subjects in sentences. Although he was doubtless influenced by this fact, he was primarily concerned with the nature of things. "And in particular," says Ross, "the fact of change drives him to distinguish between quality and substance. A quality cannot change. It is what it is and cannot become anything else; it can only be succeeded by another quality. If there is such a thing as change, as distinct from bare succession, there must be substance as distinct from qualities." [5]

The most fundamental principle of Aristotle concerning substance is that it is an *individual thing*. It is true that he speaks of universals, which characterize classes of individual substances, as "secondary" substances. But there is no doubt that the primary meaning of substance for him is that of a concrete individual thing. It is at this point that he differs most radically from Plato. Although he holds that there are nonsensible and unchangeable substances as well as sensible and changeable ones, Ideas or Forms are not among them. For universals are not, as they are for Plato, self-subsistent things with a separate existence of their own.

It is not necessary to set forth in detail Aristotle's criticisms of Plato's theory of Forms, but we shall refer briefly to a few of them because they throw light upon Aristotle's own point of view.[6] First, he rejects Plato's argument that the Forms are required to make scientific knowledge possible. Knowledge of universals *is* necessary for science, but this proves only that universals are real and not that they exist apart from individual things. In reality, the Forms of Plato are useless for the knowledge of things because they are not in them as their essence. They are simply duplicates of sensible things which cannot help to explain the existence of the latter. Second, Forms cannot account for motion and change. Since they are without motion themselves and objects are copies of them, it would seem that objects should also be without motion. Whence, then, comes the motion we actually observe in objects? Parenthetically, it should be noted that Plato realized that the Forms are not causes of motion but explained motions as due to the activity of souls. Third, if Forms contain the essence of sensible objects, they cannot exist apart from objects. The supposition that they do makes it impossible to explain the relation of Forms to particular objects which exemplify them. Plato does not really help us to explain that relation by his use of terms such as "participation" and "imitation," for "to say that they are patterns and the other things share in them is to use empty words and poetical metaphors." [7]

All of these criticisms are directed against the transcendent character of the Forms and the contrast between them and the sensible world of change or Becoming. Although Aristotle agrees with Plato in stressing the formal or structural aspect of things and regards it as the object of scientific knowledge, he holds that the universals which give form to things exist only as characteristics of individual substances. Universals are real in the sense that there is an objective foundation for them in individual substances. But they are real as immanent in and not as transcendent to things. The form of man operates in bringing into existence at birth an individual man, but it is the form of man as embodied in the father of the man. Thus, Aristotle seeks both to overcome the dualism between the transcendent Forms of the world of Being and the sensible things of the world of Becoming and to explain the changes that occur in the latter. Obviously, he is motivated by a conviction of the reality and worth of the world of Becoming, of nature and its changes. Ultimately, this conviction lies behind what is often called the "naturalism" and "empiricism" in his mature thinking, and it is the major source of the contrast between it and Plato's Idealism.

An analysis of the sensible and changeable substances of nature shows that each of them is composed of *form* and *matter*.[8] The form, *eidos,* of a substance is not one component among others; it is the essence or structure of the thing, that which constitutes it the kind of thing it is. The matter constitutes the substratum, *hypokeimenon,* in which the form is realized. Since the form of a species is identical in all the members of a species, it is the matter which is the "principle of individuation," i.e., which marks off one member of the species from another. However, there are not only sensible and changeable substances but also immaterial and unchangeable ones, and the highest of these is pure form without matter of any kind.

The world is a *hierarchy* of substances of different kinds. "Prime matter," i.e., matter which is wholly undetermined by form, nowhere exists as such; it is only postulated as an element in the nature of things and everything in nature has form as well as matter. At the bottom of the scale or hierarchy of substances are the "simple bodies" or elements of earth, water, air, and fire. These provide the matter out of which

---

[7] Aristotle, *Metaphysics*, Bk. XIII, 1079b.   [8] *Ibid.,* Bk. VIII.

minerals and tissues of plants and animals are formed. The latter, in turn, furnish the matter for other parts of plants and animals, i.e., organs, and the organs are the matter of which the body is composed. Above plants and animals is man, the highest of the animals, whose intellect in its highest aspect is incorporeal and can survive the death of the body. Still higher are intelligences which move the spheres. These are pure substances without bodies and move their spheres from without. At the top of the hierarchy is God who is pure form without matter. Thus, each substance has a definite place on the scale of being which ascends from inanimate matter to pure form.

The distinction between the form and matter of a substance exists at every moment of its history. But Aristotle is even more interested in the dynamic aspect of sensible substance, the *change* by which it passes from one state to another. This he describes as a process by which a "form," *morphē*, comes to be from its "privation," *sterēsis*, in a "substratum," *hypokeimenon*.[9] In order to account for this, he distinguishes between "potentiality," *dynamis*, and "actuality," *entelecheia*.[10] Substance A passes from the potentiality of B to the actuality of B through a process of change; e.g., an oak passes from a state of potentiality in an acorn to a state of actuality as the fully grown tree, or the will of a man changes from the potentiality to the actuality of a moral virtue. "The point is that change is not catastrophic," says Ross. "It is not the case that A which is sheerly not-B suddenly becomes B. Consider A more carefully and you will find some of the conditions of B-ness already present; if it were not so A would never become B."[11] For example, a man who has learned the art of building can build a house when he decides to do so, whereas one who has not learned it cannot do so. This means that the one has the capacity to build, while the other does not.[12] Thus, potentiality is necessary to account for change. However, A cannot pass from the potentiality of B to the actuality of B without the agency of something which is already actual. Hence actuality is prior to potentiality and potentiality is based upon actuality.[13] Above all, the potentialities of substances in nature could not be actualized without the agency of an eternal cause to set them in motion and this cause must be wholly actual. As we shall see, this is the basis for Aristotle's proof of God as the Prime Mover.

PHILOSOPHY OF NATURE

No sharp distinction can be drawn between the subjects discussed in the *Metaphysics* and the *Physics*. According to Aristotle, physics

[9] *Physics*, Bk. I, Chap. 7.   [10] *Metaphysics*, Bk. IX.   [11] Ross, *Aristotle*, p. 177.
[12] *Ibid.*   [13] Aristotle, *Metaphysics*, Bk. IX, Chap. 8.

deals with substances which are changeable. It analyzes the nature common to all natural bodies, animate and inanimate, which have in themselves a source of movement and rest. It is concerned with both the matter and the form of these bodies and with the causes in them. They are distinguished from artificial bodies such as beds or garments by the fact that there is no inherent principle of change in the latter.[14] In contrast metaphysics analyzes being as such, concerns itself with unchangeable substances as well as changeable ones, and culminates in theology which deals with God, the transcendent and immaterial First Cause.

One of the most important problems of physics is that which concerns the *causes* of change. The general term Aristotle uses for "cause" is *aitia* and it is used broadly for any essential condition or factor which is involved in change. He distinguishes four causes or factors which explain change: material, efficient, formal, and final.[15] The "material" cause, *to ex hou*, is simply the matter which is the substratum of the thing. The "efficient" cause, *to hothen hē kinēsis*, is the agent or source of motion. The "formal" cause, *to eidos,* is the form or essence of the thing which makes it what it is. The "final" cause, *to hou heneka*, is the end for which it exists. For example, the material cause of a house is the stone or wood out of which it is built. The efficient cause is the builder who by his work makes this material into a house. The formal cause is the plan which exists first in a human mind and then is realized in the structure of a house. The final cause is the purpose for which it is made, i.e., to provide a habitation. However, the efficient cause is not necessarily external to the thing that undergoes change, as it is in the case of a house. Indeed, the efficient cause is often identical with the formal cause and the final cause, which are internal or immanent in the thing. For example, the formal cause of a horse is the form or essential nature of the species horse; this is also its final cause since its end is to realize the form of the species; and it is also identical with the efficient cause insofar as the horse strives to embody its form in its activity, although the efficient cause of its coming into being is the horse which generated it.

Perhaps the most important question discussed in the *Physics* is whether changes in nature require a *teleological* as well as a mechanical explanation. Aristotle offers an argument against the materialists who sought to dispense with final causes altogether and to explain all changes as due to "necessity," *anankē*. "For thinkers," he says, "are forever referring things to necessity as a cause, and explaining that,

[14] *Physics,* Bk. II, Chap. 1.   [15] *Ibid.,* Chap. 3.

since hot and cold and so forth are what they are, this or that exists or comes into being 'of necessity.' . . . Why not say, it is asked, that Nature acts as Zeus drops the rain, not to make the corn grow but of necessity (for the rising vapor must needs be condensed into water by the cold and must then descend, and incidentally, when this happens, the corn grows), just as, when a man loses his corn on the threshing floor, it did not rain on purpose to destroy the crop, but the result was merely incidental to the raining? . . . So why should it not be a coincidence that the front teeth come up with an edge, suited to dividing the food, and the back ones flat and good for grinding it, without there being any design in the matter?" [16]

Aristotle firmly rejects this mechanical view and offers several arguments in favor of a teleological explanation of nature. The first is that natural things exist and act in a regular way, "on the whole and for the most part," and that this makes impossible an explanation of them by chance.[17] If chance were the explanation of natural things, "it ought to be a matter of chance what comes up when you sow this seed or that," whereas in each natural thing "there is always a tendency towards an identical result if nothing interferes with the process." [18] Sometimes, of course, a desirable result is brought about by luck, *tychē*. "But when the desirable result is effected invariably or normally, it is not an incidental or chance occurrence; and in the course of Nature the result always is achieved either invariably or normally if nothing hinders." [19]

Aristotle also points out that nature is like human art in that "the earlier stages in every case lead up to the final development in the same way as in the operation of art, and vice versa." Since art imitates nature and is directed by a purpose, a natural process must also be directed toward an end that is to be realized, i.e., the earlier stages are for the sake of and lead up to the later. "If, then, artificial processes are purposeful, so are natural processes, too; for the relation of antecedent to consequent is identical in art and nature." [20]

That this analogy of natural processes with the purposeful activity of art is not arbitrary, Aristotle shows by a consideration of the behavior of animals and the growth of plants. Although the works of spiders and ants are not the result of design, *technē*, some persons have raised the question whether or not they should be attributed to intelligence, *nous*, or some similar faculty.[21] Below these animals in the scale of nature, plants produce organs that serve their ends, e.g., leaves for the protection of the fruit. "Hence if it is by nature and also for a purpose that the swallow makes her nest and the spider her web, and that

[16] *Ibid.*, Chap. 8, 198*b* (Loeb ed.).   [17] *Ibid.*   [18] *Ibid.*, 199*b*.   [19] *Ibid.*
[20] *Ibid.*, 199*a*.   [21] *Ibid.*

plants make leaves for the sake of the fruit and strike down (and not up) with their roots in order to get their nourishment, it is clear that causality of the kind we have described is at work in things that come about or exist in the course of nature." [22] Thus, the adaptations of plants and animals provide empirical evidence for the view that final causes are operative not only in man but at levels below him. Of course, nature sometimes fails to attain her ends, just as there are failures in human arts like medicine. For occasional events occur which interfere with the working of teleology. These are due to chance, *to automaton,* and are "by nature" but not "according to nature," e.g., the birth of a monster.[23] But Aristotle is convinced that such failures are exceptional and that nature normally attains her ends.

This view of nature implies a different conception of necessity from that held by the materialists. There is no "unconditional" necessity in nature by which forces in matter blindly produce their effects. Rather, the necessity in nature is "hypothetical," i.e., if a purpose is to be attained certain material conditions are necessary. For example, if there is to be a saw, it must be made of iron or some similar material.[24]

This teleological interpretation of nature is not original with Aristotle. As we have seen, Anaxagoras first suggested that Mind disposes all things in nature "for the best"; Socrates tried to make this the basis for the explanation of natural events; and Plato developed it further in his cosmology.[25] Nevertheless, the contribution of Aristotle to natural teleology is an important one. While Plato had recognized the operation of final causes, he had offered no analysis of them. For he was more interested in the divine origin and the order and value of the cosmos than in the analysis of natural things, and he regarded a science of nature, the world of Becoming, as impossible. In contrast, Aristotle developed arguments for the view that final causes are indispensable and that mechanical causes are secondary to them. However, it is doubtful whether his conception of "immanent" teleology can be justified. "Plato had made use of the conceptions of a World Soul and of the Demiurge, and so was enabled to speak of ends in nature," says Copleston, "but Aristotle talks as though there were some teleological activity inherent in nature itself. He does indeed speak on occasion of *ho theos,* but he never gives any satisfactory treatment of the relation of nature to God, and what he says about God in the *Metaphysics* would seem to preclude any purposive activity in nature on the part of God." [26] Ross also regards the idea of "unconscious teleology" as un-

---

[22] *Ibid.*   [23] *Ibid.,* 199*b.*   [24] *Physics,* Bk. II, Chap. 9, 199*b.*
[25] Cf. Thomas, Chap. 1.   [26] Copleston, *History of Philosophy,* Vol. I, p. 325.

satisfactory. "Unconscious teleology implies a purpose which is not the purpose of any mind, and hence not a purpose at all." [27]

THE PRIME MOVER

In the preceding account of Aristotle's metaphysics and philosophy of nature, we have seen that nature consists of a plurality of individual substances in which different forms immanent in matter are realized by passing from potentiality to actuality through a process of change, and ends or final causes are unconsciously aimed at and normally attained. But the process in each case requires an efficient cause to set it in motion, and since actuality is prior to potentiality this moving cause must be actual. Also, in addition to the proximate moving cause, e.g., the male parent in the generation of a child, and the remote moving cause of all terrestrial processes, i.e., the sun in its course, there must be an ultimate or first moving cause.[28] As Aristotle says, "There is that which as first of all things moves all things." [29] This first moving cause or Prime Mover is the culmination of Aristotle's metaphysics and is his major contribution to theology.

His proof of the existence of the Prime Mover in Book XII of the *Metaphysics* constitutes a *cosmological argument* for God as the First Cause of all change in the world. It begins with an assertion that, since everything depends upon substances, if all substances were perishable, all things would be perishable.[30] But there are two things which must always have existed and can never cease to be, movement and time.[31] For movement "must always have existed," [32] and time cannot come into being or cease to be, "for there could not be a before and an after if time ceased to exist." [33] Moreover, movement, like time, must be continuous, since time is either the same as movement or an attribute of it.[34] The only continuous movement is movement in place, and the only continuous movement in place is circular.[35] For, as Aristotle argues in Book VIII of the *Physics*, if a thing has rectilinear motion, "the thing must turn back, and that which turns back in a straight line undergoes two contrary locomotions" and does not have a "single and continuous motion." [36] Thus, since time and motion are eternal and continuous and since the only continuous motion is circular, there must be an *eternal circular motion.*

[27] Ross, *Aristotle,* p. 186.   [28] Aristotle, *Metaphysics,* Bk. XII, Chaps. 4, 5.
[29] *Ibid.,* Chap. 4.   [30] *Ibid.,* Bk. XII, Chap. 6, 1071b.
[31] This assertion of the eternity of movement is made without proof. It indicates that Aristotle assumes the eternity of the world and is not arguing for a Creator but for an Ultimate Mover.
[32] *Metaphysics,* Bk. XII, Chap. 6, 1071b.   [33] *Ibid.*   [34] *Ibid.*   [35] *Ibid.*
[36] *Physics,* Bk. VIII, 261–262.

What is the *cause* of this motion? An eternal motion must be produced by an *eternal substance* which is capable of moving things. This substance must also exercise its capacity as a mover so that its essence must be activity. Otherwise, it would be possible for it not to exercise its capacity as a mover and motion would not be necessary and eternal. "There must, then, be such a principle, whose very essence is actuality." [37] Furthermore, if it is eternal, it must be immaterial, since matter is potentiality and involved in change and as such cannot be eternal.[38] The conclusion, then, is that there must exist an *eternal substance the essence of which is actuality; that it is immaterial; and that it imparts the eternal circular motion upon which all motion and change depend.* This conclusion is also in accord with experience. For it is "plain not in theory but in fact" that "there is something which is always moved with an unceasing motion, which is motion in a circle," i.e., the outer sphere of heaven in which the fixed stars are set.[39]

Now, the eternal substance that causes this eternal circular motion must be a *mover* which is itself *unmoved*.[40] In Book VIII of the *Physics*, Aristotle offers a proof of this statement. "It is impossible," he says, "that there should be an infinite series of movents, each of which is moved by something else, since in an infinite series there is no first term." [41] Therefore, if the first mover is moved, it must be moved not by something else, but only by itself.[42] But how can it impart motion to something without being moved itself? It can do so only if it does not move the thing in a physical way but only as an *"object of desire,"* as "the good" which is a final cause. "The final cause, then, produces motion by being loved." [43] In this way the unmoved Prime Mover produces the eternal circular movement which is the source of all motion and change. "He moves directly," says Ross, "the 'first heaven'; i.e., He causes the daily rotation of the stars around the earth. Since he moves by inspiring love and desire, it seems to be implied that the 'first heaven' has soul. . . . The motions of the sun, moon and planets are explained by the hypothesis of a 'nest' of concentric spheres each with its poles fixed in the shell of the sphere next outside it. Thus each sphere imparts its own motion to the sphere next inside it, and the prime mover, by moving the outermost sphere, moves all the others." [44] In this way all the motions and changes in the cosmos are ultimately caused by the motion imparted by the Unmoved Mover to the outermost sphere. By inspiring love or desire, he is the final cause.[45]

---

[37] *Metaphysics*, Bk. XI, Chap. 6, 1071*b*.   [38] *Ibid.*   [39] *Ibid.*, 1072*a*.
[40] *Ibid.*   [41] *Physics*, Bk. VIII, 256*a*.   [42] *Ibid.*
[43] *Metaphysics*, Bk. XII, Chap. 7, 1072*a,b*.   [44] Ross, *Aristotle*, p. 181.
[45] Aristotle, *Metaphysics*, Bk. XII, 1072*b*.

We have seen that the Prime Mover is immaterial, so that its activity cannot be physical. How, then, must it be conceived? Aristotle answers that its life is "such as the best which we enjoy and enjoy but for a short time," i.e., *thinking.*[46] This answer rests upon the assumptions that the Prime Mover must possess a mind analogous to the human mind and that the highest activity of the human mind is thinking. Aristotle does not stop in the *Metaphysics* to argue either of these points but takes them for granted. For what he is concerned to do is to show *how* the Prime Mover's thinking should be conceived. It is thought in the fullest sense which deals with what is best in the fullest sense. "Therefore it must be itself that the divine thought thinks (since it is the most excellent of things), and its thinking is a *thinking on thinking*," *noēsis noēseōs*,[47] or "thought which has *itself* for its object."[48] Aristotle regards this conclusion as necessary because the divine thinking cannot be made to depend upon something else for its object. Moreover, it is indivisible and cannot change, since change would be change for the worse. If the object of the divine thought were composite, it would change in passing from part to part of the object as in man's discursive thinking. Thus the divine "thinking on thinking" is *indivisible, intuitive,* and *unchanging.*[49]

Obviously, this description of the thinking of the Prime Mover stresses the differences between it and human thinking. The result is that the God of Aristotle is closer to the impersonal God of *Deism* than to the personal God of *Theism.* "For him, that God should know Himself, and that He should know other things, are alternatives; and in affirming the first alternative, he implicitly denies the second. Indeed, he denies explicitly much that the second would involve; he denies to God all knowledge of evil, and all transition from one object of thought to another. The result of the wish to exclude from the divine life any relation to evil and any 'shadow of turning' is the impossible ideal of a knowledge with no object but itself."[50] It is also clear that He has no concern for the world, and moves it not by any love for it, but only by its love for Him. Accordingly, there is no conception of providence in Aristotle because any interest of God in the world would be inconsistent with His perfection. The only sense in which God can be regarded as immanent in the world is that He is the cause of its change as the object of its desire.

Thus, whatever may be thought of Aristotle's cosmological argument for the *existence* of a Prime Mover as the ultimate cause of change, his conception of the *nature* of the Prime Mover and His

[46] *Ibid.*   [47] *Ibid.*, 1074*b* (italics added).   [48] *Ibid.*, 1075*a.*
[49] *Ibid.*, 1074*b*, 1075*a.*   [50] Ross, *Aristotle,* p. 183.

relation to the world has little in common with the God whom men worship and from whom they seek help.

THE SOUL

In his treatise *On the Soul,* Aristotle analyzes the nature and functions of the soul as he had analyzed in the *Physics* natural things in general and their causes. On the one hand, he opposes the view of the materialists that the soul is body and agrees with Plato that the soul is the principle of life in the body. On the other hand, he rejects the dualism of Plato's *Phaedo* and asserts that the soul is intimately related to the body as its form, the actuality of which its body is the potentiality. Man is a composite substance, the body being matter to the soul while the soul is *form* and *actuality* to the body. Thus, the soul is "the first actuality of a natural body endowed with the capacity of life." [51] Perhaps the most distinctive thing about this conception of the soul is that, while it avoids the reduction of the soul to the body and subordinates the body as matter to the soul as form and end, it also affirms the union of the body and the soul in one composite substance. They are inseparable from each other, although there may be parts which are separable "if they are not the actualities of any body whatever." [52] Aristotle's subsequent assertion that there is one such part we shall consider later.

The rejection of Platonic dualism is partly a result of Aristotle's scientific attitude toward the soul, reflecting the influence of his biological studies. It expresses his appreciation of the value of the body, and his recognition of the dependence of the soul upon the body for the exercise of its faculties.[53] Also, it is due to his "naturalistic," as contrasted with Plato's "idealistic," attitude. He had little of Plato's religious concern for the "tendance" of the soul as a spiritual being with an affinity for the supersensible world of the Forms and the gods. For him, the soul no less than the body belongs to the world of nature, and consequently it feels no sense of alienation from the body and the sensible world of time and change. Obviously, the danger of a "naturalistic" view like this is that it may lead to a denial of the uniqueness of the soul and its powers and end by embracing the reductionistic view that the soul is only a function of the body.

However, Aristotle is saved from a reductionistic view by his recognition that there are different *functions* or *powers* of the soul and that the highest of them is in its essence independent of the body. Corresponding to the different levels of living beings in the scale of nature

---

[51] Aristotle, *On the Soul,* Bk. II, Chap. 1.   [52] *Ibid.*
[53] Copleston, *History of Philosophy,* Vol. I, p. 329.

are different types of soul, and these form a series in which the higher presupposes the lower. The lowest type is the vegetative or nutritive soul, *to threptikon,* which exercises the functions of assimilation and reproduction.[54] Although these functions are found in all living beings, they exist alone in plants. The souls of animals are called sensitive and appetitive, *to aisthētikon* and *to orektikon,* because they exercise the functions of sense perception and desire which are related to the power of movement possessed by animals.[55] Imagination, *phantasia,* is the faculty by which images are presented and is dependent upon sensation although not identical with it.[56] Both of these types of soul and the functions exercised by them are inseparable from the body and hence perishable. But above them is the human soul, which includes in itself the functions of the types of soul below it but, in addition, possesses intellect, *nous.*[57] This part of the soul is receptive to all forms and hence has no form of its own but is simply a capacity or potentiality for forms, a "place of forms." [58] Hence, it is not mixed with the body. If it were, it would have some particular quality or organ, but it has none.[59]

Aristotle distinguishes between the passive intellect, *nous pathētikos,* and the active intellect, *nous poiētikos,* although he does not use the latter term himself. The *passive intellect* seems to be the receptive aspect of the intellect, upon which forms may be imprinted, while active intellect abstracts forms from images that are received by the passive intellect.[60] The *active intellect,* unlike the other parts or aspects of the soul, is separable from the body and eternal. "The active reason," says Aristotle, "is separable and impassible and unmixed, being an actuality. For the active is always of higher worth than the passive and the originative source than the matter." [61] In this passage, "separable," *chōristos,* means that the active reason is now united with the passive but can be separated from it and can survive death. The meaning of "unmixed," *amigēs,* is that it is wholly independent of the body.[62] "When it has been separated," Aristotle adds, "it is that only which it is essentially, and this alone is immortal and eternal (we do not remember, however, because this is impassible but the passive reason is perishable); and without this nothing knows." [63] Clearly this means that memory does not survive death, because the passive reason

---

[54] Aristotle, *On the Soul,* Bk. II, Chap. 2.   [55] *Ibid.*
[56] *Ibid.,* Bk. III, Chap. 3.   [57] *Ibid.,* Chap. 4.   [58] *Ibid.*   [59] *Ibid.*
[60] Copleston, *History of Philosophy,* Vol. I, p. 329.
[61] Aristotle, *On the Soul,* Bk. III, Chap. 5; cf. Ross, *Aristotle,* pp. 150–151.
[62] Ross, *op. cit.,* p. 151.
[63] Aristotle, *On the Soul,* Bk. III, Chap. 5; cf. Ross, *op. cit.,* p. 151.

upon which the circumstances of life have been impressed perishes at the death of the individual, but that the active intellect exists in its purity, or "essentially," when its association with the body is over.

However, there has never been agreement among the interpreters of Aristotle as to the identity of the active intellect. Some of them have identified it with God and have held that God in the soul illuminates that which is potentially known, as the sun's light makes objects actually seen. The argument for this view is that the active intellect is stated to be separate from matter and therefore must be the pure immaterial form, God.[64] Ross points out that there are two difficulties with this interpretation. One is that Aristotle in *On the Soul* speaks of the active intellect as existing in the human soul and that the term "separate" probably refers to the state of the active intellect only after death.[65] The other is that it is hard to reconcile the view that God is immanent in the active intellect of man with the description of Him in the *Metaphysics* as completely transcendent and as knowing only Himself.[66] Ross's own conclusion is that although the *Metaphysics* and *On the Soul* could reflect different views of Aristotle concerning God, it is more likely that the active intellect is not God, but the highest faculty of the human soul.

Copleston seems to agree with this interpretation but raises the further question whether the active intellect is regarded by Aristotle as *individual* in each man or as a principle which is *identical in all* men. If the latter, the active intellect enters into the individual man, functions in him during his life, and survives his death, while the soul of the individual perishes with his body. The argument for this view is Aristotle's statement that memory and loving and hating perish at death, since this seems to imply that the active intellect in its separate existence has no memory and hence cannot be individual. However, it does not necessarily prove that the active intellect is not individual in the state of separation; it proves only that it is not accompanied in that state by functions such as memory which accompanied it during life. And it is difficult to see how Aristotle could have thought that the active intellect of one man is numerically the same as that of another.[67]

It is probable, therefore, that Aristotle meant that the active intellect belongs to the individual human soul as its highest faculty and survives death because it is not dependent upon the body for its activity. However, his view is far from that of Christians and other

[64] Ross, *Aristotle*, p. 152.   [65] *Ibid.*, p. 153.   [66] *Ibid.*
[67] Copleston, *History of Philosophy*, Vol. I, p. 331.

theists who affirm *personal* immortality, since it is only one function of the soul, the active intellect, that survives death, while memory and love, which are essential to the life of the soul as we know it, perish with the body.

THE GOOD

When we consider Aristotle's conception of the Good, we are confronted with two different although related questions: the *metaphysical* question concerning the *status of good* or value in reality and the *ethical* question concerning the *highest good* of man. With respect to the first question, Whitney Oates has made a thorough study of all of Aristotle's writings. He points out that Plato's theory of Ideas enabled him to conceive of Being and Value as inseparable [68] and to avoid subordinating Value to Being. For the Ideas are not only forms of Being but also norms or standards of Value, and "the Idea of the Good is the most real and most valuable entity in the realm of Being." [69] Also Plato developed a teleological explanation of value in the world by picturing the divine Craftsman in the *Timaeus* as imposing Ideas upon disorderly movements in the Receptacle for the purpose of realizing good. Thus both his idealistic affirmation of the primacy of the Good and his theistic belief that the divine Mind realizes good in the world led him to claim a high status for Value in reality. In contrast, when Aristotle rejected the theory of Ideas and offered a deistic conception of the Unmoved Mover as unconcerned with the world, he developed a metaphysics in which Being was considered as primary and Value became merely a secondary aspect of Being,[70] e.g., a "quality" of individual "substances." [71] As a result, the status of Value was reduced.

Oates shows clearly that even when Aristotle conceived of value objectively as the end or final cause of substance, he was unable to develop an adequate teleological explanation of it. One reason is that "Aristotle's teleology has two aspects, one a cosmic teleology where the absolute Final Cause (the Unmoved Mover) operates as End or Purpose and the other the final cause or purpose which operates for an individual particular" and that he could not "make these two aspects cohere with each other." [72] On the one hand, he asserts an "unconscious teleology" in his *Physics* which, as we have suggested, implies a final cause immanent in a thing although it is not the purpose of any mind. On the other hand, his deistic view of the Unmoved Mover as being wholly self-sufficient and unconcerned with the world makes it impos-

[68] Whitney Oates, *Aristotle and the Problem of Value* (Princeton, N.J.: Princeton University Press, 1963), p. 49.
[69] *Ibid.*   [70] *Ibid.*, p. 56.   [71] *Ibid.*, pp. 188–196.   [72] *Ibid.*, p. 218.

sible for him to explain the final causes in things by reference to a divine purpose to realize good. With a doctrine of "creation" such as that of Plato in the *Timaeus*, it can be maintained that God has brought value into the world by His creative activity.[73] But, the realization of values through the attainment of final causes by individual substances is not effectively related by Aristotle to the Unmoved Mover as the Final Cause. Moreover, although Aristotle conceives of the Unmoved Mover as good and therefore as worthy to be the Final Cause of all change, his argument for doing so is very weak. It will be remembered that his argument for the existence of the Unmoved Mover is based exclusively upon the necessity of explaining change in nature, and it takes no account of the values realized through change. Having established the existence of such a Mover, he arbitrarily ascribed goodness to it in order to explain how it can move without being moved.

Thus, Aristotle reduces the metaphysical status of Value by subordinating it to Being, fails to relate the one Final Cause to the many final causes in the world, and does not really establish the goodness of the Unmoved Mover who is the one Final Cause. However, there is one passage in the *Metaphysics* which might seem to challenge this conclusion. It raises the question whether the universe contains the good or the best "as something separate and by itself," or "as the order of the parts," or, "in both ways, as an army does." "For the good [of an army] is found both in the order and in the leader, but more in the latter; for he does not depend on the order but it depends on him." [74] His answer is that the universe contains the good in both ways. Clearly this does not mean that the order and goodness in the universe arises from a "separate" principle of Good such as Plato's Idea of the Good, since Aristotle denies the existence of such a principle.[75] It must mean, then, that the good in the universe depends upon the Unmoved Mover which exists "separate by itself." But unless Aristotle in this passage is completely inconsistent with what he has said about the Unmoved Mover's lack of concern for the world, he cannot mean in any literal sense that the world "depends" upon the Unmoved Mover as an army depends upon its general for its order and good. For a general is the source of order and good in an army not as a self-sufficient and unconcerned being who is merely an object of desire, but as a leader who directs his army and actively seeks to realize a purpose in and through it. In contrast, the Unmoved Mover is the source of the good in the

[73] *Ibid.*, p. 252.   [74] Aristotle, *Metaphysics*, Bk. XII, Chap. 10, 1075a.
[75] Oates, *Aristotle and the Problem of Value*, p. 255; cf. Aristotle, *Nicomachean Ethics*, Bk. I.

world only in the sense that natural beings are moved by a desire for
it in some way that Aristotle does not explain. We must agree with
Oates, therefore, that the image of the general and the army perhaps
"expresses in some degree the way in which Aristotle would have liked
to articulate his theology, but which he was unable to accomplish" [76]
because he has separated Value from Being in his metaphysics. Or the
passage is an example of the influence of Plato's Theism upon Aristotle before he developed his own deistic view of the Unmoved Mover
and his relation to the world.

What, now, is Aristotle's view of the *highest good* of man? It is
expressed in his argument in Book X of the *Nicomachean Ethics* that
the highest happiness or well-being of man consists in *intellectual contemplation*. This argument presupposes Aristotle's distinction in the
Ethics between moral and intellectual virtues or excellences. Among
the intellectual virtues the highest are those of the theoretical or speculative faculty which contemplates objects that are necessary rather
than those that are contingent. Wisdom, *sophia*, unites the intuition of
first principles and the demonstration of conclusions, and is directed
toward the highest objects.[77]

Aristotle argues in the *Nicomachean Ethics* that the activity which
constitutes perfect happiness is theoretical contemplation. Some of the
reasons he offers are both interesting and illuminating. The most fundamental is that reason is the highest faculty of man and theoretical
contemplation is the highest activity of reason. Again, pleasure is an
element in happiness and philosophy is the most pleasant of human
activities since its pleasures are "pure and reliable." Moreover, the
philosopher is more self-sufficient than other men because he can think
in solitude and is less dependent on the assistance of other men. Also,
philosophy is loved for its own sake, whereas practical activity aims at
a desirable end beyond itself.[78] Finally, a life of intellectual contemplation expresses the divine element in man. Although some men counsel that we should concern ourselves with things that are human and
mortal, we should try to live at the level of the highest element in us.
Intellect is above the other elements in worth, and rules over the
others. Indeed, it is the real self in each of us, and we should live the
life suitable to our true selves rather than to something other than
ourselves.[79]

Perhaps it is in this description of intellectual contemplation as the
perfect happiness that Aristotle comes closest to expressing a religious
conception of life. Like Plato, he seems to recognize something divine

[76] Oates, *op. cit.*, p. 257.
[77] Aristotle, *Nicomachean Ethics*, Bk. VI, Chap. 7, 1141a.
[78] *Ibid.*, Bk. X, Chap. 7.   [79] *Ibid.*

in the intellectual element of the soul and urges men to exercise it and seek their happiness in it. But it is significant that he sets forth an exclusively intellectual ideal of the highest good. There is nothing corresponding to Plato's doctrine of spiritual love or aspiration, *erōs*, for beauty in the *Symposium* and the *Phaedrus*, or his view in the *Republic* that education should culminate in a vision of the Form of the Good. There is also no indication that theoretical contemplation should include the worship and contemplation of God, although Ross reminds us that, since Aristotle's *Metaphysics* culminates in theology, he may have meant to include the contemplation of the divine nature.[80] Finally, whereas Plato always links wisdom with moral virtue and political responsibility, Aristotle tends to exalt intellectual contemplation above moral and political activity. As Ross says, the moral life "constitutes a secondary form of happiness" and "helps to bring into being the higher kind," [81] but it is clear that the highest good and perfect happiness are to be found in intellectual activity alone. In short, Aristotle's ideal of the highest good for man corresponds to his conception of the Prime Mover as eternally engaged in the activity of thinking. The difference between them is that, while man contemplates the necessary objects of metaphysics, mathematics, and physics, the Prime Mover contemplates only himself.

PLATO AND ARISTOTLE

In our critical comments on Aristotle's conception of the Prime Mover, the teleology immanent in nature, the soul and its immortality, and the highest good of man, we have sought to show that he is inferior to Plato in religious feeling and insight. We may express this by saying that, as Plato is the father of ethical Theism, Aristotle is the father of Deism. We may summarize our major criticisms as follows:

1. His proof of the existence of God from the motion and change in the cosmos may or may not convince the reader that there is an eternal source of change in the world, an Unmoved Mover of some kind. But this is a metaphysical first principle and has little or nothing to do with the God of religious faith and worship. The Unmoved Mover is simply a first cause of nature which is arbitrarily endowed by Aristotle with certain attributes of God such as intellectual activity for which no evidence is offered. Its detachment and unconcern for the world bears out the judgment that it has little religious or ethical relevance.

2. Although the Prime Mover is asserted by Aristotle to be the Final Cause of all change, it is not said to be the source of the final causes which the *Physics* describes as operative in natural things. For

[80] Ross, *Aristotle*, p. 234.   [81] *Ibid.*, p. 233.

these are immanent in things and seem to point to no end beyond or
above the things themselves. Thus Aristotle nowhere shows a relationship between the *transcendent* Final Cause of the *Metaphysics* and the
immanent final causes of the *Physics*. Although he says in the *Metaphysics* that the Prime Mover is the Final Cause as an object of desire
or love, it is difficult to see how this can explain the movements of
natural things toward their ends, especially inanimate things and
plants which have no desires. And, even if this could be explained, it
would not change the fact that the Prime Mover is completely detached and indifferent to the things that move toward it as their good.

3. Aristotle's conception of the soul is somewhat more satisfactory
from both the philosophical and the religious points of view. The union
of the soul with the body to form one composite substance is in accord
with the facts of experience and with the description of man as a
psychophysiological unity found in the Bible. Also, the recognition that
there is an immaterial faculty in the soul and that it has the capacity
for a separate existence opens the door to a spiritual conception of the
soul and to the possibility of its immortality. Here the defect in Aristotle's view is a tendency, on the one hand, to emphasize the close
relation of the soul to the body with the consequent danger of
reductionism, and, on the other hand, to separate the active intellect
from the nonintellectual faculties such as memory and love and hence
to regard it alone as capable of immortality.

4. Closely connected with this intellectualist theory of the soul is
Aristotle's narrow view of man's highest good as theoretical contemplation alone. As we have seen, this eliminates or at least subordinates
moral conduct, love, and worship to intellectual activity and thus impoverishes the spiritual life.

We would conclude from these criticisms that Aristotle's main contribution to the philosophy of religion does not lie in his religious ideas
but in certain aspects of his general philosophical position. His criticism of Plato's Idealism and dualism between soul and body provides a
valuable corrective of the idealistic, otherworldly, and ascetic tendencies which have often been fostered by one side of Plato. His analysis
of nature gives worth and meaning to the natural order and presents a
teleological explanation of the world which, when grounded in the will
of God, can provide a religious interpretation of it. Finally, his analysis
of the soul is comprehensive in scope and penetrating in many of its
insights, however limited his view of the spiritual life.

These philosophical contributions of Aristotle were derived to a
considerable extent from Plato and it is a mistake to suppose that in his
mature works he completely abandoned Platonism for Naturalism. Ob-

viously, there are naturalistic elements in his later thought; [82] but he retained many of the insights of Plato, modifying them in accordance with his less religious and more worldly attitude. For this reason, it may be possible to synthesize the insights of Plato and Aristotle and at the same time to eliminate the defects of both, as Copleston suggests,[83] since the religious passion and insight of Plato are not incompatible with a full appreciation and realistic analysis of nature and man as they are.

[82] J. H. Randall, Jr., has ably emphasized these but has exaggerated them in his recent book, *Aristotle* (New York: Columbia University Press, 1960).

[83] Copleston, *History of Philosophy*, Vol. II, Chap. 34.

3 Neo-Platonism

PLOTINUS

"I am striving to give back the divine which is in me to the divine in the universe." [1] According to Porphyry, these words were spoken by Plotinus (205?–270) on his deathbed. Alongside them should be put other words reported by Porphyry to illustrate the fact that Plotinus "seemed ashamed of being in the body." He said to one who was urging him to allow a portrait of himself to be made, "Why, really, is it not enough to have to carry the image in which nature has encased us, without your requesting me to agree to leave behind me a longer-lasting image of the image, as if it was something genuinely worth looking at?" [2] Both sayings have a Platonic ring in them, insofar as they express a lofty conception of the nature and destiny of the soul and a conviction of the inferiority of the body to it.

Nevertheless, there are differences, and important ones. Plato would never have spoken of "giving back" the divine in him to the divine in the universe, as if it were to be absorbed back into its divine source; rather, he hoped for a life of the soul hereafter in company with but distinct from the gods. It is also doubtful whether he would have been "ashamed" of his body, although he insisted upon the necessity of controlling its appetites and subordinating its interests to the higher life of the soul. These differences illustrate the fact that the attitude of Plotinus toward God, the world, and the soul often diverges from that of Plato even when he uses words that show the influence of his master. While Plato has a mystical and otherworldly element in his religious philosophy, we have argued that it is subordinate to the rational and ethical elements. In contrast, mysticism and otherworldliness are at the heart of Plotinus' religious attitude, and

[1] "Porphyry On the Life of Plotinus," in *Plotinus: Enneads,* trans. Stephen MacKenna (London: Faber & Faber Ltd., 1956), Sec. 1, p. 1.

[2] "Porphyry's Life," in *Plotinus,* trans. A. H. Armstrong (London: George Allen and Unwin, 1953), Sec. 2, p. 48.

rational thought and moral activity are subordinate and instrumental to the mystical experience. It is essential, therefore, to distinguish carefully the Neo-Platonism of Plotinus from the philosophy of Plato himself. The fact is that Plotinus' philosophy, while deeply influenced by Plato, was eclectic and also owed much to Aristotle, the Stoics, the Middle Platonists, and others.

Whatever our final judgment about it may be, Plotinus' religious philosophy is worthy of careful study because it is a unique synthesis of mystical and rational elements and because of the religious passion expressed in it. Such a study is also important for an understanding of the development of Christian thought in the West. Neo-Platonism had a profound effect upon Augustine's Christian philosophy and considerable influence upon Thomas Aquinas' rational theology. Through the writings of the Christian Neo-Platonist, Pseudo-Dionysius, it entered into the stream of Christian mysticism and decisively affected the mysticism of Meister Eckhart and others. It has also been a powerful force in the modern period, helping to shape the thought of philosophers such as Schelling and stimulating the imagination of poets such as Spenser, Wordsworth, and Shelley.

THE ESTRANGEMENT OF THE SOUL

The point of departure for the philosophy of Plotinus is the tension between the suffering of the soul from the evils of existence and the pure satisfaction it experiences in certain states of contemplation. "This point of departure," says Bréhier, "is a feeling of uneasiness, the feeling that human life in its present state is a life arrested or weakened by obstacles due to the body and its passions. 'The human soul, placed in a body, is subject to evil and suffering. It lives in sorrow, desire, fear, and all forms of evil. The body is for the soul a prison and a tomb; the world, its cave or cavern!' (*Enneads* IV. 8.3) This continual feeling of dethronement is in painful conflict with the feeling that the real nature of the soul consists in being impassive and independent." [3] This tension between the actual existence of the soul and its true essence suggests that a foreign element has been added to it, as gold is covered with dirt. "It is like a man," says Plotinus, "who is plunged into the mire and no longer displays the beauty which he possessed but only the mud with which he is covered. His ugliness is due to the addition of a foreign element, and to become beautiful again it will be quite an undertaking for him to cleanse himself in order to become what he was." [4]

[3] Émile Bréhier, *The Philosophy of Plotinus* (Chicago: University of Chicago Press, 1958), p. 33.

[4] Plotinus, *Enneads*, I, 8.14; quoted by Bréhier, *op. cit.*, pp. 33–34.

Such a feeling of the estrangement of soul and of its defilement by the impure elements associated with it gave rise to a deep and widespread longing for deliverance and rebirth in the third century of the Christian era. Mystery religions such as Mithraism offered to many the promise of salvation through an ascent of the soul from the world in which it was imprisoned into a new life.[5] They developed mythical representations of the universe which pictured the ascent of the soul, after it has divested itself of impure elements, into a higher region and its enjoyment of a final union with the savior-god. In a similar manner, Plotinus conceives of the universe as divided into a lower region, "here," into which the soul has descended and in which it now lives, and a higher region, "There," to which it can ascend once more. However, he was not an adherent of any mystery religion, for he did not believe that the soul's ascent to the higher world to which it belongs could be effected by a divine redeemer. Rather, he sought to develop a philosophy in the tradition of Greek thought which would provide not only a world view but also an answer to the religious need of the soul for deliverance from evil and for fulfillment of its spiritual destiny.

THE PROCESSION FROM THE ONE

According to Plotinus, the ultimate Cause of the universe is "the One," *to hen,* or "the Good," *to agathon,* which is beyond being and thought. He seems to have been led to this conclusion, on the one hand, by the philosophical search for a unity capable of explaining the many things and values of the world, and, on the other hand, by the religious need for an eternal, unchanging, and perfect object of worship. In his philosophical quest for a principle of *unity,* he had to look above the world of matter in space and time, for every body is divided into many parts and is separated from other bodies. He discovered a principle of unity in the soul, since the soul is an organizing force in a living organism and enables its many parts to function as a whole. But the soul cannot be the ultimate source of unity, he thought, because it is not a perfect unity itself and there are many souls associated with bodies which are separated from one another. At a higher level he recognized in mind or intellect a more adequate principle of unity than soul, for in pure, intuitive contemplation it seems to be united with its objects. But it, too, is imperfect in its unity, since it has many objects and is distinguished as a subject from all of them. Therefore, "the One" which is the source of the many things in our world must be above and beyond matter, soul, and mind. It must be a transcendent principle which is completely undifferentiated in its unity. Moreover, if it is to

[5] Bréhier, *op. cit.,* pp. 34–35.

explain the many relative and imperfect values of the world as we experience it, it must be "the Good." In short, it must be both the absolutely One and the absolutely Good. As we shall see later, the religious need for an adequate object, as Plotinus interpreted it, could also be satisfied with nothing less than this undifferentiated "One" and perfect "Good."

But how does the One and the Good give rise to the *many* things and values of the world in space and time? Plotinus' answer to this question is that, while the world has not been created, it proceeds eternally from the One in a series of stages or levels. The One produces "Intellect" or "Mind," *nous*, which consists of thought and the objects of thought in an indissoluble unity and constitutes the intelligible world or Being. "Intellect" or "Mind," gives rise to "Soul," *psyche*, which belongs to the spiritual world but also mediates between it and the material world. Finally, "Soul" produces the lowest level of the world, "Matter," *hyle*, particular souls descending from the universal Soul into bodies separated from one another in space and changing in time. This procession, *proodos*, from "the One" of the three "hypostases"—"Intellect," "Soul," and "Matter"—was obviously influenced by Plato. According to Porphyry, a pupil of Plotinus, the One or the Good was derived from the "Idea of the Good" in Plato's *Republic*, Intellect or Mind from the "Craftsman" in the *Timaeus*, and Soul from the "World-Soul" in the same dialogue. Thus, Plotinus' "Trinity," which consists of the One, Intellect, and Soul and which constitutes the spiritual world in contrast to the sensible world of Matter, is clearly Platonic in origin.

However, we can understand the procession from the One and the hierarchical view of the world expressed in it only if we interpret it in the light of its *psychological origin*. For it is based upon the insight of Plato that the nature of man is the key to an understanding of the nature of the world, since he is a microcosm containing in himself all the kinds and levels of being in the macrocosm. "Plotinus' system," says Armstrong, "is predominantly psychological. . . . He does not hold that man's mind has created the order of the universe which it observes. He does hold that man's mind and soul are part of a universal mind and soul which produce and vitalize the universe and that the structure of the universal ruling principle can be deduced from the study of the ruling principle in man." [6] In other words, the stages or levels of the world are conceived by Plotinus as analogous to aspects of the human self. We can almost say that the cosmos is human nature writ large.

[6] A. H. Armstrong, *The Architecture of the Intelligible Universe in the Philosophy of Plotinus* (Cambridge, Eng.: Cambridge University Press, 1940), p. 113.

But what is the *reason* for the procession of the many from the one?
Why does not the One remain in self-sufficiency? Plotinus' answer is
similar in principle to that of Plato in the *Timaeus*. "Now when anything else comes to perfection we see that it produces, and does not
endure to remain by itself, but makes something else. . . . How then
could the Most Perfect, the First Good, the Power of all things remain
in Itself as if It grudged Itself or was unable to produce?" [7] But Plotinus describes the procession by means of analogies which show how
far his view really is from that of Plato. One of his favorite images is
that of *radiation of light*. "Everything which is moved must have some
end to which it moves. The One has no such end, so we must not
consider that it moves. . . . So if there is a second after the One it
must have to come to be without the One moving at all, without any
inclination or act of will or any sort of activity on Its part. . . . It must
be a radiation from It while It remains unchanged though the light
springs from it continually." [8] Another image is that of *water flowing*
from an inexhaustible spring. "Imagine a spring without any origin. It
supplies all the rivers with water. Yet it is not exhausted for all that. It
remains calmly at the same level, and the rivers which issue from it first
interflow before taking each its own particular course." [9]

In these and other analogies Plotinus is seeking to describe the
procession of the many from the One as an emanation from an infinite
and perfect source of being and power. Like Aristotle's Unmoved
Mover, the One gives rise to motion in everything outside it but is
itself unmoved. In the procession which originates from it, each lower
stage derives its being and power from the stage above itself and
imparts something of its own being and power to the stage below
itself. Each stage is a weakened imitation of the stage above itself
because being and power become more divided and dispersed as they
depart farther from the originative source and center.[10] From this it is
clear that Plotinus' picture of the origin of the cosmos differs from both
the biblical myth of creation in Genesis and the myth of the formation
of the cosmos in the *Timaeus*. Although his description of the procession from the One might suggest that it has taken place as a creation in
time and has involved a succession of stages, it is really an eternal and
continuous process. Furthermore, since the procession occurs without
any movement or activity on the part of the One, the latter is pictured

---

[7] Plotinus, *Enneads*, Bk. V, 4.1. The translation used here and in most of the
quotations from the *Enneads* is that of A. H. Armstrong, in *Plotinus*, which is less
poetic but clearer than the translation of Stephen MacKenna. Whenever a translation other than Armstrong's is used, it is indicated in parentheses in the footnote.
[8] *Enneads*, Bk. V, 1.6.   [9] *Ibid.*, Bk. III, 8.10 (Bréhier).
[10] Bréhier, *The Philosophy of Plotinus*, pp. 49–50.

as completely unconcerned with and unaffected by it. The One generates not by a free act of will but by necessity. It pours forth being
and power from its own inexhaustible abundance. But there is no loss
to itself, because it does not disperse itself in that which it produces.
Thus the self-sufficiency of the One and its complete detachment from
everything outside and below itself is maintained.

Although the world is a *hierarchical order* containing different
levels of being and value, there is *continuity* between each lower level
and the level above it. For the process of emanation is "an outgoing in
which unfailingly each principle retains its own seat while its offshoot
takes another rank, a lower, though on the other hand every being is in
identity with its prior as long as it holds its contact." [11] Thus being at a
higher level does not itself go down to the level of that which emanates
from it, but the latter maintains continuity and contact with it by
turning back toward it. The lower draws its being and power from the
higher, while the higher is completely unaffected by the lower. For
example, when Intellect or Mind turns back in contemplation toward
the One, it actualizes itself and its objects and is filled with the power
by which it is enabled to produce Soul. "This, when it has come into
being, turns back upon the One and is filled, and so becomes Its
contemplator *Nous*. . . . Resembling the One thus, *Nous* produces in
the same way, pouring forth a multiple power. . . . This activity
springing from being is Soul, which comes into being while *Nous*
abides unchanged." [12]

THE ONE OR THE GOOD

The One, as the cause of all things, is everywhere. But since it is
other than all things and remains in its own "seat" beyond them, it is
nowhere. It is self-sufficient, and there is no good which it seeks to
acquire because it is itself "the Good" above every good. It is lord of
itself and free, although it is what it is by necessity and could not be
otherwise. As we have seen, it is beyond being and thought. Since it is
beyond and above Mind and Soul as well as Matter, no quality or
relation can be attributed to it. For any quality or relation predicated
of it would be incompatible with its simplicity or undifferentiated
unity. "Since the nature of the One produces all things," says Plotinus,
"It is none of them. It is not a thing or quality or quantity or intellect
or soul; It is not in motion or at rest, in place or in time, but exists in
Itself, a unique Form; or rather It is formless, existing before all form,
before motion, before rest; for these belong to being and make it

[11] Plotinus, *Enneads,* Bk. V, 2.2 (MacKenna).   [12] *Ibid.,* 2.1.

multiple." [13] Even when we speak of it as "Good," we do so "not as applying a predicate to Him, saying that the Good is an attribute of His, but as saying that the Good is He Himself." [14]

Thus it is impossible to make affirmative statements about the One. Since it is utterly transcendent, simple and perfect, anything we affirm of it would involve it in multiplicity or imply deficiency in it. "Thus the One is in truth beyond all statement: any affirmation is of a thing; but the all-transcending, resting above even the most august divine Mind, possesses alone of all true being, and it is not a thing among things; we can give it no name because that would imply predication." [15] This insistence that we can affirm nothing of the One but must limit ourselves to *negative statements* had a profound influence, as we shall see,[16] upon the Christian theology and mysticism of the Middle Ages.

Can we, then, not know the One in any way? Plotinus' answer is that, while we cannot *know* it, we can *possess* it, "We do not, it is true, grasp it by knowledge, but that does not mean that we are utterly void of it. . . . unable to state it, we may still possess it. Those divinely possessed and inspired have at least the knowledge that they hold some greater thing within them though they cannot tell what it is." [17] Moreover, although speech cannot express it, it can direct the soul toward it. As Plotinus says, "in our writing and telling we are but urging towards it: out of discussion we call to vision: to those desiring to see, we point the path; our teaching is of the road and the travelling; the seeing must be the very act of one that has made this choice." [18] The nature of this "path" and the "vision" to which it leads we shall consider later.

Plotinus does not consistently maintain his negative theology. There are a few passages in which he makes *affirmative statements* about the One, although he emphasizes that they must be made in such a way as not to deny its transcendence. "Its thinking of Itself is Itself, and exists by a kind of immediate self-consciousness, in everlasting rest and in a manner of thinking different from that of *Nous*." [19] Its *thinking* is intuitive, directed solely to itself, and identical with itself so that its simplicity is not affected. Again, the One is *love*, although it loves only itself. "He is at once Lovable, and Love and Love of Himself, since He is only beautiful from Himself and in Himself." [20] Finally, we can say that the One *wills* and causes itself. "So He is not 'as he happened to be,' but as He Himself wills. . . . His being then is self-caused, self-originated. He is not 'as He happened to be' but as He wills." [21] Thus

[13] *Ibid.*, Bk. VI, 9.3.   [14] *Ibid.*, 7.38.   [15] *Ibid.*, Bk. V, 3.13 (MacKenna).
[16] Cf. Thomas, Chaps. 5, 6.   [17] *Enneads*, Bk. V, 3.14 (MacKenna).
[18] *Ibid.*, Bk. VI, 9.4 (MacKenna).   [19] *Ibid.*, Bk. V, 4.2.
[20] *Ibid.*, Bk. VI, 8.15.   [21] *Ibid.*, Bk. VI, 8.16.

Plotinus ascribes intuition, love, and will to the One, although they are to be predicated of it only in an eminent sense. It is important not to overlook this positive element in Plotinus' doctrine of the One. While he emphasizes the transcendence of the One and consequently regards all affirmations about it as inadequate, he views Mind as an imitation of it and as in a sense continuous with it. It is natural, therefore, that he should regard a self-directed intuition, will, and love as belonging to it, since his religious passion required the attribution of at least a minimum of positive activity to it as a reality worthy to be the object of worship.

We have seen that, although the One is completely self-sufficient and unaffected by the beings which emanate from it, they look back toward it as the *center* of their existence. Like Aristotle's Unmoved Mover, everything in the world is oriented toward it. There is an eloquent passage that illustrates this. "The Supreme has no desire towards us that It should centre about us; but towards It we have desire, so that we centre about It; but we do not always look. Thus a choir while singing might turn its attention away from the leader in the centre; let it face aright and it sings with beauty, present effectively. We are ever before the Supreme—cut off is utter dissolution; we can no longer be—but we do not always attend; when we do look our Term [End] is attained; this is rest; this is the end of singing ill; effectively before their leader, the singers lift a choral song that is full of God." [22] This passage expresses clearly and vividly the dependence of all finite beings, especially human souls, upon the One and the Good not only for their existence but also for the attainment of their true destiny. It is the reason for the upward movement of finite beings by which they seek to return to the One. When this movement is completed by a finite being, it participates in its ultimate Source, the One and the Good. It sings its part, however lowly, in the choral song under the divine Leader.

MIND AND SOUL

We must now consider briefly the nature of each of the stages or levels of being which emanate from the One. The first and highest stage, as we have seen, is Intellect or Mind, *nous*. The One radiates or generates Mind as a potentiality, and, as this turns back to the One in contemplation, it becomes the totality of Being in the Platonic sense of the intelligible world. It is both thought and the objects of thought, the Ideas, in indissoluble union. Unlike human thought, it does not have to

[22] Plotinus, *Enneads*, Bk. VI, ix. 8–9; quoted from G. H. Turnbull, *The Essence of Plotinus* (New York: Oxford University Press, 1934), pp. 218–219.

discover its objects or move from one to another of them by discursive reasoning; it contemplates them in intuition. Plotinus is eloquent in his description of the divine Mind in "heaven" or "There." In mythical language reminiscent of Plato's *Phaedrus,* he pictures the "gods" who "travel, always at rest, through all that higher region." "Truth," he says, "is their mother and nurse and being and food. They see all things, not those which come to be but those which really are [the Ideas] and they see themselves in them: for all things There are transparent, and there is nothing dark or opaque; everything is clear, altogether and to its inmost part, to everything, for light is transparent to light. Each There has everything in itself and sees all things in every other, for all are everywhere and each and every one is all, and the glory is un-bounded. . . . One particular kind of being stands out in each, but in each all are manifest." [23] In this passage, the "gods" symbolize Intellect or Mind; the objects they see, the things which "really are," are the Ideas or Forms of true Being; and the transparency and clarity with which they are seen describe the perfect intuitive knowledge of them by Mind. The result is a transformation of the Platonic intelligible world. It is conceived not as a realm of static Forms but as an organic living community of minds and Forms. Thus, Mind is able to represent by its unity in diversity the absolute unity and simplicity of the One.[24]

At the highest level of his soul, each person participates in this intelligible world of Mind. For there are Forms of individual persons as well as of universals in the intelligible world, so that the intellectual principle of each person which is the highest part of his soul belongs to the divine Mind. "Is there an Idea of each individual? Yes, if I and each one of us have a way of ascent and return to the intelligible, the principle of each of us is There. If Socrates and the soul of Socrates always exists, there will be an absolute Socrates, as we say, There, according to which his soul will have individuality There as well as here." [25] This is an expression of Plotinus' concern not merely for Man in the universal sense but for the soul of the individual man and is meant to ensure his status in the intelligible world.

Plotinus asserts that the whole universe "here" is modeled on the intelligible world "There," so that the heaven, the earth, and every living thing must be "There" first. Indeed, one of the considerations which seems to have led Plotinus to regard Mind as the first emanation from the One was the need to explain the forms of objects in the sensible world. "The Soul imparts to the four elements the form of the world, of which the Soul makes a gift to them. But, it is Intelligence

[23] *Enneads,* Bk. V, 8.3.   [24] Armstrong, *Plotinus,* p. 36.
[25] Plotinus, *Enneads,* Bk. V, 7.1.

which provides the Soul with the seminal reasons, just as art provides the soul of the artist with rational rules of action. Intelligence, in so far as it is form, is both the form of the Soul and that which bestows form." [26] Thus, the order of the sensible world is due to forms which have their source in Mind or the intelligible world, although Mind remains by itself and it is Soul which imposes them upon things.

This brings us to the third member of Plotinus' Trinity, universal Soul, *psyche*. As in Plato, Soul is intermediate between the intelligible world of Mind and the sensible world of Matter. But it might be more accurate to say that in different aspects it belongs to both worlds. Since it emanates from Mind and turns back to it in contemplation, it is closely related to Mind and in its higher aspect belongs to the intelligible world. But it is also active in its lower aspect in animating, forming, and ruling the material world, so that it is the source of life, order, and beauty in the visible cosmos. "The Soul," says Dean Inge, "is the centre of the Plotinian system, having affinities with every grade in the hierarchy. The human soul is a wanderer among the worlds; it may unite itself to the sphere above, and become spirit, or it may remain entangled in an environment which is below itself and beneath its true dignity." [27] The reason for this ambivalent status of the soul is that, while the universal Soul affects the world from above without being involved in it, particular souls are associated with bodies in the material world and are therefore entangled in the evils of separate and divided existence.

How does Plotinus explain this strange fact that Soul faces not only *upward* but also *downward*? His answer is not altogether consistent. Sometimes he speaks of particular souls as entering into bodies by a *necessity of nature*, although in accord with their own choice. "The inescapable rule of right (which governs their descent) is thus set in a natural principle which compels each to go in its proper order to that to which it individually tends. . . . For the universal bears heavily upon the particular, and the law does not derive from outside the strength for its accomplishment, but it is given in those who are to be subject to it, and they bear it about with them." [28] This point of view is based upon Plotinus' conception of the soul as the organizing force of bodies. Every natural being has a creative power because it has a soul mixed with its matter, and since the soul has contemplated Mind it contains in itself the order which it imposes on the matter. For this

[26] *Ibid.*, Bk. V, 9.3 (Bréhier).

[27] W. R. Inge, *Mysticism in Religion* (Chicago: University of Chicago Press, 1948), p. 116.

[28] Plotinus, *Enneads*, Bk. IV, 3.12–13.

reason, Plotinus distinguishes between a "higher soul," which remains above and participates in Mind, and a "lower soul," which leaves behind the higher soul and projects itself into particular bodies of the material world. From this point of view, the entry of particular souls into the bodies they are to animate and organize is natural and good. It is the necessary condition of the existence of the sensible world as a copy or imitation of the intelligible world.

In contrast, Plotinus sometimes speaks of a descent or *fall* of souls into matter. "The souls of men," he says, "see their images as if in the mirror of Dionysius, and come down to that level with a leap from above." [29] This fall of the souls is a source of evil to them. "But this communion with body is an evil, and its deliverance from body a good. Why? Because even if it does not belong to a particular body, when it is described as the soul of a particular body it has in some way become partial instead of universal. Its activity, though it still belongs to the whole, is no longer directed to the whole." [30] Thus, there is a tension in Plotinus' thought between two different conceptions of the soul's relation to the world. It is also important to note that the individual human soul seems to contain both the higher and the lower souls (or aspects of Soul) in itself. It is distinguished from the higher or universal Soul by its association with and involvement in a particular body, but it always remains in contact with the universal Soul and hence the intelligible world, even when it is unaware of the fact, and it can ascend to its Source if it realizes its true nature and raises its gaze from "here" to "There."

MATTER AND THE MATERIAL WORLD

"Matter," *hyle*, is the lowest stage or level produced by the process of emanation. It is conceived in Aristotelian fashion as the substratum which receives forms and endures through all changes. Since it is completely indeterminate, it can confer no qualities upon things. "The forms manifested in nature are those already contained in the Intellect that is before it, which acquires them by turning towards the Good. All differences of form, down to those of the elements, are the product of Reason and not of Matter." [31] Thus Plotinus excludes all positive reality from matter and ascribes all qualities to an action from above. Even qualities of bodies such as warmth or coldness do not depend upon matter but upon incorporeal powers, and material forces can cause nothing in the human mind or soul.[32] "Hence the things that

[29] *Ibid.*, 3.12.   [30] *Ibid.*, Bk. VI, 4.16.
    [31] T. Whittaker, *The Neo-Platonists* (Cambridge, Eng.: Cambridge University Press, 1918), p. 70.
        [32] Bréhier, *The Philosophy of Plotinus*, pp. 176–177.

seem to come into being in it (matter)," says Plotinus, "are frivolities, nothing but phantoms in a phantom, like something in a mirror which really exists in one place but is reflected in another. It seems to be filled but holds nothing; it is all seeming." [33]

Although matter is reduced to a mere shadow with no character or power of its own, it is the primary *cause of evil* in the soul. This does not imply that it is a positive principle of evil opposed to good in the Manichaean sense. Rather, it is the cause of evil because it is absolute formlessness as opposed to form, nonbeing as opposed to being.[34] It exists of necessity, since the process of emanation from the One and the Good must have a limit and this is matter which has no good in it. "Since not only the Good exists, there must be an ultimate limit to the process of going out past it, or, if one prefers to put it like this, going down or going away: and this last, after which nothing else can come into being, is the Bad." [35]

This raises a fundamental question with respect to Plotinus' philosophy: What is the status of the *material world,* the world as perceived by the senses? The answer to this question is not a simple one. In the first place, Plotinus rejects Materialism, which was well known to him in its Stoic and Epicurean forms. Against it he argues that the soul is not corporeal and that life cannot be produced by lifeless atoms or the intellect by things without understanding. The body cannot feel or think like the soul; the soul is not extended like the body; and ideas such as justice cannot be expressed in terms of extension. In the second place, Plotinus embraces a form of *Idealism* which is closer to Platonism than to modern Idealism. When we apprehend the world not through the senses or discursive thought but through intellectual intuition, the highest faculty we possess, we come into contact with reality. The phenomenal or material world of the senses is not unreal, but it possesses only an inferior kind of reality. As an actual but imperfect copy of the real or intelligible world of Mind and its Ideas, it has a kind of half-reality as "a reflection of the spiritual world in the mirror of Matter." [36] In contrast to the unity, interpenetration, harmony, eternity, and immutability of the spiritual or intelligible world, it is characterized by diversity, separation, discord, time, and change.[37] Since Matter cannot receive forms without dividing and separating them, material things must be extended in space and external to each other. Although this is a necessary condition of the material world, it

[33] Plotinus, *Enneads,* Bk. III, 6.7.   [34] *Ibid.,* Bk. I, 8.3.   [35] *Ibid.,* 8.7.
[36] W. R. Inge, *The Philosophy of Plotinus* (London: Longmans, Green, 1918), Vol. I, p. 152.
[37] *Ibid.*

makes impossible a mutual inclusion of beings like that of the spiritual world. Thus, space is the lowest level of the scale of being, "after everything else." [38]

Plotinus, then, rejects Materialism and opposes to it Idealism of the Platonic type, which regards the sensible world as possessing only an inferior reality as an imperfect copy of the intelligible world. But this does not mean that he defends a sharp dualism which sets the two worlds over against one another. Without question there is a dualistic element in his thought, as in his frequent contrast between "here" and "There" as if they were two different regions. For there is a line dividing Mind and Soul, which possess true Being or Reality, from the things of the material world, which do not possess it. However, the material world is a product of Soul, and although it is only an imperfect copy of the intelligible world, it offers us a vision of the eternal realities. If we include in the material world not only Matter but also the Soul that animates and organizes it, Plotinus affirms that "all is here that is there." [39] This is why it is possible, as we shall see, for the soul to find in the material world traces of the spiritual world and to use them as a starting point for its ascent to its true home.

Since the element of dualism in Plotinus is secondary to his idealistic view of the world, he attacks vigorously the Gnostics' conception of the world as evil, the product of a fall of the universal Soul. Of course, the material world is only an image of the spiritual world and there is much in it that is imperfect. "But could there," he asks, "be a more beautiful image? Could there be a better fire than ours, after the fire yonder? Could one conceive a better earth than this, after the earth yonder? Could there be a more perfect sphere, better ordered in its movements, after the revolution of the spiritual world?" [40] "But perhaps they (the Gnostics) will maintain that their teaching makes men escape right away from the body in their hatred of it, but ours holds the soul down to it. This is like two people living in the same fine house, one of whom criticizes the building and the architect but stays there all the same; the other does not criticize, but says the architect has built it with the utmost skill, and waits for the time to come when he will go away and not need a house any longer." [41]

It is in this spirit that Plotinus deals with the problem of *evil*. From Mind a rational law proceeds which imposes harmony on the cosmos. However, there cannot be a world below the intelligible world without a separation of its parts. Evil is a deficiency of good, and the presence

[38] Plotinus, *Enneads*, Bk. VI, 8.11 (Inge).

[39] *Ibid.*, Bk. V, 9.13 (MacKenna).

[40] *Ibid.*, Bk. II, 9.4 (Inge).   [41] *Ibid.*, 9.18.

of good in one place involves its absence in another because of their separation from each other. Natural evils such as poverty and disease, as the Stoics say, are nothing to a man of virtue, and they have a use in the order of the whole. It is true that the rule of bad men over cities and of masters over slaves is not fitting. But we must look only for the greatest perfection which is possible in a world below the intelligible world. Apart from the fact that justice is meted out not in the present life by itself but in the series of past and future lives, we cannot expect to attain happiness without adopting the proper means. For example, if men are satisfied to be fatted sheep, cowardly and unmanly, they should expect to become a prey to wolves. Moreover, war among animals and men is not wholly evil. In a world of change, animals would perish anyway if they were not destroyed by one another; and the death of men in battle is not terrible, for it is what happens to the soul not the body that counts. Even the wickedness of men has its place in the order of things, for the essence of the rational law of the world is that contraries should strive with one another, and in the world's drama the bad as well as the good must play the parts assigned to them. Thus, if we look at the world as a whole and not merely at its parts alone, it is a rational order out of which good can come. Moreover, it could not exist without matter and, as we have seen, evil necessarily results from matter. For the fall of the soul is due to its contact with matter, which does not allow it to realize all its powers. Yet without this there would be no striving after good or turning away from evil, which is a good.[42]

THE ASCENT OF THE SOUL

We have seen that the dualistic element in Plotinus is subordinated to his Idealism and that he regards the world as good on the whole despite the many evils in it. Nevertheless, there remains a tension in his thought between world-acceptance and world-rejection. Although the sensible world as a whole may be a beautiful and good image of the spiritual world, the soul of the *individual* becomes entangled in the desires of the body and alienated from its higher spiritual nature. As it surrenders to the passions of the body, it is imprisoned by it and sinks to its level. However, it has not lost contact completely with the higher Soul and the intelligible world of Mind. Therefore, it can free itself from its body and reunite itself with its Source. It can ascend from "here" to "There." How is this possible?

[42] For Plotinus' theodicy see *Enneads,* Bk. III, 2, 3; cf. T. Whittaker, *The Neo-Platonists,* pp. 77–81.

Plotinus replies that the soul must first turn away from the outer life of the senses and return to itself. "Let him who can follow and come within," he says, "and leave outside the sight of his eyes and not turn back to the bodily splendors which he saw before. When he sees the beauty in bodies he must not run after them; we must know that they are images, traces, shadows, and hurry back to That which they image. . . . Shut your eyes and change to and wake another way of seeing, which everyone has but few use." [43] Of course, a wise man will take care of his bodily health, but he must realize that his well-being is a condition of the soul and has nothing to do with the health of the body, with riches, or with rule over others. He will therefore neglect and gradually reduce these "bodily advantages" and will put away "authority and office." [44]

This is only the first stage which prepares the soul for its ascent. When it has subjected the body and renounced worldly things, the soul must begin the ascent from the sensible to the intelligible world of Mind. There are several ways by which it can rise to that level and thus return to its true self and its unity with Mind. One is the way of *dialectic*. The philosopher may be trained by mathematical studies to "accustom him to firm confidence in the existence of the immaterial," and then by dialectic he may attain knowledge of the structure of the intelligible world of Mind and unity with it in contemplation.[45] A second way is through *virtue*. Plotinus distinguishes between two kinds of virtues, "civic" and "purifying." The "civic" virtues "set us in order and make us better by giving limit and measure to our desires"; the "purifying" virtues produce in the soul "likeness to God" so that its activity may be intellectual and free from bodily affections.[46] Finally, there is the way of *beauty*. As Plato says in the *Symposium*, the soul may be led from love of beautiful bodies to love of beauty in the arts and sciences and virtues, and then "all these beauties must be reduced to unity, and he (the lover) must be shown their origin." [47]

By any or all of these ways the soul may return to its true self and attain to union with the intelligible world of Mind. But it must go higher still, because Mind participates in the One but is not the One itself. Therefore, when the soul has united itself with Mind, it is filled with eager longing for the One. It is unable to express that which it seeks in words or describe it by discursive thought which considers one thing after another, for the One is absolutely simple, beyond being and thought. But the soul can come into contact with it and know that it is present. It can "touch that Light and see It by Itself." [48] This can

[43] Plotinus, *Enneads*, Bk. I, 6.8.   [44] *Ibid.*, 4.14.   [45] *Ibid.*, 3.1–5.
[46] *Ibid.*, 2.2–3.   [47] *Ibid.*, 3.1–3.   [48] *Ibid.*, Bk. V, 3.17.

happen only if it will "take away everything," i.e., empty itself of all thoughts and desires for things other than the One.

"For no one who possesses anything else and is actively concerned with it," says Plotinus, "can see the Good or be conformed to Him. The soul must not keep by it good or evil or anything else, that it may alone receive Him, the Only one. . . . Then it sees Him suddenly appearing in itself (for there is nothing between, nor are they still two, but both are one; while He is present, you could not distinguish them; lovers and those they love here imitate this state in their longing to unite); it is not conscious of being in its body, any more, nor does it call itself anything else, man or living thing, or being, or all. . . . it seeks the Good and meets It when It is present and looks at It instead of itself; and it has no time to see who it is who looks. There it would not exchange anything in the world for This, not even if you gave it the mastery over the whole heaven, since there is nothing better, no greater good." [49] This is obviously a description of a mystical experience in which the One is present in the soul and there is nothing between it and the soul that experiences it. The union between them is so complete that the soul is not conscious of its body or even of itself. It knows that it has attained the highest good and is supremely happy. "As for all the other things in which it took delight before, position, power, wealth, beauty, knowledge, it despises them all and says so. . . . if everything else belonging to it is destroyed, it is with its full approval, so that it may be only with This; to so great happiness has it attained." [50]

There is a still more eloquent passage in which the mystical union with the One is described in unforgettable terms. "There were not two; beholder was one with beheld; it was not a vision compassed but a unity apprehended. The man formed by this mingling with the Supreme must—if he only remember—carry its image impressed upon him: he is become the Unity, nothing within or without inducing any diversity; no movement now, no passion, no outlooking desire, once this ascent is achieved; reasoning is in abeyance and all Intellection and even, to dare the word, the very self; caught away, filled with God, he has in perfect stillness attained isolation; all the being calmed, he turns neither to this side nor to that, not even inwards to himself; utterly resting he has become very rest. He belongs no longer to the order of the beautiful; he has risen beyond beauty; he has overpassed even the choir of the virtues; he is like one who, having penetrated the inner sanctuary, leaves the temple images behind him—though these become once more first objects of regard when he leaves the holies; for

[49] *Ibid.*, Bk. VI, 7.34–36.   [50] *Ibid.*

There his converse was not with image, not with trace, but with the very Truth in the view of which all the rest is but a secondary concern. . . . This is the life of gods and of the godlike and blessed among men, liberation from the alien that besets us here, a life taking no pleasure in the things of earth, the passing of solitary to solitary," [51] or, as the last phrase is often translated, "the flight of the alone to the Alone." In this striking passage as in the preceding one, all barriers between the soul and the One are transcended and the union between them is complete. The soul is in a state of absolute rest like the One itself, without desire, action, or passion. It has risen above the spiritual values of the intelligible world or Mind, for everything but the One had become a matter of secondary concern. Although it cannot sustain itself at this dizzy height and falls back to a lower level of existence, it can raise itself again through dialectic, virtue, and beauty to the level of Mind and beyond this hope for union with the One. Whenever that union occurs, the soul attains deliverance from the things of the world; it attains a godlike life.

PLOTINUS' MYSTICISM: A CRITIQUE

Plato had been content to assert the primacy of the Good among the Ideas and to picture the divine Mind (Craftsman) and World-Soul as factors in the order of the cosmos, but had not attempted to construct a metaphysical system. In contrast, Plotinus was driven by his philosophical interest in unity to develop a rational cosmology in which the world is a hierarchical system derived from the One or the Good in three distinct but related stages. In doing so, he elevated the One or the Good above the divine Mind and made it the highest reality and the object of religious worship. Thus, he denied Plato's theistic religion and substituted an abstract and impersonal principle for the concrete and quasi-personal divine Mind of the *Timaeus* who forms the world in accordance with the Ideas for the sake of good.

This was disastrous in its consequences for both Plotinus' cosmology and his religion. The main consequence for his *cosmology* was to make the First and Final Cause of the cosmos an *unknowable Reality* about which nothing can be said. As we pointed out, Plotinus supplemented his negations concerning the One with positive assertions about it as having a kind of transcendent intuition, will, and love of itself, but these assertions are not consistent with his strong insistence that the One is a simple and undifferentiated unity of which no quality can be predicated. It is obvious that the multiplicity and diversity of the world

[51] *Ibid.*, Bk. II, 9.11 (MacKenna).

cannot be explained by a simple and undifferentiated unity, and it is not surprising that Plotinus had to picture its origin from the One by means of metaphors like "radiation" and "outpouring," which are derived from impersonal natural processes and which give no reason for the existence of the world. Thus, his postulation of the One as a principle beyond Being and thought has little or no metaphysical value because it has no definite meaning.

The *religious* consequence of the elevation of the One above the divine Mind is also unacceptable. According to Plato, the highest although not the only religious object in the *Timaeus* is the divine Craftsman, who is clearly intelligent and good, and the gods, whose existence he proves in the *Laws,* care for men and exercise a kind of moral government over them. Therefore, despite his failure to attain a fully monotheistic and personal view of God, Plato laid the foundations for a theistic conception of religion centered in the imitation of intelligent and good divine beings in a life of wisdom and virtue. Instead of building on that foundation, Plotinus developed an essentially mystical and otherworldly religion centered in union with an impersonal and incomprehensible principle.

Moreover, the One is *unconcerned* with and unaffected by the many which emanate from it. It cannot be said to have any purpose in bringing Mind into existence. It is completely self-sufficient and detached in its transcendence of the world. Therefore, the ascent of the soul is exclusively a movement of its own, and there is no movement downward on the part of the One to meet it. Its movement is initiated and sustained wholly by its own longing or aspiration, *erōs,* and there is no love of God for it, *agapē,* to aid it in its ascent. As a result, Plotinus' One reminds us of Aristotle's Unmoved Mover who moves the world not by loving it but by being loved by it. The lower always looks up to the higher, while the higher never looks to the lower. It was this utter self-sufficiency of the One and its lack of concern for that which comes forth from it that seemed to St. Augustine the greatest weakness of Neo-Platonism, as we shall see. He did not find in Neo-Platonic writings, he said, the love of God for the world, the pity and care of God for the weak and erring.[52] Instead of following in the direction Plato had begun to take when he pictured the gods as having a care for men, Plotinus returned to Aristotle's conception of God as unmoved and unaffected by everything below Himself.

The result was a conception of religion which appeals to persons of a certain temperament but which is ultimately unsatisfactory. One reason for this is that Plotinus' religion is completely *individualistic.* Unlike

[52] Augustine, *Confessions,* Bk. VII, Chap. 9.

many great mystics, he was not a member of a religious community and apparently had no interest in public worship. According to Porphyry's *Life*, when one of his pupils began visiting the temples and feasts of the gods and asked Plotinus to come with him, he replied, "They ought to come to me, not I to them." [53] As an expression of the fact that God can be found within the soul, this saying is unexceptionable. But it seems also to indicate a complete indifference to the communal aspect of worship. In this connection, it is significant that he describes the experience of mystical union as a "flight of the alone to the Alone." The soul which attains the union is "alone": it has stripped off not only its interest in everything except the One but also all its relations with other persons and its concern for their good. Thus, the mystical union raises the individual soul out of the social as well as the natural world. The danger in this religious conception is that it tends toward what Inge calls "moral isolation." In a striking passage, Plotinus speaks of "vulgar and earthly persons" who cannot rise to the higher life of the spiritual world.[54] Unlike many mystics, he shows little pity for the world or sympathy for the weaknesses and sins of others. It is also significant that, although he regards the civic or political virtues as a necessary condition of order and measure, he shows little interest in political affairs and obviously regards the life of philosophic contemplation as superior to the practical life.[55] Inge points out that his motive for this was not merely freedom from the pleasures and cares of life but also invulnerability in the face of troubles from outside the self, a motive which was likewise very strong in Stoicism.[56] This desire for independence and superiority to external circumstance has a certain appeal, but it overlooks the dependence of men upon each other for their spiritual development and it emphasizes a kind of self-sufficiency which is inconsistent with their solidarity in joy and sorrow, weal and woe. Yet it was inevitable that Plotinus should seek union with the One "alone," since he conceived of the One itself as "Alone" in its self-sufficiency.

In addition to this religious individualism and moral isolation, Plotinus' conception of the mystical experience involved an *identification* of the individual with the One and a consequent loss of his consciousness of himself as a distinct being. As we shall see, this differs from the mysticism of later theistic mystics and is more akin to that of Oriental religion. The basis of it seems to be Plotinus' view that, while individuality has reality, it involves separation from others and from

---

[53] Porphyry, *Life of Plotinus*, Sec. 10, p. 49 (in A. H. Armstrong, *op. cit.*).
[54] Plotinus, *Enneads*, Bk. IV, 9.9 (Inge).
[55] W. R. Inge, *The Philosophy of Plotinus*, Vol. II, p. 164.   [56] *Ibid.*, p. 172.

the spiritual world which is its true home. Also, he presupposes that the soul of the individual has never lost its contact with the higher Soul of the world and is essentially divine. In a later chapter, we shall contrast this conception of the mystical union with that of theistic mystics. Here we shall only point out that it is incompatible with a realistic recognition of the finiteness and sin of man which separates him from God, as well as with the inescapable individuality which belongs to his existence as a finite being.

Our criticisms of Plotinus' conception of the One and of the mystical experience have been based upon the usual interpretation of the One as his God. However, some interpreters have denied this view. Dean Inge, for example, maintains that his religion centers in Mind or Spirit rather than in the One. "The Great Spirit [i.e., Mind], as the manifestation of the ineffable Godhead in all its attributes is the God of Neo-Platonism. This fact is obscured both by the completeness with which it is divested of all anthropomorphic attributes, and by the mystical craving for union with the Godhead itself [i.e., the One], which has been commonly supposed to be the starting point and goal of this philosophy. But it is only as Spirit that the Godhead is known to us as a factor in our lives. We have the power of rising above our psychic selves to share in the life of Spirit; and this communion, which may be the directing principle of our inner and outer life, is, except in rare moments of ecstasy, the highest degree of worship and spiritual joy which a human being can attain." [57]

There is some justification for this view of Plotinus, for he describes the life of Mind or Spirit in the most glowing terms [58] and says that the soul can turn its gaze toward Mind or Spirit and unite itself with it so that "there is nothing between." Also, it is true that the mystical experience seems to have been relatively rare with Plotinus—according to Porphyry, he enjoyed it four times during the years Porphyry knew him—while the ascent of the soul to the spiritual world of Mind by the ways of dialectic, virtue, and beauty is always possible for it. But mystical union with the One, however rare, is of central importance to Plotinus, and he explicitly speaks of the One as *beyond* Mind and of the longing of the soul which has risen to the level of Mind to go *further* into union with the One. From this we must conclude that Inge assimilates Plotinus' religion too closely to that of Plato, for whom the divine Mind and the Ideas of the spiritual world constitute the highest level of reality. However, Inge's interpretation is useful in calling attention to the fact that Plotinus is not only a mystic but also, like Plato, an idealist and that he regarded the attainment of union with Mind or

[57] *Ibid.*, pp. 82–83.   [58] Cf. *Enneads*, Bk. V, 1.4.

Spirit as of great importance. Indeed, the spiritual life of devotion to Truth, Beauty, and Goodness is second in importance for him only to the experience of mystical union and is an integral part of the religious life, since Mind emanates directly from the One and imitates it.

Sometimes Plotinus' conception of the *world* has been regarded as a form of Pantheism because it explains the many as products of emanation by necessity from the One and represents them as continuing to be oriented toward it as their center. Although there is an element of truth in this view, it cannot be sustained. While the many have emanated from the One and are dependent upon it, they are distinct from it and it is exalted above them in its transcendence. "It is quite true," says Copleston, "that for Plotinus the world proceeds from God *secundum necessitatem naturae* and that he rejects free creation *ex nihilo;* but it should also be remembered that for him the prior Principle remains 'in its own place,' undiminished and unimpaired, always transcending the subordinate being. . . . In other words, he tries to steer a middle course between theistic creation on the one hand and a fully pantheistic or monistic theory on the other hand." [59] On the other hand, Edward Caird interprets Plotinus as a dualist who carried to its logical conclusion the tendency toward dualism in Plato and other Greek philosophers.[60] But Caird exaggerates the dualistic element in Plotinus. There is an opposed tendency toward monism which balances it by a strong insistence upon the dependence of all the lower levels of reality upon the One and the imitation of the spiritual world "There" by the material world "here." Also, while Matter is the source of evil, it is not a positive principle opposed to the good principle, as in Gnostic dualism, but a privation. Thus, dualism does not have the last word.

Indeed, much of the appeal of Neo-Platonism to religious minds through the centuries has resulted from the fact that pantheistic and dualistic tendencies are both present in Plotinus' thought but in tension with one another, for each corresponds to a deep religious need. The pantheistic tendency arises from man's experience of the divine Reality as present in everything and therefore as near and accessible to him. In contrast, the dualistic tendency arises from the soul's experience of estrangement in the material world and its restlessness until it can return to its spiritual home. This estrangement might lead to pessimism and despair if it were not balanced by the pantheistic tendency which emphasizes the presence of God everywhere in His effects and thus

[59] Frederick Copleston, *History of Philosophy* (London: Burns, Oates, and Washbourne, 1956), Vol. I, p. 467.

[60] E. Caird, *The Evolution of Theology in the Greek Philosophers* (Glasgow: James MacLehose and Sons, 1904), Vol. II, pp. 315–316.

encourages the soul to hope for escape from its suffering and return to Him.

However, Plotinus does not always maintain the balance between the two opposed tendencies. Sometimes he seems to carry one of them to the extreme and almost to forget the other. Thus, the *pantheistic* tendency leads him to a *theodicy* which provides too easy a solution of the problem of evil, while the *dualistic* tendency results in a kind of *otherworldliness* which expresses itself in a disparagement of moral action in comparison with contemplation.

The *theodicy* of Plotinus was derived in part from the Stoics and was consistent with their pantheistic view of the World-Reason as immanent in all things and determining them for the best. Although Plotinus was not a pantheist himself, he held that the world is ordered in all of its parts by Soul in imitation of the spiritual world of Mind. It followed logically from this view that the world must be a good and harmonious system when regarded as a whole. At this point, his monistic tendency led Plotinus to a view radically different from that of Plato, for Plato did not minimize the reality of evil and insisted that the gods must not be made responsible for it. While Plotinus did not deny the existence of evil, he minimized it by asserting that it had no positive reality and that it was necessary to the good of the whole. But he was able to do so only by regarding the world in an aesthetic manner from the Olympian height of a detached spectator, to whom evil men as well as good men have their parts to play in the human drama. The difficulty with this aesthetic attitude is that it is impossible for one who is not a detached spectator but is an active participant in the conflict between good and evil. A participant must take an ethical attitude and regard moral evil not as a necessary discord in the cosmic harmony but as an enemy to the good. In contrast, Plotinus' solution of the problem of evil ignores the stubborn fact of its reality, blunts the edge of moral indignation, and weakens the sense of responsibility for opposing it.[61] If so, we must reject it despite the fact that it was accepted by as great a thinker as Augustine.[62]

On the other hand, the *otherworldly attitude* of Plotinus, which seems to contradict his optimistic view of the world as good, arises from the dualistic element in his thinking and produces a longing for escape from the evils of the world "here" into the peace and harmony which reign "There." As we shall see in a later chapter (Chap. 6), when mystical experience is complemented by a strong emphasis upon moral activity, it can be a source of spiritual power for life in the world.

[61] W. R. Inge, *The Philosophy of Plotinus*, Vol. II, p. 232.
[62] Augustine, *The Nature of the Good.*

Indeed, Bergson holds that it gives rise to an "open morality" of universal love which is world-transforming. But the religious individualism, moral isolation, and political indifference of Plotinus prevented his mysticism from having this effect. This is not surprising in view of his conception of the One as unconcerned with the world and of Mind as impersonal and without a moral purpose for man. But it helps to explain Bergson's meaning when he says that Plotinus' mysticism was not "complete." "It was granted to him to look upon the promised land, but not to set foot upon its soil. He went as far as ecstasy, a state in which the soul feels itself, or thinks it feels itself, in the presence of God, being irradiated with His light; he did not get beyond this last stage, he did not reach the point where, as contemplation is engulfed in action, the human will becomes one with the divine will. He thought he had reached the summit: in his eyes, to go further would have been to go downhill." [63] In refusing to "complete" his mystical contemplation by moral activity in obedience to the divine will, he turned away from the task of transforming the world "here" and sought refuge in the world "There," in a "flight of the alone to the Alone."

Despite this serious limitation from the perspective of ethical Theism, Plotinus' mysticism has had a deep influence upon religious imagination and feeling in the West. His view of the immanence of the divine in the soul helped to stimulate Christian thinkers like Augustine to seek for God by experience of His presence within rather than by inference from the world. His negative theology, as mediated to medieval theologians like Aquinas by the Pseudo-Dionysius, was used by them to avoid naïve anthropomorphic views and to express the transcendence of God. Above all, perhaps, the tension we have described between the pantheistic and dualistic elements in his view of God's relation to the world affected the attitude of men toward the relation of the sensible to the spiritual, the temporal to the eternal world. Eastern Orthodox theologians have always had the deep conviction, expressed in the liturgy of their Church, that the sensible world is a world of images, a visible expression of the invisible world. As Armstrong has pointed out, this "iconic" view of the world asserts that "things are neither valuable 'in themselves' nor valueless 'in themselves' but carry, simply by being what they are, a worth and significance which is given to them from something which is other, but not alien, which is their own proper perfection, and more, and which remains for ever when they pass away." [64] Although this view can lead to otherworldliness, as

[63] Henri Bergson, The Two Sources of Morality and Religion (New York: Holt, 1935), p. 210.

[64] A. H. Armstrong, "Platonism," in Prospect for Metaphysics, ed. Ian Ramsey (London: George Allen and Unwin, 1961), p. 107.

we have seen, it need not do so. For if the visible and temporal is an image of the invisible and eternal world, it participates in the values of that world and it cannot logically be regarded as an object of hate or contempt. "Platonists, of course," says Armstrong, "have a very vivid, and in my opinion realistic, sense of the troubles and frustrations of our human condition here below and are intensely aware of the precarious instability of things, the continual imminence of change and death. But because their other world is not far off in space or time, because the eternal and intelligible is present to them in its images here and now, their Platonic faith does, sometimes at least, greatly deepen their love for the fleeting goods and beauties they encounter, because they see in them the flash of an eternal excellence." [65] Doubtless it is because of this attitude to the world that Neo-Platonism has been a source of inspiration to so many English poets, such as Edmund Spenser, Henry Vaughan, and Shelley. As it has taught mystics to find God in the depths of the soul, it has stimulated the imagination of poets to see in the beauty of the world an imitation of a divine eternal Beauty.

[65] *Ibid.*, p. 109.

4 Christian Philosophy

AUGUSTINE

Augustine (354–430) tells us in his *Confessions* [1] that in his nineteenth year he was inflamed with an ardent desire for wisdom by the reading of the *Hortensius,* a lost treatise by Cicero. The pursuit of wisdom led him by devious and strange ways before it brought him to the conversion in Milan which started him on his course as a Christian philosopher and theologian. For some time he was a follower of the Manichaeans, who combined an Oriental dualistic cosmology of light and darkness with a religious belief and an ascetic discipline aimed at liberation of the soul from the power of darkness. In this sect, good was associated with light, evil with darkness, as the World Reason or "Logos" was identified with fire by the Stoics. Manichaeism seems to have appealed to the young Augustine for several reasons: its conception of God as refined material substance, light; its explanation of natural and moral evil as the result of a cosmic principle of darkness; its offer of redemption from bondage to darkness and evil; the fact that Christ, whom he had learned from his mother, Monica, to revere, was regarded as a prophet; and the claim of the Manichaeans that their teachings did not need to be accepted on authority but could be demonstrated by reason.

When he became disillusioned with the scientific pretensions of the Manichaeans, he went through a brief but painful period of Skepticism under the influence of the Academics. But Skepticism could not long satisfy a mind which was burning with a passionate desire for truth. For such a mind, the endless quest for truth, accompanied by suspension of judgment, was not enough: man's need for truth required a firm and sure possession of it. Moreover, moral decisions based upon mere probability rather than certainty concerning man's duties could

[1] Augustine, *Confessions,* Bk. III, Chap. 4. Unless otherwise noted, references to the works of Augustine are from *Basic Writings of Saint Augustine,* 2 vols., ed. Whitney J. Oates (New York: Random House, 1948).

hardly command the energies of an active will like that of Augustine. Man must *know* the truth if he is to attain the good.

It was Neo-Platonism which provided Augustine with answers to his philosophical questions and at the same time offered him a worthy object of religious devotion. He tells us in his *Confessions* [2] that "certain books of the Platonists" enabled him to conceive of God in spiritual rather than corporeal terms. At the same time, they offered him a cosmology in which the Good is the ultimate ground of all things in the visible world, the nature of every finite being is good, and evil has no substantial reality but is only a privation or defect of that which is good.[3] Finally, the Neo-Platonists awakened in him the spiritual aspiration to raise himself above the inferior and transitory things of time to mystical union with God, the eternal and unchangeable Light and Truth.[4]

However, Augustine came gradually to realize that there were limitations in Neo-Platonism. As he says in the *Confessions*, Neo-Platonism points men to the *end* of the soul's journey, i.e., union with God as unchanging and perfect Good, but it cannot show the *way* to the end.[5] The soul might on rare occasions catch a glimpse of the Good and be filled with joy—indeed, Augustine eloquently describes in the *Confessions* several of these occasions in his own experience [6]—but it could not sustain itself on those lofty heights of the spirit when images from the sensible world crowded into it and drew its attention back to corporeal things. Despite the fact that he had eagerly embraced Neo-Platonism with his intellect, his will was divided against itself, now devoting itself to the eternal Good and now being dragged downward by lust or pride. It had to be radically changed and brought into unity with itself before it could really love God and attain peace and joy. This is what his conversion in Milan, precipitated by the reading of a passage from St. Paul (Rom. 13:13–14), accomplished for him.[7] As he "put on the Lord Jesus Christ," the discord of his conflicting desires was resolved and his besetting sins of sensuality and pride began to fall away.

While Neo-Platonism had helped to provide the intellectual bridge over which Augustine passed from Manichaeism and Skepticism to Christianity, he gradually came to see the difference between the Neo-Platonic view of God and His relation to man and the view of Christianity. In the *Confessions* he tells us that he read in the "books of the

[2] *Ibid.*, Bk. VII, Chaps. 9ff.   [3] *Ibid.*, Chaps. 12–16.
[4] *Ibid.*, Chaps. 10, 17.   [5] *Ibid.*, Chap. 20.
[6] For example, his vision with his mother at Ostia, Bk. IX, Chap. 10.
[7] Augustine, *Confessions*, Bk. VIII, Chap. 12.

Platonists" that "the Word was God"—doubtless he is referring to the divine Mind or *nous* of Plotinus—"but that the Word was made flesh, and dwelt among us, I read not there" and "that in due time Christ died for the ungodly . . . is not there." [8] The Christian belief in the Incarnation implied a conception of God different from that of Neo-Platonism. The God of Christianity was not the impersonal, transcendent "One" of Plotinus but the personal God of the Bible who had stooped to man's need by manifesting His love in Christ. Moreover, man was not able to elevate himself by moral and intellectual discipline to mystical union with God and thus attain salvation for himself; his will was in bondage to self-love and only the love of God for him could awaken in him the love for God which was necessary for his salvation. These and other differences show that Augustine's conversion to Christianity not only transformed his heart and will but also had a profound effect upon his intellect. "To Plotinus," says Gilson, "he is indebted for almost all the matter and for the whole technique of his philosophy. He is indebted to the Bible for the basic Christian notions which compelled him to make the inner transformations he performed on the Plotinian theses he borrowed and to construct in this way a new doctrine which represents one of the first, and one of the most original, contributions Christianity has made to enrich the history of philosophy." [9] This somewhat exaggerates Augustine's debt to Plotinus. Although his metaphysics and theory of knowledge are fundamentally Neo-Platonic in their content, his conceptions of God, man, and history are very different and these constitute his most original contributions to philosophy. But there can be no doubt that the influence of the Neo-Platonists upon him was profound and that he never abandoned their views on many strictly philosophical matters but made "inner transformations" of them by means of his Christian beliefs.

KNOWLEDGE AND ILLUMINATION

When we examine Augustine's synthesis of Neo-Platonism and Christian faith, the first thing we notice is the *practical* and *existential* character of his conception of philosophy itself. "This is a point of prime importance if we are to understand Augustine," says Gilson, "for in his doctrine wisdom, the object of philosophy, is always identified with happiness. He wants to find the kind of good whose possession will satisfy every desire and ensure peace. Such thorough-going Eudaemonism can be explained by the fact that Augustine always re-

[8] *Ibid.,* Bk. VII, Chap. 9.
[9] Etienne Gilson, *The Christian Philosophy of Saint Augustine* (New York: Random House, 1960), p. 234.

garded Philosophy as something quite different from the speculative pursuit of a knowledge of nature. He was concerned most of all with the problem of his own destiny. For him, the important thing was to strive for self-knowledge and to learn what must be done in order to be better, and, if possible, to be happy. Speculation abounds in Augustine but its aims are always practical and its term of reference is always man. The knowledge of truth may be essential to happiness, but in Augustine truth is pursued only because truth alone can make man happy, and it is pursued only to the extent that it can make him so." [10] Thus, blessedness requires for its attainment knowledge of the good, and the purpose of philosophy is to seek for "wisdom," *sapientia*, concerning a Good which is both permanent and independent of the changes of fortune. Philosophy seeks knowledge not primarily for its own sake but for the sake of the Good, not merely to contemplate it but also to enjoy it and to love it.

If philosophy is to attain its aim of blessedness, it should be identified not with the mere search for truth but with the *possession* of it. For this reason, Augustine found it necessary, on the one hand, to refute the Skepticism which had once tempted him to despair of the truth, and, on the other, to develop a positive theory of knowledge. He deals with the skeptics in an early essay, *Against the Academics.* He denies the Academics' view that it is sufficient for the wise man to guide his actions by "probability." It is necessary for a proposition to be "like" the truth if it is to be probable, and one cannot know that it is "like" the truth unless he knows the truth itself. In reality, we do have certain knowledge. Although men make mistakes in interpreting their sense impressions, sense impressions as such never deceive us but are always true. The fact that the oar appears to be bent when it is seen in the water need not deceive us if we do not assert that it is really bent: indeed, if the laws of refraction are not to be violated, it *must* appear bent. [11] Again, we have certain knowledge of mathematical and ethical truths. For example, we know that seven and three always make ten and that we ought to render to every man his due.[12] Even if a person is deceived, the fact that he is deceived proves that he exists, since he cannot be deceived unless he exists.[13] In this argument, Augustine anticipates Descartes' famous "Cogito, ergo sum."

[10] *Ibid.*, p. 3.

[11] Augustine, *Against the Academics*, trans. John O'Meara (Westminster, Md.: The Newman Press, 1953) Vol. VI, Bk. III, Chap. 11, Sec. 26.

[12] *Ibid.*, *On Free Will*, Bk. II, Chaps. 7.21; 10.28; from Augustine, *Earlier Writings*, trans. John H. S. Burleigh, in *The Library of Christian Classics*, Vol. VI (Philadelphia: The Westminster Press, 1953).

[13] *Ibid.*, *City of God*, Chaps. 11, 26.

Augustine was not really concerned about the problem, which has troubled Descartes and other modern philosophers, whether the *external world* exists. Although he did not consider that mutable and corporeal objects are the proper objects of the intellect and regarded them primarily as a starting point for the ascent of the mind to God, he knew that in practical life we must give credence to the senses and that they add much to our natural knowledge. But he had little interest in the natural world. Since he was seeking for truth as a necessary condition of the blessedness of the soul, his primary intellectual concern was with two things: *God* and the *soul*. This is expressed in striking fashion in the *Soliloquies*. "I desire to know God and the soul," he says. "Nothing more?" reason asks. "Nothing whatever," he replies.[14]

The Platonism of Augustine's theory of knowledge is even more evident when we consider his view of *rational knowledge*. Although the objects of true knowledge must be unchanging, man can have rational knowledge of corporeal things by judging them according to eternal Ideas or standards. When he judges that one thing is more beautiful than another he does so by reference to an eternal standard or Idea of beauty; and when he judges that a line is straight or a circle well drawn, he implies a reference to the Idea of straightness or circularity. This rational knowledge is called by Augustine *scientia* to distinguish it from *sapientia* or "wisdom." Since it requires the operation of the senses and is directed to practice, it is intermediate between sense knowledge and wisdom.

What is "wisdom" and what is its relation to this rational knowledge or "science"? *Wisdom* arises when the mind turns away from the things of the senses to contemplate eternal and immutable Truth. At first sight it may seem to be nothing more than a certain kind of science, since it, too, is rational and possesses absolute certainty. However, it must be distinguished from science, which concentrates upon mutable things and tempts the mind to neglect immutable Truth. "If it [mind] were left to itself, it would, no doubt, devote all of its attention to knowing intelligibles, because it is especially at home there, in the exercise of its proper function, viz., pure contemplation, unhampered by any thought of action. But the mind is always the mind of man, i.e. it belongs to the being we have defined as 'a soul made to govern a body.' To govern a body means to live and therefore to be involved in action. It follows that man must make use of things and to do this he must know things, i.e., he must use his mind for other purposes than contemplation."[15] If we adopt Gilson's terms for these two functions of the reason, "superior

[14] *Ibid., Soliloquies*, Bk. I, 7 (*The Library of Christian Classics*, Vol. VI).
[15] Gilson, *The Christian Philosophy of Saint Augustine*, p. 117.

reason" and "inferior reason," we can say that "wisdom" belongs to
"superior reason" since it is concerned with contemplation of the eternal, while "science" belongs to "inferior reason" since it is concerned
with the mutable world and with action.[16]

Reason can function in either of these two ways and it is necessary
for man to choose between them. The decision is a fateful one. If he
chooses to exercise his "superior reason," his thought will habitually
turn toward the divine Ideas where wisdom is to be found. If he
chooses to exercise primarily his "inferior reason," he will turn toward
corporeal things in order to enjoy them and exploit them for his own
private ends.[17] The choice he makes is determined by the nature of his
will and the direction of his attention. It requires humility to submit
oneself to the eternal Ideas which are universal and common to all
minds, for to do so one must subordinate oneself to the divine order
and live as part of the whole. In contrast, one can yield to pride and
fall into that covetousness which refuses to possess things in common
with others, insists upon appropriating them for one's own satisfaction,
and exalts the part as if it were the whole. Thus, the attitudes which
give rise to wisdom and science appear to be completely opposed to
one another; and, since wisdom alone can bring blessedness, it would
seem that one must choose wisdom and sacrifice science.[18] This is not,
however, Augustine's meaning. Wisdom requires not the abandonment
but the subordination of science. Since the soul must "regulate the
body," it must also regulate temporal things in the service of the eternal and must therefore know them. When science is used in this way as
an instrument of wisdom, it is legitimate and necessary. However, it is
constantly exposed to the danger of being used by pride and covetousness to serve the private ends of the self. Thus it is ambivalent, having
one character when it is subordinated to wisdom and contemplation
and another when it becomes an instrument of appetite. Only in the
former case does it have a legitimate place between the sense knowledge of material things and the pure intuition of divine Ideas.[19]

We have pointed out that rational knowledge, or science, is made
possible by the judgment of corporeal things in relation to eternal
standards or Ideas. What is the status of these *Ideas?* Augustine accepted the Neo-Platonic view that the Ideas belong not to an impersonal realm of essences but to the divine Mind. "The Ideas," he says,
"are certain archetypal forms or stable and immutable essences of
things, which have not themselves been formed but, existing eternally

---

[16] *Ibid.*   [17] Augustine, *On the Trinity,* Bk. XII, Chaps. 14, 15.
[18] Gilson, *The Christian Philosophy of Saint Augustine,* pp. 118–121.
[19] *Ibid.,* pp. 121–123.

and without change, are contained in the divine intelligence." [20] This raises an interesting question. Does the mind when it beholds them also behold the essence of God? This is a highly controversial point in the interpretation of Augustine. Some scholars have held that, since the contents of the divine Mind must be identical with the divine essence, to see the Ideas in the divine Mind must involve an immediate intuition of the essence of God. Others have held that God actively infuses into our minds the Ideas by which we judge things and that our minds are passive with respect to them.

The difficulty of interpretation is due to the fact that the passages in which Augustine speaks of the divine "illumination" of the mind are not clear. In a passage influenced by Plato's Idea of the Good which illuminates the Ideas of the intelligible world as the visible sun illuminates the objects of the sensible world, he says that mathematical Ideas cannot be known unless they are illumined by something else corresponding to the sun and implies that this light is God.[21] In the same treatise he speaks of the Intelligible Light in, by, and through whom all intelligible things are illuminated.[22] It is clear from such passages that the divine Light somehow makes the eternal truths visible to the human mind; and obviously this illumination is made possible by the fact that God is the Truth in whom all truths participate. But how we are to conceive this divine illumination is far from clear.

According to Gilson, who has carefully analyzed the many relevant texts, Augustine does not claim that in normal as distinguished from mystical knowledge we have either an intuition of the eternal Ideas in God or the sight of God's light itself.[23] "To see the ideas of God would be to see God. Now it is evident that we do not see Him, because we find it difficult to fashion proofs for His existence which direct sight of Him would render unnecessary." [24] Nor does the divine illumination enable us to abstract concepts from sensible things, for it deals with intelligible to the exclusion of sensible objects.[25] Rather, the divine illumination makes it possible for our intellect to see the truth of its own judgment and the note of necessity it implies.[26] For example, experience can account for the formation of the idea of an arch I have seen, but the necessity and certitude of my judgment that it is beautiful cannot be explained by experience alone.[27] "Experience and not illu-

---

[20] Augustine, *De Ideis*, 2; quoted by Frederick Copleston, *History of Philosophy* (London: Burns, Oates, and Washbourne, 1956), Vol. II, p. 60.
[21] Augustine, *Soliloquies*, I, 12 (*The Library of Christian Classics*, Vol. VI).
[22] *Ibid.*, I, 3.
[23] Gilson, *The Christian Philosophy of Saint Augustine*, p. 81.
[24] *Ibid.*, pp. 81–82.   [25] *Ibid.*, pp. 82–84.
[26] *Ibid.*, pp. 86–87.   [27] *Ibid.*, p. 88.

mination tells us what an arch or man is; illumination tells us what a
perfect arch or a perfect man ought to be." [28] Gilson concludes that the
action of the divine Ideas on the mind "does not imply ontologism
because the action is essentially regulative and involves no content,
. . . for the divine idea is not knowledge which passes ready-made
from God into the mind of man; it is a law which binds him." [29] In
mystical knowledge, the mind attains a vision of the divine Ideas
and the divine light themselves.[30] But in *natural* knowledge, the divine
illumination only makes possible judgments of truth which are necessary and certain.

However, a number of Catholic thinkers have attributed "Ontologism" to St. Augustine. *Ontologism* has been defined as "an ideological
system which maintains that God and divine ideas are the first object
of our intelligence and the intuition of God the first act of our intellectual knowledge." [31] Perhaps the most distinguished representative of
this view was Malebranche, who held that our true knowledge of
things is the knowledge we have of them in their Ideas. Ideas with the
characteristics of universality, eternity, and necessity are present to our
minds. They are not derived from finite things, which are particular,
temporal, and contingent, but have their source in God and are the
divine essence itself, the infinite model of all things. "God is then
always really present to our view; we see all things, even material and
concrete things, in Him, who contains and manifests to our intelligence
their nature and existence." [32] Condemned by the Catholic Church in
the nineteenth century, Ontologism in the full sense of the term is
seldom, if ever, defended today.[33]

FAITH AND REASON

Perhaps the most important aspect of Augustine's theory of knowledge is his view of *faith* and its relation to *understanding*. Natural
knowledge can be attained by the use of the senses and reason without
the aid of faith. But the supernatural knowledge which is necessary to
salvation must be based upon faith. Augustine defines belief as "nothing else than thought accompanied by assent." [34] Far from being con-

[28] *Ibid.*, p. 90.   [29] *Ibid.*, pp. 91–92.   [30] *Ibid.*, p. 94.
[31] George M. Sauvage, "Ontologism," in *The Catholic Encyclopedia* (New
York: Robert Appleton Co., 1911).
[32] *Ibid.*
[33] However, Johannes Hessen, a Catholic philosopher, maintains that, while
Augustine was not an ontologist, he affirmed that the divine Light makes possible
an "intellectual vision of Truth" by an "irradiation" of the Ideas. See *Augustin's
Metaphysik der Erkenntnis* (Leiden: Brill, 1960), p. 187.
[34] Augustine, *On the Predestination of the Saints,* Chap. 5.

fined to the acceptance of revealed truth, it is a natural and necessary act of thought which plays a large part in life. Many of our opinions are beliefs which are based on the witness of others, and some of them are indispensable to our personal and social existence. For example, although one must believe that a certain person is one's father solely on the authority of one's mother and that a certain person is one's mother solely on the authority of the midwife and nurse, filial piety and family ties depend upon this belief.[35] In general, one believes in past events one has not seen on the authority of witnesses who have seen them and reported them. It is not different in the case of religious beliefs in historical events. Since witnesses report to me the words of Christ, the power he exerted over men's lives, and the events of his own life, why should I not believe them? Of course, my acceptance of the authority of these Christian witnesses must be based upon evidence that they are trustworthy and that belief in Christ is true. Augustine depends for this evidence largely upon the remarkable success with which Christianity spread in the first three centuries and its virtual conquest of the Mediterranean world by the time of his conversion.[36] Thus, it is reasonable that reason should not refuse the assistance of faith in its task. Will one find God if he does not seek Him with the greatest care and diligence? Will he seek Him despite all difficulties if he does not believe He exists? "Therefore do not seek to understand in order to believe, but believe that thou mayest understand; since, 'Except ye believe, ye shall not understand.'"[37]

What is Augustine's reason for insisting that faith should precede rather than follow understanding? Part of the answer is that reason is not in the state in which it was originally created. It has been distorted by sin. It cannot attain the wisdom whose object is God because it has been turned away by pride from eternal and immutable things to the temporal and changing things of the senses. Moreover, we who have deformed the image of God in ourselves cannot reform it; only God who made it can remake it. "Reason, therefore, asks help from above to do, in it and for it, things it cannot do alone. Far from despising or renouncing itself, it asks God for faith to purify the heart, so that by liberating it from the stain of sin, it may enable reason to increase its light and to become whole once again."[38] In brief, the purification of the heart by faith is a necessary condition of the illumination of the mind. Faith must transform the heart before the reason can be restored to health.

[35] Augustine, *The Usefulness of Belief*, 26 (*The Library of Christian Classics*, Vol. VI).

[36] *Ibid.*, 35.   [37] *Sermon CXXVI*.

[38] Gilson, *The Christian Philosophy of Saint Augustine*, p. 30.

It should be noted that Augustine does not question the capacity of the natural reason without faith to attain rational knowledge, e.g., the knowledge of mathematical and ethical truths. It is also true that the natural reason can attain a kind of knowledge about God. The followers of Plato, for example, "do perhaps entertain such an idea of God as to admit that in Him are to be found the cause of existence, the ultimate reason for the understanding, and the end in reference to which the whole life is to be regulated." [39] But this knowledge is imperfect and ineffective because it does not involve acknowledgment by the will and does not lead to love. Indeed, Augustine points out in his early treatise, *Of True Religion*, that in spite of their knowledge of God, the Greek philosophers did not renounce polytheism.[40]

Cushman has pointed out that the principle underlying Augustine's criticism of the classical philosophers as well as his defense of faith is the effect of the *will* on knowledge. "What is known," he says, "cannot be divorced from what is loved. At the very minimum, all cognition is directly dependent on interest, and nothing is fully known to which the consent of the will has not been given. Yet there may be awareness of reality without completed cognition of that reality. The completion of cognition lies with affection. . . . That is to say, God may be known while not being acknowledged. This is actually the center and depth of the plight of man. . . . Augustine held that, in knowing the cognitive faculty (ratio) 'takes in' according to its power, reality both eternal and temporal, but that being primarily passive or neutral it is directed to 'recognize' what it *does* recognize in virtue of the will or dominant affection of the mind. Therefore, what is not known is precisely what is not adequately loved." [41] Man has fallen under the sway of sinful pride, *superbia,* and has turned away from the love of God, *amor Dei,* to the love of self, *amor sui.* In making himself rather than God the object of his dominant affection, he has perverted his reason from its true function of contemplating the eternal Ideas and God Himself. The only remedy is for the will to be cleansed by submitting in faith to Christ and following his example of humility.

The contrast between Augustine's doctrine of the primacy of faith and Aristotelian intellectualism is striking. According to Aristotle, desire or will follows upon cognition, and the ideal of knowledge is the pure contemplation of Being without regard to practical concerns. On the other hand, Augustine maintains that knowledge involves the con-

[39] Augustine, *City of God*, Bk. VIII, Chap. 4.
[40] Augustine, *Of True Religion*, ii, 2 (*The Library of Christian Classics*, Vol. VI).
[41] Robert E. Cushman, in *A Companion to the Study of St. Augustine*, ed. Roy Battenhouse (New York: Oxford University Press, 1956), pp. 289–290.

sent of the will, so that a man's knowledge depends upon what he loves. The intellectualist refuses commitment until the reason has seen; Augustine insists that it cannot have sight until it yields commitment.[42] Since it is only the love for God which can supplant man's perverse love of himself and temporal things, faith must awaken love to bring about a renewal of the understanding of man.[43]

But Augustine never asserts that faith is the end of the quest for divine truth. Understanding should follow faith. God has said, "Unless you believe, you will not understand." This invites us not to be satisfied with a blind and immature faith but to extend it by understanding. This is the origin of the famous phrase, *fides quaerens intellectum*, "faith seeking understanding." To *believe* in God is not the last end of man; it is eternal life to *know* Him. We begin in faith and are made perfect by sight. "Faith, then, is not its own end," says Gilson. "It is merely the token of knowledge which is vaguely sketched out here below, but will be fully expanded in life eternal." [44]

Because of his view of the close relation of reason and faith, Augustine does not make a distinction between truths which are essentially *philosophical* and truths which are essentially *theological*. For all the truths necessary for blessedness, the highest good of man, are revealed in the Scriptures and must be believed. On the other hand, our reason can attain some understanding of every one of them if it seeks to do so. "All revealed truths can be known to some extent at least, but none of them can be exhausted, since they have God as their object. The difference between the various things to which our mind is applied is simply that some of them can be known clearly, others vaguely, and still others hardly at all." [45] For example, while we can understand how evil can exist in a world created by God, we cannot demonstrate or even make intelligible to ourselves the Trinity. Yet the mystery of the Trinity does not wholly escape our understanding, since we can find analogies for it in man's mind which is made in the image of God.[46] Thus Augustine does not attempt to establish, as Aquinas was to do, a line of demarcation between rational and revealed theology.

THE EXISTENCE OF GOD

It must not be thought, however, that in the realm of religious knowledge reason is limited to an exposition of the contents of faith. Since reason is the image of God and has not been destroyed by sin, it can develop rational arguments for the existence of God, although

[42] *Ibid.*, pp. 300–303.   [43] *Ibid.*, p. 307.
[44] Gilson, *The Christian Philosophy of Saint Augustine*, p. 32.
[45] *Ibid.*, p. 34.   [46] *Ibid.*, p. 36.

Augustine acknowledges that men without faith are not likely to listen to them or be persuaded by them. His most distinctive argument is from the nature of *truth* to God as its ultimate ground. It is found in his early treatise, *Of True Religion*,[47] in the form of a description of the ascent of reason from changeable things of the visible world to the rational mind within and from thence to the unchangeable being, God. But it is more fully developed in the treatise, *On Free Will*, in a dialogue between Augustine and Evodius.[48] Although both speakers in this dialogue are motivated by the desire to understand something they already believe, this does not prevent their argument from being a rational one.

The argument is based upon an analysis of the ways of knowing, which seeks to show that the highest thing in human nature is reason. The "bodily senses" enable us to perceive the qualities of corporeal objects and are superior to these objects. The "interior sense" perceives the data received by it from the bodily senses and also perceives the senses themselves.[49] It is superior to these senses since "it is in some kind of way a ruler and judge among the other senses," e.g., it judges that the eye is defective in its vision. This implies the general principle that that which judges is superior to that which is judged.[50] Above the "interior sense" is the "reason" or "intelligence" which judges both the bodily senses and the interior sense and hence is superior to them. Thus nothing can be found in human nature which is higher than reason.[51]

The next step in the argument is crucial. Augustine asks Evodius whether he would hesitate to call by the name "God" anything existing which is superior to man's reason. Evodius replies that he would, for God must not only be superior to man's reason but also be "that above which there is no superior." Augustine agrees and restates the question: "But I ask, supposing you find nothing superior to our reason save what is eternal and unchangeable, will you hesitate to call that God?"[52] When Evodius answers in the negative, Augustine shows by a Platonic analysis of knowledge that there are eternal and unchangeable truths. For there are many things which are seen by the reason of all men in common, and they are not altered by men's knowledge of them, i.e., they are objective and independent of man. These truths cannot be derived from the bodily senses. Propositions about the results of the addition or subtraction of numbers, e.g., $7 + 3 = 10$, are true not only

---

[47] Augustine, *Of True Religion*, xxix, 52–xxxi, 57 (*The Library of Christian Classics*, Vol. VI).

[48] Augustine, *On Free Will*, Bk. II.   [49] *Ibid.*, Bk. II, Chap. 3.8.

[50] *Ibid.*, Chap. 5.12.   [51] *Ibid.*, Chap. 6.13.   [52] *Ibid.*, Chap. 6.14.

now but always; the numbers themselves cannot be known by sense, e.g., the number 1 cannot be found in sensible objects each of which is also many because it is composed of parts; and there are certain and immutable laws determining the relations between numbers, although they cannot be perceived by a bodily sense.[53] Similarly, there is one wisdom concerning the highest good, without which no one is happy, and it is common to all men. It is true that there are differences between men concerning the way to happiness, but all agree in seeking happiness as their supreme good and have a notion of happiness impressed upon their minds.[54] Moreover, propositions such as "man ought to live justly"; "the worse ought to be subjected to the better"; "like is to be compared with like"; "each man should be given his due" are true, immutable, and common to all.[55]

From this analysis of mathematical and ethical truths, Augustine concludes that "there is an unchangeable truth, which contains everything that is unchangeably true" and that "it is available and offers itself to be shared by all who discern things immutably true, as if it were some strange mysterious and yet public light." [56] Moreover, it is superior to our minds, since we do not judge it but are judged by it.[57] When this truth is possessed, the supreme good is possessed with security and without change.[58] With this, the demonstration of God is complete, since it had been agreed that, if there is something above man's reason and nothing is above it, it must be God. It is identical with that Wisdom which faith declared to be begotten of the eternal Father but also equal to Him.[59] Augustine does not maintain that in seeing truths man sees the very essence of God, for one must distinguish between the Truth which is God and the truths which participate in it. But we cannot explain truths without reference to the divine Truth. They cannot be explained from the point of view of reason but oblige us to transcend it and affirm the existence of eternal and immutable Truth which is God.

It is this last step in the argument that is the most crucial one. God is asserted to exist as the ultimate source of the truths which are present to the thought of men. But, unless it is *assumed* that the eternal and immutable truths of mathematics and ethics are ideas in the divine Mind, their presence to thought is not an adequate ground for affirming the existence of God. For the fact that they seem to confront the mind as objective standards to which it must conform in its thinking might be explained in other ways, e.g., they might be regarded in

[53] *Ibid.*, Chap. 8.20–23.   [54] *Ibid.*, Chap. 9.25–26.
[55] *Ibid.*, Chap. 10.28–29.   [56] *Ibid.*, Chap. 12.33.   [57] *Ibid.*, Chap. 12.34.
[58] *Ibid.*, Chap. 14.37–38.   [59] *Ibid.*, Chap. 15.

Platonic fashion as belonging to a timeless realm of Ideas. Moreover, even if the assumption is made that the Ideas exist in the divine Mind, the only conclusion we are logically justified in drawing from the argument is the existence of an eternal and immutable Mind which is the ground of necessary and certain truths. For Augustine makes no attempt in *On Free Will* to show that this Mind is also the First Cause of the existence of all finite beings or a Personal Being in the theistic sense of the term.

When viewed as a whole, the most distinctive thing about the argument is that *it proceeds from the world to the soul and from the soul to God rather than directly from the world to God.* As Gilson expresses it, the argument moves "from the exterior to the interior and from the interior to the superior." [60] Indeed, since it infers the existence of God from the fact that man's mind is confronted by eternal and immutable truths, the argument could proceed directly "from the interior to the superior." There are also hints in Augustine's writings of the cosmological and teleological arguments, although they are not fully developed by him. For example, he points out that, although the world of the senses is always changing, it is also characterized by number, order, and measure. This must be due to the divine Wisdom which has everywhere left its mark on things.[61] But usually, even if the start of a proof by Augustine is made with sensible things, these lead the mind to the Ideas in conformity with which they were created and thus the proof passes at the second stage through the mind. Therefore, it was easy for Anselm and others later to dispense with all reference to the external world and to develop a proof for God's existence directly from the idea of Him in the mind, i.e., the "ontological" proof.

The contrast between Augustine's "ontological" method of proving God and the "cosmological" method of Aristotle is striking, and it is obviously based upon the difference between their theories of knowledge. According to Aristotle, all knowledge is derived from sensation, since the reason must abstract concepts from sensible things. From first principles or premises apprehended by intellectual intuition, the mind deduces conclusions concerning the immaterial substances of metaphysics as well as the material ones of physics. Hence the cosmological proof of the Prime Mover must start from change in the sensible world and deduce God's existence as the cause of it. We have already indicated one of the limitations of this method (see Chap. 2.) Since the evidence upon which it is based does not include the mind of man and his purpose to realize good, it can prove at the most a First Cause of

[60] Gilson, *The Christian Philosophy of Saint Augustine*, p. 20.
[61] *Ibid.*, p. 24.

physical change with little relation to the God of religion. In contrast, Augustine's Platonic theory of knowledge enables him to maintain that we know supersensible or spiritual realities such as the Ideas not by inference from the sensible world but directly through the soul. As the soul is superior to the body and knows itself better than its body, it knows other spiritual realities such as the Ideas directly, i.e., intuitively. "Why, indeed, would the soul, when its nature is spiritual like that of God, try to reach God by passing through bodies, for these are cut off from God by their very materiality?" [62] As we shall see, however, the ontological argument also has its limitations.

CREATION AND EVIL

Augustine's conception of *nature* illustrates his radical transformation of Neo-Platonism under the guidance of his Christian faith and personal experience. In contrast to the Neo-Platonic view that the world has emanated eternally and by necessity from the One and the Good, Augustine affirms the biblical doctrine of *creation* by God out of nothing. Both matter and form were created together in the beginning, and it is meaningless to ask what God did "before" the creation since the world came into existence along with time rather than in time. Things have been created by God in accordance with eternal Ideas in His mind. Augustine defines these as "principal forms or stable and unchangeable essences of things. They are themselves not formed, and they are eternal and always in the same state because they are contained in God's intelligence." [63] Creation consisted in conferring upon unformed matter, a mere "something that is nothing," the forms which give things their mode of existence.[64] Since the order and form of the creation comes from the divine Ideas, its relationship to God is one of similarity or participation. God has given things more or less being and their essences are arranged in a hierarchical order which is based on their unequal participation in Being. As the Word or Son is the image of the Father, so creatures are images which derive their unity, beauty, truth, and good from their participation in the Word. Hence, the world is an *image* which contains traces or footprints of its Maker and enables us to know in some measure His nature.[65]

Despite this Neo-Platonic emphasis upon the participation of creatures in the divine Ideas, Augustine's consciousness of man's insufficiency and need for God causes him to *limit nature* and in general to

---

[62] *Ibid.*, p. 244.

[63] Augustine, *De Div. Quaest.*, 83, 46 (Quoted by Gilson, *op. cit.*, p. 199).

[64] Gilson, *The Christian Philosophy of Saint Augustine*, pp. 204, 205.

[65] *Ibid.*, pp. 210–214.

exalt God. Gilson goes so far as to say that "when there are two equally possible solutions to one and the same problem, an Augustinian doctrine will incline spontaneously toward that which concedes less to nature and more to God." [66] An example of this is his theory that God created the primordial seeds or "seminal reasons" of living things and that everything which was to develop from them in time was already implicit in them from the beginning. According to Gilson, this theory was not meant to explain the appearance of the new by a sort of creative evolution, as has sometimes been said, for the "seminal reasons" are used to explain the stability of species rather than the evolution of new ones.[67] "It effectively rules out any suspicion of a creative efficacy in man's activity and in that of other created being." [68]

Augustine's theory of *evil* was profoundly influenced first by his rejection of Manichaean dualism and then by his controversy with the Pelagians. Against the Manichaeans he argues that the origin of evil is not to be found in a cosmic principle of evil. But it is also not to be ascribed to God. Evil arises because things have been created out of nothing and hence participate in nonbeing as well as being. As a result, they are subject to mutability. The nature of every substance, spiritual or corporeal, was created good in some degree.[69] Hence, evil must be regarded not as part of the essence of a substance but as a corruption of its perfection, a "privation of the good" which belongs to the essence of a substance.[70] This Neo-Platonic view of evil enables Augustine to explain its presence in the world without making God responsible for it. It also enables him to refute the charge that, if creation necessarily implied the existence of evil, it would have been better not to have created it. For the *natural* evils of suffering and death are compatible with belief that the creation is essentially good, since the existence of each natural being is good in itself and is succeeded after death by other beings.

The problem of *moral* evil is more difficult to solve. Man is capable of doing evil only insofar as he has freedom of choice. Why, then, has a perfect God bestowed free will upon him? Augustine's answer in his early treatise, *On Free Will,* was simple: The will is good in itself since it is a necessary condition of the good life, but it can be misused. Therefore, we should not blame God for giving free will to men; we should blame those who use it badly.[71] This implies that man falls into

[66] *Ibid.,* p. 240.   [67] *Ibid.,* pp. 206, 207.   [68] *Ibid.,* p. 207.

[69] Augustine, *On the Nature of the Good,* Chap. 3 (*The Library of Christian Classics,* Vol. VI).

[70] *Ibid.,* Chaps. 4, 10.

[71] Augustine, *On Free Will,* Bk. II, Chap. 1.3 (*The Library of Christian Classics,* Vol. VI).

sin by his own choice. When Evodius objects that the soul is often compelled by the power of natural impulse to act as it does, Augustine replies that an unworthy impulse has become dominant only because the soul has capitulated to it. Moreover, since man has free will, he can turn either toward salvation or toward reprobation, toward Christ or toward the Devil.[72] To the objection that we have inherited moral impotence from Adam's sin, Augustine replies that salvation from this is available and that God does not hold us responsible for anything we cannot possibly help.[73] However, it is well known that in his later anti-Pelagian treatises, Augustine modified this attitude toward freedom of will. Against Pelagius' view, he maintained that man's freedom not to sin was lost at the Fall, although he is still free in the limited sense of acting in accordance with his own volition. Only if God's irresistible grace is bestowed upon a man can he recover his freedom not to sin and thus his ability to obey the moral law. For grace transforms the will and enables it to do willingly from love for God what repelled it before.

It is difficult to see how irresistible grace can be compatible with *freedom of will*, so that Augustine's later view of free will is inconsistent with his earlier defense of it. His statement in his *Retractations* that his views had not changed, since he had been describing in the earlier treatise the freedom of man *before* the Fall whereas he was dealing in the later ones with man's moral impotence *after* the Fall, cannot be accepted. As David Roberts has shown, the earlier treatise "describes freedom after the Fall in terms which are incompatible with Augustine's later position; for it states that even after the Fall men are able to turn, through an act of the will, either toward Christ or toward Satan." [74] This change illustrates the fact that Augustine increasingly limited the power of creatures, especially man, and exalted the sovereignty of God. In the heat of controversy with the Pelagians, he virtually abandoned his earlier belief in man's real freedom of choice and moral capacity, in order that man might glorify God alone for his salvation. To the Pelagian assertion that man has freedom to sin or not to sin and needs no special assistance from God's grace, he opposed the doctrine that after the Fall of Adam, man lost his freedom not to sin. Although freedom of will is still part of man's created nature, sinful man is unable to will his true good without a radical reorientation of his will by the divine grace. Why, then, should he boast of his freedom to choose, when he cannot choose the good? This doctrine reflects

---

[72] David Roberts, in *A Companion to the Study of St. Augustine*, ed. Roy Battenhouse, pp. 119, 121.

[73] *Ibid.*, p. 122.　　　[74] *Ibid.*, p. 123.

Augustine's vivid memory of his own moral powerlessness in his youth and of the transformation of his will by his conversion. Therefore, he humbles man's pride and exalts God's grace. Not without reason has he been called the "doctor of grace."

MAN AND HIS GOOD

Augustine's doctrine of man and his good, like his doctrine of God, differs radically from that of Aristotle. Aristotle had based his metaphysics largely upon his analysis of the cosmos, and had considered man simply as a part of it. In contrast, Augustine's philosophy is more existential in that it arises from his reflection upon the human self and its experience. As Windelband says, it is a "metaphysics of inner experience." [75] His *Confessions,* written to describe the events of his life culminating in his conversion and the transformation that resulted from it, concentrates upon his inner development and analyzes his experience at crucial stages of his growth. And his *City of God,* written late in his life, interprets the whole of history in terms of the contrast between two opposing attitudes of the human self, love of God and love of self. Indeed, his whole philosophy revolves around man's soul and its relation to God.

In his conception of the *nature of man,* he seeks to reconcile two different world views, the Platonic cosmology with its unchanging Forms or essences and the Judaeo-Christian historical view of the world and man. When he speaks of man in *abstract* terms, he analyzes his essence in a way quite similar to that of Plato. Man is composed of soul and body; the soul is superior to the body since man is a rational soul using a mortal and earthly body; the senses and appetites distract the soul from the exercise of its highest faculty, reason; and the soul can attain its true good only by turning away from the changing and transitory things of the sensible world to the unchanging and eternal things of the spiritual world. But when he speaks of man in the *concrete* as we know him in experience, his view is more original and is expressed in the historical terms of the Bible. He describes how God created man with a nature that was good, how man destroyed his original nature by sin, and how his corrupt nature can be restored by grace. It is this concrete and historical view of man with which we are primarily concerned.

Man's destiny depends upon whether he decides to accept or reject God's rule over his life. Since it is the *will* that makes this decision, it is of central importance in the life of the self. Augustine shows that not

[75] Wilhelm Windelband, *History of Philosophy* (New York: Macmillan, 1931), p. 276.

only the acts but also the passions and the cognitive functions of the soul are under its control. The four basic *passions*—desire, joy, fear, and sorrow—are manifestations of the will, since they are movements of the soul toward a good to be attained (desire) or retained (joy), or away from an evil avoided (fear) or removed (sorrow). As Augustine says. "None of them is anything else than will. For what are desire and joy but a volition of consent to the things we wish? And what are fear and sadness but a volition of aversion from the things which we do not wish?" [76] The *cognitive* functions also depend upon the will. Sensation is possible only when the attention, which is will, fixes the sense organ upon its object, and when attention ceases the sensation also ceases. Imagination depends upon the combination and separation of images by the will. Finally, the will is the source of rational knowledge, because we seek knowledge only when we want it. [77]

It is because of this dominance of the will over passion and cognition as well as action that Augustine may be said to assert the *primacy of the will*. The tendency of Greek philosophy in the classical period was to take for granted the primacy of the intellect and the dependence of the will's acts upon it. Although Aristotle criticizes the view that knowledge is virtue and recognizes that virtues must be developed by repeated acts of the will, he still maintains the primacy of reason over will and passion and exalts intellectual contemplation over practical activity as the highest good. The Stoics had a clearer understanding of the centrality of the will and regarded its control over passion and acquiescence to circumstance as the highest good, but they held that the good will always acts in accordance with reason and that it is possible only for the wise man. Although the *fact* of will was known, therefore, the crucial importance of decision was not fully recognized by the philosophers. It is quite different with Augustine. He is certainly aware of the dignity of reason as the highest faculty of man, and he sees that it is necessary for moral conduct as well as for knowledge. But since he regards wisdom as essential to happiness and holds that it depends upon a basic choice of the will to turn away from the sensible world and toward God, he accords the primacy to the will. "Of course without intelligence there is no will, but as the will is, so are the objects of intelligence. In the drama in which we all perform, the will decides everything, for upon it depends the choice that binds us to God or cuts us off from Him forever." [78] This is why Augustine insists that sin originated not in passion or lust, *concupiscentia,* but in pride, *su-*

[76] Augustine, *City of God*, Bk. XIV, Chap. 6.
[77] Augustine, *On the Trinity*, Bk. IX, Chap. 12.
[78] Gilson, *The Christian Philosophy of Saint Augustine,* p. 237.

perbia, of an evil will which turned away from God to itself as its end and highest good, from love of God, *amor Dei*, to love of self, *amor sui*. Therefore, lust and other evil passions were not the cause of sin but the effect of a perversion of will,[79] and the passions can be purified only by a restoration of the will through conversion.

This doctrine of the primacy of will in the soul is closely related to Augustine's exaltation of *love* as the source of man's highest good. As Aristotle ascribes a natural tendency to physical bodies to be drawn to their proper places in the world by a kind of weight, Augustine speaks of a weight in the soul moving it in a certain direction. This weight is love and it moves the soul toward the object which is loved: "My weight (*pondus*) is my love (*amor*); by it I am borne whithersoever I am borne." [80] Love is an essential force in man and is always striving to attain its object. Therefore, it is useless to forbid a man to love anything, for he will always love something. The moral question is not whether he should love but what he should love.[81] This is why the Stoics were wrong to counsel "apathy" or passionlessness. For a man's passions are evil only if his love is evil, but good if it is good,[82] And, as the direction of love toward its object determines the value of his passions, it also determines the value of his will and its acts.

This insight into the power of love to move the will is the basis of Augustine's transformation of the Greek conception of the *moral virtues*. Whereas the source of the moral virtues for Plato is the control of the appetites and acts by reason aided by the "spirited" element in the soul, and the development of a moral virtue for Aristotle is due to repeated acts guided by reason, Augustine maintains that *love is the root of all the moral virtues*. For love seeks to direct the passions and acts of a man to their proper end, God, the highest Good. "The object of this love is not anything, but only God, the chief good, the highest wisdom, the perfect harmony. So we may express the definition [of the virtues] thus: that temperance is love keeping itself entire and incorrupt for God; fortitude is love bearing everything readily for the sake of God; justice is love serving God only, and therefore ruling well all else, as subject to man; prudence is love making a right distinction between what helps it towards God and what might hinder it." [83] Thus love of God, *caritas*, is not one virtue among others, it is the source of all the virtues; and as love increases, the virtues increase with it. This

[79] Augustine, *City of God*, Bk. XIV, Chaps. 11–14.
[80] Augustine, *Confessions*, Bk. XIII, Chap. 9.
[81] Gilson, *The Christian Philosophy of Saint Augustine*, p. 135.
[82] Augustine, *City of God*, Bk. XIV, Chaps. 8, 9.
[83] Augustine, *The Morals of the Catholic Church*, Chap. 15.

implies that without love, virtues are at the best imperfect. Acts which are motivated not by love but by the desire for bodily pleasure or for power and glory may appear virtuous but are not truly so.[84] For a similar reason, Augustine denies that there was ever a Roman republic, for a republic as defined by Cicero must seek the welfare of the people and be administered with justice, whereas the Romans did not worship the true God and therefore never attained justice.[85] Augustine goes so far as to say that the virtues a man seems to possess "are rather vices than virtues so long as there is no reference to God in the matter." [86] Hence the saying often attributed to him, "The pagan virtues are splendid vices."

Love is also the source of moral acts. Augustine is far from being an antinomian. He makes it clear in his anti-Pelagian treatises and elsewhere that the love of God does not abolish moral laws and rules. Rather, when God in His grace sheds love abroad in men's hearts, they are enabled to fulfill His law from love of righteousness rather than from fear of punishment.[87]

Thus, love, a gift of the divine grace, is the source of both the religious and the moral life. It is the presence of God within the soul even now; it is also a foretaste of the full possession of Him in eternal life. This immanence of God in the soul is the extreme opposite of Aristotle's view of the Prime Mover as wholly transcendent. It results from the difference between Augustine's Christian conception of God as bestowing love upon men and Aristotle's conception of Him as the object of men's love but as lacking in love for them. Yet this mystical element in Augustine's religion does not lead him to forget the distinction between the soul and God or the distance that still separates it from Him. In this life the soul seeks rest, and can find it in nothing but God. "Thou hast formed us for Thyself, and our hearts are restless till they find rest in Thee." [88] But it is only after death that we can attain the "eternal life in peace" which is the highest good.[89] In this life we must live in hope of that blessedness, *in spe,* as on a pilgrimage during which we are on the way, *in via,* to our eternal home.

THE CHRISTIAN PHILOSOPHY OF AUGUSTINE

In evaluating Augustine's Christian philosophy, we shall confine ourselves to his views on three issues: faith preceding understanding; the existence of God; the nature of man.

---

[84] Augustine, *City of God,* Bk. V, Chaps. 12–20.   [85] *Ibid.,* Bk. XIX, Chap. 21.
[86] *Ibid.,* Chap. 25.   [87] Augustine, *On the Spirit and the Letter,* Chap. 36.
[88] Augustine, *Confessions,* Bk. I, Chap. 1.
[89] Augustine, *City of God,* Bk. XIX, Chap. 11.

1. Only if we bear in mind Augustine's conception of philosoph
as a search for the wisdom which brings happiness can we understa
his conviction that *faith precedes understanding*. As we pointed out,
his restlessness and prolonged quest for wisdom before his conversion
led him through the error of Manichaeism to the Skepticism of the Academics. He finally discovered satisfactory answers to some of his philosophical questions in Neo-Platonism but found himself capable only of
viewing from afar the spiritual goal it held up before him. Thus, both
the difficulty of attaining certainty by philosophy and the powerlessness of the will to live by a spiritual philosophy were borne in upon
him by his quest for the truth through reason alone. As a result, he was
convinced that the attempt of philosophers to gain wisdom without the
aid of revelation was bound to end in doubt or disagreement. Also, he
came to believe that the attempt was caused by the sin from which he
had suffered so much: pride. From all of this he concluded that, as the
will must surrender to grace if it is to be delivered from evil, reason
must surrender to faith if it is to attain wisdom.

One of the questions which may be raised concerning this view of
the relation of faith and reason is whether it is possible to base a
philosophy upon it. Philosophy has usually been regarded in the West
as critical inquiry which rests upon reason and experience alone. In
contrast, the principle expressed by the statement *Credo ut intelligam*
seems to begin with faith and subordinate reason to it. Philosophy
seems to lose its autonomy as a rational discipline and to be confused
with theology. What defense, if any, can be offered against this criticism?

Gilson offers a partial defense by pointing out that Augustine does
not deduce his philosophical conclusions from revelation but begins
with revelation and then inquires "whether and to what extent its
content coincides with the content of reason," [90] i.e., whether its affirmations are in harmony with the conclusions reached by reason. We
may also say that he does not confine himself like a theologian to an
elucidation of Christian beliefs, but uses them as a basis for philosophical thinking about the deeper meaning and implications of these beliefs. In doing so, he shows that when they are fully understood they
illuminate man's understanding of himself and the world. For example,
in the *City of God* he shows how virtues which are based upon other
motives than love are more apparent than real, how the love of self is
the source of the injustice of states and the incessant wars between
them, and how only the love of God and neighbor can make moral virtue, political justice, and peace possible. Thus, "faith seeking under-

[90] Gilson, *The Christian Philosophy of Saint Augustine*, p. 242.

standing" involves an interpretation of the world, man, and history in terms of the Christian revelation. Of course, this does not give complete "autonomy" to the reason, for the starting point is revelation; but it does offer a broad scope for philosophical thinking and no one can read Augustine without realizing that he had an acute philosophical mind and dealt creatively with a wide range of problems.

It can also be argued that the conception of philosophy as completely autonomous is unrealistic. It expresses the attitude of modern rationalists influenced by Descartes, who claim that the philosopher should begin by doubting everything and should then establish conclusions about the world and man by pure reason. In reality, the philosopher usually starts with beliefs derived from others and from his own experience and then subjects them to the test of criticism and further experience. Moreover, when he constructs his own philosophy he does not start without presuppositions and describe the facts of experience without any clue to guide him. As Whitehead says, he starts with an "imaginative generalization" which has been suggested by one area of experience and seeks to apply it to all areas of experience in order to test its adequacy as an interpretation of reality as a whole. If so, Augustine's procedure is similar, in part, to that of other constructive philosophers, although the area of experience which was his starting point differs from that of non-Christian philosophers. And many who have not shared his Christian faith and consequently have not been convinced by his Christian philosophy as a whole have been deeply influenced by his philosophical insights.

However, the most fundamental issue for those who do not reject the very possibility of a Christian philosophy as a contradiction in terms is whether Augustine's view of the relation of faith and reason is adequate. As we shall see in the next chapter, Aquinas held a somewhat different view of that relation. While Augustine maintained that the Christian philosopher should start with faith and move toward understanding, *fides quaerens intellectum,* Aquinas held that when he functions as a philosopher he should start from experience and reason, and move toward faith. In other terms, Aquinas believed that a distinction should be made between rational theology and revealed theology ("sacred doctrine") and that the Christian philosopher in his rational theology should respect the autonomy of reason. It is significant that Jacques Maritain, a Neo-Thomist, regards Augustine's thought as closer to "infused wisdom," a gift of the Holy Spirit, than to rational wisdom or philosophy and sharply contrasts it with Aquinas' thought in this respect. "Such a 'philosophy,' which essentially presupposes faith, charity, the gifts of the Holy Ghost, the whole supernatural order, is not the task of exploring the natures of things to which tho usually called philosophers devote themselves. . . . The pec sophical instrument is not present. Once this instrument is the mind, it has its specifying object, which is the inte things, it has its own rules and light, which are those of natural reason and not of the infused gifts." [91] The point is well taken, although it is perhaps overstated. However, there is a tendency among some recent philosophers of religion to deny that a sharp line should be drawn between rational theology and revealed theology, because it would cut off the former from the beliefs of living religions and thus impoverish it.[92] Moreover, the difference between Augustine and Aquinas is not as great as it might seem, for Augustine often deals with questions such as the nature of knowledge, justice, and time, which fall outside the scope of revelation, and Aquinas is primarily a theologian who uses philosophy to serve the purpose of theology. Indeed, would it not be unrealistic to expect a philosopher who is also a Christian to keep his reason and his faith in separate compartments where they cannot influence one another?

2. Augustine's distinctive argument for the *existence of God,* as we have seen, starts from the inner experience of the soul rather than from observation of the external world. In this respect, it differs radically from the cosmological and teleological arguments of Plato and Aristotle (and later of Aquinas), which start from the motion and order of the cosmos and seek to explain them by a divine Mind. It was natural that Augustine, who had a profound experience of the presence of God in his life and was concerned only with the soul and its relation to God, should approach God from within rather than from without. In a famous prayer he says, "Et ecce intus eras et ego foris et ibi Te quarebam; . . . mecum eras et tecum non eram" ("And behold, You were within, while I was outside and sought You there; . . . you were with me but I was not with You").[93] Moreover, as a Platonist he was more certain of truths discovered within the soul by reason than of any knowledge derived by the senses from external things. Above all, he was looking not for a First Cause of cosmical change and order but for a God who could satisfy his religious and moral need for an absolute Truth and a perfect Good and thus be the source of the pure happiness and peace for which he longed. In a sense, therefore, his ap-

---

[91] Essay by Jacques Maritain in *A Monument to St. Augustine,* by Martin C. D'Arcy *et al.* (New York: Meridian Books, 1961), pp. 221, 227.
[92] William Temple, *Nature, Man and God* (London: Macmillan, 1935), Lecture I.
[93] Augustine, *Confessions,* Bk. X, Chap. 27.

proach to God is more akin to the modern approach from religious experience than to the Greek and medieval cosmological approach.

The strength of the argument is that from an intuition of eternal and unchangeable truths it moves to a divine Mind which is the source of them. Thus, it attempts to prove the personal God of Theism rather than an impersonal First Cause or Mover of the world. Moreover, it describes these truths as superior to man's reason and as norms to which it should conform in its thinking, so that the God to which they point is the ultimate ground of Value as well as of Truth. In this way, it bears some resemblance to the moral argument which was developed after Kant, since it postulates the divine Mind as the source of Truth, as the moral argument postulates the divine Will as the source of moral obligation and hence of Goodness.

The argument obviously rests upon the Platonic view that judgments concerning truth and value are possible only by reference to Ideas which may be only implicit in our minds but which function as norms or standards in all our thinking. Thus, when we judge a proposition to be true, an act to be good, or a person to be beautiful, we apply a norm of Truth, Goodness, or Beauty of which we may not be fully aware. If these norms are grounded in the divine Mind, we presuppose God's existence whenever we make any judgment, although we may think that we do not believe in Him. This is why Tillich argues that the "ontological" approach of Augustine is primary and the "cosmological" approach of Aristotle and Aquinas is secondary.[94] For God is not a "Stranger" who is absent from our experience and has to be proved by causal inference from the external world, but is present as the ultimate Ground of all our thinking and willing whenever they are governed by norms. Thus, relative and partial truths presuppose absolute Truth and relatively good acts presuppose absolute Goodness. If so, anyone who has an "ultimate concern" for Truth or Goodness implicitly acknowledges God as its Ground. This argument has considerable appeal in a time of widespread skepticism like ours, especially to persons who are not conscious of having had any religious experience in the traditional sense but who have an "ultimate concern" for truth and goodness and whose unconditional devotion to them seems to have a religious dimension.

But the weakness of Augustine's argument from truth to God is as obvious as its strength. For it presupposes both the Platonic theory of truth as conformity to eternal and unchangeable Ideas and the Neo-Platonic and Christian view that these Ideas exist in the divine Mind.

[94] Paul Tillich, in *Theology and Culture,* ed. R. G. Kimball (New York: Oxford University Press, 1959), Chap. 2.

Thus it arrives at its conclusion only by making assumpti/
many do not make. Therefore, it will not convince either/
maintain a relativistic view of truth and value or those wh
not relativistic but also not Platonic. And many who would agree ..
there are eternal and unchangeable mathematical and ethical truths
will find difficulty in the last step of the argument in which these truths
are ascribed to the Wisdom of God. Of course, the argument will have
weight for anyone who is conscious of a religious dimension in the
unconditional claims of truth upon him. However, it is incomplete as it
stands and needs to be completed by an argument which would show
that the most adequate explanation of the unconditional demands laid
upon us by truth and value is that a divine Being is the Ground both of
them and of ourselves.[95]

3. One of Augustine's greatest contributions to religious thought is
his penetrating analysis of the *nature of man*. As we have said, his view
of the *essence* of the soul and its relation to the body is Platonic. But
his insight into the *actual condition* of man, especially his love of self
and its moral and political consequences, is original and results from
his own experience. The *City of God* describes in vivid terms the
conflict between a society based upon love of self and one based upon
love of God and neighbor. The contrast between the "earthly city" and
the "City of God" is radical; it is the difference between hell and
heaven. At this point the difference between Augustine's view of man's
existence and that of Greek humanism is most striking. He accepts the
Platonic view of the soul as essentially rational in its highest part and
capable of controlling appetite and devoting itself to spiritual values
such as truth and goodness. At the same time, he emphasizes that the
love of self as manifested in sensuality and pride prevents the soul of
man as he actually is from realizing its true good and that a radical
reorientation of the will is necessary to turn it to love of God and
neighbor. Thus, he criticizes by implication the idealistic estimate of
man of the Greek humanism and lays the foundation of a Christian
humanism which affirms a high view of man's essential nature as made
by God in His own image, but is realistic in recognizing the power
of self-love in his life and the necessity for divine grace to overcome
it.

There is, however, a serious defect in Augustine's conception of
man's relation to God. Because of his own inability before his conversion to overcome the sensuality and pride which stood in the way of his
attainment of his true good and because of his interpretation of St.
Paul, he tended to minimize fallen man's moral capacity and freedom.

[95] Hessen, *Augustin's Metaphysik der Erkenntnis*, pp. 167–170.

He did not go as far as Luther who maintained that the will is in such complete bondage to sin that salvation can come "by grace alone," *sola gratia.* He insisted that after God's grace has turned man to faith, he must cooperate with God's will and fulfill the moral law from love of God. But his experience of the transforming power of God's grace in his conversion led him to exalt God's will as the ultimate cause of everything and to limit severely the capacities of His creatures. "He had had actual experience of the radical insufficiency of nature," says Gilson, "and this is the reason for his constant concern to keep within their actual limits the capacity of essences and the efficacy of their operations." [96] His argument in the anti-Pelagian treatises that after the Fall man was unable not to sin, *non posse non peccare,* and his belief that man will attain perfect freedom only when the divine grace has made him unable to sin, *non posse peccare,* attenuated man's freedom in order to exalt God's grace. Similarly, the doctrine of illumination "guarantees the maximum dependence of the intellect on God in the act of knowing." [97]

Unfortunately, this side of Augustine's doctrine of man, which culminated in the idea of "irresistible grace," had a profound effect upon Christian theology. The effect was to weaken in considerable measure Augustine's Christian humanism with its conception of the potentialities of man as a spiritual being. What was needed was to recognize the destructive power of sin in human life, as he had done, but to affirm that man continues to be in the image of God and that the divine grace assists rather than overrides man's freedom. At this point, Aquinas' principle, "Grace perfects, it does not destroy, nature," offers a more balanced and adequate view than the more pessimistic view of Augustine in his later years. However, in correcting this defect, we should not forget that Augustine's religious greatness, from the point of view of biblical Theism, is manifested precisely in his passionate emphasis upon the *grace of God* which flows from His love for man and upon the *love for God and neighbor* which it makes possible in the man of faith.

[96] Gilson, *The Christian Philosophy of Saint Augustine,* p. 240.
[97] *Ibid.,* p. 365, note 58.

5 Medieval Rational Theology

AQUINAS

The Neo-Platonic Christian philosophy of Augustine dominated Western thought for centuries after his death, and the philosophy of thinkers as late as Anselm was basically Augustinian. However, beginning about the middle of the twelfth century, the translation into Latin of a large number of Greek, Arabic, and Jewish philosophical works had a profound influence upon Christian philosophy and theology. The most important of these works were scientific and metaphysical treatises by Aristotle which had not been known before in the West. Confronted with new methods of thinking and philosophical views of the world, Christian thinkers were greatly stimulated and developed confidence in the power of the human reason. The result was a type of philosophy known as Scholasticism which flourished especially in the thirteenth century.

At first many of the ideas of Aristotle, such as the eternity and necessity of the world, shocked conservative Christian thinkers and for a time the teaching of his natural philosophy and metaphysics at the University of Paris was forbidden. However, by the middle of the thirteenth century all of his works were being taught at Paris. Thomas Aquinas (1225–1274) was largely responsible for the gradual acceptance of Aristotle as an ally rather than a rival of Christian philosophy. His commentaries on Aristotle's treatises and his use of the method of thinking and philosophical point of view of "the Philosopher" showed that Aristotelianism could be used as an aid in formulating and defending Christian truths. However, it is a mistake to suppose that Aquinas' philosophy was simply a Christianized Aristotelianism, since he was influenced by almost all of the philosophical and theological thought of his own time and his "synthesis" contains elements drawn from Neo-Platonic, Arabic, and Jewish philosophy. Moreover, he was a creative philosopher, who was not satisfied to adopt Aristotle's philosophy as he found it but transformed it in considerable measure in the light of the

97

Christian revelation. It should also be remembered that he was a theologian in his vocation and that his philosophical thinking was done to aid him in his theological studies. Indeed, his most original philosophical ideas are to be found in his theological works. In general, his philosophy is that part of his theology which he regarded as capable of rational demonstration.[1]

RATIONAL AND REVEALED THEOLOGY

According to Aquinas, theology includes both the truths about God known by reason and those known by revelation. The distinction between these two parts of theology, which have come to be known as "rational theology" and "revealed theology" (or "dogmatic theology"), is based upon the distinction between religious truths accessible to the natural reason of man and those revealed by God and contained in the Scriptures. The former can be discovered by rational inference from evidence derived from the natural order; the latter have been given to prophets and apostles by God and are to be accepted by faith. This presupposes that the natural reason is competent to demonstrate certain fundamental religious propositions but that it is incapable of demonstrating specifically Christian truths, such as the Incarnation, which are necessary for salvation. However, the fact that Christians must depend for these Christian truths upon revelation does not mean that there is a conflict between reason and faith. Since God is the Creator of both reason and faith, the revelation accepted by faith will never be contrary to reason when reason is correctly employed. "Since grace does not destroy nature, but perfects it," says Aquinas, "natural reason should minister to faith." [2]

Our concern is with Aquinas' *rational theology*. But it should never be forgotten that in his view theology also includes knowledge revealed by God and that this knowledge is necessary for salvation. Since man is directed to God as an end which "surpasses the grasp of his reason" and he must first know this end if he is to direct his intentions and actions to it, "it is necessary that certain truths about God should be revealed to him." [3] Even those religious truths which can be known by reason must also be taught to men by God, since they "would only be known by a few, and that after a long time, and with the admixture

---

[1] Armand A. Maurer, *Medieval Philosophy* (New York: Random House, 1962), p. 165.

[2] Thomas Aquinas, *Summa Theologica*, Pt. I, Q. 1, a. 8. All references to the writings of Thomas Aquinas are from *Basic Writings of Saint Thomas Aquinas*, 2 vols., ed. and annotated Anton C. Pegis (New York: Random House, 1945).

[3] *Ibid.*, Q. 1, a. 1.

of many errors, whereas man's whole salvation, which is in God, depends upon a knowledge of this truth."[4] Theology or "sacred doctrine" embraces these revealed truths as "articles of faith," and uses reason simply as a "handmaid of faith" to expound and defend them.[5] From this it is clear that for Aquinas "rational theology" has only a limited and secondary role. But it is important since it can demonstrate certain basic religious truths or "preambles of faith," e.g., the existence of God and the immortality of the soul, without the assistance of the Christian revelation. Thus, it enables Christians to argue on the common ground of reason with "unbelievers," i.e., pagans and others who do not accept the revelation in the New Testament. It also makes it possible for Christians who can understand a rational argument to *know* at least some religious truths that they had previously accepted on *faith*.

The *basic principle* of rational theology is stated in a quotation from St. Paul: "The invisible things of Him are clearly seen, being understood by the things that are made" (Rom. 1:20). "Where an effect," says Aquinas, "is better known to us than its cause, from the effect we proceed to the knowledge of the cause."[6] We cannot, of course, know the *essence* of God in this way. The reason is that, according to Aristotle, man's intellect must depend for its knowledge upon sensation. From the "sensible species" or impressions it receives through the senses, it abstracts "intelligible species" or general ideas. It then relates these ideas to one another in judgments and deduces from premises known to be true conclusions which had not been known before. Since its ideas are originally derived from sensation, it can know only that to which it is led by sensible things and it cannot be led by sensible things to see the essence of God.[7] However, this does not prevent it from inferring from sensible things the *existence* of God as their cause. "But because they [sensible things] are His effects and depend on their cause, we can be led from them so far as to know of God *whether He exists*, and to know of Him what must necessarily belong to Him, as the first cause of all things, exceeding all things caused by Him."[8] Thus, the basic principle of rational theology is that we can know God as infinite Cause from His finite effects as we experience them through the senses. In this way, we can know "whether He exists" and "what must necessarily belong to Him as the first cause of all things." For a knowledge of His essence we must wait until the life to come when God will by His grace illuminate our intellect and ena-

---

[4] *Ibid.,* Q. 1, a. 1.   [5] *Ibid.,* Q. 1, a. 8.   [6] *Ibid.,* Q. 2, a. 2.
[7] *Ibid.,* Q. 12, a. 12.   [8] *Ibid.,* Q. 12, a. 12.

ble us to attain that "vision of God" which is our "last end," i.e., our highest Good.[9]

THE EXISTENCE OF GOD: THE FIVE "WAYS"

The most important part of Aquinas' rational theology is that which deals with the *existence* of God and with the *names* which should be used to express man's knowledge of His nature. He begins his discussion of the existence of God by rejecting the view that it is "self-evident." His chief concern here is with the *ontological* argument which had been expressed in different ways by Augustine, Anselm, and others. According to Anselm's version in the *Proslogion,* men have an idea of a Being "than which no greater can be conceived." If this Being did not exist in reality, a contradiction would be involved. For then we could conceive a greater Being, one which would exist in reality as well as in the mind as idea. Therefore, He exists. In other words, the idea of such a Being implies His existence. Aquinas regards this argument as equivalent to the claim that God's existence is self-evident, since self-evident truths are those "which are known as soon as the terms are known." But the proposition "God exists" is *not* self-evident, since we cannot know that the predicate "exists" is included in the essence of the subject "God." If we knew the essence of God in this life, we could see that the predicate is the same as the subject, because the essence of God *is* His existence. But we do not know God's essence. Hence, while the proposition is self-evident "in itself," it is not so "to us." [10] Moreover, even if it were conceded that everyone understands by the name "God" a Being "than which no greater can be conceived," it would not follow that "what the name signifies exists actually, but only that it exists mentally." [11] There is no logical transition possible from "mental" to "actual" existence, from existence as an idea to existence in objective reality.

After rejecting the ontological argument, Aquinas proceeds to develop five "ways," or arguments, for the existence of God based upon knowledge of His effects. All five may be regarded as forms of the *cosmological* argument, since each of them begins with a characteristic of finite things in the visible world, or cosmos, and infers from this the existence of God as their infinite Cause. However, the fifth "way" is usually called the *teleological* argument because it starts from experience that each thing in nature moves toward an end, or "telos." In contrast to the ontological a priori argument from the *idea* of God,

---

[9] *Ibid.,* Q. 12, a. 1, 5.   [10] *Ibid.,* Q. 2, a. 1.   [11] *Ibid.,* Q. 2, a. 1.

they are all a posteriori arguments since they take their start from *experience*. But it is somewhat misleading to call them "empirical" arguments in the modern sense, because they demonstrate their conclusion by deductive reasoning without further reference to experience.

1. The first "way" starts from *motion*, by which Aquinas means any kind of change. Assuming the Aristotelian view of motion as a transition from potentiality to actuality, he asserts that everything which is moving or changing must be put in motion by something else, since it cannot actualize its potentiality itself. For the same reason, that which puts it in motion must itself be moved by something else. But we cannot go back to infinity in a series of movers which are put in motion by other movers. At some point, we must come to a mover which can put other things in motion but is not moved itself. "Therefore it is necessary," Aquinas concludes, "to arrive at a first mover, moved by no other; and this everyone understands to be God." [12]

As Mascall has pointed out, this argument seems less convincing to the modern than to the medieval mind, because modern science since the time of Newton has assumed that motion is an ultimate fact of the natural order which requires no explanation.[13] Hence, the idea that a thing cannot move without being put in motion by something else seems strange to the scientific mind. However, this does not necessarily render the argument worthless, for the fact that science takes the existence of motion for granted does not imply that it requires no philosophical explanation.[14] Another reason the argument fails to convince many is that its assumption that an infinite regress of moved movers is untenable does not seem self-evident. But the intention of Aquinas was not to demonstrate merely a *first* member of a temporal series of movers with the same status as the other members but a Mover of a different and higher order of reality. "The point is not really that we cannot have an infinite regress in the order of nature, but that such a regress in the series of moved movers would necessitate an unmoved First Mover not *in* the order of nature but *above* it." [15]

2. The second "way" starts from the order of *efficient causes* in the world of sensible things. A thing cannot be the efficient cause of itself; if it were it would be prior to itself. It must, therefore, be caused by another. In a series of efficient causes "the first is the cause of the

---

[12] *Ibid.*, Q. 2, a. 3.
[13] E. Mascall, *He Who Is* (London: Longmans, Green, 1949), p. 42.
[14] *Ibid.*, p. 43.   [15] *Ibid.*, p. 44.

intermediate cause, and the intermediate is the cause of the ultimate cause, whether the intermediate cause be several or one only." [16] Therefore, if it is possible to go on to infinity in the series of efficient causes, there will be no first efficient cause and hence no intermediate cause and no ultimate cause. Since this is not the case, we must admit a first efficient cause.[17] This argument is similar to the first, since it avoids an infinite regress of causes by positing a first uncaused cause. But is it self-evident that there can be no such regress? Modern Thomists point out that, while an infinite series of efficient causes in time is conceivable, it is necessary to posit a "first" cause not in the sense of a *temporally* first member of the series but in the sense of a *transcendent* cause of the whole series. Such a cause would not be in time, so that it is meaningless to object that there would also have to be a cause antecedent to it. But the major objection to the argument, as we shall see later, is the modern doubt whether the causal principle can be applied to the relation between the world and a cause which transcends the world and therefore cannot be experienced.

3. The third "way" is often spoken of as the argument from the *contingency* of the world and is regarded by many Thomists as the most fundamental of the arguments. We observe things in nature that come into being and pass away, so that it is possible for them to be and to not-be. Thus, it is impossible for them always to exist. If we assume that everything is contingent or can not-be, at some time there was nothing in existence. But if this were true, there would be nothing in existence now, because there would then have been nothing which could have brought things into existence. As there are things in existence now, this is absurd. Therefore, the assumption that everything is merely contingent and can not-be is false, and there must be something whose existence is necessary. If the necessity of this being is assumed to be caused by another, it is impossible to go on to infinity in a series of necessary beings. Therefore, we must admit the existence of a Necessary Being which does not receive its necessity from another but has its necessity of itself. This Necessary Being men call God.[18]

This third argument is obviously more fundamental than the first two arguments. These seek to account for the fact of motion or change and the fact of causal production in things, whereas the third seeks to account for the very *existence* of things. But, it may be asked, does the fact that the contingent things we observe have not always existed

[16] Aquinas, *Summa Theologica*, Pt. I, Q. 2, a. 3.
[17] *Ibid.*, Q. 2, a. 3.   [18] *Ibid.*, Q. 2, a. 3.

necessarily imply that at some time in the past *no* contingent beings existed, so that at that time there was nothing which could bring other things into existence and thus account for the contingent things that now exist? Only if this is the case do we have to account for the contingent things we observe by positing a Necessary Being capable of bringing them into existence. However, Aquinas' argument for a Necessary Being does not really depend upon the proposition that there was once a time when no contingent being existed, although he has stated it in such a way that it appears to do so. Even if there was never a time when no contingent things existed and they have been coming into and passing out of existence from eternity, Aquinas would still argue that the only sufficient reason that can be given for their existence is a Necessary Being. If all contingent beings derive their existence from other beings as contingent as themselves, the existence of none of them is accounted for. The essence of the argument, therefore, is that all contingent beings must receive their existence ultimately from a Being which has the power to bestow existence upon other beings because it has its existence from or of itself and thus does not have to derive it from another.

4. The fourth "way" is based upon the *degrees of perfection* in the things of the world. Some things are more and some are less good, true, noble, and the like. This presupposes the existence of a highest degree, a "maximum," of each of these perfections, "so that there is something which is truest, something best, something noblest, and, consequently, something which is most being." This is the first step in the argument. The second step asserts that this highest Being in the hierarchy of being is the cause of the being and other perfections of all other things. "Now the maximum in any genus is the cause of all in that genus, as fire, which is the maximum of heat, is the cause of all hot things. . . . Therefore, there must also be something which is to all beings the cause of their being, goodness, and every other perfection; and this we call God." [19] This argument, of course, presupposes that comparative judgments of value have a basis in objective reality. It also presupposes that goodness, truth, and other perfections are "convertible" with Being, so that that which possesses the highest degree of value also has the highest degree of Being or Reality.

The argument is distinctly Platonic in character, since it reflects the view that things in the world "participate" in perfect Being and Good. It asserts that things which possess perfections in different degrees can

[19] *Ibid.,* Q. 2, a. 3.

be explained only by positing a Being who possesses them in the highest degree, i.e., a Perfect Being. But it is another form of the cosmological argument, since it starts from man's experience of degrees of perfection in things and seeks to explain this fact by reference to a transcendent cause. "The ultimate cause of perfection," Copleston says, "must itself be perfect: it cannot receive its perfection from another, but must be its own perfection: it is self-existing being and perfection. The argument consists, then, in the application of principles already used in the foregoing proofs to pure perfections: it is not really a departure from the general spirit of the other proofs, in spite of its Platonic descent." [20] Perhaps the most serious difficulty in it is that it proves at the most a being that possesses the greatest degree of every perfection and is thus *superior* to all other beings but that it fails to prove the *supreme* Being of religion, i.e., it proves a relatively but not an absolutely greatest being. The root of the difficulty is that, if one starts from the experience of finite things which possess their "perfections" only relatively, i.e., in degrees that fall short of the maximum, it is not necessary to posit an absolutely perfect Being to explain them. For this reason, Urban argues that we must start from an intuition of absolutely perfect Being and then interpret the imperfect things of the world by contrast with it as possessing lesser degrees of perfection or value.[21] But this would be possible only if we adopted a non-Aristotelian theory of knowledge which would admit the possibility of such an intuition and would thus require a reformulation of the argument.

5. The fifth and last "way" is the *teleological* argument. It is stated in somewhat different forms in the *Summa Theologica* and the *Summa contra Gentiles*. In the former, the argument starts from the fact that things without knowledge "act for an end," as is shown by "their acting always, or nearly always, in the same way, so as to obtain the best result." Hence, they must attain their end not by chance but by design. But since they are without knowledge they cannot do so unless they are directed to their end by an intelligent being, as an arrow directed by an archer. "Therefore some intelligent being exists by whom all natural things are directed to their end; and this being we call God." [22] In the *Summa contra Gentiles* the argument is stated in broader terms and seeks to explain the order of nature as a whole. "Contrary and discordant things cannot, always or for the most part, be parts of one or-

[20] Frederick Copleston, *History of Philosophy* (London: Burns, Oates, and Washbourne, 1956), Vol. II, p. 344.

[21] W. M. Urban, *Humanity and Deity* (London: George Allen and Unwin, 1951), pp. 170, 171.

[22] Aquinas, *Summa Theologica*, Pt. I, Q. 2, a. 3.

der except under someone's government, which enables all and each to tend to a definite end. But in the world we find that things of diverse natures come together under one order, and this not rarely or by chance, but always or for the most part. There must therefore be some being by whose providence the world is governed. This we call God." [23] Thus, while the first form of the proof emphasizes the attainment of ends by natural beings without knowledge of their own to guide them, the second emphasizes the harmonious cooperation of many diverse and discordant natural beings in attaining their ends in a world order.

The influence of Aristotle's *Physics* upon the first form of the argument is obvious. As we have seen (Chap. 2), Aristotle maintains that the natural beings of each species could not actualize their potentialities "always or for the most part" in a certain manner, unless final causes or ends as well as material and efficient causes were operative within them. Similarly, Aquinas argues that natural things could not attain their ends "always, or nearly always, in the same way" unless they were directed toward them. However, while Aristotle's teleology is "immanent," Aquinas' is "external," i.e., natural beings are directed toward their ends not by an immanent principle but by a divine intelligence. The second form of his argument goes further and emphasizes the discord between natural beings of diverse natures which would result if there were no divine intelligence governing them and bringing them into one order.

There has been a tendency among Thomistic philosophers to subordinate the teleological to the cosmological arguments which precede it. Perhaps the reason is that, while it may prove the existence of an Intelligent Being wise and powerful enough to account for the attainment of ends in nature, it makes no attempt to prove that this being is identical with either a Necessary Being or a Perfect Being. Hence, it is open to the criticism that it does not prove the existence of the God of Theism but only of an Architect of the natural order. In contrast, the cosmological arguments, especially the third and fourth, prove the existence of a Being who can bestow *existence* and *value* upon finite things as well as impose order upon things already in existence. On the other hand, it is equally true that the cosmological arguments are not sufficient by themselves in that they do not arrive at the God of Theism who is an Intelligent Being realizing purposes in the world. Since the teleological argument supplements them at this point, it is essential for

[23] Aquinas, *Summa contra Gentiles,* Bk. I, Chap. 13.

Aquinas' argument as a whole. It rounds out his theistic explanation of the world by showing that God is not only the efficient cause of finite things but also an Intelligent Mind who directs them toward their ends and thus enables them to attain their good.

A full understanding of the five "ways" of Aquinas is impossible without taking a general view and noting certain features of them when considered together. The first thing to be noted is their apparent *independence* and their real *interdependence*. Each of them is a distinct and separate argument, and each is presented as sufficient by itself to demonstrate God's existence. Aquinas doubtless understood them in this way, since the Aristotelian method of deductive reasoning used in them requires that the premises of an argument and the reasoning which starts from them should be adequate by themselves to produce the conclusion. However, he proves a different aspect of the nature of God in each of the "ways," e.g., that He is an Unmoved Mover in the first and a Necessary Being in the third. To this extent, at least, the arguments are interdependent. They supplement one another, since they indicate different ways the mind may move from the world to God and lead to an understanding of different facets of His nature as manifested by different effects in the world.

Second, there are several *presuppositions* with respect to causality which underlie all of the arguments. One of these is that a cause not only precedes but produces its effect. Its relation to its effect is a necessary one, since it is the necessary condition of its effect. Therefore, it is legitimate to infer from effects of a certain kind the existence of a cause sufficient to produce them. A cause is sufficient to produce a certain kind of effect only if it possesses a degree of being and perfection at least as great as the effect, since nothing can give rise to an effect superior to itself. Indeed, as the fourth "way" makes explicit, the ultimate cause of all beings and their perfections is not merely as great as but greater than His effects. In addition, Aquinas presupposes in the first three "ways" that an infinite series of finite causes cannot provide a sufficient explanation of an effect. As we have pointed out, the reason for this is not that such a series is logically impossible. It is that even if there were an infinite series of moved movers, caused causes, and contingent beings, they would not provide a complete explanation of the effects they are intended to explain. For each member of such a series does not *produce* the effect that follows it; it merely *transmits* or communicates that which it has received from another like itself. What we need to explain the existence of a contingent being, for example, is a being which does not have to receive existence before it can communicate it to another but possesses existence of itself; and such a being cannot be a contingent being which is a member of the series but must be a Necessary Being which transcends and at the same time is the cause of the whole series.

Thus, the "ways" are expressions of a vision of the sensible world in space and time as derivative from and constantly dependent upon a transcendent Being. The fact that this Being belongs to a higher order of reality than the finite beings of the natural order is shown by Aquinas' use of terms which sharply contrast Him with them, e.g., "unmoved" and "necessary." The fact that in the second "way" he uses the term "first" for the uncaused cause has misled many of his readers, since it has suggested that God is only the first member of a temporal series and thus is of the same order as finite causes. This misunderstanding has led to the question, "If God was the first cause of nature, what was the cause of God?" But Aquinas' real meaning, as we have said, is that God is the ultimate ground of the world rather than the first member of any or every series of effects in it. Thus, the vision which inspires the proofs is that of the radical contrast between the world of sensible things which possess nothing they have not received and a transcendent Being who exists of Himself, possesses all perfections in Himself and bestows both being and value in different degrees on the world.

A common *criticism* of Aquinas' arguments is that he concludes each of them with a statement such as "This everyone understands to be God," whereas he has really proved at the most a metaphysical first principle which explains the world. It is true that none of the five "ways" proves the existence of a Being who satisfies all the needs of religious faith and worship. Obviously, neither an Unmoved Mover nor a Necessary Being nor even an Intelligent Being is all that religious people mean by the word "God." How *could* it be in view of the fact that it was arrived at not by an analysis of the beliefs of religious people but by rational inference from facts of the natural order? However, Aquinas was well aware of this. As we shall see, the "questions" in the *Summa Theologica* which follow the five "ways" seek to demonstrate other attributes of God such as intellect, will, love, justice, and mercy. Hence, if one remembers that the "ways," or arguments, for God's existence provide only the beginning, not the whole, of his doctrine of God, one will hardly be able to say that his God is *only* a "metaphysical first principle" and bears no relation to the God of religion. Perhaps the reason for the misunderstanding of him at this point is that he seems simply to *identify* the being he has proved in each of the "ways" with the Being men call "God." But in doing so he does not mean that a First Cause or Necessary Being, for example, is *all* religious men mean by "God"; he means only that they include this in their meaning of the word as one *aspect* of it. The rest of what they mean he attempts to indicate in the later questions of the treatise on God in the *Summa*.[24]

Finally, there is an assumption concerning *reason* which is evident in all of the five "ways." Although reason is dependent upon sensation for the origin of its ideas, it is capable of knowing the nature of finite beings and extending its knowledge by inference from them to the transcendent Being who is their Ground. Aquinas was a realist in his theory of knowledge, although not in his theory of Ideas or universals; he seems to have had no doubt of the power of reason to know the nature of things. Indeed, he held that reason is naturally adapted to the knowledge of being. In addition to its capacity for discursive thinking, as illustrated by the reasoning from premises to conclusions in the five "ways," it has the faculty of what may be called intellectual insight into the nature of finite beings. One of the main reasons many modern persons are not convinced by the five "ways" of Aquinas is that they have lost not only his confidence in the metaphysical capacity of reason to comprehend the nature of finite beings but also his interest in such a comprehension. They are content to stop with the scientific point of view which is interested in the description of things as they appear to the senses, or with the technological point of view which regards them merely as things to be exploited for the satisfaction of human desires. Those who are quite satisfied with the scientific description of natural phenomena and the power over nature it gives them and therefore are never led to seek for a more ultimate explanation of the world as a whole find it difficult even to take Aquinas' "ways" to God seriously.

THE NATURE OF GOD: NEGATIVE THEOLOGY

What may man know by natural reason concerning the nature of God and His relation to the world? Aquinas accepts by faith the statement in Scripture that "we shall see Him as He is" (I John 3:2) and argues that man's beatitude consists in an intellectual vision of God.[25] The natural power of the intellect cannot attain to this vision because it knows only by means of ideas which are abstracted from material things. Therefore, an intellectual vision of the essence of God is possible only if God unites Himself to the intellect by His grace and makes Himself intelligible to it, and this can occur only in the future life after the soul has been separated from the body.[26] But this does not mean

---

[24] Aquinas, *Summa Theologica*, Pt. I, QQ. 3–26.
[25] *Ibid.*, Q. 12, a. 1.   [26] *Ibid.*, Q. 12, a. 4.

that we can know nothing about God in this life. As we have seen, our intellect can be led from knowledge of the effects of God to knowledge of His existence as their cause. It can also "know of Him what must necessarily belong to Him, as the first cause of all things, exceeding all things caused by Him." [27] Since the "whole power" of God cannot be known from His effects in nature, however, we cannot know the "essence" of God in this way.

Aquinas begins his lengthy discussion of the attributes of God in the *Summa Theologica* by asserting that "we cannot know what God is, but rather what He is not," and devoting several "questions" to an analysis of "what He is not." [28] This constitutes his *negative theology*. The fundamental principle of it is that "it can be shown how God is not, by removing from Him whatever does not befit Him—viz. composition, motion, and the like." [29] Thus, we assert his "simplicity" by removing composition from Him, His "infinity" by removing everything finite, His "eternity" by removing time. Several remarks should be made about the nature and significance of this negative theology before we consider briefly a few examples of it.

The assertion that "we cannot know what God is, but rather what He is not" should not be interpreted too literally. It is a warning that we cannot know the *essence* of God in this life, not a denial that we can know anything *about* Him. Obviously, negation of "whatever does not befit" God can be made only on the basis of some knowledge, however slight, of His nature. For example, to negate all composition of Him and to affirm His "simplicity" is based upon the knowledge that He is not a corporeal being that is composed of parts but a spiritual being that is indivisible, as Aquinas indicates by citing as his scriptural authority the statement, "God is a spirit" (John 4:24).

What is the *value* of negative assertions about God? The answer is that it is only by removing from God all the imperfections of His creatures that His transcendence and otherness can be safeguarded. There has always been a tendency of the human mind to confuse God with His creatures, as in polytheism, or with the creation as a whole, as in Pantheism. By contrasting Him with created things, the negative theology emphasizes His exaltation above them, His holiness, His otherness. This is necessary not only for the sake of theoretical clarity in theology but also for the sake of religious devotion. The mystics especially have always employed negations for God in order to stress His transcendence. It seems to them that even the highest ideas men can form of God are quite inadequate to express Him, since they limit His infinite and perfect being by comparing it with finite and imperfect

[27] *Ibid.*, Q. 12, a. 12.   [28] *Ibid.*, QQ. 3–11.   [29] *Ibid.*, Q. 3, Introduction.

things. Therefore, all names predicated of God hinder rather than help the soul in its aspiration to soar above the limitations of finite existence and unite itself with God. It is well known that, although Aquinas was not a mystic himself, he had an extraordinary experience while celebrating Mass in Naples shortly before his death and that this led him to discontinue his work on the *Summa Theologica.* "All that I have written seems to me nothing but straw compared with what I have seen and what has been revealed to me." [30]

However, the negative theology is more than an expression of the mystical point of view concerning human ideas of God. Its primary theological purpose is to combat all tendencies to stress God's immanence in the world to the point of identifying Him with it or with some aspect of it. For example, some Greek thinkers had identified God with the World-Soul and a medieval thinker [31] had gone so far as to equate Him with the prime matter which is the substrate of all sensible substances. Therefore, Aquinas rejects the assertion that God enters into the composition of other things, on the ground that He is the First Cause who "rules all things without commingling with them." [32] Moreover, if man is absolutely dependent upon God as the Creator and Sustainer of his existence and as his Redeemer from all evil, God must be absolutely dependable and perfect as no finite being is. In contrast to composite things which are threatened with dissolution into their parts, He must be "simple" or indivisible, i.e., a spiritual Being. In contrast to temporal things which are always perishing, He must be "eternal," i.e., without beginning or end. In contrast to changing things which are unstable and impermanent, He must be "immutable." In contrast to finite things which are conditioned and limited by other things, He must be "infinite," i.e., unconditioned and unlimited in His being and power. Thus, the negative theology of Aquinas is not only a theological safeguard of God's transcendence but also a religious affirmation that He is worthy of man's absolute dependence upon Him, because He is above all limitations.

We shall now analyze briefly some of the attributes of God discussed in the negative theology and make a few comments on them.

1. Aquinas demonstrates the *simplicity* or indivisibility of God by showing that none of the various kinds of composition can be attributed to Him. Making use of conclusions he has arrived at in his arguments for God's existence, he has no difficulty in showing that God

---

[30] Josef Pieper, *Guide to Thomas Aquinas* (New York: Pantheon, 1962), p. 158.

[31] David of Dinant; cf. *Summa Theologica*, Pt. I, Q. 3, a. 8.

[32] Aquinas, *Summa Theologica*, Pt. I, Q. 3, a. 8.

is not a body and hence is not composed of material parts. For all bodies are moved, whereas God is the Unmoved Mover, and all bodies are potentially divisible, whereas God as First Cause is "pure act" with no potentiality. Nor is God composed of form and matter as finite substances are, because as "pure act" He can have no potentiality in Him. Nor is He composed of essence and existence—His essence *is* His existence—nor of genus and difference, nor of subject and accidents. All of these forms of composition must be "removed" from Him. For every composite thing is "posterior" to its parts and requires a cause to unite its parts, whereas nothing can be prior to or a cause of God.[33]

The chief question concerning this elimination of all composition from God is whether it is really necessary to deny of Him every form of complexity or differentiation. Obviously, the Theist must deny that He is a body, or is composed of matter and form, or that He is the result of a combination of parts brought about by some external cause. But Aquinas does not consider in his discussion of God's "simplicity" the possibility that there may be an underived complexity in God analogous to that in the mind of a person. The spiritual and indivisible character of mind is shown by the fact that it has no parts which can be separated from one another like the parts of an inanimate thing or a living body, but it has various qualities and exercises various functions which are distinguishable but not separable from one another. Is "simplicity" of this kind to be denied to God? Clearly, biblical Theism conceives of God as one in a sense analogous to the sense in which a person is one. Hence it distinguishes within His nature between His intelligence and His will, His justice and His mercy. Since He is an indivisible spiritual Being, these distinctions do not imply any conflict within His nature or prevent each of His acts from expressing His nature as a unity, but the distinctions are nonetheless real. In contrast, Aquinas regards the different attributes of God as distinctions *for our reason* but not real *in Him.* But if they do not correspond to distinctions in His nature, it is difficult to see why they should be predicated of Him. Thus, while Aquinas has rightly emphasized the fact that there is no composition of material parts in God, he has not proved that there is no distinction between His functions and attributes as a spiritual Being. It should be noted, however, that Aquinas does not, like Plotinus, deny *all* differentiation in God, as his doctrine of the Trinity of divine "Persons" shows.

2. Aquinas discusses the *perfection* and *goodness* of God immediately after His simplicity and before His infinity, immutability, and

[33] *Ibid.,* Q. 3, a. 7.

eternity. However, it is obvious that, unlike all of these, perfection and goodness do not belong to the negative theology but are positive attributes. In spite of this, we shall discuss them briefly at this point because his treatment of the infinity, immutability, and eternity of God is dependent upon his view of God's perfection.

The *perfection* of God does not designate primarily moral perfection but completeness of being. As the First Cause of all things, God is wholly actual and therefore perfect, because "a thing is said to be perfect in proportion to its actuality." [34] Having no potentiality, He lacks nothing but possesses being in the highest degree. His *goodness* is simply an aspect of this perfection of being. For the essence of the goodness of a thing is that it is desirable, and a thing is desirable only insofar as it is perfect.[35] Thus, although God is the "highest good," He is first and foremost completeness of being. It should be noted that, since His perfection is defined as pure actuality of being without any potentiality, it is incompatible with change of any kind in Him. For change is a process in which a potentiality is actualized, and this implies the presence of a lack or deficiency of some kind. As we shall see, when this Aristotelian view of God's perfection is combined with Aquinas' conception of His immutability and eternity, serious difficulties are created for anyone whose view of God is that of biblical Theism.

3. The *infinity* of God is implied in his perfection. "To be perfect and to be infinite," writes Holloway, "are not the same thing. The former posits in God the complete actuality of being and all the perfections of being; the latter removes or denies any term or limit to this being. But infinity flows from perfection: since God's Being is completely in act, there can be nothing potential or limiting within it." [36] Aquinas adds that the ancient philosophers attributed infinity to the first principle because "they considered that things flow forth infinitely from the first principle." [37] This suggests that belief in God's infinity is based in part upon the apparently inexhaustible capacity of the First Cause to produce effects, a capacity which has continued from the beginning of things to the present. More interesting than Aquinas' view of God's infinity, however, is his treatment of God's *omnipresence*. This is implied in His infinity, "for God is said to be everywhere, and in all

[34] *Ibid.*, Q. 4, a. 1.
[35] *Ibid.*, Q. 5, a. 1.
[36] Maurice Holloway, *Introduction to Natural Theology* (New York: Appleton-Century-Crofts, 1959), pp. 242–245.
[37] Aquinas, *Summa Theologica*, Pt. I, Q. 7, a. 1.

things, inasmuch as He is boundless and infinite." [38] But there is a theological problem about omnipresence which Aquinas solves in a skillful way. A theist must affirm the reality of God's presence and hence His availability for human need everywhere; but he must also guard against pantheistic confusion of Him with His creatures when he speaks of Him as being "in" all things. Aquinas avoids this by asserting that God is present in all things "not, indeed, as part of their essence, nor as an accident, but as an agent is present to that upon which it acts." [39] For this does not prevent Him from being "above all things," as His transcendence requires, "by the excellence of His nature." [40] Thus, although He is an incorporeal being and cannot be "in place" like a body, He is "in every place" by "contact of power," [41] and "inasmuch as all things are bare and open to His eyes." [42]

4. In Aquinas' view, the *immutability* and *eternity* of God are closely related and the latter follows from the former. He demonstrates God's *immutability* from the premise that He is "pure act" without potentiality. Presupposing the Aristotelian view of change as a transition from potentiality to actuality, he argues that to attribute change to Him would imply that there is potentiality in Him. He also argues that change would be incompatible with His infinity and perfection, because anything that changes "acquires something" in doing so. "But since God is infinite, comprehending in Himself all the plenitude of the perfection of all being, He cannot acquire anything new." [43] This conception of God's immutability has merit in that it preserves the transcendence of God above the mutability of His creatures and the threat of nonbeing to which it subjects them. But it does so, as we shall see, only at the cost of inconsistency with the conception of God in biblical Theism.

This will become clearer from a consideration of the *eternity* of God. Aquinas adopts the definition of eternity by Boethius: "Eternity is the simultaneously whole and perfect [i.e., complete] possession of interminable life." [44] He demonstrates the truth of this definition by showing that what is eternal has no beginning or end ("interminable") and no succession of before and after ("simultaneously whole"). Since time is the measure of motion, according to Aristotle, there can be no time in a being without motion. Therefore, there can be no beginning or end and no succession of before and after in God, since there is no motion or change in Him. But what is one to say to the

[38] *Ibid.*, Q. 7, Introduction.
[39] *Ibid.*, Q. 8, a. 1.   [40] *Ibid.*, Q. 8, a. 1.   [41] *Ibid.*, Q. 8, a. 2.
[42] *Ibid.*, Q. 8, a. 3.   [43] *Ibid.*, Q. 9, a. 1.   [44] *Ibid.*, Q. 10, a. 1.

objection that "words denoting present, past and future are applied to God in Scripture"? Aquinas' reply is that these words are applied to God "because His eternity includes all times, and not as if He Himself were altered through present, past, and future." [45]

This objection and his reply indicate the difficulty in his view of God's eternity. If eternity is without beginning or end and without succession, it is beyond time and change. If so, it is hard to see how God's eternity can "include" time, or how this is possible without His being "altered" in some sense by the changes that occur in time. Moreover, if God is in eternity beyond time and change, He can hardly be affected by the events that occur in time but must be completely detached from them. This conclusion, which is required by Aquinas' view that God is immutable in the sense that nothing new can occur to Him, is contrary to the biblical view of God's relation to His creatures in time. Clearly, in the Bible God is not unaffected by what His creatures, especially men, say and do. He hears their prayers and answers them, sees their sins and punishes them, heeds their repentance and forgives them. He is not only a God who acts but also a God who responds. He is steadfast and faithful in His purposes, but He adapts His acts to the changing situations, attitudes, and acts of His children. This view seems quite incompatible with an interpretation of God's immutability which allows for no change in Him as He responds to the changes in the lives of His children or with an interpretation of His eternity which removes from Him everything corresponding to the succession of past, present, and future in time.

This suggests the *dangers* of the negative theology. By emphasizing so strongly the transcendence of God and His otherness in relation to finite beings, it may lead to a view of God as self-sufficient and detached from the world and make it difficult to affirm perfections of Him in such a way as to give us positive knowledge of His nature. Maimonides, who was deeply influenced by the negative theology, would admit no knowledge of the positive attributes of God and insisted that even names such as "wise" and "good" should be predicated of Him only in an "equivocal" or quite different sense. Spinoza later carried this attitude to its logical conclusion when he denied that will, understanding, and other attributes could be predicated of God. Aquinas was saved from this theological agnosticism, as we shall see, by his doctrine of analogy. But in beginning his analysis of man's knowledge of God with a kind of negative theology which exaggerates His

[45] *Ibid.*, Q. 10, a. 2.

difference from His creatures, he raises a doubt in the minds of many readers whether any affirmations about God are possible in view of the gulf between Him and His creatures. How can man ascribe qualities of finite, temporal, and changing creatures like himself by analogy to such a Being? Moreover, if he overcomes these doubts and makes affirmations about God, as Aquinas did, these affirmations will have to be interpreted in such a way as to be consistent with the negative assertions which have previously been made and this will require the removal from the affirmations of most of their ordinary meaning. Thus, negative theology can, if it is pressed too far, lead *either* to a complete denial of the possibility of positive statements about God *or* to a weakening of such statements by evacuating them of meaning. This suggests that negative theology should be developed not in independence of but in close relation to the affirmative theology, if it is not to undermine or at least threaten men's positive knowledge of God and His close relationship to His creatures.

THE NAMES OF GOD: AFFIRMATIVE THEOLOGY

Following his discussion of "what God is not" in the negative theology, Aquinas introduces his *affirmative theology* by arguing that we can give a name to anything insofar as we can understand it and that we can in some measure understand or know God from His creatures as their Cause. Therefore, we can name Him from His creatures, although the names we use to signify Him will not express the divine essence.[46] These names can be applied to Him "substantially," i.e., to His substance, but they can represent Him only inadequately "as the excelling source of whose form the effects fall short, although they derive some kind of likeness thereto." [47] Some names may be applied to God only metaphorically, e.g., "stone," because they signify perfections which are present in creatures in an imperfect way. But some may be applied to Him "properly," e.g., "being," "good," and "living," because they express perfections without any imperfections as part of their meaning.[48] These names are not synonymous but have diverse meanings. For although the perfections they signify exist in God "unitedly and simply," they are "divided and multiplied" in creatures and must be apprehended by our intellect in that way.[49] With regard to "what is signified" by the names of these perfections, they are applied properly

[46] *Ibid.*, Q. 13, a. 1.   [47] *Ibid.*, Q. 13, a. 2.   [48] *Ibid.*, Q. 13, a. 4.
[49] *Ibid.*

and primarily to God, but with regard to their "mode of signification," they are applied properly and primarily to creatures.[50]

How should names of this kind be predicated of God? At first sight, it seems plausible that they should be predicated of Him and of creatures in the same sense, "univocally," since the creatures from which they are derived have a certain likeness to God. But univocal predication is impossible, because the effects of God fall short of complete likeness to Him. For example, when we apply the epithet "wise" to a man, we signify a perfection distinct from his essence and from other perfections, whereas when we apply it to God this is not the case.[51] At the other extreme, it can be argued that such names should be applied to God and His creatures in quite different senses, purely "equivocally." At first Aquinas seems to accept this view. He says that since the "distance" of some creatures from each other makes univocal predication of them impossible and God is even more "distant" from creatures than they are from each other, only equivocal predication can be applied to God and creatures.[52] But in the same article he qualifies this view in a significant way. "Neither, on the other hand, are names applied to God and creatures in a *purely* equivocal sense, as some have said. Because if that were so, it follows that from creatures nothing at all could be known or demonstrated about God; for the reasoning would always be exposed to the fallacy of equivocation." [53] Therefore, Aquinas concludes that we should predicate such names of God and creatures "in an analogous sense, that is, according to proportion," and he speaks of this form of predication as "a mean between pure equivocation and simple univocation." [54]

Since Aquinas uses this doctrine of *analogy* as the basis of his affirmative theology, it is necessary to indicate clearly its general meaning and significance. In his negative theology he had emphasized the transcendence of God and severely limited the capacity of man's intellect to know Him. If he was to apply any positive attributes to Him in an affirmative theology, he had to do so in a way consistent with his strong assertion of the transcendence and otherness of God. Therefore, he could not allow that any names derived from creatures could apply "univocally" to God because to do so would deny His "distance" from them and claim a degree of knowledge of Him which man does not possess. On the other hand, he had maintained that we can know

[50] *Ibid.*, Q. 13, a. 3.   [51] *Ibid.*, Q. 13, a. 5.
[52] *Ibid.*, Q. 13, a. 5.
[53] *Ibid.*, Q. 13, a. 5 (italics added; "some" refers to Maimonides and others).
[54] *Ibid.*

something of God as Cause from His effects, although we cannot know His essence. Therefore, he could not admit that names of perfections which include no imperfection in their meaning must be applied only "equivocally." To put it simply, univocal predication would claim too much, while "pure" equivocal predication would claim too little, for man's capacity to know God. Both would be religiously disastrous, the one by minimizing the transcendence or "distance" of God from His creatures, the other by denying all likeness between Him and them. In contrast, the doctrine of analogy is a mean between the two extremes and avoids the dangers of both. It does not permit an uncritical comparison of God with His creatures, especially man, and thus it avoids the danger of anthropomorphism; but it recognizes some likenesses between them, and thus it avoids the danger of agnosticism about the nature of God. It asserts that we know something about God from the perfections of His creatures, but it warns us that what we know is very limited. Although the names for these perfections apply properly and even primarily to God with respect to "what is signified" by them, they do not apply to Him properly with respect to their "mode of signification," for this is suitable to creatures rather than God.[55]

The Aristotelian presuppositions and the negative theology of Aquinas affect his interpretation of the positive attributes of God at many points, for they require him to conceive of God's relation to the world in a way which is in certain respects foreign to biblical Theism. The most striking expression of this conception is his argument that *there is in God no "real" relation to the world* but only a relation "in idea," so that He is not affected by His relation to the creatures as they are affected by their relation to Him. "Since, therefore, God is outside the whole order of creatures, and all creatures are ordered to Him, and not conversely, it is manifest that creatures are really related to God Himself; whereas, in God there is no real relation to creatures, but a relation only in idea, inasmuch as creatures are related to Him." [56] An implication of this is that the relation between God and His creatures involves no change in Him when changes occur in them, "as a column is on the right of an animal, without change in itself, but because the animal has moved." [57] This denial of a real relation in God to His creatures, a relation which affects Him as well as them, is probably influenced both by Aristotle's conception of the Prime Mover as completely transcendent to and unaffected by the world and by the interpretation of the "immutability" of God in the negative theology. It is

[55] *Ibid.*, Q. 13, a. 3.   [56] *Ibid.*, Q. 13, a. 7.   [57] *Ibid.*

not only inconsistent with the view of biblical Theism, but also, as we shall see, it has a profound effect upon Aquinas' conception of God's knowledge and will.

The influence of Aristotle is also manifest in his argument that the most "proper" or suitable name for God is "He who is" or "*Being.*" Although he uses as a scriptural authority God's answer to Moses' question concerning His name, "He Who Is hath sent me to you" (Exod. 3:14), his argument shows clearly the effect of Aristotle's view that "being" or "substance" is the primary category. Although he repeats his earlier proof that God's essence is the same as His being,[58] his chief argument is that all other names are less universal or more determinate than "being." "Now in this life our intellect cannot know the essence itself of God as it is in itself. . . . Therefore the less determinate the names are and the more universal and absolute they are, the more properly are they applied to God." [59] This argument is difficult to reconcile with the biblical way of speaking about God. If the "most proper" name for God is one which signifies His essence, a name indicating His personal and dynamic character would seem to be more suitable than the impersonal name "Being." It is true that "Being" is the most *fundamental* name that can be applied to God, since all other names are ascribed to Him as one who exists; but it does not distinguish Him from other beings and therefore is not the name "most proper" to Him. Modern Catholic philosophers offer a defense of Aquinas at this point. "We may wonder," writes Maurer, "whether St. Thomas is not demeaning God by saying that he is nothing but the act of being. Are there not other perfections besides being, such as life and intelligence, and is it not more perfect to live and to understand than simply to be? St. Thomas points out, however, that to live and to understand are *ways of being* included in being itself. . . . 'Being,' indeed, is the richest and most comprehensive of all terms, for it includes all perfections. Hence to say that God is Being itself is to say that he is all-perfect, or that his perfection is without limits." [60] Doubtless, it is true that for Aquinas the name "being" is rich in meaning and "includes all perfections." But it does not have such a meaning for others, and for some thinkers such as Hegel it is the poorest rather than the richest of concepts. And when its meaning is broadened to include such perfections as life and understanding and all other perfections besides, it becomes so comprehensive that it is wholly indeterminate. In

[58] *Ibid.*, Q. 3, a. 4.   [59] *Ibid.*, Q. 13, a. 11.
[60] Maurer, *Medieval Philosophy*, p. 171.

trying to say everything, it says nothing definite about the distinctive nature of the divine Being.

In addition to "being," the affirmative theology of Aquinas includes the following attributes: "knowledge," "will," "life," "love," "justice and mercy," "providence," "power," and "beatitude." Of these, we shall briefly discuss "knowledge," "will," "love," and "power," all of which are fundamental attributes of the God of Theism.

1. Aquinas demonstrates the *knowledge* of God by deducing it from the fact that He is a spiritual or immaterial being and consequently can possess the forms of all things and thus extend Himself infinitely.[61] He might also have demonstrated it by starting from the conclusion of the fifth argument for the existence of God, i.e., that "some intelligent being exists by whom all natural things are directed to their end; and this being we call God," [62] and arguing that this being must possess a knowledge of all things in order to direct them to their ends. But more important than his proof of this fundamental attribute is his analysis of its nature. God knows *Himself* primarily. He also knows things other than Himself, but He knows them *in* Himself. For in knowing Himself, He knows His power and the things to which His power extends as the effective cause of all things. Thus, He knows other things only indirectly. "He sees them," says Aquinas, "not in themselves, but in Himself, inasmuch as His essence contains the likeness of things other than Himself." [63] His assertion that God does not know other things directly or "in themselves" seems to be motivated by the fear that God's knowledge of other things would involve imperfection in Him, since Aristotle held that in knowledge the intellect is in potentiality until it is actualized by its object. This fear is groundless, he replies, because God's knowledge is not caused by other things but by His own substance, i.e., He knows them only in knowing His own substance. Obviously, there is a tension here between the biblical belief that God knows "other things," i.e., the creatures, and his own assertion in the negative theology that any potentiality in God would be incompatible with His perfection. He is able to resolve this tension only by the artificial view that God knows other things not "in themselves" but only "in Himself," so that His knowledge does not have to be actualized and involves no imperfection.

The effect of Aquinas' negative theology upon his affirmative theology is also illustrated by his argument that God's knowledge does not

---

[61] Aquinas, *Summa Theologica*, Pt. I, Q. 14, a. 1.
[62] *Ibid.*, Q. 2, a. 3.   [63] *Ibid.*, Q. 14, a. 5.

vary despite the fact that the things He knows are always changing. God's knowledge, he says, is His substance; His substance is immutable; therefore, His knowledge must be immutable.[64] This is possible because God knows things not as they are in themselves but as they are in Him. As they are in Him in an invariable manner, He can know even things that are changing by an act that is unchanging.[65] This conception of God's knowledge of things as invariable or *unchanging* is obviously necessitated by Aquinas' interpretation of the immutability of God in his negative theology. But it demands not only that His knowledge be regarded as intuitive and as including "all things together at once" [66]—a difficult conception—but also that it extend to "future contingent things" such as the acts of men. Aquinas holds that God necessarily knows all things as eternally and immutably present to His intellect. This would seem to be inconsistent with the contingency of men's acts which are the result of free choice. Aquinas replies that, although God knows future contingent things necessarily, He knows them as contingent in relation to their causes. Whether this conception is intelligible and is compatible with man's freedom of will we shall consider later. What we would point out here is that it was necessitated by Aquinas' view that God's knowledge must extend to all things, since He is "infinite"; that it involves no discursive thinking or succession in time but must be intuitive, since He is "eternal"; and that it must involve no change even when its objects are changing things and things that are future and contingent, since He is "immutable." Thus Aquinas' view of some of the most important characteristics of God's knowledge is determined by his negative theology.

2. Aquinas' analysis of the *will* of God follows the same general pattern as that of His knowledge and raises similar difficulties. The proof that there *is* will in Him is based on the assumption that "will follows intellect," i.e., that we will only what our intellect judges to be good, and that everything in nature "tends towards" its form and perfection as good. Intellectual natures tend toward the good apprehended by them, seeking to possess it and to rest in it when it is possessed. Since this tendency pertains to will, there must be will in every intellectual being and therefore in God.[67] The most significant thing in this proof is that it illustrates Aquinas' conviction of the primacy of the intellect over the will, since he assumes that will is dependent upon the apprehension of good by the intellect and seems

---

[64] *Ibid.*, Q. 14, a. 15.   [65] *Ibid.*
[66] *Ibid.*, Q. 14, a. 7.   [67] *Ibid.*, Q. 19, a. 1.

to be little more than the disposition of an intellectual being to possess and rest in its good.

Although the object of God's will is that which is good, this does not make Him dependent upon an end beyond Himself. For *God Himself is the end*, since He is in His essence good.[68] Moreover, it does not imply any potentiality and hence imperfection in Him, since His will always possesses and rests in its object, Himself as Good.[69] Thus, Aquinas is led by his view that God has no "real" relation to His creatures and that His "perfection" permits of no potentiality in Him, to center God's will upon His own good as its primary object. As a result, he argues that *God wills things other than Himself only secondarily*, as "ordained" to Himself and as participating in His goodness.[70] The parallel between this and Aquinas' view of God's knowledge of other things is obvious. "So, as He understands things other than Himself by understanding His own essence, so He wills things other than Himself by willing His own goodness." [71] However, there is also evidence of a more dynamic conception of God's will as being concerned with the good of other things in and for themselves. "For natural things have a natural inclination not only towards their own proper good . . . but also to diffuse their own good among others so far as possible. . . . Hence, if natural things, in so far as they are perfect, communicate their good to others, much more does it pertain to the divine will to communicate by likeness its own good to others as much as possible." [72] This conception of the divine will to good is more in accord with the biblical view of God which represents Him as seeking the good of His children for their own sakes. If Aquinas had followed it more consistently in his thinking about God, it might have led him to affirm that God's relation to His creatures is "real" in Him and that He is affected by them.

The will of God, Aquinas maintains, is *always fulfilled*. This assertion seems to be based upon the assumption that God's omnipotence involves absolute determinism, an assumption which may show the influence of St. Augustine upon him. "Something may escape the order of any particular agent cause," he says, "but not the order of the universal cause under which all particular causes are included. . . . Since, then, the will of God is the universal cause of all things, it is impossible that the divine will should not produce its effect." [73] The objection to this view is obvious: God's will does not seem always

---

[68] *Ibid.*   [69] *Ibid.*   [70] *Ibid.*, Q. 19, a. 2.
[71] *Ibid.*   [72] *Ibid.*   [73] *Ibid.*, Q. 19, a. 6.

to be fulfilled, e.g., His will that all men be saved. Aquinas attempts to meet this objection by distinguishing between the "antecedent" and the "consequent" will of God. "In the same way, God antecedently wills all men to be saved, and consequently wills some to be damned, as His justice exacts. . . . Hence we will a thing absolutely inasmuch as we will it when all particular circumstances are considered; and this is what is meant by willing consequently. . . . Thus it is clear that whatever God wills absolutely [i.e., consequently] takes place; although what He wills antecedently may not take place." [74] This answer, which is made necessary by the acceptance of the Augustinian doctrine of predestination,[75] is based upon an artificial distinction and is unconvincing.

The only answer that is both rationally and religiously acceptable is that His will is not fulfilled in the case of some because they do not put their trust in Him and obey Him. But this answer is based upon a conception of God's omnipotence which takes into account man's freedom to accept or reject His will, and this limits the fulfillment of it in the case of human acts. In contrast, Aquinas holds that, although these acts have "contingent" causes and God's will does not "impose necessity" upon them, they are ultimately determined by His will. By asserting that God's will is the cause not only of "the thing done" but also of "its manner of being done," i.e., that an act of human will is done from a proximate cause that is contingent, Aquinas thinks that he has saved man's freedom of choice. But this is false, since a "contingent" cause which is willed by God is just as necessary as the effect it is willed by Him to produce. Thus, God's will in the last analysis determines everything that occurs.

God's will, like His knowledge, is invariable or *unchangeable*. Although He may will a thing to be done now and something contrary to it later, His will remains permanently the same despite the fact that its effects change.[76] One difficulty with this view is that the Bible often seems to speak of changes in God's will, as when He says, "If that nation shall repent of its evil, I also will repent of the evil that I have thought to do to them" (Jer. 18:8). Aquinas replies that the reason "repentance" is ascribed to Him is that *man* "repents" or changes his purpose when he does not carry out a threat he has previously made. But the crucial question for a theist is whether God's will should be regarded as unchangeable in such a sense that it cannot respond to the changing situations and actions of men by varying its acts. In the Bible, God often seems to adapt His acts to the changing circumstances

[74] *Ibid.*   [75] *Ibid.*, Q. 23, a. 3, 5.   [76] *Ibid.*, Q. 19, a. 7.

and conduct of men, e.g., sending a flood in the time of Noah to punish the wickedness of men and promising not to carry out a threat of punishment in Jeremiah's time if the people repent of their evil ways. In other words, the Bible affirms the unchangeableness of God's will not in an absolute sense but in the sense of a steadfastness of purpose which is manifested in acts that change in response to changing conditions. But Aquinas' view of it has been distorted by the rigid and absolute conception of God's "immutability" in his negative theology as meaning that from eternity God's will has been fixed for every situation that has arisen or will arise in time and that it is affected by nothing that happens at any time. As a result, history appears to be the mere unfolding with necessity of a predetermined pattern of events which is not influenced or modified by anything man does.

3. Aquinas' conception of God's *love* in his rational theology is quite inadequate, especially from the perspective of biblical Theism. Love is defined as the movement of the will toward things apprehended as good. Since God's will always tends toward good, this implies that love exists in Him.[77] Thus love is simply another name for God's will to the good. There is no passion in it, since it belongs to His will rather than to an irrational appetite. Since all things are caused by God and are good, God loves everything that exists. But whereas our love is called forth by the goodness in things, God's love "infuses and creates goodness in things." [78] This view is in accord with the biblical picture of God's love as involving the will to good for His creatures, and it stresses the fact that the very existence of things which are good witnesses to the love of God who created them. But in eliminating from it the passion which accompanies irrational appetite, it also seems to leave out His feeling for His creatures, His care and concern for them as beings which are loved for their own sake and not merely as objects upon which good is bestowed.[79]

Another difficulty arises in connection with his view that God does not love all things equally but loves some things more than others in that He wills a greater good for them. His ground for saying this is that since God's love causes the goodness of things, "no one thing would be better than another if God did not will greater good for one than for another." [80] For example, Aquinas asserts that, although God loves sinners insofar as they *exist*, "they are hated by Him" insofar as they are *sinners*.[81] The difficulty with this view is that, whereas the New

---

[77] *Ibid.*, Q. 20, a. 1.   [78] *Ibid.*, Q. 20, a. 2.

[79] See the discussion of the "divine pathos" in Abraham J. Heschel, *The Prophets* (New York: Harper & Row, 1962), Chap. 14.

[80] Aquinas, *Summa Theologica*, Pt. I, Q. 20, a. 3.   [81] *Ibid.*, Q. 20, a. 2.

Testament describes God's love as unconditional and bestowed upon all men without regard to their worth or lack of it, Aquinas represents it as given to men in various degrees, e.g., to righteous men more than to sinners, according to the principle that better things should receive more love than others. At the same time, he also asserts that God's love is the original cause of the different degrees of good in things upon which He then bestows different degrees of love. Thus, He loves things more because they are better, but they are better because He loved them more. Apart from this apparently circular reasoning, if God's love is measured out in different degrees to different beings, it is modified by its relation to its objects, and love tends to be identified with justice which is given "to each according to his due." However, it must be admitted that Aquinas may be speaking here of the love which can be demonstrated by reason rather than love which has come to be known by revelation in the Bible. And it may be argued that it is beyond the capacity of reason to know that God's love is given equally to all, righteous and sinful alike.

4. The attribute of *power*, the last we shall consider, is treated by Aquinas in a most interesting and fruitful way. He deduces the existence of active power in God, i.e., power which acts upon something else, from the fact that God is pure actuality and therefore is an active principle which is in no way passive. But the question that concerns him most is how God's power is to be conceived as infinite, as it must be since He is infinite. This implies that He is omnipotent in the sense that He can do all things. But what is the meaning of "all" in this connection? Aquinas' answer is that God "can do all things that are possible absolutely." [82] A statement is said to be absolutely possible "if the predicate is not incompatible with the subject, as that Socrates sits," but to be absolutely impossible "when the predicate is altogether incompatible with the subject, as, for instance, that man is an ass." [83] He concludes that an absolutely impossible thing is beyond God's power not because of a defect in His power but because it is intrinsically or essentially impossible. Hence "it is more appropriate to say that such things cannot be done, than that God cannot do them." [84] For example, God cannot make the past not to have been, since that would imply a contradiction just as a contradiction is implied in saying that Socrates is sitting and not sitting.[85] Aquinas also maintains that God *can do* other things than He *has done,* because "the divine wisdom is not so restricted to any particular order that no other scheme of things could proceed from it." [86]

[82] *Ibid.,* Q. 25, a. 3.   [83] *Ibid.*   [84] *Ibid.*   [85] *Ibid.,* Q. 25, a. 4.
[86] *Ibid.,* Q. 25, a. 5.

In this interpretation of the omnipotence of God, Aquinas is at his best. In insisting that divine omnipotence does not include the power to do things that are self-contradictory and hence absolutely impossible, he is defending the view that God's power is exercised in accordance with His wisdom which is a principle of order rather than disorder. Thus he would have been opposed to the view of later "voluntarists" such as William of Ockham that God's will is not governed by His intellect and limited by principles of order and that He could by a sheer fiat of His will make stealing or adultery right.[87] On the other hand, he rejects the view that God's power is so restricted that He can do only what He actually does in the world as we know it. For this would imply that He was under the necessity of creating the world as it is and was not free to create anything other than it is. The world is a product of God's wisdom, but this does not mean that His wisdom could not have conceived other things and imposed upon them another order. Thus Aquinas guards against pantheistic doctrines like that of Spinoza, according to whom God acts from necessity and nothing was or is possible for Him but what is or will be actual. In short, he avoids the extremes of both arbitrary voluntarism and rigid determinism: God's power extends to everything which is not absolutely impossible and hence inconsistent with His wisdom, but it is not confined within the limits of what is actual.

THE CREATION AND MAN

Although Aquinas' greatest contribution to rational theology is his doctrine of the existence and nature of God, his doctrine of man and his place in the creation has also had great influence. It will be necessary, however, to deal with it very briefly and in general terms.[88]

Every being besides God exists not of necessity but by receiving its being from God who is Being-itself. God has *created* all finite beings from nonbeing or nothing, *ex nihilo*, not merely from pre-existing matter as in Plato's *Timaeus*. The question whether the world always existed or had a beginning in time cannot be answered by the natural reason of the philosopher. For the duration of the world depends upon the decision of God's will, and reason can know nothing about this. Although we know by revelation (Gen. 1:1) that the world had a beginning in time, God *could* have decided to create it with an eternal duration. In that case it would have eternally owed its whole being to Him. Thus, the proposition that the creation had a beginning in time

[87] Ockham, *Studies and Selections*, ed. S. C. Tornay (LaSalle, Ill.: Open Court, 1938), p. 180.

[88] Aquinas, *Summa Theologica*, "Creation in General," Part I, QQ. 44–49.

belongs to revealed rather than to rational theology and illustrates Aquinas' view of the limits of man's natural reason.

There was no necessity for God to create a world, for He is perfect and in need of nothing beyond Himself. He created it by a free decision of His *will*. As His will is not caused by anything, we cannot know His reason for creating a world or for creating the world as it is rather than some other possible world. However, since every actual being tends to communicate its being and since God is perfectly actual, it could be expected that He would communicate His nature as far as possible. Thus, He has created finite beings of diverse kinds according to the innumerable ways in which they can imitate His Ideas and thus participate in His being and perfection. All of these kinds of creatures are *good*, as He is good. There are natural or physical *evils* in them, but they are due to the finite character of all created things. For evil is not a being but the absence or lack in a being of something that belongs to its nature, e.g., the blindness of a man or the death of a living being. God does not cause these natural evils as such, although He incidentally causes them in that He has willed to create a world of finite beings in which defects occur. As for moral evil, it is not caused by God at all but by man's free will.

The many species of created beings are unequal to one another in their degrees of perfection. Since the infinite God could not fully express His goodness in one kind of creature, He created different kinds and ordered them in a *hierarchy* or *scale of being*. In this hierarchy, the highest rank is that of the angels, spiritual substances without which there would have been a gap in the creation and hence a break in the continuity of the creatures. Men, who are partly spiritual and partly corporeal, are below the angels and above the animals and plants. At the lowest level are the four physical elements. Thus man has an intermediate position in the scale of being between the highest level of purely spiritual beings and the lowest level of inanimate matter. Being corporeal as well as spiritual, he may be said to be the lowest of the spiritual beings. But since he is distinguished from other animal species by his possession of reason, he is the highest of terrestrial beings.

At the beginning of his "Treatise on Man" Aquinas remarks that "the theologian considers the nature of man in relation to the soul, but not in relation to the body, except in so far as the body has relation to the soul." [89] Accordingly, he concerns himself in his treatment of man primarily with the nature of the soul, its relation to the body, and its

[89] *Ibid.*, "Man," Q. 75.

"powers" or functions. In his view of the *nature of the soul* he rejects the two extremes of Platonic dualism and Materialism. Man's essence cannot be identified with the soul alone, as in the former, since one of his activities is sensation and this is not an activity of the soul by itself. Thus he is not only a soul but a being composed of soul and body,[90] so that the body is an integral part of his nature. On the other hand, the soul is not a body, as in Materialism. It is the principle of life which is found in animate but not in inanimate beings and which is the source of their movement and knowledge.[91]

The soul is a "substance" of an incorporeal kind, for its intellecual activity is "essentially an operation in which the body does not share." [92] However, it is not a "complete" substance. Since the soul is a part rather than the whole of human nature, it is the "composite" of body and soul which is a complete substance, an individual man.[93] Thus, Aquinas seeks to maintain *both* the substantial nature of the soul as capable of intellectual activity in which the body does not share *and* the fact that the complete substance of a man includes the soul and its body. This is essentially an Aristotelian view on both sides of it. For Aristotle regarded intellectual activity as the most distinctive thing about the human soul, and at the same time held that the soul is the form of the body and is therefore closely related to it. It is also Aristotelian in insisting upon the unity of the soul in spite of its different functions. Although the intellectual soul is the form of the body, it "contains virtually whatever belongs to the sensitive soul of brute animals and to the nutritive life of plants." [94] As he puts it, "neither is Socrates a man by one soul and an animal by another; but by one and the same soul he is both animal and man." [95] The fact that the intellectual soul is spiritual does not imply that its union with a corruptible body is not suitable or fitting for it. Indeed, its union with the body is indispensable to it. Since it is not naturally in possession of the truth but must gather its knowledge from things by means of the senses, it "had to be united to a body which could be the fitting organ of sense." [96]

There are obviously two sides of this view of the soul's relation to its body and at first sight they appear incompatible. On one side, the soul is *essentially spiritual* rather than corporeal, since its intellectual activity is spiritual. On the other side, the soul is the "form of the body" and is completely *dependent* upon the bodily senses for its knowledge. How can the soul be both purely spiritual in its intellectual activity and

---

[90] *Ibid.*, Q. 75, a. 4.   [91] *Ibid.*, Q. 75, a. 1.   [92] *Ibid.*, Q. 75, a. 2.   [93] *Ibid.*
[94] *Ibid.*, Q. 76, a. 3.   [95] *Ibid.*   [96] *Ibid.*, Q. 76, a. 5.

dependent upon the body? Aquinas answers by distinguishing between the soul's intellectual activity as such and the objects or contents of that activity. "The body is necessary for the action of the intellect, not as its organ of action, but on the part of the object; for the phantasm [i.e., likeness of the object] is to the intellect what color is to the sight." [97] This means that, although the intellect depends upon the senses of the body to provide it with its *objects* through the likenesses or images of them, it does not depend upon the senses as its "organ of action," i.e., for its own *activity* in knowing these objects. While the soul is united with a body in this life, it derives the objects of its knowledge from the bodily senses, but, since its intellectual activity in its essence is purely spiritual, it is possible for it to understand in another way when it is separated from its body.[98] Thus, the soul's association with and dependence upon its body is indispensable to it in its present state but is not essential to its intellectual activity in every possible state.

This solution of the difficulty, which combines Aristotelian and Platonic elements, is the basis of Aquinas' main argument for the "incorruptibility" or *immortality* of the soul. Since the soul has been shown to be a substantial or "subsistent" being, one which "has being in itself," it cannot be corrupted by the corruption of something else, i.e., its body. Therefore, if it is to be corrupted, it can only be by itself. But this is impossible for anything which is a subsistent being, which "has being in itself." "But it is impossible," says Aquinas, "for a form to be separated from itself; and therefore it is impossible for a subsistent form to cease to exist." [99] This implies that it is *essentially* immortal, although it could be annihilated by God who created it.[100] He also argues for its immortality from the natural desire of men to persist in being, on the assumption that "a natural desire cannot be in vain." This argument rests upon a teleological and optimistic view of nature as attaining the fulfillment of its ends.

The two spiritual *powers* or functions of the human soul which distinguish it from the souls of plants and animals are *intellect* and *will*. The object of the former is knowledge of the truth, of the latter attainment and enjoyment of the good. *Free will* or choice, *liberum arbitrium*, is dependent upon the former but belongs to the latter. It depends upon the fact that man possesses reason and can choose the means to the attainment of his fundamental end of happiness. Thus, as Copleston says, "St. Thomas' account of freedom is intellectualistic in

[97] *Ibid.*, Q. 75, a. 2; reply obj. 3   [98] *Ibid.*, Q. 89, a. 1.
[99] *Ibid.*, Q. 75, a. 6.   [100] *Ibid.*

character." [101] However, the decision which puts an end to deliberation is made by the will, so that freedom of choice is a power or function of the will. This account of free will illustrates the fact that, although Aquinas distinguishes between intellect and will and assigns certain functions to the one and others to the other, he is fully aware of their interdependence and cooperation.

Perhaps the most interesting thing in his analysis of intellect and will is his *intellectualism*. Unlike Augustine, who held that will is the primary function of the soul and that the direction of a man's love determines his character, Aquinas accords the primacy to the intellect and holds that the "image of God" in man is his "intellectual nature." [102] In accordance with this intellectualist view, he maintains in the *Summa contra Gentiles* that the last end or highest good of man is to be found primarily in an activity of the intellect rather than of the will. After the separation of the soul from the body, the intellect will be raised to a higher than natural power with the aid of the divine light and will be enabled to "see" God as He is in Himself.[103] This vision of God, or "beatific vision," is higher than any end attainable by the will. The reason for this exaltation of the intellectual vision of God above every activity of the will is that, as Copleston says, "absolutely speaking, the intellect is the nobler faculty, since the intellect through cognition possesses the object . . . whereas the will tends towards the object as external, and it is more perfect to possess the perfection of the object in oneself than to tend towards it as existing outside oneself." [104] However, Aquinas maintains that the vision of God in the after life will be accompanied by the fulfillment of every desire, so that the will also will attain its object, enjoyment of the Good. Thus the vision of God will make possible the complete fulfillment of all the faculties of the soul and the attainment of perfect blessedness.

This view of man's "last end" or highest good is an interesting example of Aquinas' synthesis of Aristotelian philosophy with biblical revelation. Its intellectualism has obviously been deeply influenced by Aristotle's argument in Book X of his *Nicomachean Ethics* that intellectual contemplation is the source of the highest and purest happiness of man. At the same time, it reminds one of Jesus' saying, "Blessed are the pure in heart, for they shall see God" (Matt. 5:8) and of St. Paul's faith that "Now we see through a glass darkly, but then face to face"

---

[101] Copleston, *History of Philosophy*, Vol. II, p. 382.
[102] Aquinas, *Summa Theologica*, Bk. VII, Pt. I, Q. 93, a. 4.
[103] Aquinas, *Summa contra Gentiles*, Bk. III, Chaps. 51–53.
[104] Copleston, *History of Philosophy*, Vol. II, p. 382.

(I Cor. 13:12). However, the emphasis in the New Testament is not upon an intellectual vision of God which will fulfill the need of man's intellectual nature for knowledge of the highest Truth, but upon fellowship with Him based on love, so that the "seeing" of God is clearly subordinate to the love of Him. As we have pointed out, Aquinas holds that the "vision of God" will fulfill all the desires of the soul and will be accompanied by perfect blessedness in His presence. But the Aristotelian terms in which he expresses it tend to put the emphasis upon the *knowledge* of God rather than the *love* of Him.

THE CHRISTIAN PHILOSOPHY OF AQUINAS

1. In the preceding chapter, we said that while Augustine starts from faith and moves toward understanding, Aquinas in his rational theology seems to move from reason to faith. However, this way of expressing the difference between them is misleading. We should never forget that Augustine sought understanding through philosophy before he came to faith, and that Aquinas was a man of faith before he became a philosopher and was primarily a theologian who used philosophy for theological purposes.

The picture of Aquinas' thought which is often drawn by philosophers is, therefore, a distortion of it. They describe him as beginning in a strictly rational fashion with proofs of the existence of God, proceeding in his negative and affirmative theology to demonstrate rationally God's attributes, and, after he has exhausted all that reason can tell us about God, going on to discuss the Trinity as it has been revealed to faith. Aquinas *does* follow this order in his *Summa Theologica,* and it is logically consistent with his principle ("Grace perfects, it does not abolish, nature") that he should for purposes of exposition present what can be known about God by the natural light of reason before setting forth what has been made known about Him by revelation. But this should not lead us to suppose that the rational arguments for God's existence and His attributes were not affected by the Christian revelation he had accepted by faith. This is evident in the fact that when he deals with these problems of rational theology he usually, if not always, cites as authorities passages from the Scriptures or the Fathers of the Church. Moreover, most of the conclusions he seeks to demonstrate were derived by him originally from the Christian revelation. For example, the five arguments for the existence of God are attempts to demonstrate the existence of the God of Theism in whom he had long believed, and the "names" he ascribes to God in his affirmative theology—e.g., knowledge, will, love, justice, and mercy—

are names of attributes of the personal God of the Bible. In short, although in his rational arguments as a philosopher he moves toward conclusions without any explicit reference to faith, the conclusions are those which as a Christian he has already accepted by faith. Thus the difference between Augustine and Aquinas with respect to the relation of faith and reason is not as great as might appear. Although Aquinas is more Aristotelian in his method and more systematic in his procedure than Augustine, he is no less a Christian philosopher for whom faith comes first.

2. The failure to recognize this has sometimes led to the charge that he was disingenuous, since as a Christian he already believed in God when he set out as a philosopher to demonstrate His existence. The arguments, it is said, are only "rationalizations" of that which he already believed, as the proverbial rabbit is drawn out of the magician's hat only because it has previously been put there. If this means only that Aquinas would probably not have developed arguments for the existence of the God of Theism if he had not already believed in Him, it is doubtless true. But it is not true that his demonstrations are only "rationalizations" of that belief. They are attempts to show that there are independent grounds for it in certain characteristics of the world. They seek to show that a truth which has been reached by one route, revelation, can also be reached by another and quite different route, reason. Only if it is assumed that it is not a function of philosophy to concern itself with the truth or falsity of beliefs which have originated from some other source than reasoning, can Aquinas' arguments for God's existence be dismissed as "rationalizations" of a religious belief.

The real difficulty with these arguments is that they are based upon presuppositions and employ a philosophical method which many modern thinkers do not accept. In our interpretation of the arguments we have indicated the *presuppositions:* that there is a necessary connection between an effect and its cause, so that we can infer the nature of a cause from its effect; that an infinite regress of causes, although logically conceivable, cannot satisfy the demand of reason for a sufficient explanation; and that it is legitimate to seek for such an explanation in an ultimate Cause which is transcendent to the world. As we shall see in later chapters, some or all of these presuppositions have ceased to appear self-evident to many modern thinkers such as Hume and Kant. Indeed, under the influence of science, modern naturalistic philosophers operate with presuppositions which are sharply opposed to the presuppositions of Aquinas. Moreover, the philosophical *method* employed by him, deductive reasoning from self-evident premises to necessary and certain conclusions, has ceased to commend itself to most modern philosophers. They do not consider self-evident, premises which were regarded as self-evident in the thirteenth century; they do not believe that deductive reasoning is the most suitable method for metaphysics and rational theology; and they reject the view that metaphysical conclusions which are necessary and certain are attainable.

We shall have to consider in later chapters these modern difficulties and to ask whether they can be overcome. At this point, we shall make only a few brief comments on the arguments for the existence of God. The first is that they will not be convincing or even persuasive to those whose presuppositions are those of modern naturalistic philosophy, and still less to those who hold the positivistic view that metaphysical and theological statements cannot be verified and thus are meaningless. Anyone who wishes to determine whether Aquinas' arguments are valid must, therefore, make up his mind whether the presuppositions of modern Naturalism or Positivism have superseded those of the medieval Aristotelian world view. In the second place, a distinction can and should be made between the *substance* of Aquinas' proofs and the *logical form* in which he expresses them. For one may accept the presuppositions and conclusion of the arguments as more adequate than those of modern Naturalism and Positivism but reject the method of reasoning by which they arrive at their conclusion. As we shall see, many modern philosophers regard the Thomistic arguments not as logical demonstrations which produce conclusions that are necessary and certain but as attempts to express the meaning of intuitions derived from certain kinds of experience and to develop their implications in the most adequate way which is possible. These philosophers recognize that belief in God originated not from philosophical reasoning but from these kinds of experience, e.g., the experience of the contingency and dependence of finite existence, and from intuitions arising out of them. Therefore, they hold that the function of arguments for the existence of God is not to produce belief in Him but to elucidate the experiences out of which that belief arises and to support it by setting forth evidence for it derived from other aspects of experience. In other words, these arguments do not *demonstrate* the existence of God, but *explicate* the experiences which have led men to believe in Him and seek to show that belief in Him offers the most reasonable interpretation of experience as a whole. If this is true, it is unfortunate that Aquinas makes no attempt to indicate the intuitions which lie behind the arguments, but presents them as demonstrations which should convince anyone without appealing to anything beyond the formal arguments themselves.

3. The long and comprehensive treatment of the *nature of God* by Aquinas has not received from philosophers the attention it deserves. Without question it is one of the most impressive treatises on the theistic doctrine of God which has ever been written. One of the sources of its greatness is that it attempts to synthesize the "metaphysical" or "cosmical" attributes of God emphasized by Greek philosophy with the "personal" attributes of God in the Bible. For God must be conceived as the ultimate Cause of the cosmos as well as the living God of religious faith, if man's view of Him is to be adequate. As we have seen, the "negative theology" which analyzes the metaphysical or cosmical attributes is essential to the theistic view, because the transcendence of God which distinguishes Him from all finite beings must be acknowledged as well as the more personal qualities which render Him near and dear to men. Otherwise, He will be reduced to the level of what Matthew Arnold called a "magnified non-natural man" by men who have lost a sense of His majesty and otherness.

As we have pointed out, the difficulty with Aquinas' negative theology is not that it is false or unnecessary but that it is formulated in terms of Greek philosophical conceptions which had been adopted by earlier Christian thinkers but which are inconsistent at certain points with the biblical view of God. We have seen that his conception of God's absolute independence, eternity, immutability, and perfection misinterprets the transcendence and otherness of God, and profoundly affects Aquinas' interpretation of personal attributes such as knowledge and will. This is due to the influence of Greek philosophers like Aristotle who had turned away from the anthropomorphism of the popular religion, eliminated from their idea of God all likeness to men, and exalted Him to a position of utter transcendence and detachment from the world. The effect of this influence on Aquinas' thinking is to remove God from effective relationship with the world and to evacuate personal attributes ascribed to Him of most of their meaning. But the remedy is not to reject negative theology altogether; it is to reformulate concepts such as "eternity," "immutability," and "perfection" in terms which are more consistent with biblical Theism. This task has been undertaken in our time by philosophers such as Whitehead and Hartshorne, and we shall have something to say about it in a later chapter (Chap. 13).

The other difficulty with Aquinas' conception of God concerns his use of the *doctrine of analogy*. Few would deny that his aim in proposing the doctrine, the avoidance of both uncritical anthropomorphism and agnosticism in speaking of God, is fully justified. If God is a transcendent and infinite Being, the qualities of finite beings cannot be literally ascribed to Him without degrading Him. At the same time, if religion is not to become the blind worship of an unkown Power, we must use language derived from our knowledge of the highest finite being in our experience, i.e., personality at its best, and we must use it in an analogical sense. The difficulty is that, if God is "wise" or "good," His wisdom or goodness must belong to Him in a manner which is suitable to His essence as a transcendent, infinite Being, and this must be radically different from the way in which men are wise and good. According to the interpretation of the analogy between God and finite beings as an "analogy of proportionality," God's wisdom or goodness is related to His essence as man's wisdom or goodness is related to man's essence.[105] But God's essence, according to Aquinas, is radically different from that of man: while man is a contingent being, God is a necessary being; while man is finite, God is infinite; while man is temporal, God is eternal. If so, how can we claim that an "analogy of proportionality" between God's wisdom or goodness and that of man tells us anything definite about His nature? If we knew the essence of God as we know that of man, we could know how His wisdom or goodness differs from man's and hence could form a definite idea of it. But Aquinas himself insists that we cannot know the essence of God in this life: we can know "what He is not" but not "what He is." Aquinas tells us that we are justified in applying names to God so long as we apply them with a different "mode of signification," but he does not tell us how we are to understand this difference. How, then, does "analogical" differ from "equivocal" predication?

Although the difficulty is a real one, it does not destroy the necessity of the doctrine of analogy. If we are to speak of God at all and not relapse into complete silence, we *must* apply names to Him in an analogical sense or degrade Him to the level of a finite being. This is why the doctrine of analogy is necessary. Our positive knowledge of God is limited and we deceive ourselves if we suppose that we know precisely what the terms we apply to God mean in relation to His nature. It is highly important that we apply to Him only terms which are worthy of him, i.e., terms such as "good" and "wise," which signify perfections without any admixture of imperfection in their essence. But the doctrine of analogy admonishes us to eliminate from the mean-

[105] Holloway, *Introduction to Natural Theology*, pp. 218–221.

ing of each of these terms any imperfection which is associated with it when we apply it to finite beings. Thus, the doctrine does not give us precise knowledge of the attributes of God, but it tells us that we are to remove all unworthy elements from the meaning of the terms we use for them. Although we have argued that Aquinas failed at many points in his application of the doctrine because of his Greek interpretation of the negative theology, the doctrine itself is indispensable.

4. Aquinas' conception of *man* and his *good* is both inferior and superior to that of Augustine. While Augustine had departed from the dominant Greek philosophical view in maintaining the primacy of the will over the reason, Aquinas returned to that view in his *intellectualism*. This is illustrated by his conception of freedom of choice, for he regards the will as determined by knowledge of the good.[106] This view, which Windelband calls "intellectualistic determinism," [107] has an important element of truth in it, since the will which seeks to attain good not approved by reason acts arbitrarily; but it disregards the power of passional and other nonrational aspects of the personality. Perhaps the most striking illustration of his intellectualism is to be found in his argument that the "last end" or highest good of man is the "vision of God" in the after life. As we have said, this view is closer to that of Aristotle's *Ethics* in some ways than to that of the Bible, since it is based upon the argument that intellectual contemplation is higher than moral or other activity of the will as the source of the highest good. Although the New Testament promises that men will "see" God, its emphasis is upon their love of Him.

However, Aquinas' conception of man is superior to that of Augustine with respect to the relation between *soul* and *body* and between *nature* and *grace*. We have already spoken of the way in which he followed Aristotle rather than Plato and Augustine in emphasizing the organic relation of the soul to its body and its dependence upon the body during this life, although it is spiritual in its essence and therefore immortal. This rejection of the dualism of soul and body was one of the reasons for the fact that he was less ascetic in his attitude toward life than Augustine. We have also seen that since Augustine's conversion radically transformed his whole life, it led him to a disparagement of the natural capacities of man and an exaltation of the divine grace. Aquinas softens this dualism of nature and grace by applying his fundamental principle that "Grace perfects, it does not abolish, nature" at

---

[106] Aquinas, *Summa Theologica*, Bk. VI, Pt. I, Q. 83, a. 1, 3.
[107] Windelband, *History of Philosophy* (New York: Macmillan, 1931), p. 330.

every crucial point where the relation of divine grace to human nature is involved. Thus, while Augustine argues that faith must precede understanding, Aquinas maintains that some religious truths can be attained by the natural light of reason. While Augustine claims that the moral virtues of the pagan Romans were more apparent than real since they were not motivated by love of God, Aquinas holds that "acquired virtues" such as temperance and justice can be won by repeated acts of the will. While Augustine says that there can be no justice in the state without love of God and that without justice states are only "great robber bands," Aquinas maintains that justice is possible in the state on a foundation of natural and positive law. While Augustine regards history as marked by continual conflict between the "earthly city" and the "heavenly city" as represented by the state and the Church, Aquinas takes a less tragic view of history; and he sees the state and other institutions as necessary for man's temporal welfare and the Church as cooperating with them while it leads man toward his eternal beatitude.

These and other differences are based upon a view of the *natural man* which is less dark and somber than that of the later Augustine. Man's "inclination to virtue" has been diminished by sin, and the special "gift of original righteousness" with which Adam was endowed has been destroyed by the Fall.[108] But the "rest" of virtue, the inclination of the rational nature, has not been entirely destroyed but remains, although it is in a weakened state because of the "wounds" it has received from sin.[109] This does not imply that Aquinas takes a mild and lenient view of the effects of sin. Indeed, he emphasizes that all of the powers of the soul have been wounded by it: "through sin the reason is obscured, especially in practical matters, the will hardened against the good, good actions become more difficult, and concupiscence more inflamed." [110] But his belief that the rest of the inclination to virtue in the rational nature has not been destroyed provided the basis for his view that the reason by its natural light could attain a measure of truth about God and the soul and the will by its own effort could acquire a degree of virtue sufficient for a modest personal happiness and social justice during man's life on earth.

Thus, while his conception of man's highest good, the vision of God in the future life, is no less otherworldly than that of Augustine, his general attitude toward this world and toward the possibilities of human life in history is more optimistic. Perhaps it is *too* optimistic

---

[108] Aquinas, *Summa Theologica*, Pt. II: I, Q. 85, a. 1.
[109] *Ibid.*, Q. 85, a. 2, 3.   [110] *Ibid.*

for our disillusioned age. But since it is based upon a high estimate of man's nature and potentialities even in his fallen state, it is more compatible with Christian humanism than that of Augustine. One of the most appealing things about Aquinas is that he combines an almost Greek classical view of the dignity of man with a Christian realism which is fully aware of man's sin and his need of divine grace to overcome it and fulfill his high destiny.

6 Medieval Mysticism

ECKHART

Mysticism is a form of religious experience which claims to transcend the barriers that separate most religious people from God and to attain an intimate and perfect union with Him. The mystic is not content merely to offer prayer and worship to God from time to time and to serve Him by moral obedience to His will. He longs to overcome every obstacle that stands between himself as subject and God as object, in order to become one with Him. Mysticism has sometimes been confused with Pantheism, because some mystics have been pantheists in their philosophy and some pantheists have been mystics in their religion. But Pantheism is the religious *belief* that "God is all" in some sense, a belief that may or may not be elaborated into a philosophy, while mysticism is an *experience*. It is associated, of course, with beliefs of some kind, but these beliefs may or may not be pantheistic.

Why do men become mystics? The most obvious, although not the most fundamental, reason has been the tendency of theological orthodoxy and popular religion to exaggerate the transcendence of God to the point of virtually denying His immanence in the lives of men. For example, Aquinas conceived of God's perfection and immutability in such a way as to deny that His relation to creatures was "real" to Him in the sense of affecting Him, and he denied that the "vision of God" which is the highest good of man could be attained in this life. Some of the late medieval mystics refused to accept this view. They affirmed God's immanence in the soul of man and the possibility of an experience of blessedness in this world. Mysticism also rises as a protest against ecclesiastical formalism and externalism, e.g., an extreme emphasis upon sacraments for the mediation of divine grace. Although mystics have seldom been in revolt against the Church, like religious individualists in the modern sense of the term, they have believed in the possibility and desirability of an immediate experience of God by

138

the individual and have often tended to sit loose to ecclesiastical observances.

But more fundamental than these considerations has been the dissatisfaction of mystics with the ordinary, conventional, and tepid religion of most people. Like the saints, they have not regarded religion as one interest or duty among others; it has been everything to them. They have been inflamed by a passionate desire for a perfect relationship with God. It is only when one keeps this religious intensity of the mystic in mind that one can understand the rigorous discipline he is willing to undergo in order to attain his goal or why he speaks so lyrically of his joy when he has reached it.

Is it possible to *explain* this intense and single-minded desire of the mystic for union with God? Van der Leeuw tries to account for it as due to the desire to attain *power* by breaking down the barriers of the self and becoming one with God.[1] He recognizes that the power sought by the mystic is very different from what most men mean by power, since it is won not by self-assertion but by a self-negation that is a kind of death. Through mysticism, he says, "man, by way of nothingness, constitutes himself the All."[2] There is doubtless an element of truth in this phenomenological description, for one of the consequences of the mystical union is the exaltation of the self through its participation in God. But this exaltation does not enhance the self's consciousness of its own power as a finite creature, since it is wholly the result of the power of God which pours into it. Therefore, it might be less misleading to say that the primary motive of the mystic is participation in God as the ultimate Reality and highest Good and the attainment thereby of *fullness of life*. Van der Leeuw himself speaks of the mystic's experience of "being filled with God" and points out that mysticism is related to early forms of possession or inspiration by a spiritual power. For example, the "judges" of ancient Israel were able to lead their people to victory because "the spirit of Jehovah had come upon them."[3] Thus the religious person who feels himself to be under the control of a greater power receives extraordinary power himself, whether that power takes the form of the violent activity of the "judge" or the strong conviction of the prophet. But this enhancement of spiritual and moral power is the consequence, not the motive, of the mystic's effort to attain union with God. What he seeks is perfect knowledge of God and full participation in His life.

Since many deeply religious people who are not called mystics have

[1] G. van der Leeuw, *Religion in Essence and Manifestation*, trans. J. E. Turner (London: Allen and Unwin, 1938), p. 493.
[2] *Ibid.*, p. 508.   [3] *Ibid.*, p. 487.

shared this aim in different degrees, it has been maintained that all vital or genuine religion is mystical. This is an exaggeration and would involve such a broad extension of the term "mysticism" as to rob it of any definite meaning. But it is probably true that there is a mystical *element* in all vital religion. This is important for two reasons. The first is that it explains why the mystic is able to communicate something of his experience to ordinary religious people and be understood in some measure by them. For the language of the mystic, even when he claims that his experience is ineffable, awakens a responsive feeling in most of us. This indicates that there is no absolute discontinuity between him and other religious people, as is sometimes asserted by those who regard mystics as pathological or as at least endowed with a special temperament that sets them apart from others.

The second reason is that mystical experience may commend itself as an important element in vital religion even if certain types of mysticism should be judged to be spiritually and morally one-sided and even dangerous. Many, if not all, of the great religious leaders have had experiences which were in some sense mystical. For example, St. Paul describes "visions and revelations of the Lord" in mystical terms (II Cor. 12:2–4), and repeatedly speaks of himself as being "in Christ." But although he is sometimes called a "Christocentric mystic," he is more accurately described as an apostle and missionary since intimate union with Christ is only one element in his religious life. Again, Augustine describes a mystical experience he enjoyed with his mother just before her death [4] and there is obviously a strong mystical element in his writing, but he was primarily a bishop and a theologian rather than a mystic. Examples could be multiplied indefinitely, and it is probably true that there are few religious people who have not had occasional mystical experiences of some kind.

TYPES OF MYSTICISM

One of the most serious errors concerning mysticism which has been made by philosophers of religion is to regard it as always the same and to pay no attention to its different forms. One reason for this error is the remarkable similarity between the descriptions of mystical experiences in different religions despite their independence of one another. Another reason is the tendency of some philosophers to exaggerate the extent of the similarity, because of their preference for mysticism over other kinds of religion and their belief that it is the most important evidence for the truth and value of religion. However,

[4] Augustine, *Confessions*, Bk. IX, Chap. 10.

the differences cannot be minimized without seriously distorting the facts about mysticism. Also, neglect of the differences makes it impossible to evaluate mysticism in a fair and discriminating way, since criticisms of one form of mysticism may not be applicable to a different form.

One distinction which has been made is between what Otto calls the "outward way" and the "inward way," [5] or what Stace calls the "extrovertive" type and the "introvertive" type. "The essential difference between them," says Stace, "is that the extrovertive experience looks outward through the senses, while the introvertive looks inward into the mind. Both culminate in the perception of an ultimate Unity —what Plotinus called the One—with which the perceiver realizes his own union or even identity. But the extrovertive mystic, using his physical senses, perceives the multiplicity of external material objects —the sea, the sky, the houses, the trees—mystically transfigured so that the One, or the Unity, shines through them. The introvertive mystic, on the contrary, seeks by deliberately shutting off the senses, by obliterating from consciousness the entire multiplicity of sensations, images and thoughts, to plunge into the depth of his own ego. There, in that darkness and silence, he alleges that he perceives the One—and is united with it—as the wholly naked One devoid of any plurality whatever." [6] Although the "extrovertive" is more widespread than the "introvertive" type, Stace regards it as much less important in its practical influence and philosophical implications.[7] However, he points out that mystics do not usually distinguish between the two types and that some of them, such as Eckhart, are examples of both types.[8] "The One" discovered by the "introvertive" mystic in the depths of his soul is usually identified by him with the "Unity" which "shines through" the many external objects in the "unifying vision" of the "extrovertive" mystic, so that the importance of the "outward way" should not be minimized. Moreover, the fact that the "extrovertive" type of mystical experience occurs spontaneously and requires no special technique or discipline to attain it means that it is enjoyed by a much greater number of persons than the "introvertive" type.

"Nature mysticism" is really a form of "extrovertive" mysticism, since it involves an experience of union with nature in which the self seems to become one with nature as a whole. Wordsworth feels the

[5] Rudolf Otto, *Mysticism East and West* (New York: Macmillan, 1932), Chap. 4.
[6] W. T. Stace, *Mysticism and Philosophy* (Philadelphia: J. B. Lippincott, 1960), pp. 62, 64.
[7] *Ibid.*, p. 122.   [8] *Ibid.*, p. 124.

presence of an infinite Power and Life in nature which is the source of its beauty and order,

> A presence that disturbs me with the joy
> Of elevated thoughts; a sense sublime
> Of something far more deeply interfused. . . .
> A motion of the spirit, that impels
> All thinking things, all objects of all thought,
> And rolls through all things.[9]

Zaehner denies that these lines describe a mystical experience. He admits that "there is an intimation, if you like, of something which transcends and informs transient Nature" but maintains that "it is no more than intimation" and that "there is no trace of an actual experience at all, either of union with Nature or communion with God." [10] But surely there is evidence of Wordsworth's union with nature, if not with God, in the poem just quoted and in others such as "The Prelude." To have felt "a presence that disturbs" or "a sense sublime" of a power in nature is, of course, not necessarily to have experienced "identity" with it, but it is surely more than an "intimation" and its effect upon the poet was much greater than any mere "intimation" could have had.

However, more important for our purposes than the division of the types of mysticism into "extrovertive" and "introvertive" is the division between "atheistic," "monistic," and "theistic" mysticism. This division is based not upon a difference between approaches to the Object from without and from within the self, but upon a difference between conceptions of the Object. We shall describe briefly "atheistic" mysticism and then discuss more fully "monistic" and "theistic" mysticism.

Atheistic mystics have as their goal the attainment of liberation of the self from evil into a state of fulfillment, rather than union with God. The mysticism of the Sankhya school in Hinduism is based upon a dualistic view of spirit and matter as independent and opposed realities. Matter, *Prakriti*, is the source of all multiplicity and diversity in nature, including the organs of the empirical self. Spirit, *Purusha*, is the sentient *spectator* or *witness* which is associated with the body. The goal of this philosophy is the liberation of the *Purusha* from its association with *Prakriti* in the empirical self. The discipline necessary for the attainment of this goal consists of detachment, the practice of medita-

---

[9] William Wordsworth, "Lines Composed above Tintern Abbey," 1798.
[10] R. C. Zaehner, *Mysticism Sacred and Profane* (Oxford: Clarendon Press, 1957), p. 35.

tion, and the knowledge of ultimate truth.[11] The Sankhya in its classical form is definitely atheistic. "It believes," says Hiriyanna, "in the
permanence and supremacy of spirit, but knows nothing of God." [12]
Early Buddhism is also virtually atheistic, for the gods acknowledged
by Gautama the Buddha are limited beings themselves and can play no
significant part in the salvation of men. Based upon the view that life is
suffering, it seeks release from suffering by overcoming the craving that
leads to it. Its goal, *Nirvana,* is the state of peace and joy which results
from this.

It is debatable whether the Sankhya and early Buddhism should be
regarded as forms of religious mysticism, since they do not seek liberation and fulfillment through union with a divine Power above the self.
But we may take them as examples of one form of mysticism in order
to emphasize the fact that a liberating and unifying experience is possible without union with a divine Power or Being. Such an experience is
sometimes sought by religious humanists for the sake of its psychological and moral effects. However, atheistic mysticism has had little influence in the history of religion, and we shall not consider it further.

Monistic mysticism, on the other hand, has had a profound influence, especially in the East. As the Hindu polytheism of the early
Vedic hymns lost its appeal, a monistic world view which had been
present only in embryonic form in some of the hymns developed in
India and was explicitly formulated in the Upanishads. The gods of the
early polytheism were reduced to manifestations of an impersonal cosmic principle, *Brahman.* This principle was identified with the Self,
Atman, which was experienced in certain states in the depths of the
human self. This *Brahman-Atman* or Universal Self was conceived as
the only true reality, "One without a second," while the many things
and selves of space and time were considered to be only appearances,
constituting the realm of *Maya.* As long as a person believes in the
reality of these appearances and is in ignorance of *Brahman-Atman,*
the one true reality, he cannot escape from the wheel of birth and
rebirth, *Samsara,* to which he is bound by the law of moral cause and
effect, *Karma.* If he is to win liberation, *Moksha,* from the necessity of
reincarnation, he must attain spiritual knowledge, *Vidya,* of *Brahman*
as the only reality. For only through such knowledge can he dispel the
illusory appearance of himself as a separate individual and thus break
the fetters which bind him to the things and values of the spatio-

---

[11] M. Hiriyanna, *The Essentials of Indian Philosophy* (London: George Allen
and Unwin, 1951), p. 122.

[12] *Ibid.,* p. 124.

temporal world. He can attain this spiritual knowledge by means of a vigorous physical and mental discipline, detaching himself thereby from the things of the senses and meditating upon the sole reality of *Brahman*. The culmination of this process is an intuitive realization of his identity with *Brahman-Atman* through a mystical experience of union which brings with it peace and joy.

Since the Upanishads were unsystematic and did not contain a consistent religious doctrine, several different religious philosophies were later developed which claimed to be interpretations of its teaching. Of these the most important were the "unqualified non-dualism" or strict Monism of Sankara and the "qualified non-dualism" of Ramanuja. The latter bears a considerable resemblance to Western Theism, but we are concerned here only with the Monism of Sankara because of its great influence in the East and because it provides the best example of monistic mysticism. The *Brahman* is the sole reality, according to Sankara, and the many things and persons of the spatio-temporal world constitute the realm of *Maya*. There has been much controversy as to whether these should be interpreted as wholly illusory or as possessing a sort of inferior reality as appearances of *Brahman*. If *Maya* is interpreted as a realm of illusion, a sort of dream world, the consequence is acosmism, a form of Pantheism which denies the reality of the visible cosmos and affirms the sole reality of *Brahman*. If it is interpreted as a realm of appearances of *Brahman* possessing a relative reality, the consequence is a more positive form of Pantheism in which the Brahman may be experienced as immanent in the things of time and space and they are not wholly deprived of worth.

The most striking thing in Sankara's view of *Brahman* is his denial that any qualities or relations can be attributed to it. Since man's knowledge of all qualities and relations is derived from the realm of *Maya*, the attempt to predicate any of them of Brahman provokes the reply, "No, no!" (*Neti, neti!*) In consequence, we can only say what *Brahman* is not, not what it is. It is conceived as pure Being, Consciousness, and Bliss, infinite, eternal, impersonal. However, Sankara makes a place for the personal God of popular religion, *Isvara*, since the world of the senses appears to be real to the unenlightened man. Although the philosopher in possession of spiritual knowledge of *Brahman* knows that personal qualities such as intelligence, love, and will cannot be predicated of it, the unenlightened man represents it to himself as personal, calls it "Lord," and seeks by prayer and sacrifice to enter into personal relationship with it. Thus Sankara accommodates his negative theology to the religious need of most men to worship a personal God, but he clearly regards such a God as belonging to the realm of *Maya*. Therefore liberation, *Moksha*, from the wheel of birth and rebirth must come through the intuitive realization of the identity of the individual self with *Brahman* in a mystical experience in which individuality is lost.

In contrast, *theistic* mysticism rests upon belief in a personal God who is the Creator of nature and man, and is distinct from as well as immanent in finite things and persons. It seeks union with God through purification of the will and detachment of the mind from everything which binds the self to itself and to the world. Thus, its goal is unclouded knowledge and perfect love of God, undistracted by concern for the self or any other finite thing. But it usually does not, like monistic mysticism, deny the reality of finite things and selves or maintain that the individual self can attain identity with God.

This type of mysticism has been characteristic of the three great theistic religions of the West—Judaism, Islam, and Christianity—as monistic mysticism has been characteristic of the pantheistic religions of the East, especially Hinduism and Mahayana Buddhism. However, the theistic mysticism of the West has been influenced during certain periods by Neo-Platonic philosophy and a different form of mysticism derived from that source. In some cases this has produced a type of mysticism which is basically theistic but which has elements akin to monistic mysticism. The best example of this is Meister Eckhart, (1260?-1327) one of the greatest mystics of the West. An examination of his mysticism and a comparison of it with the monistic mysticism of Sankara will throw light upon the nature of the mysticism of the West, as well as its similarities to and differences from the mysticism of the East.

MEISTER ECKHART

Eckhart's thought is complex and many influences have combined to shape it. He was a member of the Dominican order in the thirteenth century and some interpreters have regarded him as primarily a Scholastic. This is an exaggeration, but there is no doubt of the fact that at many points his ideas and his terminology were affected by Aquinas. He was also profoundly influenced by Neo-Platonism, which had been mediated to medieval Christian thinkers by the Pseudo-Dionysius and which was radically different in spirit from the point of view of Aquinas. These and other philosophical and theological views were woven into the fabric of his thought, so that he is rightly regarded as an "intellectual" mystic. It should never be forgotten that he was a Master of Theology and lectured in both Paris and Cologne. However, one of the remarkable things about Eckhart is that, although he was one of the learned doctors of his time, he was also a moving and effective preacher, like Bernard of Clairvaux, and many of his sermons are among the best of his writings. The secret behind this is that he was steeped in the New Testament and he reflects its spirit in his simple and practical piety. He was also involved in practical activity during much of his life as an administrator in his order.

The fact that he was able to combine Thomistic theology, Neo-Platonic philosophy, and simple New Testament Christianity into a unique pattern of religious thought and life is a mark of his intellectual and spiritual genius. But it is also the source of great difficulties in interpreting him, and few writers have been able to do justice to all sides of his thought. In the brief account that follows, we shall attempt only to single out some of the most important and distinctive aspects of it.

In his theory of *knowledge,* Eckhart often speaks like a Thomist. He asserts the dependence of our ordinary knowledge upon the senses and the images derived from them, the abstraction of ideas from these by the active intellect, and the discursive character of our thinking as we pass from one idea to another in the never-ending search for truth. He also accepts by faith the revelation of knowledge about Christ, the Trinity, and other truths necessary for salvation. Thus he seems to be a Thomist in his view of knowledge, both of the natural order by reason and of the supernatural order by revelation. But with respect to the knowledge of God with which he is primarily concerned as a mystic, he speaks in very different terms. For perfect knowledge of God does not come through the senses and images or through reasoning based upon them, but through the activity of God within the depths of the soul. This knowledge comes with the "birth of the Son" or "the speaking of the Word" by God in the soul. "Now haply thou wilt say: 'What is it that God does without images in the ground and essence [of the soul]?' That I am incapable of knowing, for my soul-powers can receive only in images. . . . No sooner does a man know the reason of a thing than immediately he tires of it and goes casting about for something new. Always clamoring to know, he is ever inconstant. The soul is constant only to this unknowing knowing which keeps her pursuing." [13] "Call it . . . [if] thou wilt an ignorance, an unknowing, yet

[13] *Meister Eckhart,* ed. Franz Pfeiffer, trans. C. de Evans (London: J. M. Watkins, 1924–1931), *Sermon I,* p. 7. All references which follow to the works of Meister Eckhart are from this translation.

there is in it more than in all knowing and understanding without it, for this outward ignorance lures and attracts thee from all understood things and from thyself." [14] Thus the perfect knowledge of God sought by the mystic is given to him without images and reasoning of his own. It is "unknowing," and "outward ignorance," since it provides us with no knowledge of external things or of ourselves. Yet there is more in it than in all other knowledge, for it gives us knowledge of God to which the soul is "constant" although it "tires" of knowledge of all else.

In this view, Eckhart is closer to Neo-Platonism than to Thomism in holding that we can enjoy a direct experience of God in this life and do not have to be content with knowledge about Him gained from reason and revelation. But he is a Christian rather than a Neo-Platonist at the crucial point: this knowledge cannot be attained by us through our own powers but is a gift of God wrought by His activity in the soul. What are the conditions for the reception of such knowledge by man? An answer to this question requires an understanding of his psychology.

In his *psychology* as in his theory of knowledge, Eckhart seems at first sight to be simply a Thomist. Like Aquinas, he distinguishes between the soul and its "powers" or faculties through which it acts. "Whatever the soul effects she effects with her powers. When she understands she understands with her intellect. When she remembers she does so with her memory. When she loves she does so with her will. She works them with her powers and not with her essence." [15] In addition to these higher powers of intellect, memory, and will, she possesses inferior powers such as sensation and desire by which she is related to the outside world in space and time. "Now every exterior act is linked with some means. The power of seeing is brought into play only through the eyes. . . . And so with all the other senses: their operations are always effected through some means or other. . . . For when the soul-powers contact a creature they set to, to make of the creature an image and likeness which they absorb. By it they know the creature." [16]

But here again Eckhart departs from Aquinas in his estimate of the value of these "powers" of the soul and their activities for man's relationship with God. For he regards the busy play of their activities as binding the soul to the things of the senses, the "this" and the "that" which are the worldly objects of its desires, and therefore as distracting it from perfect knowledge and single-minded love of God. "Here, the soul is scattered abroad among her powers and dissipated in the act of

[14] *Ibid.*, p. 9.   [15] Eckhart, *Sermon I*, p. 4.   [16] *Ibid.*, pp. 4, 5.

each: the power of seeing in the eye, the power of hearing in the ear, the power of tasting in the tongue, and her powers are accordingly enfeebled for their interior work, scattered forces being imperfect. It follows that for her interior work to be effective, she must call in all her powers, recollecting them out of extended things to one interior act." [17] If the soul is to find God and devote herself completely to Him, she must gather her scattered energies and interests by a process of "recollection" through which she "calls in" her powers and centers down in herself. Thus, while Eckhart accepts Aquinas' analysis of the "powers" of the soul as the necessary instruments by which she acts and relates herself to the natural world, his intense longing for union with God within leads him to stress above all her need to attain unity be curbing her activities. In this respect, he is far closer to Augustine than to Aquinas, since he is convinced that God is to be found not without but within, not "abroad" but "at home."

When the "powers" have been brought to rest, God can make himself known in the "essence" or "ground" of the soul which is its purest and noblest part. "That is mid-silence for thereinto no creature did ever get, nor any image, nor has the soul there either activity or understanding, therefore she is not aware of any image either of herself or any creature. . . . But there is no activity in the essence of the soul; the faculties she works with emanate from the ground of the essence but in her actual ground there is mid-stillness; here alone is rest and a habitation for this birth, this act, wherein God the Father speaks his Word, for it is intrinsically receptive of naught save the divine essence, without means . . . God enters the ground of the soul." [18] Thus, God makes Himself known, "speaks His Word," only in the "ground" of the soul when the "powers" have been brought to rest and the soul is completely passive. However, it should be noted that when God "speaks His Word," He pours into the "ground" of the soul such an abundance of light that it is flooded and this light "runs over into her powers and into the outward man as well." [19] Thus the "powers" and the "outward man" they serve are not destroyed by the withdrawal of the "powers" into passivity and their replacement by God's activity in the "ground" of the soul. Rather, they are transformed, redirected, and unified by the activity of God in the depth of the soul. In Aquinas' words, "Grace perfects, it does not destroy, nature."

Eckhart uses a number of different terms for the part of the soul where God makes Himself known. Since he is not attempting to give a

[17] Eckhart, *Sermon II*, pp. 11–12.   [18] *Ibid.*, *Sermon I*, p. 4.
[19] *Ibid.*, *Sermon II*, p. 10.

scientific analysis and must use physical metaphors to describe a spiritual reality, it is difficult to grasp his meaning at certain points. The "ground," he says, is "a power in the soul untouched by time and flesh, flowing from the Spirit, remaining in the Spirit, altogether spiritual. In this power is God, ever verdant, flowering in all the joy and glory of his actual self, . . . for in this power the eternal Father is procreating his eternal Son without a pause." [20] "Sometimes I have called it the tabernacle of the soul, sometimes a spiritual light, anon I say it is a spark. But now I say it is neither this nor that. Yet it is somewhat: somewhat more exalted over this and that than the heavens are above the earth. . . . It is of all names free, of all forms void: exempt and free as God is in himself. It is one and simple as God is one and simple, and no man can in any wise behold it." [21]

In the first of these passages, the "ground" is called a "power," but clearly it is not a power of the same kind as the powers of the soul we have described. Indeed, when we read that it is "untouched by time and flesh, flowing from the Spirit, remaining in the Spirit," it is difficult to see how it can be a "power" of the human soul at all or anything but the Spirit of God as present in the soul. In the second passage, Eckhart says that it is "neither this nor that" and is free of "names" and "forms," i.e., is unlike every finite thing, every "this or that," and has no determinate character or form to which a name can be given. It is one, simple and invisible like God Himself. Yet it does not seem to be the Spirit of God, since it is called a "power" of the *soul* in some sense and is a "tabernacle" *in* which the Father speaks His Word. To these perplexities must be added the question whether in calling it a "spiritual light" or "spark" Eckhart means that it *is* a "spark" of divine fire or ray of the divine "light," or a part of the human soul *in* which the divine fire and light are present inflaming and illuminating it. In other words, is it divine, or is it a human "power" in which the divine manifests itself? Or is it "by nature" a human power which "by grace" becomes divine in the mystical union? Nor is the question answered by a striking statement in one of the *Tractates:* "The spark of the soul is the light of God's reflection, which is always looking back to God." [22] For the "spark" is here regarded as a reflection of the divine light in the mirror of the soul, and it is distinguished from God by the use of the Neo-Platonic metaphor "looking back to God."

What is the *method* by which the soul withdraws its "powers" and enters into its "ground" to await the speaking of God's Word? One of

[20] *Ibid., Sermon VIII*, p. 36.   [21] *Ibid.*, pp. 37, 38.
[22] Eckhart, *Tractate VIII*, p. 338.

the most interesting things about Eckhart is that, unlike most "intro-vertive" mystics, he does not seem to have followed the "mystical way" with its three major stages of "purgation," "illumination," and "union" as described by Evelyn Underhill and other writers.[23] Rather, he seems to speak as if the mystical experience of "union" follows directly the "purgation" of the soul by its withdrawal of its "powers" into its "ground." But he has given a clear and vivid account of the method by which "purgation" is attained by the soul as it prepares itself for "union." It is the method of *detachment*, "the best and highest virtue whereby a man may knit himself most narrowly to God and wherein he is most like to his exemplar, as he was in God . . . ere God created creature," [24] i.e., like to the eternal "idea" of man in God before his creation. He extols it even above love, which for him, as we shall see, is the source of all human virtues and good works. His reasons are two. The first is that "God is bound to give himself to a heart detached" and that "detachment constrains me to admit nothing but God." [25] The object of detachment is to empty the soul in order to prepare it for God's action within it. "For a heart to be perfectly ready it has to be perfectly empty, this being its condition of maximum capacity," as anything already written on a white tablet must be erased before one writes on it.[26] In other words, "detachment" is necessary for the with-drawal of the "powers" of the soul which we have described. The second reason is that detachment is Godlike. "For that God is God is due to his motionless detachment, and it is from his detachment that he gets his purity and his simplicity and his immutability." [27] God's de-tachment was not disturbed when He created the heavens and the earth or even when the Son was made man and suffered martyrdom. For He sees all things that He will do in one eternal glance and suffers no change in Himself when He does them.[28] It will be objected that for man absolute detachment like God's is impossible and that Christ did not manifest such an attitude when He cried out on the Cross or Mary when she lamented beneath it. He replies that "what Christ and our Lady said concerning outward things was prompted by their own out-ward man, the inner man remaining in motionless detachment," as a door swings to and fro while its hinge remains in the same place without change.[29]

Eckhart insists that detachment must be carried to the point of producing absolute *stillness* and *passivity* within the soul, for the soul can contribute nothing by actions of its own to the speaking of God's

[23] Evelyn Underhill, *Mysticism* (New York: E. P. Dutton, 1949), Chap. 10.
[24] Eckhart, *Tractate IX*, p. 344.   [25] *Ibid.*, p. 341.   [26] *Ibid.*, p. 346.
[27] *Ibid.*, p. 343.   [28] *Ibid.*   [29] *Ibid.*, p. 345.

Word but must surrender itself completely to His action within it. But
it can be certain that once it has emptied itself of every sensation,
image, desire, and idea concerning itself or any other creature it will be
filled by God. As he expresses it, "God is bound to act, to pour himself
out (into thee) as soon as ever he shall find thee ready; . . . finding
thee ready he is obliged to act, to overflow into thee; just as the sun
must needs burst forth when the air is bright and clear, and is unable
to contain itself." [30] This should not be interpreted to mean that the
soul by emptying itself can *force* God to enter into it or that God is
bound by a moral law independent of His own will to do so. Eckhart
always insists upon God's freedom in His dealings with man and hence
upon His grace in giving Himself to man. Sometimes he seems to
suggest that God acts under the compulsion of a principle such as
"nature abhors a vacuum" in filling the soul that has emptied itself.[31]
But this is only a metaphor drawn from nature to express the truth that
God's grace is wholly dependable because it flows from His essence as
love. "Thou needst not call to him afar, he waits much more impa-
tiently than thou for thee to open to him. He longs for thee a thousand-
fold more urgently than thou for him: one point the opening and the
entering." [32] Thus, although the soul must prepare itself for God to
enter it, its desire for union with Him is a response to His antecedent
love for it. "God lies in wait for us therefore with nothing so much as
love. For love is like the fisherman's hook. . . . Once it takes the hook
the fish is forfeit to the fisherman; in vain it twists hither and thither,
the fisherman is certain of his catch. And so I say of love: he who is
caught thereby has the strongest of all bonds and yet a pleasant burden. . . . That we may be thus caught and freed, help us O thou who
art love itself." [33]

In Eckhart's theory of knowledge, his psychological analysis, his
praise of detachment, and his certainty that God in His love will fill the
soul which has emptied itself, it is difficult to find anything but a pure
theistic mysticism. But there are certain other points at which his views
show the effect of *Neo-Platonism* more deeply and which are very
similar to those of the monistic system of Sankara. It is this apparent
contradiction within his thought which makes him such an interesting,
if untypical, example of Christian mysticism. We shall deal briefly with
two of his views in order to illustrate the Neo-Platonic and monistic
side of his thought: his conception of God and his description of the
soul's union with Him.

According to Neo-Platonism, as we have seen (Chap. 3), the ulti-

---

[30] Eckhart, *Sermon IV*, p. 23.   [31] *Ibid.*   [32] *Ibid.*   [33] *Ibid.*, p. 25.

mate reality is an impersonal principle, "the One" and "the Good," rather than the personal God of Theism, and from it the world has emanated eternally by necessity. Man's soul, weighed down by evils due to its association with a body and its involvement in the world of matter, longs for liberation and seeks to ascend back to its original source and attain union with it. In a "flight of the alone to the Alone," it loses its consciousness of its own self as a distinct being and unites itself with "the One" and "the Good" in mystical ecstasy. In this union with "the One" it finds joy and peace. But it is unable to comprehend or describe "the One" because "the One" is an undifferentiated unity without quality or relation. Only a negative theology which refuses to apply any predicates whatever to "the One" is possible.

The effect of this Neo-Platonic mysticism, which was mediated to medieval Christian thinkers by the Pseudo-Dionysius, a Christian Neo-Platonist, is shown in Eckhart's distinction between "God," *Deus*, and "Godhead," *Deitas*. He means by "God" the personal God of Christian Theism who has revealed Himself as the Trinity, as Father, Son, and Holy Spirit. The Father has created the world through His Word according to the eternal Ideas. Since the essence of God is love, as we have seen, the Father is always seeking to give birth to His Son in the ground of every soul, as the Son was incarnate in Jesus of Nazareth centuries ago. But Eckhart holds that the soul is not satisfied by union with "God" but longs to "break through" to union with the "Godhead," and it is this which he speaks of again and again as the "eternal birth" in the soul. How does he conceive of the "Godhead" and what is its relation to "God"?

It is obvious that "God" in Eckhart corresponds to "Mind" in Plotinus, while "Godhead" in the former corresponds to "the One" in the latter. Furthermore, the "Godhead" of Eckhart is very similar to the *Brahman* of Sankara, as Otto has pointed out. It is Being, not an individual being but Being itself, pure and simple.[34] As such, it is above all conceptions and hence beyond comprehension. For it is without distinctions and formless, so that no quality or relation can be predicated of it.[35] It is a "void," a "wilderness," a "Nothing" about which nothing can be said.[36] It is eternal, indivisible, infinite, and unchanging.[37] However, that all of these are negative expressions for a positive Reality is shown by the statement, "Therefore from Being itself and by and in it are all things." [38] Finally, it is free from all activity and works, "pure knowledge, living and moving in itself." [39]

As "the One" is above "Mind" in Plotinus and *Brahman* is above

[34] Otto, *Mysticism East and West*, p. 6.   [35] *Ibid.*   [36] *Ibid.*, p. 7.
[37] *Ibid.*, p. 9.   [38] *Ibid.*, pp. 8, 9.   [39] *Ibid.*, p. 14.

Isvara in Sankara, the "Godhead" is above "God" in Eckhart. "God" and "Godhead," he says, "are as different as earth is from heaven. . . . Heaven stands a thousand miles above the earth, as the Godhead is above God. God becomes and dis-becomes." [40] The last sentence of this passage refers to Eckhart's view that, as the "powers" of the soul flow from and are withdrawn into its invisible "ground," "God" is a manifestation of the hidden "Godhead," flowing out of and returning into it. The Godhead, unlike God, is at rest and free from all work. "God works, the Godhead does not work, there is nothing to do; in it is no activity. . . . God and Godhead are as different as active and inactive." [41] Yet, paradoxically, the Godhead is also a "wheel rolling out of itself" and returning to itself in a living process.[42] For the Godhead is the ultimate Ground of all being, flowing into all things and flowing back into itself. "The Godhead flows into the Father, into the Son and the Holy Ghost, into itself in eternity and in time into creatures. It gives to each as much as it can hold: to stones existence, to the trees their growth, to birds their flight, to beasts their pleasures, to the angels reason and to man free nature. . . . God's being is first being, flowing being, fixed being, initial being and final being." [43] Hence the soul is not content to attain union with the personal, active and revealed God. It seeks union with the formless Ground which is behind and above God, plunging into the abyss of the Godhead. Speaking of a "breaking through" and an upward "thrust" of the soul, Eckhart says, "By this sudden thrust I become so rich that God is not sufficient for me, so far as he is only God and in all his divine works. . . . For there [in the Godhead] I am the immovable, which moves all things." [44] Clearly, Eckhart is seeking in language such as this to express the incomprehensible, mysterious "otherness" of God, which makes it misleading to predicate personal or any other terms of Him.

But Otto points out that Eckhart's metaphysical speculation concerning God as "Being itself" and his exaltation of the Godhead above all predicates rest upon a *theistic foundation* of simple faith and piety. The self in humility and trust seeks communion with God, surrenders itself in obedience to His will, experiences Him as merciful and forgiving love, and knows Him as the source of new being and life in the soul.[45] Even Eckhart's teaching concerning the birth of the Son in the soul is simply a mystical development from the Christian doctrine of

---

[40] Eckhart, *Sermon LVI*, quoted by Otto, *op. cit.*, p. 14.
[41] Eckhart, *Sermon LVI*, p. 143.
[42] Otto, *Mysticism East and West*, p. 170.   [43] Eckhart, *Tractate XI*, p. 366.
[44] Quoted in Otto, *op. cit.*, p. 15.
[45] Otto, *Mysticism East and West*, pp. 123–131.

union with Christ through the Holy Spirit. Therefore, it would be a mistake to suppose that in distinguishing "Godhead" from "God" Eckhart is setting up a second, impersonal God, or that in speaking of "Godhead" as "above God" he means to disparage the personal God of Christian Theism. He is only emphasizing as a mystic the infinite and ineffable depths of God when we consider not His revelation of Himself but His essence in its hiddenness. "God as the object of humble love and trust," says Otto, "in nowise disappears from his sight behind the Godhead as indwelling power. . . . The man who speaks in such a fashion of the consoling God as does Eckhart in his *Book of Divine Consolation,* and for whom mystical communion immediately turns into relationships of the most personal love, devotion and fellowship, is fundamentally a theist despite the highest flights of speculation, and is that neither by concession nor esoterically." [46]

The other respect in which Eckhart shows most clearly the influence of Neo-Platonic and monistic mysticism is in his view of the *union* of the soul with God. As we have said, the theistic mystic usually speaks of "union" rather than "identity" when he describes the intimate relations of the soul to God. But in the mysticism of the Neo-Platonists and of Sankara the soul loses its individuality and becomes identical with "the One" or *Brahman.* Eckhart often expresses himself as if this is also his view and as if the soul is deified in the mystical experience. "Because his [God's] knowing is mine," he says, "and his knowing is his substance and his nature and his essence, it follows that his substance and his nature and his essence are mine. And his substance and his nature and his essence being mine, therefore I am the Son of God. . . . I am wise and mighty just as he is, and one and the same with him. . . . Man is turned into God." [47] In another passage Eckhart says that the soul longs to become one with God and nothing but God. "She steals out of herself and so enters into the pure Being, and there concerns herself with all things as little as when she went out from God. The 'I' is reduced there to utter nought and nothing is left there but God. Yes, even God she outshines here as the sun outshines the moon, and with God's all-penetrativeness she streams into the eternal Godhead where in an eternal stream God is flowing into God." [48]

A question arises with respect to statements such as these: Does Eckhart really mean that in the mystical experience the soul or at least its "ground" is absorbed into God and becomes identical with Him?

[46] *Ibid.,* p. 135.   [47] Eckhart, *Sermon VII,* p. 33.
[48] Quoted in Otto, *op. cit.,* p. 180.

Evelyn Underhill thinks that when the Christian mystics speak of "deification," they do not mean by it "identification" with God. As she puts it, "they intend no arrogant claim to identification with God but as it were a transfusion of their selves by His Self: an entrance upon a new order of life, so high and so harmonious with Reality that it can only be called divine. Over and over again they assure us that personality is not lost, but made more real." [49] This is doubtless a correct description of the attitude of most Christian mystics, who describe the mystical union by metaphors such as the heating of iron by fire until it is white hot but does not cease to be iron. [50] But it does not necessarily apply to Eckhart whose daring "Faustian" spirit is far from typical of theistic mystics. However, there is a passage in one of the *Tractates* which seems to indicate that he did not intend to assert a complete identity with God. "In the third place let us see how the soul becomes God above grace. . . . In this exalted state she has lost her proper self and is flowing full-flood into the unity of the divine nature. But what, you may ask, is the fate of this lost soul: does she find herself or not? My answer is, it seems to me that she does find herself and that at the point where every intelligence sees itself with itself. For though she sink all sinking in the oneness of divinity she never touches bottom. Wherefore God has left her one little point from which to get back to herself and find herself and know herself as creature. For it is of the very essence of the soul that she is powerless to plumb the depths of her creator." [51] This passage is clearly describing the state of "deification," as the first two sentences show. But it denies that the soul "has lost her proper self" completely and asserts that God enables her to "find herself and know herself as creature" through her incapacity as a finite being to "plumb the depths" of God. It must be admitted, however, that many statements of Eckhart's are so extravagant that he left himself open to the charge that the soul is absorbed into God and

[49] Underhill, *Mysticism*, p. 503.

[50] One of the best examples is Bernard of Clairvaux whose mysticism of love is expressed in the symbolism of "spiritual marriage" between Christ, the Bridegroom, and the soul as Bride. Despite the intimacy of the union he describes, he always speaks of the transformation rather than the absorption of the soul in this union and thus preserves its distinction from God. "The mystical union," as Gilson says, "integrally respects this real distinction between the divine substance and the human substance, between the will of God and the will of man; it is neither a confusion of the two substances in general, nor a confusion of the substances of the two wills in particular; but it is their perfect accord, the coincidence of two willings . . . in which intention and object coincide to such an extent that the one is a perfect image of the other." Etienne Gilson, *The Mystical Theology of St. Bernard* (Wales: University College, 1933), p. 123.

[51] Eckhart, *Tractate II*, p. 282.

loses its individuality, and it is not surprising that some of them have been condemned as heretical.

The reason for the concern of many Christian theists over any identification of the soul with God is obvious: it threatens the theistic view that God is transcendent as well as immanent and that the attitude of man toward Him should be one of humility. Mystics like Eckhart have often been accused by Protestant as well as Catholic thinkers of spiritual arrogance in exalting the soul to identity with God. Otto defends Eckhart against this charge, maintaining that *exaltation* and *humility* are two "poles" of the mystic's experience and pointing out that Eckhart stresses humility as a cardinal virtue. "Eckhart's mysticism . . . grows out of the experience of the overwhelming and annihilating divine Majesty, and ends with the absolute naught and nullity of the creature." [52] Thus, Eckhart makes his exalted claim only for the "noble man," *homo nobilis*, in the soul and for it only when it has completely emptied itself and knows that it is nothing in itself. "Ours to be God by grace," he says, "as God is God by nature; ours to resign the same to God and be as poor as when we were not." [53] This suggests that exaltation and humility are polar opposites and demand each other.

Although this defense of Eckhart against the charge of spiritual pride is persuasive, it is not wholly convincing. The real charge is not that Eckhart claims deification for the soul in its own right and apart from God, but that he negates the empirical self in order to attain deification of the higher, spiritual self. Against this charge, the fact that Eckhart praised humility is not decisive. For he may have sought the virtue of humility by eliminating from the empirical ego all concern for itself and at the same time may have been affected by a spiritual pride of which he was unconscious. Whether this was the case with Eckhart no one can know. But it can hardly be denied that there is great danger of presumption in the claim of any mystic to have been exalted to the point of deification. One of the greatest advantages of theistic over monistic mysticism is that it has usually maintained that the soul continues in the mystical union to be distinguished from God.

Despite these influences of Neo-Platonism upon him, the strong emphasis of Eckhart upon *moral activity* is evidence that he was fundamentally a theistic rather than a monistic mystic. Otto has pointed out that the ethical difference between Eckhart and Sankara is cor-

[52] Otto, *Mysticism East and West*, p. 182.
[53] Eckhart, *Tractate XIV*, pp. 381, 382.

related with a basic difference between their conceptions of God. While Sankara's *Brahman* is undoubtedly a spiritual Being, as universal Consciousness, it is not a living God. In contrast to his static *Brahman*, Eckhart's God is dynamic and ceaselessly *active*. In contrast to the changeless *Brahman*, who does not work, is the God of Eckhart for whom creation and work are essential to His nature.[54] It is true that Eckhart also asserts that the Godhead is not active and does not work, so that a paradox is involved in his view. The Godhead is both at rest and in movement, both still and living, unceasingly active. Whether this paradox can be resolved may be questionable but it undoubtedly affects Eckhart's view of the mystic's life. While Sankara's goal for the self is the stilling of all activity of the self and disparagement of all works since they bind the self to the world, Eckhart advocates both "a complete inward composure and a most powerful actualization and exercise of the will." [55] He praises the stillness and repose of the soul which has detached itself from the world, but his ideal is not the quiet, contemplative Mary but the active Martha who works without ceasing. "Mary was praised for choosing the best, but Martha's life was very useful, serving Christ and his disciples. St. Thomas says the active life is better than the life of contemplation, so far as we actually spend in charity the income we derive from contemplation. It is all the same thing; we have but to root ourselves in this same ground of contemplation to make it fruitful in works, and the object of contemplation is achieved. . . . God's purpose in the union of contemplation is fruitfulness in works; for in contemplation thou servest thyself alone, but the many in good works." [56]

However, Eckhart emphasizes not so much external works done in obedience to the moral law as the *inner goodness* which results from the transformation of the soul in its depths. "Being precedes work. According to your being, so is your work." [57] The content and motivating force of this inner goodness is *love*. As Eckhart says, "Love is the form of virtue without which no virtue is virtue. . . . Wherefore we ought so to live that our whole life is love. In this disposition all practices are praise-worthy, outward or inward." [58] Thus the culmination of the mystical life is the transformation of the inner being of the self by love and the spontaneous expression of that being by works of love.

---

[54] Otto, *Mysticism East and West*, pp. 174, 175.   [55] *Ibid.*, p. 173.
[56] Eckhart, *Sermon III*, pp. 15, 16.   [57] Quoted in Otto, *op. cit.*, p. 208.
[58] Eckhart, *Tractate I*, p. 273.

MYSTICISM: AN EVALUATION

Any critical evaluation of mysticism must take account of the fact that there are fundamental differences between different types of mysticism. This is obvious in the case of the difference between atheistic mysticism and both theistic and monistic mysticism. But the difference between theistic and monistic mysticism is also very important and we shall be concerned with it at almost every point.

1. The psychological effects of the mystical experience upon the mystic himself have usually been regarded as good. The experience of mystical union is one of incomparable joy, and it has frequently been interpreted as a foretaste of eternal life.[59] The mystic feels that he has been liberated from the limitations, discords, and frustration of finite existence. His longing for union with the source of his being has been fulfilled and he has attained self-realization. Also, his joy is accompanied by a feeling of peace and serenity. The restlessness of unsatisfied desire which had thrust him into one activity after another has been stilled. As Van der Leeuw says, mysticism is a "religion of repose," [60] as contrasted with the "religion of struggle" characteristic of religious dualism. This tends to produce in some mystics an attitude of quietism which is opposed to activity. But the mystic life at its best involves an alternation between contemplation and action, as in the examples of St. Bernard and St. Teresa of Avila. After the mystic comes out of the experience of mystical union, which by its very nature can seldom be long sustained, he must deal with the problems of ordinary existence. When he does so, his activity is profoundly affected by the peace he has found during the union, and he acts with a poise and serenity lacking in most of us. Finally, many mystics have testified that the mystical union with God has helped them to unify their desires and purposes and to redirect them and bring them into harmony with the divine Will. They have learned to integrate their personality at the spiritual level and to do spontaneously what they had struggled vainly to do because of a divided will. Although theistic and monistic mystics differ radically in the way they express their personality, there can be no doubt that both types of mysticism have resulted in a unification of desires and a consequent integration of the self.

2. In spite of these psychological effects which would generally be regarded as beneficial in and by themselves, there has been much

---

[59] Cf. Augustine's account of his mystical experience in the Confessions, Bk. IX, Chap. 10.

[60] Van der Leeuw, Religion in Essence and Manifestation, p. 605.

criticism of mysticism because of certain beliefs associated with it. One of these criticisms has been aimed at what is taken to be the mystical conception of God. Although mystics have usually emphasized the immanence and accessibility of God more than other religious people, there is another sense in which they are often accused of exaggerating His transcendence. For mystics have felt the inadequacy of men's concepts and images to express the infinite nature of God and have often asserted that he is other than everything finite. Otto, who is sympathetic with mysticism, maintains that mysticism has a distinctive conception of God as "wholly other" and "without modes." "It is," says Otto, "the wholly non-rational character of this conception of God with its divergence from the intimate, personal, modified God of simple theism which makes the mystic." [61] This is one of the points at which the difference between theistic and monistic mysticism is pronounced, for Otto's statement describes Sankara's conception of *Brahman,* Plotinus' conception of "the One," and Eckhart's conception of the "Godhead" which was influenced by Neo-Platonism. But it is misleading when it is applied to most theistic mystics. Although the mystical experience has made them aware of the limitations of all images and concepts derived from finite things and persons to express fully the essence of God, they do not usually refuse to use such images and concepts to describe Him. When they use the negative theology in speaking of Him, they balance and supplement it by an affirmative theology. Indeed, it should be remembered that even a theistic mystic like Eckhart who has been influenced by the negative theology of Neo-Platonism combines negations concerning the "Godhead" with affirmations about "God." The general view of other theistic mystics does not differ substantially from that of Aquinas, i.e., that certain terms derived from persons should be predicated of God but with a clear understanding that they are to be interpreted as analogies. What is distinctive of mystics at this point is only that they are often more imaginative and daring than theologians in their use of imagery. Bernard of Clairvaux, for example, uses the erotic imagery of the Song of Songs to express the mystical union with God, and Evelyn Underhill points out that one of the images most in favor with Christian mystics is that of "spiritual marriage." [62]

Thus the theistic mystic does not have a "different conception" of God than the ordinary theist, since he shares the theist's view that God

---

[61] Otto, *Mysticism East and West,* p. 141.
[62] Underhill, *Mysticism,* pp. 163 *ff.*

is a personal Being possessing attributes such as understanding, will, and love. But he is usually more aware than the ordinary religious person that the concepts and images men apply to God are only analogies and are not to be taken literally and anthropomorphically. In this way, he combines a personal view of God with a recognition of what is often called the "suprapersonal" dimension of His nature as transcendent and infinite. Using analogies drawn from personal life and relationships, he pours into them the intense feeling of love and awe which he has experienced in the mystical union. In this way, he expresses vividly both the immanence of God in the soul as personal Love and His transcendence of everything human as infinite Power, unchangeable Light, and inexhaustible Life. Far from this being a ground for criticism of him, it may well be one of his greatest contributions to religious life and thought.

3. One of the most common criticisms of mysticism by orthodox theologians and others is that the mystical union involves identification of the soul with God. We have pointed out that monistic mystics such as Sankara assert the identity of the soul with God and that theistic mystics such as Eckhart sometimes seem to imply it. But it cannot be emphasized too strongly that theistic mysticism has usually refused to claim that the soul becomes identical with God in the mystical union. How are we to account for the fact that monistic mystics have claimed this? Insofar as the claim is not an exaggerated way of emphasizing the closeness of the union of the soul with God, it results from a misinterpretation by the mystic of his experience. This misinterpretation is due in part to the effect of a monistic philosophy upon the mystic, as in the case of Sankara. But it is also due to the psychological effect of the mystical discipline preceding the experience of union upon the mystic's later description of the union itself. For the mystical discipline involves, as we have seen, the stripping away from the soul of all its powers and activities until it becomes empty of contents, e.g., images, sensations, and ideas. It is not surprising, therefore, that the soul which has striven to become a "nothing" should itself finally be confronted by a *Brahman* or "Godhead" which seems to it "Nothing," i.e., without qualities or relations or distinctions. And it is not surprising that such a subject without content should not be able to distinguish itself from such an Object without content. Thus it is understandable that a monistic mystic like Sankara after the mystical experience should speak as if there had been no distinction but only identity between the soul and God. In contrast, the theistic mystic is aware of the fact that, however close the union between his soul and God in the mystical

experience may be, he remains a finite being distinct from the infinite God. If he uses the language of "deification," he does so only in the sense of the early Fathers who often said of the wonderful effect of the incarnation upon the faithful, "God became man in order that man might become God." Hence our conclusion is that, while monistic mystics and a few theistic mystics influenced by monistic philosophy have claimed that the soul is identical with God in the mystical union, the vast majority of theistic mystics have made no such claim and have avoided the danger of spiritual pride involved in it.[63] One of the greatest merits of Theism is its realistic recognition that man is man and God is God.

4. Another criticism which is frequently made is that all mysticism leads to world-negation. Here, again, it is important to distinguish between the different types of mysticism. On the whole, both the atheistic mysticism of early Buddhism and the monistic mysticism exemplified by Sankara *have* been world-negating, and the consequences for Indian life and thought in the past have been great. If the world of *Maya* is interpreted as illusion, its value is denied; if it is interpreted as appearance of *Brahman*, its value is at least minimized. The concern of the enlightened man is to break all the ties that bind the ignorant man to it and to identify himself with *Brahman*. This is doubtless one of the many causes of the neglect of natural science and technology for so many centuries in India, as well as of the acquiescence in economic and social evils. For it is normal to deny the reality and value of the natural order and to minimize the importance of a just social order if one believes that *Brahman* is the only reality and that only union with Him is of ultimate significance. As William Temple has pointed out, the disparagement of the material for the sake of the spiritual leads, paradoxically, not only to a neglect of the economic basis of life but also to an otherworldly view of the spiritual life.[64] For it cuts off the spiritual life from creative activity in the world. It must be admitted, however, that monistic mysticism has sometimes interpreted the natural world as an appearance of *Brahman* which possesses meaning and worth. This interpretation, which is somewhat similar to Western Idealism, has produced reverence for all living things and appreciation of the beauty and mystery of nature. Also, it must be emphasized that Hindu Monism has been profoundly influenced by Western ideals dur-

[63] Gilson, *The Mystical Theology of St. Bernard*, Chap. 5.
[64] William Temple, *Nature, Man and God* (London: Macmillan, 1935), pp. 477, 478.

ing the last century and by Gandhi's world-affirming synthesis of theistic Hinduism with social and political activity in recent years.

While the monistic mysticism exemplified by Sankara has been
world-negating, theistic mysticism has, with certain qualifications, been
world-affirming. When a theistic mystic like Eckhart is in the process of
detaching himself from the finite things and values of the world, he
tends to view them as ephemeral and worthless. Although he believes
them to be creatures made by God, they seem to him too transitory to
have real value; and, even when he loves them, his intense longing for
God causes him to regard them as hindrances to the attainment of
union with Him. But after he has attained union with God, his attitude
toward the world tends to be radically transformed. He now sees the
finite and imperfect things around him not apart from God but in
relation to Him. As such, they are endowed with meaning and worth
through their participation in Him as their Ground. As a result, the
mystic who has known God in the depths of his soul now sees Him
everywhere in His creatures. Eckhart has expressed this new attitude
toward the world in unforgettable terms. "All things are simply God to
thee who seest only God in all things. Like one who looks long at the
sun, he encounters the sun in whatever he afterwards looks at." [65] As a
result, the world which in itself is full of evil becomes a place of joy
when it is experienced in the light of God,[66] and one does not have to
wait for the vision of God in the after life to experience the state of
blessedness. As Eckhart says, "A man beholds God in this life in the
same perfection and is blessed in exactly the same way as in the after
life." [67]

Thus, while the charge that mysticism is world-negating is largely
justified when it is directed against an extreme monistic mysticism, it is
far from true of Western theistic mysticism in which union with God
can lead to an affirmation of the world because of His presence in it. If
this was the case with the mysticism of Eckhart, which was affected in
some measure by the ascetic and otherworldly attitude of medieval
Christianity, it is far more true of the theistic mysticism of the modern
period.

A closely related criticism is that mysticism is characterized by an
extreme *self-renunciation* in which the empirical self and all its powers
are denied natural expression. As a result, it is said, mysticism prevents
the development of a creative personality and the exercise of its powers
in cultural, intellectual, and artistic activity. As orthodox Christians

---

[65] Eckhart, *Sermon IV*, p. 24.   [66] Otto, *Mysticism East and West*, p. 211.
[67] Quoted in Otto, *loc. cit.*

accuse the mystics of an overweening exaltation of the self which produces spiritual pride, humanists criticize them for the opposite tendency of extreme self-negation. These two criticisms are not inconsistent with but complementary to one another, the former attacking the mystic for his "deification" of the highest and noblest part of the soul, the latter for his denial of expression to its natural powers.

Monistic mysticism like that of Sankara cannot be defended against this charge. Sankara clearly regards the empirical self as belonging to the realm of *Maya* and holds that it must be negated along with the things of the external world. But it is more difficult to evaluate the charge when it is directed against theistic mystics. There is no doubt that self-denial sometimes has been carried to the point of self-negation by theistic mystics who have been deeply influenced by medieval asceticism.[68] When this has occurred, personality has been stifled and cultural activity has been weakened. However, the purpose of self-negation in the mystical discipline is not a negative but a positive one and, as we have seen, mystics have testified that the self is unified and its spiritual powers are enhanced by the mystical experience. Many mystics have been highly creative in their lives, e.g., Meister Eckhart, Bernard of Clairvaux, and Catherine of Siena, although they usually exercised their powers in the Middle Ages in ecclesiastical activities. Thus, while theistic mysticism has sometimes led to self-negation when it has been accompanied by bodily self-mortification, it has in other cases attained self-fulfillment through the practice of self-renunciation, as in the case of Eckhart and others who have avoided bodily austerities.

5. What of the relation of mysticism to *moral conduct*? Some have argued that mysticism weakens the sense of moral responsibility by concentrating attention and effort upon union with God rather than upon the service of human needs; others have insisted that it is the source of the purest and most perfect moral goodness. Here, as elsewhere, the sharp difference of opinion is largely due to the failure to distinguish between different types of mysticism, especially the monistic and theistic types.

According to Sankara, the discipline leading up to the higher knowledge of the self's identity with *Brahman* includes the performance of duty with no desire for its worldly fruit or reward. However,

---

[68] See the description of Suso's self-mortification in William James, *Varieties of Religious Experience* (New York: Random House, Modern Library ed., 1936), pp. 301–304. For a somewhat different and more sympathetic account of Suso's mysticism see Rufus Jones, *The Flowering of Mysticism* (New York: Macmillan, 1939), Chap. 8.

after this knowledge has been attained, duty as such ceases to be required. Hiriyanna interprets this to mean not a cessation of moral activity on the part of the mystic but a replacement of duty by spontaneous service of others as "the natural expression of his felt conviction regarding the oneness of all." [69] Nevertheless, it is significant that Sankara did not regard the performance of duty as essential except as a preparation for the mystical union. Obviously, the reason is that Sankara conceives *Brahman* as impersonal and without moral qualities and does not conceive of Him as making moral demands upon those who are identified with Him.

In contrast, Christian mystics have always regarded moral activity as an essential part of the religious life. Indeed, Eckhart believed, as we have seen, that the contemplative life of Mary was inferior to the active life of Martha who poured out in good works all that she had received in contemplation. Again, the reason is obvious. Since Christian mystics have believed in a personal God whose righteous will is the source of moral demands upon His children and who is actively seeking to fulfill moral purposes in history, they have regarded moral obedience and striving as indispensable in the religious life. For their religious thinking has been shaped not only by the mystical tradition of Christianity but also by the ethical teaching of the Hebrew prophets and by Jesus' ethic of love. Indeed, Bergson rightly emphasizes that the "dynamic religion" of the West has resulted from a synthesis of the prophetic ethical ideal and the mystical experience of God as active, creative love.[70] As a result, although there have been "passive" mystics in the West, the dominant type of mysticism has clearly been "active," creative and ethical.

What is the distinctive contribution of mysticism to morality? It was pointed out that Eckhart's primary concern was the inner transformation of the soul in its depths and the spontaneous expression of its new being in works of love. He believed that only if the *being* of the soul is good, will its *doing* be good. Thus, the mystic's primary contribution to ethics is his recognition that the will is only *one* of the "powers" of the soul and that it is able to do good acts only if the soul has been transformed in its very being. His insistence that union with God is necessary to bring about this radical change in the soul provides a valuable corrective to the moral activism of many "practical" religious men.

However, since the interest of the mystic in a right relationship of

[69] Hiriyanna, *The Essentials of Indian Philosophy*, pp. 173–174.
[70] Henri Bergson, *The Two Sources of Morality and Religion* (New York: Holt, 1935), pp. 228, 229.

the self to the neighbor and to society is secondary to his religious concern, we go to prophets, moral philosophers, and others rather than to mystics for the knowledge of the *content* of morality, e.g., the duties we owe to our neighbors, the values which will fulfill their needs, and the social institutions which will best serve the common good. The ethical limitation of the mystic is that because of his consuming passion for union with God, he tends to minimize the need for such knowledge and the intellectual task of discovering it. For this reason, we cannot agree with Stace that "the ultimate source of ethical value lies in mysticism itself," [71] and that the mystical consciousness is "the *only* source from which love flows into the world." [72] Stace is right in pointing out that in the mystical experience the separateness of the individual, which divides him from others and often is the source of conflict with them, falls away and he is aware of his unity with them through his union with God.[73] But it is an error to suppose that mysticism whether monistic or theistic is the *only* source of sympathy and love and by itself an adequate foundation for morality. For example, the prophetic religion of Judaism and Christianity has been a powerful force for sympathy and love; and moral and social philosophers have provided indispensable knowledge of the way men should realize values and of the duties they should perform if their love is to be guided by intelligence.[74]

6. In our analysis of the nature of mysticism, we pointed out that the mystic is not content with conventional religion but seeks a direct, immediate experience of God. This longing for immediacy tends to make him more independent of traditional religion than most believers. This has often led to the criticism of mystics that they subordinate too much the objective side of religion to the *subjective*. This is particularly serious in the case of Christian mystics because the Christian religion is based upon a historical revelation recorded in the Scriptures and transmitted from generation to generation by the Church. Does the subjective and personal religion of the mystics weaken the objective and historical basis of religion?

The answer to this question seems to be twofold: on the one hand, the mystic's emphasis upon subjective and personal union with God *can* endanger the objective and traditional elements in religion but, on the other hand, it is indispensable in counteracting the opposite tendency of all institutional religion to degenerate into formalism and ex-

---

[71] Stace, *Mysticism and Philosophy*, p. 323.
[72] *Ibid.*, p. 327.   [73] *Ibid.*, p. 324.
[74] For the role of moral and social philosophy see George F. Thomas, *Christian Ethics and Moral Philosophy* (New York: Scribners, 1955).

ternalism. The danger of the mystic's subjectivity lies in the fact that it may lead him to neglect the historical and scriptural basis upon which the faith of the mystic as well as the ordinary believer rests. Some Christian mystics have emphasized the *present* experience of union with God so strongly that they have minimized the importance of His revelation in the *past,* and others have interpreted the scriptural record of that revelation in such a way as to distort its original meaning by imposing upon it a "spiritual" meaning congenial to the mystical type of religion. Eckhart illustrates these dangers. The historical revelation of God in the past often seems to fall into the background with him, as he emphasizes the birth of the Son in the soul here and now, and his interpretation of the biblical conception of God is weakened by his combination of it with the Neo-Platonic conception of the "Godhead."

On the other hand, the mystic's insistence upon an immediate and personal experience of union with God revitalizes religion when it has become little more than a conventional and mechanical round of observances and a habitual repetition of traditional dogmas. A religious community becomes petrified when such an objective pattern of beliefs and practices has become established and its members no longer enjoy the personal experience of God which originally gave rise to them and alone can give meaning to them. Since this occurs in every age, the mystic's consuming passion for union with God and the transformation of his life by it are needed to make the revelation of God to men in the past and the scriptural record of it relevant and meaningful in the present. We would conclude from this that the mystical and the historical, the subjective and the objective elements are complementary and must be kept in balance if religion is to maintain its continuity with the past and at the same time preserve its vitality.

7. What is the *cognitive value,* if any, of mysticism? Many would dismiss without hesitation all claims of mystics to have attained any knowledge whatever of God and His relation to man. Positivistic psychologists and philosophers believe that only propositions derived from sense experience and reasoning based upon it can give us knowledge. This is sufficient to discredit in their eyes the cognitive claims of mystics, since the mystical experience is based upon neither sensation nor reasoning. In addition, philosophical theologians like Tennant who restrict themselves to the empirical method reject these claims on the ground that the mystical experience itself has no content and that mystics "read in" the knowledge they claim to derive from it.[75] This skeptical view is partially based upon the fact that the different in-

---

[75] F. R. Tennant, *Philosophical Theology* (Cambridge, Eng.: Cambridge University Press, 1929), Vol. I, pp. 311–324.

terpretations of their experience by mystics seem to be influenced by the different religious beliefs they bring with them to it. For these and other reasons, many thinkers regard mystical experience as wholly "subjective."

In contrast, there has been a tendency among philosophers who are sympathetic toward religion but critical of organized religion based on revelation to take the cognitive claims of mystics very seriously. Both the appeal of the mystics to no authority except their own experience and the similar terms in which they describe it have impressed philosophers in a period when the claims of all special revelations are discounted. In different ways, William James in *The Varieties of Religious Experience* and Henri Bergson in *Two Sources of Morality and Religion* place this high estimate on mysticism. Perhaps the best example among more recent philosophers is Walter Stace in *Mysticism and Philosophy,* a broad and provocative examination of the philosophical implications of mysticism.

Stace's main argument rests upon the premise that we must distinguish between the mystic's "experience" and the "interpretation" of it. He holds that mystical experiences of various ages and religious traditions have been the same or similar but that different intellectual interpretations have been placed upon them under the influence of their respective religious traditions.[76] An examination of many mystics of the great religions discloses that there is a "universal core" or "nucleus" of common characteristics shared by them.[77] The essence of mysticism as expressed in this "universal core" is the experience of an "undifferentiated unity" of "pure consciousness" in which the individual self is identical with the "Universal Self." Stace admits that the theistic mystics of Judaism, Islam, and Christianity have usually denied that the union of the individual self with God involves identity with Him, but he explains this as an "interpretation" of their original "experience" which was forced upon them by the orthodox theologians of these religions because of their opposition to Pantheism.[78]

This view of the essence of the mystical experience may be correct as a description of monistic mysticism, but it does not do justice to theistic mysticism and therefore must be rejected as a description of mysticism as a whole. Stace assumes that theistic mystics have given distorted interpretations of their experience because of pressure from ecclesiastical authorities, while monistic mystics have given accurate interpretations because they have been free from such pressure. This assumption is unrealistic. It is true, of course, that Jewish, Christian,

---

[76] Stace, *Mysticism and Philosophy,* pp. 33–35.
[77] *Ibid.,* pp. 46, 47.   [78] *Ibid.,* p. 113.

and Muslim mystics have been influenced by beliefs derived from their religious traditions, and some of them have doubtless been affected by pressures from orthodox theologians or others. But Hindu and Buddhist mystics also have obviously been influenced by beliefs dominant in their religious traditions and by pressure from adherents of those traditions. The religious beliefs of mystics as well as others have usually been shaped at an early age by the Scriptures, worship and thought of the religions in which they have been brought up. Therefore, there is no ground for thinking that the interpretation by monistic mystics of their experience as one of "undifferentiated unity" and identity with the Universal Self is more accurate than the interpretation by theistic mystics of their experience as one of union with God in which the distinction of the self from Him is not lost.

If this is the case, Stace's assertion that the "universal core" as he has described it provides the basis for a pantheistic philosophy must also be rejected. For this assertion rests largely upon his acceptance of the monistic interpretation of mystical experience alone as correct. If he had taken with equal seriousness the theistic interpretation of the mystical experience of most Western mystics, he could hardly have based a pantheistic philosophy on the foundation of mystical experience.

This suggests that while the cognitive value of mystical experience should not be denied on the ground that it is merely "subjective," it is impossible to determine the nature of the object of the experience by a direct inspection of the mystical experience *alone*. This must be determined by a philosophical interpretation of experience *as a whole*. Doubtless, naturalistic philosophers and psychologists will explain away the mystic's conviction that the object of his experience is God as an illusion produced by the discipline leading up to his experience of union. But religious philosophers can argue that this discipline only prepares the psychological conditions without which the soul cannot attain union with God, but does not produce the divine Object experienced in union. One's decision between these two opposed interpretations will depend in part upon one's view of the cognitive value of religious experience in general, for mysticism is one form of religious experience and cannot be sharply separated from other forms. It will also depend in part upon the general philosophical position which one has arrived at in interpreting other aspects of experience. If so, both the denial of the cognitive claims of mystical experience and the exaggeration of those claims by making them the basis of a whole philosophy are unjustified. Rather, one should regard mysticism, along with other forms of religious experience, as offering evidence which should be taken seriously but which must be supported by other evidence before its claim to truth can be accepted.

THE MYSTICAL ELEMENT IN RELIGION

Our critical evaluation of mysticism has made it clear that there are serious *dangers* in mysticism, especially of the monistic type, but also that there are great *values* in it. Among these values are: the enjoyment by man of union with God without presuming to identity with Him; the conviction of the reality of God in the experience of union; the recognition that God transcends all man's ideas of Him and yet can in some measure be known; the enhancement of the worth of the natural world and the self in their relation to God; the revitalization of organized religion by the personal experience of God in the present; and the transformation of the moral will by the power of love in the soul. Therefore, a final question concerning mysticism arises: How can these values be preserved while avoiding the dangers we have mentioned?

The answer seems to be found in a clear acknowledgment that when mysticism even in its theistic form is regarded as the *whole* of religion it tends to lead the mystic into error but that when it is viewed as an important *element* it enriches his religious experience and raises the level of his spiritual and moral life. The inference we would draw from this is that the mystical element is valuable but that it must be supplemented and balanced by other elements in a healthy and mature religion. Baron von Hügel has indicated two of these other elements, the institutional and historical, and the rational.[79] If these elements are present in the religious life of the mystic they will guard him from the dangers we have mentioned. A critical loyalty to his religious community and its tradition will keep him from subjectivism. A sound belief concerning the nature of God and His relation to man will prevent him from accepting false speculative views about God which distort the true relation of a man to Him. Above all, a strong sense of moral responsibility will not allow him to sacrifice the service of men to his private contemplation of God. In short, mysticism is an important element but it is not the whole of vital religion.

[79] Friedrich von Hügel, *The Mystical Element in Religion* (New York: E. P. Dutton, 1909), Vol. II, pp. 387–393.

7 Pantheism

SPINOZA

Spinoza (1632–1677) stands on the borderline between the medieval and the modern worlds, looking back to the age of faith and forward to the age of science. The difficulties involved in the interpretation of his philosophy are largely due to the fact that he sought to do justice to a religious world view and ethical ideal which had come down from the past and at the same time to reinterpret it in such a way as to make it consistent with the new science. The interpretation of him is complicated further by the influence of certain classical philosophies such as Stoicism upon his thought.

As a member of the Jewish community in seventeenth-century Holland, Spinoza had studied the Hebrew Bible (the Old Testament) and later Jewish and Christian thinkers. But he had also come under the spell of modern science, its method of establishing truth and its concept of the order of nature. He had been inspired both by Giordano Bruno's pantheistic vision of the world and by the application of rigorous mathematical reasoning to nature. As a result, he rejected orthodox Judaism and was excommunicated from the synagogue. The reason for this will be clear to anyone who reads his *Theological-Political Treatise*. The claim of the Scriptures to provide us with a revelation of supernatural truth, he argues, is false. The prophets were men with vivid imaginations and a just moral sense, but we should go to them for moral ideals and examples rather than for metaphysical or theological truths. For knowledge of the world and man, we must depend upon no authority except reason, for only through reason can certain truth be attained. In one of his letters, he speaks of "the primary object of Scripture, which according to the word of Christ himself consists, of course, in loving God above all things and one's neighbour as oneself. High speculations, I believe, concern Scripture least. As far as I am concerned, I have learned none of the eternal attributes of God from

Holy Scripture, nor could I learn them." [1] Hence, Spinoza rejected the authority of revelation.

Under the influence of Descartes, he adopted the "geometrical" method of reasoning. Convinced that nature is an ordered system in which everything occurs by a necessity like the logical necessity by which the sum of the three angles of a triangle equals two right angles, he developed in his *Ethics* a metaphysical and ethical system by deductive reasoning from self-evident truths. It is with this system that we are primarily concerned, since it contains Spinoza's mature views on the nature of God, on the one hand, and on man and his good in relation to God, on the other. Before we analyze his system, however, it is necessary to indicate briefly his conception of the purpose of philosophy and of the nature of the knowledge it seeks to attain.

THREE LEVELS OF KNOWLEDGE

Although Spinoza is rightly regarded as a rationalist in his method, he was motivated in developing his philosophy by an existential concern which was similar in some respects to that of Augustine. This may seem surprising, since existentialists from Kierkegaard to Buber and Marcel have been highly critical of philosophical systems constructed by the speculative reason. Systems such as that of Hegel have seemed to them both pretentious and irrelevant to the ethical concerns of man's existence. Yet Spinoza constructed a towering and all-embracing metaphysical and ethical system and made claims for its truth which have been exceeded by those of no other philosopher.

Nevertheless, his early treatise *On the Improvement of the Understanding* makes it clear that his philosophical quest was inspired not merely by a disinterested intellectual desire for truth but also by a practical concern for perfection and happiness. He describes his disillusionment with the "vain and futile" life he has been leading and his resolution to inquire whether "there might be anything of which the discovery and attainment would enable me to enjoy continuous, supreme, and unending happiness." [2] He has learned from experience that the three things which are usually most highly esteemed by men —riches, fame, and pleasure—bring only ephemeral satisfactions or awaken hopes that are frustrated.[3] This is due to the fact that happiness is made to depend on the quality of the objects loved and that

[1] Spinoza, *Letter XXI*, p. 433. This and subsequent references to the writings of Spinoza are from *Spinoza: Selections*, ed. John Wild (New York: Scribners, 1930).
[2] Spinoza, *On the Improvement of the Understanding*, p. 1.
[3] *Ibid.*, p. 2.

worldly objects are perishable. In contrast, an eternal and infinite object would be the source of joy unmingled with sadness and therefore is greatly to be desired.[4] This discovery has led Spinoza to conceive a more perfect character than his own and to seek for means which will help him and others to attain it. It is a character based upon "the knowledge of the union existing between the mind and the whole of nature." [5] But before it can be attained, a method "must be devised for improving the understanding and purifying it . . . so that it may apprehend things without error, and in the best possible way." [6] In this early passage Spinoza foreshadows the later metaphysics, ethics, and theory of knowledge of the *Ethics*.

Although Spinoza sets forth his theory of knowledge in the *Ethics* after his metaphysical principles, it may aid in the understanding of these to deal with it first. Like Plato, he conceives of knowledge as existing at different levels and as possessing different degrees of adequacy at these levels. There are three levels: opinion, or imagination, *imaginatio;* reason, *ratio;* and intuitive knowledge, *scientia intuitiva.* The first of them, "*imagination,*" arises from the affections, or modifications of the human body by other bodies, and the reflection of these in ideas. Since these ideas are produced by the effects of other bodies upon our bodies, they are passive and vague. Moreover, they are fortuitous in the sense that they give to each individual knowledge only of bodies which affect his own body. For these reasons, they offer "inadequate" and "confused" rather than scientific knowledge. "I say expressly that the mind has no adequate knowledge of itself, nor of its body, nor of external bodies, but only a confused knowledge, as often as it perceives things in the common order of nature, that is to say, as often as it is determined to the contemplation of this or that *externally* —namely, by a chance coincidence." [7] This kind of knowledge includes not only the perception of particular objects but also universal ideas. The ideas which reflect the states produced in the body by a number of other bodies of a certain kind combine to form a composite image. In this way universal ideas such as "man," "dog," and "horse," and transcendental ideas such as "being" and "thing," have arisen. Since these are only composite images derived from the differing experiences of men, they vary from individual to individual and cannot give us scientific knowledge of things.

Although knowledge at this first level is inadequate, like "opinion" about sensible objects in Plato, it is useful for the conduct of life. Nor

[4] *Ibid.*, pp. 3, 4.   [5] *Ibid.*, p. 5.   [6] *Ibid.*, pp. 5, 6.
[7] Spinoza, *Ethics*, Pt. II, Pr. 29, Sch., p. 177.

can it be called false when it is taken in and by itself. For there is nothing "positive" in an idea itself that could make it false, but only a "privation" of knowledge. "When we look at the sun, we imagine his distance from us to be about 200 feet; the error not consisting solely in the imagination, but arising from our not knowing what the true distance is when we imagine, and what the causes of our imagination." [8] Thus, ideas of "opinion" or "imagination" are false not in themselves but in that they do not form a coherent and rational view of nature. But because they are inadequate and confused both in their content and in their arrangement, we are led into error by their partial and fragmentary character. Therefore, "it is the knowledge of the second and third, and not that of the first kind, which teaches us to distinguish the true from the false." [9]

The second kind of knowledge is called "*reason*" and arises from "common notions and adequate ideas of the properties of things." [10] These "common notions" reflect the common properties of things when they are adequately conceived. "Those things which are common to everything, and which are equally in the part and in the whole, can only be adequately conceived," "that is to say, clearly and distinctly conceived by all." [11] For example, extension and motion are properties common to all bodies. Spinoza contrasts these "common notions" with the universal ideas of the first level which are only "composite images" formed by combining ideas that are logically unrelated to each other. "Common notions" are indispensable because they provide the basis not only for science and mathematics but also for metaphysics.

If we are to understand Spinoza's rationalistic or "geometrical" method as a philosopher, we must grasp what he means by an "adequate idea." He defines it as "an idea which, in so far as it is considered in itself, without reference to the object, has all the properties or internal signs . . . of a true idea. . . . I say internal so as to exclude that which is external, the agreement, namely, of the idea with its object." [12] This means that we do not need to look for a criterion of the truth of an adequate idea in something outside it, since it is its own criterion, i.e., we know by its own internal properties that it is adequate. Thus Spinoza rejects the correspondence theory of truth which defines it in terms of the correspondence of an idea to its object. How can a man know, he asks, that an idea agrees with that of which it is the idea? His answer is that "he knows it simply because he has an idea which agrees with that of which it is the idea, that is to say, because

[8] *Ibid.*, Pr. 35, Sch., p. 181.   [9] *Ibid.*, Pr. 42, p. 187.
[10] *Ibid.*, Pr. 40, Sch. 2, p. 186.   [11] *Ibid.*, Pr. 38, p. 182.
[12] *Ibid.*, Def. IV, p. 144.

truth is its own standard." [13] The metaphysical basis for this astonishing claim to certainty is that the human mind is part of the divine intellect: "our mind, in so far as it truly perceives things, is a part of the infinite intellect of God, and therefore it must be that the clear and distinct ideas of the mind are as true as those of God." [14]

This claim is of crucial importance because it implies that knowledge of "common notions" is necessarily true. Therefore, it is not possible to doubt the truth of a self-evident proposition or the truth of a proposition which is logically entailed by it. "It follows that any system of propositions which are logically derived from self-evident axioms is necessarily true and that we know that it is true." [15] Spinoza's *Ethics* itself constitutes such a system of propositions. "The human mind," he says, "possesses an adequate knowledge of the eternal and infinite essence of God. . . . and since all things are in God and are conceived through Him, it follows that we can deduce from this knowledge many things which we can know adequately." [16] Thus Spinoza's whole system of metaphysics and ethics rests upon his assumption that we have adequate ideas which are certain and can provide us with self-evident truths, and that from these we can deduce knowledge of the nature of reality as a whole.

Since the properties grasped by "common notions" are equally present in all things, says Joachim, "science comprehends Reality under the form of necessary interconnections of content, and not as a complex or system of particular things." [17] Therefore, the second level of knowledge is in sharp contrast with the first. "It is not of the nature of reason," says Spinoza, "to consider things as contingent but as necessary," "without any relation to time, but under a certain form of eternity." [18] Whereas knowledge at the first level is personal and arbitrary, the result of things affecting us rather than of our own active thought, rational knowledge at the second level is universal and necessary. However, it has a serious limitation: it is abstract in the sense that it neglects the differences between things and the individuality of particular things. As Joachim puts it, "science begins the work of intelligible reconstruction of the world of perception, but it cannot complete it. Its analysis has allowed the breath of life to escape from the world, and its reconstruction is powerless to restore it." [19]

[13] *Ibid.*, Pt. II, Pr. 43, Sch., p. 190.   [14] *Ibid.*

[15] Frederick Copleston, *History of Philosophy*, Vol. IV, p. 235.

[16] Spinoza, *Ethics*, Pt. II, Pr. 47, Sch., pp. 194–195.

[17] H. Joachim, *A Study of the Ethics of Spinoza* (Oxford: Clarendon Press, 1901), p. 176.

[18] Spinoza, *Ethics*, Pt. II, Pr. 44, Demonst., Corol. 2, pp. 190, 193.

[19] Joachim, *op. cit.*, p. 177.

This makes it necessary to ascend to the third and highest level, "*intuitive knowledge.*" At this level, the mind returns to the individual things from which science has made its abstractions and intuits them in their essential relation to God rather than as isolated phenomena. However, it is not attained by a sudden leap but presupposes and arises from the second kind of knowledge. "Since all things are in God and are conceived through Him, it follows that we can deduce from this knowledge many things which we can know adequately, and that we can thus form that third sort of knowledge, . . ." [20] Resting upon an adequate knowledge of God or His attributes, it seeks a vision of the concrete natures of individual things, so that "the certainty and necessity of scientific demonstration unite with the immediacy and concreteness of perception." [21] Insofar as this vision of all things in God is attained, it brings with it the complete satisfaction of our emotional as well as our intellectual nature and therefore it is the basis of our highest good. "As each person therefore becomes stronger in this kind of knowledge, the more is he conscious of himself and of God; that is to say, the more perfect and the happier he is." [22] As we shall see, this is the culmination of the moral and religious as well as the philosophical quest.

"GOD OR NATURE"

We have seen that neither ordinary knowledge at the level of "imagination" nor scientific knowledge at the level of "reason" but only "intuitive knowledge" of individual things in relation to God can provide a comprehensive vision of reality and bring perfect happiness to man. We are now ready to consider how Spinoza develops his metaphysics in order to prepare the way for this vision.

The fundamental concept of Spinoza's metaphysics is *substance.* Aristotle had regarded substance as the primary category, that of which other things can be asserted but which can be asserted of nothing else itself. He had held that the world is composed of a plurality of individual substances arranged in a hierarchical order culminating in an immaterial substance, the Prime Mover. Aquinas had accepted this view of substance in the thirteenth century and it had dominated Western thought ever since. But Descartes had modified it by dividing substances into two kinds, "extended substance" and "thinking substance," which he conceived in dualistic fashion as completely different

---

[20] Spinoza, *Ethics*, Pt. II, Pr. 47, Sch., pp. 193–194.
[21] Joachim, *op. cit.*, pp. 182–183.
[22] Spinoza, *Ethics*, Pt. V, Pr. 31, Sch., p. 389.

from each other. The world is composed of a plurality of "thinking substances," or minds, and of "extended substances," or bodies, and man is made up of a mind and a body which causally interact although in their essences they have nothing in common with each other.

Now, Spinoza accepted the concept of substance as the basis of his metaphysics but radically transformed it in accordance with a *monistic* vision of the world. This is evident from the "definition" of substance which he sets down at the beginning of the *Ethics:* "By substance, I understand that which is in itself and is conceived through itself; in other words, that, the conception of which does not need the conception of another thing from which it must be formed." [23] This definition is based upon a distinction between that which is self-dependent or self-subsistent, "in itself," and that which is in something else upon which it depends for its existence. It appears similar, therefore, to Aristotle's definition of substance. But Spinoza's addition of the phrase "conceived through itself" and his explanation of substance as not needing "the conception of another thing from which it must be formed" suggests a radical difference between his conception and the traditional one. For it implies that nothing can be called a "substance" which depends upon something else as its cause, so that only a being that is necessary in the sense of "cause of itself" can be a substance. Thus, the plurality of finite substances of Aristotle and Aquinas and the two kinds of substances of Descartes must be denied the status of substances. What, then, are they?

Spinoza prepares the way for his answer to this question in the next two Definitions. "By attribute, I understand that which the intellect perceives of substance, as if constituting its essence." [24] "By mode, I understand the affections of substance, or that which is in another thing through which also it is conceived." [25] The definition of "*attribute*" as constituting the "essence" of substance as perceived by the intellect enables Spinoza to acknowledge two different ways in which "substance" is known by us and at the same time to deny the status of substance to them. For later he asserts that "thinking things" and "extended things" are either attributes of substance or affections of attributes.[26] In this way he recognizes that the division Descartes had made between "extended" and "thinking" substances corresponds to something real but reduces them to the status of "attributes" which express the essence of substance but are not substances themselves.

[23] *Ibid.*, Pt. I, Def. III, p. 94.   [24] *Ibid.*, Def. IV, p. 94.
[25] *Ibid.*, Def. V, p. 94.   [26] *Ibid.*, Pt. I, Pr. 14, pp. 107–108.

The definition of "*mode*" as an "affection" of substance, "in another thing through which also it is conceived," enables Spinoza to reduce the plurality of "substances" recognized by earlier philosophers from Aristotle to Descartes to modifications of substance. Thus, as the concept of "attribute" takes account of the distinction between mind and body, the concept of "mode" takes account of the plurality of things we experience through sense perception.[27] It should be noted, however, that Spinoza does not mean to deny reality to the many "modes" or objects of ordinary experience as if they were illusions. As Joachim says, "They are real, though their reality is dependent upon the reality of Substance in which they are." [28]

In these definitions of "substance," "attribute," and "mode," Spinoza lays down as self-evident the fundamental principles of his monistic metaphysics: there is a *substance*, which is self-dependent and upon which everything else depends; its essence consists of *attributes*, of which our minds know only two, thought and extension; and it manifests itself in many *modes*, which appear to our senses as separate but independent objects but are in reality only modifications of itself.

However, Spinoza claims to demonstrate these conclusions by his geometrical method. He argues that there can be only *one* substance. "For if there were anything by which substance could be produced, the knowledge of substance would be dependent upon the knowledge of its cause, and therefore it would not be substance," [29] since substance is by definition "conceived through itself." "In other words," as Hampshire says, "he has so strictly defined substance that nothing whose attributes are the effects of outside causes can be called a substance." [30] Therefore, it must be *cause of itself*, i.e., its essence necessarily involves its existence. It is also *infinite* in its nature. For if it were finite, it would be limited by something other than itself and would not be single or unique.[31] And since by definition "to the essence of that which is absolutely infinite pertains whatever expresses essence and involves no negation," [32] it is a "Being which consists of infinite attributes." [33] This one, necessarily existent, infinite Being, or Substance, is immediately identified with God, since God has been defined as "Being absolutely infinite, that is to say, substance consisting of infinite attributes, each

[27] *Ibid.*, Pr. 25, Corol., p. 123.
[28] Joachim, *A Study of the Ethics of Spinoza*, p. 15.
[29] Spinoza, *Ethics*, Pt. I, Pr. 6, pp. 97–98.
[30] S. Hampshire, *Spinoza* (London: Faber, 1956), p. 37.
[31] Spinoza, *Ethics*, Pt. I, Pr. 8, pp. 98–102.
[32] *Ibid.*, Pt. I, Def. VI, p. 95.
[33] *Ibid.*, Pt. I, Pr. 10, Sch., p. 102.

one of which expresses eternal and infinite essence." [34] Thus Spinoza's "demonstration" that there is only one substance and that this substance is God is *by definition.*

Spinoza's view that the "extended substance" and "thinking substance" of Descartes are not substances but two of the infinite "attributes" of the one Substance, God, is opposed to the traditional view that God is wholly immaterial since it ascribes extension to Him as one of his "attributes" and includes bodies in Him as "modes." Spinoza argues that the traditional denial of this is based on the false assumption that if God is extended He must be composed of parts and hence be capable of suffering, and imperfect.[35] But substance is indivisible and not made up of parts, so that it cannot suffer, and matter is not "unworthy of the divine nature, provided only it be allowed that it is eternal and infinite." [36] Therefore, God is the totality of all being, the infinite Being in which all finite things exist. Under the attribute of thought, He includes all minds as parts of His infinite intellect; under the attribute of extension, He includes all bodies.

Spinoza offers several proofs that *God* as he has described Him necessarily exists.[37] Three of these (the first, second, and fourth, below) are a priori in form. The *first* argues that it would involve a contradiction to suppose that God does not exist, since it has been shown that His essence necessarily involves His existence, i.e., that substance is cause of itself. The *second* asserts that if God does not exist, there must be a reason for it. But this reason cannot be found in God since He is infinite and perfect; and it cannot be found outside of Him since there is nothing outside Him. The *third* proof is a posteriori. It argues that, if only finite things necessarily exist, they have more power than the infinite Being—which is absurd. Therefore, either nothing exists, which is false since we ourselves exist, or the infinite Being also necessarily exists. The *fourth* proof argues in an a priori way from the same grounds as the third. Since ability to exist is power, the more reality a thing has the greater is its power of existence. Therefore, the infinite Being has an infinite power of existence and hence necessarily exists. Joachim maintains that not only the third, or a posteriori, proof but also the a priori proofs assume as a fact the existence of something finite, e.g., oneself. If so, the argument is that if you grant that *anything* exists, you must grant that God necessarily exists. In other words, any existent contingent being from which one starts is a fragment

---

[34] *Ibid.,* Pt. I, Def. VI, pp. 94–95.   [35] *Ibid.,* Pt. I, Pr. 15, pp. 108–113.
[36] *Ibid.,* p. 113.   [37] *Ibid.,* Pt. I, Pr. 11, pp. 103–106.

involving Reality as a whole and its contingency depends upon the necessity of that Reality, or God, so that "unless the whole is and must be, nothing can in any sense either be or be conceived." [38]

THE DIVINE CAUSALITY

This pantheistic identification of God with the one Substance which includes all things in itself has been expressed by the phrase, "God or Nature," *Deus sive Natura*. It leads Spinoza to an explanation of the causal relationship between God and finite things which is radically different from that of Theism.

First, all things which can be conceived by the infinite intellect of God must follow from the *necessity* of His nature.[39] As efficient cause of everything that exists, "God acts from the laws of His own nature only, and is compelled by no one." [40] In this sense He is a free cause, for a "free" thing has been defined as one "which exists from the necessity of its own nature alone, and is determined to action by itself alone." [41] This view of finite things as *emanating* or "flowing" from the necessity of the divine nature which is identical with its freedom is quite different from the theistic conception of creation as an act of the divine will which is free rather than necessary. It implies that God is not free to create or not to create possible things conceived by His intellect, but that every such possibility becomes an actuality by necessity. Spinoza ridicules those who think that God has freedom of will either to create or not to create or freedom to create things in addition to or different from those that actually exist. For "all things have necessarily flowed, or continually follow by the same necessity, in the same way as it follows from the nature of a triangle, from eternity and to eternity, that its three angles are equal to two right angles. The omnipotence of God has therefore been actual from eternity, and in the same actuality will remain to eternity." [42]

Second, "God is the *immanent*, and not the transitive (*transiens*) cause of all things." [43] According to the theistic view God is transcendent to and distinct from His creation, so that He acts upon it. Since Spinoza has denied that there is any substance besides God, and has argued that all things are *in* Him, he maintains that God is "the cause of the things which are in Himself." [44] However, he distinguishes the divine causal activity from the modes or finite things within which it acts by using a scholastic distinction between *natura naturans* or "God

[38] Joachim, *op. cit.*, p. 53.   [39] Spinoza, *Ethics*, Pt. I, Pr. 16.   [40] *Ibid.*, Pr. 17.
[41] *Ibid.*, Pt. I, Def. VII.   [42] *Ibid.*, Pt. I, Pr. 17, Sch.
[43] *Ibid.*, Pr. 18 (italics added).   [44] *Ibid.*

in so far as He is considered as a free cause," and *natura naturata* or "everything which follows from the necessity of the nature of God," i.e., "all the modes of God's attributes in so far as they are considered as things which are in God." [45]

Third, the existence and action of every finite thing is *determined* by another finite cause, and this cause is determined by another and this by another and so on *ad infinitum*.[46] For although God is the first cause of all finite things, they "must therefore follow from God, or from some attribute of God, in so far as the latter is considered to be affected by some mode," i.e., not immediately but through intermediate causes.[47] Thus God as *natura naturata* is a system of finite things which determine and are determined by one another. There is nothing contingent in nature but all things are determined to exist and act in a certain manner from the necessity of the divine nature.[48] Hence the *will* is not a free cause. Like every other finite thing, a volition cannot exist or be determined to action unless it is determined by another cause and this by another and so on *ad infinitum*.[49] According to this absolute determinism, every finite thing is either necessary or impossible. A thing can be called "contingent," i.e., possible, only "with reference to a deficiency in our knowledge" of the causes which produce it.[50]

Fourth, God does not seek to attain an *end* or *good* by His activity. His activity is to be conceived on the analogy of ground and consequent in geometry, all things following from the divine nature by necessity. To speak of Him as acting for the sake of the good, *sub ratione boni*, would imply that His nature is imperfect, whereas He is absolutely complete and needs to seek nothing. Hence we must not seek for the explanation of anything in the "will" of God, as if He acts for the sake of ends or final causes. The tendency to do so springs from anthropomorphic views of God's activity as due to His possession of a will and intellect like ours. But God is far more than intellect and will. Since "thought is only one of His infinite attributes, will and intellect are modes of God on the same level as other modes." [51] Besides, if intellect and will belong to God's eternal essence, they "would have to differ entirely from our intellect and will, and could resemble ours in nothing except in name. There could be no further likeness than that between the celestial constellation of the Dog and the animal which barks." [52] Finally, the idea that God acts from final causes makes

---

[45] *Ibid.*, Pt. I, Pr. 29, Sch.   [46] *Ibid.*, Pr. 28.   [47] *Ibid.*
[48] *Ibid.*, Pt. I, Pr. 29.   [49] *Ibid.*, Pr. 32.
[50] *Ibid.*, Pr. 33, Sch. 1.
[51] Joachim, *A Study of the Ethics of Spinoza*, p. 63.
[52] Spinoza, *Ethics*, Pt. I, Pr. 17, Sch.

Him dependent upon something outside His own nature "to which He looks while He is at work as to a model, or at which he aims as if at a certain mark." [53]

Why do men suppose, asks Spinoza, that all finite things work, as men do, to some end, and that God directs them to an end? His answer is that it is because man consciously seeks that which is profitable to him and does everything for the sake of the ends he seeks. Since he discovers many things in nature which further the attainment of his ends and is ignorant of their causes, he believes that "some ruler or rulers of nature exist, endowed with human liberty, who have taken care of all things for him, and have made all things for his use." [54] But mathematics, which is not concerned with ends but with essences and properties of forms, has enabled him to see that there are no ends in nature and that "final causes are nothing but human fictions." [55] The doctrine of final causes considers that which is really the cause as the effect, and vice versa; i.e., it considers the means as the effect and the end as the cause. And when we are ignorant of the causes of an event, it invites us to "fly to the will of God, the refuge for ignorance." [56]

Spinoza explains men's *judgments of value* also as a result of their anthropocentric way of looking at things. They judge that to be of greatest importance which is most useful or beneficial to them. For example, they call "good" everything which leads to their health, everything which does not, "evil." [57] Thus ideas of value, like secondary qualities such as sweet and bitter, are "nothing but modes in which the imagination is affected in different ways" and "that which to one person is good will appear to another evil." [58] In short, ideas of value do not reveal the nature of anything in itself but are relative to human desires and feelings.[59] Yet men make them the basis of complaints against God for the "imperfections" of nature. The answer of Spinoza to these complaints is simple: "For the perfection of things is to be judged by their nature and power alone; nor are they more or less perfect because they delight or offend the human senses, or because they are beneficial or prejudicial to human nature." [60]

MAN: BODY AND MIND

We are now in a position to understand Spinoza's view of *man* as "part" of nature. God's causality in finite things or "modes" is mediated by "infinite and eternal modes." The "infinite and eternal mode" in the attribute of extension is "motion-and-rest." Motion is a primary and

---

[53] *Ibid.*, Pr. 33, Sch. 2.   [54] *Ibid.*, Pt. I, Appendix, pp. 135–136.
[55] *Ibid.*, p. 137.   [56] *Ibid.*, p. 139.   [57] *Ibid.*, p. 140.
[58] *Ibid.*, pp. 141, 142.   [59] *Ibid.*, p. 142.   [60] *Ibid.*, pp. 142–143.

intrinsic property of the world as extended, although the proportions of
motion and rest in individual bodies differ and are always changing.
Hence the physical world is to be conceived as a system of bodies in
motion, complex bodies being composed of smaller bodies. As there are
more and more complex bodies, we can conceive the whole of nature
to be an individual whose parts are bodies [61] and Spinoza speaks of
this as "the face of the whole Universe." [62] Similarly, the "infinite and
eternal mode" of God in the attribute of thought is called "absolutely
infinite understanding" or "intellect." [63] For understanding or intellect
is the fundamental mode of thought, upon which other modes such as
love and desire depend.

As the human *body* belongs to the total system of bodies, the
human *mind* is a part of the "infinite intellect," so that both are parts of
nature as a whole.[64] Moreover, since nature is one system conceived
under the two attributes of thought and extension, a mode under the
attribute of thought, an "idea," corresponds to each mode under the
attribute of extension, a "body." This does not mean that there are two
chains or series of causes, mental and bodily, for there is only one order conceived in two ways. "The order and connection of ideas," says
Spinoza, "is the same as the order and connection of things." [65] This is
of fundamental importance for an understanding of the relation between mind and body. Although Spinoza says that "the human mind is
united to the body" and that we cannot understand it adequately without knowing the nature of the body,[66] mind and body are only two
aspects of the same thing. Therefore, Descartes was wrong in maintaining that there is interaction between them, and we must explain bodily
events in terms of other bodily events and not in terms of ideas, and
vice versa.

The mind, says Spinoza, is the "idea" of the body, although it is
"composed of a number of ideas" since there is an idea corresponding
to each part of the body.[67] When the human body is affected by
another body the idea, or modification, of the human body is also an
idea of the other body. But since its ideas of other bodies are mediated
by the modifications of its own body, "the ideas we have of external
bodies indicate the constitution of our own body rather than the nature
of external bodies." [68] The importance of this we have already seen,
since we pointed out that the ideas of "good" and "evil" and other

[61] *Ibid.*, Pt. II, Pr. 13, Lemma 7.   [62] Spinoza, *Letter LXIV*, p. 463.
[63] *Ibid.*   [64] *Ibid.*, *Letter XXXII*, p. 443.
[65] Spinoza, *Ethics*, Pt. II, Pr. 7, p. 149.   [66] *Ibid.*, Pr. 13, Sch., p. 157.
[67] *Ibid.*, Pr. 15, p. 165.   [68] *Ibid.*, Pr. 16, Corol. 2, p. 165.

value qualities are regarded by Spinoza as only "fictions" of our minds which reflect the effects of things upon us rather than the nature of things themselves. Also, the association of ideas "takes place according to the order and concatenation of the affections of the human body" rather than "according to the order of the intellect"; e.g., if a soldier sees the footsteps of a horse he will turn to the thought of war, whereas a country man will turn to the thought of his plow and field.[69] These facts help to explain the fact that men's ideas are so often "confused" and "inadequate," and we shall see that this has a profound effect upon their emotions. Thus Spinoza emphasizes the dependence of both the ideas and the emotions of the mind upon the body

PASSIVE AND ACTIVE EMOTIONS

We must consider more carefully the nature of the emotions, *affectus*, since Spinoza's ethics and religion rest upon his analysis of them. Most of those who have dealt with human emotions and actions, he tells us, have regarded man as standing above the ordinary course of nature. But if man is a part of nature, it is necessary to regard the affections exactly as one would deal with "lines, planes, or bodies," [70] and desires and actions are not products of free choices of the will but are as determined as bodily events. What does such an objective, naturalistic description of the emotions of man disclose?

Every individual thing in nature endeavors to persist in its own being, and this endeavor or *conatus* is its essence.[71] Man is also conscious of any change in himself to a greater or less degree of vitality or perfection. The consciousness of a change to a greater degree is pleasure, *laetitia*, to a less degree pain, *tristitia*. All other emotions are derived from these fundamental forms, i.e., from desire, pleasure, and pain. For example, "*Love* is nothing but joy accompanied with the idea of an external cause, and *hatred* is nothing but sorrow with the accompanying idea of an external cause." [72] Moreover, since our judgments of "good" and "evil" are derived from the relations of things to our desires, each one judges or estimates according to his own emotion what is good or bad, better or worse, best or worst.[73]

Now, there is a fundamental distinction between "passive" and "active" emotions. "*Passive*" emotions arise from the association of pleasure and pain with external things. For example, one is said to "love" a

[69] *Ibid.*, Pr. 18, Sch., p. 169.
[70] *Ibid.*, Pt. III, Preface, "On the Origin and Nature of the Emotions," p. 206.
[71] *Ibid.*, Pt. III, Pr. 7, pp. 215–216.
[72] *Ibid.*, Pr. 13, Sch., p. 221.   [73] *Ibid.*, Pr. 39, Sch., pp. 243–244.

person when the idea of him becomes associated with one's pleasure and heightened vitality. Since there is an accidental or contingent element in the association of pleasures and pains with particular things or persons in the experience of an individual, emotions of this kind are "passive" in the sense of dependent upon the external things with which one happens to associate pleasures and pains. "Different men may be affected by one and the same object in different ways, and the same man may be affected by one and the same object in different ways at different times." [74] In contrast, *active* emotions arise from the mind itself insofar as it is active. They depend upon "adequate" ideas, as passive emotions depend upon "inadequate" or "confused" ideas. Among the "active" emotions Spinoza emphasizes "strength of mind" and "generosity." "By *strength of mind,* I mean the desire by which each person endeavours from the dictates of reason alone to preserve his own being. By *generosity,* I mean the desire by which from the dictates of reason alone each person endeavors to help other people and to join them to him in friendship." [75] To the former are ascribed actions aiming at the advantage of the doer, e.g., temperance; to the latter, those aiming at the advantage of others, e.g., mercy.

The crucial importance of this distinction between "passive" and "active" emotions is shown by the fact that, while passive emotions are the source of human bondage and misery, active emotions are the source of human perfection and happiness. "The impotence of man to govern or restrain the affects [emotions]," says Spinoza, "I call bondage, for a man who is under their control is not his own master, but is mastered by fortune, in whose power he is, so that he is often forced to follow the worse, although he sees the better before him." [76]

MORAL PERFECTION AND HAPPINESS

Moral perfection and happiness can be attained only by liberation from the passive emotions or by a transformation of them into active ones. This liberation depends upon an intellectual advance from inadequate or confused ideas to adequate ones. For *to understand a passive emotion is to be freed from bondage to it.* "An affect [emotion] which is a passion ceases to be a passion as we form a clear and distinct idea of it." [77] For example, hatred is a passive emotion or passion, but if I understand that men act from necessity when they injure me I can overcome the hatred I feel for them. Again, "sorrow for the loss of anything good is diminished if the person who has lost it considers that

[74] *Ibid.,* Pr. 51, p. 252.   [75] *Ibid.,* Pr. 59, Sch., p. 264.
[76] *Ibid.,* Pt. IV, Preface, p. 282.   [77] *Ibid.,* Pt. V, Pr. 3, p. 369.

it could not by any possibility have been preserved." [78] Thus, reason can free us from bondage to the passions. As Hampshire has pointed out, this method is in some respects like that of modern Freudian psychology. "There can in principle be only one way of achieving sanity and happiness; the way is to come to understand the causes of our own states of mind." [79]

This implies that the *ethical ideal* for man is a life in which reason has overcome passive emotions or transformed them into active ones. Is this consistent with Spinoza's view that "good" is only a name for that which satisfies our desires and that it varies with different persons? Spinoza's answer seems to be that we form a general idea of human nature and its perfection and call men more or less "perfect" as they approximate it more or less closely. Therefore, although the terms "good" and "evil" in fact "indicate nothing positive in things considered in themselves" and are only "modes of thought," it is useful to retain them. "Good," then, means "everything which we are certain is a means by which we may approach nearer and nearer to the model of human nature we set before us," while "evil" means "everything which we are certain hinders us from reaching that model." [80] This "model" provides us with an ethical ideal that may be described as the life of reason and virtue through control of the emotions.

Spinoza offers several "remedies" for the passive emotions. An "adequate" idea of a passive emotion, he tells us, enables us to separate or detach it from the idea of an external cause, to connect it with other ideas, and thus to destroy our love or hate for the external cause with which it is associated.[81] For it makes us realize that the emotion is related to many different causes and is necessary, so that we suffer less from it.[82] Spinoza remarks that "our sorrows and misfortunes mainly proceed from too much love towards an object which is subject to many changes, and which we can never possess." [83] What is necessary, therefore, is to overcome our hate and direct our love away from the external things and persons with which it has been associated and toward a more enduring, stable, and inclusive object.

THE INTELLECTUAL LOVE OF GOD

At this point the ethics of Spinoza becomes explicitly religious. The mind, he says, can cause all of the emotions to be related to the idea of God, since an adequate idea of every emotion exhibits it as ultimately

---

[78] *Ibid.*, Pr. 6, Sch., p. 372.   [79] Hampshire, *op. cit.*, p. 142.
[80] Spinoza, *Ethics*, Pt. IV, Preface, p. 286.   [81] *Ibid.*, Pt. V, Pr. 2, p. 368.
[82] *Ibid.*, Prs. 6, 9, pp. 371–372, 373–374.
[83] *Ibid.*, Pr. 20, Sch., p. 382.

caused not by an external object but by God.[84] The joy that arises in this way is attended by the idea of God and therefore *love of God* is produced.[85] Since this love is associated with all of the emotions, it ought to occupy the mind above everything else.[86] However, one who loves God in this way cannot strive that God should love him in return, for God is not affected by any emotion of joy or sorrow and hence can love no one.[87] Spinoza adds that "this love to God is the most constant of all the affects [emotions], and that, in so far as it is related to the body, it cannot be destroyed unless with the body itself." [88] "Moreover, it begets a love towards an immutable and eternal object of which we are really partakers; a love which therefore cannot be vitiated by the defects which are in common love, but which can always become greater and greater, occupy the largest part of the mind, and thoroughly affect it." [89] This love toward God arises from that "intuitive knowledge" of which we have spoken. It is a knowledge which conceives things not insofar as they exist "with relation to a fixed time and place" but "in so far as we conceive them to be contained in God, and to follow from the necessity of the divine nature," or, as Spinoza expresses it, "under the form of eternity," *sub specie aeternitatis.*[90]

In one of the most famous passages in the *Ethics,* Spinoza describes this love of God. "From this third kind of knowledge necessarily springs the intellectual love of God.—For from this kind of knowledge arises joy attended with the idea of God as its cause, that is to say, the love of God, not in so far as we imagine Him as present, but in so far as we understand that He is eternal; and that is what I call the intellectual love of God," *amor intellectualis Dei.*[91] Moreover, since "God loves Himself with an infinite intellectual love" as He delights in His infinite perfection, "the intellectual love of the mind towards God is part of the infinite love with which God loves Himself." [92] For this love of the mind toward God is "an action by which God, in so far as He can be manifested through the human mind, contemplates Himself, the action being accompanied with the idea of Himself." [93] And, although He can love no one merely as an individual finite being, God, insofar as He loves Himself, loves men. "Hence we clearly understand," Spinoza concludes, "that our salvation, or blessedness, or liberty consists in a constant and eternal love towards God, or in the love of God

---

[84] *Ibid.,* Pr. 14, p. 378.   [85] *Ibid.,* Pr. 15, p. 379.
[86] *Ibid.,* Pr. 16, p. 379.   [87] *Ibid.,* Pr. 19, p. 380.
[88] *Ibid.,* Pr. 20, Sch., p. 381.   [89] *Ibid.,* p. 383.
[90] *Ibid.,* Pt. V, Pr. 29, pp. 387–388.   [91] *Ibid.,* Pr. 32, p. 390.
[92] *Ibid.,* Prs. 35, 36, pp. 391–393.   [93] *Ibid.,* Pr. 36, p. 392.

towards men. This love or blessedness is called Glory in the sacred writings, and not without reason." [94]

Thus Spinoza's doctrine of the intellectual love of God is the culmination of both his ethics and his religion. But the precise meaning of the doctrine is not clear. Joachim seems to take it at its face value as a statement of a deeply religious feeling of a mystical kind. "In outline, Spinoza's position is this: in the most complete thinking of which we, as intelligences, are capable, our thought is God's thought; and God's thought is God thinking so far as he constitutes the essence of our mind, i.e. God's thought is our thinking. That oneness of our intelligent being with God merges us in the divine thought and *eo ipso* most fully characterizes us or gives us our 'self.'" [95] "The mind, in its knowledge of God, is a part of God's complete knowledge of himself. And the mind, in its love of God, is a part of the complete love of God for himself." [96] In sharp contrast, Hampshire offers a naturalistic interpretation of the doctrine. "The 'Intellectual love of God,' in spite of its association with Christian and other mysticisms, is intended to be a notion with a more definite and mundane meaning. . . . To understand God must mean to understand Nature, self-creating and self-created; at the third and highest level of intuitive knowledge every individual detail of the natural world is shown related to the whole structure of Nature; the more we take pleasure, as philosophical naturalists, in tracing in detail the order of natural causes, the more we can be said to have an intellectual love of God." [97]

There is probably some truth in both of these radically different interpretations and the difficulty of deciding which is closer to Spinoza's meaning may point to an inconsistency in his philosophy. However, it seems clear that a purely naturalistic interpretation like Hampshire's is an oversimplification and that Joachim is right in taking Spinoza's religious language and concern seriously. Spinoza was a pantheist, although the naturalistic element in his Pantheism is prominent. It is true that he identifies "God" with "nature," but it is not true that one can "substitute" [98] the latter for the former wherever it occurs without losing some of Spinoza's meaning. The attribute of Thought is as important as the attribute of Extension in God, and Spinoza clearly speaks of our minds as parts of His infinite Intellect. Also, there is no reason to deny that Spinoza ascribes love to God, although it is an intellectual love rather than a passive emotion. If, then, God is charac-

---

[94] *Ibid.*, Pr. 36, Sch., pp. 392–393.   [95] Joachim, *op. cit.*, p. 294.
[96] *Ibid.*, p. 306.   [97] Hampshire, *op. cit.*, p. 169.   [98] *Ibid.*

terized by Thought accompanied by Love and our finite minds are part of His infinite Intellect, it is consistent to interpret man's "intellectual love of God" as a union of his finite mind with God in which God as immanent loves Himself and loves man as part of Himself. Moreover, the emotional side of that love no less than the intellectual side should be taken seriously and, therefore, Hampshire is not justified in simply identifying it with the intellectual satisfaction of a scientist in discovering the order of nature and the relation of the individual to it.

However, the rationalism of Spinoza's theory of knowledge and the element of Naturalism in his metaphysics make his view of the intellectual love of God very different from that of Christian mysticism. If we are to speak of it as involving a "mystical union" with God, we must bear in mind that the union Spinoza describes is very different from the mystical union of Eckhart, since the "intuitive knowledge" from which it springs depends upon "reason" or rational knowledge of the second kind and is itself intellectual. Moreover, since Spinoza's God is conceived in pantheistic terms as immanent in nature, the intellectual love of God is directed toward Him solely as present in rather than transcendent to nature. Stace maintains that, while Spinoza was a pantheist, he believed that the relation of God to the world was not one of pure identity but identity in difference, so that He is transcendent as well as immanent.[99] But this is to synthesize his Pantheism too much with Theism and cannot be sustained. Thus the mystical element in "the intellectual love of God" is distinguished from mysticism of the theistic type both by its intellectual character and by its pantheistic basis.

ETERNAL LIFE

The interpretation of Spinoza's view of eternal life is also uncertain. Many philosophers hold that he asserts eternal life for the individual only in the sense of a contemplation of things "under the aspect of eternity" in this life. On this issue Joachim and Hampshire seem to be in agreement. "For, of one thing," says Joachim, "there can be no doubt: Spinoza did *not* mean to establish for the human soul an infinitely-prolonged after-life in another world. This popular travesty of the philosophical conception of 'eternity' . . . hangs together with the very conceptions against which Spinoza's whole work is an unhesitating protest—the conception of God as a lawgiver and judge and of felicity as the 'reward' of virtue." [100] "Eternity cannot be expressed in

[99] W. T. Stace, *Mysticism and Philosophy* (Philadelphia: J. B. Lippincott, 1960), pp. 215–218.
[100] Joachim, *op. cit.*, pp. 295, 296.

terms of duration, even though it be an 'infinite' duration, i.e. one without beginning or end. . . . Eternity expresses timeless necessity of being, and has nothing to do with lasting through an 'infinitely long' time." [101] Hampshire's interpretation is similar. "Spinoza repeatedly distinguished between 'eternity' in his own sense of the word and 'everlastingness.' . . . 'after-life,' or 'survival-after-physical-death,' are expressions without any clear meaning in his philosophy." [102]

There is much in the *Ethics* which seems to support this view. But if this is all Spinoza meant, it is difficult to understand several passages in which he seems to attribute eternal existence to at least part of the mind after the body perishes. Perhaps the most important one is the following: "The human mind cannot be absolutely destroyed with the body, but something of it remains which is eternal." [103] Spinoza adds that "we feel that our mind, in so far as it involves the essence of the body under the form of eternity, is eternal, and that this existence of the mind cannot be limited by time nor manifested through duration." [104] In a later "proposition," he makes a contrast between "intellectual love" and "emotions which are related to passions only so long as the body exists," and says, "Hence it follows that no love except intellectual love is eternal." [105] This seems to contrast "passive emotions" which endure only as long as the body, and "intellectual love" which is eternal. Again, he says, "The essence of the mind consists in knowledge. The more things, therefore, the mind knows by the second and third kinds of knowledge, the greater is that part which abides." In a Scholium he adds that "it is possible for the human mind to be of such a nature that that part of it which we have shown *perishes* with its body, in comparison with the part of it which *remains,* is of no consequence." [106] Finally, he argues that "the more perfection a thing possesses, the more it acts and the less it suffers" and therefore that "that part of the mind which *abides,* whether great or small, is more perfect than the other part. For the part of the mind which is eternal is the intellect, through which alone we are said to act, but that part which, as we have shown, *perishes,* is the imagination itself." [107] In both of the last quotations, a "part" of the mind is said to "perish" with the body, i.e., the imagination which suffers passive emotions, but another "part" is said to "remain" or "abide," i.e., the intellect which acts and is more perfect.

[101] *Ibid.,* pp. 297, 298.   [102] Hampshire, *op. cit.,* pp. 171, 172.
[103] Spinoza, *Ethics,* Pt. V, Pr. 23, p. 384.   [104] *Ibid.,* Pt. V, Pr. 23, Sch., p. 385.
[105] *Ibid.,* Pr. 34, p. 391.   [106] *Ibid.,* Pr. 38, p. 395 (italics added).
[107] *Ibid.,* Pr. 40, pp. 396–397 (italics added).

From these passages we must conclude that, *although part of the mind perishes with the body, the "more perfect" part, the intellect and the intellectual love of God, remains or survives.* If so, it is eternal not only in the sense of knowing things in this life "under the aspect of eternity," but also in the sense of continuing to exist in some way after this life. However, it does not follow from this that Spinoza believed in what theists call "personal immortality." He seems to have meant that only the intellect and not the whole personality is eternal, and that it is eternal only as a mode of God's infinite Intellect. This is the interpretation of Bidney also. "The mind is partially at least immortal, as Aristotle also held, and therefore cannot be absolutely destroyed with the body. (V, 23)" [108]

But Spinoza emphasizes that we should not regard a blessed future life as a *reward for virtue* in this life. "Even if we did not know that our mind is eternal, we should still consider as of primary importance Piety and Religion." For they are based on "what reason prescribes as profitable" and even if we are ignorant of the eternity of the mind "we should consider those commands of reason as of primary importance." [109] To say that without the hope of reward and fear of punishment after death men would give themselves up to their passions is absurd. "Blessedness is not the reward of virtue, but is virtue itself; nor do we delight in blessedness because we restrain our lusts; but, on the contrary, because we delight in it, therefore are we able to restrain them." [110] The way to this "blessedness" and "peace of soul" is difficult. "But all noble things are as difficult as they are rare." [111]

SPINOZA'S PANTHEISM: A CRITICAL EVALUATION

Although Spinoza has been condemned again and again as an atheist because of his uncompromising rejection of Theism, he has also been called a "God-intoxicated man" and has had a profound influence upon many modern religious thinkers. A passage from Schleiermacher's *Addresses on Religion,* in which he praises "holy Spinoza," may help us to understand his appeal. "The contemplation of the pious is the immediate consciousness of the universal existence of all finite things in and through the Infinite, and of all temporal things in and through the Eternal. Religion is to seek this and find it in all that lives and moves, in all growth and change, in all doing and suffering. It is to

[108] David Bidney, *The Psychology and Ethics of Spinoza* (New Haven: Yale University Press, 1960), p. 364.
[109] Spinoza, *Ethics,* Pt. V, Pr. 41, pp. 397, 398.
[110] *Ibid.,* Pr. 42, p. 399.   [111] *Ibid.,* pp. 399–400.

have life and to know life in immediate feeling, only as such an existence in the Infinite and Eternal. . . . Wherefore it is a life in the infinite nature of the Whole, in the One and in the All, in God, having and possessing all things in God, and God in all." [112] In these words Schleiermacher expresses the spirit, if not the logic, of Spinoza's Pantheism. The pantheist views God as immanent in all things and seeks to experience Him in everything. He regards himself and every other finite thing as only a manifestation of the Infinite, the temporal as an expression of the Eternal, the life of the individual as part of the Whole. For him, if the finite is separated from the Infinite, it loses its meaning. Nature, as it appears to the senses at the first level of knowledge, "imagination," seems to consist of many separate, relatively independent things and persons, conditioned by and often in conflict with one another. As a result, the individual feels himself to be alienated from the world and lacks a sense of participation in a meaningful whole. At the same time, he has a feeling of dependence upon the whole and a longing for reunion with it.

This is the religious motive for the pantheist's rejection of the pluralistic view of the world as composed of separate substances and for his opposition to the dualism of popular Theism which emphasizes the transcendence of God at the cost of separating Him from nature. Every division seems to threaten the unity of the Whole and to set its parts in opposition to one another. Hence, if the pantheist is a philosopher like Spinoza, he seeks to transcend the view of the world that results from sense perception and scientific reason, the first two levels of knowledge, and to gain an intellectual intuition of God or Nature as the all-embracing and ever present source of things.

This gives the individual a sense of meaning and security based upon his participation in the eternal, immutable, and perfect Whole. It offers him an assurance that all things and events, as products of the divine causality, are beneficial, and therefore that he can accept the conditions of his existence without complaint. Whether this assurance takes the form of an affirmation that all things are the work of a cosmic Providence, as in some of the ancient Stoics, or an acquiescence in the necessity of Nature, as in Spinoza, it fosters the conviction that finite existence is endowed with meaning and value. Therefore, it is easy to see why Spinoza's Pantheism has had so much appeal for many modern thinkers. It seems to satisfy their religious need for participation in a larger Whole and to do so without demanding faith in a special revelation.

[112] Friedrich Schleiermacher, *On Religion* (New York: Harper & Row, 1958), p. 36.

There is also a scientific and philosophical motive behind the thinking of Spinoza and it greatly strengthens his appeal to many modern men. Science points to the interdependence of all phenomena, and every natural law that is discovered extends man's knowledge of the order of nature and of the way in which each thing is related to other things in the whole. As Wild says, "If we consider the human individual he turns out to be obviously dependent upon the existence of other organisms which are dependent upon the climate of the earth which is dependent upon the sun which is dependent upon the motions of the other stars et cetera, until we reach the whole universe. Only then do we seem to have a reality truly self-dependent. . . . What Spinoza is pointing to is the essential continuity of experience, the fact that reality is really one, that the sharp lines we draw between things are as a matter of fact artificial, that if we properly understand them we shall find them all to be interdependent and parts of one great interlocking system which *must* exist, since there is nothing outside it to limit it, or make it dependent." [113] Moreover, metaphysics has always sought to attain a world view which will include all aspects of reality in a system and relate them to one another and to the whole. Thus, the scientific and philosophical demand for a unity of all knowledge supports the religious concern for a unity of all being in which the individual can participate and find meaning for his life.

But the weakness of Spinoza's Pantheism as a *metaphysical theory* is also obvious. It is only by disparaging the evidence of the senses that Spinoza is able to reduce the plurality of things to the status of "modes" of one "substance" and thus to affirm a rigorous monism. Such an attitude toward the "first level'" of knowledge, "opinion" or "imagination," shows little respect for the reports of the senses and is thus fundamentally opposed to the empirical attitude of modern science as well as to common sense. Moreover, Spinoza's elaborate metaphysical system is constructed by the speculative reason by means of a purely deductive method. The certainty he claims for some of his most important conclusions, as we have seen, is founded on nothing more than "axioms" and "definitions" which he accepts as self-evident. Thus his trust in speculative reason is as uncritical as his disparagement of the senses is unjustified, and it has been thoroughly discredited in modern philosophy. While modern science seeks to describe the relations between phenomena and develops comprehensive theories, it does not lend support to a monistic philosophy which reduces the "many" to mere modes of the "one." Modern philosophers of science such as

[113] John Wild (ed.), *Spinoza: Selections,* pp. xxvii–xxviii.

Whitehead stress the existence of atomic entities, however differently they may conceive them, as well as their interdependence. And since the collapse of the ambitious metaphysical system of Hegel, modern philosophy has rejected the pretentious claims of rationalists like Spinoza to construct monistic metaphysical systems in which everything is deduced from a single principle such as Substance or Spirit.

The inadequacy of Spinoza's Pantheism as a *religious philosophy,* however, is what especially concerns us. In the first place, his strong emphasis upon the immanence of God is purchased at the price of completely denying His transcendence. This may seem an advantage to those who cannot see how God can be conceived as both immanent and transcendent and believe that His transcendence detaches Him from the world and makes him inaccessible to man. Doubtless, this was one of the reasons for the enthusiasm of Schleiermacher, Hegel, and others for Spinoza's Pantheism. But Pantheism has a fatal weakness from the religious point of view, for it is contradicted by the experience of God throughout the history of religions as "other than" finite and imperfect nature. While it is compatible with a sense of the weakness and dependence of man upon the whole of which he is a small part, it cannot account for the sense of awe in the presence of "the holy" which has been described by Rudolf Otto.

Pantheism is also incompatible with the conviction of religious men, at least since the collapse of ancient nature religion, that nature is not worthy of the absolute devotion required for religion. Despite the order and beauty as well as the power and mystery of nature, it is far from perfect; and its indifference to human values and purposes makes it impossible for nature to answer man's deepest religious needs. This is why the natural religion of Romantic poets like Wordsworth, moving and noble as it was, ultimately proved unsatisfactory.[114] Moreover, exclusive emphasis upon the immanence of God does not take seriously enough the alienation or estrangement of man from God by his sin and guilt. It is significant in this connection that Spinoza rejected all emotions which are accompanied by pain on the ground that they lessen man's sense of health and vitality, and that humility and repentance were among them.[115]

In the second place, Spinoza's vigorous repudiation of anthropomorphism made it impossible to apply any *analogies* from the human mind to God. He insists that if we ascribe *intellect* or *will* to Him because of His attribute of Thought we must bear in mind that

---

[114] Cf. Joseph Warren Beach, *The Concept of Nature in 19th Century English Poetry* (New York: Macmillan, 1936).
[115] Spinoza, *Ethics,* Pt. IV, Prs. 52, 54, pp. 332–334.

His intellect and will have nothing in common with ours except the names. It is difficult to see how, if this is the case, He can be said to love either Himself or us as parts of Himself, and this is doubtless one reason naturalistic interpreters of the "intellectual love of God" have not been able to attribute much meaning to it. In general, the denial of an intellect and a will to God which are analogous to man's is incompatible with the conception of Him as personal in any sense and hence with a personal relationship with Him. From the point of view of the religious person, this is probably the most fatal weakness in his Pantheism, because it eliminates prayer to Him, a sense of communion with Him, or any idea that we should act in obedience to His will.

Spinoza's rejection of analogies from the human mind and will in his conception of God is one of the grounds for his assertion that God's causal activity in finite things springs from the necessity of His nature rather than from the freedom of His will and that He does not cause things for the sake of good, *sub ratione boni.* This eliminates the *teleological explanation* of natural events in both the Aristotelian sense of "immanent" teleology and the Platonic and Christian sense of "external" teleology based on the purposes of God. Doubtless it was an advance in the history of physics when Galileo, Descartes, and others expelled final causes from the explanation of physical events. But Spinoza transformed a useful principle of scientific methodology into a metaphysical doctrine and prepared the way for the later naturalistic reduction of the activities of life and mind to blind and purposeless movements determined by mechanical laws. The theological consequence was to make the teleological argument for the existence of God unconvincing to many modern minds, while the religious effect was to make it difficult for men to experience the presence of God in nature.

In the third place, Spinoza's conception of *man* as simply a part of nature tends to reduce him to the status of one object among others and to minimize his uniqueness as a person. This naturalistic tendency is shown in a number of ways. Man's mind is regarded as the "idea" of his body and its dependence upon the body is emphasized. As a result it is difficult to see how the "more perfect" part of his mind, the intellect, can remain after the death of the body even as an individual mode of the infinite Intellect of God. It is also difficult to account for self-consciousness, the "idea of an idea," since Spinoza insists that there corresponds to every idea a modification of the body. And the capacity of the mind to overcome "passive emotions" by the "adequate ideas" of the intellect or to transform them into "active emotions" is put in question by his naturalistic view of the mind's relation to the body.

Spinoza's reduction of man to a mere part of nature is also inconsistent with both his religion and his ethical ideal. This is most obvious
in the contradiction between his *determinism* and his ethics. As we
have said, he offers in the *Ethics* an ethical ideal which is based upon a
concept of human perfection and which is assumed to be valid for all
men. But it is meaningless to advise men to act in a certain manner if
they are determined in their acts and cannot act otherwise than they
do. If, then, we understand by an ethical theory one which prescribes
norms for human conduct and assumes that men are free to follow
them, Spinoza's determinism rules out the possibility of such a theory.
Of course, it can be objected that he was not proposing a normative
ethic which tells men how they *ought* to act but only a descriptive
analysis of the way they *do* act when they attain virtue and happiness.
In one of his letters, he says that, although a man is "to be excused"
who cannot "govern his desires" because he is determined to be as he
is, he "is nevertheless unable to enjoy peace of mind, and the knowledge and love of God, but necessarily perishes." [116] In another letter he
denies that murderers and those who give alms are "equally good or
perfect." [117] Passages like these might seem to indicate that Spinoza in
the *Ethics* was simply describing the difference with respect to happiness and perfection between the virtuous man and the man in bondage
to his passions. But he always seems to think that through the
substitution of active for passive emotions by reason men can advance
toward happiness and perfection. Clearly, this presupposes moral striving. And in the last sentences of the *Ethics* Spinoza admits that the road
he has described is "difficult" but says that "all noble things are as
difficult as they are rare." [118] "It is all very well," remarks Copleston,
"to say that it is a change of point of view which is involved rather
than a change of conduct. Change in conduct depends for Spinoza on a
change in point of view; and how could one change one's point of view
unless one were free?" [119] We must conclude, therefore, that Spinoza
defends absolute determinism and at the same time proposes a normative ethic which is inconsistent with it.

Finally, Spinoza's conception of the divine perfection leads to a
solution of the *problem of evil* which is wholly unconvincing. He holds
that since all finite things flow from the perfect nature of God, there is
no imperfection although there are different degrees of perfection in
them. Hence, sin is nothing positive. "And therefore we shall be able to

[116] Spinoza, *Letter LXXVIII*, p. 472.   [117] *Ibid.*, *Letter XXIII*, p. 438.
[118] *Ibid.*, *Ethics*, Pt. V, Pr. 42, p. 400.
[119] Copleston, *History of Philosophy*, Vol. IV, p. 251.

find no imperfection in the decision of Adam when we consider it in itself, and do not compare it with other things which are more perfect, or show a more perfect state," for "the evil in it was no more than a privation of a more perfect state." [120] Thus, Adam's "desire for pleasure" was a "privation" or "lack" in comparison with the "better desire" of the upright man, but it "was evil only in relation to our understanding and not in relation to that of God." [121] Nor can it be said that God is the cause of evil, because it is nothing positive and God is the cause only of "everything that has essence." [122] This attempt to deny, like Plotinus and Augustine, the positive reality of evil flies in the face of man's experience of evil. It does nothing to lighten the darkness moral evil brings into the world to say that it is simply the privation or lack of a higher degree of perfection. It merely blurs the distinction between good and evil and by accepting the necessity of evil as a manifestation of God's perfection cuts the nerve of the moral effort required to overcome it. Thus it is the source of a fatal weakness in Spinoza's ethical theory. Denying the theistic view that God possesses a moral will with a purpose for man and demands that man struggle against the evil in the world, Spinoza proposes an ethical ideal of liberation from the passions by the contemplation of Nature or God. This ideal, which has something in common with ancient Stoicism, has much to commend it as an ideal of self-mastery and self-transcendence. But its power to govern the conduct of individuals is weakened by Spinoza's determinism, and its power to overcome the evil in the world is nullified by his insistence that evil is "evil only in relation to our understanding and not in relation to that of God."

[120] Spinoza, *Letter XIX*, pp. 420, 421.   [121] *Ibid., Letter XXI*, p. 428.
[122] *Ibid., Letter XXIII*, p. 436.

8 Skepticism

HUME

The Skepticism of David Hume (1711–1776) has had a powerful effect on the course of religious thought since the eighteenth century. It put in question the attempt of both rationalistic and empirical philosophers to demonstrate religious truths such as the existence of God and immortality. In doing so, it stimulated Kant to develop a critical theory of knowledge which would provide a rational justification of natural science and at the same time leave room for a reasonable belief in religion. And it has continued to this day to influence in a decisive way the approach of British empiricists to religious beliefs.

An understanding of Hume's religious Skepticism is impossible without knowledge of his religious background and his personal attitude toward religion. As Kemp Smith has pointed out, the religion which prevailed in Scotland during Hume's youth was hardly of the sort to appeal to a person of his temperament. "It was a popularized version of Calvin's teaching, retaining its darker features, and representing even these in a distorted and exaggerated form." [1] The grinding poverty, economic stagnation, and despair of the time affected the life and thought of the Church and it is not strange that "its Calvinist teaching, always grimly austere, became even more bleak and gloomy, and that its many oldtime superstitions and fanaticisms should have gained a new lease on life." [2] At an early age Hume completely abandoned the whole of Calvinist doctrine, but it always typified religion for him and his strong aversion to it affected his attitude toward religion in general. Like many others who have strongly reacted against the harsh and unlovely religion of their youth, he continued to be intellectually interested in religion until the end of his life. But after his rejection of his early religion, "religion was brought to his attention not

[1] *Hume's Dialogues concerning Natural Religion,* ed. N. K. Smith (New York: Social Sciences Publishers, 1948), p. 3.
[2] *Ibid.*

by anything in his own personal needs and convictions, but by the prominence—so surprising, as it seemed to him—with which it bulked in the lives of others, and by the strange vagaries of belief, observance, and conduct to which it gave rise." [3] Good-natured, sociable, and possessed of an equable temper, he was unable to understand the "twice-born" type of religion and was repelled by the "fanaticism" and "enthusiasm" of intensely religious people. At home in the world as it was and contented with the cultured society of Edinburgh, he seems to have been disturbed by no deep sense of sin and to have felt no need for divine aid. It is not surprising, therefore, that he not only abandoned the orthodox Calvinist doctrines but also attacked popular religion in general. He regarded it as superstitious, fanatical, and intolerant. He held that it led to the self-abasement of man before God and to the cultivation of "monkish virtues," such as humility and penance, which are contrary to human nature and happiness. He believed that the special religious duties it imposed upon men divided their attention and weakened their attachment to the ordinary moral duties of justice and humanity. [4] In short, popular religion is not only irrational and degrading in itself; it also perverts and weakens the whole intellectual and moral life of man.

However, Hume's major influence as a skeptic is not to be found in his attacks upon "popular" religion but in his criticism of "natural" religion. In the Age of Reason many thinkers had become disaffected with revealed religions such as Christianity because of the lack of agreement among religious men as to which of the alleged special revelations of the past was the true one and the lack of agreement among Christians as to which interpretation of the biblical revelation was the orthodox one. Repelled by the religious intolerance and dissension which had followed the Protestant Reformation, they advocated a religion based upon reason which could be accepted by all. It was to dispense with traditional dogmas based upon revelation and to consist of a few simple beliefs, e.g., the creation of the world by God and the distribution of moral rewards and punishments in the future life. This religion of reason was to a considerable extent founded upon the scientific view of nature developed by Newton in the seventeenth century. According to this view, God had created the world and imposed order upon it by means of immutable laws. Since the order of nature is His handiwork and a product of His intelligence, it constitutes a revelation of His power and wisdom. Thus the Newtonian picture of the natural order, which was universally accepted in eighteenth-century

[3] *Ibid.*, p. 1.   [4] *Ibid.*, p. 18.

Britain, became the basis for a teleological argument for God's existence which was somewhat different from that of Aquinas. It is this
argument with which Hume is primarily concerned in his *Dialogues
concerning Natural Religion.*

THEORY OF KNOWLEDGE

If we are to understand Hume's criticism of this argument and his
general attitude toward "natural religion," we must consider briefly his
empirical theory of knowledge. It is well known that there were two
quite different sides of the scientific method which had developed since
the time of Kepler and Copernicus. One side was mathematical and
stressed the deductive method of reasoning. It was this side which
Descartes had advocated in his *Discourse on Method* and Spinoza had
made the basis of the "geometrical" method in his *Ethics.* In general,
the Continental Rationalism which culminated in Leibniz and Wolff
took mathematical deduction from self-evident truths as its model for
philosophical reasoning. The other side of the scientific method was
empirical and emphasized observation and experimentation. Although
Newton was also a mathematician, he insisted upon verification of
his physical theories by an appeal to sense experience. This had a
decisive effect upon the British empiricists from Locke to Hume. It led
them to assert that all knowledge originates not from truths self-
evident to reason but from experience and that even the most complex
ideas are derived from what Locke called "simple ideas" of "sensation"
and "reflection" by a process of comparison and composition. One of
the results of this empirical view of the origin of knowledge was to
awaken suspicion of the validity of metaphysical speculation by abstract reasoning and to insist upon testing the meaning and truth of
every general idea by tracing it back to its origin in experience.

Hume carries this empirical theory of knowledge to the most extreme conclusions. He begins with a distinction between two kinds of
"perceptions" in the mind: "impressions" and "ideas." "Ideas" are "less
lively" perceptions derived from external and internal "impressions"
and are "copies" of them. The creative power of the mind is nothing
more than "the faculty of compounding, transposing, augmenting, or
diminishing the materials afforded us by the senses and experience." [5]
This is the case not only with our ideas of sensible objects and their
qualities, e.g., the idea of a "golden mountain," but also with our "more
sublime" ideas. Thus, the idea of God "arises from reflecting on the
operations of our own mind, and augmenting, without limit, those

[5] David Hume, *An Enquiry concerning Human Understanding* (Chicago:
Open Court, 1927), p. 16. Subsequent references to this book are to this edition.

qualities of goodness and wisdom" we find there.[6] It should be noted that the one argument Hume offers for this view applies only to our ideas of sensible objects. It is the argument that a person with a defect in the sense organ through which men receive a certain kind of sense impression will have no idea corresponding to that kind of impression, e.g., the blind man will have no idea of color, and that a person with no past experience of a certain object will have no idea of its qualities, e.g., a Laplander will have no notion of the taste of wine.[7]

The crucial importance of this presupposition that all ideas originate from impressions is very great. Impressions, says Hume, are "strong and vivid" and we do not easily fall into mistakes with regard to them. But abstract ideas are "naturally faint and obscure" and we often mistakenly imagine that a vague term has a definite idea connected with it. This suggests to Hume a way of determining the meaning of our abstract ideas. "When we entertain, therefore, any suspicion that a philosophical term is employed without any meaning or idea (as is but too frequent), we need but to inquire, *from what impression is that supposed idea derived?* And if it be impossible to assign any, this will serve to confirm our suspicion." [8] It is by applying this empirical test to the meaning of some important philosophical ideas that Hume arrives at his skeptical conclusions concerning human knowledge.

There is a second presupposition that is also very important. Reason can discern no connection between one perception and another. When the mind, therefore, passes from the perception of one object to that of another, it is determined to do so not by reason but by principles of association which unite them in the imagination. These principles, or laws of association, are "resemblance," "contiguity," and "cause and effect." Hume states this presupposition drastically in a passage of his *Treatise:* "All perceptions are distinct. They are, therefore, distinguishable and separable, and may be conceived as separately existent, and may exist separately, without any contradiction or absurdity." [9] One of the implications of this "atomistic" conception of experience is that every perception, being "distinct" and "separately existent," meets the traditional definition of a "substance" and needs no other substance to support it. Indeed, the idea of a substance becomes "nothing but a collection of simple ideas, that are united by the imagination, and have a particular name assigned to them," and the notion that there is an "unknown something" in which they inhere is groundless.[10]

[6] *Ibid.*, p. 17.   [7] *Ibid.*   [8] *Ibid.*, p. 19.

[9] Hume, *A Treatise of Human Nature,* in *Hume: Selections,* ed. Charles Hendel (New York: Scribners, 1927), Bk. I, Pt. IV, Appendix, p. 104.

[10] Hume, *A Treatise of Human Nature,* ed. Selby-Bigge (Oxford: Clarendon Press, 1958), p. 16.

This leads Hume to a skeptical conclusion with respect to our idea of external substance, or "*body*." We have an idea of an external object, or "body," which possesses both "continued existence" when it is not present to the senses and "distinct" existence independent of the mind. But our perceptions of it are interrupted when they are not present and we have no experience of anything beyond them and independent of the mind. Therefore, the idea of "body" must be ascribed neither to sense nor to reason but to imagination. It is due to the natural "propensity" of the imagination to ascribe a continuation of existence to perceptions which resemble each other despite the interruption in their appearance. A similar inference is drawn with respect to our idea of the "personal identity" of the *self*. What impression, Hume asks, can be the origin of the idea of the self as possessing identity, simplicity, and continuance in existence? He answers that he can find no such impression. "For my part, when I enter most intimately into what I call *myself*, I always stumble on some particular perception or other, of heat or cold, light or shade, love or hatred, pain or pleasure. I never can catch *myself* at any time without a perception, and never can observe anything but the perception." [11] From this Hume concludes that the self is "nothing but a bundle or collection of different perceptions, which succeed each other with an inconceivable rapidity, and are in a perpetual flux and movement. . . . The mind is a kind of theatre, where several perceptions successively make their appearance; pass, repass, glide away, and mingle in an infinite variety of postures and situations." [12] The "personal identity" we ascribe to it is a fiction of the imagination which arises from the resemblance of our perceptions as preserved in memory and from the relation of cause and effect between them.[13]

We have seen that Hume's empirical presupposition of the origin of ideas in impressions and his atomistic presupposition of the distinct and separate existence of perceptions lead him to deny the rational basis of our ideas of both external "bodies" and minds with "personal identity" and to dissolve them into collections of perceptions bound together by laws of association. This is the reason he is often called a "phenomenalist." We have now to examine briefly his application of his principles to an idea which is of fundamental importance for both science and rational theology, the idea of a "*necessary connection*" between cause and effect.

This idea is subjected to the same test as the idea of "personal identity," i.e., a search is made for an impression which could have

[11] *Ibid.*, Bk. I, Pt. IV, Sec. VI, p. 252.   [12] *Ibid.*, pp. 252, 253.
[13] *Ibid.*, pp. 260, 261.

given rise to it. Hume argues, first, that it could not have originated from a single instance of cause and effect between *external objects*. We can find no quality which makes the effect a necessary consequence of the cause; we only find that the one in fact follows the other, e.g., the impulse of one billiard ball is followed by motion in a second.[14] For the power of the sensible qualities of objects to produce effects is always hidden from us.[15] Second, the idea of necessary connection cannot be derived from any internal impression of an operation of *our minds*. The union of the mind and the body by which the former causes a change in the latter is wholly mysterious to us, so that we can have no impression of it. We are not conscious of any power in our will to bring about such a change and must learn the extent and limits of its influence upon the body from experience alone.[16] For a similar reason, we have no impression of a power in our wills to raise up a new idea and contemplate it, for the production of an idea in the mind is as mysterious as the production of a change in the body.[17]

What, then, can the impression be from which the idea of necessary connection is derived? Hume finds a clue to the answer in the fact that, although *one* instance of a particular event following upon another does not enable us to anticipate what will happen in similar cases, "when one particular *species* of event has always, in all instances, been conjoined with another, we make no longer any scruple of foretelling one upon the appearance of the other," [18] and we suppose "some power in the one by which it infallibly produces the other." [19] But why should the mere "constant conjunction" of these events give rise to the idea of a "necessary connection" between them? The answer can only be that "after a repetition of similar instances, the mind is carried by habit, upon the appearance of one event, to expect its usual attendant, and to believe that it will exist. The connexion, therefore, which we *feel* in the mind, this customary transition of the imagination from one object to its usual attendant, is the sentiment or impression from which we form the idea of power or necessary connexion." [20] In other words, the idea of necessary connection arises from the feeling of a habit in our minds, after we have experienced the constant conjunction of two events, of expecting that when one of them is presented, the other will follow it. Hume is well aware of the crucial importance of the causal relation. "On this are founded," he says, "all our reasoning concerning matter of fact or existence. By means of it alone we attain any assurance concerning objects which are removed from the present testimony of our

[14] Hume, *Enquiry concerning Human Understanding* (Open Court ed.), p. 64.
[15] *Ibid.*, p. 65.   [16] *Ibid.*, pp. 66–68.   [17] *Ibid.*, p. 70.
[18] *Ibid.*, p. 77 (italics added).   [19] *Ibid.*   [20] *Ibid.*, pp. 77, 78.

memory and senses." [21] Therefore, he takes it as an instance of "the surprising ignorance and weakness of the understanding" that the idea of necessary connection is not derived from an impression of it as an objective reality but only from an internal impression in the form of a sentiment or feeling of it which is projected into the objects.

The usual interpretation of this analysis of the causal relation has been that it is completely skeptical. But it has been pointed out by Kemp Smith and others that the skepticism of Hume concerning the necessary connection of cause and effect has to do not with its reality but with its rational justification.[22] Hume rejects the traditional view that the causal principle is self-evident or demonstrable by reason and holds that it is a "natural belief." That he did not mean to deny that events are caused is shown from a letter he wrote to one of his critics. "But allow me to tell you, that I never asserted so absurd a Proposition as *that anything might arise without a Cause:* I only maintain'd that our Certainty of the Falsehood of that Proposition proceeded neither from Intuition nor Demonstration; but from another Source." [23] In other words, the causal principle is a "natural belief" based on feeling rather than a matter of rational knowledge. That this idea of necessary connection corresponds to a real causal relation between the events is shown by a passage in which Hume speaks of "a kind of pre-established harmony between the course of nature and the succession of our ideas." [24] Nature in her wisdom has not entrusted the inference from like causes to like effects to "the fallacious deductions of our reason" but has based it upon an "instinct or mechanical tendency" which "carries forward the thought in a correspondent course to that which she has established among external objects." [25] Thus Hume does not deny the truth of the idea of causal connection or of the knowledge of nature which it makes possible.

This throws much light upon the meaning of Hume's skepticism with respect to our ideas of external "body" and "personal identity" as well as "necessary connection." In the last section of the *Enquiry* he distinguishes between "excessive" and "mitigated" skepticism. Although he maintains that the rational arguments for "excessive" or thoroughgoing skepticism are convincing, he admits that "no durable good can ever result" from it and that "all human life must perish" if its principles were to prevail.[26] Therefore, he proposes a *"mitigated"* skepticism

[21] *Ibid.,* p. 79.
[22] N. K. Smith, *The Philosophy of David Hume* (London: Macmillan, 1941), Chap. 17.
[23] Quoted by Smith, *The Philosophy of David Hume,* p. 413.
[24] Hume, *Enquiry,* p. 55.   [25] *Ibid.,* p. 56.   [26] *Ibid.,* p. 170.

in which the doubts of excessive skepticism would be "corrected by common sense and reflection." [27] This "mitigated" skepticism would curb the imagination which delights in "whatever is remote and extraordinary" and would limit inquiry to "such subjects as are best adapted to the narrow capacity of human understanding." [28]

What are these subjects? The first is the abstract science of mathematics which is concerned with quantity and number and in which alone demonstration is possible.[29] The second consists of sciences which deal with "matters of fact or existence." In these sciences propositions are incapable of demonstration because there is no matter of fact the negation of which involves a contradiction.[30] Hence they must be proved by causal arguments based entirely on experience.[31] In other words, the only subjects which are within "the narrow capacity of human understanding" are *mathematics* and the *empirical sciences* of nature and man. What does this imply for *metaphysics* and *theology?* Hume's answer is devastating: "If we take in our hand any volume of divinity or school metaphysics, for instance; let us ask, *Does it contain any abstract reasoning concerning quantity or number?* No. *Does it contain any experimental reasoning concerning matter of fact and existence?* No. Commit it then to the flames: for it can contain nothing but sophistry and illusion." [32]

Thus Kemp Smith is justified in holding that the traditional view of Hume as a skeptic who denied the existence of bodies, of selves, and of causal relations is false. Rather, Hume's purpose was to show that, although we have assurance that these are real, the source of that assurance is not reason but natural beliefs resting upon feeling. Hence he is a skeptic in the sense of maintaining the narrow limits of reason, restricting its capacity to attain *rational* knowledge by demonstration to the "relations of ideas" in mathematics. But his primary aim is a positive one, to show that our assurance of "matters of fact" such as the existence of bodies, selves, and causal relations is based upon *natural belief* rather than knowledge. As Kemp Smith expresses it, the central thing in his teaching is not skepticism but "the doctrine that the determining influence in human, as in other forms of animal life, is feeling, not reason or understanding." [33] This is why he is a "mitigated" rather than an "excessive" skeptic, correcting the negative conclusions of skepticism by "common sense." Thus his primary "intentions" are positive and his skepticism is subordinate to them.[34]

[27] *Ibid.,* p. 171.   [28] *Ibid.,* p. 172.   [29] *Ibid.,* p. 173.   [30] *Ibid.,* p. 174.
[31] *Ibid.*   [32] *Ibid.,* p. 176.
[33] N. K. Smith, *The Philosophy of David Hume,* p. 11.
[34] J. A. Passmore, *Hume's Intentions* (Cambridge, Eng.: Cambridge University Press, 1952), Chaps. 1, 8.

But it is important to note that they are positive only with respect to natural beliefs concerning nature and man. For Hume makes it very clear, as we have seen, that the "remote and extraordinary" subjects dealt with by metaphysics and theology are beyond "the narrow confines of our understanding" and that their claims to provide us with knowledge of matters of fact are nothing more than "sophistry and illusion." In short, our examination of Hume's theory of knowledge leads to the conclusion that while he accepted the natural beliefs of common sense and knowledge from the empirical sciences about nature and man, his skepticism concerning knowledge in metaphysics and theology of anything *beyond nature and man* is not "mitigated" but complete. However, we must test this conclusion by considering his *Dialogues concerning Natural Religion.* Since it was revised shortly before his death and published posthumously, we may take it as expressing his mature views on theology.

THE EXISTENCE AND NATURE OF GOD

The major subject dealt with in the *Dialogues* is the "natural religion" of the eighteenth century. There are three principal speakers who differ greatly in their points of view. This makes the interpretation of the argument very difficult, as it is not immediately certain whether Hume's own views are expressed by one of the speakers alone or whether different aspects of his thought are represented by two or all three of them. Philo is the representative of Skepticism, Demea of rigid orthodoxy, and Cleanthes of philosophical Theism. It has usually been held that Philo, the skeptic, speaks for Hume, because his views are presented in a forceful way and appear to be similar, at least during most of the *Dialogues,* to the skeptical views expressed by Hume in the works we have been examining. However, Cleanthes, the theist, bases his argument on an empirical theory of knowledge which has much in common with Hume's theory; he is treated by Philo with respect; and in the concluding part of the *Dialogues* Philo seems to move closer than before to his position. Demea's position of "rigid, inflexible orthodoxy" does not seem to be taken very seriously. Although Philo obviously expresses Hume's skeptical views, we have seen that there is a more positive side of his philosophy which emphasizes "natural beliefs," and it is possible that Cleanthes represents this side of his mind. We shall return to this question after we have examined the argument itself.

The *Dialogues* are concerned mainly with the *teleological argument.* Although Demea laments the fact that Cleanthes makes no use of "a priori" arguments and in Part IX offers an "a priori" argument of his own, Philo and Cleanthes agree that only "a posteriori" arguments starting from experience are worthy of consideration. Thus they approach the problem with the same empirical presuppositions concerning knowledge, although their conclusions are opposed to one another.

Cleanthes' statement of the teleological argument shows the influence of the Newtonian view of nature and the origin of its order in the divine mind. "Look around the world: Contemplate the whole and every part of it: You will find it to be nothing but one great machine, subdivided into an infinite number of lesser machines, which again admit of subdivisions, to a degree beyond what human senses and faculties can trace and explain. All these various machines, and even their most minute parts, are adjusted to each other with an accuracy which ravishes into admiration all men, who have ever contemplated them. The curious adapting of means to ends, throughout all nature, resembles exactly, though it much exceeds, the productions of human contrivance; of human design, thought, wisdom, and intelligence. Since therefore the effects resemble each other, we are led to infer, by all the rules of analogy, that the causes also resemble, and that the Author of nature is somewhat similar to the mind; though possessed of much larger faculties, proportioned to the grandeur of the work, which he has executed. By the argument *a posteriori,* and by this argument alone, we do prove at once the existence of a Deity, and his similarity to human mind and intelligence." [35] This argument by Cleanthes rests upon the similarity of nature to a great machine made up of smaller machines, all of which are adjusted to one another as means to ends, and upon the analogy between the order of nature so constituted and machines or other products of human design. It infers that the cause of the order of nature resembles the cause of these human products, that "the Author of Nature is somewhat similar to the mind of man." [36] Thus it moves from an analogy between two effects, a human product and the order of nature, to an analogy between the known cause of the one and the unknown cause of the other.

The most obvious weakness of the argument, as Philo points out, is that the *analogy* between natural order and a human machine or product such as a house is so remote that we are not justified in inferring an analogy between their causes. [37] But a more fundamental weakness is that we have no basis in experience for drawing *any* inference concerning the cause of natural order. If the connection between an effect and its cause can be known only through repeated experiences of their

[35] Hume's *Dialogues concerning Natural Religion* (ed. N. K. Smith), p. 143.
[36] *Ibid.,* p. 143.   [37] *Ibid.,* p. 144.

constant conjunction and the habit in our minds of expecting the one to follow the other, an inference from the order of nature regarded as an effect to a divine Mind regarded as its cause is unwarranted. "When two *species* of objects have always been observed to be conjoined together, I can *infer* by custom, the existence of one wherever I *see* the existence of the other: And this I call an argument from experience. But how this argument can have place, where the objects, as in the present case, are single, individual, without parallel, or specific resemblance, may be difficult to explain. . . . To ascertain this reasoning, it were requisite, that we had experience of the origin of the worlds; and it is not sufficient surely, that we have seen ships and cities arise from human art and contrivance." [38] "Have worlds ever been formed," asks Philo, "under your eye?" [39] The point, of course, is that, since there is not a "species" of worlds known to us but only a "single" one, there have not been repeated experiences of worlds being formed by a divine Mind. Hence there is no basis in experience for regarding our world as the effect of such a cause.

Other criticisms by Philo are directed against the inference that the cause of natural order resembles a *human mind* rather than some other cause known to us. "Thought, design, intelligence, such as we discover in men and other animals, is no more than one of the springs and principles of the universe, as well as heat or cold, attraction or repulsion, and a hundred others, which fall under daily observation. It is an active cause, by which some particular parts of nature, we find, produce alterations in other parts. But can a conclusion, with any propriety, be transferred from parts to the whole? Does not the great disproportion bar all comparison and inference? From observing the growth of a hair, can we learn anything concerning the generation of a man?" [40] Since human mind is only one of the many "springs" or "active causes" in nature, one "part" of an immense and complex whole, how can we learn anything about the cause of nature as a whole from it? Even if it were logically permissible to make the operations of one part upon another the basis for a judgment about the origin of the whole, would it not be strange to select so *small* and *weak* a part as the human mind rather than some other part? As Philo puts it, "Why select so minute, so weak, so bounded a principle as the reason and design of animals is found to be upon this planet? What peculiar privilege has this little agitation of the brain which we call thought, that we must thus make it the model of the whole universe? Our partiality in our own favour does indeed present it on all occasions:

[38] *Ibid.*, pp. 149, 150.   [39] *Ibid.*, p. 151.   [40] *Ibid.*, p. 147.

But sound philosophy ought carefully to guard against so natural an illusion." [41] "We do not even know that the inhabitants of other planets possess minds similar to our own, so that mind may be confined merely to this small corner." [42] But even if it were found to be present everywhere in the universe and its activity elsewhere were greater than on the earth, this would not prove that it was the cause of the formation of the universe.[43]

As we shall see, this criticism rests upon a certain view of the human mind and its place in nature. But here we must note how Philo presses his criticism of mind as the proposed cause of natural order still further. If mind is alleged to be the cause, he asks, must we not inquire concerning the cause of this cause? Since an idea of the mind depends upon causes, reason tells us that "a mental world, or universe of ideas, requires a cause as much as does a material world, or universe of objects." [44] "Have we not the same reason to trace that ideal world [in the divine Mind] into another ideal world, or new intelligent principle? But if we stop, and go no farther; why go so far? . . . How can we satisfy ourselves without going on *in infinitum?*" [45] Of course, the theist will reply that the divine Mind requires no cause beyond itself and that it arranges its own ideas. But Philo is not satisfied with this reply and asks, "Why is it not good sense to say, that the parts of the material world fall into order of themselves, and by their own nature?" [46] "It were better, therefore, never to look beyond the present material world." [47]

Philo here seems to be moving beyond mere criticism of the theistic explanation of natural order and suggesting a *naturalistic* explanation as an alternative. He suggests as its cause "an eternal, inherent principle of order." "How could things have been as they are were there not an original, inherent principle of order somewhere, in thought or in matter? And it is very indifferent to which of these we give the preference. Chance has no place on any hypothesis, sceptical or religious. Everything is surely governed by steady, inviolable laws." [48] This seems to mean that the order of nature should simply be accepted as a given fact, that it is due to an "inherent" principle of order rather than to a transcendent divine Mind, and that it operates by necessity according to immutable laws.

Having proposed this naturalistic explanation in a general form, Philo proceeds to indicate specific ways in which the "eternal, inherent

[41] *Ibid.*, p. 148.   [42] *Ibid.*   [43] *Ibid.*   [44] *Ibid.*, p. 160.   [45] *Ibid.*, p. 161.
[46] *Ibid.*, p. 162.   [47] *Ibid.*   [48] *Ibid.*, p. 174.

principle of order" might be conceived. Since the world resembles an animal or a vegetable more than a machine, may it not have had its origin in animal generation or vegetable growth, hatched out as from an egg or growing as from a seed? [49] He admits that he cannot explain the operation of generation or vegetation but points out that the theist is in the same difficulty since he cannot explain the operation or internal structure of the mind. After all, animals spring from generation with as great certainty as a house is built by design. "These words, *generation, reason,* mark only certain powers and energies in nature whose effects are known, but whose essence is incomprehensible; and one of these principles, more than the other, has no privilege for being made a standard to the whole of nature." [50] *Instinct* and *vegetation* are also causes of similar effects and there may be other principles of order in parts of the universe unknown to us. "Any one of these four principles above mentioned (and a hundred others which lie open to our conjecture) may afford us a theory, by which to judge of the origin of the world; and it is a palpable and egregious partiality, to confine our view entirely to that principle, by which our own minds operate." [51] When it is objected that animals and vegetables could not, without thought to guide them, give rise to order, Philo replies that we see them doing so all the time, for an animal or tree bestows order and organization on its offspring without being conscious of it.[52] Nor can it be shown that this order "proceeds ultimately from design" unless it can be proved that "order is, from its nature, inseparably attached to thought, and that it can never, of itself, or from original unknown principles, belong to matter." [53] Moreover, animal generation in one respect has a positive advantage over reason. In our experience reason "arises from" generation rather than generation from reason, reason never being found except in an animal body but animal bodies often being found without reason.[54]

In addition to animal generation, vegetable growth, and instinct, Philo mentions still another alternative to mind as the possible cause of natural order, "the old Epicurean hypothesis" of a finite number of atoms undergoing transformations during an infinite time and finally settling into an orderly world which preserves stability in its forms.[55] Although this is justly regarded as "the most absurd system," it might be brought by a few alterations "to bear a faint appearance of probability." [56] Of course, there are disadvantages in it, but *all* systems of

[49] *Ibid.,* pp. 176, 177.   [50] *Ibid.,* p. 178.   [51] *Ibid.*   [52] *Ibid.,* p. 179.
[53] *Ibid.*   [54] *Ibid.,* pp. 179, 180.   [55] *Ibid.,* p. 182.   [56] *Ibid.*

cosmogony are bound to be imperfect. Philo's purpose in bringing
forward this and other hypotheses has not been to champion any of
them but only to show that each of them has some plausibility but
none of them is convincing. The conflict between them can never be
resolved and they merely "prepare a complete triumph for the sceptic."
"A total suspense of judgment is here our only reasonable resource." [57]

But Philo is not content to challenge the teleological explanation of
natural order by the criticisms we have mentioned. He also argues that
the teleological explanation, even if it were able to show that the most
probable cause of natural order is a mind analogous to that of man,
could not prove that that mind possesses the *attributes* ascribed to the
God men worship. The principle behind Cleanthes' argument has been,
"Like effects prove like causes." If this principle is valid, the Mind that
may be proved by the argument must be like the human mind.[58] Philo
triumphantly points out the damaging consequences of this conclusion. "*First*, By this method of reasoning, you renounce all claims to
infinity in any of the attributes of the Deity. For as the cause ought
only to be proportioned to the effect, and the effect, so far as it falls
under our cognisance, is not infinite; what pretensions have we, upon
your suppositions, to ascribe that attribute to the divine Being? . . .
Secondly, You have no reason, on your theory, for ascribing *perfection*
to the Deity, even in his finite capacity; or for supposing him free from
every error, mistake, or incoherence in his undertakings. . . . At least,
you must acknowledge, that it is impossible for us to tell, from our
limited views, whether this system contains any great faults or deserves
any considerable praise, if compared to other possible, and even real
systems. . . . And what shadow of an argument, continued Philo, can
you produce, from your hypothesis, to prove the *unity* of the Deity. A
great many men join in building a house or ship, in rearing a city, in
framing a commonwealth: Why may not several Deities combine in
contriving and framing a world? This is only so much greater similarity
to human affairs." [59]

Hume had offered a similar argument in *An Enquiry concerning
Human Understanding* against the theistic belief in a *particular providence* and a *future state*.[60] "When we infer any particular cause from
an effect, we must proportion the one to the other, and can never be
allowed to ascribe to the cause any qualities, but what are exactly

[57] *Ibid.*, pp. 186, 187.   [58] *Ibid.*, p. 165.

[59] *Ibid.*, pp. 166, 167 (italics added).

[60] Hume, *An Enquiry concerning Human Understanding* (Open Court ed.),
Sec. XI.

sufficient to produce the effect. . . . But if we ascribe to it further qualities, or affirm it capable of producing other effects, we can only indulge the license of conjecture, and arbitrarily suppose the existence of qualities and energies, without reason or authority." [61] What are the implications of this principle for the problems of providence and a future life? Clearly, the main implication is that, if the gods are the authors of the existence of the world, "they possess that precise degree of power, intelligence, and benevolence which appears in their workmanship, but nothing farther can ever be proved." [62] "The supposition of farther attributes is mere hypothesis; much more the supposition, that, in distant regions of space or time, there has been, or will be, a more magnificent display of their attributes, and a scheme of administration more suitable to such imaginary virtues. We can never be allowed to mount up from the universe, to Jupiter, the cause; and then descend downwards, to infer any new effect from that cause." [63] But this is precisely what religious persons have done who have argued from the gods as causes to their supposed effects, "presuming that a more perfect production than the present world would be more suitable to such perfect beings as the gods." [64] Having argued from the appearances of things that the gods are their causes, they then "come backward" and argue that there must be "a fuller display of (their) particular attributes." [65] For example, they assert that there is a providence or governor of the world who guides the course of events, punishes the wicked, and rewards the virtuous in a "more particular" way than appears in the ordinary course of events.[66] And, not content with such a "particular providence" in this life, they "render this life merely a passage to something farther; a porch, which leads to a greater, and vastly different building; a prologue, which serves only to introduce the piece, and give it more grace and propriety." [67] These ideas they have derived from their own imagination and not from the facts of experience, so that they are nothing more than a mere possibility which cannot be inferred by reason from the effects we actually observe.[68]

It is by a similar line of reasoning that Philo argues in the *Dialogues* that the effects in nature from which we infer a Mind as their cause do not warrant us in bestowing upon it the attributes of the God men worship, e.g., infinity, perfection, and unity. For although nature is immense, it is finite; although it is impressive, it is not perfect; al-

[61] *Ibid.*, pp. 143, 144.   [62] *Ibid.*, p. 144.   [63] *Ibid.*, p. 145.
[64] *Ibid.*, p. 146.   [65] *Ibid.*, p. 147.   [66] *Ibid.*, p. 148.   [67] *Ibid.*, p. 149.
[68] *Ibid.*

though it constitutes a system, it could have been produced by the co-operation of several minds rather than one. And this leads to another and still more important point: if we look carefully at the world as it is, we must ask whether its Author is even *good*. In Part X of the *Dialogues* Philo describes vividly and in detail the many different evils, natural and moral, which bring suffering into the lives of men.[69] Can Cleanthes, after considering all of these, "assert the moral attributes of the Deity, his justice, benevolence, mercy, and rectitude, to be of the same nature with these virtues in human creatures"? [70] "Epicurus's old questions are yet unanswered. Is he willing to prevent evil, but not able? then is he impotent. Is he able, but not willing? then is he malevolent. Is he both able and willing? whence then is evil?" [71]

Cleanthes acknowledges that this is a serious and, if true, perhaps a fatal objection to Theism. "If you can make out the present point and prove mankind to be unhappy or corrupted," he says, "there is an end at once of all religion. For to what purpose establish the *natural* attributes of the Deity, while the *moral* are still doubtful and uncertain?" [72] But he denies the accuracy of Philo's description of the misery and wickedness of man as "exaggerated" and "contrary to fact and experience." [73] "Health is more common than sickness: Pleasure than pain: Happiness than misery. And for one vexation which we meet with, we attain, upon computation, a hundred enjoyments." [74] Philo strongly disputes this optimistic judgment but does not rest his whole case upon his own more pessimistic view. Rather, he holds that his objection will stand even if human happiness exceeds human misery in this life. If God possesses infinite power, wisdom, and goodness, as theists affirm, "why is there *any* misery at all in the world?" [75] Even if one admits that human misery may be *compatible* with God's infinite power and goodness, it is impossible to prove that these pure and unmixed attributes exist in Him from "the present mixed and confused phenomena, and from these alone." [76] If a person were antecedently assured when he was brought into the world that it was the work of a benevolent Being, he would be disappointed to find it so full of evil, but he would realize that he was too ignorant to comprehend the reason for it and would not abandon his belief.[77] But if, as is the case with regard to man, he is not antecedently convinced of this but has to form his belief from the appearances of things in the world, he will never find a reason to accept such a view.[78] For what picture of the world does one form

[69] Hume, *Dialogues* (ed. N. K. Smith), pp. 192–198.   [70] *Ibid.*, p. 198.
[71] *Ibid.*   [72] *Ibid.*, p. 199 (italics added).   [73] *Ibid.*, p. 200.   [74] *Ibid.*
[75] *Ibid.*, p. 201.   [76] *Ibid.*   [77] *Ibid.*, p. 204.   [78] *Ibid.*

when one examines closely the "prodigious variety and fecundity" of living beings? Philo's answer is unforgettable. "How hostile and destructive to each other! How insufficient all of them for their own happiness! How contemptible or odious to the spectator! The whole presents nothing but the idea of a blind nature, impregnated by a great vivifying principle, and pouring forth from her lap, without discernment or parental care, her maimed and abortive children!" [79] What conclusion should one draw from this with respect to the original cause of nature? Certainly, not that it is perfectly good in the sense of benevolent; nor that it is perfectly bad or malevolent; but that it is neither good nor bad. "The true conclusion is, that the original source of all things is entirely indifferent to all these principles, and has not more regard to good above ill than to heat above cold, or to drought above moisture, or to light above heavy." [80]

We have now reviewed the major criticisms of the teleological argument by Philo and have seen that they all express in different ways his belief that the theistic explanation of natural order is based upon an *illegitimate use of the causal principle.* (1) We are not justified in inferring from the one instance of a world we have experienced to the nature of its cause, for we have not experienced the constant conjunction of a divine Mind with the origin of worlds. (2) Moreover, there is no sufficient reason to think that its cause was a mind like our own rather than animal generation, vegetable growth, or some other principle we have observed producing effects in nature. For the ultimate cause may have been "an eternal, inherent principle of order" in nature rather than a divine Mind beyond her. Therefore, a decision between possible cosmogonies is beyond the narrow capacity of our reason and we should suspend judgment with respect to them. (3) Finally, even if we should decide in favor of a Mind as the most probable hypothesis, we would have no justification for ascribing attributes such as infinity, perfection, unity, and, above all, moral goodness to it, so that we would not have proved the existence of the God men worship.

In the closing part of the *Dialogues,* the conclusions are drawn from the argument as a whole. It is here that we are faced squarely with the baffling problem, already mentioned, as to whether Philo or Cleanthes is the major spokesman for Hume or whether both are important as representatives of different sides of his mind. As Kemp Smith has said, throughout most of the *Dialogues* the center of interest is Philo's assault from different angles upon the teleological argument

[79] *Ibid.,* p. 211.   [80] *Ibid.,* p. 212.

and upon the conclusions about God which have been drawn from it by theists. Moreover, the defense of the argument by Cleanthes is phillosophically weak, often amounting to little more than further affirmations and illustrations of the point that only mind can be the source of natural order. Also, Philo's objections reflect Hume's skeptical attitude toward reason when it goes beyond common sense and science and concerns itself with metaphysical and theological questions. Above all, his objections are in line with Hume's view of the nature and limits of causal explanation and his naturalistic view of mind and its place in nature as expressed in his other works. It is not surprising, therefore, that Smith and many other philosophers have considered Philo to be Hume's major spokesman and have regarded Cleanthes as important only when he agrees with Philo.

However, a number of philosophers have rejected this view and have argued that at the end of the argument Hume is closer to Cleanthes' philosophical Theism than he is to Philo's Skepticism. The major evidence for this interpretation is found in Part XII of the *Dialogues*. For Philo takes a position there which at first sight seems to contradict what he says in the earlier parts of the book and to agree with the position of Cleanthes. After his lengthy and various criticisms of the teleological argument, he abruptly changes his tone at the beginning of Part XII and seems to minimize the difference between his Skepticism and the philosophical Theism he has been attacking. However, Smith thinks that the change is more apparent than real. Is he right in thinking so? To answer that question let us examine Philo's remarks for ourselves.

"You are sensible," he says to Cleanthes, "that, notwithstanding the freedom of my conversation, and my love of singular arguments, no one has a deeper sense of religion impressed on his mind, or pays more profound adoration to the divine Being, as he discovers himself to reason, in the inexplicable contrivance and artifice of nature. A purpose, an intention, or design strikes everywhere the most careless, the most stupid thinker; and no man can be so hardened in absurd systems, as at all times to reject it." [81] As if to emphasize his acceptance of Cleanthes' teleological argument despite his criticisms of it, he refers to the Copernican system of astronomy and to Galen's analysis of the anatomy of the human body to illustrate the point that "all the sciences almost lead us insensibly to acknowledge a first intelligent Author," [82] and he asks "to what pitch of pertinacious obstinacy must a philosopher in this age have attained who can now doubt of a supreme intelli-

[81] *Ibid.*, p. 214.   [82] *Ibid.*, pp. 214, 215.

gence?" [83] Unless he is speaking with his tongue in his cheek, Philo seems in this passage to be accepting the conclusion of the teleological argument and to be dismissing his previous criticisms of it as unconvincing. Moreover, this seems to be borne out by an earlier statement at the end of Part X: "In many views of the universe and of its parts, particularly the latter, the beauty and fitness of final causes strike us with such irresistible force, that all objections appear (what I believe they really are) mere cavils and sophisms; nor can we then imagine how it was ever possible for us to repose any weight on them." [84] In view of these statements, may not Hume have accepted the *conclusion* of the teleological argument as a "natural belief" even if he rejected the *argument* for it as logically unconvincing and vulnerable to the criticisms Philo has directed against it?

However, Philo's next statement gives us pause and makes us realize that his apparent agreement with Cleanthes' conclusion may not mean what it seems at first sight to mean. For he now suggests that the dispute between theists and atheists is mainly a "dispute of words" having to do only with "the degree of a quality," i.e., mind, in God. The theist, while insisting rightly that there is a "considerable resemblance," admits that there is also a "vast difference" between the divine Mind and human minds.[85] The atheist emphasizes the immense difference, but if he is asked whether "there be not a certain degree of analogy among all the operations of nature, in every situation and in every age; *whether the rotting of a turnip, the generation of an animal, and the structure of human thought be not energies that probably bear some remote analogy to each other*," he will "readily acknowledge it." [86] If he is then asked "if it be not probable, that the principle which first arranged, and still maintains, order in this universe, bears not also some remote inconceivable analogy to the other operations of nature, and *among the rest to the economy of human mind* and thought," he must reluctantly assent.[87] If so, the dispute between the theist and the atheist is merely a verbal one, since the theist admits that the divine intelligence is "very different" from human mind, while the atheist admits that there is "some remote analogy" between them.[88]

The importance of these passages is shown by the fact that at the very end Philo returns to the same points. "If the whole of natural theology, as some people seem to maintain, resolves itself into one simple, though somewhat ambiguous, at least undefined proposition,

---

[83] *Ibid.*, p. 215.   [84] *Ibid.*, p. 202.   [85] *Ibid.*, p. 217.
[86] *Ibid.*, p. 218 (italics added).   [87] *Ibid.*   [88] *Ibid.*, p. 227.

*that the cause or causes of order in the universe probably bear some
remote analogy to human intelligence:* If this proposition be not capable of extension, variation, or more particular explication: if it afford
no inference that affects human life, or can be the source of any action
or forbearance: And if the analogy, imperfect as it is, can be carried no
farther than to the human intelligence; and cannot be transferred with
any appearance of probability, to the other qualities of the mind: If
this really be the case, what can the most inquisitive, contemplative, and religious man do more than give a plain, philosophical assent to the proposition, as often as it occurs; and believe that the
arguments on which it is established, exceed the objections which lie
against it?" [89]

How are we to interpret Philo's attitude as he expresses it in these
passages? Has he really come over to Cleanthes' position, as some
interpreters have held? Or has he made no real concession to that
position, as Kemp Smith and others seem to think? In our opinion, he
has accepted a part, but by no means the whole or even the most
important part, of the theistic view of Cleanthes.

In the first place, Philo's admission at the end of Part X that "the
beauty and fitness of final causes strike us with such irresistible force"
as to make objections appear as "mere cavils and sophisms" does not
imply that he has abandoned his earlier skeptical criticisms of the
teleological argument. It may be interpreted in the light of Hume's
view as a "mitigated skeptic" that we should accept certain truths as
"natural beliefs" although we have no rational basis for claiming to
have knowledge of them. If so, his reference to the "irresistible force"
of final causes means that, while his previous criticisms of them are still
logically valid, they are psychologically too weak to prevent the acceptance of teleology as a "natural belief" of the imagination.

In the second place, Philo's argument in Part XII that the dispute
between the theist and the atheist is merely a verbal one asserts a
supposed agreement between them but on the basis of a bare minimum of belief. While the atheist is brought to admit that there is an
analogy between the cause of natural order and the *human mind,* an
analogy is also asserted between that cause and other natural operations such as *animal generation* and *vegetable growth.* This seems to
imply that among the possible causes of natural order animal generation and vegetable growth have a claim to acceptance as well as mind.
For Philo represents the atheist as admitting only that the cause of
natural order bears "some remote inconceivable analogy to the other

[89] *Ibid.*

operations of nature, and *among the rest* to the economy of human mind and thought." Hence, Philo seems to be admitting only that a mind resembling our own is *one* of the causes of natural order but not necessarily that it is more important than animal generation and vegetable growth whose claims to be the cause he has defended earlier. This is hardly Theism.

In the third place, Philo uses the adjective "remote" several times to weaken the analogy between the mind which is one of the causes of natural order and the human mind. He also weakens it by the use of other terms. The analogy is "inconceivable," and the proposition that asserts it is "somewhat ambiguous, at least undefined." [90] Mind is spoken of as "the cause or causes of order," which implies that its unity should not be asserted. The cause or causes "probably" bear an analogy to mind.[91] Above all, the proposition that asserts this "remote analogy" is "not capable of extension, variation, or more particular explication," and it can "afford no inference that affects human life." [92] For Philo maintains his earlier view that *moral goodness* should not be ascribed to the cause of nature, so that no moral inferences are to be drawn from the admission that it bears a remote analogy to human mind. This is the meaning of Philo's insistence that the analogy "can be carried no farther than to the human intelligence, and cannot be transferred, with any appearance of probability, to the other qualities of the mind." [93]

In view of these considerations, it is very dubious whether Philo's position at the end of the *Dialogues* should be called "Theism." He has conceded to Cleanthes that the order of nature suggests teleology with an "irresistible force" that is psychologically stronger than the criticisms of reason and that the cause (or causes) of this order "probably bear some remote analogy to human intelligence." But there is also an analogy to "other operations of nature." And he has emphasized again and again the remoteness of the analogy to mind and has refused to admit that the cause has either unity or moral goodness. We must conclude, therefore, that the *volte face* of Philo at the beginning of Part XII of the *Dialogues* is more apparent than real. While the conclusion (if not the arguments) of Cleanthes has apparently been accepted by him as a "natural belief," it has been so qualified and weakened as to be both ambiguous in its meaning and useless for the purposes of religion and morality. If so, while Cleanthes as well as Philo may be regarded as a spokesman for Hume, his constructive contribution to the conclusion is small.

[90] *Ibid.*   [91] *Ibid.*   [92] *Ibid.*   [93] *Ibid.*

The last sentence of the *Dialogues*, in which the reporter of the discussion, Pamphilus, offers his judgment on the views expressed by the participants, should not be allowed to change this conclusion. He says, "Upon a serious review of the whole, I cannot but think, that Philo's principles are more probable than Demea's; but that those of Cleanthes approach still nearer to the truth." [94] Since Pamphilus was the youthful "pupil" of Cleanthes and was regarded as his "adopted son," [95] he would be expected to sympathize with Cleanthes' point of view; and in any case he was a "mere auditor" of the discussion whose competence to judge at a philosophical debate is not evident.[96] Also, Philo's professed longing at the end for a special revelation to compensate for the unsatisfactory results of "natural religion" must not be taken seriously. He speaks of "a longing desire and expectation, that Heaven would be pleased to dissipate, at least alleviate, this profound ignorance, by affording some more particular revelation to mankind and making discoveries of the nature, attributes and operations of the Divine object of our Faith. A person, seasoned with a just sense of the imperfections of natural reason, will fly to revealed truth with the greatest avidity. . . . To be a philosophical sceptic is, in a man of letters, the first and most essential step towards being a sound believing Christian." [97] Apart from the fact that this pious statement expresses a desire for rather than a belief in a special revelation, there is no evidence that Hume had ever accepted the Christian revelation since his youthful rejection of Calvinism. His attitude toward popular religion which is based on special revelation is always hostile, as we pointed out at the outset. Moreover, in the pages immediately preceding the passage we have just quoted he makes a severe indictment of the "pernicious consequences," intellectual, moral, and political, of popular religion.[98] He admits that there are no such consequences in the case of "true religion," but this is limited to a few "philosophical theists" who alone merit the divine "favor," while "philosophical sceptics" are entitled to the divine "indulgence." [99] If he regards himself as one of these few "philosophical theists," it is only in the very minimal sense defined by Philo at the end of the *Dialogues*. And philosophical *Theism* of this highly attenuated kind is barely distinguishable from philosophical *Naturalism*, which explains the order of nature not by a transcendent divine Mind but by "an eternal, inherent principle (or principles) of order."

[94] *Ibid.*, p. 228.   [95] *Ibid.*, p. 130.   [96] *Ibid.*, p. 128.
[97] *Ibid.*, pp. 228–229.   [98] *Ibid.*, pp. 219–226.   [99] *Ibid.*, pp. 226, 227.

HUME'S SKEPTICISM: CONTRIBUTIONS AND LIMITATIONS

It is recognized by most modern philosophers that Aquinas' arguments for the existence of God are based on presuppositions derived from Greek philosophy, especially the metaphysics and theory of knowledge of Aristotle. The fact that many philosophers now regard his arguments as unconvincing is largely due to the fact that they no longer accept the presuppositions on which they were based. It is not so clearly recognized, however, that Hume's attack upon the "natural religion" of his time was *also* based upon presuppositions concerning the origin and nature of knowledge which he took for granted and made no attempt to prove because of the dominance of Newton in science and Locke in philosophy. Therefore, before the conclusion is accepted that Hume's criticisms of the "natural religion" of his time have destroyed rational theology of every kind, these presuppositions should be critically examined.

Since this task has already been performed by many philosophers from Thomas Reid through T. H. Green to Kemp Smith and others in our time, it will not be necessary for us to undertake it once more. It will suffice for our purpose simply to mention some of Hume's presuppositions as an empiricist before passing on to remarks concerning the criticisms of natural religion he based upon them. The first is that "nothing is ever really present to the mind but its perceptions or impressions and ideas," and that "'tis impossible for us so much as to conceive or form an idea of anything specifically different from ideas and impressions." [100] Hume states this presupposition in a radical form. "Let us fix our attention out of ourselves as much as possible: Let us chace our imagination to the heavens, or to the utmost limits of the universe; we never really advance a step beyond ourselves, nor can conceive any kind of existence but those perceptions, which have appear'd in that narrow compass." [101] This means that we can never break out of the charmed circle of our own "perceptions" and attain knowledge of objects independent of our minds. Although this presupposition was derived from Descartes and Locke, neither of them drew the extreme conclusion of Phenomenalism from it as did Hume. In criticism, it need only be said that realistic philosophers before and after Hume have rejected it and that almost all natural scientists have agreed with them.

The second and third presuppositions are closely related and may

[100] Hume, *A Treatise of Human Nature*, Bk. I, Pt. II, Sec. VI (Oxford Edition).
[101] *Ibid.*, pp. 67, 68.

be mentioned together. Hume presupposed that all "ideas" are derived from external and internal "impressions" and that any abstract idea which cannot be traced back to a specific impression is to be regarded with suspicion since it is probably fictitious. As we have indicated, he offers no proof of this sweeping generalization except to show that a complex idea of a *sensible* object such as a "golden mountain" is derived from external impressions. With regard to this presupposition, modern philosophers from Kant on have pointed out that it does not account for the form or structure of experience and that its acceptance would make science impossible, since science uses many concepts and principles which do not originate from impressions.

The third presupposition is that all of our perceptions are distinct from each other and separately existent, so that we have knowledge of no connections or relations between them. This makes it necessary for Hume to maintain that both substances which seem to endure through their changes and causal relations between objects are products of feeling and imagination by means of laws of association. This "atomistic" view of experience, when combined with the first two presuppositions, is the root of Hume's Skepticism. It has been refuted by many philosophers, both idealistic and realistic, and is completely false. The objects of our experience include not only our perceptions but also the relations between them; indeed, we apprehend relations along with their terms. It is only when we analyze our experience into its constituent parts that we regard it not as a continous whole but as a collection of atomic parts independent of each other.

The fact that these presuppositions are all extremely dubious (and incompatible with the claims of science as well as philosophy to give us knowledge) should make us wary of Hume's criticisms of "natural religion" in the *Dialogues* insofar as these criticisms are based upon them. However, this should not blind us to the truth and importance of some of his criticisms and the necessity for a sound rational theology to take account of them.

One of the most surprising things about the "natural religion" which Hume is criticizing through the skeptic Philo is the *limited range of the evidence* it uses as the basis for its theistic conclusion. In contrast to Aquinas, the theist Cleanthes depends exclusively upon the teleological argument from natural order which was so popular in his time. The result was that other evidence from nature which was regarded as important by Aquinas and evidence from morality upon which Kant based his Theism were completely neglected. To most modern theists, a rational belief in God arises first not so much from the evidence for design in nature as from the moral consciousness, existential concern for meaning and value, and religious experience. Cleanthes says nothing whatever about evidence of these kinds derived from the distinctive experiences of man as a spiritual being. It was only with Kant's ethical theology, Schleiermacher's religion of feeling, and Hegel's philosophy of spirit that philosophers of religion began to pay serious attention to the spiritual nature and experience of man as evidence for the existence and nature of God.

Hume has pointed out with great skill and force the logical flaws in this narrowly based "natural religion" of his time. The analogy between natural order and a machine or other product of the human mind is obviously remote. There is a somewhat closer analogy between the order of the "lesser machines" or parts of nature and the order of a human machine. As Cleanthes points out, in an organ such as the eye many parts are delicately and precisely adjusted to one another and to the end of the whole organ, vision; and the anatomy of the human body as a whole does often give the impression of a complex and smoothly running machine. However, the analogy is not close enough to justify without further argument the inference that there is an analogy between the cause of an organ or an organism and the human mind which is the cause of a machine. While an organism attains its ends like a machine through the cooperation of its parts, it does so by means of a principle of order immanent in it. "The organic," says Kemp Smith, "is not only organized; it is self-organizing. Organisms are self-developing, self-maintaining, self-regulating, self-propagating. Their 'form,' that is to say, is as native and natural to them as is the 'matter' of which they are composed. In an artificial product, on the other hand, the form, so far from being native to it, depends for its existence on an external artificer . . . through the external fitting together of bodies antecedently shaped and formed." [102] It is for this reason that Philo can argue from the organization of animals or plants to animal generation or vegetable growth as the cause of natural order, since organisms seem to depend for their order not upon the imposition of form from without but upon an inherent principle of order within.

There is plausibility in this naturalistic explanation of natural order, but whether it is an adequate explanation is another question. For the fact that there is an immanent principle of order in organisms may not be self-explanatory but may demand explanation itself, i.e., it may be the proximate but not the original and ultimate cause. In short, Philo's criticism is convincing against the form of the teleological argument

[102] *Hume's Dialogues concerning Natural Religion* (ed. N. K. Smith), p. 102.

proposed by Cleanthes, since this assumes that the matter in organisms is passive and inert like inanimate matter and therefore has no internal organizing principle. But it is not conclusive against later forms of the argument which seek for an ultimate cause of the inherent order of organisms in a directive Mind at work throughout and within the evolutionary process.[103] Thus, Philo's naturalistic alternative to Theism is possible as an explanation of natural order, but as an ultimate explanation it is doubtful whether it is as probable as the theistic one.

The most fundamental issue raised by Philo in his criticism is whether it is legitimate to use the causal principle at all in attempting to explain natural order. Not only the teleological argument but also the cosmological arguments presented by Aquinas are based on the presupposition that from the characteristics of the world we can infer the existence of a cause which is distinct from the world. Philo attacks this presupposition on the Humian ground that the idea of necessary connection between a cause and its effect arises only from the constant conjunction in our experience of two "species" of objects, whereas we have experienced only one world and have not experienced any worlds coming into being following their causes. This view of the causal principle was derived by Hume from early modern science. It is not for the philosopher of religion to decide whether it is adequate for contemporary science, although this may be doubted. But he does have the right to inquire whether it is adequate for the purpose of philosophical explanation. "The physicist," says Copleston, "is not concerned, for instance, with the problem of the logical and ontological status of the principle that everything which begins to be does so through the agency of an extrinsic cause. . . . But the philosopher does ask this question." [104] If he does not accept Hume's atomistic analysis of experience and view of the origin of connections between the objects of experience, he cannot be satisfied with the view that we have only a natural belief but no knowledge of the connection between cause and effect. For one thing, we are conscious of the causal power of our will in producing bodily movements and bringing ideas before the attention. Hume is quite right in saying that we do not know *how* it does so, but we know *that* it does so.

Of course, Hume's skepticism with respect to the idea of necessary connection may be unjustified and yet he may be right in denying that

---

[103] Cf. F. R. Tennant, *Philosophical Theology* (Cambridge, Eng.: Cambridge University Press, 1928–1930), Vol. II, Chap. 4; and Teilhard de Chardin, *The Phenomenon of Man* (New York: Harper & Row, 1959).

[104] Frederick Copleston, *History of Philosophy* (London: Burns, Oates, and Washbourne, 1956), Vol. V, p. 287.

we can legitimately extend causal explanation beyond the limits of our experience to a transcendent cause, the divine Mind. And it is obviously true that we have never *experienced* a world—or worlds—being produced by a divine Mind. The question for philosophy is whether we have a right to *infer* such a transcendent cause, on the ground that it offers the most adequate explanation of the world. Whether we have such a right cannot be decided merely by reference to the radical empiricist dogma that we have knowledge only of that which we have experienced. The question must be decided by reason in the light of all the evidence. However, when the theist affirms the existence of a divine Mind as the cause of nature, he should recognize that such a transcendent Being should be spoken of as a "cause" only in an analogical sense. For it is obvious that we cannot know the mode of operation of a transcendent Being beyond our experience. We cannot assume, for example, that the divine Mind *precedes* its effects in time or *ceases* to act upon them after they have come into being. Indeed, Theism has usually maintained that the divine causal activity is concomitant with its effects and continues to be the sustaining Ground of them. Thus, Philo's criticism of the application of the causal principle to a transcendent Mind is unjustified but serves a useful purpose by warning us to think of God's causal activity in creating and sustaining the world as only an analogy.

Whatever one may think of Hume's analysis of the causal relation and his restriction of it to objects of experience, one of his major *contributions* to the philosophy of religion is his insistence that it is logically impossible to prove an infinite and perfect Being by causal inference from a finite and imperfect world, or a morally good Being from a world in which good and evil are mixed. At the beginning of Part XI of the *Dialogues,* Cleanthes admits that this is the case and draws the only conclusion that a strict empiricist like himself could draw, i.e., that theists should revise the traditional concept of God in order to bring it into line with the facts. "If we preserve human analogy," he says, "we must forever find it impossible to reconcile any mixture of evil in the universe with infinite attributes; much less, can we ever prove the latter from the former. But supposing the Author of Nature to be *finitely perfect* though far exceeding mankind; a satisfactory account may then be given of natural and moral evil, and every untoward phenomenon be explained and adjusted. . . . And in a word, benevolence, regulated by wisdom and limited by necessity, may produce just such a world as the present." [105] Whether this solution of

---

[105] Hume, *Dialogues,* ed. N. K. Smith, p. 203 (italics added).

the problem of imperfection and evil in the world is ultimately satisfactory we shall not consider here. What is essential is that the theist
should honestly recognize that, if the only evidence we have concerning the nature of God is derived from the natural order, as in the
teleological argument of Cleanthes, we are warranted in inferring at
the most a great Mind but not an infinite, perfect, and good one. For,
as Philo says, we have a right to infer from given effects only such a
cause as is sufficient to produce them and we should not bestow upon it
attributes which are not required by those effects. The same argument
is employed in the *Enquiry* against the belief in a "particular providence" and a "future state" superior to anything we experience here
and now, and it is equally valid there. However, this is not conclusive
against the ascription of "infinite attributes" to God. What it does is to
make clear that the basis of belief in the infinity, perfection, and goodness of God must be broader than evidence drawn from the natural
order. It must also include, for example, evidence from the religious
experience of God as infinite and perfect and the moral consciousness
of Him as righteous will demanding moral goodness of men.

Thus the teleological argument by itself can prove at the most the
probability of the existence of a divine Mind, and it cannot prove that
He possesses infinity, perfection, or moral goodness. Both of these
limitations accentuate the point we made at the beginning of our
evaluation, i.e., that the "natural religion" criticized by Philo rests upon
too narrow a foundation. Unless the religious experience of God as
infinite and transcendent to the world is taken into account, it is impossible to justify His infinity and perfection. Unless His will is also encountered in conscience as making moral demands upon men which go
beyond the requirements of social morality, we have no adequate
ground for ascribing moral goodness to Him. Thus the most basic
objection to the "natural religion" of Cleanthes is that it rests the case
for Theism upon evidence which is limited and takes no account of the
primary evidence which has led men to belief in Theism. Hume has
rendered a valuable service in pointing out this weakness.

We have indicated that the Skepticism of Hume was subordinated
to a positive intention. His intention was to establish the moral and
social sciences on the foundation of a science of human nature as
Newton had established the natural sciences on other foundations before him.[106] Although he was not a materialist, his conception of
human nature was a naturalistic one. His *Naturalism* is especially evident in his view of the self or mind and its relation to nature, and this

---

[106] J. A. Passmore, *Hume's Intentions*, Chap. 1; Hume, *Enquiry*, pp. 11, 12.

view profoundly affected his attitude toward the teleological argument and Theism in general. For Hume, the human mind is simply a "part" of nature and is entitled to no "peculiar privileges" in preference to other parts in explaining natural order. It "arises from" animal generation, since it is associated with and dependent upon a body. It is "weak" and confined to a "small compass," being found in only one animal species on one planet. The order of the ideas in a divine Mind when it forms a design requires a causal explanation no less than the natural order it is invoked to explain. In short, mind is simply one natural "principle" and "operation" among many. His reduction of the mind to the status of a relatively insignificant part of nature is a manifestation of the general naturalistic bias of Hume's thinking. It is also a result of his empirical method of analyzing the self. Since he does not discover any "impression" from which the idea of the "personal identity" of the self can be derived, he reduces our knowledge of it to a succession of ideas, volitions, and feelings which resemble and are causally related to one another. This does not prevent him from accepting the reality of the self as a "natural belief" but it does prevent him from affirming that there is a spiritual principle which is the ground of its identity and consequently its continuity.

This naturalistic view of human mind helps to explain Philo's reluctance to accord a privileged position to mind as the cause of natural order. He cannot accept the theistic view that there is a primary analogy of the original cause with human mind because he does not recognize the *uniqueness and pre-eminence of mind in the world*. He does not acknowledge its capacity to govern its thinking by logical laws and its willing by moral laws quite different from the physical and biological laws governing the rest of nature, or its freedom of will and creativity, or its transcendence of its past and present by anticipation of the future. Only one who fully appreciates this uniqueness of human mind and the pre-eminence in nature which results from it is likely to accept the theistic view that the world cannot be explained by reference to anything less than mind. Of course, it is true that animal generation and vegetable growth are also causes of natural order, as Philo says, but we should not overlook the striking differences between the kind of order they are able to create and that which is created by the human mind. An animal is able by instinct to build a nest or to spin a web and carry out other patterns of activity again and again; and it can transmit to its offspring the same form or organization it has received from its parents. But the human mind also has the capacity to modify and transcend the form man receives from his parents by realizing new potentialities; and it can transform its natural environment and create a distinctively human environment through the culture and social institutions it produces and transmits from generation to generation. Therefore, it is neither arbitrary nor a sign of human conceit to give mind a privileged position among possible causes of natural order.

Underlying most of Philo's criticisms of the theistic position we have been considering is Hume's phenomenalist theory of knowledge and consequent unwillingness to accept any *metaphysical interpretation* of ultimate reality. Although he held that we can have certain knowledge of "relations of ideas" in mathematics and can make generalizations which are probably true concerning "matters of fact" in the natural and social sciences, metaphysics and theology are beyond the "narrow compass" of our understanding. One's final estimate of Hume's religious skepticism, therefore, will depend upon whether one accepts his view that we cannot attain knowledge which goes beyond phenomena. This is not the place for a critical consideration of his phenomenalism and rejection of metaphysics. If one starts with the presuppositions of Hume that "nothing is ever really present to the mind but its perceptions" and that these are distinct and separate from one another, it is logically impossible to affirm a world view of any sort. However, we pointed out at the outset that these presuppositions are false. If so, Hume's complete skepticism about metaphysical and theological views may be set aside, and we may consider the relative merits of Theism, Naturalism, and other world views.

In this connection, it is relevant to point out that, while the phenomenalist tries to dispense with metaphysical views, he is unable in practice to avoid them. It is not necessary for him to have a comprehensive metaphysical "system" like Spinoza's or a theological "system" like Aquinas'; but life imposes upon every person the necessity of making decisions with respect to fundamental metaphysical and religious issues such as the nature of mind and the relation of mechanism to teleology. Fearful of falling into error, the phenomenalist may attempt to suspend judgment permanently and refuse to take a definite stand on such issues. But it is impossible consistently to maintain this attitude. As Hume admitted, the skeptic is forced by the realities and exigencies of life to put aside his doubts with respect to the existence of external objects, selves, and causal connections; for our experience of objects, persons, and their interaction gives rise to natural beliefs which we cannot deny without disastrous results. What Hume failed to see was that on basic metaphysical issues like those we have just mentioned we are also required to make up our minds and commit ourselves to one side or the other. For we are under the necessity of discovering unity in our experience by relating different kinds of objects and events to one another and ourselves to the world around us in order that we may have at least a general picture of the world and our place in it to guide us in our thinking and conduct.

The proof that this is inescapable is that even persons who are innocent of philosophical reflection always think and act in accordance with presuppositions which are derived from general beliefs about the world and man. Hume himself is no exception to this rule. Although he is critical of all philosophical and religious theories, his world view is fundamentally that of modern Naturalism, as we have seen. Philo's conception of the human mind and his reference to an "eternal, inherent principle of order" in nature are expressions of a general tendency to consider the world as an eternal system of natural "energies" and "operations" whose order is a product of necessity in accordance with immutable laws. Since he is not a materialist who reduces mind to a form of bodily motion, he is willing to admit that mind is one of the "principles" of order in nature. But his general metaphysical position is clearly that of Naturalism, and his gesture in the direction of philosophical Theism at the end of the *Dialogues* is a feeble one.

Our conclusion is that Hume's contribution to the philosophy of religion is largely negative. His criticisms of the teleological argument of his time and of the uncritical use of the causal principle in ascribing "infinite attributes" to God were very valuable. By criticisms such as these he made it clear that the "natural religion" of the eighteenth century was based upon evidence which was too narrow and limited in its scope and that a much broader view of experience than that of radical Empiricism was necessary to support it. But his naturalistic view of the self and the world, as well as his phenomenalistic theory of knowledge, made it impossible for him to make any positive contribution to a constructive philosophy of religion.

9 Critical Philosophy

KANT

The influence of Immanuel Kant (1747–1804) upon both philosophy of religion and Protestant theology during the last century and a half has been immense. It is no exaggeration to say that his criticisms of metaphysics and rational theology in the *Critique of Pure Reason* have been one of the main causes of the repudiation of both metaphysics and theology by philosophers, which found its most extreme expression in the Logical Positivism of the last generation. At the same time, the more constructive part of his religious thought, his substitution of ethical theology in the *Critique of Practical Reason* for the rational theology he had rejected, has opened up a new approach to religious problems for theistic philosophers. The effect of his thought, especially on its negative side, upon Protestant theologians has been equally great. For liberal theologians after Schleiermacher have tended to accept his criticisms of rational theology as final and have sought to reconstruct religious thought on the foundation of religious experience and moral values, and Christian theology on the basis of historical revelation.

The general effect of these developments in philosophy and theology has been a gradual separation of reason and faith which has led in our time to the indifference or hostility of naturalistic and positivistic philosophy to religion, on the one hand, and the repudiation of philosophy by neo-orthodox theology as irrelevant or dangerous, on the other. It is true, of course, that Absolute Idealism, which developed out of Kant, attempted a constructive synthesis of philosophy and religion which strongly affected nineteenth- and early-twentieth-century thought in Europe and America. But it is not too much to say that this ambitious form of speculative philosophy had ceased to wield any substantial influence upon either philosophy or theology by the end of World War I.

It is obvious, therefore, that the contemporary philosopher of religion must examine carefully and critically Kant's negative attitude toward rational theology in his first *Critique* and his attempt to substitute an ethical theology for it in his second *Critique*. In his examination of these major works, it is essential for him not to separate Kant's philosophy of religion from his theory of knowledge. It is also necessary for him to consider Kant's treatment of teleology in nature and its theological implications in the *Critique of Judgment*.

In his Critical Philosophy, Kant seeks to reconcile the scientific view of nature formulated by Newton in the seventeenth century with his own profound conviction, derived largely from Christianity, that there is a moral order which transcends the world of the senses. He had had a strong interest in the sciences since his matriculation in the university at the age of sixteen and accepted without reservation the dominant Newtonian conception of nature. On the other hand, he had been deeply affected by Pietism in his family and school. As C. C. J. Webb has pointed out, German Pietism emphasized "moral earnestness and strict discipline," "the urgency of the moral law written upon our hearts," "the 'radical evil' in human nature," and the necessity of "a complete change of orientation" for the good life.[1] These features of Pietism had a permanent and positive effect upon Kant's thought and life. On the other hand, there are many evidences of "a reaction from the atmosphere of over-strained absorption in private spiritual experience"; and his preference for natural rather than revealed religion may have been partly due to a revulsion against the "fanaticism" and "enthusiasm" of those whose piety was more favorable to religious feeling than to moral rectitude or clear thought.[2] It was inevitable, therefore, that there should develop a conflict in his mind between the Christian beliefs of his youth and the scientific view of the world which was dominant in his time. Despite this, he maintained the fundamental beliefs of ethical Theism throughout his life, and one of his major concerns was to find a way to reconcile them with modern science.

KANT'S THEORY OF KNOWLEDGE

That Kant was concerned with metaphysics as well as science and ethics is shown by the fact that one of the main purposes of the *Critique of Pure Reason* was to examine the claim of reason to give us knowledge of supersensible realities which transcend the world of nature. He had accepted the rationalistic metaphysics of Leibniz and Wolff in his "pre-critical" period but the reading of Hume had "awak-

[1] C. C. J. Webb, *Kant's Philosophy of Religion* (Oxford: Clarendon Press, 1926), p. 20.
[2] *Ibid.*, pp. 20, 21.

ened" him from his "dogmatic slumber." In the Preface to his first *Critique*, he drew a sharp contrast between logic, mathematics, and natural science, all of which had attained knowledge upon which there was general agreement, and metaphysics, which had never been able to reach agreement in its conclusions and consequently had alternated between periods of dogmatic pretension and skeptical distrust of reason. Why had these sciences flourished and attained certainty in their results, while metaphysics had languished and all of its efforts had come to nothing? The importance of this question to Kant was that metaphysics had claimed to be able to demonstrate the most cherished beliefs of mankind: God, freedom, and immortality. Kant had come to believe that this claim was unfounded and that the belief in God, freedom, and immortality had quite other grounds than speculative philosophy. Therefore, he warned that his critical examination of reason would lead to a denial of the claim of metaphysics to give us knowledge of religious truths but affirmed that it would prepare the way for the establishment of them on the more solid ground of rational faith. "I have therefore," he said, "found it necessary to deny knowledge, in order to make room for faith." [3]

In order to understand Kant's criticism of metaphysics and rational theology in the *Critique of Pure Reason,* it will not be necessary to present in detail his general theory of knowledge. However, it is essential to indicate the nature of the question he raises and the general character of the answer he offers. The question is: "What are the capacities and limitations of man's reason in his quest for knowledge?" Kant holds that an answer to this question must be based upon a thorough "critique" or critical examination of the "powers" of reason in its theoretical or cognitive function. More especially, he is concerned to determine the rational basis of the universal and necessary truths which the sciences have presupposed and which metaphysics also claims to offer. Since universal and necessary knowledge can never be gained by induction from experience alone, there must be an a priori element in it, i.e., concepts and principles which are independent of experience. For example, the principle that "every alteration must have a cause" and the concept of substance are indispensable to scientific knowledge of the world. Therefore, although Kant is convinced that "all our knowledge *begins* with experience," as empiricists like Hume had claimed, "it does not follow that it all *arises* out of experience." [4]

---

[3] Immanuel Kant *Critique of Pure Reason,* trans. N. K. Smith (London: Macmillan, 1929), B. 30. Hereafter, references to the *Critique of Pure Reason* will be to the N. K. Smith translation.
[4] *Ibid.,* B. 1 (italics added).

The a priori element which our own reason "supplies from itself" is Kant's primary concern in the *Critique of Pure Reason*.

Kant sees no problem concerning the possibility of a priori judgments that are "analytic," i.e., judgments in which the predicate merely explicates the subject without adding anything to it. Their truth depends upon the law of contradiction, since their denial involves a logical contradiction. His problem is limited to the possibility of a priori "synthetic" judgments, i.e., judgments in which the predicate amplifies the subject and which therefore extend our knowledge. Mathematics, natural science, and metaphysics alike consist of propositions which are not only *a priori* but also *synthetic*, i.e., judgments which do not arise from our experience and yet claim to add something to our knowledge. For example, the judgment in arithmetic "5 + 7 = 12" and the judgment in physics "every event has a cause" are *synthetic* a priori judgments, since in neither case can the predicate be found by analysis of the subject to be contained in it. Hence, the general question of the *Critique* is: "How are synthetic judgments a priori possible?" More specifically, how are such judgments possible in mathematics? in natural science? and in metaphysics? [5]

The key to an understanding of his answers to these questions is found in the assumption behind his "Copernican revolution" in the theory of knowledge. As Copernicus had assumed that the earth moves around the sun rather than the sun around the earth, Kant suggests the hypothesis that for objects to be known they must conform to the mind, not the mind to objects. This does not imply that the mind creates its objects in knowing them but that things cannot become objects of knowledge unless they conform to certain conditions imposed by the cognitive faculties of the mind. It assumes that the mind is active rather than passive in the process of knowing and that it adds something of its own. What does it add? Kant's general answer is that, while the *content* of our knowledge is derived from sense experience, the *form* is imposed by reason and that this provides the a priori element in our knowledge. "Our knowledge," he says, "springs from two fundamental sources of the mind; the first is the capacity of receiving impressions (receptivity for impressions), the second is the power of knowing an object through these representations. . . . Through the first an object is *given* to us, through the second the object is *thought* in relation to that [given] representation." [6] The first of these "powers" or faculties he calls *sensibility*, the second *understanding*. Their cooperation is indispensable to all knowledge of objects. "Without sensibility

[5] *Ibid.*, B. 20, 21, 22.   [6] *Ibid.*, B. 74.

no object would be given to us, without understanding no object would be thought. Thoughts without content are empty, intuitions without concepts are blind." [7] In order to answer the question concerning synthetic a priori judgments, therefore, it is necessary to analyze these two cognitive faculties of our reason.

Kant's analysis of *sensibility* in the *Critique* [8] discloses that, although it is the faculty of receptivity through which objects are presented to us by means of impressions, it also contains "forms of intuition," *space and time,* and imposes these upon all its impressions. Hence, it is impossible for us to experience objects except as they conform to space and time as forms of our sensibility. Our sense impressions are ordered in relation to one another in space and they occur in succession to one another in time. But they are ordered in these ways, not because space and time are objective realities in which objects are located and events occur, but because they are subjective forms which we bring with us to all sense experience and by means of which we relate our impressions to one another. As such, they are a priori "forms of intuition" belonging to our "sensibility." In a manner we cannot here describe, Kant argues that it is these forms of space and time which make the synthetic a priori propositions of mathematics possible.

Similarly, his examination of the *understanding* [9] as the faculty of thinking the objects of experience discloses the fact that it possesses *categories* such as substance and cause by means of which it relates the "manifold" of sense impressions to one another and organizes them into a coherent whole of objects of experience. These categories are not innate ideas but forms of synthesis belonging to our understanding and brought into play when impressions are presented to it by our sensibility. By means of these "categories" and the "principles" of understanding through which they are applied to sense impressions, experience as a coherent and organized whole of objects in space and time is rendered possible. Since these "categories" and "principles" belong to our understanding as forms of its synthesizing activity and are brought with it to its task of thinking all objects presented to it, they are a priori. Hence, we know in advance the general *form* which all objects of experience must take, since our understanding can think them only by imposing its categories upon them and making them conform to its own structure. Of course, the *content* of our knowledge of objects cannot be anticipated in this way but must come to us through experi-

[7] *Ibid.,* B. 75.   [8] *Ibid., Transcendental Aesthetic.*
[9] *Ibid., Transcendental Analytic.*

ence. Natural laws, for example, must be discovered by empirical observation and inductive generalization. But synthetic a priori judgments such as "Every event must have a cause" and "The quantity of
matter remains constant through all changes" are derived from the
categories and principles of our understanding.[10] Since a priori judgments such as these are necessary conditions of the possibility of experience as an orderly whole and therefore of natural science, they
provide the answer to the question: "How is pure science of nature
possible?"

In broad outline, then, the main *positive* result of the critical examination of sensibility and understanding is that synthetic a priori
judgments of mathematics and natural science are possible by means of
the forms of sensibility and categories and principles of understanding
which are imposed by reason upon the manifold of impressions. But
Kant also draws an important *negative* conclusion from this analysis, a
conclusion which has a decisive effect on his thinking about metaphysics in general and rational theology in particular. Since space,
time, and the categories are applicable only to objects presented by
"sensuous intuition," he argues, we can have knowledge only of things
as they appear to us, *phenomena*, while "things-in-themselves,"
noumena, are forever beyond our capacity to know. If we had the
power of nonsensuous or intellectual intuition, it might be possible for
things-in-themselves to be presented to us and be known by reason.
But since that power is lacking in us, only sensible objects can be
known and supersensible or transcendent objects are beyond the reach
of reason. Two of Kant's reasons for asserting the existence of things-in-
themselves despite the fact that they cannot be known are interesting.
The first is that it is necessary to account for that which is given in
experience.[11] The second is that, as we shall see, reason possesses
certain "Ideas," such as freedom and God, which do not correspond to
objects in the world of phenomena but which suggest transcendent
objects in the world behind phenomena.[12] Thus, while our faculties of
sensibility and understanding make mathematical and scientific knowledge of the sensible world of phenomena possible, reason can know

[10] The justification for asserting that, although they are subjective in the sense
of being forms of synthesis of our understanding, they can give us knowledge of
objective reality is that they constitute objects from the multiplicity of sense
impressions, that without them experience as a coherent and organized whole of
objects in space and time would be impossible. This is the main point of Kant's
difficult "transcendental deduction of the categories," which is not so much a
deduction as a *justification*.

[11] A. C. Ewing, *A Short Commentary on Kant's Critique of Pure Reason*
(London: Methuen, 1938), p. 191.

[12] *Ibid.*, p. 195.

only *that* there are things in themselves beyond phenomena but not *what* they are.

METAPHYSICS AND RATIONAL THEOLOGY

The implications of this restriction of knowledge to phenomena for *metaphysics* are obvious. They are worked out in the "Transcendental Dialectic" of the first *Critique* which examines the claims of *reason* to give us knowledge of transcendent or supersensible objects. It should be noted that "reason" is used in this connection not for the reason *as a whole* but for that *faculty* of reason which "seeks for the *unconditioned* which makes possible the totality of conditions for any given conditioned." [13] As logic seeks for the ultimate ground of the premises from which a conclusion is drawn, "reason" seeks for something unconditioned behind conditioned objects as their ultimate ground.

There are three of these *Ideas* of "reason" which serve this function, and it is with these that metaphysics, as Kant interprets it, is primarily concerned. First, there is the Idea of a permanent ego, or subject, conceived as a spiritual substance, or *soul*. It is the purpose of "Rational Psychology" to demonstrate the existence and immortality of such a substance. Second, there is the Idea of the *world* as the totality of the causal sequences of phenomena. This is the Idea with which "Rational Cosmology" is concerned. Third, there is the Idea of *God* as the supreme reality (*ens realissimum*) which is the ultimate presupposition or ground of all phenomena. This is the "Ideal" which "Rational Theology" attempts to demonstrate. Kant examines each of these Ideas in turn to determine its validity.

Kant maintains that the Idea of Rational Psychology, i.e., that of a permanent, identical, spiritual substance or *soul*, involves "paralogisms" or logical fallacies. He had argued that the "transcendental unity of apperception" or "I think" must accompany all representations if objects of experience are to be known. But to say that such a *logical subject* is a presupposition of the possibility of knowledge is not to affirm the existence of a *spiritual substance* or *soul*. In order to know that such a substance exists, we would need to have a nonsensuous intuition of it, and we possess only the capacity for sensuous intuitions.

Moreover, I have no right to infer from the fact that I distinguish myself as a thinking being from other things outside myself, including my body, that there is an *immaterial* and therefore an *immortal* soul. Kant admits that I do distinguish myself from external objects in this

---

[13] Kant, *Critique of Pure Reason*, B. 379.

way. "But I do not thereby learn," he says, "whether this consciousness of myself would be even possible apart from things outside me
through which representations are given to me, and whether, therefore, I could exist merely as thinking being (i.e. without existing in
human form.)" [14] However, he is not afraid that this rejection of the
metaphysical proof of immortality will jeopardize men's belief in it,
for he holds that the belief has never really been based upon "merely
speculative proof."

These and other criticisms of the Idea of Rational Psychology are
based upon the assumption that we have no nonsensuous intuition of a
substantial soul. This assumption leads Kant to a conclusion concerning
the self that is very serious: the self can be known only as an *empirical
ego* composed of psychical states or phenomena succeeding one another in time and determined by the law of causality. Thus, the self as
known becomes merely an object in the phenomenal world of nature.
It is true that a "logical subject" or "I think" must also be presupposed
to make knowledge, including the knowledge of this empirical ego,
possible. But nothing further can be said about the self, and the main
point of the "paralogisms" is that we cannot know it as a substantial,
spiritual, immortal reality.

As the reason commits "paralogisms," or fallacies, when it seeks to
demonstrate propositions about the soul in Rational Psychology, it falls
into "antinomies," or contradictions, when it comes to grips with problems concerning the *world* in Rational Cosmology. For example, it is
able to prove both the "thesis" that "the world has a beginning in time
and is also limited as regards space" and the "antithesis" that "the
world has no beginning and no limits in space; it is infinite as regards
both time and space." [15]

The most interesting of these "antinomies" for our purposes is the
third, since it deals with the question of *freedom*, one of the major
metaphysical ideas with which Kant is concerned. The "thesis" argues
that causality in accordance with laws of nature is not the only causality but that "it is necessary to assume that there is another causality,
that of freedom." [16] The "antithesis" argues that "there is no freedom;
everything in the world takes place solely in accordance with laws of
nature." [17] The proof of the thesis is that, if there is no other causality
than that according to laws of nature, there can be no first beginning
and the series of causes cannot be completed.[18] The proof of the

[14] *Ibid.*, B. 409.   [15] *Ibid.*, B. 454, 455.   [16] *Ibid.*, B. 472.   [17] *Ibid.*
[18] *Ibid.*, B. 474.

antithesis is that a spontaneous or free cause would be contrary to the causal law and would make the unity of experience impossible.[19] Kant remarks that the thesis and antithesis represent two different and conflicting interests of reason. The thesis is favored by the "practical interest" in the beginning of the world and the freedom of the will as "foundation stones of morals and religion," as well as by the "speculative interest" in the completion of the task of causal explanation.[20] The antithesis, on the other hand, is favored by no practical interest but is demanded by the "speculative interest" in extending our certain knowledge by investigating the laws of nature.[21]

Kant suggests that the antinomy cannot be resolved so long as Rationalism and Empiricism, which are motivated by these conflicting interests, maintain their positions. But if the point of view of his Critical Philosophy is adopted and a distinction is made between phenomena and things-in-themselves, a solution is possible. For *both* thesis *and* antithesis can be true, the former with respect to things-in-themselves and the latter with respect to phenomena. We can say that our wills are *free* in their acts as things-in-themselves, although we cannot demonstrate the fact, but their acts are causally *determined* as phenomena. This is possible if the self in its "intelligible character" belongs to the realm of things-in-themselves and exercises freedom by acting in accordance with moral rather than natural laws, while in its "empirical character" it belongs to the realm of phenomena and its acts are determined by antecedent causes.[22] In this way, both the practical interest of morality in freedom and the speculative interest of science in determinism can be maintained. Kant concedes that this solution does not establish the *reality* of freedom, since we do not have knowledge of things-in-themselves; but it shows that "causality through freedom is at least *not incompatible* with nature." [23] Thus, the way is left open for an affirmation of the reality of freedom if it can be shown to be necessary on other than theoretical grounds, i.e., as a presupposition of moral action.

After his critical examination of the claims of Rational Psychology and Cosmology, Kant turns to the third branch of metaphysics, Rational Theology. The Idea of reason with which Rational Theology is concerned is the idea of "the most real Being," *ens realissimum*, which is the unconditioned condition of the possibility of everything that exists. Since it contains in itself all possible perfections, it is "the most perfect Being," *ens perfectissimum*. It is one, simple, individual Being.

[19] *Ibid.*, B. 475.   [20] *Ibid.*, B. 495.   [21] *Ibid.*, B. 496.
[22] *Ibid.*, B. 561–585.   [23] *Ibid.*, B. 586.

Finally, it is a necessary Being and the ultimate cause of all finite beings. The question faced by the critical philosopher is whether this Being is only an Idea of reason or whether it is also *real*. To answer this question, Kant considers in turn the three arguments of Rational Theology for the existence of God: the ontological, cosmological, and teleological arguments. In view of his conclusion that our knowledge is restricted to phenomena, it is not surprising that he is critical of these traditional arguments.

The *ontological* argument is regarded by Kant as the most fundamental, since it starts from the idea of a Perfect Being and the other arguments must finally depend upon it if they are to arrive at the existence of such a Being. Anselm had argued that we have in our minds the idea of a being than which no greater can be conceived and that to deny the existence of such a being outside our minds corresponding to this idea would involve a contradiction; and Descartes had insisted that the idea of a Perfect Being, or God, implies His existence with the same necessity as the sum of the angles of a triangle must equal two right angles. Thus the ontological argument is an a priori one, moving from the concept of God to His existence. "It is declared," says Kant, "that it [the concept of the *ens realissimum*] possesses all reality, and that we are justified in assuming that such a being is possible. . . . Now [the argument proceeds] 'all reality' includes existence; existence is therefore contained in the concept of a thing that is possible. If, then, this thing is rejected, the internal possibility of the thing is rejected—which is self-contradictory." [24]

In criticism, Kant points out that if "God exists" is an *analytic* proposition, the assertion of existence in the predicate adds nothing to the subject so that we have "nothing but a miserable tautology." [25] Of course, if existence is surreptitiously introduced into the idea of a being, the conclusion can be drawn that it exists. But then one is only asserting the tautology that an existent being exists. "I can draw the conclusion," says Copleston, "that the being exists from its concept or idea only because I have already put existence into the idea, thus begging the whole question." [26] In reality, Kant argues, propositions asserting existence are *synthetic* rather than analytic and therefore can be denied without contradiction. Of course, if we reject the predicate while retaining the subject, a contradiction results. "But if we reject subject and predicate alike, there is no contradiction; for nothing is then left that can be contradicted. To posit a triangle, and yet to reject its three angles, is self-contradictory; but there is no contradiction in

[24] *Ibid.*, B. 625.   [25] *Ibid.*, B. 626.
[26] Copleston, *History of Philosophy*, Vol. VI, p. 296.

rejecting the triangle together with its three angles. The same holds true of the concept of an absolutely necessary being. If its existence is rejected, we reject the thing itself with all its predicates; no question of contradiction can then arise." [27]

The root of the error, Kant says, lies in the assumption that existence is a "real predicate" which adds something to the other predicates or attributes of a thing. "*'Being'* is obviously not a real predicate; that is, it is not a concept of something which could be added to the concept of a thing. It is merely the positing of a thing, or of certain determinations, as existing in themselves." [28] Therefore, if we say "God is" we do not add a new predicate or attribute to the concept of God.[29] "Otherwise stated, the real contains no more than the possible. A hundred real thalers do not contain the least coin more than a hundred possible thalers. . . . For the object, as it actually exists, is not analytically contained in my concept, but is added to my concept . . . synthetically." [30]

If, then, the proposition "God exists" is a synthetic judgment in which the predicate is not a "real predicate" or attribute *contained in* the subject but is *added to* it, there is no contradiction involved in denying it. The conclusion Kant draws from this is that it is logically impossible to pass from the mere *idea* or concept of a being to its *existence,* but that there must be evidence in experience to justify the assertion that it exists. In the case of objects of the senses, we can attain this evidence either immediately or through inferences connecting them with perception. Unfortunately, the existence of God cannot be known in this way because He is not a sensible object capable of being perceived by the senses. Therefore, "we can no more extend our stock of [theoretical] insight by mere ideas, than a merchant can better his position by adding a few noughts to his cash account." [31]

In contrast to the ontological argument, the *cosmological* argument is a posteriori, inferring the existence of God as a necessary Being from experience of the contingency of the world. "It runs thus: If anything exists, an absolutely necessary being must also exist. Now I, at least, exist. Therefore, an absolutely necessary being exists." [32] Kant maintains that in this argument there lies hidden "a whole nest of dialectical assumptions" which are unwarranted. For example, it takes for granted that the causal principle can be applied to a cause which is beyond the sensible world of phenomena, whereas the *Critique* has shown that the categories and principles of the understanding such as causality have

[27] Kant, *Critique of Pure Reason,* B. 626.   [28] *Ibid.,* B. 627.
[29] *Ibid.*   [30] *Ibid.*   [31] *Ibid.,* B. 630.   [32] *Ibid.,* B. 633.

meaning and application only to objects of experience.[33] Also, it assumes the impossibility of an infinite series of causes in the sensible world. But this conclusion is not justified "even within the world of experience, still less beyond this world in a realm into which this series can never be extended." [34]

In attacking these assumptions, Kant is only repeating criticisms Hume had already made in his *Dialogues*. But in a third criticism he goes further. When the cosmological argument has arrived at the conclusion that there is a necessary being, the conception of that being is found to be indeterminate. In order to determine the properties of the necessary being, the argument then asserts that only the concept of the *ens realissimum* can determine it completely and concludes that that being, i.e., the Supreme Being, necessarily exists. "What properties this [necessary] being may have, the empirical premise cannot tell us. Reason therefore abandons experience altogether, and endeavours to discover from mere concepts what properties an absolutely necessary being must have. . . . Now, these, it is supposed, are nowhere to be found save in the concept of an *ens realissimum;* and the conclusion is therefore drawn that the *ens realissimum* is the absolutely necessary being. But it is evident that we are here presupposing that the concept of the highest reality is completely adequate to the concept of absolute necessity of existence; that is, that the latter can be inferred from the former. Now this is the proposition maintained by the ontological proof. . . . Thus the so-called cosmological proof owes any cogency which it may have to the ontological proof from mere concepts." [35]

This last criticism seems to be invalid, if the cosmological argument claims only to prove the existence of a necessary being without determining its nature. Of course, if it claims also to prove that the necessary being is the Supreme or Perfect Being, as Kant seems to think, it can complete its proof only by identifying the former with the latter. But if not, it does not need to prove the existence of a necessary being a priori from the idea of a Perfect Being, since it has already proved its existence as the cause of the contingent beings in the world.[36] However, Kant is pointing out a limitation of the cosmological argument: it proves at the most the existence of a necessary being but cannot determine the nature of that being. This leaves it uncertain whether the argument has proved the existence of the God men worship, i.e., a Perfect Being.

The third argument for the existence of God is the *teleological* or

[33] *Ibid.*, B. 638.   [34] *Ibid.*   [35] *Ibid.*, B. 635.
[36] Frederick Copleston, *History of Philosophy*, Vol. VI, p. 299.

"physico-theological" argument. It starts from experience of the order of nature. "This proof," says Kant, "always deserves to be mentioned with respect. It is the oldest, the clearest, and the most accordant with the common reason of mankind." [37] He even says that it would be "utterly vain to attempt to diminish in any way the authority of this argument" and that "one glance at the wonders of nature and the majesty of the universe" is sufficient to dispel any doubts suggested by speculation.[38]

Nevertheless, Kant cannot approve its claim to have established the certainty of its conclusion without the need for further support from other sources. What those other sources are we shall see when we consider the *Critique of Practical Reason*. In the first *Critique*, Kant confines himself to pointing out certain logical flaws in the argument which prevent it from being adequate in and by itself. Unlike Hume, he admits that "if we are to specify a cause at all, we cannot here proceed more securely than by analogy with those purposive productions of which alone the cause and mode of action are fully known to us." [39] But he points out that, since the argument proves the contingency of the form but not of the matter of the world, it can only lead to "an architect of the world who is always very much hampered by the adaptability of the material in which he works, not a *creator* of the world to whose idea everything is subject." [40] Moreover, the argument can prove at the most, as Hume has said, the existence of a cause "proportioned" to the order and purposiveness actually observable in the world but not the omnipotence, supreme wisdom, and perfection of this cause.[41] Therefore, it shifts its ground and infers from the contingency of natural order the existence of a *necessary Being*, as in the cosmological argument, and then passes on to the concept of a *Perfect Being*, as in the ontological argument. Thus the teleological argument rests upon the cosmological and the cosmological upon the ontological.

Since the cosmological and teleological arguments have been shown to have logical flaws in them and to fall back upon the ontological argument to complete themselves and since the ontological argument has been shown to be fallacious, Kant concludes that the attempt of Rational Theology to demonstrate the existence of God has failed. However, the results of his critical examination of it have not been wholly negative. Rational Theology, he points out, may be of great value in correcting and making consistent the concept of a Supreme Being. For if the *existence* of such a Being could be established in some

[37] Kant, *Critique of Pure Reason*, B. 652.   [38] *Ibid.*   [39] *Ibid.*, B. 654.
[40] *Ibid.*, B. 655.   [41] *Ibid.*, B. 656.

other way "it would be of the greatest importance accurately to determine this concept on its transcendental side, as the concept of a necessary and supremely real being, to free it from whatever . . . is out of
keeping with the supreme reality, and at the same time to dispose of all
counter-assertions, atheistic, deistic, or anthropomorphic." [42] "Thus,
while for the merely speculative employment of reason the supreme
being remains a mere *ideal*, it is yet an *ideal without a flaw*, a concept
which completes and crowns the whole of human knowledge." [43] In
this way, Kant concludes his critique of Rational Theology on a more
positive note than has usually been recognized. In indicating that the
Idea of God developed by Rational Theology may prove indispensable
if His existence can be established on other grounds, he looks forward
to the reconstruction of theology on a moral basis in the *Critique of
Practical Reason*.

However, Kant's general verdict on the claims to knowledge of all
three branches of metaphysics—Rational Psychology, Cosmology, and
Theology—is negative. The Ideas of Reason, he says, have only a
"regulative," not a "constitutive," function. For we cannot attain
knowledge of things-in-themselves by means of the categories and
principles of our understanding. While the Ideas of Reason have an
indispensable regulative function of directing the understanding toward the attainment of the greatest possible extension and unity of its
knowledge,[44] they can never give us knowledge of objects which transcend the world of phenomena.

THE FIRST CRITIQUE: AN EVALUATION

A critical evaluation of Kant's conclusions in the first *Critique*, especially with respect to Rational Theology, must be based upon a general
estimate of his theory of knowledge. For our purposes, it is not necessary to consider his vindication of the possibility of synthetic a priori
judgments in mathematics and natural science. It is generally recognized that his great achievement in this constructive part of his task is
his insistence that knowledge of objects can be obtained only by the
cooperation of sense and understanding. This enables him to avoid the
extreme positions of Empiricism and Rationalism and to do more justice than either of them to both experience and reason as the major
sources of our knowledge.

Unfortunately, in making his synthesis he fell into several kinds of
dualism which led him to limit the capacity of reason for knowledge to

[42] *Ibid.*, B. 669.   [43] *Ibid.*, B. 670.   [44] *Ibid.*, B. 673.

the world of phenomena. The first of these is a dualism between *sensibility* and *understanding*. This vitiates his interpretation of both the empirical and the rational elements in knowledge. Sensibility is defined as "receptivity," the capacity to receive representations of objects, and it is conceived as presenting to our minds a "manifold" of impressions. In sharp contrast, understanding is defined as the "spontaneity" or constructive capacity of the mind in thinking objects, and it is conceived as synthesizing this manifold of impressions. Thus, the sensibility is passive, receiving a welter of impressions ordered only in the forms of space and time, while the understanding actively judges objects by means of its categories and thus constitutes them. Since the understanding *imposes* a form, or structure, of its own upon unorganized sense impressions, the reader is left with the question whether the form which is imposed corresponds to anything in the impressions themselves. At this point Kant goes too far in the direction of Rationalism by ascribing too much to the reason. The constructive activity of the understanding does not *constitute* objects by imposing a form of its own upon impressions but responds to the form discovered by experience in the objects and makes it explicit. Its function is not to constitute but to *interpret* objects. This implies that the categories it uses in its interpretation are not a priori in Kant's sense of "independent of experience" but are based upon qualities and relations discovered in the objects by experience.

But if Kant ascribes too much to the understanding with respect to the form of knowledge, he ascribes too much to the *sensibility* with respect to the *content*. At this point, he goes too far in the direction of Empiricism. Like Hume, he holds that "all our knowledge begins with experience," [45] so that the origin of all the content of our knowledge is in sense impressions. The only way we can perceive objects and present them to the mind is by sensuous intuition. Although there may be other rational beings with the capacity for nonsensuous or intellectual intuition, e.g., God, man's reason possesses only a sensuous intuition. Consequently, the only objects which can be perceived by us are sensible ones.

This narrow view of the experience of objects which limits it to sense impressions leads to another kind of dualism, that between *phenomena* and *things-in-themselves*. Kant maintains that we know objects only as they *appear* to our senses and can never know them as they are *in themselves*. Since we can know objects only as sensuous

[45] *Ibid.*, B. 1.

intuition presents representations of them to the mind, we can never push aside the veil of phenomena and know things-in-themselves. This conclusion is as unwarranted as the assumption upon which it rests, i.e., that all knowledge of objects is derived from sense experience. We know not merely the *appearances* of things but things-in-themselves *in* and *through* their appearances. Of course, our knowledge of them can never be exhaustive, because of the complexity of their structure, qualities, and relations. For this reason, the distinction between appearance and reality is a useful one, reminding us that our knowledge of an object, whether physical or mental, is never complete and must be corrected and supplemented by further knowledge. But the distinction does not justify us in setting up a dualism between phenomena and things-in-themselves and thus asserting that we can have knowledge of the former but are forever shut out from knowledge of the latter.

There is also a third dualism which arises from the dualism between sensibility and understanding and between phenomena and things-in-themselves. It is the dualism or at least the contrast between the *understanding,* which is "constitutive" of objects, and the *reason,* which is only "regulative" in its function. If Kant had not regarded the understanding as *constituting* objects by means of its categories and principles, the sharp contrast between it and the reason which only regulates or directs the understanding in its effort to attain unity and completeness in its knowledge could have been avoided. For the categories of the understanding would have been conceived as performing a function essentially like that of the Ideas of Reason. The categories would have been conceived as interpreting objects of experience as *parts* of an organized whole, Ideas of Reason as completing the task of interpretation by offering the most adequate explanation possible of the *whole.* Although Kant sometimes seems to approach this positive view of the Ideas of Reason, his usual attitude toward them is highly critical. For example, he speaks of the "transcendental illusion" that the Ideas can give us knowledge of things-in-themselves. "In defiance of all the warning of criticism, it carries us altogether beyond the empirical employment of categories and puts us off with a merely deceptive extension of pure understanding," [46] and "even after its deceptiveness has been exposed, [it] will not cease to play tricks with reason and continually entrap it into momentary aberrations ever and again calling for correction." [47]

As we have seen, this negative attitude toward the Ideas of Reason

[46] *Ibid.*, B. 352.   [47] *Ibid.*, A. 298, B. 355.

in metaphysics and Rational Theology is largely the result of Kant's dualism between phenomena and things-in-themselves and his more fundamental dualism between sensibility and understanding. Only if these dualisms are uncritically accepted—and we have given reasons for thinking that they should not be—is it necessary to accept the conclusion that metaphysics and Rational Theology are impossible.

His rejection of metaphysics and Rational Theology was also due to his reaction against the dogmatism of the rationalistic metaphysics of Wolff and others. He was fully justified in denying the claim of this dogmatic Rationalism to demonstrate propositions in metaphysics with the same certainty as mathematicians demonstrate propositions in geometry. Although we have argued that the Ideas of metaphysics are necessary in order to complete the interpretation of objects by the categories, the scope of metaphysics is more comprehensive than that of science, for metaphysics seeks to interpret reality as a whole, while science is limited to natural phenomena. This means that its task is never finished and that dogmatism is out of place. Furthermore the propositions of metaphysics, unlike scientific propositions, are not verifiable by an appeal to sense experience. This is largely responsible for the failure of any metaphysical theory to win agreement as the sciences are able to do. However, this does not make metaphysics any the less valuable and necessary. For the Ideas of metaphysics are required for the interpretation of reality as a whole and decisions with respect to basic metaphysical issues are inescapable despite the fact that they cannot be logically demonstrated or experimentally verified.

Thus, Kant was justified in unmasking the pretensions of rationalistic metaphysics. Unfortunately, he could conceive of no other kind of metaphysics and therefore denied altogether the possibility of attaining knowledge of things-in-themselves. Yet he himself had shown the way to another kind of metaphysics. As the justification for the application of the *categories* of understanding to objects of the senses is that they are necessary conditions of the interpretation of natural phenomena, so the justification for the use of *Ideas* of reason in metaphysics is that they are necessary conditions of the interpretation of reality as a whole. Kant did not see this because he could not escape from the assumption of Empiricism that knowledge is limited to objects through the senses. As a result, he was able to expose the excesses of rationalistic metaphysics but could not replace it by a less dogmatic metaphysics of his own.

Thus, Kant's criticisms of Rational Psychology, Cosmology, and Theology are not conclusive, although they indicate weaknesses in the metaphysics of his time. The Ideas of the soul, freedom, and God are indispensable for the interpretation of reality if other aspects of experience than those dealt with by science are taken into account.

1. With respect to Rational Psychology, it seems clear that the idea of the *soul* or mind as a spiritual reality which is identical with itself through the succession of its changing states is indispensable for the interpretation of activities such as thinking and willing and dispositions such as moral virtues. Whether it should be called a "substance," and if so in what sense, is doubtless a question which needs to be reconsidered in the light of modern philosophy of mind, and the question of its "immortality" cannot be answered as simply as Wolff thought. But it is impossible to accept Kant's view that we know only the "empirical ego" which consists of psychical states succeeding one another in time and causally connected with one another. As Kant himself emphasized, knowledge would be impossible if there were not an "I think" which accompanies all objects of experience and binds them together in one consciousness, and in self-consciousness we are aware that this is a spiritual reality. Similarly, moral activity and character would be unintelligible if there were no spiritual reality which is identical with itself through its states. The fact that we cannot have a sensuous intuition of it is irrelevant because it is a spiritual being rather than a sensible object.

2. With respect to Rational Cosmology, we have seen that Kant's solution of the "antinomy" between the thesis of *freedom* and the antithesis of *determinism* is that both can be true if freedom is ascribed to the noumenal self and determinism to the phenomenal or empirical self. This solution is ingenious but unconvincing. That an act should be both noumenally free as the timeless product of a transcendental self and phenomenally determined as the product in time of an empirical self determined by natural laws is unintelligible. As Ewing says, "That the self can be subject to this peculiar dual causality is a difficult doctrine and from the nature of the case cannot be made clear." [48] It "cannot be made clear" because it banishes freedom from the phenomenal self whose acts are known to a hypothetical noumenal self whose acts cannot be known because it is a thing-in-itself. Also, it is incredible that an act should be *both* completely determined by antecedent events and predictable from the "empirical character" of the self *and* free as an expression of its timeless "intelligible character." "A solution is rendered impossible," Kemp Smith says, "by the very terms in which he formulates the problem. If the spiritual and the natural be opposed to one another as the timeless and the temporal, and if the natural be further viewed as a unitary system, individual moral free-

[48] Ewing, *A Short Commentary on Kant's Critique of Pure Reason*, p. 230.

dom is no longer defensible." [49] If we are to defend freedom, there-fore, we must not accept Kant's view of nature (including mind) as a "unitary system" in which every event is determined by natural laws and we must insist that freedom belongs to the empirical rather than the noumenal self.[50]

3. It is impossible to evaluate fully Kant's criticisms of the tradi-tional proofs of the existence of *God* until we consider his reconstruc-tion of theology in the second *Critique*. However, most philosophers of religion would agree with him that these proofs are not *demonstrations* whose conclusion is certain, for he has indicated logical flaws and limitations in the ontological, cosmological, and teleological proofs as they were formulated in his own time. The question remains, however, whether one or more of them can be reformulated in such a way that the existence of God can be shown to be the most *adequate explana-tion* of the world when all aspects of experience are taken seriously and when the claim to certainty is abandoned.[51] Since Kant could not conceive a kind of Rational Theology which would be more modest in its claim than that of the dogmatic Rationalism of his time, he did not consider this question. However, we shall see that in the second and third *Critiques* he made valuable contributions to the later develop-ment of such a Rational Theology.

ETHICAL THEOLOGY

In his *Critique of Practical Reason*, Kant attempts to reconstruct theology on an ethical foundation. Having attacked the "pretensions" of theoretical reason to *demonstrate* the existence of God, freedom of the will, and immortality of the soul, he seeks to restore *rational belief* in them as "postulates of practical reason." Since he bases his argument upon his conception of morality as formulated in his *Groundwork of the Metaphysics of Morals*, it is necessary to indicate briefly the nature of that conception.

The good will, says Kant, is characterized by its form. It is good in itself and not merely in relation to something else such as happiness.

---

[49] N. K. Smith, *A Commentary to Kant's "Critique of Pure Reason"* (London: Macmillan, 1918), p. 518.

[50] Ewing, *op. cit.*, p. 239.

[51] For example, although the criticisms of the ontological argument by Kant have been regarded by most modern philosophers as conclusive, there has recently been a revival of interest in the argument, and several interesting defenses of it have been made from different points of view. One of these may be found in Norman Malcolm's essay on "Anselm's Ontological Arguments" in *Knowledge and Certainty* (Englewood Cliffs, N.J.: Prentice-Hall, 1963), and another in Charles Hartshorne, *The Logic of Perfection* (La Salle, Ill.: Open Court, 1962), Chap. 3.

For it seeks in all its acts to conform to the moral law from the motive of respect for that law, doing its duty for duty's sake. Moral laws are not derived from experience of the good and bad consequences of different kinds of acts; they are laid down a priori by the practical reason. They are not "hypothetical" imperatives conditional upon the adoption of certain ends or objects of desire; rather, they are derived from a "categorical imperative" which imposes duties upon us unconditionally. We should always act in accordance with these laws whether they agree with our natural inclinations and conduce to our happiness or not. Kant expresses the categorical imperative in such a way as to emphasize the universal validity of moral laws. "Act only on the maxim whereby thou canst at the same time will that it should become a universal law." [52] Again, since man as a rational being is an end in himself, i.e., an end which possesses absolute and not merely relative value, the categorical imperative can be formulated in another way. "So act as to treat humanity, whether in thine own person or in that of any other, in every case as an end withal, never as means only." [53] Finally, since every rational being should always have the ideal before him of a kingdom of ends in which each person treats every other person as an end in himself, he should act as though he were through his maxims laying down universal laws for a Kingdom of ends.[54]

It was because Kant conceived of morality in this rigorous and lofty fashion that he could make it the foundation of religious beliefs. If he had regarded moral conduct in a Utilitarian manner as merely a means to nonmoral ends such as happiness or in modern sociological terms as conformity to the moral rules of a particular society, he could hardly have spoken of "reverence" for the moral law. "Two things," he says, "fill the mind with ever new and increasing admiration and awe, the oftener and the more steadily we reflect on them: *the starry heavens above and the moral law within.*" [55] Because of this reverence for the moral law, Kant regarded the consciousness of duty in the presence of it as the ground for belief in a supersensible or noumenal world and in the dignity of human persons as members of it as well as of the phenomenal world of nature. The origin of duty, he says, "can be nothing less than a power which elevates man above himself (as a part of the world of sense), a power which connects him with an order of things that only the understanding can conceive. . . . It is, then, not to be wondered at that man, as belonging to both worlds, must regard his

---

[52] *Kant's Critique of Practical Reason and Other Works on the Theory of Ethics,* trans. T. K. Abbott (London: Longmans, Green, 1923), p. 38. Hereafter references to the *Critique of Practical Reason* will be to the Abbott translation.
        [53] *Ibid.,* p. 47.   [54] *Ibid.,* p. 57.   [55] *Ibid.,* p. 260.

own nature in reference to its second and highest characteristic only with reverence, and its laws with the highest respect." [56]

Man's knowledge that he is free is also bound up with his relation to the moral law. His *freedom* is not the freedom of indeterminism; it is the freedom to determine his actions by moral laws which the practical reason lays down instead of being determined by natural laws, as things in the sensible world are. Indeed, the ground of our knowledge (the *ratio cognoscendi*) of freedom is our consciousness of being subject to the categorical imperative. In the third "antinomy" of the first *Critique* Kant had argued that theoretical reason cannot prove freedom but that it leaves open the possibility of free or spontaneous causality. What remained for the theoretical reason a possibility is for the practical reason a reality. The fact that I am under obligation to do my duty implies that I am capable of doing it. "I ought, therefore I can." For the practical reason, in imposing moral laws upon the will, must presuppose that the will is free in the sense of being able to determine its acts by these laws instead of being determined by natural causes. Without "transcendental freedom," in the sense of independence of both external and internal natural causes, no moral law would be possible.[57] Thus, man's relation to the moral law enables him to know the reality of freedom, for freedom is a presupposition or condition of man's obedience to the moral law. As such, it is the first and most fundamental of the "postulates" of practical reason.

Are there other presuppositions of morality? In answering this question, Kant speaks of the "totality of the object" of the reason as the *summum bonum*.[58] The "supreme good," *supremum bonum*, is virtue, since virtue through conformity to the moral law is the "supreme condition" of everything desirable.[59] But it does not follow from this that virtue is the complete good, since this also includes happiness. Hence, the "complete" or "highest good," *summum bonum*, must include both virtue and happiness. Moreover, it requires the distribution of happiness "in exact proportion" to virtue, since virtue is "the worth of the person and his worthiness to be happy." [60] "Hence this *summum bonum*," says Kant, "expresses the whole, the perfect good, in which, however, virtue as the condition is always the supreme good, since it has no condition above it; whereas happiness, while it is pleasant to the possessor of it, is not of itself absolute and in all respects good, but always presupposes morally right behavior as its condition." [61]

Kant recognizes the difficulty involved in combining such hetero-

[56] *Ibid.*, p. 180.   [57] *Ibid.*, p. 190.   [58] *Ibid.*, p. 203.   [59] *Ibid.*, p. 206.
[60] *Ibid.*   [61] *Ibid.*, pp. 206, 207.

geneous elements as virtue and happiness in the *summum bonum*. The desire for happiness cannot be the cause or motive for virtue, as we have seen; and virtue does not always produce happiness, which depends upon the harmony of our desires with nature. But this "antinomy" admits a solution. Happiness in proportion to virtue is not unattainable unless one supposes that existence in the sensible world is the only existence available to man and that he must depend upon his own power alone to attain the *summum bonum*. But man may exist also as a noumenal reality in the supersensible world; and there may be a "mediate," if not an "immediate," causal connection between virtue and happiness through the agency of "an intelligent author of nature." [62] If this can be shown to be the case, the *summum bonum* will be seen to be a "true object" of the moral will and the moral law will have "objective reality." [63]

We are now in a position to understand Kant's arguments for the immortality of the soul and the existence of God as "postulates of the practical reason." *Immortality* must be postulated in order to make possible the attainment of virtue, the supreme condition and the primary element in the highest good, by perfect obedience to the moral law. Although the moral law demands such perfect obedience or "holiness," no person is capable of attaining it at any time in the sensible world. Therefore, "it can only be found in a *progress in infinitum* towards that perfect accordance" and "it is necessary to assume such a practical progress as the real object of our will." [64] "Now, this endless progress is only possible on the supposition of an *endless* duration of the *existence* and personality of the same rational being (which is called the immortality of the soul). The *summum bonum*, then, practically is only possible on the supposition of the immortality of the soul; consequently this immortality, being inseparably connected with the moral law, is a postulate of pure practical reason." [65] Kant adds that, although endless progress toward moral perfection is not the same as attainment of it, "the Infinite Being, to whom the condition of time is nothing, sees in this to us endless succession a whole of accordance with the moral law" and finds in it the holiness His justice requires.[66] Again, although a person cannot have complete assurance of perseverance throughout an endless duration, he may derive from the moral progress he has already made a "comforting hope," and "a prospect of a blessed future." [67]

[62] *Ibid.*, p. 211.   [63] *Ibid.*, p. 218.   [64] *Ibid.*   [65] *Ibid.*, pp. 218, 219.
[66] *Ibid.*, p. 219.   [67] *Ibid.*, p. 220.

Several comments on this argument may be made. Kant's view that it is impossible for anyone to attain moral perfection at any time in his life indicates a tension between his perfectionism with respect to the moral goal and his realism with respect to man's ability to reach it. His moral realism results from his view of the "radical evil" in human nature which is due to the opposition of our sensuous to our rational nature.[68] Duty is usually, if not always, contrary to our natural inclinations. Endless moral progress is made possible by immortality, but moral perfection is infinitely remote and therefore can never be attained. Hence we can hope for and entertain a *prospect* of an unending future, but the future life, it would seem, can hardly be a blessed life because the goal is never fully *attained*. Also the future state of the soul is described in moral rather than religious terms. According to the Christian view of eternal life, it is characterized by communion with God and His children. Although Kant refers to the "Infinite Being" who imputes to a person perfect virtue even if he has only made progress toward it, there is no mention of fellowship with God or other persons as a source of joy. Happiness is regarded as having its source solely in one's virtue.

Apart from doubts in connection with these points, one difficulty is certain to occur to anyone who reflects upon the argument. Even if one accepts the assumption that moral perfection is *demanded* by the moral law, what ground is there for the belief that this demand must be *satisfied* and therefore that an endless duration of time will be made available? Is it not possible that, while moral perfection is required of man, the present life offers him the only opportunity to attain it, and that if he cannot attain it in time he can never attain it at all? When this difficulty arises it becomes obvious that Kant is making a basic assumption in the argument which he does not make explicit. It is the assumption that the natural order, in accordance with which death threatens to prevent the attainment of moral perfection, is subordinate to the moral order. Since this subordination can only be brought about through the agency of a Being who is the ground of both the natural and the moral orders and has the power to harmonize them, it requires the further assumption of the existence of God. Thus the argument for the postulate of immortality is defective in that it says nothing about the existence of God which is presupposed by it. Only if this religious presupposition is made explicit does the moral argument produce conviction. But when it *is* made explicit, the immortality of the soul becomes not merely a "postulate of the practical reason" on strictly moral

    [68] Cf. Kant, *Religion within the Limits of Reason Alone*, trans. T. M. Greene and H. H. Hudson (New York: Harper & Row, 1960), Bks. I and II.

grounds but also a corollary of religious faith in a righteous and power-ful God who is the source of the natural order, has a moral purpose for man, and wills that man shall attain that purpose.

The postulate of the existence of *God* is also required, Kant argues, as a presupposition or condition of the attainment of the *summum bonum.* But it is the second rather than the first element of the *summum bonum,* i.e., happiness in proportion to virtue, which God is required to make possible. Since man is not the cause of nature but is only a part of it, he cannot by his own power bring nature into harmony with his moral purpose in order to assure happiness for him-self in proportion to his virtue. "Happiness," says Kant, "is the condi-tion of a rational being in the world with whom *everything goes ac-cording to his wish and will.*" [69] "Accordingly, the existence of a cause of all nature, distinct from nature itself, and containing the principle of this connection, namely, the exact harmony of happiness with morality, is also postulated." [70] What must be the nature of this cause? It must be a Supreme Being who possesses a *moral* character and is also the cause of nature by *intelligence* and *will,* i.e., God.[71] Therefore, it is necessary to presuppose the existence of God. The existence of God is not necessary either as a basis of obligation, since this would deny the autonomy of the practical reason, or because of the inability of man to obey the moral law without the aid of divine grace. The existence of God is postulated solely in order to harmonize the natural order with the moral end of man and thus to make possible the attainment of happiness in proportion to virtue.

Kant interprets Christianity as setting forth doctrines of the *summum bonum,* immortality, and God similar to his own. Christi-anity, too, demands moral perfection. However, conscious of "a con-stant propensity to transgression," it offers man a hope of immortality in order that he may progress toward perfection. Also it represents the world in which men strive to obey the moral law "as a *kingdom of God,* in which nature and morality are brought into a harmony foreign to each of itself, by a holy Author who makes the derived *summum bonum* possible." [72] This purely ethical interpretation of Christianity is qualified only by a passing reference to the "hope that if we act as well as it is in our *power to do,* then what is not in our power will come in to our aid from another source, whether we know how this may be or not." [73] But this oblique reference to divine Grace is not further devel-

[69] *Critique of Practical Reason* (Abbott trans.), p. 221.
[70] *Ibid.*
[71] *Ibid.,* p. 222.   [72] *Ibid.,* pp. 225, 226.
[73] *Ibid.,* p. 225.

oped. Kant's description of religion is exclusively ethical. Religion is *"the recognition of all duties as divine commands, not as sanctions, that is to say, arbitrary ordinances of a foreign will and contingent in themselves,* but as essential *laws* of every free will in itself, which, nevertheless, must be regarded as commands of the Supreme Being, because it is only from a morally perfect (holy and good) and at the same time all-powerful will and consequently only through harmony with this will, that we can hope to attain the *summum bonum* which the moral law makes it our duty to take as the object of our endeavours." [74]

Obviously, Kant's argument for the postulate of the existence of God is open to criticism.

1. The basic premise of the argument is that practical reason requires not only virtue but also happiness in exact proportion to virtue. Is this premise consistent with the spirit of morality at its best? In the earlier stages of Hebraic religion, there was a strong conviction that virtue would and should be rewarded with prosperity and happiness. But hard experience gradually taught the greatest prophets, such as Jeremiah, that the wicked prosper and the righteous often suffer. The Book of Job passionately affirmed that innocent as well as guilty men suffer and concluded with Job's reaffirmation of faith in God despite the fact that he could not see how his suffering as an innocent man was to be justified. Satan had cynically asked the Lord, "Doth Job fear God for nought?" (Job 3:9.) Job's refusal to repudiate his faith in the face of great adversity showed that the answer was, "Yes." Is this consistent with Kant's view that virtue must be accompanied in exact proportion by happiness if moral effort is to be meaningful? For the religious man, at least, the answer must surely be, "No." Thus Kant's view that virtue must be accompanied by happiness or the moral life will be jeopardized must be rejected. There is a sense in which Spinoza is right when he says, "Virtue is its own reward." Kant's error lay in the acceptance of a hedonistic view of happiness and in the attempt to combine it with the nobler and truer view that spiritual contentment rather than natural happiness is the proper accompaniment of virtue.

2. Whatever may be thought of Kant's assumption concerning the relation of virtue to happiness, the argument for God which he bases upon it is religiously unsatisfactory. For that argument comes perilously close to treating God as a mere instrument or servant of man's effort to obtain happiness in proportion to his virtue. "The hope of happiness," Kant says, "first begins with religion only." [75] Of course

----

[74] *Ibid.*, p. 226.   [75] *Ibid.*, p. 227.

Kant insists again and again that the condition of happiness is virtue, "worthiness to be happy," and that only those who have attained virtue have any claim upon God for happiness. Since religion must regard moral laws as divine commands, God is primarily concerned with the moral condition under which happiness is to be deserved. However, it cannot be denied that even when the misleading impression of God as a sort of "celestial errand boy" is removed, Kant's view is religiously inadequate. The "autonomy" of the practical reason, as Kant conceives it, requires that men perform their duties solely from respect for moral laws they have imposed upon themselves, so that God's will is not to be taken into account when man determines his duties. Moreover, man does his duties and strives for virtue primarily, if not wholly, by his own efforts, with only a vague hope of assistance from divine Grace if he does all that is in his power and hence deserves to be helped. And worship of God for His own sake, without relation to moral conduct, plays no part. For these reasons, the relation of man to God is an almost wholly external one, as in eighteenth-century Deism. God appears to function only as the original Author of the natural and moral orders and the just Judge who dispenses happiness to those who have earned it. Schleiermacher was completely justified in rejecting this moralistic conception of God and religion.

THE COGNITIVE STATUS OF THE POSTULATES

Now that we have presented Kant's arguments for freedom, immortality, and God as "postulates of the practical reason," we must examine the *cognitive nature* and *status* of these "postulates." What is their relation to the knowledge attained by theoretical reason? Do they provide us with knowledge or with something that falls short of knowledge? Kant's answers to these questions are not entirely clear.

First, *what* is a "postulate of practical reason"? "These postulates," says Kant, "are not theoretical dogmas but suppositions practically necessary; while then they do (not) extend our speculative knowledge, they give objective reality to the ideas of speculative reason in general (by means of their reference to what is practical), and give it a right to concepts, the possibility of which it could not otherwise venture to affirm." [76] This asserts that the postulates are "suppositions" which it is "practically necessary" to affirm and which bestow "objective reality" upon ideas that the theoretical reason cannot demonstrate. Unlike the

[76] *Ibid.*, p. 229.

categories and principles of the understanding which are presuppositions of the *knowledge of objects,* the postulates are presuppositions of
moral action and hence "practically" rather than "theoretically" necessary. They may be described as convictions or beliefs which must be
assumed by the practical reason as conditions of morality. More specifically, the postulates are presuppositions or conditions without which
the attainment of the *summum bonum* as the ultimate object of the
moral will would not be possible and the meaning of moral effort
would be called in question. Freedom is a presupposition of moral
action itself, for moral action "ought" to be done, and therefore "can"
be done. On the other hand, immortality and God are presuppositions
of the realization of the ultimate object or end of moral action, the
summum bonum.

Second, what *justification* is there for accepting these presuppositions despite the fact that the theoretical reason was shown in the first
Critique to be incapable of proving them? Kant's answer to this question rests upon his view of the relation of the practical to the theoretical reason. The practical reason, he says, has "primacy" over the theoretical reason. When one speaks of the "primacy" of one thing over
another or others, one refers to "the prerogative belonging to one, of
being the first determining principle in the connexion with the rest," or,
where two or more interests are involved, "the prerogative of the interest of the one in so far as the interest of the other is subordinated to it,
while it is not postponed to any other." [77] Every faculty of the mind
has an interest which "calls it into exercise," the interest of the theoretical faculty consisting in cognition of objects and that of the practical faculty consisting in the direction of the will to its final and complete end.[78] Thus, in asking whether "primacy" should be accorded to
the practical or to the theoretical reason, Kant is asking which of them
has the right by virtue of its superior interest to subordinate the other
to itself.

Kant's answer is that theoretical or speculative reason can and
should accept the postulates, since they have to do with what practical
reason sees to be necessary conditions for obedience to the moral law
and hence are "*inseparably* attached to the *practical* interest." [79] Furthermore, theoretical reason should "try to unite them with its own
concepts," [80] although the propositions of the latter are handed over to
it as from a foreign source and seem strange to it. Why? The answer is
that if the theoretical reason did not accept them from the practical

[77] *Ibid.,* p. 216.   [78] *Ibid.*   [79] *Ibid.,* p. 217.   [80] *Ibid.*

reason, reason would fall into conflict with itself. Moreover, "since all interest is ultimately practical, and even that of speculative reason is conditional, it is only in the practical employment of reason that it is complete." [81] This last sentence, which Kant does not elaborate, is the crux of the argument. It seems to mean that, while the interest of the *theoretical* reason in *truth* is only "conditional," that of the *practical* reason in *good as a whole* is "complete" and therefore superior, since it includes the intellectual value of truth and subordinates it to the moral value of goodness. This interpretation is conjectural but it seems to be borne out by the famous statement at the beginning of the *Metaphysic of Morality:* "Nothing can possibly be conceived in the world, or even out of it, which can be called good, without qualification, except a Good Will," [82] for that statement is followed by a sentence in which intelligence and other talents of the mind are said to be only conditionally good.[83] Thus Kant's justification of the "primacy" of the practical reason is that its interest in the *moral* value of virtue and happiness in proportion to it is superior to the *intellectual* value of knowledge, since the former is unconditional while the latter is merely conditional and must be limited by the requirements of the former.

However, Kant jealously safeguards the claim of theoretical reason to provide us with knowledge by limiting the claim of the practical reason to *extend* our knowledge to transcendent or supersensible objects. Our knowledge, he says, is extended by practical reason "only in a practical point of view." [84] We can know that there *are* objects corresponding to our ideas of freedom, immortality, and God, but we cannot know their *nature*. For example, we can know that there is freedom, but "how freedom is possible, and how we are to conceive this kind of causality theoretically and positively, is not thereby discovered." [85] Since we do not have a nonsensuous intuition which could present to us the transcendent objects affirmed by the postulates, we can have "thoughts" of them but these are not "cognitions"; we can know "that they have objects" but cannot gain "a cognition of these objects." [86] Thus the primacy of the practical reason only warrants us in *thinking* transcendent objects as objectively real but not in claiming to *know* them.

However, this restriction is difficult to reconcile with the assertion by Kant that when theoretical reason has accepted these ideas from practical reason it will "think those objects by means of the catego-

---

[81] *Ibid.,* p. 218.   [82] *Ibid.,* p. 9.   [83] *Ibid.*   [84] *Ibid.,* p. 231.
[85] *Ibid.* (italics added).   [86] *Ibid.,* p. 232.

ries." [87] For example, the idea of God can be determined by predicates derived from man's nature, i.e., understanding and will, provided that we eliminate everything that belongs to these as we empirically observe them in ourselves.[88] Thus the categories "enable us to *conceive the supersensible* definitely, only so far, however, as it is defined by such predicates as are necessarily connected with the pure *practical purpose* given *a priori* and with its possibility." [89] If we can apply the categories and predicates derived from human personality to them, how can it be denied that we "know" them? The only possible answer is that Kant, under the influence of his narrow restriction of "knowledge" to phenomena in the first *Critique,* is unwilling to admit that we "know" noumena. Perhaps Kant's real meaning is that, while the categories can be applied to noumena and can give us vague knowledge, they cannot be applied in the schematized form necessary to give us full knowledge of objects.

As a result, the "postulates" have a peculiar and ambiguous status with respect to their cognitive value. They extend our knowledge but "only from a practical point of view." Does that mean that they *do* or that they *do not* really extend our knowledge? They are presuppositions, conditions of morality. Does that mean that we must definitely affirm them to be true, or, as some interpreters of Kant have held, that we must act "as if" they were true? The answer is not certain, but Kant seems to be asserting that the postulates have a kind of intermediate status between knowledge and ignorance, since we know *that* their objects exist, but not *what* they are. Yet, as we have seen, he also seems to claim a limited knowledge by means of the categories of *what* they are.

The problem is further complicated by a striking passage concerning the role of will in affirming the postulates: "The righteous man may say: I *will* that there be a God, that my existence in this world be also an existence outside the chain of physical causes and in a pure world of the understanding, and lastly that my duration be endless; I firmly abide by this, and will not let this faith be taken from me; for in this instance alone my interest, because I must not relax anything of it, inevitably determines my judgment." [90] The introduction of a sort of "will to believe" in this passage may be merely an elaboration of what he said earlier about the primacy of the practical reason because of the superiority of its interest. But at least he seems to be asserting a right

[87] *Ibid.,* p. 234.   [88] *Ibid.,* pp. 234, 235.   [89] *Ibid.,* p. 239.
[90] *Ibid.,* p. 241.

to believe in immortality and God which is exercised by the will in behalf of its moral interest. Thus the ambiguity of the cognitive status of the postulates is due not only to the fact that they enable us only to *think* without knowing their objects but also to the fact that even to think them requires pressure from the *will* upon the theoretical reason.

It is this ambiguity concerning the cognitive value of the postulates which makes it difficult to assert that Kant substituted for the rationalistic metaphysics he had criticized in the first *Critique* another kind of theistic metaphysics which was based primarily upon the moral will of persons seeking to realize purposes and using the natural order as a sphere of activity. Copleston argues that Kant did develop such a metaphysics. "It is metaphysics," he says, "based on the moral consciousness of the law and obligation. It does not provide us with an intuition of supersensible reality. . . . But there are, none the less, reasoned positions in regard to supersensible reality." [91] This is true, but we must not forget the ambiguity in Kant's view of the postulates. Even if "ways of thinking" supersensible realities be admitted to be ways of *knowing* them, Kant will not allow that they extend our theoretical knowledge, and they are affirmed only with the aid of a will to believe. It might be more accurate, therefore, to say that Kant arrived at insights that would have provided him with invaluable principles for the construction of a theistic metaphysics, but that he was inhibited from carrying out the task. Why?

One of the reasons, as we have said, was that he rejected the dogmatic metaphysics of his time. But Kant was also inhibited by his *dualism* between *theoretical* and *practical reason*. The distinction between the theoretical and the practical functions of reason is a real one, and it is as old as Aristotle. But Kant misconceives these functions when he limits the theoretical reason to *cognition of objects* and the practical reason to *legislation for action*. The effect of this sharp division of functions is a dualism of what *is* and what *ought to be,* existence and value. Once this dualism has arisen, it is difficult to overcome it. Since the moral laws laid down by practical reason are regarded as ideal principles, it is difficult to establish a connection between them and existence, and therefore to know their significance for an understanding of reality. Although they are objective in the sense of universally valid for men as rational beings, they correspond to nothing in the phenomenal world and hence appear to be merely rational ideals. If they had been regarded by Kant not as a priori principles laid down

---

[91] Copleston, *History of Philosophy,* Vol. VI, p. 343.

by practical reason without reference to experience but as derived in part from an analysis of human nature and its values as disclosed in experience, it would have been possible for him to acknowledge their theoretical as well as their practical significance. Thus they would have been viewed as discoveries of the reason which have practical value for the guidance of moral action but also theoretical value for the interpretation of reality as a whole.

That Kant was not far from a recognition that the existence of persons confronted by moral imperatives can extend our theoretical knowledge of reality as a whole is shown by his postulates. He realized that, while moral laws are laid down for man's action as a member of the supersensible world, they affect his life as a member of the sensible world. Although they originate in the world of noumena as *ideal* principles, they demand to be realized in the *existent* world of nature and history. Thus, they provide a bridge between the ideal and the real world, the "ought" and the "is," spirit and nature. As such, they offer us a key for the interpretation of both realms and their relation to one another. Kant was willing to affirm this as a matter of *practical faith,* but he had begun by separating legislation for action by the practical reason so sharply from knowledge of objects by the theoretical reason that he could not allow the postulates to extend *knowledge* of the latter. The result was that he laid himself open to the charge, undoubtedly false, that he was really an agnostic who permitted himself and others a little wishful thinking about God and immortality in order to strengthen the foundations of morality.

NATURAL TELEOLOGY

Kant's attempt in the first two *Critiques* to reconcile Newtonian science with the requirements of morality and religion resulted in four major conclusions: (1) knowledge of *natural phenomena* by theoretical reason is possible through the cooperation of sensibility and understanding, so that the claims of mathematics and natural science to give us knowledge are justified; (2) knowledge of noumena or *things-in-themselves* is impossible, so that the claims of metaphysics and rational theology to give us knowledge of transcendent objects is unwarranted; (3) knowledge of universal *moral laws* by practical reason is valid as the basis of moral conduct; and (4) *rational beliefs* or *postulates* of practical reason are necessary as presuppositions of morality, i.e., God, freedom, and immortality, but we can only "think" and not "know" them. We have seen that these postulates provided the basis for a new theistic metaphysics but that Kant was hampered by his presuppositions in performing this task. We have now to inquire whether he succeeded in his last great work, the *Critique of Judgment,* in breaking out of the limitations imposed by these presuppositions and overcoming the dualism between the natural and the moral order, the order of necessity and the order of freedom, which had resulted from them.

That Kant was seeking for a way to overcome, or at least to mitigate, this dualism is shown by his introduction to the *Critique of Judgment.* Speaking of "the great gulf that separates the supersensible from phenomena," he says that the faculty of judgment "furnishes the mediating concept between the concept of nature and that of freedom." [92] What is this "mediating concept"? It is the concept of a *purposiveness of nature.* This means that judgment, by means of the concept of purposiveness in nature, can make it possible to think of nature in such a way that it will be compatible with the possibility of attaining moral ends.[93]

The faculty of judgment is defined by Kant as "the power of thinking the particular as being contained in the universal." For science to be possible, we need not only the universal laws or principles of the understanding but also special empirical laws and their connections with one another. Physics, for example, requires not only the universal law of causality but also particular causal laws and their relations to one another. Since these laws are not given to the faculty of judgment, all that the judgment can do is to look for them in experience. In doing so, it acts on the principle that nature is a system governed by particular laws which are intelligible to the human mind and possess unity as if they had their common ground in a divine mind. This principle of judgment is "the purposiveness of nature in its variety," says Kant. "That is, nature is represented by means of this concept, as if an Understanding contained the ground of the unity of the variety of its empirical laws." [94] However, judgment in making use of this a priori principle is "reflective" rather than "determinant," since it is a necessary condition not of objects themselves but of reflection in its investigation of objects.

Kant raises the question whether there *is* an "objective purposiveness" of nature, i.e., whether there are natural objects which are intelligible only through the kind of causality we ascribe to purposes. In answering this question, he dismisses cases of what he calls "relative"

[92] Kant, *Critique of Judgment,* trans. J. H. Bernard (London and New York: Macmillan, 1931), pp. 38, 39. Hereafter references to the *Critique of Judgment* will be to the Bernard translation.

[93] Copleston, *op. cit.,* Vol. VI, p. 349.   [94] *Ibid.,* p. 352.

or "external" as distinguished from "inner" purposiveness. Cases of such purposiveness, especially in relation to man, can easily be found, e.g., the Laplander is served by reindeer who are sustained by dry moss scratched out from under the snow.[95] But external purposiveness of this kind is only relative and hypothetical, not absolute. It can be asserted only in relation to the being for which it is advantageous and only on condition that that being is in itself a purpose of nature.[96] This is Kant's answer to the anthropocentric teleology of the eighteenth century.

We must, therefore, look further and consider what Kant calls "natural purpose." His analysis of a "natural purpose" is one of his most significant contributions in the *Critique of Judgment*. First, a thing is a natural purpose if it is "both cause and effect of itself." [97] For example, a tree generates another tree of the same genus and so "produces itself generically"; it also develops itself by transforming the matter it receives from outside until the matter has become its own product, and so it "produces itself as an individual." [98] Furthermore, the maintenance of any part of a tree "depends reciprocally on the maintenance of the rest," e.g., the leaves are produced by the trees but in turn support it.[99] Second, things as natural purposes are "organized beings" or organisms. The parts are possible only through their relation to the whole and they are combined in such a way that they are cause and effect of each other.[100] "In such a product of nature," Kant says, "every part not only exists *by means of* other parts, but is thought of as existing *for the sake of* the others and the whole, that is, an (organic) instrument—because it is an organized and self-organizing being." [101] As such, it is unlike a machine in that it possesses a "formative power" by which it organizes its materials; and, unlike a product of art, it is not shaped by an artificer external to it but organizes itself from within.[102] Here, again, Kant makes a decisive break with eighteenth-century teleology which tended to regard natural order too simply as analogous to a product of human art.

Organized beings or *organisms* are the only beings in nature, Kant maintains, which can be regarded as *natural purposes* and can provide the basis for a teleology. For in them "every part is reciprocally purpose (end) and means and nothing can be ascribed to a blind mechanism of nature." [103] Why is mechanical causality unable to explain such organized beings? The answer is that the principle of mechanical causality can tell us only that the parts of the organism have combined

[95] Kant, *Critique of Judgment*, p. 271.   [96] *Ibid.*   [97] *Ibid.*, p. 274.
[98] *Ibid.*   [99] *Ibid.*, p. 275.   [100] *Ibid.*, pp. 276, 277.
[101] *Ibid.*, pp. 277, 278.   [102] *Ibid.*, pp. 278, 279.   [103] *Ibid.*, p. 280.

from necessity, but it leaves their relation to one another and to the whole unexplainable.[104] Thus mechanical causality cannot explain "why the parts of our objects should be related to one another in such a way that it seems as if each of them existed only for the sake of the others and the whole to which they all belong, as if each of them existed not merely *through* the others but also *for* the others." [105] In other words, while mechanism regards every complex object as a mere aggregate, we assume in the case of an organism that every part of it is related to the whole. Moreover, we cannot stop with the concept of natural purpose in particular organized beings. This concept leads necessarily to the Idea of the whole of *nature as a system governed by purposes* to which all the mechanism of nature must be subordinate.[106] Even things which are unpleasant to us and contrary to our purposes, such as vermin and mosquitoes, must be interpreted with the aid of this Idea.

However, the scientist must limit himself to speaking of a "purpose of nature" and refuse even to consider whether such a purpose is "designed or undesigned." [107] For the teleological judgment is only "reflective" in the sense that it does not positively attribute purposes to natural objects as a particular kind of causality but "only adds for the use of the Reason a different kind of investigation from that according to mechanical laws in order to supplement the inadequacy of the latter even for empirical research into all particular laws of nature." [108] While we may speak in physics of the "wisdom," "economy," "forethought," or "beneficence" of nature, we must not make her an intelligent being or place another intelligent Being above her as her Architect.[109]

Thus Kant finds himself confronted by an *antinomy,* or contradiction. In its reflection on nature, judgment may proceed from two different maxims, the first of which is suggested by the causal principle of the understanding used in knowing objects of experience and the second by experience of the peculiar characteristics of organisms. These two maxims seem to be incompatible. On the one hand, reason seems to be required to explain *all* natural products by mechanical laws, but, on the other hand, it must explain *some* of them, i.e., organized beings, by final causes. Can this antinomy be overcome? Kant holds that, if the two maxims or principles of judgment are regarded as "constitutive," they definitely contradict one another. On the

---

[104] H. W. Cassirer, *Commentary on Kant's Critique of Judgment* (London: Methuen, 1938), p. 323.

[105] *Ibid.,* p. 323.   [106] Kant, *Critique of Judgment,* p. 284.

[107] *Ibid.,* pp. 288, 289.   [108] *Ibid.,* p. 290.   [109] *Ibid.*

other hand, if they are both regarded as merely "regulative" principles of investigation, they involve no contradiction. The reason is that in the first case they are treated as "determinant," in the second as merely "reflective." To treat them as "determinant" is to assume that we are judging about things in themselves, but to treat them as "reflective" is to assume that we are judging about phenomena. By making use of both maxims as "regulative" principles and restricting their application to phenomena, we leave open the question as to the ultimate cause of natural forms in things-in-themselves. Moreover, "it is left undecided whether or not in the unknown inner ground of nature, physico-mechanical and purposive combination may be united in the same things in one principle." [110] For rational beings with cognitive faculties different from ours might know the real causes of things as we do not and be able to unite the two principles of explanation in a way we cannot conceive. All we can say, therefore, is that for minds with cognitive faculties like ours, teleological explanation is necessary to supplement mechanical explanation in investigating these beings.[111]

This is Kant's solution of the antinomy, or contradiction, between mechanical and teleological principles of explanation. It consists in restricting the application of both of them to phenomena and refusing to make any decision about the applicability of either to things in themselves. Thus the "objective purposiveness" of organisms, analyzed so penetratingly by Kant, is denied metaphysical significance and is reduced to the status of a regulative principle for scientific investigation. This is confirmed by his rejection of all metaphysical "systems" or theories with respect to the purposiveness of nature, both those, such as Spinoza's Pantheism, which have maintained that all natural purposiveness is "undesigned," and those, such as Leibniz's Theism, which have maintained that natural purposiveness is "designed." [112] However, Kant speaks of Theism as "superior to all other grounds of explanation." [113] One might think that this would have been sufficient ground for accepting the explanation of purposiveness in terms of design by God as, at the very least, the most adequate "system" or theory. Why was Kant unwilling to draw this conclusion? The answer is that it involves "a Being such as cannot be given us in experience" [114] and that "we do not, properly speaking, *observe* the purposes in nature as designed." [115] Here, again, we observe the effect of Kant's narrowly empirical view of knowledge as restricted to objects of which we can have a sensuous intuition, a view which prevents him from making any

[110] *Ibid.*, p. 296.   [111] *Ibid.*, p. 297.   [112] *Ibid.*, pp. 302–305.
[113] *Ibid.*, p. 305.   [114] *Ibid.*, p. 308.   [115] *Ibid.*, pp. 311, 312.

metaphysical judgments. Although he seems to be convinced that the mechanical explanation of organisms is insufficient and that a teleological explanation is necessary, he is inhibited from affirming this by his agnosticism about transcendent objects beyond experience. Hence he insists at one moment that a teleological explanation of organic beings is necessary while at another moment he suggests that this may be due to the nature of our cognitive faculties and that a mind differently constituted might see things in a different way.

Indeed, both views are expressed within a single paragraph. "It is indeed quite certain," he says, "that we cannot adequately cognize, much less explain, organic beings and their internal possibility, according to mere mechanical principles of nature; and it is absurd for men to make any such attempt or to hope that another Newton will arise in the future, who shall make comprehensible to us the production of a blade of grass according to natural laws which no design has ordered. We must absolutely deny this insight to men." [116] There could hardly be a more emphatic statement of the necessity for a teleological explanation of organisms. And yet, what follows? "But then how do we know that in nature, if we could penetrate to the principle by which it specifies the universal laws known to us, there *cannot* lie hidden (in its mere mechanism) a sufficient ground of the possibility of organic beings without supposing any design in their production? Probabilities here are of no account when we have to do with judgments of pure Reason." [117] Swinging back and forth between these two positions, Kant concludes that we cannot judge objectively whether there really are purposes in organized beings and whether a Being acting according to design is the Author of the world.[118]

Thus Kant to the end refused to grant reason the power to know transcendent objects of which we have no sensuous intuition. In view of his acceptance of the postulate of the existence of God as intelligent Author of nature, he must have personally believed in the teleological explanation of the natural order, especially of organisms. But so deep was his suspicion of reason when it seeks to know things-in-themselves that probable reasoning was not enough to establish truth concerning them. Nothing less than certainty was sufficient. Thus a prisoner of both his empirical denial of nonsensuous intuition and his rationalistic refusal to acknowledge anything less than certain as knowledge, he could only decline to draw any metaphysical conclusion from the powerful evidence for natural teleology he had himself advanced, since "probabilities here are of no account."

[116] *Ibid.*, pp. 312, 313.   [117] *Ibid.*, p. 313.   [118] *Ibid.*

Finally, Kant raises the question whether natural teleology can provide the basis for a teleological argument for the existence of God. His answer is that, at the most, the teleological argument can establish an intelligent World Cause or Architect of nature, but it can tell us nothing about the properties of such a being except what is disclosed by experience of its effects. Therefore, we must derive the concept of an Infinite or Perfect Being from a quite different source than natural teleology.[119] Thus "physico-theology" is serviceable only "as a preparation (propaedeutic) for Theology; and it is only adequate to this design by the aid of a foreign principle on which it can rely." [120] This "foreign principle" is, we are not surprised to learn, morality. The basis of belief not only in the existence of God but also in an ultimate purpose of nature is to be found in ethical theology rather than in natural teleology. Thus Kant insists upon the primacy of moral theology over natural teleology, and ascribes only a subordinate function to the latter. His view seems to be that moral theology is "sufficient in itself" but that natural teleology can "confirm incidentally" the conclusions of moral theology.

This suggests that, if Kant had not been prevented by his epistemological assumptions and metaphysical agnosticism from affirming without reservations a teleological view of nature, he might have been able to combine his a priori moral argument for the existence of God with an a posteriori teleological argument. Since he had a more profound understanding of the nature of organisms than most eighteenth-century thinkers, he could have developed a more adequate teleological argument than that which was criticized by Hume and himself. If he had carried out this constructive task, he might have seen that "Rational Theology" and "Ethical Theology" are not mutually exclusive, as he usually seems to imply in the first and second *Critiques,* but that each needs to be supplemented by the other. Although the teleological argument may be able to establish an "intelligent World Cause" of natural order and purposiveness, such a Being cannot be identified with the Perfect Being required by Theism without arbitrarily attributing to Him qualities such as moral goodness for which nature by itself provides insufficient evidence. The moral argument supplements the teleological at this crucial point by offering evidence from the moral consciousness and activity of man for the attribution to Him of such qualities as the Ground of the moral order. On the other side, the moral argument, despite Kant, is *not* "sufficient in itself" to prove that God is

[119] *Ibid.,* p. 364.   [120] *Ibid.,* p. 369.

the Ground of the natural order and has the power to subordinate it to moral purposes. To establish this, the teleological argument is indispensable and is thus an invaluable supplement to the moral argument. Although Kant's presuppositions did not allow him to develop such a constructive position, he often gives the impression in the third *Critique* of trying to break through the restraint they imposed upon him in order to do more justice to the religious implications of natural organisms as well as of the moral order.

THE THREE CRITIQUES: RETROSPECT

In our critical analysis of Kant's three greatest works, we have seen that in certain respects he was typical of the Age of Reason. For example, because of his purely rational and ethical view of religion, he was unable to do justice to the personal relationship of man with God in worship and feeling. We have also pointed out that the theory of knowledge he developed in the *Critique of Pure Reason* was weakened by his dualism between sensibility and understanding and between understanding and reason. Under the influence of the Newtonian view of science and of British Empiricism, he was led to exalt the scientific knowledge of phenomena and to reject the metaphysical interpretation of reality as a whole. If he had been able to conceive the possibility of a kind of metaphysics less pretentious than that of Continental Rationalism, he might have been able to supplement his criticisms of the traditional metaphysics and rational theology by constructing a theistic metaphysics on more solid foundations. But his uncritical acceptance of the dogma of Empiricism that we can know only objects experienced through the senses, together with his reaction against the excesses of Rationalism, prevented him from realizing this possibility.

In his *Critique of Practical Reason*, however, Kant transcended the limitations of the Age of Reason by his recognition that the unconditional nature of moral imperatives and the capacity of man as a rational being to impose them upon his conduct presuppose the existence of supersensible realities which transcend the sensible world of phenomena. He also saw that the obligation of man to obey these imperatives could provide the ground not only for the assertion of freedom but also for a rational faith in God and immortality as presuppositions of the attainment of the highest Good. The "ethical theology" which resulted from this insight had a profound influence on nineteenth-century Protestant theology, e.g., Ritschl followed Kant in the view that religious belief is moral in its nature. Later theistic philosophers were led by his example to substitute arguments for God based upon the moral and spiritual life of man for the traditional arguments based upon nature.[121] Thus, in theological circles of the nineteenth century and in some philosophical circles of the early twentieth century, the constructive side of Kant's thought in the second *Critique* outweighed the destructive effect of his criticisms of rational theology in the first *Critique*.

However, the glaring weaknesses in the arguments for God and immortality as postulates, the ambiguous nature of the claims of these postulates to give us knowledge, and the dualism of the theoretical and practical reason which cut the postulates off from support by the theoretical reason aroused the suspicion of most philosophers that they were merely products of wishful thinking intended to encourage moral conduct. Moreover, the naturalistic and positivistic tendencies in philosophy which followed the decline of Idealism led many philosophers of the nineteenth century to take more seriously Kant's restriction of knowledge to natural phenomena in the first *Critique* than the more constructive aspect of his thought in the second *Critique*. Thus, while the positive side of his philosophy (his ethical theology) had considerable influence upon theologians, the negative side (his attack upon metaphysics and rational theology) influenced the philosophers more strongly. Morever, even in the Protestant theology of the last generation Kant's virtual dismissal of rational theology has had more effect than his substitution of ethical theology for it, since the dominant tendency in Neo-orthodoxy has been to depend upon revelation alone and to dispense with philosophical support altogether. Thus the result of Kant's critical philosophy has been quite different from that which he intended. *While his intention was only to "deny reason in order to make room for faith,"* [122] *his critical philosophy has strengthened the tendency to limit knowledge to the scientific description of natural phenomena and to discredit not only rational theology but also the rational faith which was to replace it.*

Finally, we pointed out that in the *Critique of Judgment* Kant sought to overcome the dualism of the first and second *Critiques* between the phenomenal world of objects governed by natural law and the moral order of persons determining their acts by freedom. He did so by analyzing the purposive character of organisms and thereby suggesting a broader view of nature than that of Newton. At this point, as in his analysis of morality, he sought to break out of the narrow limita-

---

[121] E.g., W. R. Sorley, *Moral Values and the Idea of God* (Cambridge, Eng.: Cambridge University Press, 1931) and A. E. Taylor, *The Faith of a Moralist* (London: Macmillan, 1951).

[122] Kant, *Critique of Pure Reason*, B. 30.

tions imposed by his theory of knowledge. To a certain extent, he succeeded in doing so by his insistence upon the necessity of teleological as well as mechanical causality in explaining living organisms and by his suggestion that there may be an ultimate purpose of nature as a whole which is grounded in a divine Mind. If he had followed this way of thinking to its logical conclusion, he could have developed a theistic metaphysic based upon morality, on the one hand, and the purposiveness of nature, on the other. But at the crucial point his empirical bias against the admission of any kind of knowledge which goes beyond phenomena made him draw back and assert that teleological judgments are "reflective" rather than "determinant" of things-in-themselves. As a result, although he achieved fame as a great critical philosopher who clipped the wings of reason, he failed to construct the theistic philosophy for which he had laid the foundations by his profound insight into the morality of human persons and the purposiveness of living organisms.

10 Absolute Idealism

HEGEL

Although Hegelian Idealism had a profound influence upon British and American philosophy until World War I, as the names of Bradley and Royce should remind us, few philosophers since that time have taken Hegel (1770–1831) seriously. In the twenties and thirties naturalists and realists at least paid him the honor of attacking his idealistic metaphysics and theory of knowledge. But after logical empiricists turned away from metaphysics, theology, and ethics and analytical philosophers began to confine themselves to linguistic analysis, most philosophers have not even taken the trouble to read Hegel. If he is dealt with at all in the history of philosophy, it is only as one who forgot Kant's warnings about the limits of reason and indulged in arbitrary metaphysical speculations, or as one whose "system" must be studied just enough to understand Kierkegaard's attack upon it. The recent appearance of J. N. Findlay's *Hegel: A Re-examination* indicates that in some circles this neglect of a great thinker by philosophers is beginning to be challenged, but the antirational and anti-idealistic temper of our age is not favorable to a rediscovery of him.

Theologians of the neo-orthodox type have not forgotten Hegel, but they have repudiated him. Because of the influence of his view of God as immanent in man and his attempt to interpret the biblical revelation in terms of his own philosophy, they have regarded him, along with Schleiermacher, as the evil genius of nineteenth-century Liberal theology. When they read him, they read him through the eyes of Kierkegaard whose views were in many respects antithetical to his own. In short, Hegel's philosophy of religion is now seen by most philosophers as a sort of odd relic of the Age of Rationalism and by most theologians as a horrible example of the compromise of Christianity with philosophy in the Age of Liberalism.

This is unfortunate, for Hegel's philosophy of religion is **a** classic example of the idealistic interpretation of religion in the West and corresponds in certain ways to the monistic religious philosophy of the

East. Although few Western religious philosophers are likely to accept his idealistic metaphysics or theory of knowledge, some of his insights into the nature of religion and its place in the spiritual life are profound, even if one-sided. For this reason, we shall direct our attention primarily to his philosophy of spirit and shall attempt to show how his philosophy of religion is an expression of his view of Absolute Spirit and its relation to the finite spirit of man. However, it will be necessary to speak briefly of his logic and philosophy of nature, the other major parts of his system, since we can understand his philosophy of spirit only in relation to them.

LOGIC AND THE DIALECTICAL METHOD

The *Logic* of Hegel consists of a critical examination of the concepts, or "categories," which have been developed by man's reason for the interpretation of his experience. Kant in his first *Critique* had shown that the reason is able to attain universal and necessary knowledge of the objects of experience by imposing upon sense impressions certain categories or forms of the understanding for the purpose of synthesizing them into an ordered whole. The post-Kantian idealists attempted to "deduce" the categories necessary for an interpretation of experience, but they refused to limit themselves to the twelve categories of Kant and repudiated Kant's limitation of knowledge by the categories to phenomena. Hegel's *Logic* must be understood as such an attempt. It is unlike formal logic in that it is concerned not only with the form but also with the content of thought. Consequently, its analysis of the categories involved in thinking is also an analysis of metaphysical theories in relation to the different categories they employ as keys to the interpretation of reality as a whole. For example, Hegel's analysis of the category of "substance" contains a criticism of the metaphysics of Spinoza on the ground that it regards the many things of experience as only "modes" of one "Substance," Nature or God, but does not account for the differentiation of the One into the many. The reason it is unable to do so, Hegel insists, is that this "Substance" is not interpreted as "Subject," i.e., as a spiritual reality capable of self-determining, free, creative activity governed by purpose. This illustrates the way in which reason in the *Logic* moves from lower to higher, from abstract to concrete, categories of thought and metaphysical interpretations of reality. The movement culminates in the "Absolute Idea" or Spirit, which is the highest category and as such the key to reality as a whole.[1]

[1] G. W. F. Hegel, *Logic*, trans. William Wallace, in *Encyclopedia of the Philosophical Sciences* (Oxford: Clarendon Press, 1894).

The method by which Reason proceeds in this advance from lower to higher categories of thought is *dialectic*. The dialectical method was employed by Kant to show that the reason which seeks to answer metaphysical questions about the world falls into contradiction with itself, e.g., it can prove both the "thesis" that causality in the form of free activity exists and the "antithesis" that every event is the necessary effect of antecedent causes. In contrast, the dialectical method has a positive value for Hegel, since it corresponds to the tension of opposites in reality and discovers behind this tension an underlying identity. The process is as follows: A "thesis" is advanced, but when it is critically examined it shows its one-sidedness and inadequacy. Its "antithesis" suggests itself, but this in turn discloses that it is lacking. Hence Reason is forced to go beyond both the thesis and the antithesis to a "synthesis" which sets them aside but at the same time preserves the truth in each of them. As Hegel expresses it, they are *aufgehoben,* i.e., annulled, but taken up into the more concrete and adequate view of the synthesis. But the synthesis itself is now seen to be inadequate; an antithesis to it is set forth which is likewise one-sided; and another synthesis emerges. Thus Reason moves through one conflict of opposites after another to higher and higher categories until it arrives at the highest, the "Absolute Idea."

In this connection it is important to note that Hegel's view of the relation of "Understanding," *Verstand,* and "Reason," *Vernunft,* is quite different from that of Kant. Kant had distrusted the pretension of the Reason to go beyond the knowledge of phenomena to a knowledge of things-in-themselves. In contrast Hegel maintains that the Reason can know things-in-themselves and thus can attain metaphysical knowledge. The *Understanding* apprehends its objects by means of abstract concepts which are distinct from one another, so that it sees them as opposed and even contradictory to one another. But concepts which are opposed to one another, e.g., freedom and necessity, indicate different aspects of experience and hence are capable of being combined by Reason in a synthesis. For *Reason* realizes that in thinking about concrete reality the law of contradiction is not the last word but that there may be an identity between opposites. "The contradictions which are held fast by the Understanding are not hard abstractions, but moments in a living process. . . . It [dialectic] resolves contradictions which for the Understanding are incapable of resolution, as it continually allows concepts which negate one another to arise and be united again." [1] In this way the dialectical movement through contra-

<hr>

[1] Erik Schmidt, *Hegel's Lehre von Gott* (Gutersloh: G. Bertelsmann, 1952), pp. 87f.

diction to synthesis is motivated by the drive of Reason to overcome oppositions and attain to unity of knowledge. "Understanding is the power of distinction but it cannot bind together again the concepts it has distinguished. . . . The power of synthesis, the combination of thesis and antithesis into a higher unity is speculation," [2] and speculation is a function of Reason.

As we shall see, the importance of this distinction between Understanding as the faculty of abstraction which leads to contradictions and Reason as the faculty of synthesis which overcomes them cannot be overestimated. We shall illustrate later its significance for Hegel's philosophy of religion by reference to his treatment of the relation between the finite and the infinite.

The *Logic* culminates in the *Absolute Idea,* which is the unity of subject and object in self-consciousness. In ordinary thinking the object stands over against the subject as something other than and opposed to it. In theoretical activity the subject seeks to overcome the otherness of the object by discerning its universal aspects which make it intelligible to reason; and in practical activity it seeks to transform the object in order to bring it into harmony with the purposes of the subject. In the "Absolute Idea" this otherness and opposition of the object are overcome, and the unity of the subject and object in self-consciousness is attained. "Absolute Idea" is the logical expression for the "Absolute Spirit," the fundamental principle of Hegel's metaphysics.

SPIRIT AND ITS MANIFESTATIONS

What does Hegel mean by "Spirit," *Geist?* In the first place, it is not merely "substance" but *"subject."* We know Spirit in ourselves as consciousness of objects and in its fullest development as consciousness of itself or self-consciousness. It includes not only the subject but also the objects of consciousness, and, indeed, the subject apart from the contents of its consciousness is only an abstraction. For this reason, Hegel may be called an "objective" idealist, since he does not reduce reality, like Berkeley, to minds and their ideas but regards the objects of mind as also real, although only in relation to mind. Second, Spirit is a form of *rational activity,* a process in which objects of experience are made to yield universal meanings. As Findlay puts it, "It is the activity which disengages universality and unity from particularity and plurality, and which interprets the latter through the former." [3] Thus, Spirit is ra-

[2] *Ibid.,* p. 91.

[3] J. N. Findlay, *Hegel, A Re-examination* (London: Allen and Unwin, 1958), p. 41.

tional. However, it is not the reason of the self in its particularity but the Reason which is common to all selves which performs this task. Therefore, Spirit is also *universal*. This is why Spirit expresses itself most fully in experiences which are governed by intersubjective, universal norms, e.g., logical thinking and moral action.[4] But, third, Spirit is also *individual* as well as impersonal and universal. "It is as essential, therefore, for Spirit to be wedded to particular finite contents and to determinate places in the world, as it is for it to be freely ranging and 'infinite,' since it is only by being the former that it can be the latter." [5] For Spirit requires the particularity of sense experience and impulse as raw material for Reason to organize and control.

The fourth and perhaps the most distinctive thing in Hegel's conception of Spirit is that it must be confronted by that which is *other* than and *opposed* to itself, that which seems to limit its realization of its purposes. At this point Hegel was influenced by Fichte's view that the Self, or Ego, "posits" that which is other than itself, the "non-Ego," in order that its moral activity may encounter something that resists it and may overcome that resistance. This is necessary if the Ego which is moral will is to exercise its energies and realize itself. Hegel adopts this view, but modifies it in two important respects. He complains that for Fichte the union of the Ego and the non-Ego never becomes a present reality but always remains an object of endless striving. On the contrary, he says, the Absolute Spirit continually overcomes the resistance of the other and brings it into unity with itself, so that its purposes are realized here and now and always. Further, while for Fichte the aim of the positing of the non-Ego is the moral fulfillment of the Ego, for Hegel it is the attainment of *self-consciousness*. This aim can be realized only in the process of overcoming the opposition of the things and persons which are the objects of the Spirit's theoretical and practical activity. In this process the Spirit does not impose anything upon them which is alien to their nature but makes explicit what they implicitly or potentially are. But it is only by patiently and often painfully overcoming their apparent opposition to itself that Spirit can come to self-consciousness. As Hegel puts it, the Spirit requires "the seriousness, the suffering, the patience, and the labour of the negative." [6] Moreover, the result of the process of overcoming oppositions cannot be separated from the process itself, so that the life of the Spirit combines painful struggle with blessed repose.

⁴ *Ibid.*, pp. 42*f*.   ⁵ *Ibid.*, p. 43.
⁶ G. W. F. Hegel, *Logic*, trans. Wallace, in *Encyclopedia of the Philosophical Sciences* (Oxford: Clarendon Press, 1894), quoted from Findlay, *Hegel, A Reexamination*, p. 45.

The culmination of Hegel's concept of Spirit is his affirmation that *"Absolute Spirit" is the only and absolute Reality and hence the Truth. Nothing in nature or man can be understood unless it is viewed as a manifestation of Spirit.* The "Absolute Idea" in which the *Logic* culminates is only the form of Spirit and as such is an abstraction apart from its realization in the world. Therefore, the *Logic* is only the first part of Hegel's system as presented in his *Encyclopedia of the Philosophical Sciences* and is followed by the second and third parts, the *Philosophy of Nature* and the *Philosophy of Spirit,* which deal with the manifestation of the Absolute Idea in nature and finite spirit. "God," says Hegel, "has two revelations, as Nature and Spirit. Both these divine formations are temples of God that He fills by His presence. God as an abstraction is not the true God: only as the living process of positing His other, the World, . . . and first, in the union with His other, as Spirit, can He be subject." [7]

Of these two "revelations," *nature* is the Absolute Idea in the form of "externality." Natural objects and events are external to one another in space and time and appear to be wholly other than the subject which seeks to know them. Therefore, nature is implicitly Spirit, i.e., it shows anticipations of and is the raw material for Spirit, but in its immediate form it seems to be the antithesis of the spiritual. Since it has a need to go beyond itself to Spirit, however, it manifests itself in a series of levels each of which arises out of what is below it. [8]

The second and higher "revelation" is *spirit* as it is manifested in man. Hegel deals with it under three forms: "subjective," "objective," and "absolute" spirit. "Subjective" spirit is spirit as it emerges from nature. It is finite, individual consciousness, which has within itself the possibilities of all forms of conscious awareness and activity, theoretical and practical, but has not yet brought them to fulfillment. [9] "Objective" spirit is spirit as expressed or embodied in the world of laws and ethical institutions, i.e., family, civil society, and state, which constitute the conditions of true rational freedom. It reaches its perfection in the moral life, which Hegel conceives primarily as participation in the "ethical substance" of the nation: obedience to its laws and customs, and acceptance of the duties required by one's station in it. [10] However, although morality seems to be determined by the demands of the

---

[7] Hegel, *Philosophy of Nature,* in *Encyclopedia,* quoted in Findlay, *Hegel, A Re-examination,* p. 269.

[8] *Ibid.,* pp. 270–272.

[9] Hegel, *Philosophy of Mind,* trans. Wallace, in *Encyclopedia of the Philosophical Sciences* (Oxford: Clarendon Press, 1894), Sec. I.

[10] *Ibid.,* Sec. II.

state, Hegel holds that the basis of both the state and its morality is religion. Thus religion is more fundamental than morality, although it must never be divorced from it.

"Absolute" Spirit is the highest level of the life of the human spirit, and "the subjective and the objective spirit are to be looked on as the road on which this aspect of reality or existence rises to maturity." [11] In *art, religion,* and *philosophy* the human spirit comes to consciousness of its unity with the Absolute Spirit and at the same time the latter comes to consciousness of itself. Absolute Spirit in these three forms of experience expresses its consciousness of itself in progressively more adequate forms: in art, in sensuous form; in religion, in the "quasi-pictorial" form of ideas; and in philosophy, in concepts of speculative reason. Thus Spirit at its highest level of Absolute Spirit becomes conscious of itself and knows itself as the one and only reality of which nature and finite spirit are manifestations. As such, it is the end or final cause of the world toward which all things strive, like Aristotle's Prime Mover which moves everything as the object of desire or love. It is also the efficient cause or ground of everything, like the God of Theism, insofar as it posits nature and finite spirit as other than itself, and they have no reality independent of it.

THE ESSENCE OF RELIGION: KNOWLEDGE vs. FEELING

It is only when we keep in mind Hegel's conception of Absolute Spirit as the ultimate and unconditioned reality which manifests itself in nature and the human spirit that his interpretation of religion becomes intelligible. *In its essence, religion is man's consciousness of God, his elevation of himself as finite spirit to union with God the Infinite, Absolute Spirit.* Through this consciousness of the eternal, man raises himself above the evils and limitations of his temporal existence, so that religion is "that region in which all the enigmas of the world are solved, all the contradictions of deeper-reaching thought have their meaning unveiled, and where the voice of the heart's pain is silenced —the region of eternal truth, of eternal rest, of eternal peace." [12] Since in religion man places himself in relation to the unconditioned and unlimited God who is the beginning and end of all things, the spirit "unburdens itself of all finiteness, and wins for itself final satisfaction and deliverance." [13] Here the emphasis is upon the union of the finite spirit with the Infinite Spirit and upon deliverance thereby from the perplexities, suffering, and restlessness of temporal existence into rest

[11] *Ibid.,* Sec. III.
[12] Hegel, *Philosophy of Religion,* trans. Rev. E. B. Speirs and J. Burdon Sanderson (London: K. Paul, Trench, Trubner and Co., 1895), Vol. I, p. 1.
[13] *Ibid.*

and peace. Finitude, temporality, and suffering rather than sin and guilt seem to be the primary evils from which deliverance is sought, and religion offers the assurance that man can be freed from these evils in this life. As Hegel puts it, "Whatever awakens in us doubt and fear, all sorrow, all care, all the limited interests of finite life, we leave behind on the shores of time," and "man, lifted out of the hard realities of this actual world, contemplates it as something having only the semblance of existence." [14]

The implications of this optimistic view for the problem of history and providence we shall consider later. Obviously, it rests upon his metaphysical Idealism and simply expresses that Idealism in religious terms. Man's existence is characterized by finitude with all its limitations and by temporality with all its restless striving and pain. This implies that, although he is spirit, he is estranged from the Absolute Spirit and needs to be delivered from the evils of that estrangement. But there seems to be no insurmountable obstacle which can prevent him from overcoming these evils. Indeed, he can through religion overcome them so completely that the "hard realities" of time are seen to have only "the semblance of existence." This way of thinking is possible only for an idealistic monist, one who believes that the only true reality is the Absolute Spirit, that the finite spirit of man is in its essence one with that Spirit, and that the estrangement between them is not too great to be overcome. Since the Absolute Spirit has put forth the world of nature and finite spirit from itself in order to overcome their opposition and thereby attain consciousness of itself, the finite spirit is not required to elevate itself to union with the Absolute Spirit by its own efforts alone, for the Absolute Spirit is immanent in it and is drawing it back to itself. This is why Hegel can say that religion is not only man's consciousness of God but also God's consciousness of Himself in and through man's consciousness of Him, as man's "intellectual love of God" for Spinoza is also God's love for Himself.

Since this view of the nature of religion is largely determined by Hegel's idealistic philosophy, it is not surprising that he regards religion as identical with philosophy in its *content* and different from it only in its *form*. The content or subject of both is the Absolute Spirit and the union of the finite spirit with it. As the interest of philosophy is not merely theoretical knowledge of *truth* but knowledge of the Absolute Spirit which brings *deliverance* from the evils of finite existence, the interest of religion is not merely *faith* in the Absolute Spirit but *knowledge* of it as true. Indeed, religion is primarily a *form of knowledge,* although it also expresses itself in worship and conduct.

[14] *Ibid.*

This is the explanation of Hegel's polemic against every attempt of theologians to make *faith* independent of reason. They are right in basing faith upon the revelation contained in the Scriptures, he concedes, but they should recognize that reason is required to interpret the meaning of the revelation and that it must use philosophical concepts for that purpose. "Thought explicitly contains categories, principles, premises, which must make their influence felt in the work of interpretation. . . . It is, indeed, the sense contained in the words which is supposed to be given. The giving of the sense means, however, the bringing forward of the sense into consciousness, into the region of ideas; and these ideas, which get their determinate character elsewhere, then assert their influence in the exposition of the sense supposed to be contained in the words." [15] Moreover, faith and philosophical inquiry cannot exist side by side in watertight compartments. "The human spirit in its inmost nature is not something so divided up that two contradictory elements might subsist together in it. If discord has arisen between intelligent insight and religion, and is not overcome in knowledge, it leads to despair, which comes in the place of reconciliation." [16]

Hegel is also strongly opposed to the Romantic view of religion represented by the early Schleiermacher, i.e., that religion is a form of *feeling*. He makes several trenchant criticisms of this view. Feelings may be of very different kinds, and whether a religious feeling is true and good or false and evil depends upon its content.[17] Furthermore, if a person appeals to feeling instead of reason to justify his faith, community between him and others is impossible since he can come to no understanding with them about the object of his feeling. As Hegel says, "If one person says you ought to have such feelings, another may reply, I simply *have not* those feelings; as a matter of fact, I *am* not so constituted." [18] Again, while feeling is an element in religious experience, it must be nourished and made permanent by means of ideas if it is not to vanish or lose all definite content.[19] While the content of religious experience is present first in feeling, "in the heart," it is there only in "a hidden and developed mode." Finally, it is a feeling of the self as well as of the religious object and may therefore become self-centered unless attention is centered on the religious object through clear knowledge of the latter.

In these criticisms of the theory of feeling, Hegel is not denying

---

[15] *Ibid.,* p. 29.   [16] *Ibid.,* p. 49.   [17] *Ibid.,* p. 130.   [18] *Ibid.,* p. 132.
[19] *Ibid.,* p. 134.

that feeling has a place in religion. He is saying that man as a rational being cannot be content with a vague, indefinite feeling of the divine, but must have knowledge of the divine object if his feeling is to be a true and worthy one and if it is to be a permanent element in his experience. He is also warning that to identify religion with feeling encourages the natural tendency of the self to subjectivity and thus prevents it from losing itself in the religious object, God. While these criticisms of the Romantic theory are largely justified, it cannot be denied that Hegel tended to exalt the element of knowledge in religion too highly and to reduce the element of feeling at times to a very minor position. Pfleiderer points out that he is here misled by "the error of passing from one form to another as the higher," whereas "there is in truth a purely positive relation of co-existence and interaction of several equally essential forms of mind." [20] What is needed for mature religion, as John Wesley said, is a *union* of "knowledge and vital piety."

HEGEL AND THE ENLIGHTENMENT

Hegel is also opposed to the tendency of the philosophers of the Enlightenment to reject all positive religion and especially the doctrines of the Church. "God is a living God, who is acting and working," he says. "Religion is a product of the Divine Spirit; it is not a discovery of man, but a work of divine operation and creation in time." [21] Therefore, the hostile attitude of the Enlightenment toward *historic religions* is not justified. Philosophers must recognize that, although religions "often enough exhibit the most distorted, confused, and abortive ideas of the divine Being," "there must be reason in them, and amidst all that is accidental in them a higher necessity." [22] Therefore, philosophers should respect the historic religions as "moments" in the development of the Absolute Spirit toward self-consciousness and distinguish the rational from the accidental element in them.

The fundamental cause of the religious skepticism of the Enlightenment, Hegel maintains, was a narrow rationalism based upon the abstract thinking of the Understanding. As we have seen, he holds that the Understanding is unable to overcome the contradictions it discerns between opposing ideas. Since religion expresses its beliefs in the "ideas" of ordinary thought, it opens itself to attacks from the Understanding. For example, the terms "Son" and "begetting" are figures derived from a natural relation and only approximately indicate the

---

[20] Otto Pfleiderer, *The Philosophy of Religion on the Basis of History*, trans. A. Stewart (London: Williams, 1886–1888), Vol. II, p. 91.

[21] Hegel, *Philosophy of Religion, op. cit.*, Vol. I, p. 33.   [22] *Ibid.*, p. 78.

relation of the first and second "Persons" of the Trinity. Again, in the idea of creation, the relation of God to the world is conceived as external and the connection between them is not represented as a necessary one.[23] Similarly, the attributes of God are expressed in ordinary thought as qualities which are distinct and related only in an external way, and it is easy for the Understanding to point out apparent contradictions between them, e.g., between His kindness and His justice, His power and His wisdom.[24] These defects in the "ideas" of religion make it necessary for the speculative Reason to transform them into the "concepts" of philosophy and to demonstrate their unity and necessity.

Perhaps the best example of the way Understanding emphasizes contradictions in ordinary religious thought and Reason overcomes these contradictions by philosophical thought is to be found in Hegel's treatment of the relation between the *finite* and the *infinite*. From the point of view of the Understanding, the finite and the infinite stand in antithesis to each other. The infinite is regarded simply as the "not-finite" and hence "remains over against the finite as an *Other* and so itself a finite." [25] This is what Hegel calls the "false infinite." Its religious inadequacy is not only that it conceives of the infinite God as really finite but also that it separates Him from and sets Him over against man. Hegel develops his speculative philosophical doctrine of the "true infinite" to overcome this dualistic error. "The concept of the true infinite," says a recent German writer, "is the fundamental principle (*Grundgedanke*) of the Hegelian philosophy. All further concepts of his metaphysics of the Absolute are nothing more than developments, particular illustrations of the concept of the true infinite. It is directed against the dualism of God-World, which subjects the infinite to an insurmountable limit." [26] Since ordinary faith speaks of the infinite God as separated from the world by a gulf and understanding conceives of the infinite in an abstract way, both fail to do justice to the true infinity of God.[27]

In contrast to the view of both faith and understanding that the finite stands opposed to the infinite, Hegel affirms "the indissoluble unity of the two." [28] "The finite," he says, "is therefore an essential moment of the infinite in the nature of God, and thus it may be said it is God Himself who renders Himself finite, who produces determinations within Himself. . . . God creates a world, God determines; out-

---

[23] *Ibid.*, p. 148.   [24] *Ibid.*, pp. 157f.   [25] *Ibid.*, p. 183.
[26] Schmidt, *Hegel's Lehre von Gott*, p. 153.   [27] *Ibid.*, p. 154.
[28] Hegel, *Philosophy of Religion*, Vol. I, p. 197.

side of Him there is nothing to determine. He determines Himself
when He thinks Himself, places an Other over against Himself, when
He and a world are two. . . . But the truth is that this finiteness is
only an appearance, a phenomenal shape in which He has or possesses
Himself. . . . Thus, then, the finite is a moment of the Divine Life." [29]
"What is true is the unity of the infinite, in which the finite is
contained." [30] Thus, although the finite appears as other than and
opposed to the infinite, God, it is in reality a necessary manifestation of
His life and is contained in Him as a moment. "If God does not have
the finite in Himself," says Schmidt, "it stands as independent over
against Him, and then the infinity of God is a false infinity and God is
Himself finite and limited. Thus, the finite can be conceived only as a
transitory moment in God Himself. . . . God is at once the movement
to the finite and the overcoming of the finite." [31]

In this manner Hegel's concept of the "true infinite" denies all
dualism between God and the world. Indeed, it simply states what is
implied by his idealistic monism with respect to God's relation to the
world. Although Absolute Spirit is the one and only reality, it must put
forth that which appears as other than itself in order to come to consciousness of itself. It must be not only "in itself" but also "for itself" in
order that it may "return" to itself and be "in and for itself." Thus, the
finite world of nature and human spirit is essential to the self-realization of the infinite Spirit, God. But it must not be conceived as outside
God and independent of Him, for this would set it in opposition to
Him and make it impossible for it to unite itself with Him.

PANTHEISM OR PANENTHEISM?

Does this not imply a pantheistic view of God's relation to the
world, as is often said? If God contains the finite world as a moment in
Himself, is not the transcendence of God denied? Hegel was very
sensitive to the charge that his view, like Spinoza's, was pantheistic and
there is no doubt that he wished to avoid pantheism. In his *Encyclopedia*, he took "the new piety and the new theology" to task for
claiming that "philosophy has too much of God—so much so that,
if we believe them, it asserts that God is everything and everything is
God." [32] They cannot show, says Hegel, "that *any one philosopher, or
any one man,* had really ascribed substantial or objective and inherent

[29] *Ibid.*, pp. 198f.   [30] *Ibid.*, p. 200.
[31] Schmidt, *op. cit.*, p. 154.
[32] Hegel, *Philosophy of Mind, op. cit.*, p. 184.

reality to *all* things and regarded them as God." [33] Indeed, the Pantheism of the Hindus and of Spinoza, instead of identifying God with everything finite, tends to deny the reality of the finite altogether and to assert that God is the sole reality. In contrast, while Hegel's philosophy also emphasizes unity, it is not the abstract unity of mere identity but a concrete unity which manifests itself in the many finite things of the world.[34] This is not to identify God and the world, because it bestows upon the many finite things of the world a reality, although not an ultimate reality, by regarding them as necessary "moments" in the life of God.

Although this passage is not wholly clear, Hegel obviously means to contrast his own view that God distinguishes the world from Himself and at the same time contains it in Himself with both the popular "Pantheism" which is supposed to identify Him with the totality of finite things ("everything") and the genuine Pantheism of the Hindus and Spinoza which tends toward acosmism by reducing finite things to mere appearances. He is not a "pantheist" in the popular sense, because for him finite things have no substantial, independent reality of their own; but he is also not a pantheist of the acosmical type, because he holds that finite things are created "other" than God and at the same time are contained in Him as "moments." "He teaches," says Schmidt, "the identity of God and the world, but this identity is for him no abstract identity of the understanding, no abstract unity in which all differences are negated. Hegel teaches a concrete unity, in which the differences are preserved as essential moments. . . . God is the omnipresent Subject; and thus He has the world which stands over against Him eternally in Himself." [35]

But although Hegel rejected Pantheism, he was even more strongly opposed to the dualism of the orthodox theology of his time. His own view is best understood as an attempt to combine the truth contained in both Pantheism and orthodox Theism, avoiding the acosmical tendency of the former and the dualistic tendency of the latter. It has been described as "dialectical Panentheism. . . . All comes from God and all is in God; all is created by God and all remains as a moment in Him. God is the movement toward the world and the annulment (*aufhebung*) of the world." [36] However, whether this description of Hegel's position as "Panentheism" really enables him to refute the main criticism of those who have charged him with "Pantheism" is another matter. Panentheism as well as Pantheism is opposed to traditional

---

[33] *Ibid.*, p. 185.   [34] *Ibid.*, pp. 192f.
[35] Schmidt, *Hegel's Lehre von Gott*, p. 189.   [36] *Ibid.*, p. 193.

Theism. For even when Theism has avoided dualism by stressing the immanence as well as the transcendence of God, it has never been willing to accept the view that God contains the world in Himself. To assert that the world is a moment in the divine life is to involve God in its finitude and temporality, or, to put it otherwise, to introduce its finitude and temporality into Him.[37] Thus it fails to preserve the transcendence of God over the world and consequently His perfection and holiness. At the same time, the world as a "moment" in the life of God is endowed with a rational, ideal, and necessary character it does not possess. The implication for Hegel's conception of man's nature and relation to God is equally dubious from the theological point of view, for it seems to make the human spirit identical in essence with God and thus to encourage man's pride.

ESTRANGEMENT AND RECONCILIATION

We have seen that, while Hegel respected the positive religions of history and sought to vindicate the doctrines of Theism by changing its *form*, his reinterpretation of the theistic view of God's relation to the world and man tends also to distort its *content*. A brief examination of his reinterpretation of the Christian doctrine of "estrangement," *Entfremdung*, and "reconciliation" or "atonement," *Versöhnung*, will illustrate the same tendency and help to explain the sharp reaction of recent Neo-orthodoxy against his theology.

The profound influence of Christianity upon him is shown by the fact that he calls it both the "revealed" and the "absolute" religion and regards it as the crowning stage in the historical evolution of the religious consciousness. It is even more evident in the seriousness with which he takes the distinctive Christian beliefs. That his acceptance of the truth of these beliefs is more than nominal is shown by the fact that his idealistic metaphysics was developed to a considerable extent under their influence. In this respect, his attitude is radically different from that of Kant and other philosophers of the Enlightenment who had sought to develop a purely "natural" religion and hence had eliminated every distinctive belief of Christianity as a revealed religion of redemption.

He praises the doctrine of the *Trinity* on the ground that God is not an abstract and undifferentiated One like the Allah of Islamic monotheism but a living, concrete, spiritual Being who distinguishes Himself as "Father" from Himself as "Son" and returns to unity with Him-

[37] *Ibid.*, p. 194.

self as "Holy Spirit." The doctrine, he holds, is identical with the fundamental insight of his idealistic philosophy, that the Absolute Spirit is eternally "in itself," differentiates itself from its "other" and is thus "for itself," and returns to itself in self-consciousness "in and for itself." [38] At the same time, Hegel defends the doctrine of the Trinity against the criticism of the Understanding that "we are required to conceive of three units as only one unit"; [39] for this is to take number as a "category of finitude" too literally. He also warns against the association of the term "person" with the isolated, independent subject, which is quite separate and different from other persons, for this suggests that there are "three Gods." [40]

Hegel also takes seriously the Christian doctrine of man, his *estrangement* from God, and his need for redemption. There is, he points out, a division between man's essence or true nature and his existence. The basis of this division is his consciousness of the distinction between his particular, finite self and his universal nature as spirit. The will of man is a particular will, moved by natural and sensuous impulses. The natural man is therefore self-centered. When evil is spoken of as the "original sin" which began with Adam, this really refers not to an individual man, the first, but to man as man. For man as man possesses consciousness and from this necessarily arises a feeling of independence over against the universal. This division of the spirit within itself is the source of pain and sorrow in it. It feels itself to be out of harmony with the Absolute Spirit, with its own nature, and with the world. This feeling of unhappiness manifests the need of the finite, estranged spirit for *reconciliation* or atonement through the removal of the contradiction within it. But it is not able to bring this about by itself, for it is itself involved in the contradiction which must be overcome.[41] How, then, can it be reconciled to its true spiritual nature from which it is alienated?

Hegel's answer is that only through the atoning activity of the Absolute Spirit can the finite spirit be reconciled to it and thereby to itself. This was possible only through a manifestation of the unity of the divine nature with human nature in a man. "Man," says Hegel, "can only know himself taken up, accepted in God insofar as God is to him not a strange being, his relation to whom is merely outward, but insofar as he knows that in God his own being as spirit, as freedom, as subjectivity, is affirmed. But this essential unity of the divine nature with human nature can only be brought home to the consciousness of man, can only become an immediate certainty to him, by God appear-

[38] Hegel, *Philosophy of Religion, op. cit.*, Vol. III, pp. 11, 12.
[39] *Ibid.*, p. 23.   [40] *Ibid.*, pp. 24f   [41] *Ibid.*, pp. 45ff.

ing as man and man as God." [42] In other words, the unity of the human spirit with the divine Spirit could become a certainty to all men only if it appeared in the visible form of an individual man who was at the same time known to be "the absolute Idea, the Son of God." [43] Thus, the idea of the *divinity of Christ* was an inner necessity, once the religious consciousness had arrived at an awareness of the need for reconciliation.

But the *historical form* in which the idea of atonement or reconciliation was clothed is of secondary interest to Hegel. Although it was only in the historical form of an individual man that atonement could have appeared to men as something which had actually taken place and could therefore have been known as an objective truth, atonement is not merely an event which occurred at a particular time and in a particular man in the past. For the idea of atonement is true for *all* men at all times and needs only to be appropriated by each person in a subjective process. After the death of Christ, the coming of the *Holy Spirit* made it possible for Christians to see the Atonement as an event which not only had taken place in Christ but also was taking place in their own lives as a present reality. In the Church and through the activity of the Holy Spirit they were able to give up their independent, self-centered existence, and experience union with God.[44] Moreover, this subjective process in their lives manifested itself outwardly by its effects upon the world, either through a negative renunciation of the world or through a more positive penetration and transformation of the world by moral and social activity.[45]

Even from this brief sketch of Hegel's interpretation of the Christian doctrines of the Trinity, estrangement, and reconciliation it is obvious that he attempts to do full justice to these doctrines. Indeed, one of the most interesting things in his philosophy of religion is that he does not confine himself to the problems of "Rational Theology" as it had been conceived from Aquinas to Kant but seeks like Anselm to vindicate by reason the truth of the Christian faith and the theological beliefs derived from it.

But while he shows in this way the possibility of a philosophical approach to Christian theology, he also illustrates the dangers of such an approach for both philosophy of religion and Christian theology. As a philosopher of religion he did not succeed in proving the necessity of Christian doctrines such as the Trinity and the Atonement by reason.

[42] *Ibid.*, p. 108.   [43] *Ibid.*, p. 73.
[44] Pfleiderer, *The Philosophy of Religion on the Basis of History*, Vol. II, pp. 111*f*.
[45] *Ibid.*, pp. 112*f*.

He merely expressed these doctrines in the abstract concepts of his own idealistic philosophy; and he was able to do this in a plausible manner only because he had originally developed his philosophy to a considerable extent under the influence of these doctrines. Moreover, he accommodated the Christian doctrines of God, sin, and Atonement to his idealistic metaphysics at the cost of changing their content and meaning. Since we are not concerned in this book with problems of theology as such, we shall only point out that to most theologians today Hegel seems to treat the union of the divine with the human nature in Christ primarily as a mere historical example of a universal truth, so that the uniqueness of God's reconciling act in Christ is minimized. At this point, Hegel is still under the spell of the eighteenth-century view that the particular historical events through which God has revealed Himself are "accidental" and that what is really "essential" is the universal truth which reason finds to be illustrated in them. Thus Hegel's philosophical interpretation of Christian doctrines such as the reconciliation of man to God through Christ has satisfied neither philosophers nor theologians, the former because it seeks to demonstrate the necessity of those doctrines in a circular manner by means of a philosophy which is largely based upon them, the latter because it does not do justice to the uniqueness of the redemptive acts of God in history.

EVIL AND PROVIDENCE

Perhaps the greatest weakness of Hegel as a philosopher of religion, however, is to be found in his treatment of the problems of evil and providence. The problem of *evil* for him as a monistic idealist may be stated in the form of a question: if the Absolute Spirit is good and if it is the one true reality, how can there be evil in the world? Hegel's general answer to this question, insofar as it refers to sin and moral evil, is that the Fall of man was a necessity due to his nature as a finite being. Man, he holds, could become spirit only by asserting his freedom and his independence. Therefore, sin was a necessary condition of his spiritual development. Since this view explains sin as a necessity of man's nature which was created by God, it makes God responsible for it and absolves man himself from responsibility and guilt. This seems to be incompatible with the view of biblical Theism that man's created nature was good and that his Fall was due not to a necessity of his nature but to a misuse of his freedom.

Hegel's treatment of the problem of *providence* and *history* raises even more serious difficulties. Most of these result from his view that providence determines the whole course of history and thus imposes necessity upon all human events. In his *Philosophy of History* he pours scorn upon the popular "peddling" view of providence which tends to restrict its operation to the lives of individuals. Rather, it is effective in the whole of world history, including peoples and states.[46] For this reason, he rejects the idea that God acts in a secret way and hence cannot be known, for His hand can be seen everywhere in history. He also denies that God's almighty power is not in complete control of the course of events. Since the Absolute Spirit is the true reality, and nature and finite spirit are but manifestations of it, everything occurs by necessity and nothing by chance.[47] "What is rational is real, and what is real is rational." Thus everything that occurs is a result of the rational plan of God. "For the divine reason is not something which is to be fulfilled only in the distant future but something which at every time has already been fulfilled. The Idea always has the power to carry itself through." [48] This does not mean that human activity and striving for ideals is useless. The divine purpose for the world is always fulfilled but never wholly fulfilled. As Schmidt puts it, "The world at any given time is as it ought to be, as God will have it; but God never wills the world to be just as it is but wills its further development." [49]

Despite this optimism about history, Hegel is aware of the dark side of life, the sorrow and evil in the world. Indeed, when it is looked at from the human point of view, it seems tragic. But when we view it from the divine perspective, we can be certain that God's will is done. His right transcends all earthly and human rights and his laws need not correspond with our desires. While individuals often suffer wrong, they serve as means to the progress of world history. The divine Reason uses the selfish passions and immoral actions of men, especially "heroes" or "world-historical individuals," to serve its purposes.[50] "This may be called the *cunning of reason*—that it sets the passions to work for itself, while that which develops its existence through such impulsion pays the penalty, and suffers loss. . . . The particular is for the most part of too trifling value as compared with the general: individuals are sacrificed and abandoned." [51]

There is a certain grandeur in this philosophy of history which pictures the Absolute Spirit or God as governing the whole course of events, great and small alike, and making the evil as well as the good acts of men serve its purposes. It is the antithesis of positivistic views which see no unity or purpose in events and of naturalistic views which

[46] Hegel, *Philosophy of History*, trans. J. Sibree (New York: Willey Book Co., 1944), Introduction, pp. 13f.
[47] *Ibid.*, pp. 12f.   [48] Schmidt, *Hegel's Lehre von Gott*, p. 197.
[49] *Ibid.*, p. 198.   [50] Hegel, *Philosophy of History*, pp. 29–32.
[51] *Ibid.*, p. 33.

regard the dominant force in history not as the divine purpose but as the irrational desires of man such as greed and the will to power. But although it is a religious view of history, there are fatal defects in it. It deprives men of real freedom by treating their passions and actions as necessary effects of the divine will. It subordinates the individual, his interests, and his happiness, to the universal purposes of the Absolute Spirit in a ruthless or heartless way. It fosters a sort of optimism about the conquest of good over evil here and now which breeds complacency and a conservative acceptance of things as they are. Finally, it transforms faith in the reality of providence into a pretended knowledge of its workings in the lives of individuals and peoples. But it is presumptuous for man to claim to know the detailed plan of God in His rule of the world. As Schmidt says, "The God of history is a hidden God." [52] That Hegel did not see this is doubtless due to his supreme confidence in the capacity of speculative reason to "go beyond" faith and dispel the mysteries of God's nature and His relation to the world. This is the Achilles heel of his impressive philosophy of religion and it has made him vulnerable to sharp attacks by both philosophers and theologians from his day to our own.

HEGEL: CONTRIBUTIONS AND LIMITATIONS

Hegel's greatest contribution to the philosophy of religion was probably his insistence, in contrast to the emphasis of Schleiermacher on feeling and of Christian theologians on faith, that *reason* has an important function in spiritual religion. It is impossible, he maintains, for man as a rational being to be content with a vague religious feeling alone; he must clarify the content or object of his feeling in order to make it definite, eliminate unworthy elements and communicate it to others. Also, man cannot avoid seeking to understand the meaning of his faith and to overcome any inconsistency between different parts of it. Therefore, he must use his reason, making explicit what is only implicit in his religious feeling and bringing his religious beliefs into a coherent pattern. Although the language of religion is mainly pictorial and concrete, any attempt to make its meaning precise and to communicate it to others requires an interpretation of it in the conceptual language of philosophy. This is possible because religion is not only feeling or faith but also knowledge of reality. Thus, although Hegel goes too far in defining religion as a form of knowledge, he is an effective critic of irrational emotionalism and fideism in religion.

Hegel also recognized that *oppositions* between religious concepts

---

[52] Schmidt, *op. cit.*, p. 201.

are often due to the tendency of "understanding," which is always on the alert for contradictions, to regard apparent contradictions as real ones which cannot be overcome. As we have seen, the "understanding" thinks in abstract terms, separating and opposing to each other distinguishable aspects of a concrete reality, whereas "reason" can often show that there is a unity beneath the diverse aspects of such a concrete reality as Spirit. One of the best examples of this is to be found in the doctrine of the Trinity. Hegel points out that in the Age of Reason "understanding" saw a contradiction between the assertion that God is "one substance" and the assertion that he is "three persons." This was natural because it took the "persons" in an abstract way to be referring to distinct beings and rightly insisted that one Being cannot also be three beings. But "reason" makes it clear that the doctrine does not mean to separate the "persons" into distinct beings but regards them as eternal aspects or modes of the one divine Being. Although there are other statements of Hegel's concerning the Trinity and other doctrines which are open to criticism, the point we have just mentioned is an important one and has implications for the theory of religious language which is being widely discussed in our time. For it is now recognized by students of religious language that there are "paradoxes" in the language of Theism, e.g., the assertion that God is both transcendent and immanent, but that they are not necessarily contradictions.

Another major contribution of Hegel is his insistence, in opposition to the Age of Reason, that the philosopher of religion must take seriously the actual *religions of history* and their claims to truth. Although he did not have a profound knowledge and appreciation of other religions than Christianity, he did not suppose, like the unhistorical thinkers of the eighteenth century, that the reason of the philosopher could discover the truth about God and His relation to man and could then substitute it as a "natural religion" for the "revealed religions" of the past. Indeed, his conception of the philosophy of religion was based on the assumption that the philosopher must study the historical development of the religious consciousness in its different forms, and he made a serious effort to understand the Christian religion and to develop its implications, although we have seen that he misinterpreted it at a number of points.

For these and other reasons, Hegel must be regarded as one of the most important philosophers of religion of the last century. Unfortunately, his supreme confidence in the speculative capacity of the reason led him, as it had led Spinoza, to an excessive *rationalism* which soon provoked a violent reaction because of its pretensions. We have already indicated some examples of this rationalism. In affirming that philosophy is a higher stage of development of the Absolute Spirit than religion, he left the impression that it is necessary to "go beyond" faith to reason or, to put it otherwise, that what religion says in concrete language philosophy says better in abstract concepts. He also attempted the impossible task of demonstrating by reason the truth of the Christian doctrines of God, man, Christ, and reconciliation, and he seemed to imply that, since the philosopher can show these doctrines to be necessary and universal truths by reason, the historical basis of them in particular events is not really essential. Furthermore, in arguing that Providence is in complete control of history and that its operation is clearly manifest to reason everywhere, he seemed to claim a kind of omniscience for the human reason—at least his own—in discerning the necessity and rationality of events. These examples are sufficient to illustrate the fact that, if one of his main contributions is his recognition of the importance of reason in religion, one of his greatest defects is his excessive rationalism.

Other defects which must also be mentioned are due to his *monistic Idealism*. This is manifest especially in his tendency to regard every form of dualism as relative and to overcome every form of opposition by dissolving it in a higher unity. The fundamental principle of his metaphysical Idealism, of course, is that the dualism between the subject and the object of knowledge is not ultimate, that thought and reality are one. This theory of knowledge does not sufficiently recognize the contingency and independence of the objects given to reason. As a result, Hegel's Idealism, which regards nature and man as manifestations of the one Absolute Spirit, has been rejected by almost all philosophers because it denies the independence of objects which stand over against the subject and reduces them to appearances of the Absolute Spirit.

Our primary interest, however, is in the implications of this monistic Idealism for religion. For one thing, it leads to a denial of the kind of distinction between God and the world which has been asserted by Theism in its doctrine of Creation. For Hegel maintains that the world is not "other" than God in an ultimate sense but is contained in Him as a necessary "moment" or stage in His life, since He must go out of Himself into His "other" in order to attain self-consciousness. This results in the "panentheistic" view of God's relation to the world we have described, a view which virtually denies the transcendence of God in the theistic sense of the term. Again, the relation of man to God is that of the participation of finite spirit in the Absolute Spirit and the virtual identification of the former with the latter. This view, on the one hand, seems to reduce God to the level of man by stressing His immanence, and, on the other hand, exalts man but at the same time minimizes his freedom and independence by treating him as an instrument of God's self-realization.

Finally, the influence of Hegel's monistic Idealism is shown in his conception of religion. The essence of religion, he holds, is the elevation of the finite spirit and its deliverance from the cares and sorrows of time into the peace and rest of eternity. This is attained through the process of reconciliation by which the finite spirit abandons its independent and self-centered existence and identifies itself with the Absolute Spirit, realizing for itself in the present the union with God exemplified by Christ in the past. This is a noble conception of religion, but it is inadequate from the theistic point of view. For reconciliation, as it is conceived in biblical Theism, involves not so much the *identification* of the finite with the infinite Spirit as the *obedience* of the individual self to the divine Will. In other terms, Hegel's conception of the religious life is primarily *ontological* rather than *ethical*, for it emphasizes the union of the finite with the Infinite rather than faith in God and service of His will. This conception, when combined with Hegel's view of Providence as determining all historical events so that the real is one with the ideal, tends to encourage a complacent acceptance of the world as it is instead of stimulating moral effort to overcome the evil in it in cooperation with the will of God.

11 Christian Existentialism

KIERKEGAARD

Kierkegaard (1813–1855) is one of the most difficult of modern religious thinkers to interpret. The difficulty arises in part from his brilliant but involved and subtle style, in part from the complexity of his thought. But it is due also to the fact that it is almost impossible to classify him as a thinker and therefore to know by what norms to judge his work. Sometimes he is the imaginative and sophisticated writer of "aesthetic" treatises, describing ways of life with irony and penetrating psychological insight. Sometimes he speaks as a prophet criticizing his age for its mediocrity, its indifference to the spiritual, its submergence of the individual in the mass. Sometimes he speaks in the manner of a Christian preacher or teacher, addressing "edifying discourses" to the faithful. Sometimes he appears to be a Christian theologian, not a systematic expositor of the major doctrines of the faith, but a polemicist attacking distortions of them and an apologist presenting them in vivid and unusual language as possibilities for unbelievers. Sometimes, finally, he engages in dialectic as a philosopher, attacking the dominant "system" and proposing "subjective thinking" as an alternative. It is because he plays all of these roles in different works that rationalistic and naturalistic philosophers are usually irritated by him and dismiss him as an imaginative but violent prophet denouncing bourgeois society, or as a theologian with extreme views on religion, or, worst of all, as a brilliant but erratic thinker who might have become a genuine philosopher if he had not been a religious fanatic and an irrationalist.

If we are to understand and evaluate correctly his contributions to the philosophy of religion, we must take him as he is. Although he does not fit neatly into any of our categories, we shall find that there are valuable insights in his writings which must be taken seriously by religious philosophers. At the same time, we shall be forced to recognize that these insights are expressed in ways that are often extreme and sometimes false and dangerous.

SOCRATES vs. HEGEL

Although Kierkegaard was influenced in his philosophical thinking by several of his contemporaries such as Schelling,[1] his view of philosophy was dominated by his sharp reaction against Hegel's Idealism and by his admiration for Socrates. A brief analysis of his attitude toward these philosophers will help us to understand his own philosophical position.

His respect for Socrates was based upon the fact that Socrates had turned away from speculation about the cosmos and concerned himself with ethics, had abandoned the search for knowledge of the objective world for the sake of knowledge of himself and his good. In doing so, he had shown that his primary concern was for his own existence as an individual. Of equal importance was the fact that Socrates had professed his ignorance of the truth, regarding himself as a philosopher not because he possessed truth but because he loved it. In his humility, he recognized the limits of man's ability to know. In the quest for truth, he employed dialectic as a "midwife," seeking through dialogue with another to help him bring to birth the truth and requiring him always to decide for himself. Moreover, Socrates was profoundly religious in spirit. Although he was a pagan, he understood his mission as a philosopher in religious terms, obeyed the voice of the "daimon" within him, and died rather than escape from Athens and abandon his philosophical vocation. Finally, his intellectual humility, moral concern, and religious seriousness were graced by a wonderful gift of irony. He lived his philosophy, and his life was never dull.

In contrast, Hegel's speculative philosophy is indifferent to the existence of the individual and distracts him from his ethical task. For one thing, he subordinates at every point the *individual* to the *universal*. In his theory of knowledge, the individual is only a particular expression of the universal, the concept. In his metaphysics, he reduces the individual spirit to a manifestation of the universal Spirit or Absolute. In his ethics, he treats the self simply as a member of the state whose duties are to be determined not by his own conscience but by his station in society. And in his philosophy of history, all individuals, even great men who have played creative roles, are regarded as mere instruments used by the "cunning" of the World Reason for its uni-

[1] Cf. Walter S. Ruttenbeck, *Søren Kierkegaard, Der Christliche Denker und Sein Werk* (Berlin & Frankfurt/Oder: Trowitsch und Sohn, 1929).

versal purposes. To Kierkegaard, all of this is precisely the opposite of the truth, for existence is always that of individuals.

Again, Hegel's *rationalism* fosters exaggerated claims for man's reason. In his *Logic*, he claims to exhibit the dialectical process by which reason moves in a necessary order from one concept to another until it has developed a comprehensive system of concepts which culminates in "the Idea." Moreover, this process is supposed by Hegel to correspond to the structure and movement of the Absolute Mind itself and hence to comprehend Ultimate Reality. Kierkegaard attacks this pretentious claim on several grounds. The most fundamental is that logic is concerned with abstractions rather than concrete realities. Thought deals with possibilities, not with real beings. "Thought attains only to being as it is thought [*l'être pensé*], that is, the possible and the past. Abstraction can master reality only by transforming it into possibilities and thereby suppressing it." [2] This has two implications with respect to the possibility of a "system."

The first is that "a logical system is possible" but only at the cost of avoiding the inclusion of anything which has to do with existence. It is illegitimate, for example, to introduce movement into logic, as Hegel claims to do, for logic cannot explain movement. Rather, movement is the presupposition of both thinking and being, and it cannot be explained. In fact, logic "is indifferent to existence in the sense of actuality," and it is an "exhibition of ventriloquism" when the logician surreptitiously produces "the content of reality" as Hegel claims to do.[3] Moreover, the claim that a logical system has a beginning which is absolute and hence without presuppositions is false. For the beginning is reached by means of a process of reflection, and, since reflection is in its nature infinite, it can be brought to a stop and a beginning made only by a resolution of the will.[4] This means that the whole logical system, although it deals only with concepts, rests upon an act of the will on the part of an existent thinker, and this cannot be included in the system. Yet a logician such as Hegel tends to "forget that he is an existing individual," that he is an "empirical ego" as well as a "pure ego" or logical thinker. As a result, a logical system is possible, but only at the cost of "a kind of dying away from the self." [5]

The second implication of the abstractness of logical thinking is that "an existential system is impossible." [6] A system requires finality,

[2] Jean Wahl, *Études Kierkegaardiennes* (Paris: J. Vrin, 1949), p. 114.
[3] Kierkegaard, *Concluding Unscientific Postscript*, trans. David Swenson and Walter Lowrie (Princeton, N.J.: Princeton University Press, 1941), pp. 99–101.
[4] *Ibid.*, pp. 101–103.   [5] *Ibid.*, pp. 106f.   [6] *Ibid.*, p. 107.

while "existence is precisely the opposite of finality." [7] Existence is becoming, and only the past is complete and can be included in a system. If a man were God, forever complete in His eternity and yet including all existence within Himself, he could overcome this limitation and possess a system which would comprehend existence as a whole. But he is only an individual existing in time and as such he must strive persistently for the truth and can never complete the task. Moreover, while the Hegelian idealistic system culminates in "the Idea" as the identity of subject and object, the unity of thought and being, existence is characterized by their separation. [8] Kierkegaard ironically suggests that speculative philosophers like Hegel forget this limitation of their thought as finite, existing individuals, and imagine themselves to be "infinitely great." They think they have overcome the conditions that bind men to the earth, and can fly. But this is "a privilege reserved for winged creatures, and perhaps also shared by the inhabitants of the moon—and there perhaps a System will find its true readers!" [9]

Finally, the Hegelian system is a *monistic* one which stresses identity, the identity between thought and being, inner and outer, subject and object, ideal and real, and even divine and human. Although it recognizes the existence of difference and opposition, it minimizes and relativizes them. Continuity and unity are discovered everywhere and all differences are reconciled in the whole. In contrast, Kierkegaard sees the world as characterized not by identity, continuity, and harmony but by difference, discontinuity, and unresolved tension. The oppositions cannot be conjured away, the contradictions remain despite every attempt of the dialectic to overcome them. In consequence, the Hegelian philosophy seems to Kierkegaard to gloss over or even to suppress the difficulties and tensions of existence, to "make things easy." By its conclusion that "the real is the ideal and the ideal is the real," it shows clearly that it is a philosophy which sanctifies things as they are.

Thus Kierkegaard is radically opposed to Hegel's subordination of the individual to the universal, his rationalistic pretension that he has comprehended all reality in his system, and his complacent monism.

But it is the *ethical* and *religious* implications of Hegel's philosophy to which Kierkegaard most strongly objects. If the individual is merely a manifestation of the universal Spirit, if his freedom lies only in accepting the destiny imposed upon him, if the ideal is the real and things are as they should be, the nerve of moral effort is cut. The

[7] *Ibid.*   [8] *Ibid.*, p. 112.   [9] *Ibid.*, pp. 112f.

attitude of the individual becomes one of acquiescence, complacent acceptance of things as they are, conformity to the group. Decision involving a real choice between alternatives is ruled out. In consequence, man forgets that he is responsible for becoming himself by his free choices and his constant striving. He is content to become one of the crowd, conforming to the group and reflecting the spirit of the age. In short, he ceases to make ethical decisions and thereby ceases to be an individual.

The *religious* implications are equally disastrous. The Hegelian philosophy is incompatible with the transcendence of God which is affirmed by Christianity. Since it regards the Absolute Spirit as immanent in man and as realizing itself in and through the spirit of man, it virtually identifies the divine with the human. The doctrine of the Incarnation of God in Christ becomes merely a symbol of the union of the divine and the human as a universal truth. Sin becomes only a necessary "moment" or stage in the development of the finite spirit and is overcome when the finite spirit realizes its identity with the Absolute Spirit. To Kierkegaard, all of this seemed nothing less than a pantheistic caricature of Christianity, a relapse into the pagan religion of immanence. By denying the transcendence of God and the awful gulf between God and man opened up by man's sin, it seemed to make a real Incarnation unnecessary. Thus, while Hegel and his disciples claimed to be defending Christianity, they were really seeking to "go beyond" faith and dissolving Christian doctrines into mere symbols of the universal truths of the Hegelian philosophy.

THE INDIVIDUAL AND HIS EXISTENCE

It is in the light of his Socratic conception of philosophy and his opposition to the Hegelian system that we must understand Kierkegaard's own attitude toward philosophical reflection on religion in general and Christianity in particular. Before we analyze this attitude, however, it is necessary to clarify his theory of existence, since this determines his view of the limitations of philosophy and the nature of faith.

Most modern philosophers have used the term "existence" in the Kantian sense, with reference to an actual thing which exists in time and space and hence is an object of experience. It is contrasted with "essence," which refers to a possibility that can be defined but that may or may not have an actuality corresponding to it. As we have seen, Kierkegaard used this distinction in attacking Hegel's identification of thought with being, on the ground that logic cannot pass from the possibilities dealt with by thought to concrete reality. However, "existence" also has a more distinctive meaning for Kierkegaard since it refers to the existence of the individual *human self*. What are the characteristics of existence in this sense? First, existence is becoming. Becoming is a movement, conceived in Aristotelian fashion as a transition from potentiality to actuality. The self is not something which is, but something which becomes what it is. Since becoming occurs in time, existence involves temporality. But, second, the existence of the individual is a becoming which differs radically from natural process or change. For the becoming of the self is not a result of causes operating upon it but a task which is to be carried out by itself, a task which requires constant effort. Therefore, existence involves choice, and freedom is essential to it. The self is confronted again and again by alternatives between which it must choose. Decision is absolutely necessary to it. It cannot divest itself of its responsibility or refuse the exercise of its freedom. Thus will rather than reason is the center of the self for Kierkegaard, and ethical decision assumes a crucial importance for him.

But it would be a great mistake to interpret this radical insistence upon the responsibility of the self to choose itself in the sense of contemporary existentialists like Sartre, for whom "existence precedes essence" and the self makes itself by its arbitrary decisions, creating its own essence out of nothing as if it were God to itself. For Kierkegaard the individual is to become what it *is*, to actualize the potentiality which has been *given* to it. This brings us to the religious dimension of the individual's existence. For the true relation of the self to itself implies its *relation to God*. To put it another way, it is only when the self relates itself to God or is grounded in God that it is properly related to itself. The true authentic self is the self which is conscious of itself "before God." It is this relationship of the temporal self to the eternal God which is the ultimate source of its passion. For passion is the sign that the finite self is related not only to itself but also to the infinite.

At this point, the difference between Kierkegaard and Hegel with respect to the nature of man is evident. Like Hegel, Kierkegaard accepts a spiritual rather than a naturalistic view of the self. "Man is a spirit. But what is a spirit? Spirit is the self. . . . Man is a synthesis of the infinite and the finite, of the temporal and the eternal, of freedom and necessity, in short it is a synthesis. A synthesis is a relation between two factors." [10] The language is Hegelian and the definition of man as

---

[10] Kierkegaard, *The Sickness unto Death*, trans. Walter Lowrie (Princeton, N.J.: Princeton University Press, 1941), p. 17.

a synthesis of opposites is essentially a Hegelian one. But the difference from Hegel in the sentence that follows is striking: "So regarded man is not yet a self." [11] "This dramatic letdown," says Bretall, "brings out exactly the difference between S.K. and the Idealist philosophers, whose definition of man he can adopt in principle, but upon which he immediately throws a different light by insisting that man is actually not at all what he is in principle—that his *existence* is not only at variance with his ideal nature, but really its polar opposite. Man is not a unity, but a disunity; he is not his true self, which means that he is not a *self* at all." [12] For man is in contradiction with himself. When as a subject he makes himself an object in self-consciousness, he discovers that his actual self, or empirical ego, falls short of his ideal self. In his case, despite Hegel, the ideal is not the real. Through imagination he reaches out toward the ideal, seeks to unite himself with the infinite and eternal. But he is never able to achieve the "synthesis" or union for which he longs; he is destined as an existent being to strive toward but never attain it. As Kierkegaard says, "Life itself consists precisely in such striving, which indeed is the very hallmark of the life of man, who is compounded of the finite and the infinite. The conception of positive completeness is chimerical. No doubt it is possible that logic has such completeness . . . but subjectivity is existential, hence consists in contradiction and becoming and if it exists at all exists in striving." [13]

STAGES ON LIFE'S WAY: AESTHETIC AND ETHICAL

Thus the fulfillment of the self is not a given fact but a goal to be attained. This is the assumption behind Kierkegaard's phenomenological analysis of the three *stages of life*, "aesthetic," "ethical," and "religious," through which men pass on their spiritual pilgrimage. He means by "stage" a mode or sphere of human existence which is based upon a certain attitude and manifests definite characteristics. The three stages are related to each other as ascending steps on the way to an authentic human existence, the ethical being higher than the aesthetic and the religious higher than the ethical. But the ascent from one to another is not made by a smooth transition, like the advance from one point on a road to the next. The stages are discontinuous, and it requires a choice or decision of the self to ascend from a lower to a

---

[11] *Ibid.*

[12] Robert Bretall (ed.), *A Kierkegaard Anthology* (Princeton, N.J.: Princeton University Press, 1946), p. 340.

[13] Quoted from the "provisional edition" of the *Concluding Unscientific Postscript* in Hermann Diem, *Kierkegaard's Dialectic of Existence*, trans. Harold Knight (Edinburgh: Oliver and Boyd, 1959), p. 39.

higher stage. That which determines the order of the three stages is the principle that the highest kind of life is that which possesses the greatest "inwardness" and "passion," and the greatest passion is generated by devotion to an absolute end.

The *aesthetic* stage is the mode of life which is characterized by interest in the "immediate." The aesthetic man lives for a succession of momentary experiences. His present experience bears little or no relation to his past and future experiences, so that there is no continuity in his life. That which he seeks is pleasure or enjoyment for himself, and whether it is sensual or more refined pleasure is secondary. Since every pleasure soon palls, his life is always threatened with boredom and he must use the method of "rotation" to discover ever new sources of pleasure.[14] Also, a man at the aesthetic stage must not allow himself to be committed to any cause or to form a permanent attachment to any person. He preserves a complete independence, breaking off any relationship which threatens to involve him in responsibility for another. Above all, he does not allow love to trap him into marriage. The sensualist may find an intense pleasure in erotic love, but he does not commit himself to a permanent union.[15]

Since a life consisting of nothing but a series of momentary pleasures has no purpose to give it unity, the aesthetic life leads to despair. Therefore, the realization of the self can be attained only by going beyond it to the *ethical* stage, the basis of which is obedience to duty or conformity to universal laws. Its superiority to the aesthetic stage is shown by the fact that it brings continuity and stability into life. For example, the responsible love of the ethical man in marriage is superior even in pleasure to the romantic love of the aesthetic man, because it makes possible the repetition of love and unites present enjoyment with recollection of past and hope for future joys. Love and duty are not opposed to one another, for love intends permanence, and fidelity strengthens that intention.[16] Moreover, the ethical stage is more inward than the aesthetic, since it is based upon the active and free decision of the individual rather than upon external conditions. Its essence is the voluntary subordination of the individual to universal moral laws. Thus the "tragic hero" of morality is a person like Agamemnon who sacrificed his daughter for the common good or Brutus

---

[14] Kierkegaard, *Either/Or*, Vol. I, trans. David Swenson and Lillian Swenson (Princeton, N.J.: Princeton University Press, 1941); "The Rotation Method," pp. 231–249.

[15] *Ibid.*, "The Diary of the Seducer," pp. 249–372.

[16] *Ibid.*, Vol. II, trans. Walter Lowrie, "The Aesthetic Validity of Marriage," pp. 3*ff*.

who put to death his son in obedience to the laws of the state.[17]

But despite the sense of responsibility to others and the inwardness of the ethical life, it cannot be the final stage but must give way to the religious stage. Kierkegaard offers several reasons for this view. The first is that the ethical attitude "favours the tendency we all have to lose ourselves in the crowd, to become a passive element in the multitude," [18] so that our moral norms tend to coincide with public opinion or custom even when it is commonplace or perverse. The second is that there are exceptional cases in which it is impossible to discover a moral law that is adequate. For example, the moral law seemed to demand that Kierkegaard keep his promise to Regina Olsen and marry her, but he was convinced that he should not do so. Again, when Abraham believed that God had commanded him to sacrifice his son Isaac, the divine command was opposed to the moral law against murder. In such a case, a higher "telos" or end requires a "teleological suspension of the ethical." [19] The ethical is not superseded when this occurs, but it must be "reduced to a position of relativity" because of "an absolute duty toward God." The third reason is that the ethical sets before man an abstract ideal and assumes that he is capable of attaining perfect virtue by realizing it. But this overlooks the moral weakness of man when confronted by the law and the powerlessness of the ideal to overcome it, as St. Paul said (Rom., chap. 7).

For these reasons, the realization of an authentic self is possible for an individual only if he enters into a relationship with God by faith and thus passes into the *religious* stage. However, the ethical is not abolished, it is only "dethroned" at the religious stage. "The ethical is and remains," Kierkegaard writes, "the highest task for every human being. . . . The ethical is the very breath of the eternal." [20] The importance of the ethical for him is shown by the fact that the Epistle of James was one of his favorite books in the Bible, and one of his own books bears the title *Works of Love.* But while the ethical must be preserved in the religious life, it must be dethroned from the supreme position and subordinated to the religious. What is the nature of the religious stage?

[17] Kierkegaard, *Fear and Trembling,* trans. Walter Lowrie (Princeton, N.J.: Princeton University Press, 1941), p. 69.

[18] R. Jolivet, *Introduction to Kierkegaard,* trans. W. H. Barber (London: F. Muller, 1950), p. 136.

[19] Kierkegaard, *Fear and Trembling,* pp. 79ff. For an acute criticism of this view, see Martin Buber, *Moral Principles of Action,* ed. Ruth Nanda Anshen (New York: Harper & Row, 1952), Chap. 13.

[20] *Concluding Unscientific Postscript,* pp. 135f.

THE RELIGIOUS STAGE

First, religion is defined by Kierkegaard as a relationship of the individual to *eternal happiness* as his absolute "telos" or highest good. The emphasis upon eternal happiness in this statement should not be interpreted in a eudaemonistic sense. For Kierkegaard's ethical seriousness led him to conceive of the relationship of the individual to his highest good not in terms of the satisfaction but in terms of the transformation of the individual. "The pathos which adequately corresponds to an eternal happiness," he says, "consists in the transformation by which everything in the existence of the individual is altered, in and through his mode of existence, so as to bring it into conformity with this highest good." [21] Moreover, if eternal happiness is the highest good, "all finite satisfactions are volitionally relegated to the status of what may have to be renounced in favor of eternal happiness." [22] For it requires *absolute devotion* and should not be regarded merely as one of the many good things to be sought. Above all, one should expect no finite advantage from the religious relationship. "In the finite sense there is nothing whatever to gain and everything to lose. In the life of time the *expectation* of an eternal happiness is the highest reward, because an eternal happiness is the highest *telos;* and it is precisely a sign of the relationship to the absolute that there is no reward to expect, but suffering to bear." [23]

Second, this absolute relationship to the absolute end requires a relative relationship to the *relative ends* or goods of existence.[24] To live for the absolute end only "once in a while," treating it as only one good among others, is to make it relative. "The task is therefore to exercise myself in the relationship to the absolute *telos* so as always to have it with me, while remaining in the relativities of life." [25] Absolute devotion to the highest good, eternal happiness, does not mean that the individual must become indifferent to the finite or even that he must express his religious inwardness by acting in a way outwardly different from others. "True inwardness demands absolutely no outward sign." [26] This is essentially a Protestant point of view, based on the conviction that the religious life does not demand the abandonment of relative goods and withdrawal from the world into a cloister. However, Kierkegaard was more keenly aware than most Protestant thinkers have been that worldliness or preoccupation with relative goods threatens absolute devotion to the absolute end. For this reason, he

[21] *Ibid.,* pp. 348f.   [22] *Ibid.,* p. 351.   [23] *Ibid.,* p. 360.   [24] *Ibid.,* p. 365.
[25] *Ibid.*   [26] *Ibid.,* p. 370.

understood the attraction of the monastic ideal. "He admits," says Roberts, "that, as compared with a self-satisfied Protestantism which has compromised with the world, monasticism is incomparably superior. . . . Monasticism is mistaken not because it protests against this complacent attempt to combine worldly success with Christianity, but because it thinks that inwardness can be achieved by getting rid of the external world." [27] After all, the individual cannot by entering a monastery escape from the temptations of finite existence; and he can attain inwardness while participating in ordinary life and its values.

Third, the maintenance at one and the same time of an absolute relationship to the absolute end and a relative relationship to relative ends involves great difficulty, and for this reason *suffering* is an essential element in the religious life. As Kierkegaard puts it, "The distinguishing mark of religious action is suffering." [28] This has nothing to do with misfortune, for the religious man experiences suffering even when misfortune is entirely absent. Rather, it is an inescapable aspect of the religious life in all circumstances, and, while the "aesthetic" man avoids suffering as wholly evil, "the religious man believes that it is precisely in suffering that life is to be found." [29] For this reason, Kierkegaard speaks with the greatest irony of the "religious orator" who helps others to minimize their suffering by painting "a cheerful picture of better times in prospect" and the man who claims that since he has learned to "keep close to God" his business prospers, he is happily married, and his children are well and strong.[30] Suffering is absolutely essential because "the individual is in his immediacy absolutely committed to relative ends" and suffering is involved in "dying away from immediacy." [31] Only in this way can he attain the absolute relationship to the absolute end which is demanded of faith. Thus, suffering is a negative sign of something positive, i.e., absolute devotion to eternal happiness in the face of the natural tendency to exalt the relative values of existence in time. However, there is also a suggestion of something different here. Suffering, he says, expresses "the principle that the individual can do absolutely nothing of himself, but is as nothing before God," that "self-annihilation is the essential form for the God-relationship," and that it is his religious task "to become wholly nothing and to exist thus before God." [32] This is an ascetic side of Kierkegaard's attitude toward suffering and may reflect the influence of

---

[27] David Roberts, *Existentialism and Religious Belief*, ed. Roger Hazelton (New York: Oxford University Press, 1957), p. 111.
[28] *Concluding Unscientific Postscript*, p. 387.   [29] *Ibid.*, p. 390.
[30] *Ibid.*, pp. 398f.   [31] *Ibid.*, p. 412.   [32] *Ibid.*

medieval monasticism. However, he explicitly rejects the medieval tendency to inflict suffering upon the self by "flagellations," because he who tortures himself "counts his acts of self-torture as being something." [33] Religious earnestness is to shorten one's hours of sleep and not spare oneself in order to uproot selfishness—but without thinking that one has achieved something by oneself and without outwardly manifesting one's inwardness.

Fourth, the "decisive" expression of religious feeling or "pathos" is *guilt*. In seeking an absolute relationship with his absolute end and enduring the suffering that is essential, the religious man must *begin* with a clear recognition that his condition is one of guilt and that he can never escape from that guilt. When he enters into the absolute relationship, he is eager in his enthusiasm "to be off like Icarus, soaring up to an ideal task." [34] But in this he deceives himself, for "guilt is the expression for the strongest self-assertion of existence." [35] Moreover, he cannot throw the blame for his guilt upon existence itself since he is himself responsible for it as a free being,[36] and he cannot minimize the degree of it by comparing it with the guilt of others or by thinking childishly that he is guilty only now and then in relation to particular acts.[37] For in his absolute relationship he must judge himself by the highest standard and regard himself as "totally or essentially guilty." [38] Since his consciousness of guilt expresses his recognition of his responsibility for and misery in his estrangement from God, he should not try to escape from the eternal recollection of his guilt by any "lower satisfaction" such as that derived from "self-inflicted penance." [39] It is only by accepting the burden of total guilt without mitigation that he can maintain the absolute relationship.

Kierkegaard designates the religion he has been describing up to this point as "religiousness A" and distinguishes it from "religiousness B" which is his term for "the specifically Christian religiousness." The distinction he has in mind is not that between the religion of pagans and the religion of Christians, for *religiousness A* is the religion not only of pagans but also of "everyone who is not decisively Christian, whether he be baptized or no." [40] Rather, it is the difference between the religion of *immanence*, pagan and Christian, and the religion of *transcendence*, which is true Christianity. Speculative philosophy, Kierkegaard remarks, regards "religiousness A" as higher than "religiousness B" because it is the religion of immanence, while "Christianity is not content to be an evolution within the total definition of

[33] *Ibid.*, p. 414.   [34] *Ibid.*, p. 469.   [35] *Ibid.*, p. 470.   [36] *Ibid.*
[37] *Ibid.*, pp. 472f.   [38] *Ibid.*, p. 471.   [39] *Ibid.*, p. 482.   [40] *Ibid.*, p. 495.

human nature." [41] This gives us a clue to the meaning of the distinction. Hegelian speculative philosophy regarded the individual self as a manifestation of the Absolute Spirit and held that the individual needed only to develop the divine potentialities within himself in order to become one with God. The only condition of an absolute relationship to eternal happiness for such a philosophy is inward appropriation by the individual of his relationship with God.

In contrast, *religiousness B* is based upon a conviction of the transcendence of God and the individual's estrangement from Him. It can arise only when the consciousness of guilt has attained its greatest depth and has passed over into the *consciousness of sin* before God. At that point the individual is aware that he needs to relate himself through faith to that which is not immanent in but outside himself. "In religiousness B," says Kierkegaard, "the edifying is a something outside the individual, the individual does not find edification by finding the God-relationship within himself. . . . The paradoxical edification corresponds therefore to the determination of God in time as the individual man; for if such be the case, the individual is related to something outside himself." [42] Hence the object of faith in "religiousness A" is the Eternal which is immanent in the individual, but the object of faith in "religiousness B" is the Eternal God who is transcendent but has entered into time in a particular man, so that faith is conditioned and called forth by something outside the individual.

Thus the individual passes from "religiousness A" to "religiousness B" when he sees himself as a sinner before God and realizes that he is separated by an abyss from Him. It is only then that he knows himself as he really is and turns to God in repentance and faith. As Kierkegaard says, "All ways come together at one point, the consciousness of sin-through that passes 'the way' by which He draws a man, the repentant sinner, to Himself." [43] In short, the consciousness of sin is the necessary condition of becoming a Christian. But a man cannot attain this condition by himself. It is only through God's revelation of Himself in the Incarnation that a man can become aware of the depth of his sin. Only then is faith possible for him.

Finally, Kierkegaard's view of religion is almost completely *individualistic*. His interest is in the relationship of the individual with God, and participation in the religious community is definitely subordinate to this. Until almost the end of his career he participated in public

---

[41] *Ibid.*, p. 496.

[42] *Ibid.*, p. 498.

[43] Kierkegaard, *Training in Christianity*, trans. Walter Lowrie (Princeton, N.J.: Princeton University Press, 1944), p. 155.

worship and preached now and then, but he was suspicious of the "crowd" even in a congregation of the Church. Moreover, his emphasis upon faith as inward and personal made it impossible for him to appreciate the importance of fellowship with others and the necessity of the tradition of the Church in nourishing and strengthening the faith of the individual and assisting him in the practical expression of it in his life. For Kierkegaard, the Christian must stand in isolation face to face with God as revealed in Christ, for he had a "profound distrust of all mediational agencies except Christ Himself." [44] Moreover, he warns over and over against the tendency of the Church to make it easy to be a Christian. In its doctrines it conceals the risk and paradox involved in faith. In its ethic it softens the demands of New Testament Christianity by adapting it to contemporary attitudes and practices. It offers objective assurances to the believer, such as baptism and orthodoxy of belief, to save him from insecurity. In doing so, it encourages him to think that his doubts and temptations can be overcome by leaning on something outside himself instead of by inward struggle. As Roberts says, "He protested against any institutional security which might conceal the fact that churchmen remain existing persons in history, subject to fallibility, uncertainty, and the possibility of temporal defeat." [45] Thus, religion was for him a relation of the individual in which he stands "before God" in almost complete isolation from others and makes his decisions in passionate inwardness. His violent and extreme attack upon Christendom at the end of his career, therefore, was only the culmination of the religious individualism which had characterized his attitude during most of his life.

"PHILOSOPHICAL FRAGMENTS": REASON AND FAITH

We are now ready to consider the two works in which Kierkegaard deals most directly and fully with the problem of the relation of reason to faith in the religious life, *Philosophical Fragments* and *Concluding Unscientific Postscript*. The first is a pseudonymous work under the name of Johannes Climacus, and uses the method of "indirect communication." The second is a sequel or "postscript" to the first and professes only to complete it. In reality, it contributes a new and more detailed study of the problem.

Despite the fact that *Philosophical Fragments* claims to be a "piece," Kierkegaard is well aware that the "project of thought" he is offering under his pseudonym is a radical one. He claims that it "makes

[44] Roberts, *Existentialism and Religious Belief*, p. 90.
[45] *Ibid.*, pp. 91f.

an advance on Socrates" with respect to the question, "How far does Truth admit of being learned?" According to the doctrine of recollection proposed by Socrates in Plato's *Meno*, learning is interpreted as a kind of remembering, and one who seems to be ignorant of a truth needs only a reminder to become conscious of what he already knows. "Thus the Truth is not introduced into the individual from without, but was within him." [46] This doctrine determined Socrates' conception of his function as a teacher. He played the role of a midwife because he realized that this was the highest relation one being could have to another.[47] For the teacher's relation to the learner with respect to essential Truth can only be that of an "occasion" or stimulus, since the Truth is within each individual and does not have to be communicated to him from outside. Therefore, the fact that I have been instructed by Socrates or some other human teacher "can concern me only historically," [48] but it "cannot concern me with respect to my eternal happiness" since I already possessed the Truth within myself.[49] Similarly, the "moment" which was the occasion of my learning can have no absolute importance for me since "I have known the truth from eternity." It should be noted that Kierkegaard is here referring only to essential Truth, the religious and ethical Truth upon which a man's eternal happiness depends, and that this consisted for Socrates of the eternal Ideas with which the soul has an affinity.

Kierkegaard now offers his "project of thought" or imaginative hypothesis which is to "make an advance" on this Socratic view of learning the Truth. If we suppose that the learner before he met the teacher was *not* in possession but was destitute of the Truth, the moment when he came to know it would have a decisive and permanent significance for him. Moreover, if the learner was in error and was departing from rather than seeking the Truth, he would have to be given not only the Truth but the condition for receiving it. For his condition would be that of being not merely outside of but opposed to the Truth, a condition for which he was himself responsible, a condition of guilt caused by sin. The recognition of this nonrational factor in error puts the relation of the learner to the teacher in a very different light. For it requires a divine, not a human, Teacher to give the learner the condition necessary for understanding when his error is due to sin and is actively opposed to the Truth. Obviously, Kierkegaard is presupposing here the Augustinian-Reformation view that sin has corrupted or distorted all of

[46] Kierkegaard, *Philosophical Fragments*, trans. David Swenson (Princeton, N.J.: Princeton University Press, 1936), p. 6.
   [47] *Ibid.*   [48] *Ibid.*, p. 7.   [49] *Ibid.*, p. 8.

man's faculties and that he cannot know the Truth upon which his eternal happiness depends until his understanding as well as his will and heart have been transformed by divine grace. Accordingly, he rejects the suggestion that the learner can free himself from the bondage to error and sin by his own will, for he has lost control of his will.

The Teacher who frees the learner from the error due to his sin and gives him the "condition" for understanding the Truth must be more than a Teacher. He must be Savior and Redeemer because he saves the learner from his bondage and redeems him from the captivity into which he has plunged himself.[50] Furthermore, the effect upon the learner is not merely that he learns the Truth he did not know before but also that he becomes a man of a different quality, "a new creature," who has undergone a "new birth" or "transition from non-being to being."[51] Hence, the "moment" of his liberation from error and sin assumes decisive significance, it is "the Fullness of Time."[52] In this difference of attitude toward the "Teacher" and toward the "moment" of learning the Truth, Kierkegaard sees the fundamental contrast between Socrates and Christian faith. The Greek philosopher assumed that the Truth was within a man and could be discovered by his own efforts with the help of another person who merely served as a stimulus for his thinking. In contrast, Christians have learned that man is in error and cannot lay hold of the Truth by his own powers but must have it bestowed upon him and be enabled to understand it by God. Hence his relation to the divine "Teacher" must be wholly different from his relation to any human teacher and his relation to the "moment" of learning the Truth must have "decisive" significance for him since it brings about a transformation of his whole nature.

In a beautiful passage obviously inspired by the New Testament, Kierkegaard completes his "project of thought" by pointing out that the divine Teacher can bestow the Truth and thus manifest His love for the learner only by a "descent," by becoming equal to him through taking the form of a servant and by suffering all things like the humblest of men.[53] But what especially concerns the philosopher of religion is his view of the way in which the learner must receive the Truth that is thus offered to him. Briefly, he must receive it by what Kierkegaard calls a "new organ" and this "new organ" is *faith*. Why is faith necessary for this purpose?

According to the "project of thought," the divine Teacher has given

[50] *Ibid.*, p. 13.   [51] *Ibid.*, p. 14.   [52] *Ibid.*, p. 13.   [53] *Ibid.*, p. 25.

the Truth to the learner by taking on the form of a man. Thus, the eternal has entered into time in a particular historical event. But the learner must be able to apprehend the meaning of this historical event, if he is to appropriate the Truth that has been revealed in it. How can he come to understand the meaning of this event which is decisive for his eternal happiness? It cannot be understood immediately through the senses, since the senses can present to him only the content of the event. They can never apprehend its meaning as to the entrance of the eternal into time. This requires an interpretation which is uncertain, for a historical event occurs from freedom rather than from necessity, and the manner of its becoming, its "how," can never be known with certainty. Therefore, the learner needs an "organ for the historical," an organ which can negate this uncertainty. Faith is this "organ," since "faith believes what it does not see." [54] Moreover, the uncertainty or doubt can be overcome only by a free act, an act of will.[55] As Kierkegaard puts it, "Belief is not a form of knowledge, but a free act, an expression of will." [56]

This view of faith as the "organ" for apprehension of the meaning of historical events refers, of course, to the historical event of the Incarnation. It is obviously crucial, therefore, for an understanding of Kierkegaard's conception of the nature of the Christian faith and its relation to historical knowledge. He holds that faith implies doubt or uncertainty and at the same time negates it by affirming certainty. However, it does so not by knowledge but by will. "Belief and doubt are not two forms of knowledge, determinable in continuity with one another, for neither of them is a cognitive act; they are opposite passions." [57] *Belief is occasioned by the historical facts; but it is not inferred from them by an act of knowledge, it is affirmed by an act of will.* Therefore, Kierkegaard maintains that "the contemporary disciple" of Jesus had no advantage over the disciples of later generations with respect to faith in him, for the meaning of the facts was uncertain to both, and both had to overcome their doubts by an act of will. The only difference between them is that the "contemporary disciple" believed by virtue of his immediate experience of the events, while his successors of later generations and today believe by virtue of his testimony. "But no contemporary can believe by virtue of this immediacy alone, and neither can any successor believe solely by virtue of the testimony to which he has access." [58]

In our analysis of the *Philosophical Fragments,* we have been con-

---

[54] *Ibid.,* p. 67.   [55] *Ibid.*   [56] *Ibid.,* p. 68.   [57] *Ibid.,* p. 69.
[58] *Ibid.,* p. 70.

cerned up to this point to set forth and interpret the contrast between the Socratic and the Christian points of view with respect to the way a person learns the Truth, which is the source of his eternal happiness or salvation. As we pointed out at the beginning, the Christian point of view is presented by the author only as a hypothesis and no attempt is made to defend its truth. It must be accepted, if at all, by faith.

However, there is a short chapter in which an attempt is made to show that the confidence of Greek (and modern) philosophers in the power of reason to discover religious Truth is not well founded and that a divine revelation of the Truth apprehended by faith is necessary. Despite the lack of clarity of some parts of this "metaphysical crotchet" it is necessary to examine it because it contains a frontal attack on the attempt of philosophers to prove the existence of God by *reason* and thus supports the view that the Truth must be revealed by the divine Teacher and received by *faith*.

There is a "supreme passion of the Reason," says Kierkegaard, which proves to be its undoing and leads man to doubt even his knowledge of himself. It is the passionate attempt to discover something that thought cannot think, "the Unknown" which we call "God," [59] and it has led to the development of proofs for the existence of God. Like Kant, Kierkegaard argues that these proofs fail to attain their purpose.

1. In beginning a proof of the existence of God, he argues, I *presuppose* it not as doubtful, but as certain. Otherwise, I would not begin, because I would realize that it would be impossible to prove Him if he did not exist.[60] Hence the proof becomes merely "an additional development of the consequences that flow from my having assumed that the object in question exists." [61] At another point, he says that, if it is undetermined at the beginning whether God exists or not, the thinker will never begin, "partly from fear of failure, since God perhaps does not exist, and partly because he has nothing with which to begin." [62] There seem to be two different reasons offered here for thinking that the conclusion of the proof must be presupposed from the beginning. The first is psychological, i.e., "fear of failure" if one is not already certain of the conclusion. Doubtless Kierkegaard is right in thinking that this prevents many persons from attempting to prove God's existence, but it may be disregarded here because psychological obstacles as such do not affect the logical validity of a proof. The second reason is more important. Kierkegaard says that unless the thinker presupposes God's existence he "has nothing with which to

<hr>

[59] *Ibid.*, p. 31.   [60] *Ibid.*   [61] *Ibid.*   [62] *Ibid.*, p. 34.

begin." This seems to mean that unless he starts from premises or facts in which God's reality is perceived to be already present, he cannot arrive at God's existence at the conclusion. To put the point in another way, one cannot derive from premises in which God is unknown a conclusion in which His existence is affirmed as known. He makes a somewhat similar point when he argues that existence must be *given* rather than *proved*. "Thus I always reason *from* existence, not *toward* existence. . . . I do not, for example, prove that a stone exists, but that some existing thing is a stone." [63]

It may be pointed out that some recent philosophers have insisted that the proper method of philosophy in general is not to infer the unknown from the known but to make explicit and clear what is already known in an implicit and vague way.[64] And Austin Farrer asserts that rational theology should start from experiences in which God is already present but in a hidden way, "crypto-theism," and should proceed by analysis of these experiences to Theism.[65] If these philosophers are right, Kierkegaard's criticism of the traditional proofs as merely developing a presupposition made at the beginning may be accepted as containing an important truth. But this does not imply that they are useless, for to make explicit that which is only implicit in experience is to bring it into the clear light of consciousness and make possible a definite commitment to it.

2. A second general criticism of the proofs is that it is impossible for the existence of God to emerge in the conclusion "without any breach of continuity." "As long as I keep my hand on the proof, i.e. continue to demonstrate," says Kierkegaard, "the existence does not come out, if for no other reason than that I am engaged in proving it; but when I let the proof go, the existence is there. But this act of letting go is surely also something; it is a contribution of mine. Must not this also be taken into account, this little moment, brief as it may be—it need not be long, for it is a leap." [66] Perhaps Kierkegaard's point may be put in the form of a question: "How am I to be certain when my demonstration is complete and I do not need to bring forward more arguments or facts? In other words, how can I ever know that my argument is sufficient to enable me to draw the conclusion that God exists without having to leap over a gap between the last stage of

[63] *Ibid.*, p. 31 (italics added).
[64] R. G. Collingwood, *An Essay on Philosophical Method* (Oxford: Clarendon Press, 1933), pp. 161–164.
[65] Austin Farrer, *Finite and Infinite* (Westminster, Md.: Dacre Press, 1943), p. 10.
[66] *Philosophical Fragments,* pp. 33*f.*

the argument and the result?" It will be remembered that one of Kier-kegaard's criticisms of a logical system is that a *beginning* can be made only by stopping the infinite process of reflection. Similarly, any dem-onstration of the existence of God is bound to be inconclusive, since His existence never emerges with such certainty that reason is finally satisfied and needs no further arguments or evidences. Hence the phi-losopher must "let the proof go" and make a "leap" to the conclusion although he is not certain that it has really emerged.

Here again Kierkegaard has expressed an important insight. It is only in logical and mathematical reasoning that the conclusion "emerges" from the premises with such certainty that no discontinuity is felt. In all reasoning concerning matters of fact or existence, the conclusion "emerges" with less than absolute certainty and requires a decision that is not necessary and involves a risk of error. However, it does not follow that the decision in the case of proofs for the existence of God is arbitrary and that the proofs are therefore useless, but only that they should not be conceived in rationalistic fashion as producing a conclusion which is as certain as that of a mathematical demonstra-tion.

3. Although Kierkegaard discusses the *ontological* argument, he adds little to Kant's criticisms of it. He does point out, however, that Spinoza's assertion that "the more perfect a thing is by virtue of its nature, the more being it has" is really only a tautology. Spinoza had said that "by perfection I understand only reality of being." But if "perfection" is *defined* in this way as "reality of being," it is tautologous to say that "the more perfect a thing is, the more it is." [67] As a result, Spinoza evades the difficulty involved in the ontological argument which seeks "to introduce God's ideal essence dialectically into the sphere of factual existence." [68]

4. Kierkegaard's criticism of the *teleological* argument, however, differs somewhat from that of Kant. It is impossible, he says, to pass from known effects to the existence of the unknown cause of them. For example, how could I prove the existence of Napoleon from his deeds, unless I already assumed it? Since there is no absolute or necessary relationship between these deeds and that particular person, some other great general might have performed them.[69] With respect to the existence of God, if we know only the effects of some unknown cause and have no antecedent knowledge as to who (or what) the cause is, we cannot demonstrate that the unknown cause is God rather than

[67] *Ibid.*, p. 32.   [68] *Ibid.*, p. 33.   [69] *Ibid.*, p. 32.

something else. As Hume would say, "Why might not some other principle than a divine Mind have been the cause?"

Kierkegaard also points out that the existence of God cannot be
inferred from His "works" in the world without running the risk that
something terrible may happen which would overthrow the proof. This
implies that the teleological proof is based upon a *selection of the
evidence* which emphasizes the favorable and neglects the unfavorable
facts. "From what works then do I propose to derive the proof? From
the works as apprehended through an ideal interpretation, i.e. such as
they do not immediately reveal themselves. But in that case it is not
from the works that I prove God's existence. I merely develop the
ideality I have presupposed and because of my confidence in *this* I
make so bold as to defy all objections, even those that have not yet
been made." [70] Thus the teleological argument illustrates the general
criticism to which we have already referred: it cannot succeed without
presupposing the existence of God from the beginning.

Kierkegaard concludes his "metaphysical crotchet" by arguing that
Reason is also inevitably baffled in its efforts to know the *nature* of the
unknown God. The Unknown is a "limit" to Reason and a "torment for
passion." But the reason cannot get beyond the limit in any way, for
God is the "absolutely different" and "the Reason cannot even conceive
an absolute unlikeness." [71] Here Kierkegaard makes plain the assumption which underlies his whole treatment of the possibility of knowing
God: God is not merely "the Unknown," He is also "the absolutely
different" who is wholly other than man. This implies that Reason
cannot conceive Him because there is nothing even remotely like Him
which could serve as an analogy for Him. Because of its passion for
knowledge of "the Unknown," Reason cannot accept this negation and
tries to reduce the difference between God and man. But it succeeds
only in substituting a likeness for the unlikeness and thus deceiving
itself.

The conclusion Kierkegaard draws from this complete failure of
Reason to prove the existence of God and to know His nature is that it
confirms the necessity for a divine Teacher to give man the Truth he
cannot attain by his own reason. The truth has been given in the form
of the "Absolute Paradox" that God has done away with the "absolute
unlikeness" between Himself and the learner, and has assumed an
"absolute likeness" by taking on the form of a servant.[72] Reason, says
Kierkegaard, could not have discovered this paradox, cannot under-

[70] *Ibid.*, p. 33.   [71] *Ibid.*, p. 35.   [72] *Ibid.*, p. 37.

stand it when it is proclaimed, and will always raise objections to it. But its failure to know the Unknown, he implies, prepares it to "come together in a mutual understanding with the Paradox" when the latter is accepted by faith.[73]

"CONCLUDING UNSCIENTIFIC POSTSCRIPT": SUBJECTIVE THINKING

The *Concluding Unscientific Postscript* is one of the longest and most ambitious of Kierkegaard's works. Published under the pseudonym of Johannes Climacus but with an acknowledgment by Kierkegaard of his own responsibility for its publication, it claims to be "unscientific." "*In the end*," he wrote in his *Journal*, "*all corruption will come about as a consequence of the natural sciences. . . .* But such a scientific method becomes especially dangerous and pernicious when it would encroach upon the sphere of spirit. Let it deal with plants and animals and stars in that way; but to deal with the human spirit in that way is blasphemy, which only weakens ethical and religious passion." [74] It seems clear from this statement that the primary source of the "corruption" he has in mind here is not the natural sciences as such but the application of the scientific method employed in them to the human spirit. In any case, that which he attacks in the *Postscript* is not these sciences but the dominance of the scientific method of "objective thinking" in historical investigation and speculative philosophy.

The book purports to be a "postscript" to the *Philosophical Fragments*. The problem with which Kierkegaard is to deal in its general form is: "Is it possible to base an eternal happiness upon historical knowledge?" When it is expressed in its Christian form, it becomes: "How may I, Johannes Climacus, participate in the happiness promised by Christianity?" [75] Thus, the primary question has to do not with the *truth* of Christianity but with the individual's *relation* to it, i.e., it is not a theoretical but an "existential" question. However, since many in his time seemed to be more concerned with the question as to whether Christianity could be proved to be true by historical inquiry or speculative philosophy, Kierkegaard devotes a considerable part of his argument to this theoretical question. He calls it "the objective problem concerning the truth of Christianity" and one of his major purposes in

[73] *Ibid.*, p. 39.
[74] Quoted by Walter Lowrie, in the editor's Introduction to *Concluding Unscientific Postscript*, p. xv.
[75] Kierkegaard, Introduction, *Concluding Unscientific Postscript*, trans. Swenson and Lowrie, p. 20.

the book is to show that it is impossible to prove the truth of Christianity either by historical inquiry or by philosophical reasoning. Only after completing this negative part of his task does he turn to the primary "subjective problem" which has to do with "the relation of the subject to the truth of Christianity" or "the problem of becoming a Christian."

Dealing first with the attempt to prove the truth of Christianity by the *historical method,* Kierkegaard attacks the biblical scholars who assume that by the methods of biblical criticism they can answer the question whether God really entered history in Jesus of Nazareth. His primary criticism of these scholars is that "the greatest attainable certainty with respect to anything historical is merely an *approximation,*" and that "an approximation, when viewed as a basis for an eternal happiness, is wholly inadequate." [76] The task of the historian is an endless one. Since new evidence is constantly being discovered, historical research can attain at best a high degree of probability in its conclusions. In consequence, the biblical scholar is tempted by his desire for certainty to postpone indefinitely his decision concerning the truth about Christ, and his life runs out before he has made up his mind. Moreover, as the biblical critic becomes more and more engrossed in his scholarly task, his passionate existential interest in his personal relation to his eternal happiness through Christ becomes weaker and weaker until it finally vanishes. For the objective, scientific approach to the problem gradually produces a contemplative attitude which takes the place of a passionate religious interest. "Passion and reflection." says Kierkegaard, "are generally exclusive of one another." [77] Finally, the results of biblical criticism are irrelevant with respect to faith, for faith is not derived from historical facts. Favorable results are irrelevant because even if one could attain certainty about the historical facts they could not produce faith, while unfavorable results do not relieve a person of his responsibility for not becoming a believer in Christ.

Similar criticisms are directed against the attempt of Grundtvig and others to determine Christian doctrine with certainty by basing it on the authority of the Church as a present reality or the influence of Christianity in the past. For this gives rise to the same kind of historical uncertainty as that which is involved in biblical criticism. Thus, every attempt to prove the truth of Christianity on historical grounds is doomed to failure. Lessing was fully justified in saying that "accidental historical truths can never serve as proofs for the eternal truths of

[76] *Ibid.,* p. 25.   [77] *Ibid.,* p. 540.

the reason," and in concluding from this "that the transition by which it is proposed to base an eternal truth upon historical testimony is a leap." [78] The individual's eternal happiness depends upon his relation to a past historical event, but the meaning of this event must be apprehended by faith rather than proved by reason.

We may deal more briefly with Kierkegaard's criticism of the *philosophical* attempt to prove the truth of Christianity. The main object of his attack is the effort of Hegel to identify the historical beliefs of Christianity with the eternal and universal truths of his own philosophy. But Kierkegaard's criticisms are also leveled against speculative philosophy in general. His most fundamental criticism is that philosophy in its objectivity is wholly indifferent to the eternal happiness of the philosopher and everyone else.[79] The question of his personal happiness cannot even arise for the speculative philosopher "because his task consists in getting more and more away from himself so as to become objective, thus vanishing from himself and becoming what might be called the contemplative energy of philosophy itself." [80] Moreover, while the existing thinker may *strive* for the eternal truth, he is only a temporal being and can never *attain* his goal. Therefore, Lessing's saying is to be approved: "If God held all truth in his right hand and in his left the lifelong pursuit of it under the condition of always and eternally erring, and said to me, 'Choose!' I would humbly choose the left hand and say, 'Father, give! the pure truth is for Thee alone!' " [81] For only God can know completely the eternal truth; it is the destiny of man always to strive toward it.

Having shown that both historical scholarship and philosophical speculation fail in their attempt by "objective thinking" to prove the truth of Christianity, Kierkegaard proceeds in the main part of the *Postscript* to argue that "subjective thinking" alone can enable one to appropriate religious truth. It is this part of the book which is of most interest to the philosopher and it is necessary to examine it carefully.

Kierkegaard bases his argument for *subjective thinking* upon the conviction that "the ethical is and remains the highest task for every human being," [82] so that knowledge of the ethical alone is essential for the existence of the individual. The ethical task is the task of becoming subjective, and subjective thinking is necessary for the fulfillment of this task. For example, subjective thinking is indispensable in answering the question: "What does it mean to be immortal?" [83] Of course, it is possible to turn this into a learned question and gather the opinions

---

[78] *Ibid.*, pp. 86–90.   [79] *Ibid.*, p. 53.   [80] *Ibid.*, p. 54.   [81] *Ibid.*, p. 97.
[82] *Ibid.*, p. 135.   [83] *Ibid.*, p. 152.

of the wisest and best about it. "But the question of immortality is essentially not a learned question, rather it is a question of inwardness, which the subject by becoming inward must put to himself." [84] "Immortality," Kierkegaard adds, "is the most passionate interest of subjectivity; precisely in the interest lies the proof." [85] Therefore, he praises Socrates for leaving the answer to the question of immortality uncertain in the *Phaedo* but staking his life on it and facing his death with passionate hope for it. "On this 'if' he risks his entire life, he has the courage to meet death, and he has with the passion of the infinite so determined the pattern of his life that it must be found acceptable —if there is an immortality. . . . The bit of uncertainty that Socrates had, helped him because he himself contributed the passion of the infinite." [86]

This example will help us to understand Kierkegaard's conception of "subjective truth" and the "subjective thinking" which is necessary to attain it. Since thought and being are not identical but are separated for an existing individual, two ways of looking at truth are possible, one of which emphasizes the objective and the other the subjective side of the relationship between the object and the knower. "For an objective reflection the truth becomes an *object*, something objective, and thought must be pointed away from the subject. For a subjective reflection truth becomes a matter of appropriation, of inwardness, of subjectivity, and thought must probe more and more deeply into the *subject* and his subjectivity." [87] Kierkegaard offers his definition of subjective truth in sharp contrast with objective thinking and truth: "*When the question of truth is raised in an objective manner, reflection is directed objectively to the truth, as an object to which the knower is related. Reflection is not focussed upon the relationship, however, but upon the question of whether it is the truth to which the knower is related. If only the object to which he is related is the truth, the subject is accounted to be in the truth. When the question of the truth is raised subjectively, reflection is directed subjectively to the nature of the individual's relationship; if only the mode of this relationship is in the truth, the individual is in the truth even if he should happen to be thus related to what is not true.* Let us take as an example the knowledge of God. Objectively, reflection is directed to the problem of whether this object is the true God; subjectively, reflection is directed to the question whether the individual is related to something in such a man-

---

[84] *Ibid.*, p. 154.   [85] *Ibid.*, p. 155.   [86] *Ibid.*, p. 180.
[87] *Ibid.*, p. 171 (italics added).

ner that his relationship is in truth a God-relationship." [88] Of course, this applies only to ethical and religious truth which alone is "essential," and has no application to the "accidental" truths of science which must be regarded from the objective point of view. [89]

Now, this definition, which seems to be so completely opposed to the usual conception of truth, *could* be read merely as a strong way of asserting that, *in addition to* the question of the objective truth with respect to God, it is important to raise the question whether the knower is in the true—in the sense of right—relationship to God. It would then be simply a useful reminder that it is not enough for a religious man to have true knowledge *about* God as an object, but that the way he relates himself *to* God personally should also be true in the sense of conforming to the ideal relationship between a person and God. However, Kierkegaard appears not to accept this interpretation which would bring together the objective and subjective approaches to religious truth. He explicitly rejects the view that the truth is to be found "on neither side, but in the mediation of both." [90] The combination of objective and subjective thinking with respect to God must be ruled out because objective truth remains uncertain and the attempt to attain it involves a postponement of decision.

Since one must decide, then, *between* objective and subjective thinking, "anyone who has not been demoralized with the aid of science" must decide for the latter. [91] This leads Kierkegaard to his most extreme statement of the superiority of subjective over objective thinking. "If one who lives in the midst of Christendom goes up to the house of God, the house of the *true God*, with the true conception of God in his knowledge, and prays, but prays in a false spirit; and one who lives in an idolatrous community prays with the entire passion of the infinite, although his eyes rest upon the image of an idol; where is there most truth? The one prays *in truth* to God though he worships an idol; the other prays *falsely* to the true God, and hence worships in fact an idol." [92]

Two things should be noted in this well-known passage. In the first place, the reason given by Kierkegaard for his paradoxical conclusion has to do with the *way* in which each relates himself to the object. This is shown by the use of adverbs and adverbial phrases, e.g., "in truth," "in a false spirit," and "falsely." *"The objective accent,"* says Kierkegaard, *"falls on* WHAT *is said, the subjective accent on* HOW *it is said."* [93] Clearly Kierkegaard means to emphasize primarily the neces-

[88] *Ibid.*, p. 178n.   [89] *Ibid.*   [90] *Ibid.*   [91] *Ibid.*, p. 179.
[92] *Ibid.*, pp. 179f. (italics added).   [93] *Ibid.*, p. 181.

sity for a personal appropriation of religious truth by means of a right relationship to the object and the hollowness and meaninglessness of a merely formal assent to the truth which makes no difference in one's life. In effect, he is saying, "When philosophy speaks of truth as 'conformity of thought and being' it omits the most important dimension of truth, at least of ethical and religious truth. Real conformity with being requires the involvement of the whole self, not the intellect alone. A man does not really know the truth unless he affirms it with *passion* and wills to *live* by it. If so, does not one who intellectually comprehends only a small part of the truth about God but lays hold of it with his whole self possess it more than one who intellectually grasps it more fully and clearly but is indifferent to it? The one is *in* the fragment of truth he knows, the other is *outside* the truth he assents to but does not make his own."

The second thing which should be noted is that Kierkegaard does not deny that there is an objective truth about God. This is evident from the fact that he speaks of the Christian as praying to "the true God, with the true conception of God in his knowledge," and of the other as worshiping an "idol." He was an orthodox Christian in his beliefs and would not have dreamed of saying that the subjective truth of the idolater made his conception of God as true as that of the Christian. To understand the paradox which is expressed in the statement, we must remember Kierkegaard's conception of his special mission. Living in Christendom at a time when everyone professed to be a Christian and regarded it as easy to be one, Kierkegaard made it his mission to challenge this complacent assumption. He did so by emphasizing the paradoxical character of the faith and the costliness of the life of the true Christian. He assumed that most of his readers, like himself, already accepted the doctrines of Christianity as true. But he sought to show how much *more* than mere intellectual assent to these doctrines is involved in being a Christian. Therefore, we cannot agree with Höffding's statement that Kierkegaard's view of subjective thinking was the same as Feuerbach's, i.e., "that Theology is Psychology." [94] Kierkegaard *begins* not with his own subjectivity, but with the revelation of Truth by the divine "Teacher" as a *given fact,* and his subjective appropriation of this is a *response* to it as an objective reality.

This becomes clear in the next passage in which Kierkegaard offers a striking definition of subjective truth. "An objective uncertainty," he

---

[94] Harald Höffding, *Kierkegaard als Philosoph* (Stuttgart: F. Frommann, 1896), p. 75.

says, "held fast in an appropriation-process of the most passionate inwardness is the truth, the highest truth available for an existing individual. At the point where the way swings off . . . there objective knowledge is placed in abeyance. Thus the subject merely has, objectively, the uncertainty; but it is this which precisely increases the tension of that infinite passion which constitutes his inwardness. The truth is precisely the venture which chooses an objective uncertainty with the passion of the infinite." [95] What is meant by speaking of the "passionate inwardness" of this process of appropriation? Kierkegaard seems to mean that the doubt which is aroused by the "objective uncertainty" increases the passion with which it is affirmed as subjective truth. Since this doubt is overcome not by knowledge but by faith, the definition of subjective truth we have just quoted is "an equivalent expression for faith." "Faith," says Kierkegaard, "is precisely the contradiction between the infinite passion of the individual's inwardness and the objective uncertainty. . . . If I wish to preserve myself in faith, I must constantly be intent upon holding fast the uncertainty, so as to remain out over the deep, over seventy thousand fathoms of water, still preserving my faith." [96] There could hardly be a more vivid expression of the fact that "subjective truth," or faith, can be maintained only by a constant effort of the will and that this is necessary because doubt due to the "objective uncertainty" of what is embraced is never overcome and remains very strong. Kierkegaard glories in this doubt on the ground that it increases the intensity of faith and the "passionate inwardness" with which it is affirmed.

The "objective uncertainty" of that which is affirmed as true by subjective thinking, or faith, gives it a *paradoxical* character. "When subjectivity, inwardness, is the truth," says Kierkegaard, "the truth becomes objectively a paradox." [97] This seems to mean that the object or content of that which is affirmed as subjective truth is a paradox to reason. "The eternal truth has come into being in time; this is the paradox." [98] "The absurd is—that the eternal has come into being in time, that God has come into being, has been born, has grown up and so forth, precisely like any other individual human being, quite indistinguishable from other individuals." [99] This "absolute paradox" is the source of the most profound inwardness.

Speculative philosophy tries to do away with this "absolute paradox" and its absurdity by seeking objective truth rather than accepting

[95] *Concluding Unscientific Postscript*, p. 182.   [96] *Ibid.*   [97] *Ibid.*
[98] *Ibid.*, p. 187   [99] *Ibid.*, p. 188.

subjective truth, or faith. What is the result? It attains only probability and forfeits the certainty which the individual requires for his eternal happiness. Every attempt of reason to escape from the "absolute paradox" or the "absurd" by making it probable is bound to fail and the only result is to make it impossible to believe. The truth is that Christianity is a mystery. It was "never intended to be understood"; indeed, "the maximum of understanding which comes in question is to understand that it cannot be understood." [100] Therefore, when the speculative philosopher claims to comprehend the truth of Christianity, he does not really understand it; he simply "abrogates the paradox." [101] Thus, it is impossible to "believe with the understanding"; rather, "with the understanding directly opposed to it, the inwardness of faith must lay hold of the paradox." [102] Indeed, faith seems to require the understanding chiefly in order to overcome its opposition and deepen its own passionate inwardness. The understanding also serves a useful purpose in discerning nonsense and preventing the Christian from believing it.[103] But in relation to faith its primary function is purely negative. The Christian believes "against the understanding." He uses the understanding to discover its own limits and thereby to become aware of what is incomprehensible to it, but it is faith and faith alone which has the positive function of appropriating the truth and it does so not "with" but "against" the understanding.

KIERKEGAARD: PRO AND CON

A critical evaluation of Kierkegaard's contribution to the philosophy of religion must start from that which is the primary fact of man's existence for him: the self before God. Like Augustine, he is concerned with two realities: the soul and God. He shows little interest in the natural environment of man or the scientific description of it, on the one hand, or in the historical development and social institutions of man, on the other. Rather, he centers his attention upon man as a spiritual being and above all upon the ethical and religious aspects of the spiritual life.

How does he conceive of God and His relation to the self? As Ruttenbeck points out, the religious thought of Kierkegaard is characterized by a *dualism between God and man*.[104] This is expressed most clearly in his statement, "There is an eternal qualitative difference between God and man." What does this imply with respect to God? The answer is that Kierkegaard stresses, above all, God's *grandeur* or

---

[100] *Ibid.*, p. 192.   [101] *Ibid.*, p. 200.   [102] *Ibid.*, p. 201.
[103] *Ibid.*, p. 504.   [104] Walter S. Ruttenbeck, *Søren Kierkegaard*, p. 133.

sublimity. "God is the Sovereign, the unconditioned Majesty and not 'merely a highest superlative of human majesty.'" [105] He is an all-consuming Fire who awakens fear and trembling.[106] He confronts man with an unconditional demand, "Thou shalt," and man has no right to ask why, for that would be to deny His authority.[107] We must humble ourselves before Him, and we owe Him unconditional obedience and adoration.[108] "For we are nothing before God and we draw nearer to Him the more we abase ourselves before Him." [109] God is also *love,* and His sublimity and love are bound up together. But the primary fact of his philosophy of religion and his interpretation of Christianity is his exaltation of God to a position of utter transcendence in the presence of whom man should feel himself to be nothing. Thus his view of God represents a strong repudiation of the pantheistic tendency in Hegelian Idealism and a return to the orthodox Christian view of God as transcendent and personal.

However, Kierkegaard's interpretation of the Christian conception is an extremely one-sided one, since the biblical doctrine of God as immanent in the Creation has almost completely disappeared. As a result, the supernatural is separated from the natural, grace from nature, as by a great chasm. This one-sided emphasis on God's transcendence was due in part to Kierkegaard's profound experience of God's holiness and otherness, in part to his strong tendency to exaggerate difference and discontinuity rather than similarity and continuity. Now, the religious consciousness, as Rudolf Otto has shown, is always aware of the mysteriousness and otherness of God.[110] The religious man feels himself to be in the presence of a holy, transcendent being or power, before whom he must abase himself. But it also affirms the presence of God in nature and man. Certainly the Bible expresses over and over an awareness of His wisdom and power in nature and asserts that man was made in His image. If so, it is an exaggeration to think that He is "wholly other" than His creatures or that there is an "absolute qualitative difference" between Him and man.

Closely related to this error is another, which affects his view of the relation of faith to reason. It is the insistence that every transition in the spiritual life, e.g., every advance from one "stage" to a higher one, involves a "leap." This is true of the transition not only from the "aesthetic" stage to the "ethical" but also from the "ethical" to the "religious."

---

[105] *Ibid.,* p. 141.   [106] *Ibid.*   [107] *Ibid.*   [108] *Ibid.,* p. 142.   [109] *Ibid.*
[110] Rudolf Otto, *The Idea of the Holy,* trans. John W. Harvey (London: Oxford University Press, 1933), Chaps. 1–6.

One may accept Kierkegaard's emphasis upon discontinuity and crisis in spiritual development as a necessary corrective of the tendency of Hegelian philosophy to minimize the breaks and smooth out the transitions that occur. There *are* qualitative differences between the "stages" of life and the transition from one to another *does* involve a radical break with what has gone before. But Kierkegaard has been led by his stress on difference and discontinuity to a view of the "leap" which divorces it too much from what has preceded it.

The importance of this for an evaluation of his religious thought becomes apparent when one considers his view of the *nature of faith*. Faith is described by Kierkegaard as the result of an act of will which cannot be rationally justified and therefore appears completely arbitrary. As we have seen, this is the case both with belief in the existence of God and belief in immortality. Kierkegaard not only denies the validity of all proofs of God's existence; he rejects the search for proofs as an evidence of doubt. Similarly he heaps scorn upon philosophers who have offered "three proofs" of immortality and commends Socrates who risked everything on the hope for immortality of which he was "objectively uncertain." Parenthetically, he does not mention the fact that in the *Phaedo* Socrates offers several arguments for immortality himself, although he does not claim that they are logically demonstrative.

The line between truth and error on this point is difficult to draw. Kierkegaard seems to think that we must choose between two positions with respect to "proofs" of God, uncritical acceptance of them as demonstrative and complete rejection of them as fallacious. But a third view is possible, i.e., that they are valuable not as logical demonstrations but as interpretations of certain kinds of experience which seem to indicate the presence of a divine reality. Kierkegaard does not even consider this possibility and consequently rejects the teleological and ontological arguments as useless. Hence an affirmation of God's existence is possible for him only by a "leap" of faith which is made by an act of the will and which receives no support from the understanding. Why does he overlook the third possibility we have just described?

The reason seems to be that his conception of the knowledge which reason seeks is essentially a rationalistic one. A rational argument leading to a conclusion which falls short of certainty, he assumes, can give us no knowledge at all. On this point, his criticism of the "objective thinking" of reason in history and philosophy as merely an "approximation-process" is significant. In consequence, he holds that we can obtain no "objective truth" in the religious sphere and must be content with "subjective truth," or faith. This is to overlook the fact that, while reason may never *attain* certain knowledge of God, it is important for it to *approximate* more and more closely to the truth by a patient effort to correct its errors and clarify its understanding. Moreover there is a kind of "informal inference," to use Newman's term, which is based upon the convergence of many lines of evidence toward a conclusion.[111] This cannot produce logical certainty in the conclusion— indeed, such certainty is unattainable in any field outside of logic and mathematics—but it may provide strong support for belief in God.

Thus, while rational argument cannot take the place of faith, it can make faith more reasonable and avoid the conflict between faith and reason which arises when the will affirms beliefs "against the understanding." In rejecting constructive reasoning of every kind on questions of religious belief, Kierkegaard is driven to accept belief in God without any support whatever from reason. His insistence that an act of will is necessary to overcome doubt and make faith possible is a clear indication of the arbitrariness of a "leap" of faith which is not supported by evidence of any kind. He seems to think that faith is more *intense* when it is affirmed against opposition from the understanding and that this produces a deepening of *inwardness*. Since he also holds that the spiritual level of a person is determined by the depth of his "passionate inwardness," he infers that a faith which embraces a "paradox" with its absurdity is the highest faith. This is very doubtful, to say the least. It is true that it requires a greater effort of *will* to maintain a belief which appears to be contrary to the understanding than one which appears to be supported by it, and this effort may be a sign of passionate interest or desire to believe. But it does not follow from this that the depth of faith depends upon the amount of effort and passion required to maintain it. Of course it is true, as theologians from Luther to Tillich have stressed, that faith can be maintained in the face of strong doubt—as Job reaffirmed his faith in the face of God's apparent injustice to him. But faith *despite doubt* must be distinguished from faith *contrary to reason*.

Since we are concerned with Kierkegaard's philosophy of religion rather than with his interpretation of Christian theology, we cannot discuss his view that the entrance of the Eternal into time in the Incarnation is a sheer "*paradox*." However, it is legitimate for a philosopher of religion to point out fallacies in Kierkegaard's arguments against historical inquiry as a method of approach to these doctrines. For the same assumptions about the limitations of reason are operative

[111] John Henry Newman, *An Essay in Aid of a Grammar of Assent* (New York: The Catholic Publishing Society, 1870), Pt. II, Chap. 8, Sec. 2.

here as in his criticism of proofs of the existence of God and they lead him to similar negative conclusions.

1. It is true, as Kierkegaard says, that *historical inquiry* involves an "approximation-process" which never ends and that new evidence may at any time modify established views of the Jesus of history. Historical science can never establish certainty; it must always be content with the highest probability attainable. But if the Christian faith is a response to the historical events recorded in the Gospels, it is essential to establish as clearly as possible the nature of those events. The fact that certainty is unattainable does not make historical inquiry less essential for Christians who take seriously the historical basis of their faith. It is true that a mere historical knowledge of the facts about Christ is not a sufficient basis for faith in him, for an interpretation of the facts which involves risk of error is also required. But it does not follow from this that historical investigation of the facts about him is unessential. For unless the *interpretation* affirmed by faith is to be completely arbitrary, it must be consistent with the *facts* as they can be known. The "contemporary disciple" of Jesus enjoyed no decisive advantage over the disciples of later generations since faith was as necessary for him as for them, as Kierkegaard says. But since they must depend for the facts upon the record in the Gospels and cannot assume that it is an accurate account in all respects, they have a responsibility to examine the records as carefully as possible in order to establish the facts.

2. Kierkegaard's depreciation of the importance of historical inquiry about Christ sometimes leads him to speak as if the historical *facts* about him are unimportant for faith. Yet, as David Roberts has pointed out, "The human figure—the form of a servant, the renunciation of power and prestige, freedom from guilt and anxiety—is, from Kierkegaard's standpoint, singularly *appropriate* for expressing the nature of God. . . . And if the historical manhood was an appropriate medium of revelation as, say, the life of a scoundrel or a despot never could be, then the historical details cannot really be a matter of indifference." [112] "This can be seen still more clearly if one faces the problem which would arise if historical research established with high probability facts about Jesus that were unfavorable to faith, for example, that he never existed or that he was a scoundrel." [113] In reality, Kierkegaard himself assumed the truth of the Gospel account of Jesus, at least in its broad outlines, for the beautiful parable in *Philosophical Fragments* concerning the king who loved the poor maid and de-

[112] *Existentialism and Religious Belief,* p. 84.   [113] *Ibid.,* p. 88.

scended to her level to marry her was clearly inspired by the Gospels. Of course, the truth of the faith in Christ does not depend upon the *details* of the life and teachings of Jesus as recorded in the Gospels, and that faith has been maintained by Christians who have held different views about many of these details, e.g., whether Jesus was really born of a virgin and whether most of the teachings attributed to him in the Fourth Gospel were really spoken by him. But there is an obvious connection between the general account of the Jesus of history in the Gospels and the faith of Christians in him, and if the substantial truth of that account should be discredited by historical study, the faith would have to be modified if not abandoned by honest Christians.

Thus the conclusion we arrive at with respect to Kierkegaard's criticism of historical study in relation to the Christian faith is similar to our conclusion with respect to his attack upon philosophical argument concerning the existence of God: although "objective thinking" is not adequate by itself to demonstrate the truth of the Christian or any other faith, it is indispensable if "subjective thinking," or faith, is not to be a blind and arbitrary "leap" without support from experience and reason.

This brings us to a criticism which has been implied in what we have said about philosophical reflection and historical inquiry: *"objective thinking" should be regarded as an ally rather than an enemy of "subjective thinking,"* or faith. As we have seen, Kierkegaard treats "objective truth" in the religious sphere as an *alternative* to "subjective truth" rather than as a *preparation* and *support* for it. As we pointed out earlier, he did not mean to deny that the Christian conception of God is true and the pagan conception false; his concern was that objective truth should be not only assented to but personally appropriated by Christians. But in refusing to accept the view that both objective and subjective truth are essential, he sometimes speaks as if the former is so secondary as to be unimportant. The most striking example of this is his statement that "if only the mode of this relationship is in the truth, the individual is in the truth even if he should happen to be thus related to what is not true." [114] This is almost equivalent to saying that all that counts is sincerity and that truth does not matter. Although Kierkegaard was not indifferent to the truth about God, as we have pointed out, the statement we have quoted is so extreme as to lay him open to the charge. It should be emphasized, therefore, that although truth is *for* a subject, it must be *about* an object. To deny this with

[114] *Concluding Unscientific Postscript*, p. 178.

respect to religious truth would be to fall into the pit of subjectivism. Moreover, it is arbitrary to separate the subjective activity of personal appropriation from the object toward which it is directed and to assume that the quality of the former is not affected by the nature of the latter. Can the inward attitude in worship be sound when it is directed toward an illusion or an idol?

The criticisms we have offered should not be allowed to blind us to the *profound insights* of Kierkegaard into the spiritual life in general and the ethical and religious "stages" in particular. One of his greatest contributions to the philosophy of religion is undoubtedly his penetrating and realistic analysis of *existence*. In this analysis he corrected the tendency of Hegel and later collectivistic thinkers like Marx to subordinate the individual to the state, the class, the crowd, the *Zeitgeist* of a historical era, or the impersonal Absolute Spirit or Reason. He reasserted the irreducibly personal nature of human existence and safeguarded the distinction of the individual from God which is essential to the personal relationship with Him affirmed by ethical Theism. At the same time, he understood the dynamic character of man's existence as becoming in time, and the fact that freedom and decision are necessary conditions of that becoming. Moreover, unlike some of the twentieth-century "atheistic" existentialists, he has an essentially spiritual view of man and recognizes that a truly human existence is impossible without self-transcendence, that the finite and temporal spirit of man must be grounded in and responsible to the infinite, eternal God. Thus whatever one may think about his theology, his insight into the *nature of man* is profound.

Again, although we have emphasized the errors in his criticism of historical inquiry and philosophical reflection, his attack upon the excesses of "historicism" and "speculative philosophy" furnished an invaluable corrective to the dominant *Rationalism* of his time. His criticisms of Hegelian Idealism are among the most penetrating that have been made. Their philosophical value lies not so much in the dialectical acuteness with which he indicated particular defects of the "system" as in the clarity and force with which he showed the utter incompatibility of Rationalism in any form with the temporal existence and limitations of a finite thinker. Similarly, his attack upon the attempt of Hegel to reinterpret Christianity and assimilate it to his own philosophy was thoroughly justified. In repudiating so violently the alliance of Protestant theology with Hegelian Idealism, Kierkegaard was ahead of his time and anticipated the reaction against that alliance that was to come later. Moreover, while we have pointed out that he failed to consider the possibility of any kind of metaphysics other than the Hegelian, his criticisms of the "system" of Hegel constitute a useful warning against the general tendency of philosophers to forget the limitations of reason.

Closely related to this is another and more positive contribution of Kierkegaard's, his insistence upon the necessity of *subjective thinking*. He remarks in the *Postscript* that there are two kinds of "madness," one of which results from such an excess of subjectivity that the individual is isolated from his fellows and the world, while the other emphasizes objectivity so strongly that the thinker ceases to be an individual, existing being. He was one of the first to see and expose the dangers of the "madness" of objectivity which has developed in the modern world from an almost exclusive emphasis upon the scientific method. Regarded as a warning against this kind of madness and the impoverishment of life to which it leads, his criticisms of "objective thinking" are invaluable. Moreover, his recognition that in ethical and religious thinking a passionate interest in God and one's relationship to Him is essential to personal appropriation of the Truth reminds us that for religion God is not primarily an *object of knowledge*. Rather, He is the Being with whom we are *ultimately concerned* as the source of meaning and value in our existence. This implies that to "know" Him in a religious sense the whole self must be involved, heart and will as well as mind. Under the influence of modern Rationalism and its ideal of objectivity it is easy to forget that only through faith as personal commitment of the whole self can man "know" God as the Bible understands that term. For if God is personal, He is a Subject as well as an Object, and to *know about* Him through objective knowledge is at best a beginning of the process by which we can come to *know* Him.

Theodor Haecker has pointed out that Kierkegaard's conception of subjective truth departs radically from the dominant European conception of *truth* as a property of judgments in their relation to objects. Although Kierkegaard does not contradict this conception, he regards it as an abstraction from truth in the concrete sense of the word since it rests upon a separation of the intellect from everything else in man. "Whereas the order and procedure in European philosophy . . . proceeds from the world through the person, who is but an empty relative point, back to the world . . . he wishes to go from the person over the things to the person and not from the things over the person to the things." [115] This emphasis upon the primacy of the subjective and

[115] Theodor Haecker, *Søren Kierkegaard*, trans. Alexander Dru (London and New York: Oxford University Press, 1937), pp. 25f.

personal in a world that has come to be dominated more and more by the objective and impersonal is perhaps Kierkegaard's greatest contribution to philosophy and it has in our own century begun to have the profound influence it deserves.

12 Naturalistic Humanism

FEUERBACH and DEWEY

The major rival of Theism in the twentieth century is neither Pantheism nor Idealism but the Naturalistic Humanism which developed in the nineteenth century. Since the publication of Feuerbach's *The Essence of Christianity* in 1841, this humanistic philosophy of religion has gained many followers in intellectual circles. In certain respects Communist ideology has been affected by it, despite the official opposition of the Communist Party to all forms of religion, for Marx and Engels were profoundly influenced by Feuerbach during the period when they were breaking away from Hegelian Idealism. In Western Europe and America also, humanistic religion has had a considerable effect. It has given rise to new religious communities and has permeated the thinking of many Liberal Protestants in a number of churches. However, it has expressed itself primarily as an unorganized movement among individuals who have rejected the traditional religion of Church and synagogue. The extent of its influence is difficult to determine. Although those in the West who openly profess belief in it are a small minority, many educated people inside as well as outside the churches are in sympathy with it and accept it insofar as they accept any form of religion at all. Moreover, there are many forces at work in our scientific, technological, and industrial age which favor its growth.

NINETEENTH-CENTURY HUMANISM:
FEUERBACH

The greatest representative of Naturalistic Humanism in the nineteenth century was Ludwig Feuerbach (1804–1872). His importance in modern religious thought is shown by the fact that many of his criticisms of traditional religion have been repeated in the twentieth century by humanists such as John Dewey. Feuerbach's uncompromising hostility to the supernatural and his vivid and vigorous style have made him one of the most effective religious iconoclasts of the modern world. But the real secret of his influence is the psychological insight with which he grasped the unconscious motives behind much, if not all, traditional religion and the enthusiasm with which he embraced the nineteenth-century faith in man.

Although Feuerbach had studied with Hegel at Berlin, he turned against the speculative philosophy of the master and sought to use the *empirical method* of science in his own philosophy. He based his philosophy of religion upon a study of the historic religions, interpreted psychologically as expressions of human nature. His generalizations about religion, he claimed, were "no *a priori*, excogitated propositions, no products of speculation," but were derived from "the known manifestations of human nature, in particular of the religious consciousness." [1] Thus in his theory of knowledge he placed himself in direct opposition to Hegel, calling himself a "realist" who "generates thought from the *opposite* of thought, from Matter, from the senses." [2] Speculative philosophy, he said, "makes religion say only what it has itself thought," but "I constitute myself only its listener and interpreter, not its prompter." [3] As we have seen, Hegel was not indifferent to the facts of religious history, as this implies. One may also question whether Feuerbach was always merely a "listener and interpreter" and never a "prompter," as he claimed to be. For one can see on every page the effects of his "realistic" theory of knowledge, which is based on sense perception, upon his interpretation of religion.

As he was a realist or empiricist in his theory of knowledge, he was a *naturalist* in his metaphysics. The effect of this on his interpretation of religion was to close his mind to the possibility that the object of religious faith and worship is a supernatural Being. At the beginning of his career he was not a materialist. Hook has shown that in 1838 he made a sharp attack upon a contemporary form of Materialism and called himself an "Idealist in the sense of one who does not accept the view that everything is material or that intellectual activity can be fully explained by means of physical categories." [4] In *The Essence of Christianity* a few years later he still acknowledged the reality of man's mind and its distinction from nature below the level of man. Although the use of water in baptism "reminds us of our origin in Nature, an origin which we have in common with plants and animals," the use of bread and wine in the Lord's Supper symbolizes the fact that we are also

[1] Ludwig Feuerbach, *The Essence of Christianity* (New York: Harper & Row, 1957), p. xxxiii.
[2] *Ibid.*, p. xxxv.   [3] *Ibid.*, pp. xxxvf.
[4] Sidney Hook, *From Hegel to Marx* (New York: Reynal, 1936), p. 237.

distinguished from the plants and animals and that "Nature needs man, as man needs Nature." [5] Indeed, he goes so far as to say that "in bread and wine we adore the supernatural power of mind, of consciousness, of man," since they are, "as to their materials, products of Nature, as to their form, products of man." [6] Perhaps this assertion that man's mind cannot be reduced to nature and that "Nature needs man" reflects the influence of Hegel's Idealism. In any case, it enables Feuerbach in *The Essence of Christianity* to accept the view of natural science that man is part of nature but at the same time to regard him as being worthy of devotion. In the latest stage of his career, he abandoned this attitude and embraced a completely materialistic view.[7]

The importance of Feuerbach's sensationalistic Empiricism and his Naturalism is that they led him to dismiss without hesitation the claim of traditional religion that faith should be centered in a supernatural Being. If there is no reality beyond and above nature and man, religious people *must* be deceived in thinking that there is a supersensible and supernatural Being who confronts them in their experience. Feuerbach does not attempt to prove this fundamental point; he simply assumes that the natural world in space and time which is experienced through the senses and described by the sciences constitutes the whole of reality. It follows from this assumption that that which *appears* to the religious person to be a supernatural Being *must* be a natural one.

Nevertheless, Feuerbach insists that his basic intention in his work is a *positive* rather than a merely negative one. "Certainly, my work is negative," he says, "but, be it observed, only in relation to the un-human, not to the human elements of religion." [8] He reduces theology to anthropology but it is in order to "exalt anthropology into theology." [9] He means by this that his criticism of traditional religion based upon faith in God has the positive purpose of replacing it by a religion based upon *love for man*. Thus, that which in religion occupies the first place, i.e., God, is in truth second, and "that which to religion is the second, namely, man . . . must therefore be constituted and declared the first. If human nature is the highest nature to man, then practically also the highest and first law must be the love of man to man." [10]

This humanistic view of religion is supported by Feuerbach's analysis of the *essence* of religion. "Religion, at least to the Christian," he says, "is the relation of man to himself, or more correctly to his own

---

[5] Feuerbach, pp. 276f.   [6] *Ibid.*   [7] Hook, *op. cit.*, pp. 267f.
[8] Feuerbach, *The Essence of Christianity*, p. xxxvi.
[9] *Ibid.*, p. xxxviii.   [10] *Ibid.*, pp. 270f.

nature (i.e., his subjective nature); but a relation to it viewed as a nature apart from his own. The divine being is nothing else than the human being, or rather, the human nature purified, freed from the limits of the individual man, made objective . . . i.e. contemplated and revered as another, a distinct being. All the attributes of the divine nature are, therefore, attributes of the human nature." [11] This is admitted, he asserts, in relation to the attributes, or *predicates*, of the divine nature, but it is denied in relation to the *subject* of the predicates.[12] But it is inconsistent to deny the objectivity of the divine attributes, e.g., personality and goodness, and refuse to deny it of the subject of these attributes.[13] "If thou doubtest the objective truth of the predicates, thou must also doubt the objective truth of the subject whose predicates they are. If thy predicates are anthropomorphisms, the subject of them is an anthropomorphism too." [14] This seems to mean that we know a "subject" only as disclosed by its qualities, or "predicates," and that, if love, goodness, and other "predicates" are acknowledged to be human, the "subject" of these must also be human.

This denial of the objective reality of God is based, at least in part, on a *psychological assumption*. "Man is nothing without an object. . . . But the object to which a subject essentially, necessarily relates, is nothing else than the subject's own, but objective, nature. . . . Whatever kind of object, therefore, we are at any time conscious of, we are always at the same time conscious of our own nature; we can affirm nothing without affirming ourselves." [15] This assertion, for which no proof is offered, leads Feuerbach to a conclusion concerning knowledge, which is of the greatest importance: "Man cannot get beyond his true nature." [16] If so, Feuerbach argues, "consciousness of God is self-consciousness, knowledge of God is self-knowledge." In other words, whereas "the object of the senses is out of man, the religious object is within him." [17] In this argument, Feuerbach seems to be using the Hegelian idealistic theory of knowledge, according to which the object of knowledge is really identical with the subject, to prove that the object of the religious consciousness is identical with the subject, i.e., man. However, he does *not* apply the idealistic theory to the objects of sense experience, which he interprets in a realistic manner as "out of man." In this way, he uses an idealistic principle to turn Idealism upside down, denying the reality of that which to Hegel was most real,

[11] *Ibid.*, p. 14.   [12] *Ibid.*   [13] *Ibid.*, p. 17.   [14] *Ibid.*   [15] *Ibid.*, pp. 4, 6.
[16] *Ibid.*, p. 11.   [17] *Ibid.*, p. 12.

the Absolute Spirit or God, but asserting the reality of that which to Hegel was only an appearance, sensible objects.

The only other argument Feuerbach offers for his view that the essence of religion is man's consciousness of his own nature as divine is an *historical* one. The development of religion, he says, is concomitant with the development of human culture, and at every stage men's ideas of the Divine reflect their ideas of their own nature. "So long as man is in a state of nature, so long is his God a mere nature-god—a personification of some natural force. . . . The later, more cultured artists of Greece were the first to embody in the statues of the gods the ideas of dignity, of spiritual grandeur, of imperturbable repose and serenity. But why were these qualities in their view attributes, predicates of God? Because they were in themselves regarded by the Greeks as divinities." [18] It should be noted that historical facts of this kind could have been interpreted as meaning not that the divine nature is only man's ideal nature but that man has to interpret the divine nature by analogy with the highest qualities he is aware of in his own experience. Why did Feuerbach not interpret them in this way?

The answer is probably to be found in his belief that he had discovered the *psychological explanation* of religion, and it is this explanation which is the most important aspect of his theory. The clue to it is the paradoxical fact that, although the attributes of God are derived from ideal qualities of human nature, they are *alienated* by man from himself when they are ascribed to God. "To enrich God, man must become poor; that God may be all, man must be nothing. But he desires to be nothing in himself, because what he takes from himself is not lost to him, since it is preserved in God." [19] He alienates reason, goodness, and other qualities from himself and ascribes them to God because he wants to receive them back from God without the limitations and imperfections that accompany them in himself. "Man—this is the mystery of religion—projects his being into objectivity, and then again makes himself an object of this projected image of himself thus converted into a subject," or, more simply, he *projects* by imagination a divine being as "a means of human salvation." [20] "God acts, that man may be good and happy. Thus man, while he is apparently humiliated to the lowest degree, is in truth exalted to the highest. Thus, in and through God, man has in view himself alone. It is true that man places the aim of his action in God, but God has no other aim of action than the moral and eternal salvation of man: thus man has in fact no other

[18] *Ibid.*, pp. 20f.   [19] *Ibid.*, p. 26.   [20] *Ibid.*, p. 29.

aim than himself." [21] In brief, man "projects" ideal qualities such as intelligence and goodness from his own nature into an imaginary God because he is aware of his own imperfections and hopes that these ideal qualities will be returned to him in perfect form. Feuerbach also expresses this psychological explanation of religion in terms of what is today called "wish fulfillment." "Nature, this world, is an existence which contradicts my wishes, my feelings. Here it is not as it ought to be; this world passes away; but God is existence as it ought to be. . . . God is the fulfiller, i.e. the reality, the fulfillment of my wishes." [22]

In *The Essence of Christianity*, which we have been considering, Feuerbach applies his theory of the nature and psychological explanation of religion to the major beliefs of Christianity. Perhaps the best way to test his theory is to summarize his interpretations of these beliefs and then to subject them briefly to critical examination.

1. *God* as such is not at the heart of the Christian faith, Feuerbach contends. God is only a projection of the reason or understanding of man. As reason, he has no desires or passions, knows nothing of the suffering of the heart.[23] He is merely a metaphysical principle, conceived as an unconditioned and unlimited cause of all things.[24] But a God who has only the nature of the understanding cannot satisfy the needs of religion. Even moral perfection, the highest attribute ascribed to God as such, cannot satisfy religious need because it demands a similar perfection from man which he is unable to attain.[25] It is only love that can be a "substantial bond" between God and man. "Love is God himself, and apart from it there is no God. Love makes man God and God man." [26] Thus the God of Christianity is not merely understanding or moral perfection, but love, human, forgiving love.

2. The *Incarnation*, says Feuerbach, is "the practical, material manifestation of the human nature of God." [27] "God became man out of mercy: thus he was in himself already a human God before he became an actual man; for human want, human misery, went to his heart. . . . Man was already in God, was already God himself, before God became man, i.e. showed himself as man. How otherwise could God have become man?" [28] The love from which God sent His Son is simply love to man and this love is God. "But is not love to man human love? . . . Who then is our Savior and Redeemer? God or Love? Love; for God as God had not saved us, but Love, which transcends the difference between the divine and human personality." [29] Thus,

---

[21] *Ibid.*, p. 30.   [22] *Ibid.*, p. 174.   [23] *Ibid.*, p. 34.
[24] *Ibid.*, Chap. 2.   [25] *Ibid.*, pp. 46f.   [26] *Ibid.*, p. 48.
[27] *Ibid.*, p. 50.   [28] *Ibid.*   [29] *Ibid.*, p. 53.

the "nucleus of truth" in the doctrine of the Incarnation is simply that God is identical with human love. The central point of Christianity, the love of God to man in Christ, is the same as the love of man to himself made into an object.[30]

3. In similar fashion, Feuerbach interprets the doctrines of *Creation* and *Providence* in human terms. In the doctrine of the Creation, man affirms the divinity of the subjective, unlimited will as fancied by the imagination. Creation out of nothing is the highest expression of omnipotence, which is simply "subjectivity exempting itself from all objective conditions and limitations." [31] Thus it is in the same category as miracle and, indeed, it is the first and greatest of the miracles. The doctrine of Providence is interpreted in similar terms. "Belief in Providence is belief in a power to which all things stand at command to be used according to its pleasure, in opposition to which all the power of reality is nothing. Providence cancels the laws of Nature; it interrupts the course of necessity, the iron bond which inevitably binds effects to causes; in short, it is the same unlimited, all-powerful will that called the world into existence out of nothing." [32] But the religious meaning of the doctrine lies not only in this affirmation of omnipotent Will but also and primarily in its relation to man. "It is for man's sake that Providence makes of things whatever it pleases: it is for man's sake that it supersedes the authority and reality of a law otherwise omnipotent." [33]

4. What is the meaning of *prayer*? It expresses "the certainty that the inmost wishes of the heart have objective validity and reality, that there are no limits, no positive obstacles to human feeling, that the whole world, with all its pomp and glory, is nothing weighed against human feeling." [34] When man addresses God as "Thou" and expresses his deepest wishes to Him, he excludes from his mind the idea of the world in which every effect has a natural cause and affirms his petitions with the conviction that "the power of the heart is greater than the power of nature." [35] Thus "in prayer man adores his own heart, regards his own feeling as absolute." [36]

5. In the belief in *heaven* or personal immortality, man declares openly his wishes and reveals his egoistic concern with his own existence alone. The religious man conceives of the future life as like the present one but with all the imperfections of the latter removed, so that "the joys of heaven are the same as those of earth, only that they are freed from the limits and contrarieties of this life." [37] Thus the

---

[30] *Ibid.*, p. 58.   [31] *Ibid.*, pp. 101f.   [32] *Ibid.*, p. 103.
[33] *Ibid.*   [34] *Ibid.*, p. 121.   [35] *Ibid.*, p. 123.   [36] *Ibid.*, p. 125.
[37] *Ibid.*, p. 182.

interpretation of heaven is similar to the interpretation of God, the Incarnation, Creation, Providence, and prayer: "The beginning, middle and end of religion is man." [38]

6. Feuerbach's treatment of what he calls "the contradiction between faith and love" throws into high relief the basic issue between traditional religion based upon *faith* in God and humanistic religion centered in *love* for man. While the "essence" of religion is the identity of the divine with the human, he says, its "form" affirms a distinction between them. Thus, while love identifies man with God, faith separates him from God. Since God is simply a projection from man, the separation of man from God by faith means the separation of man from man and consequently "the unloosening of the social bond." [39]

In a sustained polemic against *faith* in God, Feuerbach maintains that it depends upon a special revelation from God and inevitably leads those who accept it to become narrow, exclusive, and intolerant toward others.[40] Since it is specific in its character, it necessarily becomes fixed as dogma and leads to the condemnation and persecution of unbelievers.[41] "All the horrors of Christian religious history, which our believers aver not to be due to Christianity, have truly arisen out of Christianity, because they have arisen out of faith. . . . for faith claims for itself only what is good, everything bad it casts on the shoulders of unbelief, or of men in general." [42] And this is not all. For faith is exalted above the laws of natural morality, and duties toward God come into conflict with common duties toward man.[43] Even when faith inclines man to do good, "he does good not for the sake of goodness itself, not for the sake of man, but for the sake of God." [44] Thus, although Christianity speaks much of love, its love is "tainted" and "limited" by faith.[45] Since Christian love is based upon faith in Christ, it is subordinate to faith and is particular rather than universal.

In contrast, true *love* for man needs no special authority because it is a universal law of nature based on the unity of the human species. "The idea of love is an independent idea; I do not first deduce it from the life of Christ; on the contrary I revere that life only because I find it accordant with the law, the idea of love." [46] It follows from this apotheosis of love to man that all *social relations*, e.g., of husband and wife, brother and brother, friend and friend, are in themselves religious. "Life as a whole is, in its essential, substantial relations, through-

---

[38] *Ibid.*, p. 184.   [39] *Ibid.*, p. 247.
[40] *Ibid.*, pp. 248–250.   [41] *Ibid.*, pp. 252–256.   [42] *Ibid.*, pp. 257*f*.
[43] *Ibid.*, p. 260.   [44] *Ibid.*, p. 262.   [45] *Ibid.*, p. 264.
[46] *Ibid.*, p. 266.

out of a divine nature." [47] The relations of marriage, friendship, and civil law are sacred in themselves and do not need to be consecrated by religion.[48] Similarly morality "has always its ground of sacredness in itself" and needs no "support from above." [49] Even eating and drinking ought to be religious acts and we ought to be grateful to nature and man for providing water, bread, and wine for our use. But it is only when reason has destroyed the "illusion" of religion that men will be able to "vindicate to common things an uncommon significance, *to life, as such, a religious import.*" [50]

Feuerbach seemed to believe that religion in its traditional or "false essence" was already dying in his time and that the day of religion in its humanistic or true essence was dawning. "Religion has disappeared, and for it has been substituted, even among Protestants, the *appearance* of religion—the Church—in order at least that 'the faith' may be imparted to the ignorant and undiscriminating multitude," so that only "the *external signs* of the faith are in vogue." [51] He was confident that "Christianity has in fact long vanished, not only from the reason but from the life of mankind, that it is nothing more than a *fixed idea*, in flagrant contradiction with our fire and life assurance companies, our railroads and steam-carriages, our picture and sculpture galleries, our military and industrial schools, our theatres and scientific museums." [52] The shell of Christianity as an organized religion survived, and men from habit continued to repeat its formulas and to go through its ceremonies; but the faith in God which had made it a living thing had died. Should not an age in which man was progressing so remarkably in science, technology, industry, education, and culture banish the illusion of God and give all the glory to Man?

FEUERBACH: A CRITIQUE

Any critical evaluation of Feuerbach's philosophy of religion must center upon his psychological explanation of religion, on the one hand, and his application of it to the doctrines of Christianity, on the other. His *psychological theory*, which is similar in some ways to that which was developed later by Freud, has had great influence in the last century. The reason is obvious: to a considerable extent it corresponds to the reality of childish, self-centered religion.[53] It is not only primi-

[47] *Ibid.*, p. 271.   [48] *Ibid.*, pp. 271f.   [49] *Ibid.*, p. 274.   [50] *Ibid.*, p. 278.
[51] *Ibid.*, p. xxxix.   [52] *Ibid.*, p. xliv.
[53] *Cf.* Gordon Allport, *The Individual and His Religion* (New York: Macmillan, 1950), Chap. 2.

tive religion in which the principle behind sacrifices and offerings to the gods may be expressed by the saying "*Do ut des* (I give that You may give)." One of the major contributions of Feuerbach is his trenchant, if one-sided, analysis of this side of religion, and the development of psychoanalysis since his time has laid bare some of its pathological consequences.

The theory also throws light upon the human side of religion in general. This may be frankly admitted by religious believers without accepting Feuerbach's interpretation of it as a proof that religion is both egoistic and illusory. For religion has a subjective as well as an objective side, a human as well as a divine pole. Since it is a relationship between man and God, it expresses the nature, limitations, and needs of man as well as his conception of the character and requirements of God. The longing for salvation or deliverance from the evils and imperfections of man's temporal existence is an essential part of every religion, and man looks for fulfillment of this longing to the Being or beings he worships as divine. This requires from him both an acknowledgment of his own weakness and imperfection and a belief in the power and perfection of the Divine.

Insofar as Feuerbach emphasizes this human and subjective side of religion and indicates how it affects religious beliefs, he has furthered our understanding of religion; and few have shown as effectively as he how often it takes the form of a childish and self-centered exploitation of the Divine by men to satisfy their own desires. But the basic question is whether he has not distorted the nature of religion by reducing it entirely to this subjective factor in its egoistic form and denying that there is also an objective reality present to man in the religious experience, a divine Being who is other than himself and is worthy to be worshiped and served for His own sake. The answer to this question will depend upon one's conception of religion and upon one's metaphysical point of view. It cannot be settled by evidence such as Feuerbach offers from the history of religions, because the psychological factors are subject to different interpretations. While psychology can throw light upon the nature of the subjective factor in religion, it cannot answer the question whether there is an objective reality corresponding to it. For psychology is a descriptive science which is competent to deal only with human experience as such, and the nature of the objects of experience must be determined in other ways.

The value and the limitation of Feuerbach's theory may be tested by a critical examination of his interpretation of *Christian doctrines*. That there is truth in some of his ideas concerning Christian beliefs no one can deny. He sees clearly that the most distinctive thing in the

Christian doctrine of *God* is not that He is an infinite, unconditioned Mind which is the first cause of the world but that He is characterized by love. It is also doubtless true that the main object of faith and worship for many Christians is the *Son* rather than the Father, because it is the Son who manifests and mediates God's love to man and thereby brings salvation to them. Moreover, it must be admitted that, although the doctrines of *Creation* and *Providence* assert the power of God as manifested in nature and history, they possess religious value for many Christians because of their belief that God exercises His power primarily if not exclusively for the benefit of men. This is not as obvious in the doctrine of Creation as in the doctrine of Providence, since man is only a small part of the Creation while he is involved in the whole of history. But it is now generally recognized by Old Testament scholars that belief in the Creation of the world arose later than belief in God's mighty acts in history on behalf of His chosen people and was subordinate to the latter. Again, *prayer* for many Christians does consist, mainly if not wholly, of petitions for temporal blessings and for the means of grace necessary to win eternal salvation. And belief in personal *immortality* is often motivated primarily by the natural desire to survive, to escape from the limitations of earthly existence, and to enjoy reward hereafter for virtue and merits acquired here. Finally, Feuerbach's sharp criticism of *faith* as leading to dogmatism and intolerance and as weakening morality and love rather than strengthening them is valid when it is leveled against a faith which is identified with dogmas alone and which is regarded as sufficient by itself without works of love. In his interpretation of these and other Christian doctrines, Feuerbach penetrates beneath the surface of men's professed beliefs to their deeper desires and motives and shows how far the actuality of their religion falls short of its ideal. Like Marx who pointed out the way religion has been used by the dominant class in society to justify its power and privileges, like Nietzsche who showed how "love of neighbor" has often become a weak and sentimental thing, he has done service to organized religion by his merciless exposure of its weaknesses.

But his almost exclusive concern to ferret out these weaknesses leads to a caricature of Christian beliefs at many points. Since he is prevented by his Naturalism from taking any of these beliefs seriously, he searches for unconscious motives for them in human nature. And, since he regards emotion and desire as the primary elements in human nature, he inevitably finds these motives in irrational wishes and feelings. Christian beliefs, he thinks, *cannot* have arisen out of the experience of God in nature and history as interpreted by men of moral and spiritual insight; they *must* be mere projections of the imagination to fulfill men's wishes and express their feelings. But if one does not view Christian beliefs from the perspective of Naturalism, one sees that Feuerbach distorts their meaning at every point.

1. Although it is true that the doctrine of God as infinite Mind and moral Will is secondary in popular Christianity to the doctrine that He is Love, it is also true that the Bible and Christian thought affirm that He is Creator of the world and Judge of men. The belief that God is Love and that He is merciful toward men becomes sentimental and leads to self-indulgence only when Christians forget that He is also the infinite and eternal Lord of nature and that He demands righteousness of His children.

2. The doctrine of the Incarnation does not mean that Christ offered love and forgiveness to men without requiring anything from them. He preached the "good news" of the Kingdom of God, but also repentance, amendment of life, and obedience to the law of love. The fact that Christ made severe moral demands upon his followers renders absurd the claim that the Christian life consists merely of a passive acceptance of blessings from above.

3. The doctrines of Creation and Providence have a much deeper meaning than that which Feuerbach ascribes to them. Belief in the Creation means not only that God has power over nature to fulfill men's needs but also that the world is good and that man is a creature who is responsible to his Creator for all that he is and does. Belief in Providence means not that God controls the course of history solely for the benefit of man but that He has a purpose for history and that man must subordinate his personal desires to that purpose.

4. Prayer does not consist exclusively of petitions for earthly blessings and heavenly rewards; indeed, at its higher levels it rises far above this to intercession for one's fellows and the world, praise and adoration of God in and for Himself, and communion with Him as the highest Good. Although it includes the petition, "Give us this day our daily bread," it also rises at its highest point to complete self-renunciation, "nevertheless not my will, but thine, be done" (Luke 22:42).

5. Personal immortality is not, to thoughtful and mature Christians, a demand for reward hereafter; it is an expression of hope for the completion after death of the spiritual pilgrimage begun in this life and for the continuation of fellowship with God.

6. Finally, faith in its essence is not a set of dogmas which separate believers from unbelievers and limit love for men. It is trust in God and should be an occasion for gratitude to Him rather than an ex-

cuse for condemnation of unbelievers. And its primary and indispensable expression is in the fruits of love.

Thus Feuerbach's psychological theory of the origin of religion has value in indicating the importance of the subjective side of religion, i.e., its concern for human needs, and the extent to which childish and popular religion has been perverted by making the Divine a mere servant of man. But the theory is a result of Feuerbach's naturalistic view of the world and his almost exclusive preoccupation with the perversions of religion rather than the product of a genuinely scientific study of the history and psychology of religions. Its application to Christianity, as could have been expected, leads to a penetrating insight into the weaknesses of many Christians but an almost complete distortion of the essence of Christianity itself.

THE HUMANISM OF JOHN DEWEY

In his essay in Volume II of *Contemporary American Philosophy*, John Dewey (1859–1952) included a paragraph on his attitude toward religion. He remarked that "while the conflict of traditional religious beliefs with opinions that I could myself honestly entertain was the source of a trying personal crisis, it did not at any time constitute a leading philosophical problem" and said that this was due to "a feeling that any genuinely sound religious experience could and should adapt itself to whatever beliefs one found oneself intellectually entitled to hold." [54] This is a significant statement and makes it clear that when he set forth his views on religion in *A Common Faith* a few years later he was dealing with a subject which had always been of minor interest to him as a philosopher and was presenting views of it which would "adapt" it to a philosophy that had been developed under the influence of other interests.

Like Feuerbach, his positive view of religion is asserted in sharp opposition to traditional religion, especially Christian Theism, and to idealistic philosophies such as that of Hegel. But whereas Feuerbach bases his criticism primarily upon a historical and psychological analysis of traditional religion, Dewey criticizes the latter primarily on the ground that it is inconsistent with the modern world view based on science and that it stands in the way of social progress. However, he echoes several of Feuerbach's criticisms and simply makes more explicit the philosophical Naturalism based on science which has been characteristic of religious Humanism for the last hundred years.

[54] John Dewey, in *Contemporary American Philosophy*, Vol. II, ed. G. P. Adams and W. P. Montague (New York: Macmillan, 1930), p. 19.

Dewey begins the argument of *A Common Faith* by asserting that men are divided today into two camps, those who believe in the supernatural and those who think that scientific and cultural progress has discredited it. There is a third possibility, he suggests, the separation of "the religious aspect of experience" from all association with the supernatural.[55] Thus, at the outset he ranges himself with those who are opposed to religion centered in the *supernatural*. One of his reasons for doing so is the great diversity of religious beliefs and practices in the past. This suggests that religions are relative to particular states of culture and that the "achievements and aspirations" of our culture may require a radically different kind of faith from faiths of past cultures. Would it not be wise, therefore, to "wipe the slate clean and start afresh" by freeing the religious aspect of experience from "all historic encumbrances"?[56] Another reason Dewey offers for abandoning the supernatural is that he thinks there are no grounds in experience for belief in it. The effort of some Protestant theologians to ground belief in God in religious experience, for example, he regards as unconvincing. He does not doubt that the reports of religious experience and its transforming effects are authentic but argues that the explanation of these facts as due to a supernatural cause is not "inherent in the experience itself." Religious experiences with similar effects are explained in other cultures by reference to different causes.[57]

But it is a third objection to belief in the supernatural that is most distinctive of Dewey. Traditional religion, he says, has converted men's "moral faith" in *ideal ends* into the belief that these ends are already realized in a transcendent reality. "Faith that something should be in existence as far as lies in our power is changed into the intellectual belief that it is already in existence. When physical existence does not bear out the assertion, the physical is subtly changed into the metaphysical. In this way, moral faith has been inextricably tied up with intellectual beliefs about the supernatural."[58] This philosophical idea is fostered by the psychological tendency to believe that what we antecedently desire is already realized in ultimate reality despite appearances to the contrary.[59] This criticism is worked out in more detail by Dewey in *The Quest for Certainty*. In earlier stages of civilization, he says, when men did not have knowledge of the means to control events, they were powerless to realize their ideal ends. This fostered a tendency to believe in the realization of these ends in God and in a heaven above the earth. It also encouraged the development of idealis-

[55] John Dewey, *A Common Faith* (New Haven: Yale University Press, 1934), pp. 1f.

[56] *Ibid.*, p. 6.   [57] *Ibid.*, pp. 12f.   [58] *Ibid.*, pp. 21f.   [59] *Ibid.*, p. 22.

tic philosophies from Plato to Hegel. "It will not be denied, I suppose, that the chief aim of those philosophies which I have called classical, has been to show that the realities which are the objects of the highest and most necessary knowledge are also endowed with the values which correspond to our best aspirations, admirations, and approvals. This, one may say, is the very heart of all traditional philosophic idealisms. . . . It is difficult for men to see desire and choice set earnestly upon the good and yet being frustrated, without their imagining a realm in which the good has come completely into its own, and is identified with a Reality in which resides all ultimate power." [60] But while this Idealism has given men consolation, it has also distracted their attention and diverted their energy from the task of realizing their ends and values by their own effort.[61] It has led to the separation of knowledge from practice, the exaltation of knowledge above practice, and the failure to seek intelligent methods of realizing values.[62]

With the rise of modern science, this religious and philosophical attempt to ground men's highest values in an ultimate Reality began to be challenged, since science found no evidence for such a relationship between value and a transcendent Reality. As a result, modern philosophy has sought to resolve the conflict between the traditional view and science. Philosophers like Hegel have tried to resolve it by proving that man's values are manifestations of the Absolute Spirit, the ultimate Reality. Others like Kant have sought to show that there are two realms, the realm of phenomena described by science and a higher realm of moral values known by another method.[63] But all of these efforts have failed because they are incompatible with modern science.

This brings us to Dewey's most fundamental criticism of traditional religion: its beliefs cannot be verified by and indeed are inconsistent with the *scientific method*, which is the only method of attaining real knowledge in any field. "The mind of man is being habituated to a new method and ideal: There is but one sure road of access to truth—the road of patient, cooperative inquiry operating by means of observation, experiment, record and controlled reflection." [64] This is a more basic source of conflict between religion and science than clashes between particular beliefs of the former and new discoveries of the latter, for acceptance of the scientific method as the *only* method of knowing requires the "surrender of the whole notion of special truths that are

---

[60] John Dewey, *The Quest for Certainty* (London: George Allen and Unwin, 1930), p. 34.

[61] *Ibid.*, p. 36.   [62] *Ibid.*, pp. 36, 40.   [63] *Ibid.*, Chap. 3.

[64] *A Common Faith*, p. 32.

religious by their own nature, together with the idea of peculiar ave-
nues of access to such truths." [65] We can no longer divide knowledge
into two different kinds which are attained by quite different methods,
for present gaps in knowledge attained by the scientific method may
reflect only a temporary limitation which may be overcome by science
in the future.[66] Moreover, allegiance to this method is irreconcilable
with even a minimum of belief that has been fixed and can never be
modified.[67] Above all, while the scientific method is public and yields
conclusions that can be verified by everyone, alleged knowledge derived from a special kind of "religious experience" is private and
limited to those who have enjoyed the experience.[68]

Thus "knowledge" gained from religious experience or historic revelation is subjective, unverifiable, and unmodifiable by further experience. It must be dismissed, therefore, as a product of the "idealizing
imagination" symbolizing ideal ends or values. The conclusion is similar to that of Feuerbach: the Divine is a projection of human values
and ideals by the imagination. But it has been arrived at not by psychological analysis but by restriction of knowledge to what can be
discovered and verified by the scientific method.

We must also mention briefly criticisms of traditional religion
which are of a more *practical* kind. "Men have never fully used the
powers they possess to advance the good in life, because they have
waited upon some power external to themselves and to nature to do
the work they are responsible for doing." [69] This attitude is an expression of pessimism concerning human nature and its powers; it may also
produce an excessive optimism due to confidence that faith will be followed at once by a regeneration of the self.[70] This criticism is very
important to Dewey because of his strong interest in moral activity and
social change under the guidance of intelligence. It is also related to his
criticism that traditional religion has led to evil consequences because
its distinction between the supernatural and the natural has been accompanied by a distinction between "religious" and "secular" interests.
Dewey admits that in liberal religions the separation of "sacred" from
"profane" values has been largely overcome, but he holds that there is
still a tendency to divide man's interests and efforts between two sets
of values. This is incompatible with the revolutionary change in the
status and function of religion in the modern period as a result of the
emancipation of human activities from control by ecclesiastical institu-

---

[65] *Ibid.*   [66] *Ibid.*, p. 33.   [67] *Ibid.*, pp. 34f.   [68] *Ibid.*, p. 39.
[69] *Ibid.*, p. 46.   [70] *Ibid.*, p. 47.

tions and the growth of secular interests unrelated to any church. The process of breaking down the dualism between sacred and profane should be carried further and men should devote *all* of their energies to the realization of possibilities of value in nature and human life.

Opposed to this modern tendency is the theological view that human nature has been corrupted by sin and is incapable of realizing the good. Dewey's answer to this objection throws light upon his own view of *human nature* and helps to explain his complete lack of sympathy for Christianity as a religion of redemption. The belief in man's corruption by sin, he says, overlooks the fact that positive values have emerged from human nature.[71] This suggests that the real source of social evils is not man's sin but his ignorance of the causes of these evils and his failure to apply intelligence in the struggle against them.[72] What is needed, therefore, is not supernatural aid but "the development of social intelligence" and an application of it to social evils similar to the application of natural science to human disease.[73] Thus the basis of Dewey's practical criticisms of traditional religion is his optimistic view of human nature, his confidence in man's power to overcome social evils, and his conviction that dependence upon supernatural aid prevents him from using his own will and intelligence in overcoming them.

What is the *conception of religion* which Dewey proposes in the place of traditional religion? In brief, he proposes to substitute for "religion" what he calls "the religious." The noun "religion" always designates a special set of beliefs and practices and some kind of institutional organization, whereas the adjective "religious" refers not to any "specifiable entity" of this kind but to "attitudes that may be taken toward every object and every proposed end or ideal."[74] More specifically, it refers to attitudes which do not affect "particular modes of conduct" only but involve an "adjustment" of the whole self and consequently are capable of enduring through many changes of circumstance.[75] The imagination has an indispensable role to play in bringing about such an attitude and thus making possible the unification of the self with itself and with the world. "The idea of a whole, whether of the whole personal being or of the world, is an imaginative, not literal, idea. . . . Hence the idea of a thoroughgoing and deepseated harmonizing of the self with the Universe (as a name for the totality of conditions with which the self is connected) operates only through imagination."[76]

[71] *Ibid.*, p. 74. [72] *Ibid.*, p. 76. [73] *Ibid.*, p. 77. [74] *Ibid.*, pp. 9f.
[75] *Ibid.*, p. 15. [76] *Ibid.*, pp. 18, 19.

The process by which the imagination effects this unification of the self and the world is not only intellectual but also practical. It sets up "ideal ends" for the self which are acknowledged to have a rightful claim to authority over the self's choices and actions.[77] When these ideal ends are so inclusive that they unify the self, the attitude toward them is religious, since they control its destiny and thus have the same function as the unseen powers of traditional religion. However, faith in them does not involve belief that they must prevail, for their claim upon our devotion is based wholly on their intrinsic nature.[78] They include not only moral values but also friendship, beauty, and knowledge, indeed, all ends that are inclusive enough to contribute to the unification of the self. "Any activity pursued in behalf of an ideal end against obstacles and in spite of threats of personal loss because of conviction of its general and enduring value is religious in quality." [79] *Thus "the religious" is primarily an attitude of devotion to ideal ends set up by the imagination to govern the choices of the self and to bring about its unification with itself and the world.*

There is a secondary element in this humanistic view which has some importance. As a philosophical naturalist, Dewey emphasizes the fact that man is a part of nature and that he is dependent upon his natural and social environment for the realization of his ideal ends. "The essentially unreligious attitude is that which attributes human achievement and purpose to man in isolation from the world of physical nature and his fellows." [80] The acknowledgment of this dependence Dewey calls *"natural piety,"* and he maintains that it is "an inherent constituent of a just perspective in life." [81] This conception of "natural piety" is closely related to the unusual meaning Dewey gives to the word "God." Although most naturalistic humanists have been unwilling to use the word because of its traditional meaning, he suggests that it may be used to denote "the unity of all ideal ends" to which one is supremely devoted.[82] It may also be used with a broader meaning. "But this idea of God, or of the divine, is also connected with all the natural forces and conditions—including man and human association—that promote the growth of the ideal and that further its realization. . . . It is this *active* relation between ideal and actual to which I would give the name 'God.'" [83] Dewey justifies this peculiar use of "God" primarily on practical grounds. A clear idea of the union of ideal ends with actual conditions can arouse emotion, unify interests,

---

[77] *Ibid.,* pp. 20, 21.   [78] *Ibid.,* p. 23.   [79] *Ibid.,* p. 27.   [80] *Ibid.,* p. 25.
[81] *Ibid.,* p. 26.   [82] *Ibid.,* p. 42.   [83] *Ibid.,* pp. 50, 51.

and direct action.[84] It can also express man's sense of dependence on the world and its support for his aspirations. While "militant atheism" lacks natural piety and regards the world as indifferent or hostile to man, "use of the words 'God' or 'divine' to convey the union of actual with ideal may protect man from a sense of isolation and from consequent despair or defiance." [85] Although we cannot claim that the universe is "friendly to man" in an unqualified sense, we *can* say that it is favorable to the emergence and growth of his ideal ends.[86]

THEISM vs. RELIGIOUS HUMANISM

In *A Common Faith* Dewey has given us one of the most persuasive statements of the case for Naturalistic Humanism. He states with clarity and conviction the four major themes of that view of religion: its rejection of the supernatural; its naturalistic view of the world based on science; its high view of man as part of nature but unique in his possibilities; and its ethical and social idealism. Moreover, he presents these themes in such a way that the negative and polemical aspects of his argument are seen to rest upon a positive attitude toward man's ideals and a sincere devotion to his welfare.

There is an important element of truth in his statement of each of the four themes of Humanism. No one can deny that it is impossible to prove the major beliefs of Theism with certainty, that religious experience has been interpreted in different ways, or that belief in the supernatural has often led to the disparagement of natural values and human effort. Furthermore, a naturalistic world view has its positive attractions, e.g., the fact that our knowledge of nature through sense experience is in general trustworthy, that we are conscious of ourselves as natural beings and of our values as bound up with natural conditions, and that science provides us with dependable knowledge of the means to realize our ends. Again, while traditional religion has often seemed to be pessimistic in its view of man, Humanism puts its major emphasis upon his dignity and worth. Finally, few persons have been more deeply concerned than Dewey with man's realization of his moral and social possibilities through intelligence and effort. For these reasons, Dewey's religious attitude doubtless offers a possible alternative for those who cannot accept traditional religion in any form for intellectual or practical reasons.

Nevertheless, it fails both in its criticisms of traditional "religion" and in its proposal of "the religious" as a substitute.

[84] *Ibid.*, pp. 51, 52.   [85] *Ibid.*, p. 53.   [86] *Ibid.*, pp. 55, 56.

1. Dewey's *criticisms of traditional religion* are not convincing. An example is his denial of the value of Christian "religious experience" as evidence for a personal God on the ground that the interpretation of religious experience differs in different cultures. "Taoists, Buddhists, Moslems, persons of no religion including those who reject all supernatural influence and power, have had experiences similar in their effect." [87] This objection is not supported by a comparative analysis of the quality and effects of the religious experiences characteristic of the four religions and of unbelievers mentioned by Dewey. He simply asserts without proof that the experiences in all five groups are "similar in their effect." Moreover, his negative conclusion concerning religious experience is based on the false assumption that there has been no unity among the higher religions with respect to the presence in religious experience of a transcendent Being. Of course, there have been different *interpretations* of this Being, but this does not prove that it is merely subjective.

2. Dewey's objection that traditional religion ascribes "antecedent reality" to ideal ends or values because of wishful thinking and that this prevents men from realizing them by their own efforts has an element of truth in it, but taken as a whole it is false. The truth in it is that Theism affirms that ideal ends or values are grounded in Reality in the sense that they are not merely subjective expressions of human desire or feeling but are based upon the will of God who is a Perfect Being. While they are only ideal possibilities *for men,* they are eternally real *for God* as objects of His will and purpose. But the eternal reality of ideal ends for God need not weaken man's will to realize them in his own life by striving. Man is man and not God; and, if ideal ends are to be realized in *his* life, it must be by his own effort, with the aid of divine grace. This has always been the view of Theism, although some theologians have stressed so strongly man's dependence on God's grace for his highest good that the necessity of his own effort has fallen into the background. Moreover, the fact that ideal ends are eternally real for God strengthens rather than weakens man's striving to realize them, for if he believes that he is not alone in his concern for them but that he is supported by God's will and power he will face obstacles and opposition with more courage. It is easy to make this recognition by man of his dependence upon God appear as a mere manifestation of weakness, but it need not lead to passivity and it tends to strengthen moral effort.

Nor is the belief that ideal ends are grounded in God's will and

[87] *Ibid.,* p. 12.

hence already in a sense real a mere product of human desire. In addition to the experience of divine grace by religious persons, there are reasons of a general character for thinking that man's ideal ends and his spiritual nature have their origin in a divine Being who is spiritual in character and who wills that men shall realize good in their lives. It is difficult to account for either the emergence of persons or their aspirations to realize spiritual values in any other way. In contrast, Dewey's naturalistic view of man and his ideal ends reduces them to by-products of natural forces and laws which are blind and purposeless. Although he rejects the "mechanical" type of Naturalism and recognizes that man possesses possibilities beyond those of other natural beings, he does not believe that nature is a product of mind and purpose.

3. Ultimately, the Naturalism of Dewey rests upon a dogmatic and arbitrary restriction of knowledge to that which can be discovered and verified by the scientific method. There is no valid reason for accepting this *absolutization of the scientific method*. It results from the fact that natural science has had remarkable success in describing the phenomena of the natural world and has enabled technology to further man's welfare and comfort. But it does not provide us with knowledge of all aspects and dimensions of reality. While it has shown itself adequate to deal with the inanimate world and with the physical and chemical aspects of the biological world, it cannot account for the purposiveness and organization of living organisms or the intellectual and moral activity of persons. Of course, life and mind are embodied and have physical manifestations which science can investigate by its method, but this does not mean that their unique characteristics and capacities can be exhaustively known by the scientific method. Hence the attempt to exalt that method by denying the value of all other methods is simply an example of "methodological imperialism" and of the intellectual pride that leads to it. If so, the naturalistic philosophy of Dewey must be rejected, since his primary reason for embracing it is that the scientific method has nothing to say about any reality which is not publicly observable and verifiable by everyone as a thing or event in space and time. Thus Dewey's criticisms of traditional religion lose their force when one sees that they depend upon his Naturalism and that this in turn is simply a consequence of his uncritical and exclusive devotion to the scientific method.

4. This brings us to his proposal that we substitute *"the religious"* for "religion." Clearly, if there is nothing higher in reality than man and his ideal ends, it is inevitable that his religion should be a humanis-

tic one. For this reason, it is not surprising that in the modern age of skepticism Naturalistic Humanism should become a substitute for religion in the traditional sense. However, it is significant that most persons who can find meaning and purpose in their lives by devoting themselves to the realization of values such as truth, beauty, and justice do not speak of such devotion as "religious." Does this mean that Naturalistic Humanism is not a form of religion but a substitute for religion developed by modern intellectuals who have been aware of the value for man of the traditional religion they have abandoned and are seeking to preserve as much of that value as is compatible with Naturalism?

If the question were only a linguistic one, it might not be very serious. A philosopher often uses words like "religious" with meanings radically different from those they possess in ordinary usage. But the point of the question is not merely that "religious" has ordinarily been used in relation to belief in a transcendent Being or Power in some sense; it is also that to use such a term for devotion to man's "ideal ends" is misleading. It suggests that the *attitude* and the *effects* of Naturalistic Humanism are the same as those of traditional religion although the *object* of devotion is entirely different, so that nothing of value is lost when the religious attitude is directed toward a human rather than a superhuman object. Again and again Dewey says that the association of the religious attitude throughout the history of religion with belief in and worship of the supernatural is not essential to it, so that if that association is broken the nature of the religious attitude will continue unchanged. He regards the beliefs and practices of historic religions as "encumbrances" and holds that the essence of the religious attitude would not be modified by their removal but would be freed from a burden of adventitious accretions. But as Otto and others have pointed out, religion has always centered in the experience of "the holy," that which is other than and transcendent to everything natural and human. It is not true, therefore, that the direction of religious devotion to the human and natural world would only relieve religion of unessential "encumbrances"; it would transform it into something essentially different from what it has been throughout its history. For the quality and essence of an attitude cannot be defined in abstraction from its object, and it is bound to change when it is directed toward a radically different object.

Moreover, if the religious attitude is changed, its *effects* on human life will change. It is true that one of the effects of traditional "religion" has been the "unification" of the self with itself and its world and that "the religious" attitude of devotion toward ideal ends also has a tendency to unify the self. But the *kind* of unification it produces differs from that produced by traditional religion. For it unifies the self by means of ideal ends constructed by the imagination, so that the self achieves its unification by its own effort. In contrast, traditional religion has achieved unification by relating the self in faith and devotion to a transcendent Being and subordinating its desires to His purpose. Thus the self does not have to depend on its own effort alone to achieve its unification; it is unified with itself and the world through its relation to God. In addition, traditional religion has given man an assurance that he is not alone but that the transcendent Being beyond nature and humanity is akin to him and that he can have communion with Him. Thus not only the nature but also the effects on man of the religious attitude are profoundly modified when its object ceases to be God and becomes man's own ideal ends.

5. Another criticism concerns Dewey's view of the relation of man's ideal ends to nature and his use of the word "God" to express that relation. Since the Hebrew prophets arrived at ethical monotheism, the word "God" has been used to mean an Infinite and Perfect Being who is Creator of nature and whose Providence governs history according to His purposes. To Dewey, however, "God" is simply a name for the relation of ideal ends to those natural and social forces which further them. The difficulty is that, although such a "God" is greater than man in power, It is in no sense superior to man in value, so that worship of It is impossible. Nor does It have the religious value of the God of Pantheism, since It is identified not with Nature as a whole conceived as perfect but only with those aspects of nature and society which support man's ideal ends. Hence an "intellectual love of God" like Spinoza's, which dwarfs man's pride and at the same time enables him to participate in the perfection of Nature as a whole and attain thereby a kind of "blessedness," is quite impossible. Thus the "God" of Dewey has the religious value of neither the God of Theism nor the "God" or "Nature" of Pantheism.

6. Perhaps the most fundamental difficulty with Naturalistic Humanism is that *it proposes to men a religious object which does not warrant absolute devotion*. One can love man; one can respect him; but can one give absolute devotion to him? Can one put one's faith in his ideal ends or in him as possessing absolute worth? It is significant that Naturalistic Humanism does not speak of the "worship" of man or of his ideal ends and that there is no place in it for prayer unless one identifies prayer with meditation for the purpose of strengthening de-

votion to ideal ends. Since worship and prayer have always been integral elements of the religious life, this will seem to many a sufficient reason for rejecting "the religious" as a substitute for "religion."

But is it even possible to put "faith" in man and ideal ends? In answering this question in the negative, one need not accept the pessimistic view of man as wholly corrupted by sin or deny that there is much that is good in him. For the question is not whether he is totally evil or partially good and capable of being made better, it is whether he and his ideal ends are worthy of absolute trust. In the nineteenth and early twentieth centuries, many educated men in the West found it possible to answer this question affirmatively. For the achievements of Western man in science, technology, social reform, and other fields were substantial and belief in progress toward an earthly Utopia seemed justified. But in the latter half of the twentieth century it is no longer possible to have such unbounded faith in man. Two world wars and the threat of universal destruction by a third have made men aware of the *power of evil* in human nature and of the limits of their ability to overcome it. It is not merely that they have witnessed the cruelties of dictators and the follies of masses perverted by them. They have also come to realize that men are corrupted even by their loyalty to "ideal ends" if there is no absolute perspective from which they can be judged. As Hartshorne has pointed out, man's lust for arbitrary power, political or otherwise, is dangerous and needs to be curbed. "Whence is the curb to come? From pure reason and humanitarian sentiment? From education? This notion might be plausible but for one circumstance. Emotions are conquered, as Spinoza taught us, by other emotions; and it cannot be that any group of intellectuals can impose humanitarian ideals upon average egoistic mankind unless it can point to an object of admiration and devotion emotionally more stimulating, not merely than each man is to himself, but also more moving than are the objects of devotion furnished to most men by the groups to which they belong, such as family or nation. Without God as a real individual above man, what can each of us concretely realize as so great and so definite that his individual and collective egoisms are humbled in its presence?" [88]

Nor is it sufficient to say that the trouble lies in the failure to develop and use "social intelligence," for men's desires blind them to the truth and lead them to use the knowledge gained by the social as well as the natural sciences to serve their own individual and collective

[88] Charles Hartshorne, *Beyond Humanism* (New York: Harper & Row, 1937), p. 31.

interests. It should give us pause that the ideology which is the greatest source of danger in our time has much to say about "ideal ends" such as "the classless society" and that many Americans make the "ideal end" of "liberty" an excuse for irresponsibility and self-indulgence. But apart from these dangers, man's ideal ends cannot qualify as a worthy object of absolute devotion. Such devotion requires an absolute object, an Infinite and Perfect Being who unites power and goodness in Himself. *Man is neither infinite nor perfect, and his ideal ends are worthy of devotion only insofar as they are subordinated to the purposes of One who is both.*

13 Process Philosophy

WHITEHEAD

It is generally agreed that Alfred North Whitehead (1861–1947) was one of the greatest philosophers of the present century. After attaining eminence in Great Britain as a mathematician, logician, and scientist, he accepted a call from the Department of Philosophy at Harvard University. Then in his sixties, he spent the rest of his life in America. In less than ten years he published three major works which established his reputation as a philosopher with wide-ranging interests and remarkable capacity for imaginative generalization. These were *Science and the Modern World* (1925) in which he attacked the limitations of the modern scientific mentality and the materialistic philosophy to which it had led; *Process and Reality* (1929) in which he developed his own philosophy of organism and his conception of God and the world; and *Adventures of Ideas* (1933) in which he applied his fundamental insights to the problems of civilization. In addition, he published a number of smaller books of a less technical nature, of which the most important for the philosophy of religion were *Religion in the Making* (1926), *Modes of Thought* (1938), and the Ingersoll Lecture on *Immortality* (1941). In presenting an account of his contributions to the philosophy of religion, we shall confine ourselves mainly to the three major works and to *Religion in the Making*, but shall refer also from time to time to other works.

SCIENCE AND THE MODERN WORLD

Many persons who find Whitehead's metaphysics so difficult as to border on the unintelligible or so speculative as to appear fanciful have been deeply influenced by his analysis of the limitations of "scientific materialism" and his demonstration that recent developments in science require a quite different world view. Although he had prepared the way in earlier works for his radical reinterpretation of science, it was in *Science and the Modern World* that he first presented in general terms the conclusions he had reached about modern science and began to develop a philosophy more adequate to the recent revolution in science.

In the Preface he remarks that "men can be provincial in time, as well as in place" and raises the question "whether the scientific mentality of the modern world in the immediate past is not a successful example of such provincial limitation." [1] Greek philosophers, especially Plato and Aristotle, regarded nature as a rational and teleological order.[2] Medieval thinkers insisted upon the rationality of God, "conceived as with the personal energy of Jehovah and with the rationality of a Greek philosopher," and were certain that every detail in nature was ordered by Him.[3] But these older ways of thinking have been set aside by the science of the last three centuries. The result has been "scientific materialism" which "presupposes the ultimate fact of an irreducible brute matter, or material, spread throughout space in a flux of configurations. In itself such a material is senseless, valueless, purposeless. It just does what it does do, following a fixed routine imposed by external relations which do not spring from the nature of its being." [4]

Whitehead regards this scientific materialism as due to a confusion of abstractions, which are of course essential for scientific investigation, with the concrete facts of experience. He calls this "the Fallacy of Misplaced Concreteness," the "error of mistaking the abstract for the concrete." [5] The advantage in restricting attention to a set of abstractions is that one can deduce conclusions concerning the relationships between them, but the disadvantage is that one abstracts from or excludes things which may be important.[6] Since every science must confine itself to selected aspects of the world and pay no attention to other aspects, philosophy is absolutely necessary for an understanding of the whole. As a "critic of abstractions," philosophy "harmonizes" the abstractions of the special sciences by assigning them to their proper positions in relation to each other and "completes" them by comparing them with concrete intuitions of the world such as those which are expressed in poetry and religion.[7] The main purpose of *Science and the Modern World* is to offer a thorough criticism of the abstractions of modern science and to prepare the way for a more adequate philosophy than scientific materialism.

One of Whitehead's criticisms is directed against the theory of

[1] Whitehead, *Science and the Modern World* (New York: Macmillan, 1925), p. ix.

[2] *Ibid.*, p. 11.   [3] *Ibid.*, pp. 17, 18.   [4] *Ibid.*, p. 24.   [5] *Ibid.*, p. 72.
[6] *Ibid.*, p. 82.   [7] *Ibid.*, p. 122.

"simple location." According to Newton, the mass of a material body remains permanent during its changes of motion in time. It is also assumed that matter "can be said to be *here* in space and *here* in time, or *here* in space-time, in a perfectly definite sense which does not require for its explanation any reference to other regions of space-time." [8] Thus the transition of time has nothing to do with its character. The conclusion drawn from this by seventeenth-century scientists was that "the world is a succession of instantaneous configurations of matter." [9] Whitehead holds that this is an example of "the Fallacy of Misplaced Concreteness." Moreover, it makes great difficulties for induction, since it implies that nothing in the present fact inherently refers either to the past or to the future.[10] As we shall see, Whitehead maintains that present facts not only are related to past and future facts, but also are partially constituted by their relation to the former and partially constitute the latter by their relation to them.

Another abstraction of modern science and philosophy is that which has to do with the categories of *substance* and *quality*. Whitehead admits that these categories are necessary for our ordinary thinking but regards them as products of abstraction which present us with simplified views of matters of fact.[11] It is natural when we observe something with qualities such as hard, round, blue, and noisy, to speak of a "substance" or substratum of which these are "predicates." [12] But difficulty arises concerning the status of qualities such as color and sound, and early modern physicists regarded these qualities not as facts in external nature but as "merely motion in material," i.e., light and sound waves.[13] Therefore, they distinguished between "primary qualities" such as mass, which are essential qualities of material substances, and "secondary qualities" such as color and sound, which are only qualities in the mind projected into these substances.[14] The consequence was that nature was deprived of the qualities which give it meaning and value. "Nature is a dull affair, soundless, scentless, colourless; merely the hurrying of material, endlessly, meaninglessly." [15] Whitehead maintains that this view of nature is unbelievable and has arisen only because we have taken abstractions to be concrete realities.[16] Also the sharp distinction of Descartes between material substance and mental substance or mind with its quite different qualities has led to a *dualism* which has made the relation between body and mind wholly inexplicable. To escape from this dualism, two kinds of

[8] *Ibid.*, p. 69.   [9] *Ibid.*, p. 71.   [10] *Ibid.*, p. 73.   [11] *Ibid.*, p. 74.
[12] *Ibid.*, p. 75.   [13] *Ibid.*, pp. 75, 76.   [14] *Ibid.*, p. 77.   [15] *Ibid.*
[16] *Ibid.*, p. 78.

monists, the materialists who "put mind inside matter" and the idealists who "put matter inside mind," have arisen.[17] Whitehead regards
dualism, materialism, and idealism as all alike mistakes due to the "Fallacy of Misplaced Concreteness." [18] As we shall see, he holds that both
material and mental substances are abstractions and that what we call
bodies and minds are highly complex societies composed of entities
which are organic in nature.

The *mechanism* of modern science has also resulted from the confusion of abstractions with concrete realities. A line of Tennyson's

"The stars," she whispers, "blindly run"

illustrates the problem. "Each molecule blindly runs. The human body
is a collection of molecules, therefore, the human body blindly runs,
and therefore there can be no individual responsibility for the actions
of the body." [19] This doctrine of determinism, which is contrary to
man's moral intuitions, applies only to abstract entities. The answer to
it is not vitalism which accepts mechanism throughout the whole of inanimate nature but holds that it is partially overcome within living
bodies; it is the view that reality as a whole is composed of organisms
rather than material atoms. "The concrete enduring entities are organisms, so that the plan of the *whole* influences the very characters of the
various subordinate organisms which enter into it." [20] Thus, the electron "runs within the body—in accordance with the general plan of
the body, and this plan includes the mental state." [21]

Again, the *theory of evolution,* which has been widely interpreted
in materialistic terms, is really inconsistent with materialism. Matter, as
it is understood by materialism, is incapable of evolution. "Evolution,
on the materialistic theory, is reduced to the role of being another
word for the description of the changes of the external relations between portions of matter. . . . There can merely be change, purposeless and unprogressive." [22] Moreover, the theory of evolution has usually emphasized only one side of the development of organisms: their
adaptation to a given environment, their struggle for existence, and
natural selection.[23] But there is another side which has been neglected: creativeness, the capacity of societies of cooperating organisms to create their own environment. Thus "friendly help" as well as
"struggle for existence" is a factor in evolution.[24] Moreover the application of the concept of organisms which is necessary for an explana-

[17] *Ibid.,* p. 79.   [18] *Ibid.*   [19] *Ibid.,* p. 109.   [20] *Ibid.,* p. 111   [21] *Ibid.*
[22] *Ibid.,* pp. 151, 152.   [23] *Ibid.,* pp. 157, 158.   [24] *Ibid.,* p. 159.

tion of evolution should not be confined to the biological realm, but
should be extended to the physical realm as well since there is no
discontinuity between the two realms.

Whitehead points out that the Romantic poets of the nineteenth
century such as Wordsworth and Shelley refused to accept these abstractions of scientific materialism. "Both Shelley and Wordsworth em-
phatically bear witness that nature cannot be divorced from its aesthetic values; and that these values arise from the cumulation, in some
sense, of the brooding presence of the whole onto its various parts." [25]
They had an intuitive apprehension of nature as consisting not of
material atoms with simple location but of organisms which are intimately related to each other so that the whole of nature is involved in
each one of them. They also restored to nature the *values* which had
been regarded by scientific materialism as subjective like the secondary
qualities. Thus the nature poetry of the Romantic poets was "a protest
on behalf of the organic view of nature, and also a protest against the
exclusion of value from the essence of matter of fact." [26]

Finally, the recent revolution in physics has opened the way for a
new theory of *matter*. The concept of mass has been transformed into
the concept of energy. The quantum theory assumes that "an electron
does not continuously traverse its path in space" but "appears at a
series of discrete positions in space which it occupies for successive
durations of time." [27] Since electrons and protons are now regarded as
the fundamental entities of which the material bodies of ordinary experience are composed, this discontinuity requires us to revise our ideas
of matter. Whitehead suggests that, as a steadily sounding note or a
steady color is the outcome of vibrations, so we may conceive each
primordial element as "an organized system of vibratory streaming of
energy," which manifests itself during a period of time.[28] Since matter
in the traditional sense has been eliminated, Whitehead thinks that the
explanation of matter must be found in a new doctrine of *organism*
and that the energy of the physicist is only an abstraction from the
concrete fact of organism.[29]

The starting point for this doctrine of organism is the fact that,
while things are *separated* by space and time, they are also *together*
even if they are not contemporaneous in space and time.[30] While a thing
is in a sense in one place and in no other and endures through a certain
period and no other, it does not have "simple location," [31] for volumes

[25] *Ibid.*, pp. 122, 123.   [26] *Ibid.*, pp. 132, 133.   [27] *Ibid.*, p. 50.
[28] *Ibid.*, pp. 51, 52.   [29] *Ibid.*, p. 53.   [30] *Ibid.*, p. 90.   [31] *Ibid.*

of space and durations of time do not have independent existence but exist within a totality, and their relations to their environment are essential to their nature.[32] Each volume and duration "takes account" of or "mirrors" in itself every other. This *interrelatedness* of all things in space and time is made possible by the "prehension" or "apprehension" by each of all the others, so that a natural entity is a gathering together of things into the unity of a prehension. A concrete fact or actual entity is a "process," and nature is a "structure of evolving processes."

THE NATURE OF RELIGION

Before we consider the metaphysical system developed by Whitehead as an alternative to scientific materialism, it will be well to deal briefly with his conception of religion. In *Science and the Modern World*, he made it clear that he regarded religion as important and that religious intuition must be taken into account along with scientific description by the philosopher. "The fact of the religious vision, and its history of persistent expansion, is our one ground for optimism. Apart from it, human life is a flash of occasional enjoyments lighting up a mass of pain and misery, a bagatelle of transient experience." [33] In *Religion in the Making* he offered an equally high estimate of religion. "Religion can be, and has been, the main instrument of progress." [34] However, this does not imply that there are no shortcomings in religion or that it has always been good rather than bad. He speaks of the "melancholy record of the horrors which can attend religion," e.g., human sacrifice, superstition, bigotry, and hatred. "Religion is the last refuge of human savagery. The uncritical association of religion with goodness is directly negatived by plain facts." [35]

Because of its great importance for human life and the frequency with which it has been perverted to evil ends, it is essential that religion should not be divorced from reason and allowed to become a matter of blind emotion. Religious experience and belief must be accompanied by emotion if they are to have a transforming power in life, but they must be expressed in terms which are compatible with scientific knowledge. Whitehead holds that the conflict between religion and science ought not to be a cause for alarm, since they have different functions and deal with widely different aspects of reality. "Science is concerned with the general conditions which are observed to regulate physical phenomena; whereas religion is wholly wrapped up in the

[32] *Ibid.*, pp. 91, 92.   [33] *Ibid.*, p. 268.
[34] Whitehead, *Religion in the Making* (Cleveland and New York: World, 1960), p. 36.
[35] *Ibid.*

contemplation of moral and aesthetic values." [36] When there is a clash
between them, it should be regarded as an "opportunity for further
development," not as a "disaster." [37] For both religion and science
have always been in a state of development, and neither of them
should claim finality at any stage for the formulations of its truths. One
of the major reasons for the decline of religion in the West has been
the defensive attitude of religious thinkers toward the new scientific
theories of the modern period, and it cannot regain its old power unless
it is willing to face change without fear. "Its principles may be eternal, but the expression of those principles requires continual development." [38] Therefore, religion and science alike must be patient in the
face of apparent contradictions between them at any given time and
seek a reconciliation which will do justice to both.

What is the *nature* of religion? There are a number of "definitions"
of religion in Whitehead's works, and no one of them should be taken
by itself as offering his view of its essence. In *Religion in the Making*,
he speaks of religion as "a transforming agency," "a force of belief
cleansing the inward parts," [39] and emphasizes the fact that a man's
character and conduct depend upon his beliefs when they are sincerely
held.[40] This leads him to one of his definitions of religion. "Religion is
the art and theory of the internal life of man, so far as it depends on
the man himself and on what is permanent in the nature of things. This
doctrine is the direct negation of the theory that religion is primarily a
social fact. . . . Religion is what the individual does with his
own solitariness. . . . Collective enthusiasms, revivals, institutions,
churches, rituals, bibles, codes of behavior, are the trappings of religion, its passing forms. . . . But the end of religion is beyond all
this." [41] Because of this definition of religion in terms of the individual
and his solitariness and the depreciation of its social aspects as mere
"trappings" and "passing forms," Whitehead has often been accused of
an extreme *individualism* in his view of religion and a blindness to the
importance of the religious community in shaping the "internal life" of
the individual and in transmitting to others the religious insights of
creative individuals. There is much truth in this charge, because
Whitehead was interested in religion primarily as a transforming
power in the lives of individuals. He seemed to think that religion is
essentially social only in its more primitive phases, which are dominated by ritual and emotion, and in its decadent phase, when it "sinks

[36] *Science and the Modern World*, p. 258.   [37] *Ibid.*, p. 259.
[38] *Ibid.*, p. 263.   [39] *Religion in the Making*, p. 15.   [40] *Ibid.*, p. 15.
[41] *Ibid.*, p. 16.

back into sociability." [42] In contrast, "rational religion" makes belief the central element governing both thought and conduct, and this is an achievement of creative individuals such as the Hebrew prophets, the Buddha, and Christ.[43]

However, Whitehead's religious individualism is qualified by his recognition that the higher religions are concerned not only with "the value of an individual for itself" but also with "the value of the diverse individuals of the world for each other" and "the values of the objective world." [44] For the individual self cannot attain value "till it has merged its individual claim with that of the objective universe. Religion is *world-loyalty*. The spirit at once surrenders itself to this universal claim and appropriates it for itself." [45] It should also be noted that a religion such as Buddhism or Christianity could become universal only by breaking the ties that bound it to a particular nation and becoming the religion of individual persons. Therefore, Whitehead's conception of religion is better understood if the two definitions we have considered are placed side by side and allowed to qualify each other: "Religion is what the individual does with his own solitariness"; and "Religion is world-loyalty."

Thus religion is concerned with the attainment of value by individuals in and by themselves, but also in relation to other individuals and the world. But we must consider another definition if we are to come to the heart of the matter. "Religion is the vision of something which stands beyond, behind, and within, the passing flux of immediate things; something which is real, and yet waiting to be realised; . . . something which is the ultimate ideal, and the hopeless quest." [46] In *Process and Reality*, this conviction that religion is concerned with *permanence* and *change* is vividly expressed. Referring to the Psalms and the saying of Heraclitus that "all things flow," he asserts that "the flux of things is one ultimate generalization around which we must weave our philosophical system." [47] But there is a "rival" generalization which "dwells on permanences of things—the solid earth, the mountains, the stones, the Egyptian Pyramids, the spirit of man, God." [48] The union of these two antithetical ideas is expressed in the opening line of a hymn:

---

[42] *Ibid.*, pp. 22, 23.   [43] *Ibid.*, p. 30.   [44] *Ibid.*, p. 58.
[45] *Ibid.*, p. 59 (italics added).
[46] *Science and the Modern World*, pp. 267, 268.
[47] Whitehead, *Process and Reality* (New York: Macmallan, 1929), p. 317.
[48] *Ibid.*, p. 318.

Abide with me; fast falls the eventide.

Whitehead sees in these words a formulation of the problem of meta-physics. "Permanence can be snatched only out of flux; and the passing moment can find its adequate intensity only by its submission to per-manence." [49]

Whitehead's concern as a philosopher with the problems of perma-nence and flux, order and change, is closely related to his conviction that religion seeks the *realization of value* in the midst of time and the *conservation of value* after it is realized. "The purpose of God," he says, "is the attainment of value in the temporal world." [50] This pur-pose can be reached only if He is an eternal principle of order who transcends the flux of events and provides the final cause which guides every creature in the process of attaining new value. At the same time, He must be the source of an order in which the new values which are ever being created in time are saved from loss. As we shall see, White-head's metaphysics culminates in a solution of this problem.

But while he insists that the philosopher must ask what metaphysi-cal principles require with respect to the nature of God apart from the beliefs of existing religions, he also asserts that his argument must take into account our *religious and moral intuitions.*[51] In *Adven-tures of Ideas* he indicates clearly the source and nature of the religious and moral intuitions which have influenced him most deeply. The source is "certain historical occasions scattered irregularly within a period of about twelve hundred years, from the earlier Hebrew proph-ets and historians to the stabilization of western theology by Augus-tine." [52] The nature of the intuitions he derives from this source is indicated by what he regards as the three culminating phases of this historical development: the conviction of Plato that the divine element in the world is a persuasive rather than a coercive agency; [53] the exemplification of this truth in the life of Christ; [54] and the affirmation of the "direct immanence" of God in Christ and in the world through the doctrine of the Trinity.[55] Thus Whitehead's conception of God and His relation to the world is in part an attempt to express ethical and religious intuitions derived mainly from Platonism and Christianity. As we shall see, however, he does not always express these intuitions in terms a traditional Platonist or Christian would use, but reformulates them in terms required by his own philosophic and religious vision.

[49] *Ibid.*, p. 513. [50] *Religion in the Making*, p. 97.
[51] *Process and Reality*, p. 521.
[52] Whitehead, *Adventures of Ideas* (New York: Macmillan, 1938), p. 211.
[53] *Ibid.*, p. 213. [54] *Ibid.*, p. 214. [55] *Ibid.*, p. 216.

WHITEHEAD'S METAPHYSICS

In *Process and Reality,* Whitehead developed the constructive suggestions of earlier works such as *Science and the Modern World* and *Religion in the Making* into an elaborate metaphysical system in which he sought to do justice to science and religion, fact and value, and efficient and final causes. Unlike many recent philosophers, he believed that "speculative philosophy" was indispensable. Defining it as "the endeavour to frame a coherent, logical, necessary system of general ideas in terms of which every element of our experience can be interpreted," [56] he describes its method in terms which seek to do justice to both the empiricists' demand for knowledge based on experience and the rationalists' belief in the ultimate rationality and coherence of all reality. It must start from observation of particular facts of experience, make "a flight in the thin air of imaginative generalization" like an airplane, and then return to earth for "renewed observation" of the facts.[57] Thus its method is not that of deduction of conclusions from clear and certain premises, but that of descriptive generalization, and its conclusions are tentative rather than final. Moreover, the philosopher must not assume that only experiences which can be expressed in clear and distinct ideas are important, but must pay special attention to vague experiences on the fringes of consciousness.

According to Whitehead, the world consists of a plurality of *actual entities.* Whatever else exists depends upon and must be explained by reference to these. The world is not made up, as Descartes held, of material and mental substances, whose essence is unchanging through the changes in their qualities. Such "substances" are abstractions rather than concrete actualities, i.e., each of them is complex and composed of many actual entities. An actual entity is not a substance but a *process,* whose being is constituted by its becoming. It is an individual unit of becoming which completes itself and is succeeded by other such units. All actual entities are individualizations of a generic activity which Whitehead calls "creativity." *Creativity* is not itself an actual entity; it is the creative activity exemplified by all actual entities. Thus, an actual entity is a process, an instance of the creativity of the world which is perpetually bringing forth novelty.

How does an actual entity come into existence? It creates itself by a process of *concrescence* or growing together of "data" or "objects" which it absorbs into its being. These are in part other actual entities which have come into being in the past and perished. For when an

---

[56] *Process and Reality,* p. 4.   [57] *Ibid.,* p. 7.

actual entity has completed its process of becoming, it ceases to be active and becomes an "object." It can then be "objectified" as one of the data or objects of later actual entities. Objects of another kind which Whitehead calls "eternal objects" also enter into the constitution of an actual entity. The nature of these "eternal objects" we shall consider later.

What is the essence of actual entities? "Each actual entity," says Whitehead, "is conceived as an *act of experience* arising out of data. It is a process of 'feeling' the many data, so as to absorb them into the unity of one individual satisfaction." [58] His basic reason for accepting this "subjectivist principle" is that that which is primary in actual human experience offers the key to the nature of reality. Although Greek philosophers were "objectivist" in the sense that they based their conception of reality on such statements as "This stone is grey," what is really primary in our actual experience is illustrated by the statement, "*My perception* of this stone is grey." [59] Hence Whitehead asserts that "apart from the experience of subjects there is nothing, nothing, nothing, bare nothingness." [60] However, he differs from modern idealists in holding that the essence of the "act of experience" of actual entities is not consciousness or judgment but something more primitive, *feeling*. As he puts it, "the primitive feeling is sympathy, that is, feeling the feeling *in* another and feeling conformally *with* another." [61]

Thus his view of the nature of actual entities is clearly a form of *panpsychism*. One of his main reasons for this view is that our minds as experiencing subjects are closely related to our bodies which are parts of the world of nature. This indicates that human experience is "a fact within nature" and that the external things with which it interacts cannot be essentially different from it. Moreover, animals and plants seem to have "a vague feeling of causal relationship with the external world," e.g., "a jellyfish advances and withdraws" and "a plant grows downwards to the damp earth and upwards towards the light." [62] This suggests that experience or feeling at different levels is found in all living organisms, and the principle of the continuity of nature requires its existence at a very low level in physical bodies as well.

Although actual entities are subjective in their nature, each of them is related through its feelings of objects to the world of which it is a part. Through them it perceives the actual entities in its environment and they exercise a causal influence on it. Indeed, all entities in the universe have the potentiality for being objects or elements in the experience of each actual entity and contributing to its internal

---

[58] *Ibid.*, p. 65 (italics added).   [59] *Ibid.*, p. 241 (italics added).
[60] *Ibid.*, p. 254.   [61] *Ibid.*, p. 246.   [62] *Ibid.*, p. 268.

constitution. The activity by which it creates itself consists of the *prehension* or grasping of its objects and the inclusion of them as part of its own essence. "Prehension" is defined by Whitehead as "a process of 'feeling' the many data, so as to absorb them into the unity of one individual 'satisfaction.' " [63] It should be noted that a prehension may be either *positive* or *negative*. A "positive" prehension is one which includes an object in an actual entity as contributing to its internal constitution, while a "negative" prehension is one which excludes an object from it.[64] Thus an actual entity is a process in which positive and negative prehensions or feelings are integrated into a novel unity of experience.

It is also necessary to distinguish between "physical" and "conceptual" prehensions or feelings. A *physical prehension* is one whose object is another actual entity which has completed its process of becoming and ceased to be a subject of experience. Through a physical prehension an actual entity is causally affected by a past actual entity by means of the "reproduction" or "re-enaction" of its feeling. The feeling of the actual entity in process of becoming has a *"subjective form"* or affective tone which "conforms" to the subjective form of the feeling of the past actual entity. As Whitehead expresses it, "the subjective form of a physical feeling is re-enaction of the subjective form of the feeling felt. . . . There is a flow of feeling." [65] This makes possible the *continuity* of novel actual entities in the present with actual entities which have perished. Thus the latter attain what Whitehead calls *objective immortality;* for actual entities which have ceased to be subjects cannot act in the present, but as objects they can condition the nature of present actual entities.

A *conceptual prehension* or feeling is one which grasps an *eternal object.* "Eternal objects" are "forms of definiteness" and have a role somewhat similar to that of Plato's Ideas or Forms. They are "eternal" in the sense of timeless, and universal in the sense of being potentially present in many actual entities. They have "ingression" into actual entities in the sense of being present in them as "forms of definiteness." But they do not exist apart from all actual entities in a Platonic realm of Ideas or Forms. Rather, they are "components" of actual entities, "potentials" for the determination of them, although they are neutral with respect to the particular actual entities they are to inform. They are "given" to present actual entities as objects by virtue of their existence as ingredients of past actual entities.[66]

The importance of these eternal objects is that they "constitute the

[63] *Ibid.,* p. 65.   [64] *Ibid.,* p. 66.   [65] *Ibid.,* pp. 362, 363.
[66] Ivor Leclerc, *Whitehead's Metaphysics* (London: George Allen and Unwin, 1958), Chap. 7.

potentialities of definiteness for any actual existence." [67] As Whitehead says in a Platonic passage, "the things which are temporal arise by their participation in the things which are eternal." [68] This participation results from a *decision* by each actual entity to receive into itself certain eternal objects and to exclude others from itself. Such a decision involves a selection from the multiplicity of eternal objects or possibilities. In making it, the actual entity is guided by an end or ideal for itself which Whitehead calls its *subjective aim*. The origin of this subjective aim we shall indicate later.

Through *conceptual prehensions* an actual entity includes in itself the eternal objects which are to give definiteness to it. Thus, an actual entity has both a "physical pole" and a "mental pole," since it creates itself out of both physical prehensions of past actual entities and conceptual prehensions of eternal objects. Under the guidance of its subjective aim it integrates these physical and conceptual prehensions into a novel unity of experience.

The aim of all actual entities is *intensity of experience*. This requires the elimination from each actual entity of objects which are mutually incompatible and frustrate one another, as well as the inclusion of others which are compatible but in contrast with one another, as in the pattern of contrasts in the aesthetic experience. Thus *satisfaction* is attained in a unity of feeling, and *value* is realized. Since every actual entity aims at value through the achievement of such a unity of feeling, value is an essential aspect of reality. "Everything has some value for itself, for others, and for the whole." [69]

Each actual entity is an individual, a unit of becoming distinct from all others. In this respect, Whitehead's metaphysics is a form of *atomism* and the world consists of a succession of individual, atomic units of becoming. However, these atomic actual entities are internally related and enter into the constitution of each other, so that his position is more accurately described as *organic pluralism*. The world consists of a plurality of individual organisms which are organically related to one another.

Finally, a group of actual entities which share certain common characteristics is described by Whitehead as a *society*. A *physical object* of ordinary experience is a society composed of units such as electrons, each of which is itself a society made up of a succession of actual entities. A *person* is also a society consisting of a succession of "occasions of human experience" genetically related to each other. The

[67] *Process and Reality*, p. 63.   [68] *Ibid.*
[69] Whitehead, *Modes of Thought* (New York: Macmillan, 1938), p. 151.

existence of any such society is dependent upon a wider social environment which is favorable to it. This wider environment is characterized by *laws of nature,* which are not externally imposed upon the actual entities in it but simply define the characters common to them. There is nothing immutable about the laws of nature in our special "cosmic epoch" because they may cease to exist if the society decays, and they are quite compatible with the freedom and creativity of actual entities which are guided by their own subjective aims.

In this brief outline of Whitehead's metaphysics, we have seen that the world consists of a plurality of actual entities, each of which is a process of becoming through the integration of data into a novel unity of feeling; that each actual entity receives its data through physical feelings of past actual entities and conceptual feelings of eternal objects or forms of definiteness; that these feelings are integrated under the guidance of a subjective aim in a process which culminates in a satisfaction; that when it perishes it attains objective immortality as a potential datum or object for succeeding actual entities; that the aim of every actual entity is intensity of feeling and thus the realization of value; that this requires order based upon the dominance of common characteristics in enduring societies of actual entities; and that these societies require a favorable wider social environment with natural laws which are neither necessary nor immutable.

GOD AND THE WORLD

We have deliberately postponed consideration of Whitehead's concept of God because it can be understood only in relation to the metaphysical principles we have been describing. The fact that the concept of God and His relation to the world is fully treated only in the last two chapters of *Process and Reality* must not deceive the reader into thinking that it is a mere "addendum" to Whitehead's metaphysical system. That it is required by the metaphysical system developed in the earlier parts can best be shown by returning to his concept of the "subjective aim," or "ideal," which is necessary to guide an actual entity throughout the process of concrescence until it has attained its "satisfaction."

According to the "ontological principle" that the reasons for things must be sought in actual entities, the subjective aim of a temporal actual entity must be derived from some actual entity. It cannot be given by the temporal actual entity to itself because it is presupposed as the guiding principle of that actual entity from the beginning of its process of concrescence. Nor can it be derived from any of the past actual entities which provide objects or data, for they cannot bring into being a present actual entity which will not merely reproduce themselves in its characteristics but will be a novel synthesis. Therefore a *unique actual entity* of some kind must be admitted as the source of the subjective aims of all temporal actual entities and thus of their value and order. Both "creativity," which is the generic nature of all actual entities, and the "eternal objects," which provide "pure potentials" for actual entities, are neutral or indeterminate with respect to the "forms of definiteness" which are to characterize particular actual entities if the maximum intensity of feeling and value is to be realized by them. Therefore a unique actual entity is indispensable as the source of their "subjective aims."

This unique actual entity is *God.* As Whitehead conceives God, He is a concrete actual entity and, like all actual entities, has both conceptual and physical prehensions. Thus, there are two aspects of His nature, and Whitehead by abstraction considers each of them by itself. When he does so, he calls the "conceptual" aspect the "primordial nature" and the "physical" aspect the "consequent nature." But it is essential not to be misled by this distinction into supposing that these "natures" are actual entities themselves. The unity of God as a concrete actual entity of which the "natures" are only aspects should always be borne in mind.

The *primordial nature* refers to God's "conceptual envisagement" of eternal objects, accompanied by an "appetition" or "urge towards realization" of them in actual entities. Whitehead also speaks of the primordial nature of God as "the unconditioned conceptual valuation of the entire multiplicity of eternal objects" which brings about a "graduation of the relevance of eternal objects" for each actual entity.[70] In this way, God in His primordial nature is the source of all the subjective aims of temporal actual entities. The subjective aim of each actual entity is derived from God by means of a "hybrid physical prehension" in which God is objectified by one of His conceptual feelings of eternal objects. Thus an eternal object or ideal is presented to the actual entity as a "lure for feeling" and a "potential for actualization." Hence God is the source of order and value in the world. However, it should not be forgotten that God does not create temporal entities. They create themselves. God's function is to provide the ends or final causes which guide them in the process of self-creation. His purpose is "depth of satisfaction" or the "evocation of intensities."

God in His primordial nature is infinite, eternal, and unchanging.

---

[70] *Process and Reality,* p. 46.

But He is "deficient" in that His feelings are purely conceptual, so that He is lacking in fullness of actuality and in consciousness. Therefore, He requires other actual entities for His completion or fulfillment. This means that, like other actual entities, His nature is "dipolar," possessing both a "mental pole" consisting of conceptual feelings of eternal objects and a "physical pole" containing physical feelings of temporal actual entities. As His primordial nature constitutes the mental pole, His *consequent nature* constitutes the physical pole, since it "originates with physical experience derived from the temporal world." [71] "The consequent nature of God is conscious; and it is the realization of the actual world in the unity of his nature, and through the transformation of His wisdom." [72] In other words, the consequent nature of God consists of His experience of temporal actual entities "integrated with" or "woven upon" the conceptual experience of His primordial nature.[73]

Thus the defects of God's primordial nature are overcome in His consequent nature. The "completion" of His nature is attained through His physical prehension or feeling of the world. While His primordial nature is unchanging, His consequent nature is "incomplete" and in a sense grows, "moving onward and never perishing" as it is affected by "the creative advance of the world." [74]

While God is completed or fulfilled by His experience of the world, the world is perfected and "saved" as it enters into His conscious experience. This is Whitehead's answer to the religious problem of the *conservation of value*. As we have seen, he conceives of religion as being concerned primarily with the realization of value, on the one hand, and the conservation of value, on the other. The realization of value is initiated by God in His primordial nature through the provision of subjective aims as final causes for all temporal actual entities. The conservation of value is attained through the reaction of the world upon God and its effect upon Him in His consequent nature. For the world is felt by Him without "loss" or "obstruction" in "a unison of immediacy." [75] He prehends all temporal actual entities into the unity of His experience "woven by rightness of feeling into the harmony of the universal feeling." [76] Thus he conserves their value by receiving them in His "everlasting" consequent nature. Moreover, by supplementing His physical feelings of them by appropriate conceptual feelings ("rightness of feeling"), he overcomes the evil which accompanies and obstructs the value in them. The eloquent passage in which this process of conservation and transformation is described deserves to be

[71] *Ibid.*, p. 524.   [72] *Ibid.*   [73] *Ibid.*   [74] *Ibid.*, pp. 524, 525.
[75] *Ibid.*, p. 524.   [76] *Ibid.*, p. 525.

quoted. "The revolts of destructive evil, purely self-regarding, are dismissed into their triviality of merely individual facts; and yet the good they did achieve in individual joy, individual sorrow, in the introduction of needed contrast, is yet saved by its relation to the completed whole. The image—and it is but an image—the image under which this operative growth of God's nature is best conceived, is that of a tender care that nothing be lost. The consequent nature of God is his judgment on the world. He saves the world as it passes into the immediacy of his own life. It is the judgment of a tenderness which loses nothing that can be saved. It is also the judgment of a wisdom which uses what in the temporal world is mere wreckage." [77]

However, Whitehead's discussion of the *problem of evil* is so brief and his language is often so metaphorical that his meaning is not wholly clear. The evil in the world is ascribed by him to the temporal actual entities and not to God, so that God is always regarded in Platonic fashion as the source of good but never of evil. Although God helps to determine the nature of actual entities by presenting them with their "subjective aims," they create themselves and are therefore responsible for the "revolts of destructive evil" against the good. However, the nature of the process by which God "saves" the world is not entirely clear. "He saves the world," says Whitehead, "as it passes into the immediacy of his own life." [78] This means that in some way the values realized by actual entities are saved by being included in the experience of God as a "completed whole." But does it mean that the world is transformed and the evil in it overcome, or only that it is included in the harmony of God's experience? The method by which it is "saved" is said to be rationality rather than force. "The sheer force of things lies in the intermediate physical process—God's role is not the combat of productive force with productive force, of destructive force with destructive force; it lies in the patient operation of the overpowering rationality of his conceptual harmonization." [79] This reflects the Platonic view that the divine Mind seeks to overcome the recalcitrancy of "necessity" by "persuasion" rather than by force. But the "overpowering rationality of his conceptual harmonization" seems to be effective not in transforming the *world* and overcoming its evil but in harmonizing its discords in the experience of *God*. That this is the implication of Whitehead's words seems to be borne out by his statement that God is "the poet of the world, with tender patience leading it by his vision of truth, beauty, and goodness," [80] for this suggests that His action upon the world is primarily that of a final cause presenting

[77] *Ibid.*   [78] *Ibid.*   [79] *Ibid.*, pp. 525, 526.   [80] *Ibid.*, p. 526.

it with ideals as "lures for feeling" rather than that of a creative and re-demptive will.

Since God includes prehensions, or feelings, of all the temporal actual entities of the world, each in its own individuality, Whitehead speaks of His consequent nature as both a "multiplicity" and a "unity." It is "composed of a multiplicity of elements with individual self-realization." Each temporal actual entity is received into God's nature, but there is a "transmutation of that temporal actuality into a living, ever-present fact." [81] For example, that which corresponds in His nature to an "enduring personality" which is a "route of occasions" in the temporal world is "an even more complete unity of life in a chain of elements for which succession does not mean loss of immediate unison." [82] This seems to mean that the successive experiences of a person in time are received in the consequent nature of God in such a way that his past is conserved along with his present in the unity of God's experience. The implication of this for immortality we shall con-sider later.

Whitehead also speaks of God as *superject*, i.e., as an "object" which is prehended by temporal actual entities. "The consequent na-ture," he says, "itself passes into the temporal world according to its gradation of relevance to the various concrescent occasions," and in doing so "the creative action completes itself." [83] The meaning of this becomes clear only if we bear in mind that it is not the primordial nature of God by itself which is the source of subjective aims of actual entities. For God as determined in his consequent nature by His pre-hensions of the past world of an actual entity is the object of the "hybrid physical feeling" from which the subjective aim is derived. In this way, God's conceptual prehension can offer a possibility which is relevant to that particular actual entity, a "real" rather than an "ab-stract" potentiality.[84] Thus the consequent nature becomes a "super-ject" and "passes into the temporal world," for "each temporal actuality includes it as an immediate fact of relevant experience." [85]

But what this implies with respect to the *attitude* of God toward the world is not wholly clear because of the poetic religious images Whitehead uses to express it. "The kingdom of heaven is with us today. The action of the fourth phase [i.e., of God as "superject"] is the love of God for the world. It is the particular providence for particular occasions. What is done in the world is transformed into a reality in

[81] *Ibid.*, p. 531.   [82] *Ibid.*   [83] *Ibid.*, p. 532.

[84] William Christian, *An Interpretation of Whitehead's Metaphysics* (New Haven: Yale University Press, 1959), p. 377.

[85] *Process and Reality*, p. 532.

heaven [i.e., the consequent nature] and the reality in heaven passes back into the world. By reason of this reciprocal relation, the love in the world passes into the love in heaven, and floods back again into the world. In this sense, God is the great companion—the fellow-sufferer who understands." [86] Do these religious metaphors mean that God in His consequent nature as symbolized by "the kingdom of heaven" literally acts upon the world and that He does so from "love" for it? or that His action is a "providence" for particular actual entities? or that God is really a "companion" to and "fellow-sufferer" with them? Although these religious images seem to suggest a view of God and His relation to the world similar to that of biblical Theism, we shall see that their meaning is not certain.

When both the primordial and the consequent natures of God are taken into account as aspects of His nature as a concrete reality, it is easy to see that God and the world are *interdependent*, each requiring and being required by the other. Here Whitehead is sharply opposed to the medieval Christian view that God is the transcendent Creator of the world and that it is completely dependent upon Him but He is not dependent in any way upon it. According to this view, there is "an entirely static God, with eminent reality, in relation to an entirely fluent world, with deficient reality." [87] This view is inconsistent with the fundamental intuition at the heart of religion, "of permanence in fluency and of fluency in permanence." [88] The problem of how to conceive the relation between "permanence" and "fluency" in such a way as to express this religious intuition is solved by regarding the temporal world, when perfected by its reception and transmutation in the consequent nature of God, as a fulfillment of the appetition of the primordial nature of God.[89] In the light of this relation between permanence and fluency several antitheses are stated by Whitehead. Perhaps the most striking is: "It is as true to say that God creates the World, as that the World creates God." [90] In another passage, Whitehead speaks of "the dynamic effort of the World passing into everlasting unity, and of the static majesty of God's vision, accomplishing its purpose of completion by absorption of the World's multiplicity of effort." [91] Thus God is dependent upon the World for His temporal and changing completion as the world is dependent upon Him for its completion. This implies that there is a "growth" of God in his consequent nature as He is affected by the world's "creative advance into

[86] *Ibid.*   [87] *Ibid.*, p. 526.   [88] *Ibid.*   [89] *Ibid.*, p. 527.   [90] *Ibid.*, p. 528.
[91] *Ibid.*, p. 530.

novelty." Indeed, like the world, God never "reaches static completion." [92] He is "reality"; but He is also "process." He is "actuality"; but
He is also "potentiality."

Thus, while God in His primordial nature is eternal, in His consequent nature He is involved in *time* and *change*. According to the
theistic view of Aquinas, the eternity of God means not only that He is
without beginning or end but also that there is no succession of before
and after in His experience corresponding to the past, present, and
future of events in time. He is perfect in the sense of completely actual,
with no potentiality in Him yet to be actualized. In contrast, Whitehead "takes time seriously." He introduces it into the nature of God as
well as the world, since God in His consequent nature changes in
response to the changes in the world and actualizes new possibilities in
His experience. Although He is "complete" and "unchanging" in His
primordial nature, He is "incomplete" and ever "changing" in his consequent nature as he is affected by the world. Whitehead is well aware
that this view conflicts with the traditional notion of a "static God"
unaffected by the changes in the world, but he regards this notion as
an error resulting from the dualism which stressed God's transcendence
at the cost of separating Him from the world. In contrast, his view
emphasizes the *immanence* of God in the world, and the immanence of
the world in God. Only in this way, he thinks, can God "save" the
world by initiating the realization of values in it, conserving the values
which have been realized, and supplementing and transmuting the
destructive forces of evil as He receives the world into the unity of His
experience. Thus the religious significance of Whitehead's view that
God is involved in time and change is obvious. It is an answer to the
threat of meaninglessness which arises from the fact that all finite
actual entities perish. "In this way," says Whitehead in the concluding
sentence of *Process and Reality*, "the insistent craving is justified—the
insistent craving that zest for existence be refreshed by the ever-
present, unfading importance of our immediate actions, which *perish*
and yet *live for evermore*." [93]

But the question arises as to whether Whitehead in emphasizing so
strongly that God is affected by the world and is involved in time and
change negates the *transcendence* of God. Clearly, he denies that God
is the "eminent reality" of medieval theology who is utterly transcendent to and other than the world. He argues that the existence and
nature of such a Being would be utterly unknowable and stresses the

[92] *Ibid.*, p. 529.   [93] *Ibid.*, p. 533 (italics added).

immanence of God as illustrated by Christ's saying, "The Kingdom of Heaven is within you." [94] This does not mean, however, that God is wholly immanent. He transcends temporal actual entities in the sense that in His primordial nature He is eternal, aboriginal, and independent of them. He transcends them in the sense that the infinite multiplicity of eternal objects conceptually envisaged by Him is never exhausted by their realization in the world. Above all, He transcends them, as Christian has pointed out, by the perfection of His experience in its scope, quality and intensity, and by the unlimited extension and effect of His influence upon actual entities and His preservation of temporal achievements.[95] But Whitehead's conception of God's transcendence is very different from that of biblical Theism, which stresses God's majesty and holiness and the complete dependence of the world upon Him. This is most obvious in Whitehead's explicit denial that God is the creator of finite actual entities.

It should be evident from what we have said that Whitehead is *not* a *pantheist.* Unlike Spinoza, he is a pluralist rather than a monist. Although the actual entities are bound together by internal relations so that he can speak of his philosophy as "organic pluralism," he is nonetheless a pluralist. Actual entities which create themselves can hardly be regarded as mere "modes" of one substance or "appearances" of one Absolute Reality. The fact that he speaks of "creativity" as the "generic nature" of all actual entities and the "universal of universals" [96] should not be allowed to mislead us. As we have seen, he makes it perfectly clear that "creativity" is not an actual entity but a name for the universal fact that all actual entities are examples of creative activity. Moreover, the very fact that he regards God as *an* actual entity who transcends *other* actual entities by virtue of the fact that He exists for Himself as an individual is decisive against any claim that universal "creativity" is Whitehead's God and that he is therefore a pantheist.

Is he, then, a *panentheist?* According to Panentheism ("all in God"), the world is in God, but God also transcends the world. Charles Hartshorne maintains that God as a concrete actuality "includes" the world in Himself, while His abstract essence is independent of and transcendent to the particular actual entities of the world. Is he right in attributing this view to Whitehead? We would agree with William Christian that he is not.[97] For one thing, God does not literally "include" or "contain" the world in Himself. Although He prehends or

[94] *Religion in the Making,* pp. 68–70.
[95] Christian, *An Interpretation of Whitehead's Metaphysics,* p. 381.
[96] *Ibid.,* p. 31.   [97] Christian, *op. cit.,* pp. 372, 373.

feels temporal actual entities, He experiences them as objects. This implies that He does not include their feelings as such in Himself, although He conforms to, supplements, and transmutes them as He prehends them in His consequent nature. As Whitehead puts it, His "tenderness loses nothing *that can be saved*." [98] Hence God transcends the world not only in His "abstract essence," as Hartshorne maintains, but also in His "concrete actuality," i.e., His experience.

From considerations such as these Christian concludes that "Whitehead's theory of God and the world is somewhat nearer traditional theism than panentheism is." [99] God is not *identical* with the world as in Pantheism, nor does He *include* it as in Panentheism. Rather, His activity is "conditioned" by the world, but is not "determined" by it, so that He is intimately *related to* the world, as in Pantheism and Panentheism, but at the same time *transcends* it, as in Theism. However, Whitehead's view of God is so different in several respects from the traditional Theism which has developed under the influence of Judaism and Christianity that it would probably be wise not to speak of him without qualification as a "theist." That which distinguishes his view from the Theism of the Judaeo-Christian tradition is not his criticism of popular supernaturalism on the ground that it ascribes arbitrary power to God and refers anything perplexing to the direct decree of His will, for many theologians have made the same criticism. Nor is it the fact that he denies the immutability of God in His consequent nature and insists that there are changes in His experience as He responds to the changing world, for theistic theologians such as F. R. Tennant have taken the same view.[100] Rather, that which separates him from traditional theists, liberal as well as orthodox, is his uncertain attitude toward the view of God as *personal*. On the one hand, in *Religion in the Making* he seems to associate belief in the personal nature of God with uncritical supernaturalism and to think that there is no direct intuition of God as a person in religious experience.[101] There is no widespread agreement among the different religions in support of the belief. For the alleged intuition of God as personal occurs only in "exceptional moments" and is "unable to maintain itself at all emotional temperatures amid great variety of environment," [102] whereas "the concept of a rightness of things, partially conformed to and partially disregarded," [103] is supported by a wide consensus. The conclusion seems

---

[98] *Ibid.*, p. 525 (italics added).   [99] *Ibid.*, p. 406.

[100] F. R. Tennant, *Philosophical Theology* (Cambridge, Eng.: Cambridge University Press, 1929), Vol. II, pp. 147–149.

[101] *Religion in the Making*, pp. 60, 66.   [102] *Ibid.*, p. 63.   [103] *Ibid.*, p. 65.

to be that religious experience suggests an impersonal rather than a personal concept of God.

On the other hand, in *Process and Reality*, published three years later, Whitehead uses such terms as "love of God," "great companion," and "particular providence." What are we to make of this? In one passage he refers to the image of God's "tender care that nothing be lost" as "but an image." This seems to suggest that terms which ascribe personal qualities or relations to God should be interpreted metaphorically. On the other hand, Christian points out that for Whitehead "God is an actuality that exists through time without loss of immediacy" and that His unity is "a continuing unity *within* an individual immediacy," a view which seems to be in accord with the ordinary idea of personality.[104] Moreover, Whitehead makes statements about God which seem to require that He be conceived as personal. Apart from the religious images we have mentioned, the description of His primordial nature as "conceptual envisagement" and "appetition," the ascription of "consciousness" to His consequent nature, and the reference to His "wisdom," "purpose," and "love" are meaningless unless He is regarded as personal at least in an analogical sense. Therefore, Christian's conclusion is probably justified that Whitehead rejects *both* "simple attribution of personality to God" *and* the view that He is "the impersonal order of the universe," and that "he proposes his theory as a view that avoids both extremes." [105] At the very least, the influence of the theistic conception of God upon him was profound, despite his strong reaction against the interpretation of it by popular supernaturalism and medieval theology.

Perhaps one of the main reasons for Whitehead's reluctance to affirm explicitly the personal character of God may be found in a certain aspect of his metaphysics. He holds that God is an "actual entity" and that the same "categoreal conditions" must apply to Him as to other actual entities, although He differs in important respects from other actual entities.[106] In contrast, "personality" is not one of the basic "categories" of Whitehead's metaphysics; the idea of a "personal order" or society of actual entities is a "derivative notion." [107] Nevertheless he ascribes personal attributes to God again and again. "The consciousness which is individual in us," he says, "is universal in him: the love which is partial in us is all-embracing in him." [108] Indeed, that which he emphasizes most, perhaps, is that God is characterized not by

[104] Christian, *An Interpretation of Whitehead's Metaphysics*, p. 411.
[105] *Ibid.*, p. 410.   [106] *Process and Reality*, p. 28.   [107] *Ibid.*, p. 51.
[108] *Religion in the Making*, p. 152.

force but by *love*. He criticizes sharply the "Semitic" and medieval view of God as an Oriental king who rules His subjects by force and rejects it as inconsistent with the life and teachings of Christ. Original Christianity, he says, "dwells upon the tender elements in the world, which slowly and in quietness operate by love; and it finds purpose in the present immediacy of a Kingdom not of this world." [109] This emphasis upon God's love rather than power, persuasion rather than arbitrary will, is one of the best illustrations of Whitehead's synthesis of Platonic and Christian elements in his religious thought. It seems to justify Christian's view that, although Whitehead's conception of God and the world is hardly that of traditional Theism, it is "somewhat nearer traditional theism than panentheism is." [110]

The fact that Whitehead regards personality not as a basic "category" for the interpretation of ultimate reality but as a derivative notion may also help to explain why he does not seem to take seriously the theistic hope for *personal immortality*. Although in *Religion in the Making* he asserts that he is neutral on the question of personal immortality and seems to leave it open,[111] in *Process and Reality* he is silent on the matter and in his later Ingersoll Lecture on *Immortality* in 1941 he seems to rule it out. We should not be misled on this point by his concept of "objective immortality." As we have seen, this means only that every actual entity is effective beyond its activity as a subject, in the sense that it can become an object or datum for later actual entities when it has perished. In this way an actual entity helps to determine future actual entities after its own immediacy has been lost, and it is also prehended, or felt, by God in His consequent nature. In this sense and to this extent, God "loses nothing that can be saved." But that which is preserved is the actual entity not in its immediacy as a subject but only as an object. Thus it seems clear that he does not affirm *personal* immortality. In his Ingersoll Lecture on *Immortality* he speaks of "a coordination of many personal individualities as factors in the nature of God." [112] This means that whatever is of value in the experiences of persons is "saved" by entering into the experience of God in His consequent nature. He also speaks of a contribution of persons to the good of future beings in the world. "What does haunt our imagination is that the immediate facts of present action pass into

---

[109] *Process and Reality*, p. 520.   [110] Christian, *op. cit.*, p. 406.
[111] *Religion in the Making*, p. 107.
[112] Whitehead, "Immortality," lecture delivered in 1941; in *The Philosophy of Alfred North Whitehead*, ed. Paul A. Schilpp (New York: Tudor, 1951), Sec. 14, p. 694.

permanent significance for the Universe." [113] Thus, he simply reasserts his doctrine of the "objective immortality" of all actual entities in entering as "objects" or "data" into the experience of God, on the one hand, and temporal actual entities, on the other. As Victor Lowe expresses his meaning, "a quality, derived from the man's life and purified in the harmony of God's experience, contributes good to the world for evermore. More precisely, *every* occasion of *every* temporal creature has this immortality in God and thence in the temporal world." [114] Whatever one may think about this doctrine of *objective* immortality, it is clearly not *personal* immortality in the theistic sense of the term.

WHITEHEAD'S RELIGION AND METAPHYSICS

Whitehead's contribution to the philosophy of religion in our time has been unique. This has been due in part to the fact that he combined a respect for the primary religious and moral intuitions of men, especially in the creative period between the Hebrew prophets and Augustine, with an independent philosophical approach to some of the most important religious problems. Few philosophers have had his profound appreciation of religion and at the same time his realistic understanding of its shortcomings. Philosophers such as Hume have allowed their disillusionment with the actual religion around them to turn them against religion in general and to blind them to its transforming power in human life. Although Whitehead was obviously repelled by some aspects of historical religion, he was able to distinguish between the actual and the ideal and to appreciate the creative religious insight and moral greatness of the Hebrew prophets, Plato, and Jesus. Also, if one may judge by his statements concerning the importance of religion and the moving language he frequently uses in speaking about it, he did not write as a detached spectator but as one who understood religious experience from the inside.

One of Whitehead's major contributions to recent religious thought has been his emphasis upon the *cosmical element* in religion.[115] In contrast to much modern theology and philosophy of religion, which has seemed, like Augustine, to be concerned only with God and the soul and has regarded nature as little more than a background for man, he has been profoundly interested in cosmology. By his vision of God's intimate relation to the world, he has helped men to recover that

---

[113] *Ibid.*, Sec. 17, p. 697.

[114] V. Lowe, *Understanding Whitehead* (Baltimore, Md.: Johns Hopkins Press, 1962), p. 107.

[115] J. S. Bixler, "Whitehead's Philosophy of Religion," in *The Philosophy of Alfred North Whitehead*, ed. Paul A. Schilpp, p. 492.

natural piety toward the creation which has been all but destroyed by scientific naturalism, technology, and the exploitation of nature. He has done this in several ways. The first is by his effective criticism of the materialistic interpretation of modern science which reduced nature to material atoms in external relation to one another and without value or purpose. For this has opened the way to an understanding of nature as a dynamic, creative, and purposive sphere for the realization of meaning and value. Again in his constructive theory of the cosmos he has shown that the scientific description of efficient causes and the religious and moral concern for final causes are compatible, since mechanism and teleology, fact and value are woven together in the fabric of natural events. In doing so he has also made it clear that, although the final causes, or "subjective aims," of things are immanent in them and bring "satisfaction" to them, the ultimate explanation of them and of the values realized through them must be found in an eternal and infinite Mind with a creative Eros for the good. Furthermore, Whitehead has described the close relations of man with other creatures, emphasizing his dependence upon the body and the natural environment for the internal constitution of his nature. Thus he has shown that man is a part of nature, a product of the evolutionary process, and akin to all living things, however pre-eminent he is by virtue of his consciousness and rationality.

Although his interpretation of the principle of continuity leads Whitehead to an inadequate view of human personality, as we shall see, his stress upon the unity of man with nature has been a salutary corrective for modern man's pride and is quite compatible with Theism. At the same time, he has insisted upon man's freedom and rationality and has refused to explain him in reductionistic fashion as a mere result of efficient causes. "The individual enjoyment is what I am in my role of a natural activity, as I shape the activities of the environment into a new creation, which is myself at this moment; and yet, as being myself, it is a continuation of the antecedent world. If we stress the role of the environment, this process is causation. If we stress the role of my immediate pattern of active enjoyment, this process is self creation." [116] Finally, in his emphasis upon the fact that God would be "incomplete" in His nature unless He could fulfill His purpose to realize values in the world and that the values which are realized in it are everlastingly conserved in the unity of His experience, he ascribes religious worth to the world and a permanent significance to its values in the sight of God.

[116] *Modes of Thought*, p. 228.

What are we to say about Whitehead's general understanding of the *nature of religion?* We have pointed out that he had little sympathy with the social or institutional side of religion and conceived of it almost exclusively as a personal experience of men in their solitariness. Also, his own religious experience seems to have been of the "once-born" type described by William James and he has little appreciation of the "twice-born" type. There is no indication that he ever went through a religious crisis, passing from the doubt and despair of the divided soul through conversion into peace and joy. The term "sin" seldom, if ever, occurs in his writings. "As for sin," writes Victor Lowe, "I don't think Whitehead discusses it anywhere." [117] Lowe seems to think that this was because "he did not conceive of God as omnipotent or issuing decrees" as a King wielding absolute power over His subjects.[118] But the sense of sin is not necessarily based upon such a conception of God, and it consists in a state of alienation from God and not mere disobedience to His "decrees." Probably the reason he did not mention sin was that, although he experienced tragedy in his personal life, his religious experience seems to have been that of "healthy-minded" men who have not known the depths of doubt and despair. It is significant that, although he often speaks of God as "saving" the world from the loss of value in the flux of time, he never speaks of Him as "saving" men from sin and guilt.

This does not mean that Whitehead has no conception of *salvation.* On the contrary, he emphasizes the fact that God persuades each temporal actual entity toward an aim beyond itself. In his discussion of "adventure" and "peace" as two of the qualities of a civilized society, this is very evident. "A race preserves its vigour," he says, "so long as it harbours a real contrast between what it has been and what it may be; and so long as it is nerved by the vigour to adventure beyond the safeties of the past." [119] And "adventure" must be supplemented by the transcendence of self-centeredness. Hence "peace," which is "the harmony of the soul's activity with ideal aims that lie beyond any personal satisfaction," [120] and which therefore involves "a surpassing of personality," [121] is indispensable. This is a high ideal of human life. The main question which may be raised concerning it is: Does it not rest upon a rather optimistic estimate of man's moral and spiritual capacity to respond to "ideal aims" and to overcome self-centeredness?

We have been considering Whitehead's general attitude toward religion. We must now turn to some questions concerning his *meta-*

[117] Lowe, *Understanding Whitehead*, p. 112.   [118] *Ibid.*, p. 112.
[119] *Adventures of Ideas*, p. 360.   [120] *Ibid.*, p. 371.   [121] *Ibid.*, p. 367.

physics, since his conception of God and His relation to the world is an integral part of his metaphysical system. The first question we would raise is whether the conclusion he draws from his "subjectivist principle" as to the subjective nature of all actual entities is justified. It should be noted that, although he regards all actual entities as units or subjects of experience whose essence is feeling, he does not deny that there are important differences between stones, plants, animals, and men with respect to the nature of the feelings of the actual entities which compose them. For example, a stone is a "society" composed of low-grade actual entities which repeat one another and attain little novelty. The actual entities which compose an animal are more creative because their subjective aims play a more important role. Man differs from the animals by virtue of the greater complexity and intensity of his feelings. Nevertheless, the generic nature of all actual entities is essentially the same, so that there is continuity between physical, biological, and human actual entities. This, of course, is a form of *panpsychism.* How are we to evaluate it?

It has an immediate appeal to those who are repelled by the scientific materialism which Whitehead criticized so effectively in *Science and the Modern World.* At first sight it seems to be an effective answer to the materialistic reduction of life and mind to configurations of matter, since it asserts that matter itself is organic in character. If the principle of continuity requires that there should be only one kind of actuality, it seems at least as reasonable to reduce matter to low-grade organisms as to reduce life to high-grade matter. Indeed, it seems *more* reasonable because it is difficult to see how biological organisms could have developed in the course of evolution if they had been composed of anything less than organisms. Nevertheless, the argument for panpsychism is inconclusive and it must be regarded as a *speculative theory* which may or may not be true. Whitehead's main argument for accepting the "subjectivist principle," i.e., that the speculative philosopher must take as his starting point the concrete experience of man and generalize this by extending it to all other beings, is unconvincing. It is true that a metaphysician must start with some *aspect* of experience which seems to him of primary importance and take it as a key for the interpretation of experience as a *whole.* But this does not necessarily require the conclusion that there is only one kind of reality. Only if the principle of continuity means that there are no fundamental differences between actualities which appear to be different does this conclusion follow. But it is very doubtful whether the principle of continuity should be interpreted in this way. After all, there are boundaries which mark off the objects of the different sciences from each other, e.g., biology from physics and both from psychology, although it may be difficult to classify certain "borderline" objects. And one of the major issues in metaphysics concerns the proper interpretation of the principle of continuity.

The only way to test the theory of panpsychism is to apply Whitehead's own criterion for the truth of a metaphysical theory: Is it "adequate" to *all* the facts of experience? Doubtless, if the terms "experience" and "feeling" are used in a broad sense, the theory is applicable to animals as well as human beings, at least in the sense that they have "experience" and "feeling" of some kind. It may also be applicable to plants, since they seem to "take account of" objects in their environment. But does it correctly describe the components of *physical objects* such as stones? It must be said at once that there is no evidence that the "enduring objects" such as electrons and protons which compose the atoms in such physical objects consist of actual entities of a subjective kind. Although the recent revolution in physics has outmoded the traditional view of matter, Whitehead's theory that the primary entities are organisms constituted by prehensions, or feelings, is a philosophical speculation which is based largely on his interpretation of the principle of continuity. Since the time of Aristotle, animal organisms have been distinguished from inanimate objects by their capacity to move themselves, to reproduce themselves, and to experience external objects through sensation and appetition. Whatever may have been the cause of their "emergence" from inanimate objects, they have emerged and possess characteristics which those objects do not seem to have. Moreover, there is no positive evidence that the actual entities which compose the electrons and protons of a "society" such as a stone create themselves out of feelings of the objects in their environment or are guided by subjective aims in doing so.

In the case of human beings or *persons*, Whitehead's panpsychism is not "adequate" for a quite different reason. Obviously, persons *are* subjects of experience, grow by feeling objects of their environment, and are guided by subjective aims or ends. The difficulty in this case is not that the theory claims *too much* for them, as in the case of stones, but that it claims *too little*. For it seems obvious that a human "person" is more than a succession of actual occasions of which the later "inherit" from the earlier. A person is identical with himself and possesses unity and continuity with himself throughout the succession of his experiences. As Kant pointed out, knowledge of objects is possible only by virtue of the fact that impressions are held together in a unity of consciousness, and this presupposes the existence of a mind with personal identity. Similarly, moral decision must be the act of a self whose will is identical and continuous with itself through time, and a person cannot be held morally responsible for an act at a later time unless he is identical with himself during the intervening period. In *Adventures of Ideas* Whitehead showed that he was aware of these difficulties. "In our account of human experience," he wrote, "we have attenuated human personality into a genetic relation between occasions of human experience. Yet personal unity is an inescapable fact. . . . Any philosophy must provide some doctrine of personal identity. "[122] But he does *not* provide such a doctrine, except to say that "our consciousness of the self-identity pervading our life-thread of occasions, is nothing other than knowledge of a special strand of unity within the general unity of nature" and that the general principle behind it is "the immanence of the past emerging in the present."[123] Thus Whitehead's panpsychism does not offer an "adequate" account of human persons. This may be one reason he was so reluctant to speak of *God* as personal, although he ascribed characteristics to Him which seem to presuppose His personal nature. For one who had such an "attenuated" concept of human personality could hardly take "personality" as the key to the nature of God.

Another criticism of Whitehead's metaphysical system is that his reaction against the traditional concept of unchanging substance has led him to *subordinate reality to process*. An example of this is his view that each actual entity is an atomic unit which creates itself out of the data or objects prehended by it. This idea of *self-creation* is ultimately unintelligible and has no warrant in experience. In the case of a person, an actual occasion or unit of experience comes into existence not through its own creative activity but as a phase of the continuous experience of an enduring subject or self which is already in existence. Similarly, the actual entities which compose a living organism come into existence as parts of an enduring whole and are dependent upon the whole for their creation. If so, enduring things or substances such as human persons and animal organisms cannot be mere "societies" of atomic actual entities each of which has created itself, since the actual entities which constitute them depend upon them for their own origin. This implies that creativity, which is conceived by Whitehead as the generic character of every actual entity, is really an activity of enduring things.

[122] *Ibid.*, pp. 239, 240. [123] *Ibid.*, p. 241.

Also, *continuity* in time cannot be explained adequately by "the identity of subjective form inherited conformally from one occasion [i.e., actual entity] to the other." [124] It requires the existence of enduring things which change but are relatively permanent through their change. This implies that in the world, both as a whole and in its parts, "process" presupposes "reality." Whitehead recognizes the primacy of reality insofar as his solution of the problem of "flux" and "permanence," especially the conservation of value, rests upon God's eternal character in His primordial nature and His everlasting character in His consequent nature. But he also speaks of "creativity" as the "ultimate notion of the highest generality at the base of actuality" and of God's primordial nature as "a creature of creativity," as well as "a condition of creativity." [125] In this sense, "process" seems to be primary, and unchanging "reality" secondary. The implications of this for Whitehead's conception of God and His relation to the world we shall see.

GOD AND THE WORLD

Whitehead's view of God and the world, as it is developed in *Process and Reality* is his most distinctive and important contribution to the philosophy of religion. Although he makes no attempt to demonstrate the *existence* of God, he offers an argument for His existence based upon metaphysical considerations and upon the religious intuitions of men. Three phases of this argument may be distinguished but they should not be separated.

The first is the *cosmological* phase. In both *Science and the Modern World* and *Process and Reality* he argues that God is required as a *principle of limitation* or *concretion* who selects from the boundless multiplicity of possibilities conceptually envisaged by Him those which are relevant or appropriate for each actual entity. This part of the argument is similar to the traditional cosmological argument in that it infers from contingent being the existence of a necessary Being, but it differs in that God is inferred to account for the "forms of definiteness" of contingent beings rather than for their existence. Since Whitehead does not speak of God as the sole cause of the existence of actual entities, the question can be raised whether the cosmological phase of his argument is not subject to the same criticisms as Plato's myth of the shaping of the cosmos through the imposition of eternal Forms by a divine Craftsman upon a Receptacle which is independent of Him, i.e., that it conceives of God as an Architect rather than a Creator and implies a dualism between Himself and the medium ("creativity") in

[124] *Ibid.*, p. 239.
[125] *Process and Reality*, p. 47.

which He works. However, its strength lies in the recognition that the determinate forms exemplified or realized in nature must be explained. It is difficult to avoid Whitehead's view that a multiplicity of "eternal objects" or possibilities must be postulated to account for the empirically observed forms of things and that these must be capable of "exemplification" or "ingression" in different things. Moreover, since these are only possibilities and do not possess a causal power of their own, we must explain the fact that some of them rather than others are exemplified in each particular thing, so that a selection of these from among the multiplicity of possibilities is necessary. This selection can be best explained by an eternal or primordial Mind which envisages the whole range of possibilities and selects those which are "relevant" or suitable for each particular actual entity. And this Mind must be infinite if it is to be capable of the "conceptual envisagement" of the boundless multiplicity of possibilities.

In considering this cosmological phase of the argument, we have abstracted from the fact that the forms of things are related to the *ends* or *values* realized by them. This is the basis of the second phase of Whitehead's argument, which is a *teleological* one. As we have seen, actual entities are guided by "subjective aims" in the process of becoming and these cannot be provided by themselves or by other temporal actual entities. Therefore Whitehead argues that there must be a primordial Mind which not only "envisages" but also has an "appetition" for the eternal objects and a "purpose" to realize them in the world. His motive in doing so must be creative *"erōs"* or "love" which seeks to attain the maximum of "value" in all actual entities. Therefore He presents to each of them the "subjective aim" which is "relevant" to it and thereby initiates its process of becoming. In this way only can the final causes or ends of things be accounted for.

In the development of this teleological phase of the argument Whitehead was influenced by the fact that actual entities which arise in time do not necessarily reproduce or re-enact those which have preceded them, although "low-grade" ones such as those which compose physical objects seem to do so. At the level of living organisms and human persons, there is a continual emergence of novelty. This suggests that creative activity guided by final causes or ends must be at work, for efficient causes from the past tend merely to reproduce themselves in their effects. The most adequate explanation of these final causes or ends and of the novelty they make possible is that they are presented by God as "ideals" or "lures for feeling" to the actual entities. The empirical grounds Whitehead offers for this conclusion are strong. We are conscious of the presence of such ideals or ends in our own experience and to deny their existence would make human conduct unintelligible. That plant and animal organisms are affected by final causes is also shown by a study of the evolutionary process. In *The Function of Reason* Whitehead argues that the struggle for existence and adaptation to environment cannot explain "the fact that organic species have been produced from inorganic distributions of matter, and the fact that in the lapse of time organic species of higher and higher types have evolved." [126] The "upward trend" of evolution, which is in sharp contrast to the "degradation of energy" in physical nature, suggests that organisms seek not only to "live" but also to "live well" and to "live better" and therefore that they are moved by an urge toward the attainment of ends.[127] "Mental experience is the organ of novelty, the urge beyond." [128]

The third phase of the argument is necessary to complete it. It maintains that God is required if the values realized in the world are to be "saved" from loss. The actual entities of the world require for their "completion" that God in His consequent nature should include them in the everlasting unity of His experience. Also, if God not only affects the world but is affected by it, it is necessary for the "completion" of His nature. Thus, while the world requires God for its "completion," He requires the world for His "completion." Both requirements are met by the *conservation of values* of the world in God's consequent nature. "In this way God is completed by the individual, fluent satisfactions of finite fact, and the temporal occasions are completed by their everlasting union with their transformed selves." [129]

This argument for God as the conserver of the world's value in His consequent nature obviously rests not only on the metaphysical requirement that God's nature should be completed, but also on the religious intuition that the good attained in the world is "saved" from loss by God. That this religious intuition has influenced the argument is shown by Whitehead's assertion that " 'everlastingness' is the content of that vision upon which the finer religions are built—the 'many' absorbed everlastingly in the final unity." [130] Therefore the argument is likely to be fully convincing only to those who believe that the religious vision that achievements of value will not be engulfed in the flux of time is true. However, the metaphysical argument has force in itself. If the cosmological-teleological argument has led to the conclusion that the ultimate cause of the world's order and value is God's purpose to realize the maximum of value, it would seem to follow that He can

---

[126] Whitehead, *The Function of Reason* (Boston: Beacon Press, 1958), p. 7.
[127] *Ibid.*, p. 8.   [128] *Ibid.*, p. 33.   [129] *Process and Reality*, p. 527.
[130] *Ibid.*

fulfill that purpose only by conserving the world's value everlastingly. Whether the value of human persons is adequately conserved by their "objective immortality" in the unity of God's experience rather than "personal immortality" in fellowship with Him is another question.

We have now considered the three phases of Whitehead's argument for the existence of God and have found that although they are not formal "proofs" they are very persuasive. However, it is probable that his most distinctive and influential contribution to the philosophy of religion is his criticism of certain aspects of the traditional theistic conception of the *nature of God* and his constructive suggestions for the development of an alternative view. Unfortunately, he did not develop these suggestions very fully and they have given rise to different interpretations at certain points, but the main outlines of his view are fairly clear.

Medieval Theism represented God in terms which were to a considerable extent derived from Greek philosophy. As we have seen, Aquinas interpreted the perfection, eternity, immutability, knowledge, will, and power of God in ways which at certain points can hardly be reconciled with the biblical view of Him (see Chap. 5). He described God's perfection as complete actuality without potentiality of any kind; His eternity and immutability as excluding all succession in time and all change; His knowledge as including even future contingent events; His will as the ultimate cause of all events, even contingent and evil ones; and His power as limited only by absolute impossibility. Thus God's perfection is that of "static completion," and, while the world is wholly dependent upon Him, He is dependent upon it in no way. Whitehead called in question this medieval conception of God which continued to dominate modern orthodox theology up to the twentieth century. As Hartshorne has argued in *The Divine Relativity* and other works, Whitehead insisted that God is related to the world as it is related to Him, so that He is not wholly independent of it but needs it for His "completion" as it needs Him for its "completion." Therefore His perfection must be reinterpreted in such a way as to admit "incompletion" or potentiality in His nature, His eternity in such a way as to be compatible with succession in His experience, and His immutability in such a way as not to exclude change. This makes it possible to conceive of His consequent nature as growing with the "creative advance of the world" so that His experience is constantly being enriched by the effect of the world upon Him.[131] Also His will must not be

---

[131] Charles Hartshorne has shown that it is possible to accept Whitehead's doctrine of God's "relativity" to the world and yet to maintain the "absoluteness" of His essence and to ascribe "incompletion" or potentiality to Him without denying the perfection of His essence. For while Whitehead describes the *con-*

conceived as the sole cause which determines all things, for temporal actual entities create themselves and are responsible for the evil they do. And although His power is manifest in the realization of value in the world and the conservation of it in His own experience, He fulfills His purpose not by force but by persuasion, presenting ideals as "lures for feeling" to actual entities.

However, there are certain *difficulties* in Whitehead's conception of God. The first is that his emphasis upon the "incompletion" or potentiality in God's nature and upon His involvement in time and change is so excessive that it endangers the *transcendence* of God. Although he maintains that God's primordial nature is eternal, unchanging, infinite, and in a certain sense perfect, it must be remembered that the primordial nature is only an aspect of His nature. Therefore these "metaphysical" attributes, which have traditionally expressed God's transcendence of the world and the perfection of His nature, tend to become secondary to the attributes which express His dependence upon the world. As a result, the danger arises of a return to the immanentism of Hegelian Idealism, which affirmed that the Absolute Spirit realizes itself and comes to self-consciousness only through its manifestation in the world, or even to Theistic Naturalism, which seems to regard God as nothing more than the value-producing aspect of the creative process itself. Whitehead does not succumb to this danger because he maintains God's transcendence of the world as an individual actual entity who affects the world at every point. But, as we have pointed out, in developing a pluralistic atomism of actual entities whose being is their becoming and in treating continuity and endurance as products of the relations between these entities, he subordinates permanence to change, reality to process in his metaphysics. Similarly, in emphasizing God's "relativity" to the world and His dependence upon the world for His "completion," he puts in jeopardy God's immutability and perfection. God *is* related to and dependent upon the world in the sense that His love and purpose for the world are essential to His nature. But His nature as a concrete reality is eternally and immutably what it is. Thus, while the *contents* of His experience change with and are enriched by the "creative advance" of the world, His *nature* itself

---

sequent nature of God as relative to the world and as changing with its "creative advance," he regards the *primordial nature* as the absolute, independent, and unchanging "abstract essence" of God. There are difficulties in this view, but it shows that Whitehead's conception of God is, at least to a certain extent, "available" for religious purposes. Whether it is also "adequate" for them is the question we are now considering. Cf. Charles Hartshorne, *The Divine Relativity, Reality as a Social Process*, and other books, as well as his essay "Whitehead's Idea of God" in *The Philosophy of Alfred North Whitehead*, ed. Paul A. Schilpp.

does not change. The problem of the relation between permanence and change, actuality and potentiality in God's nature has yet to be worked out in a satisfactory way. But it may be predicted that the Theism of the future will not abandon the Greek and medieval emphasis upon the eternity, immutability, and perfection of the transcendent God, but will seek a way to reinterpret them and synthesize them with the insistence of Whitehead and Hartshorne upon His intimate relation to the world and its profound effect upon Him.

Another difficulty with Whitehead's conception of God is his subordination and at times disparagement of the *moral side* of religion and his lack of appreciation for the Hebraic emphasis upon God's *moral will*. When he criticizes the representation of God as a "ruthless moralist" in Judaism, Christianity, and Islam, he contrasts it with Christ's view of the divine love which is "a little oblivious as to morals." [132] These statements may be interpreted merely as a criticism of the belief that God imposes moral laws upon men by the arbitrary fiat of His will and enforces them by ruthless punishment. If so, they are justified when directed against the legalistic perversions of religious morality which have been all too common in Judaism and Christianity. But they manifest a lack of sympathetic understanding of the attitude of the Hebrew prophets and lawgivers, who believed that grateful obedience was due to God's will not as an arbitrary despot but as one who had shown His love for His people in the past (Deut. 6:20–25; 8:11–20). Even if this were not the case, the association of religious morality with arbitrary will is not *essential* to it.

What is the source of Whitehead's disparagement of the moral aspect of religion? One of the sources is his *theory of value*, especially aesthetic value. God's purpose in presenting subjective aims to actual entities is the attainment of "intensity of feeling" and consequently the realization of aesthetic value. In *Adventures of Ideas* five "qualities" which Whitehead regards as essential for civilization are discussed: beauty, truth, art, adventure, and peace.[133] It is significant that moral goodness is not among them. This is in sharp contrast to the view of Plato that morality is fundamental to the unity of the state and the happiness of its citizens. Of course, Whitehead does not regard morality as unimportant. Moral codes, although relative to the circumstances of a particular environment, witness to an "ideal beyond personal limitations" or an "aim at social perfection." [134] But morality is, it seems, an instrumental rather than an intrinsic value. Beauty, "the

---

[132] *Process and Reality*, p. 521.
[133] *Adventures of Ideas*, p. 353.   [134] *Ibid.*, p. 375.

mutual adaptation of the several factors in an occasion of experience" to produce "the perfection of harmony," [135] is the only "self-justifying" value. "The teleology of the Universe is directed to the production of Beauty." [136] "Thus Beauty is left as the one aim which by its very nature is self-justifying." [137] In contrast, morality is a means for the promotion of "aesthetic value," a necessary condition for the maximizing of value experience of every kind. In *Modes of Thought*, it is defined as "the control of process so as to maximize importance" or "the aim at greatness of experience in the various dimensions belonging to it," [138] and "importance" and "greatness of experience" are interpreted in aesthetic terms such as intensity and harmony of experience.

The religious objection to this view of morality is not only that it seems to subordinate moral conduct to aesthetic values but also that it makes no mention of a *moral order* based upon God's will and of the obligation of men to act in accordance with it. Such a moral order need not consist of a code of laws or rules which prescribe or prohibit specific kinds of acts; it may consist, rather, in general principles which are applied with freedom and flexibility to the changing situations of human life. Whitehead himself refers to two such principles, "the generality of harmony" and "the importance of the individual." [139] But he does not seem to regard these principles as belonging to a moral order based upon God's will, nor does he speak of them as moral demands which are universally binding upon men.[140] In contrast, ethical Theism insists that, while God in His love may be "a little oblivious to morals" in the sense of mere obedience to moral codes, He makes moral demands upon the individual which are not less but more rigorous than those of any code of moral laws. When this is overlooked and the love of God for men is separated from His demands upon them for love and justice toward one another, the conception of God as love is itself weakened. Is it possible that Whitehead, in his reaction against the notion of God as imposing His will upon men like an "imperial ruler," has confused this notion with the quite different idea of Him as moral will motivated by love and requiring justice, mercy, and humility from His children (Mic. 6:8)?

---

[135] *Ibid.*, pp. 324, 325.   [136] *Ibid.*, p. 341.   [137] *Ibid.*, p. 342.
[138] *Modes of Thought*, p. 19.
[139] *Adventures of Ideas*, p. 376.
[140] On the other hand, William Christian has questioned (in correspondence with George F. Thomas) whether Whitehead "denies the intrinsic value of moral conduct." He thinks "it would be possible to work out a set of doctrines involving the concept of moral order from Whitehead's scheme, e.g., doctrines of judgment, providence, etc. But he certainly does not make much of this explicitly."

A final question with respect to Whitehead's conception of God concerns his depreciation of the concept of divine *power*. As we have seen he rejects the doctrine of the omnipotence of God, i.e., the possession by God of all power and His causal determination of all events, on the ground that this would deprive temporal actual entities of their freedom and make God responsible for the evil they do. Most modern theists would agree with him on this point, although many would assert that it involves a self-limitation by God in the use of His power rather than an external limitation on His power. But the question we are raising concerns his Platonic view that God does not "rule" the world by "force" but affects it by "persuasion," i.e., by setting "subjective aims" before actual entities. Daniel Day Williams puts it this way: "If he avoids the Despot, is his God too weak?" [141] "The question to be raised," Williams says, "is whether Whitehead's account of the divine causality leaves God without concrete power in the world. . . . He sets certain limits to the creatures and absorbs the world's activities in a certain way. But does he act with power to transform the world beyond presenting it with an ideal aim?" [142] "My question concerns the divine initiative in history and the way in which it is exercised. Does God only listen or does he speak?" [143] For Whitehead, God is primarily the *Final Cause* of the realization of values in the world and the *Conserver* of its values when they have been realized. But He is not the *Creator* upon whose power the existence of actual entities depends, since they create themselves. Nor is He the *Redeemer* of the world who transforms His creatures by the power of His grace and brings new life to them. In this respect, Whitehead is closer to Platonic than to Jewish and Christian Theism. As a result, his conception of God, noble as it is, lacks something of the majesty of the transcendent God of the Bible, who combines love for men with the moral demand for justice and mercy and uses His power in history and beyond history to fulfill His purpose for the creatures He has made.

[141] Ivor Leclerc (ed.), *The Relevance of Whitehead's Metaphysics* (London: Allen, 1961), p. 365.
[142] *Ibid.*, p. 368.   [143] *Ibid.*, p. 3.

14 Philosophical Theology

TILLICH

Since coming to the United States from Germany in 1933, Paul Tillich (1886–   ) has come to be recognized as one of the foremost philosophical theologians of our time. He had been a professor of theology at Marburg and elsewhere and a professor of philosophy at Frankfurt before he came into conflict with the Nazis and was dismissed from his position. Called to Union Theological Seminary in New York as Professor of Philosophical Theology, he quickly established himself as a prominent figure in theological circles. After the publication of the first volume of his *Systematic Theology* in 1951 and a volume of essays by various authors entitled *The Theology of Paul Tillich* in 1952, he became still more widely known. His concern to speak in terms relevant to our time and intelligible to the lay mind led to the publication of a number of small books such as *The Courage to Be* and *Dynamics of Faith*. The second volume of the *Systematic Theology*, his most important work, appeared in 1957, and the third volume was published in 1963.

Tillich has not only been one of the most influential American theologians; he has also had a considerable effect upon the philosophy of religion and has had much to do with the recent revival of interest in that subject. Although it is with the philosophical aspect of his work that we shall be mainly concerned, it must not be forgotten that he is primarily a theologian. Like Aquinas, he has used philosophy to serve the purposes of theology. It is difficult, therefore, to separate his philosophy from his theology. However, it is possible to consider certain of his doctrines apart from the rest of his system without doing too great violence to them. We shall attempt to do this, confining ourselves to his doctrines of reason and revelation, on the one hand, and being and God, on the other hand. We shall concentrate mainly upon his treatment of these doctrines in the first volume of the *Systematic Theology*, but shall also consider relevant parts of several other books. Although it will be necessary to refer to the theological aspects of the doctrines, we shall concern ourselves primarily with the way they are related to his philosophical position.

PHILOSOPHY AND THEOLOGY: THE METHOD OF CORRELATION

For many years Tillich has attempted to reconcile the approaches of philosophy and theology to the nature of reality. As one who has been both a professor of theology and a professor of philosophy, he has been acutely conscious of the difference between them and of the fact that many theologians and philosophers believe any collaboration between them to be impossible. In one of his most revealing small books, he faces squarely both the belief of many theologians that biblical religion and philosophy are opposed to each other and the objections of logical positivists to metaphysical questions concerning being.[1] To both of these groups he opposes his own conviction that there is "an ultimate unity and a profound interdependence" between biblical religion and the philosophical quest for reality. "*Against* Pascal I say: The God of Abraham, Isaac and Jacob and the God of the philosophers is the same God." [2]

His belief that philosophy and theology are "interdependent" in seeking an answer to the nature of being underlies Tillich's *method of correlation*. Philosophy and theology, he holds, are both interested in reality as a whole but approach it from different perspectives and by different methods. "Philosophy deals with the *structure* of being *in itself;* theology deals with the *meaning* of being *for us.*" [3] This results in a difference of attitude. While the philosopher seeks to maintain a "detached objectivity" toward being, the theologian is "involved" in the object and his attitude is existential.[4] Another difference between the philosopher and the theologian has to do with the sources upon which they depend. Whereas the philosopher looks at the "whole of reality" rather than a "particular place" to discover the structure of being, the theologian derives his knowledge from "the *logos* manifesting itself in a particular historical event." [5] Finally, whereas the philosopher deals with the categories of being in relation to the material described by them, the theologian considers them in relation to the quest for "salva-

[1] Paul Tillich, *Biblical Religion and the Search for Ultimate Reality* (Chicago: University of Chicago Press, 1955), pp. 1, 15.

[2] *Ibid.,* p. 85.

[3] Paul Tillich, *Systematic Theology,* Vol. I. (Chicago: University of Chicago Press, 1951), p. 22 (italics added).

[4] *Ibid.,* pp. 22, 23.   [5] *Ibid.,* p. 23.

tion" or the "New Being." Because of these differences [6] Tillich maintains that there can be no conflict between philosophy and theology but also no synthesis of them. A common basis for both conflict and synthesis is lacking.[7] However, he admits that there is also a "convergence" of philosophy and theology, since the philosopher has an "ultimate concern" whether he is conscious of it or not; and the theologian can make clear the universal validity of his ultimate concern only in an attitude of detachment.[8]

The "method of correlation" is a method of relating philosophy and theology in the quest for ultimate reality. "The method of correlation," says Tillich, "explains the contents of the Christian faith through existential questions and theological answers in mutual interdependence." [9] "Theology formulates the questions implied in human existence" and then correlates them with the answers provided by divine revelation.[10] The analysis of the human situation must be a philosophical one, although it is performed by a theologian. The eyes of the theologian making such an analysis are "partially focused by his ultimate concern," but his act of seeing is "determined only by the object as it is given in his experience." [11] However, the content of the answers cannot be derived from the philosophical analysis. Only the form in which they are expressed is dependent upon the questions.[12]

The purpose of the method of correlation is to show the *relevance* of Christian theology to the human situation as expressed in culture and analyzed by philosophy. Tillich remarks that a theology which presents the Christian message as "a sum of revealed truths which have fallen into the human situation like strange bodies from a strange world" is inadequate, because "man cannot receive answers to questions he has never asked." [13] This statement throws light not only upon the purpose of the method of correlation but also upon Tillich's general *intention* as a philosophical theologian. The last generation has been characterized by a divorce between philosophy and theology. Philosophy has tended to confine itself in Europe largely to existential analysis of man's condition or, in England and America, to logic and linguistic analysis, dismissing the perennial problems of metaphysics as unreal and reducing the problems of theology to the analysis of religious language. Theology under the leadership of Barth has denied that philosophy should substantially affect the interpretation of the Christian message. Tillich has set himself squarely against this separation of phi-

[6] *Ibid.*, p. 24.   [7] *Ibid.*, pp. 26, 27.   [8] *Ibid.*, pp. 24, 25.   [9] *Ibid.*, p. 60.
[10] *Ibid.*, p. 61.   [11] *Ibid.*, pp. 63, 64.   [12] *Ibid.*, p. 64.
[13] *Ibid.*, pp. 64, 65.

losophy and theology and has argued that they are interdependent and should be correlated with one another. A synthesis of them is impossible because of their differences, but they are not opposed to one another when each performs its proper function. Philosophy can analyze the structure of being and raise questions that are implied by human existence and must be answered if man is to find meaning in his life. But it cannot answer these questions. The answers can be found in revelation and formulated by theology. But they will go unheeded if men are not aware that they are relevant to the questions raised by human existence. Therefore philosophical analysis is necessary to formulate the questions and theology is necessary to provide the answers.

Thus Tillich is not content to present the Christian revelation, like Barth and other dogmatic theologians, without concerning himself with the question whether men can see its relevance to their questions and needs. He seeks to be an "apologetic," or "answering," theologian speaking to an age which is groping for meaning but has not found answers to its deepest questions. In correlating theology with philosophy he is not merely seeking to make it philosophically respectable or to show that it can be philosophically demonstrated. Rather, his intention is to show that the Christian revelation is not contrary to reason but fulfills it by answering ultimate questions that reason can raise but cannot answer. In a sense, his purpose is similar to that of Thomas Aquinas, but his way of carrying it out is very different. For his view both of reason and of revelation is more critical than that of Aquinas. As a post-Kantian philosopher, he is more aware of the limits of reason in answering ultimate questions. As a post-Reformation theologian, he refuses to accept any particular interpretation of the Christian revelation as authoritative and absolute. He has also been influenced by the Existentialism of Kierkegaard and is fully aware of the involvement of both man's reason and his religion in the "ambiguities" of his existence. Hence he does not attempt to make a modern synthesis of reason and revelation which will bring them into harmony with one another. But the task he has set himself is an important one. For he has sought honestly and persistently to understand the questions of contemporary men and to formulate Christian answers in terms which will be relevant to them. It is this resolute effort to understand and speak to the contemporary mind which is the source of his wide influence.

The method of correlation obviously rests upon the assumption that philosophy is capable of raising questions concerning human existence which it is unable to answer. Accordingly, the function of philosophy is *critical* rather than *speculative*. It can analyze the categories and principles which, in Kant's terms, "make experience possible," [14] but it cannot present a complete system of reality, forgetting the finitude of the human mind,[15] as Hegel tried to do. On the other hand, it cannot avoid the question of being and thus reduce philosophy to logic and theory of knowledge, as Logical Positivism does, for this would make it irrelevant to life.[16] Therefore, critical philosophy is "more modest" than speculative philosophy but "less modest" than positivistic philosophy. It aims at an "ontology" or doctrine of being which analyzes the structures of being we encounter in experience, not at a "metaphysics" which explains the world by a transcendent realm beyond it. Obviously, such a critical philosophy presupposes a basic confidence in the capacity of reason to discover the *structure of being* by phenomenological analysis, but denies the power of reason to grasp *being-itself*.

Another presupposition of the method of correlation is that a theologian can analyze the structure of being with the "detached objectivity" of a philosopher, i.e., without being influenced by his theological commitment. Can a theologian who has discovered ultimate reality in "Jesus as the Christ" deal with the categories of being as they appear in nature and history without considering their meaning for him and their relation to his quest for salvation? Critics have pointed out that the ontological analysis he offers is not accepted by philosophers who have not been deeply influenced by Idealism, e.g., logical positivists and naturalists. This does not prove that he did not make his philosophical analysis with as much objectivity as he could, but it raises the question whether it is possible to separate a philosophical analysis of being and human existence from the theological commitment (or lack of one) of the person who makes it.

Indeed, it must be said that Tillich's sharp distinction between philosophy and theology exaggerates the differences between them and rests upon a theoretical analysis of what has been claimed to be the *essence* of each rather than a concrete examination of the *actual* thinking of philosophers and theologians. Of course philosophy has been theoretical in its interest in the structure of reality. But it is not true that philosophers have been indifferent to the meaning of reality for man or lacking in existential involvement. Tillich recognizes this but explains it as due to the presence of a theological element in the thinking of the great philosophers. This is a tacit admission that, although philosophy and theology may be so *defined* as to be mutually exclusive, one and the same person may combine theoretical and existential concerns so that they are not mutually exclusive *in fact*. Exam-

[14] *Ibid.*, pp. 18, 19.   [15] *Ibid.*, p. 19.   [16] *Ibid.*, pp. 19, 20.

ples of this among philosophers are numerous, e.g., Plato, Spinoza, Kant, and Whitehead; and some of the greatest theologians have also been philosophers, e.g., Augustine and Aquinas. It is true that some philosophers have limited themselves to logical and epistemological problems, but Tillich himself regards them as "too modest" in their claims for philosophy. Indeed, he has virtually conceded in *Dynamics of Faith* the abstractness of his distinction between philosophy and theology. "The historically most significant philosophies show not only the greatest power of thought but the most passionate concern about the meaning of the ultimate whose manifestations they describe." [17]

It is not surprising, therefore, that Tillich himself does not keep his philosophical analysis of the "questions" and his theological statement of the "answers" as separate as his method of correlation would require. In the philosophical sections of the *Systematic Theology*, his formulation of the questions at certain crucial points is that of a philosopher who is also a theologian, and in the theological sections his formulation of the answers is partly determined by the philosophical point of view from which he has stated the questions. As we shall see, this is particularly true in the case of his treatment of being and God, and it has provoked some sharp criticisms by theologians who have asserted that his ontology largely determines the content as well as the form of his doctrine of God. For example, Kenneth Hamilton maintains that the "congruity" of the questions with the answers in his system has been made possible only by taking his ontology as certain and authoritative and then making the answers given by theology fit the questions.[18] In our opinion, this underestimates the influence of Christian theology upon Tillich's thought and seems to imply that he is only a philosopher who has forced theology to conform to his system without much regard for what it actually says. We should prefer to say that, since he has been both a philosopher and a theologian throughout his career, his philosophy and theology have developed together and have profoundly affected one another. In view of this fact, it is natural that his philosophy should not be confined to a formulation of the questions implied by human existence and that the answers offered by his theology should be deeply influenced by his philosophy.

REVELATION AND FAITH

Since Tillich holds that theology depends for its answers upon revelation and revelation is received by faith, it is necessary to consider

[17] Paul Tillich, *Dynamics of Faith* (New York: Harper & Row, 1957), p. 92.
[18] Kenneth Hamilton, *The System and the Gospel* (London: S.C.M. Press, 1963), pp. 119–121.

briefly the nature of revelation, the kind of truth it offers, and the reception of it by faith. In the *Systematic Theology* Tillich deals with the nature and truth of revelation, and in *Dynamics of Faith* he analyzes the state of faith.

Revelation is the manifestation of the "mystery" of being-itself or the ground of being, as mediated through an objective "miracle" or "sign-event" and as received through "ecstatic reason." [19] There are two sides of revelation, negative and positive. The negative side is the revelation of the "abysmal" element in the ground of being through the "shock" that occurs to the mind when it experiences the threat of nonbeing.[20] The positive side is the revelation of "the power of being, conquering nonbeing." [21] Since there is a revelation only if there is someone who receives it, it includes not only the objective occurrence or "miracle" but also the subjective reception of it in the "ecstasy" of reason.[22] *Ecstasy* occurs when the mind is shaken by the "shock" at the threat of nonbeing. But it is not a negation of reason; it is the state in which reason is "beyond itself, that is, beyond its subject-object structure." [23] It opens a "new dimension" of knowledge in relation to the mystery of being.[24] The *miracle* or objective event in which the mystery of being is revealed is a "sign-event" which is astonishing but is not the result of a supernatural interference. Anything can become a medium of revelation, since every person or thing participates to some degree in being-itself, e.g., natural objects, historical events, and persons.[25] The *ground* of revelation is God as He manifests Himself, i.e., the "Word" or *logos*. The *purpose* of revelation is not merely the enlightenment of men's minds but their transformation so that they can attain the "New Being." [26]

Tillich is concerned not merely with revelation in *general,* but with the *concrete* revelation in "Jesus as the Christ." As a theologian, he is committed to the belief that this special revelation has *finality.* By "final" revelation he means not only "the last genuine revelation," but also the "decisive" one which is the "criterion" of all the others. The justification for the claim of the Christian revelation to finality is that in "the picture of Jesus as the Christ" there are present two qualities that are necessary in one who is to be the medium of final revelation: "his maintenance of unity with God and his sacrifice of everything he could have gained for himself from this unity." [27] He was not only united with the ground of being without separation throughout the ambigui-

---

[19] *Systematic Theology*, Vol. I, p. 110.   [20] *Ibid.*   [21] *Ibid.*
[22] *Ibid.*, p. 111.   [23] *Ibid.*, p. 112.   [24] *Ibid.*, p. 114.   [25] *Ibid.*, p. 118.
[26] *Ibid.*, pp. 144–147.   [27] *Ibid.*, p. 135.

ties of existence, but was also through the surrender of his finitude "completely transparent to the mystery" of that which he revealed.[28] Therefore, the revelation of the "New Being" in him is universally valid for the existence of every person and is the center and source of meaning for all history.[29]

The *faith* by which man receives the divine revelation is defined by Tillich as "the state of being ultimately concerned." The "content" or object of one's ultimate concern makes an unconditional demand upon the self but also promises it an ultimate fulfillment.[30] Although the "content" may be something finite such as the nation or economic power, such an object is idolatrous because it cannot make good its promise of ultimate fulfillment. Faith is an act of the whole personality and involves all of its functions, rational, volitional, and emotional.[31] To identify it exclusively with one of these functions results in a "distortion" of it; e.g., the emotional conception of faith disregards its cognitive element and the element of commitment. The source of faith is an immediate "awareness" of the infinite and unconditional to which man belongs.[32] It is *certain* insofar as it consists of this awareness. However, it is *uncertain* about the concrete content or object of its ultimate concern. Since there is no immediate awareness of this and it is mediated by something finite, i.e., the "sign-event" or "miracle" which is the objective side of revelation, acceptance of it by faith involves a risk. Therefore, *doubt* is a necessary element in faith.[33] Since no finite reality can express the ultimate and unconditional directly, the *language* in which faith is expressed is necessarily symbolic.[34] A symbol "points beyond itself while it participates in that to which it points." [35] Thus, the identification of the object of ultimate concern with a concrete divine being, e.g., Apollo or Yahweh, is affirmed by faith and expressed symbolically.[36]

Is there *truth* in faith? If so, what kind of truth? Tillich protests against the "intellectualistic distortion" of faith as a form of knowledge for which there is a low degree of evidence so that it is only more or less probable.[37] Faith is not a form of theoretical knowledge at all, and the certitude it possesses is not based on reasoning but is existential in character.[38] But this does not imply that faith makes no claim to truth, for faith is not opposed to reason but is "reason in ecstasy." "Reason is the presupposition of faith, and faith is the fulfillment of reason." [39]

[28] *Ibid.*, p. 133.   [29] *Ibid.*, pp. 136, 137.   [30] *Dynamics of Faith*, p. 1.
[31] *Ibid.*, p. 4.   [32] *Ibid.*, p. 9.   [33] *Ibid.*, pp. 19, 20.   [34] *Ibid.*, p. 44.
[35] *Ibid.*, p. 45.   [36] *Ibid.*, pp. 46, 47.   [37] *Ibid.*, p. 31.
[38] *Ibid.*, pp. 33–35.   [39] *Ibid.*, p. 77.

However, the truth of faith is quite different from scientific and historical truth. While science describes the structures and relations in the
world and history concerns itself with the origins and relations of
events, faith does not offer information about facts but interprets the
meaning of facts from the point of view of an ultimate concern.[40]
Therefore, there can be no conflict between the truth of faith and
scientific or historical truth because it is in a different "dimension of
meaning" from both of them. For the same reason, faith cannot "guar-
antee" the truth of historical assertions, e.g., the claim that Moses was
the author of the Pentateuch or the story of the virgin birth of Christ,
for historical truth must be established by historical research.[41]

Thus faith is the reception by the whole person of a revelation of
the ultimate and unconditional in the finite. Affirming with risk the
presence of the ultimate in something concrete, it expresses itself in
symbols which point beyond themselves to the ultimate. Although it
contains no truths about the facts of nature or history, it offers truth
concerning another "dimension of meaning," the ultimate. The crucial
importance of faith is that it receives the final revelation in Jesus as the
Christ which provides the answers of theology to the questions raised
by philosophy. The most fundamental of these answers is the Christian
doctrine of *God* which gives the answer to the question raised by
being. In the rest of this chapter we shall concern ourselves with this
question and answer.

THE STRUCTURE OF BEING

The ontological question, says Tillich, is "the question of being as
being" or "the character of everything that is insofar as it is."[42] It
arises in the "shock" of possible nonbeing as expressed in the question:
"Why is there something; why not nothing?"[43] The question arises
because man belongs to being and knows its power in himself but is
also separate from it in his finitude. Moreover, the transitoriness of all
things and their isolation from one another drive him to search for the
ultimate reality which is the ground and power of being in everything.[44] The doctrine of being, "ontology," consists of principles, categories, and concepts which are a priori in the sense that they constitute the structure of experience and therefore are presupposed in every
actual experience.[45] There are four levels of these ontological principles
and concepts. We shall deal briefly with each of these levels.

[40] *Ibid.*, p. 86.   [41] *Ibid.*, pp. 87, 88.
[42] *Systematic Theology*, Vol. I, p. 163.   [43] *Ibid.*
[44] *Biblical Religion and the Search for Ultimate Reality*, pp. 11, 13.
[45] *Systematic Theology*, Vol. I, p. 166.

The first is the "basic ontological structure," *self* and *world*. Man discovers this, of course, in his own experience as a "self" having a "world" to which he "belongs." He can take this experience of himself and his world as a key to the understanding of the structure of reality as a whole because he is the being in whom all levels of being are united and accessible.[46] In other words, since man is a microcosm in whom all levels of the world are present, he experiences directly in himself the structure of being as a whole. Since he experiences himself as a self having a world, "selfhood or self-centeredness must be attributed in some measure to all living beings, and, in terms of analogy, to all individual *Gestalten* even in the inorganic realm. One can speak of self-centeredness in atoms as well as animals, wherever the reaction to a stimulus is dependent on a structural whole." [47] But although self and world are correlative concepts, the human self is not completely bound to its environment but transcends it by knowing and willing according to universal ideas and norms.[48]

This basic ontological structure underlies the *subject-object structure* of reason. In terms which remind one of Hegel, Tillich distinguishes between "subjective reason," which is "the rational structure of the mind," and "objective reason," which is "the rational structure of reality." [49] Although these "correspond" to each other, he offers no philosophical interpretation of their relationship and is content to reject extreme views of it. "Reductive naturalism" tries to derive the subject from the object, but this dehumanizes man and destroys his essential subjectivity.[50] "Deductive idealism" attempts to derive the object from the subject, but with no success.[51] The "philosophy of identity" avoided these extreme views, but it failed because the relation between subject and object is that of polarity rather than identity.[52] Tillich's conclusion is that the basic ontological structure must simply be "accepted." Reason cannot answer the question: "What precedes the duality of self and world, of subject and object?" [53]

Although the subject-object structure is present in all knowledge of being and we cannot avoid speaking of God as an "object" of knowledge, Tillich maintains that He is not an "object" in the ontological sense, i.e., in His essence. For God as the "ground of being" is "beyond" or "precedes" the subject-object structure. The crucial importance of this for Tillich's conception of God will appear later.

The second level of ontological concepts is that of the "ontological elements," which consist of three pairs of elements in polarity with each other. They are: "individualization and participation," "dynamics

[46] *Ibid.*, p. 168.   [47] *Ibid.*, p. 169.   [48] *Ibid.*, p. 170.   [49] *Ibid.*, p. 75.
[50] *Ibid.*, p. 173.   [51] *Ibid.*, p. 174.   [52] *Ibid.*   [53] *Ibid.*, p. 175.

and form," and "freedom and destiny." The first element of each pair corresponds to "self" and the second to "world" in the basic ontological structure. Obviously, it is because the basic structure of being is "self" confronted by "world" that being can be interpreted as containing *individuals* which are self-centered but also *participate* in their environment, are *dynamic* or active but have *form,* and are *free* but limited by *destiny* as parts of the world. This implies a teleological interpretation of reality. Indeed, it is often said that although Tillich rejects the attempt of "deductive idealism" to derive the object from the subject, he is fundamentally an idealist influenced by Hegel and Schelling in his philosophy.[54] At the very least, it must be said that he gives self, its individuality, its dynamics or activity, and its freedom a place of such importance that he is closer to Idealism than to Naturalism in his ontology.

Individualization is characteristic not only of every self but of every being.[55] But the individual self also *participates* in its environment. Man as a rational being "participates in the universe because the universal structures, forms, and laws are open to him." [56] Moreover participation is the basis of relations in the world and makes knowledge possible through the participation of the knower in the known.[57] Above all, the source of the awareness of God is the participation of the finite in the infinite, as we have seen.

The second polarity of ontological elements is that of *dynamics* and *form.* Every being has a "form" and that which is formed is "dynamics." Dynamics is neither something that is nor something that is not but is "the potentiality of being." [58] Potentiality is a factor not only in the life-process in general but also in the depth of the divine life. Therefore, Tillich rejects the Thomistic doctrine that God is "pure actuality," *actus purus,* since this implies a static rather than a living God.[59] In man's experience dynamics and form appear as "vitality" and "intentionality." Vitality, "the power which keeps a living being alive and growing," is conditioned by intentionality, which is the relation to "meaningful structures" that are objectively valid.[60] Thus the dynamic character of being implies the tendency of everything to transcend itself and yet to conserve its own form. In this way Tillich seeks to do justice both to creativity, which is emphasized by modern thinkers like Bergson, and to permanence, which was primary in the classical view.

[54] For the idealistic element in his epistemology see the essay by Dorothy M. Emmett in *The Theology of Paul Tillich,* ed. Charles W. Kegley and Robert W. Bretall (New York: Macmillan, 1952), pp. 206–208.
[55] *Systematic Theology,* Vol. I, p. 175.   [56] *Ibid.,* p. 176.   [57] *Ibid.,* p. 178.
[58] *Ibid.,* p. 179.   [59] *Ibid.,* p. 180.   [60] *Ibid.*

The last pair of polar ontological elements is that of *freedom* and *destiny*. Tillich rejects the tendency of determinists and indeterminists to set freedom and destiny over against each other and insists upon their interdependence.[61] Freedom is man's capacity to determine his acts "neither by something outside him nor by any part of him but by the centered totality of his being." [62] Destiny is the basis of the centered self and decision arises out of it. "Destiny is not a strange power which determines what shall happen to me. It is myself as given, formed by nature, history, and myself. My destiny is the basis of my freedom." [63] This polarity of freedom and destiny is present in everything, even in organic things. Thus Tillich seeks to do justice both to the existentialist emphasis upon the freedom and responsibility of the self and the determinist emphasis upon the limitations imposed by nature and history upon the self's determination of its acts.

We have now completed our outline of the "basic ontological structure" and polar "ontological elements" in Tillich's doctrine of being and can turn to the characteristic of being which is most important for the formulation of the question of God: *finitude*. What is finitude and how does it raise the question of God?

"Being, limited by nonbeing," says Tillich, "is finitude. Nonbeing appears as the 'not yet' of being and the 'no more' of being." [64] Everything which is finite is "mixed" with nonbeing in the sense that "it is being in process of coming from and going toward nonbeing." [65] The "nonbeing" of which he speaks here is "dialectical nonbeing." There is a meaning of nonbeing which has no relation to being at all, *ouk on* in Greek, and a meaning which has a dialectical relation to being, *mē on* in Greek. While Parmenides conceived of nonbeing as *ouk on* and thus excluded the whole world of becoming from being, Tillich maintains that Christianity cannot dispense with the concept of "dialectical nonbeing" as that which has the potentiality of being.[66] Moreover, God's own being must include dialectical nonbeing or potentiality in itself, if He is to be regarded as "living" and as concerned with the processes of life and history in finite beings.[67] For life and history necessarily involve the actualization of potential being. Also, the evil which arises in life and history must be accounted for by reference to this dialectical nonbeing insofar as it resists being. In short, dialectical nonbeing is that which both provides the potentiality of being and, in the case of finite beings, resists or threatens being.

Anxiety arises from man's awareness of his finitude. Since it is not the result of fear of a special object but arises from the general threat

---

[61] *Ibid.*, p. 182.   [62] *Ibid.*, p. 184.   [63] *Ibid.*, pp. 184, 185.
[64] *Ibid.*, p. 189.   [65] *Ibid.*   [66] *Ibid.*, p. 188.   [67] *Ibid.*, pp. 188, 189.

of nonbeing, it is always present.[68] Its omnipresence is shown by an analysis of the four major *categories*, or "forms of finitude." Each of them expresses being but also the nonbeing which threatens it. Uniting affirmative and negative elements, each expresses both anxiety and courage.[69] (1) *Time* is transitory, the present being only a moment between past and future. The fact that everything is engulfed by it in its movement is the negative element in time which gives rise to anxiety. On the other hand, time is creative, ever producing that which is new. This is the affirmative element in it which gives man courage to accept temporality. The question it raises is: What is the ultimate foundation for this courage? (2) Every being needs a *space*, both a physical location and a social sphere of influence, and strives to provide and preserve its space. But a finite being must eventually lose every space it has ever had. The anxiety to which this gives rise is balanced by the courage to affirm the space it has and to face the threat of losing it. How is such a courage possible? (3) *Causality* affirms the power of being as that which precedes a thing and makes it real. But the fact that every finite thing depends upon something else as cause of its existence is also a source of anxiety, since "the same contingency which has thrown man into existence may push him out of it." [70] What is the source of man's courage to accept his contingency? (4) Finally, every finite being has a *substance*, something relatively unchanging and self-contained which endures beneath its appearances. On the other hand, it is subject to continuous change, which reveals its lack of substantiality and threatens it with the final loss of its substance at death. How is the courage to face and accept this loss possible? [71]

The negative element in finitude also shows itself in the way the polar character of the "ontological elements" opens them to the threat of nonbeing.[72] For in finite beings the polar elements tend to draw away from each other and destroy the unity of the whole.[73] Thus, the tension between individualization and participation can give rise either to a self-centeredness which produces loneliness or to a collectivization which leads to the loss of individuality,[74] as Tillich has shown in detail in *The Courage to Be*.[75] Or the tension between dynamics and form can lead to the loss of creativity in "rigid forms" or the destruction of all forms in a "chaotic formlessness." [76] Or the tension between free-

[68] *Ibid.*, p. 191.   [69] *Ibid.*, pp. 192, 193.   [70] *Ibid.*, p. 196.
[71] *Ibid.*, p. 198.   [72] *Ibid.*   [73] *Ibid.*   [74] *Ibid.*, pp. 199, 200.
[75] Paul Tillich, *The Courage to Be* (New Haven: Yale University Press, 1952), Chaps. 4, 5.
[76] *Systematic Theology*, Vol. I, pp. 199–200.

dom and destiny can threaten man with the loss of his freedom or the loss of his destiny.[77] Thus, finitude is characterized not only by anxiety over the loss of *being* in all of the categories, but also by anxiety over the loss of *essential being* and meaning through the disruption of the polar elements in the self and its consequent disintegration.

Although finite being is threatened with disruption and self-destruction in this manner, the tension between the polar elements does not *necessarily* lead to destruction. Nevertheless, Tillich maintains that existence *universally* involves a distortion of essential being.[78] On the one hand, Christianity affirms the essential goodness of the creation; but on the other hand, it emphasizes "the split between the created goodness of things and their distorted existence." [79] This distinction and contrast between *essence* and *existence*, the created and the actual world, is "the backbone of the whole body of theological thought." [80] For the threat of nonbeing either as loss of being or as loss of meaning characterizes all human existence, gives rise to anxiety, and drives man to raise the question of an ultimate source of courage to accept and overcome his anxiety.

NATURAL THEOLOGY AND THE QUESTION OF GOD

We are now ready to consider the way in which this philosophical analysis of existence gives rise to the "question" of God. It should be noted, first, that *Tillich rejects the traditional arguments of natural theology for the existence of God.* For one thing, he maintains that the concept of "existence" is not applicable to God. God is beyond essence and existence because He is the creative ground of both. Also, as the creative ground He cannot participate in the tensions and disruptions of existence.[81] This attitude toward the existence of God seems to rest on the assumption that the term "existence" should be used exclusively in a Kantian and Kierkegaardian sense for finite objects and persons in space and time with all their limitations. For another thing, he maintains that the traditional arguments are a failure as arguments.[82] In the cosmological and teleological arguments, he asserts, "God is derived from the world" and therefore "cannot be that which transcends the world infinitely" but must be simply "a missing part of that from which

---

[77] *Ibid.*, p. 200. [78] *Ibid.*, p. 202. [79] *Ibid.*, pp. 203, 204.
[80] *Ibid.*, p. 204. [81] *Ibid.*, p. 205. [82] *Ibid.*, p. 204.

he is derived." [83] But Tillich does not develop these brief criticisms, and it must be said that he does not make an adequate examination of the possibility of reformulating one or more of the traditional arguments before dismissing them as a failure. The conclusion at which he arrives is that the traditional arguments are of value only as "expressions of the *question* of God which is implied in human finitude." [84] They "elaborate" the question of God but cannot answer it.[85] The answer must come, as we have seen, not from philosophy but from theology.

In order to understand Tillich's negative attitude toward the traditional arguments for God, it is necessary to bear in mind that he is in the Augustinian rather than the Thomistic tradition in his approach to the knowledge of God. This is made clear in an important essay on "Two Types of the Philosophy of Religion," in which he distinguishes between the "ontological approach" of Augustine and the "cosmological approach" of Aquinas, between "the way of overcoming estrangement and the way of meeting a stranger." [86] According to the "ontological approach," man is estranged from God in his existence, but he is not separated from Him and can overcome his estrangement because he and God essentially belong to each other. In contrast, the "cosmological approach" regards God as a "stranger" to man, One who has no essential connection with him, so that man can have no certain knowledge of Him and can be separated from Him.

The *ontological* or Augustinian approach affirms that man is immediately aware of the unconditional with certainty, so that he does not need to infer its reality.[87] As Augustine asserted, eternal and unchangeable Truth is present in the quest for knowledge and even doubt presupposes it.[88] It constitutes the unconditional element in all theoretical activity, the "*verum ipsum,* the true-itself as the norm of all approximations to truth." [89] Again, Kant pointed out in his "moral argument" that there is an unconditional element in the practical activity of reason, the "*bonum ipsum,* the good-itself as the norm of all approximations to goodness." [90] And both "the true-itself" and "the good-itself" are manifestations of "*esse ipsum,* being-itself as the ground and abyss of everything that is." [91] Thus, the ontological argument does not prove the existence of God as *a* being, but it points to

[83] *Ibid.,* p. 205.   [84] *Ibid.*   [85] *Ibid.,* p. 206.
[86] Paul Tillich, *Theology of Culture* (New York: Oxford University Press, 1959), Chap. 2.
[87] *Ibid.,* p. 23.   [88] *Ibid.,* pp. 12, 13.
[89] *Systematic Theology,* Vol. I, p. 206.   [90] *Ibid.,* p. 207.   [91] *Ibid.*

the immediate awareness of an unconditional or ultimate element in man's encounter with reality. For this reason it is of fundamental importance for philosophy and theology.

In contrast, the *cosmological* approach of Aquinas maintains that the rational way to God is not through an immediate awareness but through argument. It rests upon the assumption that God is a "stranger" in the sense that He is not present in our experience, so that we have to try to demonstrate His existence and attributes from His effects in the world which are known to us.[92] This approach, which is based on the Aristotelian view that all knowledge begins from the senses, gives rise to arguments which produce probability rather than certainty.[93] Their failure leads to a cleavage between philosophy and theology and consequently to the "self-destruction" of religion. However, if the ontological approach is accepted as the basis of the philosophy of religion, a subordinate use of the cosmological approach can be made in order to show how the unconditional element of which we are immediately aware can be recognized in nature and culture.[94] For the "cosmological argument" from contingent being to a necessary Being raises the question of God as being-itself, capable of conquering non-being and making courage in the face of anxiety possible.[95] And the "teleological argument" from the order of nature to an Intelligent Being expresses the question of God as the ground of meaning, capable of overcoming the threat of meaninglessness and making courage possible.[96] Thus, although they cannot answer the question they raise, by raising it they "drive reason to the quest for revelation." [97] This seems to mean that they make clear the need of man for God to give him courage to face his anxiety, so that man is prepared to accept the revelation of God by faith.

We would raise a basic question concerning Tillich's treatment of the traditional arguments of natural theology: Is philosophy really limited to raising the question of God, or may it also provide at least the foundation for an answer by showing that belief in the God of Theism is *reasonable* even if not *demonstrable?* Tillich does not consider the latter possibility. Like Kant, he seems to think that if the traditional arguments cannot demonstrate God with certainty, they have no value at all as arguments and therefore can provide no support for belief in God. Yet he himself seems to go beyond a mere elaboration of the "question" of God in his assertion that the ontological argu-

[92] *Theology of Culture*, pp. 16, 17.   [93] *Ibid.*, p. 18.   [94] *Ibid.*, pp. 26, 27.
[95] *Systematic Theology*, Vol. I, p. 209.   [96] *Ibid.*, p. 210.   [97] *Ibid.*

ment expresses an immediate awareness of the ultimate or unconditional element in reality and that this shows the question of God to be "possible." Can it show this unless the immediate awareness of the ultimate or unconditional is regarded as an awareness of God as real? Doubtless, an intuitive awareness of this kind is not a *proof* of God's existence, but is it not important as part of the *evidence* for God? Again, it may be asked whether the cosmological and teleological arguments should be dismissed without a more careful consideration than Tillich has given them. As we have seen, Whitehead accepted a form of these arguments on scientific and philosophical grounds. And Austin Farrer and F. R. Tennant have shown that they can be reformulated in less rationalistic terms than those in which they were expressed in the time of Hume or Kant.[98] In contrast, Tillich regards these arguments merely as expressions of man's existential need for an ultimate source of courage. When he says that because of the threat of nonbeing to man "the question of God *must* be asked," [99] the "must" seems to express only an existential necessity for man rather than a rational necessity grounded in the nature of the world. If so, is it not subject to the criticism which is often made of Kant's "postulates" of practical reason, i.e., that it is only an expression of a human wish or need and has no support from reality?

Thus, while Tillich is doubtless right in thinking that the traditional arguments cannot demonstrate the existence of God, it may be possible to formulate them in such a way as to offer reasonable grounds for belief in Him. Tillich's failure to recognize this possibility makes the distance between philosophical "question" and theological "answer" wider than it actually is. As a result, the acceptance by faith of the "answer" God is more ungrounded in reason than it need be.

GOD AS BEING-ITSELF

Following his philosophical analysis of being and the question of God implicit in human finitude Tillich presents the theological answer to the question: *God as being-itself.* The meaning of "God," he says, is "that which concerns man ultimately." [100] Since anything about which a man is to be ultimately concerned must be encountered in reality or imagination, the more concrete a thing is, e.g., a person, the greater is the possible concern about it. On the other hand, if it is to be really

---

[98] Austin Farrer, *Finite and Infinite* (Westminster, Md.: Dacre Press, 1943), Pt. III, and F. R. Tennant, *Philosophical Theology* (Cambridge, Eng.: Cambridge University Press, 1937), Vol. II, Chap. 4.

[99] *Systematic Theology*, Vol. I, p. 208.   [100] *Ibid.*, p. 211.

ultimate, it must transcend everything concrete and finite.[101] The conflict between these demands for *concreteness* and *ultimacy* produces an inner tension in man's idea of God and provides a key to the changes in the idea of God in religious history.[102] It explains why "gods" have been conceived both as concrete beings which can be described in the categories of finitude and as beings with qualities which transcend those of finite beings, e.g., immortality and overwhelming power.[103] An analysis of the divine as "the holy" leads to a somewhat similar conclusion. For "the holy," on the one hand, is the *transcendent* which is the "abyss" and "ground" of being, but, on the other hand, it is mediated through concrete *objects* or *beings* of various kinds which point to the divine beyond themselves but become idolatrous or demonic if regarded as holy in themselves.[104]

Tillich presents a typology of religions which is based largely on the tension between the requirements of concreteness and ultimacy in the divine or holy. *Polytheism* is an expression of the religious demand for concreteness in the divine. *Monotheism* is the product of a reaction against this concreteness and it emphasizes ultimacy. *Mysticism,* a form of monotheism which emphasizes the element of ultimacy in a radical way by transcending all concrete expressions of the divine, undergoes a "philosophical transformation" and appears as "idealistic monism." This philosophy, in which the many finite things disappear in the unity of being, leads to *Pantheism* in its view of God.[105] Although Tillich expresses his sympathy with Pantheism and mystical religion, he asserts that they are dangerous unless they are combined with "exclusive monotheism" which emphasizes the absolute transcendence of God.[106] The danger of mysticism and Pantheism, the swallowing up of the many finite beings in the one infinite Being, is "overcome" in *Trinitarian Monotheism*, which balances the opposed demands for ultimacy and concreteness by combining "the structural oneness of everything within the absolute" with the "manifoldness of the real." [107]

This typology of religions is important because it prepares the way for Tillich's bold attempt to synthesize the *mystical* and *pantheistic* conception of God as "being-itself" with the *theistic* conception of Him as transcendent. God, he says, is not "a being alongside others or above others" but "being-itself." [108] This assertion, which is obviously derived from the mystical and pantheistic side of his synthesis, is based upon Tillich's view that to call God "a being" is to subject Him to

---

[101] *Ibid.*   [102] *Ibid.*   [103] *Ibid.*, p. 212.   [104] *Ibid.*, p. 216.
[105] *Ibid.*, p. 233.   [106] *Ibid.*, p. 234.   [107] *Ibid.*, p. 235.   [108] *Ibid.*

categories which apply only to finite beings, especially space and substance.[109] Even when He is regarded as the "highest" or "most
perfect" or "most powerful" being, He is placed alongside other beings
although elevated above them.[110] Therefore, God should not be called
"a being," but "being-itself" or the "ground of being." As "being-itself,"
God is "the power inherent in everything, the power of resisting
nonbeing." [111] He is immanent in the sense that "everything finite participates in being-itself," but He is also transcendent in the sense that
He "transcends every being and the totality of beings." [112] Hence, He is
both "creative" as the power of being and "abysmal" as infinitely transcending all beings.

Since God as being-itself is the ground of the structure of being, He
is not subject to that structure. However, we cannot speak of anything
except in terms of elements of the structure of being. These can provide us with symbols which point to the ground of being. The only
nonsymbolic statement we can make about God is that He is being-
itself, for this statement does not "point beyond itself" but "means what
it says directly and properly." [113] Everything else which is said about
Him must be *symbolic*, since every concrete assertion about Him must
be drawn from some "segment" of finite experience which points beyond itself to Him.[114] As we have seen, a segment of finite reality can
become the basis for a symbolic assertion about the infinite because
every finite thing participates in the infinite, being-itself.[115] In Volume
II of his *Systematic Theology*, Tillich goes even further and qualifies
the assertion that one statement about God is nonsymbolic, i.e., that
He is being-itself. Although we must speak nonsymbolically about God
"in terms of a *quest* for him," he says, we must combine symbolic with
nonsymbolic elements when we "try to *formulate* that for which we
ask." [116] Thus, when we speak of God as "being-itself," we speak
both "ecstatically" and "rationally," i.e., both symbolically and nonsymbolically, at the same time.[117]

We have seen that God is not "subject" to the polar ontological
elements of which He is the "ground." For within the divine life, each
ontological element includes its polar opposite without tension and the
threat of disruption. However, there is a difference between the first
and second elements in each polarity with respect to their power to
symbolize the divine life.[118] "The elements of individualization,

[109] *Ibid.*   [110] *Ibid.*   [111] *Ibid.*, p. 236.   [112] *Ibid.*, p. 237.
[113] *Ibid.*, p. 238.   [114] *Ibid.*, p. 239.   [115] *Ibid.*
[116] Tillich, *Systematic Theology*, Vol. II (Chicago: University of Chicago
Press, 1957), p. 9 (italics added).
[117] *Ibid.*, p. 9.
[118] *Systematic Theology*, Vol. I, p. 243.

dynamics, and freedom represent the self or subject side of the basic ontological structure within the polarity to which they belong. The elements of participation, form, and destiny represent the world or object side." [119] Although both sides are rooted in the divine life, man uses as symbols for that which is his ultimate concern terms taken from his own being as a self. Therefore, the first side of each polarity expresses the existential relationship between God and man. The importance of this emphasis upon "the self or subject side" of the polarities as the primary source of symbols is that it provides a justification for using *personal* qualities, actions, and relations in speaking about Him.

Thus, while the assertion that God is "being-itself" rather than "a being" expresses the *pantheistic* and *mystical* element in Tillich's conception of God, the principle that the primary symbols for Him should be derived from "the self or subject side" of the structure of being expresses the *theistic* element. We must now examine the way Tillich combines these two elements in his synthesis.

SYMBOLS FOR GOD

1. *God as living.* The first symbolic assertion Tillich makes about God is that He is *living.* Life is the process in which potential becomes actual being. Since there is no distinction between potentiality and actuality in God, we cannot speak of Him as "living" in a nonsymbolic sense, but we *can* say that He is living in the sense that He is "the ground of life." [120] Tillich criticizes Aquinas' view of God as "pure actuality" and the antithetical modern view of Him as "becoming." He rejects the Thomistic view because it denies the dynamic character of God and makes His creativity in history impossible.[121] But the modern doctrine must also be rejected because it subjects God to a process which is completely open to the future.[122] Against both views he asserts that, while there is a dynamic element of "becoming" as well as a static element of "rest" in God, there is no potentiality which is not actualized, for the "not yet" is always balanced by an "already" in Him.[123] But, we would ask, is it possible to affirm both that there is an "eternal process" in God *and* that "there is no distinction between potentiality and actuality" in Him? Is a "not yet" which is always "balanced" by an "already" really a "not yet," a potentiality, at all?

2. *God as personal.* Perhaps the most controversial issue raised by Tillich concerns the use of the symbol "personal" for God. Man views the divine life as "personal, dynamic, and free," he says, because "God

---

[119] *Ibid.*   [120] *Ibid.*, p. 242.   [121] *Ibid.*, p. 246.   [122] *Ibid.*, p. 247.
[123] *Ibid.*, p. 246.

is man's ultimate concern and therefore stands in analogy to that which man himself is." [124] He does *not* say that these symbols derived from man's personal life are *essentially* more adequate to describe God's nature than symbols derived from the "world or object side" of the polarities would be; he says only that they are more "powerful" for symbolizing man's ultimate concern in his existential *relationship* with God. Moreover, he asserts that the "world or object side" of the polarities is "included," at least implicitly, in the "self or subject side" from which the personal symbols are taken. What is the meaning of the symbol "personal," then, when it is applied to God?

"The symbol 'personal God' is absolutely fundamental," says Tillich, "because an existential relation is a person-to-person relation. Man cannot be ultimately concerned about anything that is less than personal." [125] He adds that to speak of God as personal "means that God is the ground of everything personal and that He carries within himself the ontological power of personality. He is not a person, but he is not less than personal. . . . Ordinary theism has made God a heavenly, completely perfect person who resides above the world and mankind. The protest of atheism against such a highest person is correct. There is no evidence for his existence, nor is he a matter of ultimate concern." [126] It is quite clear from this that, *while Tillich regards the symbol "personal God" as necessary for an existential person-to-person relationship with God, he rejects the traditional theistic view that God is a personal Being distinct from the world.* To say "God is personal" means only that as being-itself He is in some undetermined way "the ground of everything personal" and "not less than personal."

3. *God as spirit.* The influence of St. Paul, on the one hand, and modern Idealism, on the other, is evident in Tillich's strong emphasis upon this symbol. "God *is* spirit. This is the most embracing, direct, and unrestricted symbol for the divine life. It does not need to be balanced by another symbol, because it includes all the ontological elements." [127] Spirit is the fulfillment of life. Tillich speaks of "the urge of life to become spirit, to fulfil itself as spirit." [128] In the recently published third volume of his *Systematic Theology,* he speaks of spirit as arising out of a "constellation" of psychological conditions and constituting a new "dimension" in the "multidimensional unity of life." [129] As the fulfillment of life, it unites "power" and "meaning" and includes all the ontological elements in union with one another. Therefore the

[124] *Ibid.,* p. 243.   [125] *Ibid.,* p. 244.   [126] *Ibid.,* p. 245.   [127] *Ibid.,* p. 249.
[128] *Ibid.*
[129] Paul Tillich, *Systematic Theology,* Vol. III (Chicago: University of Chicago Press, 1963), pp. 25–28.

manifestation of the "Divine Spirit" or the "Spiritual Presence" in the human spirit is the source of the "New Being" or "salvation" in man's life.[130] Also, the symbol of spirit provides the philosophical presupposition for the Christian doctrine of the *Trinity*.[131] "Through the Spirit," says Tillich, "the divine fulness is posited in the divine life as something definite [i.e., the "logos"], and at the same time is reunited in the divine ground." [132] This Trinitarian conception of God is the basis for Tillich's view of the relation of the *infinite* to the *finite*. "God is infinite because he has the finite (and with it that element of non-being which belongs to finitude) within himself united with his infinity." [133]

4. *God as immanent and transcendent.* To say that the finite is "within" the infinite indicates the close relation of the world to God. Does it imply Pantheism, as some of Tillich's critics have charged? The answer is that like Hegel he seeks to synthesize the pantheistic element of immanence with the theistic element of transcendence in a way that seems to point to *Panentheism* rather than Pantheism. "God is immanent in the world as its permanent creative ground and is transcendent to the world through freedom. Both infinite divinity and finite human freedom make the world transcendent to God and God transcendent to the world." [134] This interpretation is based upon Tillich's highly controversial view that, although man is created good in his essential being, he universally actualizes himself at the cost of becoming estranged from God. "Fully developed creatureliness," he says, "is fallen creatureliness. . . . Seen from one side, this is the end of creation. Seen from the other side, it is the beginning of the fall." [135] He insists that this does not imply the necessity of the Fall because it is the product of individual freedom as well as universal destiny. However, many of his theological interpreters have not agreed with him on this point.[136]

In the second volume of the *Systematic Theology*, Tillich points out that his view differs from both "supranaturalism" and "naturalism," which he seems to equate with naturalistic Pantheism. "Supranaturalism" separates God from all other beings and transforms His infinity into finiteness by making Him an individual substance and a cause alongside other causes.[137] "Naturalism" of Spinoza's type iden-

---

[130] *Ibid.*, Pt. IV, Chaps. 2, 3.   [131] *Ibid.*, Pt. IV, Chap. 4.
[132] *Ibid.*, Vol. I, p. 251.   [133] *Ibid.*, p. 252.   [134] *Ibid.*, p. 263.
[135] *Ibid.*, p. 255.
[136] *Ibid.*, p. 256. For a criticism of Tillich's view of the relation of the Fall to the Creation see the essay by Reinhold Niebuhr in *The Theology of Paul Tillich*, ed. Charles W. Kegley and Robert W. Bretall (New York: Macmillan, 1952).
[137] *Systematic Theology*, Vol. II, p. 6.

tifies God with the essence, unity, and power of being. Hence it denies the "infinite distance" between finite things and their infinite ground as disclosed in the experience of the holy.[138] A third view, which Tillich defends, is in a sense intermediate between these two extremes: God is the creative ground of being, but He transcends that of which He is the ground. "He stands *against* the world insofar as the world stands against him, and he stands *for* the world thereby causing it to stand for him." [139] But the transcendence of God does not mean that He is "above" the world.

Thus, although Tillich affirms the transcendence of God against Pantheism, he does not accept the traditional theistic view that God is transcendent to the world as its Creator who is distinct from it. For God is not "a being" distinct from other beings but "being-itself," and finite beings are contained within although they are also transcended by Him. The fundamental philosophical question this raises is how it is possible for finite beings both to be *within* God and to assert their freedom *against* Him; the fundamental religious question is whether it does justice to the infinite *distance* or *gulf* between God and creatures which Tillich himself says is disclosed in the experience of God as "the holy."

5. *God as eternal and temporal.* Tillich, like Whitehead and Hartshorne, rejects the Thomistic view of God as eternal in a sense which excludes time from the divine life. "The divine eternity includes time and transcends it." [140] God is essentially related to time, but in His life the moments of time are not separated from one another; for eternity is symbolized as an "eternal present" not in the sense of "simultaneity" but as "moving from past to future without ceasing to be present," so that the future is open and the new can happen in history.[141] Faith in God as eternal in this sense gives man the courage to face his anxiety over the past and the future, since the separated moments of time are united in eternity.[142] Also, this faith is the ground of the certainty of man's participation in *eternal life.* "The hope of eternal life is based not on a substantial quality of man's soul but on his participation in the eternity of the divine life." [143]

6. *God as knowledge and will.* In the light of Tillich's attitude toward the theistic view of God as a personal being, it is not surprising that he says very little about God's knowledge and will. The polarity of dynamics and form, he says, is expressed in classical theology as the polarity of will and intellect, and modern thought agrees with Duns

---

[138] *Ibid.*, p. 7.   [139] *Ibid.*   [140] *Systematic Theology*, Vol. I, p. 257.
[141] *Ibid.*, p. 275.   [142] *Ibid.*, p. 276.   [143] *Ibid.*

Scotus against Aquinas that will rather than intellect has the primacy because it is the dynamic element.[144] But "will" and "intellect" in their application as symbols to God "express infinitely more than the mental acts of willing and understanding as these appear in human experience. They are symbols for dynamics in all its ramifications and for form as the meaningful structure of being-itself." [145] Moreover, since God cannot be brought under the subject-object structure involved in knowledge, the *"omniscience"* of God does not mean "the faculty of a highest being who is supposed to know all objects." [146] To speak of the divine knowledge is only a symbolical way of saying that "nothing is outside the centered unity of his life; nothing is strange, dark, hidden, isolated, unapproachable. Nothing falls outside the *logos* structure of being. . . . The abysmal quality cannot swallow the rational quality of the divine life." [147] The most remarkable thing about this analysis of the divine knowledge and will, apart from its brevity, is its ambiguity. This is not surprising, since knowledge and will can have no meaning except as functions of a personal being. Since Tillich has denied that God is *a* being, the "divine knowledge" seems to mean nothing more than the inclusion of everything in the rational structure of the divine spiritual life in some vague and indeterminate sense.

7. *God as directing creativity or providence.* "Faith in providence," says Tillich, "is faith 'in spite of'—in spite of the darkness of fate and of the meaninglessness of existence," and it "gives meaning to historical existence in spite of never-ending experiences of meaninglessness." [148] This chastened conception of providence is in sharp contrast to what Tillich calls the "teleological optimism" which tries to demonstrate that all things are so ordered as to serve human happiness.[149] It is also opposed to the "dialectical" view of Hegel and Marx which emphasizes conflict as an essential factor in history but affirms that providence triumphs either in the present or in the future.[150] Amidst the catastrophes of the twentieth century, the individual asks whether there is a possibility of believing in a personal fulfillment. Tillich answers that God directs everything toward its fulfillment. But his view of this "directing activity" differs radically from the traditional theistic view. Providence works through the freedom of man and the structure of creatures in general. "Providence is 'the divine condition' which is present in every group of finite conditions and in the totality of finite conditions. It is not an additional factor. . . . It is a quality of inner

---

[144] *Ibid.*, pp. 247, 248.   [145] *Ibid.*, p. 247.   [146] *Ibid.*, p. 278.
[147] *Ibid.*, p. 279.   [148] *Ibid.*, p. 264.   [149] *Ibid.*, p. 265.
[150] *Ibid.*, pp. 265, 266.

directedness present in every situation. The man who believes in providence does not believe that a special divine activity will alter the
conditions of finitude and estrangement. He believes, and asserts with
the courage of faith, that no situation whatsoever can frustrate the
fulfillment of his ultimate destiny, that nothing can separate him from
the love of God which is in Christ Jesus (Romans, chap. 8)." [151] Since
this view of providence, he says, is not connected with "special events
or special expectations" and does not cherish utopian hopes for history,
it does not lead to disappointment and cynicism. [152]

8. *The divine love and justice.* Although Tillich's conception of
divine love is expressed in ontological terms, it is in general accord
with that of biblical Theism. Love, he says, is the unity of the trend
toward *separation* and the trend toward *reunion* in the life-process.
Since reunion presupposes separation, love cannot be realized where
there is no individualization and is fully realized only in man. [153] That
which is distinctive of the *agapē* type of love in the New Testament is
the affirmation of the other unconditionally or apart from his qualities,
the acceptance of the other in spite of resistance, and the willingness to
suffer for and forgive him. [154] This type of love can be asserted of God
symbolically because He works for the fulfillment of every creature
and seeks to bring into unity with Him all who are separated. [155]
Justice is not opposed to love, but is an expression of it. For it "acknowledges and preserves the freedom and the unique character of the
beloved" and "neither forces him nor leaves him." [156] It is true that
justice resists and condemns those who are unjust, but this is due to the
reaction of love against that which violates it. [157] Moreover, the divine
love manifests itself as *grace* toward those who have violated justice,
giving fulfillment to the separated and accepting the unacceptable. [158]
Thus the divine love as manifested in grace and reconciliation is the
ultimate answer to the question implied in the finitude, disruption, and
estrangement of human existence. [159]

The symbol of the love of God is "Father." For the term "Father"
expresses the originating, sustaining, and directing creativity of God, as
well as His activity in justifying man by His grace. [160] But as love is
accompanied by justice, the symbol "Father" must be balanced by the
symbol "Lord." For "Lord" expresses the power, majesty, rule, and
justice of God; and God must remain Lord and Judge in spite of the
reconciling power of His love. [161]

---

[151] *Ibid.*, p. 267.   [152] *Ibid.*, p. 268.   [153] *Ibid.*, pp. 279, 280.
[154] *Ibid.*, p. 280.   [155] *Ibid.*, p. 281.   [156] *Ibid.*, p. 283.   [157] *Ibid.*
[158] *Ibid.*, p. 285.   [159] *Ibid.*, p. 286.   [160] *Ibid.*, p. 287.   [161] *Ibid.*, p. 288.

THE COURAGE TO BE AND THE GOD ABOVE GOD

Although Tillich concludes his discussion of God in the *Systematic Theology* with these primary biblical symbols derived from personal qualities and relations, we are still left with the question: Do these and other symbols of a personal character indicate the *nature* of God or only express the way in which men inevitably experience their *relationship* with Him because they are personal? In *The Courage to Be* this question becomes acute. Defining "courage" as "the self-affirmation of being in spite of the fact of nonbeing," Tillich inquires into the basis of the "courage to be" in the face of the anxiety of fate and death, guilt and condemnation, and emptiness and meaninglessness. His general answer is that there must be a "religious root" for the courage to be, since it depends upon faith in the power of being-itself.[162] But when he asks what *kind* of religious faith is required, his answer differs from the usual Christian answer.

Our period, he says, is one in which the anxiety of doubt and meaninglessness produces a more radical despair than that produced in earlier periods by the anxiety of death or guilt. In anxiety over death or guilt, meaning and certainty could still be affirmed so that a basis for the courage to be could be provided either by mystical participation in being-itself or by personal encounter with the God of Theism. For many in despair over radical doubt and meaninglessness, however, this is not possible. The only possible answer for those in such a situation is that the acceptance of despair itself involves faith, since there is an affirmation implicit in negation.[163] "The vitality that can stand the abyss of meaninglessness is aware of a hidden meaning within the destruction of meaning." [164] The basis of this assertion seems to be the "ontological approach" of Augustine which we discussed earlier. As Augustine held that doubt would be impossible without the presupposition of Truth, so Tillich maintains that despair in the face of radical doubt and meaninglessness implies the presence, although hidden, of being-itself as the source of meaning.

But the faith which arises in this situation is not the faith of mystical religion or the faith of theistic personal encounter; it is *"absolute faith."* "It is simply faith, undirected, absolute. It is undefinable, since everything defined is dissolved by doubt and meaninglessness." [165] While the "power of acceptance" is experienced, "there is nobody and nothing that accepts." [166] Nevertheless, absolute faith "opens up" or

[162] *The Courage to Be*, p. 156.   [163] *Ibid.*, pp. 174, 175.   [164] *Ibid.*, p. 177.
[165] *Ibid.*, p. 176.   [166] *Ibid.*, p. 177.

"shows" the nature of being, since it is an experience of being affirming itself against nonbeing.[167] "Courage participates in the self-affirmation of being-itself, it participates in the power of being which prevails against nonbeing." [168]

Although "absolute faith" does not have a special or concrete content, it has a content. Its content is the *"God above God,"* and this God "transcends the theistic idea of God." [169] Although mystical religion must also be "transcended" because it plunges directly into the ground of being and leaves behind the world of finite meanings, it seems clear that the "God above God" is closer to the "Godhead" of the monistic mystics than to the personal God of Theism.[170] When traditional theistic symbols such as "providence" and "forgiveness" have "lost their power," absolute faith can re-establish the courage to be. *"The courage to be is rooted in the God who appears when God has disappeared in the anxiety of doubt."* [171]

Some readers have interpreted "absolute faith" in the "God above God" to mean that Tillich has renounced Christian Theism. Therefore, in Volume II of the *Systematic Theology,* published after *The Courage to Be,* he sought to correct the misinterpretation of his "God above God" as "a dogmatic statement of a pantheistic or mystical character." [172] Asserting that the statement was *not* a "dogmatic" but an "apologetic" one, he indicated that it was meant to speak to those in a state of radical doubt about all religious language, including the name "God." "But such an extreme point," he added, "is not a space within which one can live. The dialectics of an extreme situation are a criterion of truth but not the basis on which a whole structure of truth can be built." [173] Unfortunately, he did not elaborate this brief statement, but it constitutes a warning against the hasty assumption of some readers that in *The Courage to Be* he was giving up the role of the Christian theologian and abandoning the use of Christian symbols for God.

BEING AND GOD: A CRITIQUE

As we have indicated, Tillich's intention as a philosophical theologian has been to correlate the questions raised by philosophical analysis with answers derived from Christian theology and thus to show the relevance of the Christian revelation to contemporary life. With this intention everyone who believes that philosophical reflection has an important role to play in theological thinking must be in sym-

---

[167] *Ibid.,* pp. 178, 179.   [168] *Ibid.,* p. 181.   [169] *Ibid.,* p. 182.
[170] *Ibid.,* p. 186.   [171] *Ibid.,* p. 190.
[172] *Systematic Theology,* Vol. II, p. 12.   [173] *Ibid.*

pathy. Moreover his great influence in recent years is evidence that he has succeeded in speaking effectively to contemporary man. The question we must now ask is whether his position is philosophically and theologically adequate.

1. We have pointed out that his professed limitation of philosophy to the raising of questions implied in existence is unjustified. Such a limitation may give rise to no objections from theologians with little or no appreciation of the value of the philosophical approach to religion; and it has the merit, from the apologetic theologian's point of view, of showing the relevance of Christian doctrines to the questions and needs of contemporary men. But philosophers will not be satisfied with it. They will naturally feel that if philosophy is competent to raise questions, it must be capable of giving at least partial answers to them. This will be the case especially with philosophers who do not accept Tillich's restriction of the function of philosophy to the phenomenological analysis of the structure of being and his consequent rejection of speculative philosophy or metaphysics. As we have seen, one of the consequences of his rejection of metaphysics is that he dismisses without sufficient consideration the traditional arguments for the existence of God and insists that they only raise the "question" of God. Since he offers no arguments of his own, his phenomenological analysis of being leaves Theism without sufficient rational support. As a result, the minds of his readers are not prepared by that analysis for the "answer" of God offered by theology. Thus he does not really show that "faith is the fulfillment of reason." He presents God as the answer to man's existential need for the courage to be but not to his theoretical demand for truth.

Paradoxically, if Tillich shows too little confidence in the capacity of reason in metaphysics and natural theology, he seems to have too much confidence in the ontology which he himself develops by his phenomenological analysis of being. The influence of the Idealism of Schelling and Hegel upon this ontology is very strong. Although Tillich rejects "deductive Idealism" as a metaphysical theory which attempts to derive nature from mind, he asserts a correspondence between the "subjective reason" of the self and the "objective reason" in the world, states that "spirit" is the "most embracing, direct, and unrestricted" symbol for God, and bases his interpretation of the Trinity upon an idealistic interpretation of divine Spirit. Yet he offers little argument for this idealistic interpretation of being and God and seems to regard it as the necessary result of a purely objective phenomenological analysis, although it is rejected by most philosophers and theologians of the twentieth century.

This is unfortunate in view of the fact that the influence of his ontology upon his conception of God is crucial with respect to its content as well as its form. For example, it is one of the main sources of his Panentheism, which seeks to synthesize Pantheism and Theism by affirming both that God contains the many finite things within Himself and that He transcends them by His freedom. This does not really do justice to the transcendence and otherness of God, since it views God as the Ground rather than the Creator of the world who is distinct from His creatures. Nor does it safeguard the freedom of the human self, since it interprets man's estrangement from God as the result of universal destiny as well as individual freedom. This unstable compromise between Pantheism and Theism results from Tillich's uncritical acceptance of an idealistic ontology which refuses to emphasize the distinction between God and the world because of the fear that it will lead to dualism.

2. It is his idealistic ontology which is also mainly responsible for his view that God is not "a being" but "being-itself." Several critical comments on this view should be made. The first is that responsible theologians have never considered God to be merely one being alongside of but superior to other beings. One of the main purposes of "negative theology" has been to emphasize the "ontological distance" between God and all finite beings, i.e., the fact that God is a necessary, infinite, eternal, and perfect Being whose mode of being is radically different from that of finite beings. It is true that many Christians have thought of Him in such a way as to remove or reduce this "distance" between Him and other beings, imagining him as localized in heaven "above" finite creatures and having the appearance of a human father. But this is merely an example of the human all-too-human tendency to domesticate God and make Him a means to human ends, and it has nothing to do with the Christian conception of Him. Again, the theistic conception of God as a being *distinct* from the world does not imply that He is *separated* from it, as Tillich insists. It is true that Christians have often failed to maintain the balance between God's transcendence and His immanence and have fallen into a dualistic kind of "supranaturalism." As a corrective of this tendency Tillich's criticism of "supranaturalism" is valuable. But the essence of the biblical view of God's transcendence is not that He is "above" or "beyond" or "separate" from the world, but that He is "distinct" from it as its Creator and Sustainer upon whom it depends. When Christians have been true to the biblical view, they have always emphasized His immanence or what Tillich calls His "Spiritual Presence" as the source of human fulfillment or "New Life." [174]

[174] *Systematic Theology*, Vol. III, Pt. IV, Chap. 2.

Tillich's strong and repeated insistence that God is not "a being" but "being-itself" is partly motivated by his conviction that God as the object of "ultimate concern" must be "ultimate" as well as "concrete." This requires us, he thinks, to conceive Him as beyond all limitations and, since every finite being is subject to limitations, as "being-itself" rather than "a being." The most obvious difficulty with this view is that, if we are to use the philosophical term "being-itself" to interpret the religious term "God," it should have a meaning which would warrant us in using it for this purpose. But "being-itself" seems to have no definite meaning. Moreover, "power of being" and "ground of being" are equally indefinite and are regarded by Tillich himself as "symbolic notions" which cannot explain its literal meaning.[175] In other words, "being-itself" is ineffable in the sense that no positive and direct assertions can be made about it, since this would subject it to the structure and limitations of being.[176] But if "being-itself" has no definite meaning, it can affirm God's "ultimacy" only at the cost of denying His "concreteness" and making Him unknowable.

3. Again, the attitude of Tillich toward the symbol *"personal God"* is ambiguous. Although he says that it is "absolutely fundamental because an existential relation is a person-to-person relation," we have seen that he does not affirm God to be personal in His own nature. He says only that "God is the ground of everything personal and that he carries within himself the ontological power of personality." [177] This ambiguity seems to be due, in part, to his tendency to identify "personality" with "individuality" and to think of it as opposed to "participation." But such an identification is based upon a misconception of personality. That which characterizes personality in man is not only that it belongs to an individual with an existence distinct from that of other beings but also that it has an almost unlimited capacity to participate in the beings and values of the world. Tillich himself has stressed this fact in his criticism of the modern individualistic and romantic courage to be "as oneself," which narrows and impoverishes the self by separating it from others.[178] But if human personality requires the widest possible participation for its development, why should personality in God be regarded as incompatible with His universal participation?

Probably Tillich has been influenced at this point by the difficulty of conceiving personality except in human terms. A human person is limited to a body, localized in space, and separated from other beings.

---

[175] W. L. Rowe, "The Meaning of 'God' in Tillich's Theology," *Journal of Religion* (Oct., 1962), p. 284.

[176] *Ibid.*, p. 285.   [177] *Systematic Theology,* Vol. I, p. 245.

[178] *The Courage to Be,* Chap. 5.

As a result, he participates in other beings only in a very imperfect way. In contrast, if God is infinite, it is necessary to think of Him not only as a personal *center* of knowing, willing, creating, and saving activity, but also as present and active *everywhere*. For this reason, some theists have said that personality should be ascribed primarily to God and is present in man only in a secondary and imperfect sense. Others have said that God is "personal, and more than personal" or that He is "suprapersonal." Still others have preferred to combine "personality" with "spiritual" in speaking of God in order to stress both His transcendence as a personal center of activity and His immanence or participation in everything.

Despite the difficulties, it can hardly be denied that Christian theology, which Tillich claims to be interpreting, has always maintained that God is "personal" not only as the ground of personality in man but also in His own nature and activity. Since this term is derived from our experience of human persons and is associated with the imperfections of personality in ourselves, it may be wise in speaking of God to use it with great reserve and careful qualification. What is essential from the theistic point of view is not that men should *call* God "a person" but that they should ascribe personal *attributes* and *actions* to Him, e.g., knowledge, will, and purpose. We have pointed out that many philosophers from Plato to Whitehead have maintained that the most adequate explanation of the order and value of the world is to be found in a divine Mind which is seeking to realize Good, and we know of no mind which does not belong to a personal being. In contrast Tillich seems to interpret the "knowledge" and "will" of God merely as general symbols for the "form" and "dynamics" of the divine spiritual life. Moreover his interpretation of *providence* raises a serious question about his view of the "personal" attributes and acts of God. As we have seen, he denies that providence requires the "special activity" of God in history and defines it as a general quality or condition of "directedness" in situations. Doubtless he is right in asserting that providence works through the freedom of man and other general structures of being. But it does not follow from this that there is no *special* divine activity in particular historical situations and that providence is only a *general* "divine condition" in all situations. To the biblical writers, from the prophet Isaiah to the Apostle Paul, providence is not a general "condition" immanent in everything. They regard God as a transcendent Being distinct from His creatures and capable of acting in and upon them in special as well as general ways. To deny this is to deny His acts of revelation and redemption as interpreted by the historical and prophetic writers of the Bible.

4. One of the sources of Tillich's interpretation of such personal terms for God is his view of *religious symbols*. As we have seen, he holds that symbols for God must be taken from finite beings, since these participate in God as being-itself and point beyond themselves to Him. However, finite beings are subject to the structure of being while God transcends it, so that symbols derived from them must be affirmed and negated at the same time when they are applied to God. This conception of religious symbols implies that the meaning of all of them is infected with ambiguity. Perhaps Tillich would admit this but would reply that the ambiguity cannot be avoided without absolutizing things which are relative by identifying the divine object of ultimate concern with something finite. But in safeguarding the "ultimacy" of God in this way he has put in question the meaning of everything "concrete" and definite which theists assert about God.

As a result, his view of the cognitive value of symbols for God differs from the traditional doctrine of analogy, although he asserts that it is based on the "analogy of being." As we have said (Chap. 5), Aquinas asserts that names which are predicated of God apply "properly" and even "primarily" to Him with respect to "what is signified" by them, although their "mode of signification" is different.[179] He explicitly rejects the view that names applied analogously to God signify only "His relationship to creatures" and argues that they apply to Him "substantially." [180] For this reason, Tillich's symbolic view of names for God is not identical with the classical doctrine of analogy, since he does not maintain that names such as "goodness" and "wisdom" can be applied "substantially" to God with respect to "what is signified" by them.

Tillich's assertion that symbols must be negated as well as affirmed when they are applied to God seems to be an expression of the *mystical* element in his religion. As we have shown (see Chap. 6), Christian mystics such as Eckhart who have been influenced by Neo-Platonism have distinguished between the personal "God" of Theism and the "Godhead" which is experienced in the mystical union. They have also asserted that in speaking of the "Godhead" only negations are appropriate. It is obvious that when Tillich refers to God as the "abyss" and when he describes the object of "absolute faith" as the "God above God," he shows the influence of this Neo-Platonic mystical tradition rather than Christian Theism. According to Plotinus and his followers, "the One" transcends all of its finite manifestations and no quality or relation found in them can be predicated of it. When Tillich speaks of "being-itself" as "beyond" the polarities which characterize the struc-

[179] Aquinas, *Summa Theologica*, Q. 13, a. 3.   [180] *Ibid.*, Q. 13, a. 2.

ture of being, e.g., the "split" between subject and object, he reflects this monistic mysticism. As the "ground of being," God can be symbolized by terms derived from the structure of being. But as the "abyss" of being He cannot be expressed by symbols but can only be experienced in a mystical union. The result is that the value of Christian symbols for God, such as knowledge, will, and providence, is put in question.

Theologians have always recognized that the meaning of the divine revelation is accompanied by mystery, that the "revealed God" remains a "hidden God." However, this does not imply that knowledge, will, and providence cannot be ascribed to Him unambiguously. It means that we do not know the "mode of signification" of these terms when applied to Him. What is at stake, therefore, is not whether our knowledge dispels all mystery concerning Him and enables us to comprehend His essence completely—no intelligent Christian theologian would claim that this is the case—but whether we have analogical knowledge of personal and other attributes of His nature which do not need to be negated as well as affirmed.

However, those who make much of categories and analogies derived from personal existence need constantly to be reminded of the limitations of these and of the necessity of defining them in terms which are worthy of Him. As Tillich says at the end of Volume I of his *Systematic Theology*, the ego-thou relationship with God is not the only one, for we often feel the mystery of God's power, eternity, unchangeableness, and infinity. We need the mystic to warn us that even our best words can only point in the direction of the living God but can never contain Him.

5. Although we have emphasized the philosophical and theological limitations of Tillich's conception of God, we would conclude by recognizing the greatness of his *contribution* in refusing to accept the separation of theology from philosophy and in seeking to relate the God of Abraham, Isaac, and Jacob to the God of the philosophers. To deny the identity of the God of religion with the ultimate reality which philosophy strives to know is to eliminate the cosmic dimension of His being and to confine Him to the function of serving human needs. For this reason, Tillich's insistence upon the necessity of a philosophical doctrine of being for the interpretation of theological doctrines must be approved, however inadequate one may consider his own idealistic ontology to be for that purpose.

In general, Tillich's most distinctive and fruitful insights have been in the area of the relation of *theology and culture*. He has long been concerned with problems not only on the boundary between theology and philosophy but also on the boundary between theology and art, psychoanalysis, and politics. In short, he has had a deep and abiding concern that religion should be related in a creative way to culture and that the separation of the sacred from the profane should be overcome. "Religion," he has said, "is the substance of culture, culture is the form of religion." [181] Heywood Thomas is doubtless right in saying that this formula is more true of a primitive society than it is of modern culture.[182] But if Tillich's statement is taken not in a descriptive but in a normative sense, it expresses perfectly his own strong conviction that religion should underlie "secular" life as the "substance" which gives meaning to all cultural interests and activities.

Thus Tillich is in the tradition of Christian thinkers who have sought to come to terms with Western culture. As Augustine interpreted Christian beliefs in the light of Neo-Platonism and Aquinas with the help of Aristotelianism, Tillich has presented his theology from the perspective of German Idealism, Mysticism, and Existentialism. There is danger in the effort of a theologian to relate the beliefs of a historical religion to a particular philosophy. For every philosophical system is only an approximation to the truth about ultimate reality, and the correlation of theology with any philosophy runs the risk of distorting it at some points. It is easy to see, therefore, why many theologians, fearful that their faith may be obscured or undermined by philosophical interpretation, should regard philosophy as an enemy rather than an ally. But the danger of this negative and defensive attitude for religion is greater than the risk involved in facing honestly the problems raised by philosophy. This is why Tillich, despite the dubious aspects of his system, deserves a place of honor among contemporary religious thinkers for his creative work during a long career on the boundary between theology and philosophy.

---

[181] *Theology of Culture*, p. 42.
[182] J. Heywood Thomas, *Paul Tillich: An Appraisal* (Philadelphia: Westminster Press, 1963), p. 179.

Epilogue
SOME PRESENT TENDENCIES

We have been dealing in the last three chapters with religious philosophies of the twentieth century. The influence of these three philosophies upon religious thought in our time has been considerable: Humanism among scientists who have rejected traditional religion but have retained a religious attitude; Process Philosophy among philosophers and theologians who have not broken with Theism but are seeking to reinterpret it in terms of a recent metaphysical theory; and Philosophical Theology among theologians who are concerned to make their faith relevant to contemporary culture. All three involve a departure to some extent from traditional Theism, a departure which is of course radical in the case of Humanism. In this respect they differ sharply from Neo-Thomism which is still dominant in Catholic philosophical circles. But they all have in common and share with Neo-Thomism a basic confidence in the capacity of philosophy to deal with religious problems and to arrive at constructive conclusions which can have significant effects on human life.

However, it would be misleading to assert that any of these recent religious philosophies is dominant in contemporary philosophy, at least outside Protestant and Catholic institutions. Since World War I several philosophical tendencies have developed which have manifested skepticism about the capacity of reason to work out a constructive religious philosophy. These tendencies were prepared for by several religious philosophies which we have analyzed in previous chapters, e.g., Hume's Skepticism, Kant's Critical Philosophy, and Kierkegaard's Existentialism. But they have also been strengthened by the rapid growth of religious skepticism during the nineteenth century. Franklin Baumer has shown that in the nineteenth century, the skeptical tradition "moved into a new phase which was both qualitatively and quantitatively different from the previous phases," [1] a phase which was dramatically expressed by Nietzsche's statement, "God is dead!" From various sources strong arguments against religion were advanced: social, scientific, anthropological, psychological, economic, and historical.[2] As a result, the Victorian age was an age of religious perplexity and doubt, and many abandoned belief in God altogether. However, Baumer points out that the nineteenth century was also an Age of Faith. Its religious skepticism did not involve a denial of the existence of ultimate truths, the capacity of reason to discover them, and, above all, the worth and power of man. Indeed, it was accompanied by a touching faith in man and a virtual deification of Society, Science, and Culture.[3] In contrast, the religious skepticism of the twentieth century rejects the Victorian faith in man no less than the traditional faith in God.

This recent religious skepticism has been accompanied by a revolution in philosophy in both Europe and America which has brought about a profound distrust of metaphysics and natural theology. As a result, the religious and philosophical climate in our time makes the task of the philosopher of religion very difficult. The revolution in philosophy has also presented new opportunities because it has raised new issues and modified the terms in which the perennial issues are now being discussed. It is possible at the conclusion of this book only to deal briefly with three of these contemporary philosophical tendencies: Analytical Philosophy, Religious Existentialism, and Atheistic Humanism.

ANALYTICAL PHILOSOPHY

The importance of Analytical Philosophy is indicated by the fact that it now dominates the departments of philosophy in most of the large universities of England and the United States. Although there are considerable differences between the analysts, they agree in holding that the function of philosophy is the clarification of concepts and statements by analysis rather than the construction of comprehensive metaphysical theories. Unlike the special sciences, philosophy can give us no new knowledge of facts. Hence it depends upon the "first-order" statements of ordinary language and the sciences and confines itself to "second-order" statements which clarify the meaning of these. Thus its task is the analysis of language, although analysts assume that in this way they can attain knowledge of reality.

[1] Franklin L. Baumer, *Religion and the Rise of Scepticism* (New York: Harcourt, Brace, 1960), p. 129.
  [2] *Ibid.*, Chap. 3.   [3] *Ibid.*, pp. 162–164.

Linguistic analysis is not new; indeed, a great deal of philosophy since the time of Socrates has consisted of the analysis of concepts. What is new is the claim of some analytical philosophers that philosophy is primarily, if not exclusively, linguistic analysis. In consequence they maintain that philosophers should take a more modest view of their task than they did in the past. They should not be expected to offer answers to the perennial problems of man concerning the world, morality, and religion. For their task is not to give guidance to men as they face the ultimate questions of life but to deal with more limited problems by minute and rigorous analysis. Because of this modest conception of their function, analysts have usually expressed their views in single articles or collections of articles by different authors rather than in books.

Although Analytical Philosophy in England began with G. E. Moore and Bertrand Russell, it came into prominence there only with the Logical Positivism of A. J. Ayer in his *Language, Truth and Logic.*[4] According to the logical positivists, the propositions of formal logic and pure mathematics are "analytic." Since they simply state the implications of certain definitions and premises, they are "tautologies" which give us no information about the existent world. In contrast, "synthetic" propositions, which do give us information about existent things, are empirical hypotheses. The criterion of the meaning of these is their empirical verifiability, in the sense that observation-statements derived from them must be capable of being verified, at least in principle. The implications of this principle of verification are devastating. Since metaphysical, theological, and ethical statements cannot be empirically verified, they are declared to be nonsensical and meaningless. As Frederick Ferré has pointed out, the application of "verification analysis" to religious statements has led to various attempts to deny their meaningfulness or their distinctive character as assertions about reality.[5] The challenge of Logical Positivism to the claim of religious assertions to truth, therefore, is obvious, and H. J. Paton has charged it with attempting to exercise a "linguistic veto" on the philosophy of religion.[6]

However, few analysts of the present time would accept the positivist's restriction of meaning to statements capable of meeting the test of empirical verification. Under the influence of the later Wittgenstein's insistence that there are many "language-games" which serve different

[4] London: V. Gollancz, 1936.
[5] Frederick Ferré, *Language, Logic and God* (New York: Harper & Row, 1961), Chaps. 2–4.
[6] H. J. Paton, *The Modern Predicament* (London: George Allen and Unwin, 1955), Chap. 2.

functions and that the meaning of any statement is to be found in its "use" in a particular language game,[7] most linguistic analysts of today do not dismiss religious statements as meaningless and are willing to analyze them as they are used by religious people. This has prepared the way for several attempts by religious philosophers in England and America to analyze religious statements in order to show that they are assertions about reality and to indicate what is unique about them.[8]

Also there has recently been a recognition by linguistic philosophers that metaphysics is necessary. A volume of essays entitled *The Nature of Metaphysics* has been edited by D. F. Pears [9] and a small volume of "descriptive metaphysics," *Individuals*, has been published by P. F. Strawson.[10] Although metaphysics as conceived by these linguistic philosophers is much more limited and modest than metaphysics as conceived by philosophers like Whitehead who have developed comprehensive systems, it is clear that some of the analysts are beginning, however cautiously, to grapple with metaphysical questions. Thus analytical philosophy seems to have broken through the narrow limitations imposed by Logical Positivism; recent linguistic analysts have recognized that religious language is meaningful and must be analyzed in its own terms; and some of the analysts are once more showing an interest in metaphysics. As a result, natural theology, which along with metaphysics has been under a cloud for a generation, now faces a more promising future.[11]

However, the insistence of Logical Positivism that propositions about existence must be capable of empirical verification if they are to be meaningful reflects a widespread tendency of our time to restrict knowledge to the world of nature and man as described by the sciences. This tendency, which is largely due to the impressive development of science and technology, has led to a profound skepticism about the possibility of attaining knowledge of any transcendent reality. "How many people there are, as we know by experience," says Copleston, "whose practically spontaneous attitude towards theology and metaphysics is that of believing that they are dreams and moonshine. . . .

[7] Ludwig Wittgenstein, *Philosophical Investigations,* trans. G. E. M. Anscombe (New York: Macmillan, 1953), Part I: 7, 10, 23.

[8] E.g. Frederick Ferré, *op. cit.*, Chaps. 5, 11; Ian Crombie, in *New Essays in Philosophical Theology,* ed. Antony Flew and Alasdair MacIntyre (New York: Macmillan, 1955); Ian Ramsey, *Religious Language* (New York: Macmillan, 1957).

[9] London: Macmillan, 1957.   [10] London: Methuen, 1959.

[11] A recent collection of essays by Christian philosophers advocates a return to a kind of metaphysics and natural theology which will avoid the defects of the rationalistic deductive systems of the past and will be based upon intuitions arising from experience. See *Prospect for Metaphysics,* ed. Ian Ramsey (London: George Allen and Unwin, 1961).

We are no longer troubled by apparent discrepancies between scientific theories and *Genesis:* for we have a better idea now of the nature of scientific theories and hypotheses, on the one hand, while on the other hand every sensible person realizes that the Bible was not designed to be a handbook of astronomy or of any other branch of science. But it is none the less true that the growth of our industrialized, technical civilization, governed predominantly by economic values, has produced a type of mind which is 'naturally' closed to the Transcendent, to metaphysics and to theology." [12] The result of this tendency is that, although most analytical philosophers have rejected Logical Positivism, many of them still distrust reason when it attempts to deal with metaphysical or religious questions.

RELIGIOUS EXISTENTIALISM

It has been the fashion of British and American philosophers, especially the analysts, to dismiss Existentialism as an expression of the disillusionment and despair of postwar Europe. Because of its preoccupation with the description of states of mind or feelings such as anxiety, some have refused to accept it as philosophy and have relegated it to the status of psychological analysis of the human condition. And because several leading existentialists have also been literary men, e.g., Sartre and Marcel, others have treated it as a sort of passing literary fad, a German and French aberration. It is no longer possible to minimize a philosophical movement which has had such a great influence in Europe. Least of all can philosophers of religion do so. Religious existentialists such as Buber, Jaspers, and Marcel have contributed important insights to the philosophy of religion. And Heidegger has not only affected the theology of Bultmann and Tillich but also provided much of the basis for the atheistic Existentialism of Sartre and the atheistic Humanism of Camus.

The primary category or point of reference of Existentialism is human "existence." Man is viewed not as a thing among other things, as in Naturalism, nor as a pure subject shut up in its own inner states, as in Descartes. Rather, his consciousness is essentially "intentional" and "open" toward what is other than himself, since his being is "being-in-the-world." The primary task of philosophy is to give a phenomenological description of man's "existence" in his "world," intuitively apprehending the essence of the phenomenon which it is analyzing and suspending judgment with respect to all metaphysical questions con-

[12] Frederick Copleston, *Contemporary Philosophy* (London: Burns, Oates and Washbourne, 1956), p. 32.

cerning it. However, the ultimate purpose of an existentialist philosopher like Heidegger in making such an analysis of man's existence is
ontological, to understand the nature of being as it discloses itself in
man.

From its beginning with Kierkegaard, Existentialism has reacted
violently against the rationalism of modern science and philosophy.
When rationalism under the influence of science has led to Naturalism,
it has reduced man to an object in a world of objects and thus has denied the importance of his subjectivity. When it has led to monistic
Idealism, it has subordinated the individual person to the universal
Spirit or Mind immanent in him and has denied his freedom. In both
cases, what is distinctive about man's existence has been eliminated.
Although Kierkegaard attacked rationalism in its idealistic form, recent
existentialists have been more concerned with it in its naturalistic form.
They have pointed out that Naturalism, which results from the objective
description of the world by the sciences, reduces it to an impersonal
system of laws, strips it of the meanings and values it has for man,
treats man as an anonymous spectator without a soul, and denies his
relationship to anything which transcends the natural order. In attacking it, they have sought to get beyond the abstract concepts of scientific rationalism and to return to reality in its concreteness and especially to human existence in its uniqueness.

The method existentialists have used in carrying out this task is
to broaden the concept of experience, which has been restricted by
empiricists to sense experience, to include affective, volitional, and
other forms of experience. By phenomenological analysis of these experiences, usually regarded by rationalists as irrational, existentialists
have sought to show that they are revelatory of important aspects of
human existence capable of being known in no other way. For example,
Heidegger uses the term *Befindlichkeit* to indicate a "state-of-mind" or
"mood" which makes manifest "how one is, and how one is faring." [13]
He maintains that, although philosophy has usually regarded such affective states as mere "accompanying phenomena" of quite secondary
importance, they disclose the nature of man's existence and his relation
to the world and himself. Anxiety, *Angst*, is a basic "state of mind"
which has particular significance. That in the face of which one is
anxious is not something definite, as in the case of fear, but "Being-in-
the-world as such"; [14] and that about which one is anxious is his own
"potentiality-for-Being," i.e., his possibility of attaining authentic ex-

[13] Martin Heidegger, *Being and Time*, trans. John Macquarrie and Edward
Robinson (New York: Harper & Row, 1962), pp. 172, 173.
[14] *Ibid.*, p. 231.

istence.[15] Through anxiety one may realize that his concern for the things of ordinary life does not constitute the meaning and value of his life. Faced with the end of his life in death, he may come to understand that what counts is what he himself will do with the possibilities confronting him.

According to Karl Jaspers, philosophy is, as it has always been, concerned with Being. But it is not a universal science which takes the whole of reality rather than a limited field as its province. For a science must deal with a determinate type of object, whereas Being cannot be "objectified," turned into a determinate object.[16] Thus the problem of Being does not arise on the scientific level, since science is limited to the world of objects. Rather, it arises on the level of human existence, as man seeks to discover himself. Being is the Transcendent, and man discovers it because he is himself a transcending being, conscious of his limits but also of his movement toward the transcending of them. In "limit-situations," Grenzsituationen, such as the realization of death, a man can become conscious of himself as limited but at the same time of the enveloping or encompassing presence of Being as the ground of his being and of all beings. He cannot have a rational proof of the existence of the Transcendent, and he cannot apprehend it as an object. But he can in his freedom affirm his relationship to it by an act of "philosophic faith" and thereby attain authentic existence for himself.[17] However, philosophy cannot give a description of the Transcendent which will be universally valid. A metaphysical system or religion has value as a subjective deciphering, a "cipher" of Being, but it cannot be regarded as final.[18] Since Being cannot be objectified, it cannot be known; it can only be affirmed by faith. The influence of Kant and Kierkegaard is obvious in this denial of the possibility of metaphysics and natural theology, on the one hand, and the affirmation of faith in the Transcendent (although not in the form of the Christian faith), on the other.

The value of such existentialist analysis of human existence and affirmation of the Transcendent is that they challenge the complacency of modern scientific and philosophical rationalism, which has tended to reduce man to the status of an object in a world of objects and to deny the reality of the Transcendent altogether. But the effectiveness of this challenge has been seriously weakened by the existentialists' distrust of conceptual thought. They have usually maintained that concepts separate man from Being rather than help to bring him close to it. As a result, they have believed that experience rather than conceptual

[15] Ibid., pp. 231–232.   [16] Copleston, Contemporary Philosophy, p. 157.
[17] Ibid., p. 163.   [18] Ibid., p. 164.

thought is the way to know concrete reality and consequently have depended upon intuition rather than rational argument for knowledge of Being, or God. This accounts for the fact that they have had great difficulty in passing from phenomenological analysis of human existence to a metaphysical interpretation of Being, or God.

Although Heidegger asserted in *Being and Time* that his phenomenological description of human existence was to lead to an ontology or doctrine of Being, it is well known that he has been unable to carry out his purpose successfully in his later works. Again, since Jaspers holds that the Transcendent, or God, is apprehended only in a personal act of transcending and not objectively, he refuses to describe Him in universally valid terms. Therefore there can be no natural theology which offers grounds for the belief that He exists and possesses certain attributes.[19] As Copleston points out, this is the consequence of Jaspers' exaggeration of the dangers of "objectification." But we cannot avoid "objectifying" the Transcendent if we are going to talk about it at all.[20] Because Jaspers refuses to do so, he has to "leave assertion and denial of God's existence as two subjective possibilities without any adequate examination of the objective grounds for the alternative which he himself certainly adopts."[21] Similarly, Buber is critical of every philosophical or theological attempt to develop a concept of God because of his fear that this would make an object of Him which would become an idol preventing an "I-Thou" relationship with Him.[22]

Thus, although existentialists like Heidegger have made a valuable contribution to the phenomenological analysis of man's existence, and religious existentialists like Jaspers have shown how man's experience of his finitude makes him aware of his relation to the Transcendent, their distrust of conceptual and objective thinking has made it impossible for them to develop a positive metaphysics or natural theology.

ATHEISTIC HUMANISM

While Analytical Philosophy has been influenced by the skeptical conclusions of Hume, and Existentialism by the criticisms of metaphysics and natural theology by Kant and Kierkegaard, the Atheistic Humanism of Albert Camus is a product of more recent philosophical developments, especially Nietzsche's dramatic proclamation that "God is dead" and the attitude toward reason of the existentialists. It has little in common with the Naturalistic Humanism of Dewey, which emphasizes devotion to human ideals and values and entertains op-

[19] *Ibid.*, pp. 223, 224.   [20] *Ibid.*, p. 224.   [21] *Ibid.*, p. 225.
[22] Martin Buber, *Eclipse of God* (New York: Harper & Row, 1952), Chap. 3.

timistic hopes for the future of mankind. Dewey never abandoned the nineteenth-century belief in progress through the extension of science, education, and social reform, while Camus expresses the disillusionment of the postwar period in Europe.

Camus has given classic expression to the radical skepticism and atheism of this period in his concept of "the absurd." In *The Myth of Sisyphus*, he asserts that a feeling of the absurdity of existence can arise in various ways: from the pointlessness of daily routine, the temporal nature of life, the indifference and hostility of nature to man's values and hopes, and, above all, the inevitability of death.[23] Although the reason naturally seeks for clarity about the world and human life, it can find no meaning in either. That which constitutes the absurd is not merely the irrationality of the world but the contradiction between its irrationality and man's desire for clarity. "But what is absurd is the confrontation of this irrational and the wild longing for clarity whose call echoes in the human heart." [24] Naturally, this conclusion is repugnant to man and he seeks to escape from it. For example, religious existialists like Kierkegaard and Jaspers who have joined in the "attack on reason" have tried to escape from its logical conclusion by a leap of faith, the former affirming God beyond the world and the latter leaping from the finite to the Transcendent. But this is to deny reason by making it a mere instrument of desire, i.e., it is wishful thinking. The fact is that there is neither "logical certainty" nor "experimental probability" in that which is affirmed by faith; and since it transcends human reason, it is incomprehensible.[25]

What consequences should be drawn from the absurdity of the world and life? Suicide is not the solution, because it involves resignation and a surrender to the absurd. The absurd can have meaning for man only if he maintains his consciousness of it and revolts against it. "That revolt gives life its value. Spread over the whole length of a life, it restores its majesty to that life. . . . the sight of human pride is unequalled." [26] This is why Camus takes Sisyphus, whom the gods have condemned ceaselessly to roll a rock to the top of a mountain only to have it fall back of its own weight, as an example of the "absurd hero." Although he was forced to spend his life in futile and hopeless labor, he maintained his consciousness of his wretched condition and his rebellion against it. Hence he was superior to his fate and we can imagine him happy. "The struggle itself towards the heights is enough to fill a man's heart." [27]

[23] Albert Camus, *The Myth of Sisyphus*, trans. Justin O'Brien (New York: Random House, Vintage Books, 1955), pp. 10–12.
[24] *Ibid.*, p. 16.   [25] *Ibid.*, p. 30.   [26] *Ibid.*, pp. 40, 41.   [27] *Ibid.*, p. 91.

What kind of a life will the "absurd man" live? Since the world is godless and there are no absolute values, there is no moral obligation. In general, the ethic of the absurd man is one of quantity rather than quality. Although all experiences are ultimately without meaning, what counts for him is "not the best living but the most living, . . . the quantity and variety of experiences." [28] The illustrations Camus offers of the kinds of life an absurd man may choose include not only Don Juan but also the conqueror who commits himself to a historical struggle and the creative artist who expresses his intuitions of the world.[29] In *The Plague* Camus even portrays a sort of atheistic saint. But whatever kind of life the absurd man chooses, he will realize the ultimate equivalence of all actions, maintain his freedom, and entertain no false hopes that he can find an ultimate meaning in his life.[30]

Camus' conviction of the absurdity of human life is based in part upon his radical skepticism concerning the capacity of reason to satisfy its longing for clarity and his unwillingness to accept any belief which is not completely comprehensible to reason. It is obvious that at this point he has been affected not only by the "attack on reason" of the existentialists to whom he refers but also by the passion for absolute lucidity and certainty which has been a powerful factor in French philosophy since Descartes' emphasis upon "clear and distinct ideas." Indeed, one might argue that he exemplifies the generalization that a skeptic is a disillusioned rationalist who began by making excessive claims for reason, because of his failure to recognize the finitude of everything human.

But there are other factors besides philosophical skepticism involved in Camus' view of life as absurd. It is due also to the frustration of man's desire for values which will not be transitory and for life which will not be swallowed up by death. Like many other thinkers of our time, he is obsessed by the problem of evil. Unlike more optimistic humanists, as for example Dewey, the realization of values such as truth, beauty, and justice does not seem to him sufficient to give meaning to life in view of the fact that time and death will engulf them all. Also, since he has no faith in God and a future life, he can find no satisfaction in serving a divine purpose and can entertain no hope of

[28] *Ibid.*, p. 45.   [29] *Ibid.*, pp. 51–57.

[30] We have based our account of Camus' skepticism and atheism exclusively upon *The Myth of Sisyphus*, which was written in 1940. However, it should be pointed out that in some of his later essays such as *Return to Tipasa* (1952) and *The Artist and His Time* (1953) and in his novel *The Plague* (1948), Camus gave expression to a moving humanistic attitude which combined an almost Greek love of beauty, a deep feeling for nature, a compassion for man in his suffering, and an identification with the struggle for justice of our time.

fulfillment beyond death. As a result, the only meaning he can discern in life is a succession of experiences which are as great in quantity and variety as possible.

There is still another factor in Camus' indictment of life as absurd. As we have seen, the absurd man refuses to escape from absurdity by a leap of faith and wills to maintain his consciousness of the absurd and to rebel against it. Moreover, he attains worth and even nobility by persisting during his whole life in his rebellion, and his "pride" and "scorn" make him "happy." Clearly, there is something of the Romantic spirit here, and at times the defiance seems rather strident. But there is also something appealing in Camus' eloquent description of the courage of the absurd man, powerless to escape from his fate but winning a victory over it by proudly rebelling against it.

However, there is another side of the matter. The "revolt" of Camus' absurd man represents one of the culminating phases of modern man's self-sufficiency and self-assertion. Since the Renaissance, modern man has increasingly insisted upon his autonomy and has refused to be limited in any sphere of social and cultural activity by restraints imposed upon him in the name of religion and morality. The Communist revolution, which has sought to stamp out religion as an opiate of the people and traditional morality as a product of the bourgeoisie, has simply carried this attitude to an extreme. In the same spirit, Sartre assumes almost without argument that "God is dead," repudiates objective values, and exalts the unfettered freedom of the individual to create himself. Father John Courtney Murray has recently attributed this radical atheism of our time to an assertion of man's will that God be absent. "If God is present, man is being made by God, and he is being made a man, a being with an essence and a nature. Therefore, man is not free to make himself *ex nihilo*, out of a nothingness of nature and essence. . . . God must be declared dead, missing, absent. The declaration is an act of the will, a basic will to the absence of God." [31]

As an explanation of the militant atheism of the Communists and of Sartre, there is much truth in this statement. Doubtless it also throws some light upon the atheism of Camus. But it probably exaggerates the extent to which contemporary atheism on both sides of the Iron Curtain is a consequence of a conscious act of the will. The atheism of Camus is a product of the skepticism which began with the exaltation of the scientific method of attaining knowledge and which has decisively affected philosophy since the seventeenth century. Other factors of a more practical kind have strengthened the appeal of this skepticism,

[31] John Courtney Murray, *The Problem of God* (New Haven: Yale University Press, 1964), p. 117.

e.g., the disaffection with the Church in the Age of Revolution because of its association with absolute monarchy and feudalism and the materialism which resulted from the Industrial Revolution in the nineteenth century. Thus the radical atheism of today is the culmination of a long intellectual and social development in which men have not so much *willed* the absence of God as *lost* their belief in His presence, partly through their distrust of their capacity to know Him and partly through their preoccupation with the development of their own powers and the mastery of the world around them.

However, the radical skepticism and atheism of Camus is not typical of contemporary Western thought. In our brief analysis of Analytical Philosophy and Existentialism, we have seen that the dominant tendency in both is not atheism or nihilism but skepticism concerning the capacity of reason to prove the Transcendent. As Baumer has said, our age is an Age of Skepticism, but it is also an "Age of Longing." [32] Men have been disenchanted with the idols of the nineteenth-century religion of man and are seeking "a new transcendental faith." [33] If they are to be successful in finding such a faith, whether new or old or a blend of old and new, it will have to be a faith which is in accord with their experience and which commends itself to reason as consistent with all that they know. Therefore, philosophy of religion must continue to play an important, even if secondary, role in religious life and thought, as it has since the time of Plato.

[32] Baumer, *Religion and the Rise of Scepticism*, Chap. 4.
[33] *Ibid.*, p. 191; Baumer here quotes Julien Delattre.

Bibliography
Index

Bibliography

GENERAL

Burnet, John, *Greek Philosophy*, Part I: "Thales to Plato." London, Macmillan, 1924.

Burtt, E. A., *Types of Religious Philosophy*. New York, Harper and Brothers, 1939.

Copleston, F., *A History of Philosophy*, Vols. I, II. London, Burns, Oates and Washburn; Vols. III–VII. Westminster, Md., The Newman Press; 1946–1963.

Gilson, E., *Reason and Revelation in the Middle Ages*. New York, Scribners, 1938.

———, *The Spirit of Mediaeval Philosophy*. New York, Scribners, 1936.

Mackintosh, H. R., *Types of Modern Theology*. London, Nisbet, 1952.

Maurer, A. A., *Medieval Philosophy*. New York, Random House, 1962.

Thilly, F. and Wood, L., *History of Philosophy*. New York, Holt, 1957.

Windelband, W., *History of Philosophy*. New York, Macmillan, 1931.

PLATO

The Dialogues of Plato, 2 vols., trans. by B. Jowett, intro. by Raphael Demos. New York, Random House, 1937.

Cornford, F. M., *Plato's Cosmology*. New York, Humanities Press, 1952.

———, *Plato's Theory of Knowledge*. London, Paul, 1935.

———, *The Republic of Plato*. New York, Oxford University Press, 1943.

Crombie, Ian, *An Examination of Plato's Doctrines*. London, Routledge, 1930.

Cushman, Robert, *Therapeia*. Chapel Hill, University of North Carolina Press, 1958.

Demos, Raphael, *The Philosophy of Plato*. New York, Scribners, 1939.

Grube, G. M. A., *Plato's Thought*. London, Methuen, 1935.

Ritter, C., *The Essence of Plato's Philosophy*. London, George Allen and Unwin, 1933.

Ross, W. D., *Plato's Theory of Ideas*. Oxford, Clarendon Press, 1953.

Shorey, Paul, *The Unity of Plato's Thought*. Chicago, University of Chicago Press, 1904.

Solmsen, F., *Plato's Theology*. Ithaca, Cornell University Press, 1942.

Taylor, A. E., *Plato, The Man and His Work*. New York, The Dial Press, 1929.

ARISTOTLE

Works, trans. by J. A. Smith and W. D. Ross. Oxford, Clarendon Press, 1908.

Grene, Marjorie, *A Portrait of Aristotle*. Chicago, Chicago University Press, 1963.

Jaeger, Werner, *Aristotle*, trans. by R. Robinson. Oxford, Clarendon Press, 1948.

Mure, G. R. G., *Aristotle*. New York, Oxford University Press, 1932.

Oates, Whitney, *Aristotle and the Problem of Value*. Princeton, Princeton University Press, 1963.

Owens, J., *The Doctrine of Being in the Aristotelian Metaphysics*. Toronto, University of Toronto Press, 1951.

Randall, J. H., Jr., *Aristotle*. New York, Columbia Press, 1960.

Ross, W. D., *Aristotle*. London, Methuen, 1930.

PLOTINUS

Plotinus, trans. by A. H. Armstrong. London, Allen, 1953. *The Enneads*, trans. by Stephen MacKenna. London, Faber, 1956.

Armstrong, A. H., *The Architecture of the Intelligible Universe in the Philosophy of Plotinus*. Cambridge, Cambridge University Press, 1940.

Bréhier, Emil, *The Philosophy of Plotinus*. Chicago, University of Chicago Press, 1958.

Caird, E., *The Evolution of Theology in the Greek Philosophers*, Vol. II. Glasgow, James MacLehose and Sons, 1904.

Inge, W. R., *Mysticism in Religion*. Chicago, Chicago University Press, 1948.

——, *The Philosophy of Plotinus*, 2 vols. London, Longmans, Green and Co., 1918.

Whitaker, T., *The Neo-Platonists*. Cambridge, Cambridge University Press, 1918.

AUGUSTINE

Basic Writings of St. Augustine, 2 vols., trans. and edited by Whitney J. Oates. New York, Random House, 1948; *The Library of Christian Classics*, Vol. VI, "Earlier Writings," trans. by John H. S. Burleigh. Philadelphia, The Westminster Press, 1953; *Against the Academics*, trans. and annotated by John O'Meara. Westminster, Md., The Newman Press, 1950.

Battenhouse, Roy, ed., *A Companion to the Study of St. Augustine*. New York, Oxford University Press, 1956.

Bourke, V. J., *Augustine's Quest for Wisdom*. Milwaukee, Bruce, 1945.

Boyer, C., *Christianisme et Neo-Platonisme dans la Formation de Saint Augustin*. Paris, Beauchesne, 1921.

D'Arcy, M. C., ed., *A Monument to St. Augustine*. New York, Meridian Books, 1961.

Gilson, E., *The Christian Philosophy of St. Augustine*. New York, Random House, 1961.

Hessen, Johannes, *Augustin's Metaphysic der Erkenntnis*. Leiden, Brill, 1960.

O'Meara, J. J., *The Young Augustine*. London, Longmans, 1954.

Portalié, E., *A Guide to the Thought of St. Augustine*, trans. by Ralph J. Bastian from article in *Dictionnaire de Théologie Catholique*. Chicago, H. Regnery Co., 1960.

AQUINAS

Basic Writings of Saint Thomas Aquinas, 2 vols., ed. and annotated by Anton C. Pegis. New York, Random House, 1945.

Copleston, F., *Aquinas*. Baltimore, Penquin Books, 1957.

Garrigou-Lagrange, R., *God: His Existence and His Nature*, 2 vols., trans. by B. Rose. St. Louis, B. Herder, 1934–1936.

Maritain, J., *St. Thomas Aquinas, Angel of the Schools*. London, 3rd ed., 1946.

Mascall, E., *He Who Is*. London, Longmans, 1949.

Patterson, R. L., *The Concept of God in the Philosophy of Aquinas.* London, Allen, 1933.

Pegis, A. C., *St. Thomas and the Problem of the Soul in the Thirteenth Century.* Toronto, St. Michael's College, 1934.

Sertillanges, A. D., *Foundations of Thomistic Philosophy,* trans. by G. Anstruther. St. Louis, B. Herder Book Co., 1931.

MEISTER ECKHART

Meister Eckhart (sermons and treatises), trans. by R. Blakney. New York, Harper, 1941; *Meister Eckhart,* ed. by Franz Pfeiffer and trans. by C. de Evans. London, J. M. Watkins, 1924–1931.

Clark, J. M., *The Great German Mystics, Eckhart, Tauler and Suse.* Oxford, Basil Blackwell, 1949.

————, *Meister Eckhart, An Introduction to the Study of his Works.* London, Nelson, 1957.

James, William, *Varieties of Religious Experience.* New York, Modern Library, 1936.

Jones, Rufus, *The Flowering of Mysticism.* New York, Macmillan, 1939.

Otto, Rudolph, *Mysticism, East and West.* New York, Macmillan, 1932.

Stace, W. T., *Mysticism and Philosophy.* Philadelphia, J. B. Lippincott Co., 1961.

Underhill, E., *Mysticism.* New York, Dutton and Co., 1949.

Von Hügel, F., *The Mystical Element in Religion.* New York, Dutton and Co., 1909.

Zaehner, R. C., *Mysticism Sacred and Profane.* Oxford, Clarendon Press, 1957.

SPINOZA

The Chief Works of Benedictus Spinoza, trans. by R. H. M. Elwes. New York, Dover, 1951; *Spinoza, Selections,* ed. by John Wild. New York, Scribners, 1930.

Bidney, David, *The Psychology and Ethics of Spinoza.* New Haven, Yale University Press, 1960.

Hallett, H. F., *Benedictus Spinoza: The Elements of His Philosophy.* New York, Oxford University Press, 1957.

Hampshire, S., *Spinoza.* London, Faber, 1956.

Joachim, H., *A Study of the Ethics of Spinoza.* Oxford, Clarendon Press, 1901.

McKeon, R., *The Philosophy of Spinoza.* New York, Longmans Green, 1928.

Parkinson, G. H. R., *Spinoza's Theory of Knowledge.* Oxford, Clarendon Press, 1954.

Roth, L., *Spinoza.* London, Benn, 1929.

Wolfson, H. A., *The Philosophy of Spinoza,* 2 vols. Cambridge, Harvard University Press, 1934.

HUME

Hume's Dialogues Concerning Natural Religion, ed. by N. K. Smith. New York, Social Sciences Publishers, 1948; *An Enquiry Concerning Human Understanding.* Chicago, Open Court, 1927; *A Treatise on Human Nature,* ed. by Selby-Bigge. Oxford, Clarendon Press, 1958; *Hume, Selections,* ed. by Charles Hendel. New York, Scribners, 1927.

Hendel, C. W., *Studies in the Philosophy of David Hume.* Princeton, Princeton University Press, 1925.

Laird, J., *Hume's Philosophy of Human Nature.* London, Methuen, 1932.

Passmore, J. A., *Hume's Intentions.* Cambridge, Cambridge University Press, 1952.

Smith, N. K., *The Philosophy of David Hume.* London, Macmillan, 1941.

KANT

Critique of Judgment, trans. by J. H. Bernard. New York, Macmillan, 1931;
Critique of Practical Reason and Other Works on the Theory of Ethics, trans.
by T. K. Abbott. London, Longmans Green and Co., 1923; *Critique of Pure
Reason,* trans. by N. K. Smith. London, Macmillan, 1929, 1930; *Religion within
the Limits of Reason Alone,* trans. by T. M. Greene and H. Hudson. New York,
Harper Bros., 1960.
Caird, E., *The Critical Philosophy of Immanuel Kant,* 2 vols. New York, Mac-
millan, 1909.
Cassirer, H. W., *Commentary on Kant's Critique of Judgment.* London, Methuen,
1938.
England, F. E., *Kant's Conception of God.* London, Allen and Unwin, 1929.
Ewing, A. C., *A Short Commentary on Kant's Critique of Pure Reason.* London,
Methuen, 1938.
Kroner, R., *Kant's Weltanschauung,* trans. by J. E. Smith. Chicago, University of
Chicago Press,
Lindsay, A. D., *Kant.* London, Benn, 1934.
Paton, H. J., *The Categorical Imperative.* Chicago, University of Chicago Press,
1948.
Smith, N. K., *A Commentary to Kant's 'Critique of Pure Reason.'* London, Mac-
millan, 1918.
Webb, C. C. J., *Kant's Philosophy of Religion.* Oxford, Clarendon Press, 1926.
Weldon, T. D., *Introduction to Kant's Critique of Pure Reason.* Oxford, Clarendon
Press, 1945.

HEGEL

Early Theological Writings, trans. by T. M. Knox. Chicago, University of Chicago
Press, 1948; *The Logic of Hegel; Hegel's Philosophy of Mind,* trans. by W. Wallace (from *Encyclopedia of the Philosophical Sciences.* Oxford, University Press,
1894); *Philosophy of History,* trans. by J. Sibree. New York, Willey Book Co.,
1944; *Philosophy of Religion,* trans. Rev. E. B. Speers and J. Burden Sanderson.
London, K. Paul, Trench, Trubner and Co., 1895; *The Phenomenology of Mind,*
trans. by J. Baillie. London, George Allen and Unwin, 1961.
Caird, E., *Hegel.* London, W. Blackwood and Sons, 1883.
Findlay, J. M., *Hegel: A Reexamination.* London, Allen, 1958.
Pfleiderer, Otto, *The Philosophy of Religion on the Basis of History,* trans. by A.
Stewart, Vol. II. London, Williams, 1888.
Reyburn, H. A., *The Ethical Theory of Hegel.* Oxford, Clarendon Press, 1955.
Royce, Josiah, *Lectures on Modern Idealism.* New Haven, Yale University Press,
1919.
Schmidt, Erik, *Hegel's Lehre von Gott.* Güttersloh, G. Bertelsmann, 1952.
Stace, W. T., *The Philosophy of Hegel.* New York, Dana, 1955.

KIERKEGAARD

Journals (Selections), trans. by A. Dru. London, Oxford University Press, 1938;
Stages on Life's Way (1940); *Fear and Trembling* (1941); *The Sickness Unto
Death* (1941); *The Concept of Dread* (1944); *Training in Christianity* (1944),
trans. by Walter Lowrie. Princeton, Princeton University Press; *Either/Or,*
Vol. I, trans. by D. and L. Swenson, Vol. II, trans. by Walter Lowrie. Princeton,
Princeton University Press, 1941; *Philosophical Fragments,* trans. by D. Swen-

son. Princeton, Princeton University Press, 1930 (Introducton and Commentary by Niels Thulstrup in 2nd ed., 1962); *Concluding and Unscientific Postscript,* trans. by D. Swenson and Walter Lowrie. Princeton, Princeton University Press, 1941.

Bretall, Robert, ed., *A Kierkegaard Anthology.* Princeton, Princeton University Press, 1946.

Collins, J., *The Mind of Kierkegaard.* Chicago, H. Regnery Co., 1953.

Diem, Hermann, *Kierkegaard's Dialectic of Existence,* trans. by Harold Knight. Edinburgh, Oliver and Boyd, 1959.

Haecker, T., *Søren Kierkegaard,* trans. by A. Dru. New York, Oxford University Press, 1937.

Heinecken, Martin, *The Moment Before God.* Philadelphia, Muhlenberg Press, 1956.

Jolivet, R., *Introduction to Kierkegaard,* trans. by W. H. Barber. London, F. Miller, 1950.

Lowrie, W., *Short Life of Kierkegaard.* Princeton, Princeton University Press, 1942.

Roberts, David, *Existentialism and Religious Belief,* ed. by R. Hazelton. New York, Oxford University Press, 1957.

Ruttenbeck, Walter, *Søren Kierkegaard, Der Christliche Denker und Sein Werk.* Berlin, Trowitsch und Sohn, 1929.

Wahl, Jean, *Études Kierkegaardiennes.* Paris, J. Vrin, 1949.

FEUERBACH

Das Wesen der Religion. Leipzig, Kroner, 1908; *The Essence of Christianity.* New York, Harper and Bros., 1957.

Engels, Friedrich, *Ludwig Feuerbach and the Outcome of German Classical Philosophy.* New York, International Publishers, 1941.

Hook, Sidney, *From Hegel to Marx.* New York, Reynal, 1936.

Jodl, F., *Ludwig Feuerbach.* Stuttgart, F. Fromman, 1904.

Nüdling, Gregor, *Ludwig Feuerbach's Religionsphilosophie.* Paderborn, Schöningh, 1936.

DEWEY

The Quest for Certainty. London, G. Allen and Unwin, 1930; *Experience and Nature.* Chicago, Open Court, 1925; *A Common Faith.* New Haven, Yale University Press, 1934.

Hook, Sidney, *John Dewey, an Intellectual Portrait.* New York, John Day, 1939.

Hendel, C. W., *John Dewey and the Experimental Spirit in Philosophy.* New York, Liberal Arts Press, 1959.

Schilpp, P. A., ed., *The Philosophy of John Dewey.* Evanston, Northwestern University Press, 1939.

WHITEHEAD

Science and the Modern World. New York, The Macmillan Co., 1925; *Process and Reality.* New York, The Macmillan Co., 1929; *Adventures of Ideas.* New York, The Macmillan Co., 1938; *Religion in the Making.* Cleveland, The World Publishing Co., 1926; *Modes of Thought.* New York, The Macmillan Co., 1938; *The Function of Reason.* Boston, Beacon Press, 1958; *Dialogues of Alfred North Whitehead,* recorded by L. Price. London, M. Reinhardt, 1954.

Christian, William, *An Interpretation of Whitehead's Metaphysics.* New Haven, Yale University Press, 1959.

Emmet, D. M., *Whitehead's Philosophy of Organism.* London, Macmillan, 1932.

Hartshorne, Charles, *The Divine Relativity*. New Haven, Yale University Press, 1948.

Johnson, A. H., *Whitehead's Theory of Reality*. New York, Dover, 1962.

Leclerc, Ivor, *Whitehead's Metaphysics*. London, G. Allen and Unwin, 1958.

———, ed., *The Relevance of Whitehead's Metaphysics*. London, Allen, 1961.

Lowe, V., *Understanding Whitehead*. Baltimore, Johns Hopkins Press, 1962.

Schilpp, P. A., ed., *The Philosophy of Alfred North Whitehead*, esp. essays by Seelye Bixler and Charles Hartshorne. New York, Tudor Publishing Co., 1951.

TILLICH

The Courage to Be. New Haven, Yale University Press, 1952; *Biblical Religion and the Search for Ultimate Reality*. Chicago, Chicago University Press, 1955; *Dynamics of Faith*. New York, Harper and Bros., 1957; *Theology of Culture*. New York, Oxford University Press, 1959; *Systematic Theology*, 3 vols. Chicago, University of Chicago Press.

Hamilton, Kenneth, *The System and the Gospel*. London, S. C. M. Press, 1963.

Kegley, C. W. and Bretall, R. W., eds., *The Theology of Paul Tillich*. New York, Macmillan, 1952.

Martin, B., *The Existentialist Theology of Paul Tillich*. New York, Bookman Associates, 1963.

Tavard, G. H., *Paul Tillich and the Christian Message*. New York, Scribners, 1962.

Thomas, J. H., *Paul Tillich: An Appraisal*. Philadelphia, Westminster Press, 1963.

EPILOGUE

Ayer, A. J., *Language, Truth and Logic*. London, Gollancz, 1936.

Baumer, Franklin, *Religion and the Rise of Scepticism*. New York, Harcourt Brace, 1960.

Buber, Martin, *Eclipse of God*. New York, Harper, 1952.

———, *I and Thou*, trans. by R. G. Smith. New York, Scribners, 1938.

Camus, Albert, *The Myth of Sisyphus*, trans. by Justin O'Brien. New York, Random House, 1955.

Copleston, Frederick, *Contemporary Philosophy*. London, Burns and Oates, 1956.

Ferré, Frederick, *Language, Logic and God*. New York, Harper, 1961.

Flew, A. and MacIntyre, A., *New Essays in Philosophical Theology*. New York, Macmillan, 1955.

Heidegger, Martin, *Existence and Being*. Chicago, Henry Regnery and Co., 1949.

———, *Introduction to Metaphysics*, trans. by Ralph Manheim. New Haven, Yale University Press, 1939.

———, *Being and Time*, trans. by John Macquarrie and Edward Robinson. New York, Harper and Row, 1962.

Hepburn, R. W., *Christianity and Paradox*. London, Watts and Co., 1958.

Jaspers, Karl, *The Perennial Scope of Philosophy*, trans. by Ralph Manheim. New York, Philosophical Library, 1949.

———, *The Way to Wisdom*, trans. by Ralph Manheim. New Haven, Yale University Press, 1955.

Mitchell, Basil, ed., *Faith and Logic*. London, Allen, 1957.

Murray, John Courtney, *The Problem of God*. New Haven, Yale University Press, 1964.

Pears, D. F., ed., *The Nature of Metaphysics*. London, Macmillan, 1960.

Wittgenstein, Ludwig, *Philosophical Investigations*, trans. by G. E. Anscombe. New York, Macmillan, 1953.

Index